Professional Discipline and Healthcare Regulators

a legal handbook

Available as an ebook at www.lag.org.uk

The purpose of the Legal Action Group is to promote equal access to justice for all members of society who are socially, economically or otherwise disadvantaged. To this end, it seeks to improve law and practice, the administration of justice and legal services.

Professional Discipline and Healthcare Regulators

a legal handbook

SECOND EDITION

Jon Whitfield QC, Gemma Hobcraft,
Althea Brown, Amanda Hart, Eloise Power,
Louise Price, Nicole Ridgwell, Sue Sleeman
and Tom Stevens

LAG the access to justice charity
Legal Action Group
2018

This edition published in Great Britain 2018
by LAG Education and Service Trust Limited
National Pro Bono Centre, 48 Chancery Lane, London WC2A 1JF
www.lag.org.uk

First edition 2012 by Christopher Sallon, Jon Whitfield, Gemma Hobcraft, Steve Broach, Amanda Hart, Eloise Power, Louise Price, Nicole Ridgwell and Sue Sleeman

British Library Cataloguing in Publication Data
a CIP catalogue record for this book is available from the British Library.

Print ISBN 978 1 908407 52 8
ebook ISBN 978 1 908407 53 5

Typeset by RefineCatch Limited, Bungay, Suffolk
Printed in Great Britain by Hobbs the Printers, Totton, Hampshire

This book remains dedicated to the memory of Arsineh Gaspariance, a long-term colleague and friend of many at Doughty Street Chambers who sadly passed away in 2012. Whilst the passing of time perhaps reduces the impact, it does not diminish the loss. There will always be times when, despite huge determination, positivity and bravery, there is still only so much that current medicine can or, at times, ought to do.

Foreword to the first edition

by The Hon Mr Justice Collins

As the introduction pertinently points out, the regulation of healthcare professionals is in a state of flux. This is described as a practical handbook. So it is, and a very useful one, not only for practitioners who are instructed in hearings before the various disciplinary bodies or on appeal to a tribunal or court but also for those who take part in such hearings or undertake preparatory work for them in various capacities.

The focus is on five regulators. They deal with many thousands of professionals and, since the sanctions which may be imposed can affect the ability of those professionals to work, there is not only a need to act fairly but also a need to comply in particular with Article 6 of the European Convention on Human Rights. This should not lead to any real problems provided the legal principles, helpfully set out in the first chapter of this book, are properly applied. But it is essential that all those who are in any way involved in or are likely to be involved in the disciplinary processes applicable should be aware of the material principles.

Unfortunately, although the procedures are broadly intended to produce not only fairness to all parties but decisions which are made within a reasonable time, they are not identical in each of the five regulators. However, the legal principles to be applied are common to all. There are now a considerable number of cases in the Administrative Court which have set out those principles. Many of these are unreported and so the citations in chapter one are particularly valuable for anyone who needs to know how to deal with particular issues which may arise in individual cases.

A real concern, which stems from the increase in the workload of the regulatory bodies, is that there are substantial delays and hearings can take far too long. The two problems to an extent go together. But delays and lengthy hearings not only increase costs but also increase the pressure on registrants who are involved, particularly if they are subjected to interim orders or are in fact innocent. All those involved should take all steps which can reasonably be taken to narrow the issues and to avoid prolixity in hearings. A degree of firmness by chairmen of panels, with an input from legal advisors, is in my view desirable and it is surely in the interest of the various professionals that unnecessary delays and lengthy hearings should be avoided. This handbook gives practical advice which will enable cases to be prepared and presented in as efficient a manner as possible in order to achieve as speedy a process as is compatible with fairness. And the advice deals with the particular requirements of the procedures laid down for the regulatory body in question.

The final chapter deals with the Independent Safeguarding Authority which, albeit not directly regulatory, may make orders against those who work with vulnerable individuals and who have been found guilty of criminal offences or whose conduct has been such that regulatory sanctions have been imposed upon them. It focuses on the barring scheme and provides valuable advice and information.

Whatever changes may be made, the legal principles applicable will remain the same. Furthermore, the advice on how to prepare and present cases will continue to be of the greatest assistance. I have no doubt that this handbook is a necessary aid not only for practitioners but for all who are or are likely to be involved in regulatory proceedings. I am accordingly happy to commend it.

Mr Justice Collins
Administrative Court
Royal Courts of Justice
London
July 2012

Introduction

The changing face of healthcare regulation

It was said in the introduction to the first edition of this book that 'the regulation of professional discipline for healthcare professionals, commonly referred to as fitness to practise proceedings, is (like many other areas of law) in a fairly constant state of flux.' This remains an apt description for the introductory words to this second edition.

In October 2017, the Department of Health launched a consultation on the future of professional regulation: *Promoting professionalism, reforming regulation*. The foreword states affirmatively that the 'regulation of healthcare professionals must change in order to protect patients, to support the transformation of our healthcare services and to meet future challenges. It needs to be faster, simpler, better and less costly.' The consultation states that the regulatory system for healthcare professions:

> . . . is a historical patchwork, periodically mended and amended, with different aspects of the resulting regulatory regime reflecting the particular concerns and constraints of the time they were reformed. As a result, there is inconsistency, in both practice and legislation.

The consultation makes plain that there is a need for 'a UK-wide system of professional regulation that contributes to the delivery of this ambition and supports the development of high quality professionals. This needs to be complemented by a culture that enables professionals to learn from their experiences, including from their mistakes. All too often professionals encounter a culture of blame rather than learning.'

The consultation also raises questions about the need to examine which professions need to be regulated on a statutory footing and highlights that consideration may need to be given to reducing the number of regulators:

> There is no clear rationale for the current position of having nine regulatory bodies. Some regulators have a large number of registrants and others have relatively few. Research suggests that efficiencies begin to accrue when a regulatory body has a registrant base of between 100,000 and 200,000. Five of the regulatory bodies are smaller than this, contributing to additional costs of the regulatory system. In order to simplify the system, foster greater consistency and reduce costs, the four UK governments believe there is need for radical change. The four governments would be keen to understand what form a system containing a reduced number of regulations (possibly to three or four) might take.

The four regulators with more than 100,000 registrants are currently: the Nursing and Midwifery Council, the Health and Care Professions Council, the General Medical Council and the General Dental Council. Perhaps by the time a third edition of this book is being drafted the shape of the book will look very different in terms of both regulators and approach to regulation. Time will tell.

The result of consultation should be watched with interest, because it may go some way to providing a consistent regulatory law skeleton but the flesh and clothing will likely remain much akin to the current 'spot the difference' scenario of the regulators – on first glance they all appear very similar, but once the differences have been pointed it is impossible to ignore them. We hope this book will assist readers with learning how to spot the difference between them so that an adviser can feel confident before any of the regulators that is the subject of this book.

In the introduction to the first edition, it was also noted that the elephant in the room in relation to healthcare regulators remains the need for there to be, and for there to be seen to be, a greater separation between the regulator as investigator, prosecutor and adjudicator. Various regulators have made attempts to create more space between these functions. Since the first edition was published, perhaps the most significant structural change has been the move to operational tribunal services – to promote independence between investigation and adjudication stages of fitness to practise proceedings – to ensure independent decision-making. The Medical Practitioners Tribunal Service (MPTS) and the Health and Care Processions Tribunal Service (HCPTS) are now the adjudication arms for the cases brought by the General Medical Council (GMC) and the Health and Care Professions Council (HCPC).

Other significant changes are the growing use – particularly at the MPTS – of Legally Qualified Chairs (LQCs) in lieu of a tribunal sitting with a legal assessor and also that the General Medical Council now also have a right of appeal against MPTS decisions in appropriate cases. This has recently caused considerable press interest in the case of the Dr Bawa-Garba where the GMC appealed the Tribunal's decision to suspend the doctor for 12 months, resulting in her being erased from the register by the High Court.

The Government provides the legislative framework governing regulation for healthcare professionals. The relevant statutes provide the regulators with their duties and powers. Internal procedures and processes are for the regulator to decide upon in consultation with interested parties. There are numerous health regulators, each with their own nuanced practices and procedures, but with broadly the same approach to professional disciplinary proceedings/fitness to practise cases. This can make it difficult for those representing registrants to remember the specific detail of whether hearings are conducted in three discrete stages, two stages or before a 'Health Committee', a 'Conduct and Competence Committee' or a 'Fitness to Practise Panel' or indeed a tribunal. Terminology matters and an understanding of the specific rules is obviously a cornerstone to effective representation of registrants.

The rules, as in any area of law, only provide so much detail – what practitioners or advisers starting out in this area need (and others who may be experienced before one regulator, but appearing for the first time before another) is the detail between the rules – for example, how to advise a registrant to respond at an investigation stage, what to expect on the first day of a hearing, what is meant by insight or impairment, or what mitigation might be of most use at the sanction stage – just a few of the issues addressed in relation to each of the six regulators that are the subject of this book.

Aims of the book

This book aims to be a practical handbook setting out the preparation, practice and procedure for professional disciplinary hearings before six healthcare regulators: the General Medical Council (GMC), the Nursing and Midwifery Council (NMC), the Health and Care Professions Council (HCPC), the General Dental Council (GDC), the General Optical Council (GOC) and the General Pharmaceutical Council (GPhC) (herein, 'the Councils'). The object is to provide lay advisers, registrants, trade union officials and lawyers new to this area of law with a handbook which covers the relevant law applicable to professional discipline cases before these Councils. It can be used as a self-contained guide by those running or advising on such a case. It also provides clear guidance on general principles relating to the health care regulators that are the subject of this book, as well as a chapter on judicial review and appeals in the regulatory context.

Scope of the book

A practical book needs to be relatively portable. To ensure portability (and completion!) it was simply not possible to address every single health regulator within this edition. Therefore, as indicated, six regulators are the focus of this book – as found in Part 2 of the book:

- The General Medical Council (GMC) responsible for regulating doctors.
- The Nursing and Midwifery Council (NMC) – the regulator for nurses, midwives and health visitors.
- The Health and Care Professions Council (HCPC) which currently regulates 16 health and care professions – arts therapists, biomedical scientists, chiropodists/podiatrists, clinical scientists, dieticians, hearing aid dispensers, occupational therapists, operating department practitioners, orthopists, paramedics, physiotherapists, practitioner psychologists, prosthetists/orthotists, radiographers, social workers in England and speech and language therapists.
- The General Dental Council (GDC) which regulates dentists, dental nurses, dental technicians, clinical dental technicians, dental hygienists, dental therapists and orthodontic therapists.
- The General Optical Council (GOC) which regulates optometrists, dispensing opticians, student opticians and optical businesses.
- The General Pharmaceutical Council (GPhC) which regulates pharmacists, pharmacy technicians and pharmacist premises in Great Britain.

Nothing should be read into the importance or lack of importance of those regulators included or not included. This book could, for example, have included chapters on other healthcare regulators subject to PSA oversight.[1] The fact that it does not only reflects the practical need to limit the book length and the key experience and expertise of the author group.

Structure of the book

Part 1

In a change from the first edition and in recognition of the utility of chapter 1 and the growing volume of High Court case-law, chapter 1 has now become chapters 1, 2 and 3. Breaking down the general backbone of the book into more easily navigable sections, these chapters collectively cross-cut all the healthcare regulators featured within this book (and others not featured). There is a detailed account and analysis of the law in this field, relevant extracts from case-law and commentary on the applicability of the European Convention on Human Rights to these regulators:

- chapter 1: General principles and preliminary matters; human rights, charges, abuse of process;
- chapter 2: Hearings (interim orders and full hearings), evidence and procedure;
- chapter 3: Outcomes, findings and sanctions.

The stress of proceedings that can strip an individual of their only known profession and livelihood are not to be underestimated and the importance of substantive and procedural safeguards are fundamental. Amongst a vast range of topics, there is also guidance on the move by some regulators to Legally Qualified Chairs and the new rights of appeal available to certain regulators as well as guidance on the most recent Supreme Court decision on dishonesty.[2]

Part 2

Chapters 4–9 are the regulator-specific chapters, with one chapter dedicated to the specific rules and procedures of each Council. Providing a roadmap through GMC (chapter 4), NMC (chapter 5), HCPC (chapter 6), GDC (chapter 7), GOC (chapter 8) and GPhC (chapter 9) proceedings with reference to rules, practice, convention, tactics and procedure. As indicated, above, these can be read stand-alone, but all provide cross-referencing back to the relevant paragraphs of Part 1 (chapters 1, 2 and 3) to allow quick reference to further detail relating to case-law and the application of general principles across the regulators.

Utilising judicial review and appeal mechanisms can be a vital tool for a registrant who considers that there were procedural or substantive concerns with how their hearing occurred or what decision was made. Registrants also need to be aware that the Professional Standards Authority can appeal a decision of a regulator and there is now a move for regulators

1 The General Chiropractic Council (GCC), the General Osteopathic Council (GOsC) and the Pharmaceutical Society of Northern Ireland (PSNI).

2 *Ivey v Genting Casinos Ltd* [2017] UKSC 67.

themselves to be able to appeal decisions. Chapter 10 provides guidance on when judicial review or an appeal may be appropriate.

Due to the practical emphasis of this book, readers may find that further research is necessary on the law itself especially in new, developing, specialist or complex areas.

Enormous gratitude is due to LAG (especially Esther Pilger) for supporting this publication and to everyone who read, bought or used the first edition. We hope the second edition proves useful.

The law is stated as known at November 2017. Where possible, reference has been made to more recent law at proof stage.

Jon Whitfield QC, Gemma Hobcraft, Althea Brown, Amanda Hart, Louise Price, Sue Sleeman and Tom Stevens

Members of the professional discipline and regulatory team
Doughty Street Chambers
November 2017

Authors

Jon Whitfield QC spent 30 years as a leading practitioner in crime dealing with cases of terrorism, homicide and fraud. During this time he developed a particular interest in mental health, leading to his sitting as a judge in mental health tribunals since 2002. Increased contact with medical and regulatory issues led to his advising in MPTS proceedings, where he has sat as a legal assessor since 2007 and latterly as a Legally Qualified Chair. Jon now advises in proceedings before the MPTS, NMC, GPhC and GOsC. His wealth of experience across these and other regulators gives him both a very detailed and a broad comparative knowledge of healthcare regulation. Jon was lead author for chapters 1, 2 and 3.

Gemma Hobcraft specialises in healthcare law, particularly professional discipline, and represents a wide range of medical and healthcare practitioners, including doctors, nurses, midwives, pharmacists, psychologists and physiotherapists in fitness to practise proceedings before their regulators. She also specialises in the health-related aspects of public law including judicial reviews and statutory appeals. Gemma has a particular interest and expertise in reproductive health rights. For nine years prior to coming to the Bar, Gemma was heavily involved in advocacy for young people's sexual and reproductive rights at the local, national and international level. She was a lay member of the Human Fertilisation and Embryology Authority (HFEA) from 2008 to 2015. Gemma was lead author for chapter 4 on the General Medical Council.

Althea Brown is a specialist in professional disciplinary regulation, employment and discrimination law. She is regularly instructed in cases before healthcare regulators including the GMC, GDC, HCPC, NMC and GPhC. She is also instructed in cases before the Financial Conduct Authority and Solicitors Disciplinary Tribunal. Althea has represented registrants facing all manner of alleged breaches of professional standards, whether by lack of competence, gross negligence or misconduct. Examples range from serious allegations of dishonesty, drug dependency, alcohol abuse, inappropriate relationships and violent assault to poor record keeping, plagiarism and mental health difficulties. Althea was the lead author of chapter 8 on the General Optical Council.

Amanda Hart is a specialist in regulatory and employment law. She has over 10 years' experience of representing nurses and midwives in NMC fitness to practise proceedings, and represents other health professionals and teachers in their disciplinary proceedings. Amanda also specialises in employment and discrimination law representing claimants at employment tribunals, in the Employment Appeal Tribunal and the Court of Appeal. Prior to being called to the Bar, Amanda was a national union official for the National Association of Teachers in Further and Higher Education. Amanda was co-author, with Nicole Ridgewell, of chapter 5 on the Nursing and Midwifery Council.

Eloise Power is a barrister at Serjeants' Inn Chambers specialising in clinical negligence, product liability, regulatory law and public law. She has a particular interest in appellate work: she represented the GDC in *Ninian Peckitt v General Dental Council* [2016] EWHC 1803 (Admin) and *Manuel Nunez Martinez v General Dental Council* [2015] EWHC 1223 (Admin). She represents the lead claimant in the JJML Pelvic Organ Prolapse Products Litigation (the trans-vaginal mesh litigation). Eloise is the author of two chapters of *Medicolegal Issues in Obstetrics and Gynaecology* (to be published by Springer). She is a pupil supervisor and a member of the Gray's Inn advocacy faculty. Eloise is the lead author of chapter 7 on the General Dental Council.

Louise Price specialises in regulatory and employment law and in her practice regularly deals with the interplay between employment tribunal claims and professional regulatory proceedings. She also acts in public law matters with a focus on the rights of the individual in community care and education contexts. Prior to joining Doughty Street Chambers, Louise had worked for the International Labour Organization and domestically as a specialist adviser for Citizens Advice. Louise was the lead author of chapter 10 on appeals and judicial review.

Nicole Ridgewell is a solicitor with Ridouts Professional Services Plc. She advises providers of health and social care on a range of regulatory matters and represents individual practitioners before their regulatory bodies. She previously worked in various legal roles for the Royal College of Nursing, advising registered nurses and healthcare assistants on referrals to the Nursing and Midwifery Council and the Disclosure and Barring Service, as well as discrete matters of public law and personal injury. Nicole regularly writes for health and social care publications, and presents at conferences on health and social care matters. Nicole was co-author, with Amanda Hart, of chapter 5 on the Nursing and Midwifery Council.

Sue Sleeman is an employment and regulatory law practitioner. She regularly appears before a variety of professional disciplinary tribunals and regulatory bodies, representing individuals facing allegations of misconduct and lack of competence. While the majority of her regulatory work is on behalf of health professionals, including nurses, midwives, physiotherapists and paramedics, she also represents other professionals such as teachers, college lecturers and social workers. Before coming to the Bar, Sue worked in the trade union movement, initially as a lay representative in UNISON and later for the NUT and the Chartered Society of Physiotherapy. Sue's employment practice is claimant-based and in the main she acts for trade union members bringing claims in the employment tribunals for unfair dismissal, discrimination and whistleblowing. Sue was lead author on chapter 6 on the Health and Care Professions Council.

Tom Stevens is a criminal defence specialist who represents defendants in complex and serious cases from high-value frauds and sexual offences to those involving extreme violence and multi-handed drug trafficking cases. He is a contributory author to *The Drug Offences Handbook*. Alongside his criminal defence work Tom has gained extensive experience in the field of professional discipline, having advised and represented registrants before a wide range of healthcare regulators, including the GMC, NMC and HCPC. Tom is also frequently instructed to appear on behalf of the GDC before their FTP and HC Committees. Tom was the lead author for chapter 9 on the General Pharmaceutical Council.

The editorial team would like to thank Christopher Sallon QC and Steve Broach for their contribution to the first edition of this book and their continued support for the second edition.

Contents

Table of cases

British Dental Association v General Dental Council [2014] EWHC 4311 (Admin)	10.79
Brozicek v Italy (A/167) (1990) 12 EHRR 371, (1990) Times, January 3, ECtHR	1.85
Bryant v Law Society [2007] EWHC 3043 (Admin), [2009] 1 WLR 163	3.249
Bultitude v Law Society [2004] EWHC 1370 (Admin)	3.249
Burrows v General Pharmaceutical Council [2016] EWHC 1050 (Admin)	3.191–3.193
C plc v P and Attorney-General (intervenor) [2007] EWCA Civ 493, [2008] Ch 1	1.296
Casey v General Medical Council [2011] NIQB 95	8.187
Chandrasekera v Nursing and Midwifery Council [2008] EWHC 3528 (Admin)	8.204
Chandrasekera v Nursing and Midwifery Council [2009] EWHC 144 (Admin)	3.211
Chaudhury v General Medical Council [2002] UKPC 41, [2004] Lloyd's Rep Med 251	9.99, 9.328
Chauhan v General Medical Council [2010] EWHC 2093 (Admin)	1.98, 1.218, 2.97, 2.217, 5.132
Cheatle v General Medical Council [2009] EWHC 645 (Admin), [2009] LS Law Medical 299	2.224, 2.226, 3.8, 3.56, 3.57, 3.152, 3.178, 3.180, 4.51, 5.275, 5.282
Christou v Haringey LBC [2013] EWCA Civ 178, [2014] QB 131	1.305–1.307
Christou v Nursing and Midwifery Council [2016] EWHC 1947 (Admin)	5.86
Clarke v General Optical Council [2017] EWHC 521 (Admin), (2017) 155 BMLR 192	1.207–1.210, 3.127–3.130, 3.385, 5.304
Cohen v General Medical Council [2008] EWHC 581 (Admin), [2008] LS Law Medical 246	1.96, 1.98, 1.209, 1.210, 2.217, 2.224, 2.226, 2.387, 3.8, 3.22, 3.50, 3.52, 3.72, 3.129, 3.130, 3.177, 3.235, 4.51, 4.201, 4.202, 5.275, 5.282, 9.205, 9.307
Connelly v Director of Public Prosecutions [1964] AC 1254, [1964] 2 WLR 1145, HL	1.159, 1.300
Council for Healthcare Regulatory Excellence v Nursing and Midwifery Council and Grant [2011] EWHC 927 (Admin), [2011] ACD 72	1.209, 3.5, 3.6, 3.125, 3.129, 3.165, 3.309, 4.232, 5.282, 5.283, 8.130, 9.100
Council for the Regulation of Healthcare Professionals v General Dental Council and Fleischmann [2005] EWHC 87 (QB), (2005) Times, February 8	3.214, 3.221, 4.232, 5.305, 6.88
Council for the Regulation of Healthcare Professionals v General Dental Council and Marshall [2006] EWHC 1870 (Admin), (2006) 92 BMLR 36	3.104
Council for the Regulation of Healthcare Professionals v General Medical Council and Biswas [2006] EWHC 464 (Admin)	3.10, 9.299

General Medical Council v Krishnan [2017] EWHC 2892 (Admin), [2018] ACD 9	3.248
General Medical Council v Makki [2014] EWHC 769 (Admin)	2.84
General Medical Council v Narayan [2017] EWHC 2695 (Admin)	13.138
General Medical Council v Nwachuku [2017] EWHC 2085 (Admin), (2017) 158 BMLR 161	3.317, 3.318, 10.79
General Medical Council v Pembrey [2002] EWHC 1602 (Admin), [2002] Lloyd's Medical Reports 434	1.41
General Medical Council v Qureshi [2014] EWHC 775 (Admin)	2.75
General Medical Council v Razoq [2010] EWHC 2258 (Admin)	2.76
General Medical Council v Sheill [2006] EWHC 3025 (Admin)	4.95, 8.134
General Medical Council v Spackman [1943] AC 627, [1943] 2 All ER 337, HL	3.78
General Medical Council v Srinivas [2012] EWHC 670 (Admin)	2.14–2.16
General Medical Council v Theodoropoulous [2017] EWHC (Admin)	13.290
General Medical Council v Visvardis. *See* General Medical Council v Adeogba	
Georgieva v Nursing and Midwifery Council 2017 GWD 11-156	5.132
Ghosh v General Medical Council [2001] UKPC 29, [2001] 1 WLR 1915	1.42, 1.46, 1.82, 2.310, 3.117, 3.126, 3.199, 3.345, 3.346, 10.97
Gian and Mohd-Yusoff v Crown Prosecution Service [2009] EWCA Crim 2553, [2010] Crim LR 409	2.394
Giele v General Medical Council [2005] EWHC 2143 (Admin), [2006] 1 WLR 942, [2005] 4 All ER 1242	3.232, 3.295, 4.217, 5.301, 9.329
Giwa-Osagie v General Medical Council [2013] EWHC 1514 (Admin)	3.183, 3.184
Glencore Energy UK Ltd v Revenue and Customs Commissioners [2017] EWHC 1476 (Admin), [2017] STC 1824	10.57, 10.58
Goodchild-Simpson v General Medical Council [2014] EWHC 1343 (Admin), (2014) 139 BMLR 128	3.85
Goodwin v Health and Care Professions Council [2014] EWHC 1897 (Admin)	1.70
Gray v Police Appeals Tribunal [2016] EWHC 1239 (Admin)	1.314
Guest v General Medical Council [2013] EWHC 3121 (Admin)	2.363
Gulamhusein v General Pharmaceutical Council [2014] EWHC 2591 (Admin)	9.162
Gupta (Prabha) v General Medical Council [2001] UKPC 61, [2002] 1 WLR 1691	3.96, 3.97, 3.100, 3.118, 3.139, 3.289
H (minors) (sexual abuse: standard of proof), *Re* [1996] AC 563, [1996] 2 WLR 8, HL	2.373, 2.377, 2.382, 5.262
Haikel v General Medical Council [2002] UKPC 37, [2002] Lloyd's Rep Med 415	1.178, 3.218
Hameed v Central Manchester University Hospitals NHS Foundation Trust [2010] EWHC 2009 (QB), [2010] Med LR 412	2.311–2.313
Harford v Nursing and Midwifery Council [2013] EWHC 696 (Admin), [2013] Med LR 179	2.408, 5.14
Harry v General Medical Council [2012] EWHC 2762 (QB)	2.50, 2.90, 8.135
Hayat v General Medical Council [2014] EWHC 1477 (Admin)	3.122, 3.123
Hayat v General Medical Council [2017] EWHC 1899 (Admin)	2.365, 5.157
Hazelhurst v Solicitors Regulation Authority [2011] EWHC 462 (Admin), [2011] NPC 29	3.135

Richards v Law Society [2009] EWHC 2087 (Admin)	1.101
Richardson v Redpath Brown & Co Ltd [1944] AC 62, [1944] 1 All ER 110, HL	2.298
Robinson v Solicitors Regulation Authority [2012] EWHC 3054 (Admin)	3.124
Roomi v General Medical Council [2009] EWHC 2188 (Admin)	1.97, 1.218, 1.299, 2.97, 4.80, 6.76
Rowe and Davis v United Kingdom (28901/95) (2000) 30 EHRR 1, 8 BHRC 325, ECtHR	1.250, 1.251
Royal Brunei Airlines Sdn Bhd v Tan [1995] 2 AC 378, [1995] 3 WLR 64, PC (Brunei)	3.250–3.253, 3.257, 3.258
Royal College of Veterinary Surgeons v Samuel [2014] UKPC 13	3.278, 3.279
Roylance v General Medical Council (No 2) [2000] 1 AC 311, [1999] 3 WLR 541, [1999] Lloyd's Rep Med 139, PC	3.35, 5.277, 8.120, 8.121
Rylands v General Medical Council [1999] Lloyd's Rep Med 139	3.26, 4.36
S v General Medical Council [2007] EWHC 3257 (Admin)	3.156, 3.157
Sacha v General Medical Council [2009] EWHC 302 (Admin)	1.316
Sadler v General Medical Council [2003] UKPC 59, [2003] 1 WLR 2259	3.35, 3.63, 3.64, 3.343
Saha v General Medical Council [2009] EWHC 1907 (Admin), [2009] LS Law Medical 551	3.9
Salha and Abusheikha v General Medical Council [2003] UKPC 80, [2004] ECDR 12	1.115, 3.105, 4.143
Sandler v General Medical Council [2010] EWHC 1029 (Admin), [2010] Med LR 491	2.46, 2.47, 2.54, 5.86, 8.132
Sarkodie-Gyan v Nursing and Midwifery Council [2009] EWHC 2131 (Admin)	3.53, 3.84, 4.51, 5.282
Schmidt v Secretary of State for Home Affairs [1969] 2 Ch 149, [1969] 2 WLR 337, CA	10.78
Schodlok v General Medical Council [2015] EWCA Civ 769, [2015] Med LR 409	3.43, 3.44
Scott v Solicitors Regulation Authority [2016] EWHC 1256 (Admin)	3.330
Secretary of State for Business, Innovation and Skills v Weston [2014] EWHC 2933 (Ch), [2014] BCC 581	1.312
Secretary of State for the Home Department v AF (FC) and another and one other action [2009] UKHL 28, [2009] 3 WLR 74	1.269
Selvanathan v General Medical Council [2001] Lloyd's Rep Med 1, (2001) 59 BMLR 95, PC	3.102, 3.107
Selvarajan v General Medical Council [2008] EWHC 182 (Admin), [2008] LS Law Medical 193	1.49, 1.79, 1.169, 1.181–1.184, 1.319, 3.147
Shah v General Pharmaceutical Council [2011] EWHC 73 (Admin)	3.198
Sharma v General Medical Council [2014] EWHC 1471 (Admin)	2.382, 3.255
Sheill v General Medical Council [2008] EWHC 2967 (Admin)	1.93
Shepherd v Law Society [1996] EWCA Civ 977	3.73
Siddiqui v General Medical Council [2013] EWHC 1083 (Admin)	3.161
Singleton v Law Society [2005] EWHC 2915 (QB)	1.117, 1.145, 1.146, 1.153
Smith v Bar Standards Board [2016] EWHC 3015 (Admin), [2017] ACD 6	2.132–2.134, 3.389
Solicitors Regulation Authority v Chan [2015] EWHC 2659 (Admin)	1.138, 3.324, 3.340

Table of statutes

Table of statutory instruments

Table of international legislation

Table of guidance

GOC Guidance

GPhC Guidance

HCPC Guidance

HCPTS Guidance

MPTS Guidance

NMC Guidance

Professional Standards Authority

Abbreviations

ADR	alternative dispute resolution
ASA	Advertising Standards Authority
ASBO	anti-social behaviour order
BACP	British Association for Counselling and Psychotherapy
BDA	British Dental Association
BMA	British Medical Association
BSB	Bar Standards Board
CCC	Conduct and Competence Committee
CEA 1995	Civil Evidence Act 1995
CET	continuing education and training
CHRE	Council for Healthcare Regulatory Excellence
CJA 2003	Criminal Justice Act 2003
CJPOA 1994	Criminal Justice and Public Order Act 1994
Copine	Combating Paedophile Information Networks in Europe
CPD	continuing professional development
CPIA 1996	Criminal Procedure Investigations Act 1996
CPR	Civil Procedure Rules 1998
CPS	Crown Prosecution Service
CPSM	Council for the Professions Supplementary to Medicine
CQC	Care Quality Commission
CRB	Criminal Records Bureau
CRHP	Council for the Regulation of Healthcare Professionals
DA 1956	Dentists Act 1956
DA 1984	Dentists Act 1984
DBS	Disclosure and Barring Service
DOH	Department of Health
DPA 1998	Data Protection Act 1998
ECHR	European Convention on Human Rights
ECtHR	European Court of Human Rights
FOIA 2000	Freedom of Information Act 2000
FTP	fitness to practise
FTPC	Fitness to Practise Committee
FTPT	fitness to practise tribunal
GCC	General Chiropractic Council
GDC	General Dental Council
GMC	General Medical Council
GOC	General Optical Council
GOsC	General Osteopathic Council
GPhC	General Pharmaceutical Council
GSCC	General Social Care Council
GTCE	General Teaching Council for England
HC	Health Committee
HCA	healthcare assistant
HCPC	Health and Care Professions Council
HCPTS	Health and Care Professionals Tribunal Service
HPC	Health Professions Council

HSCA 2008	Health and Social Care Act 2008
HSWPO 2001	Health and Social Work Professions Order 2001 SI 2002 No 254
IBB	Independent Barring Board
IC	Investigation Committee
ICAEW	Institute of Chartered Accountants in England and Wales
ILEX	Institute of Legal Executives
IOP	Interim Orders Panel
IOT	interim orders tribunal
ISA	Independent Safeguarding Authority
ISP	Indicative Sanctions Policy
LRMP	List of Registered Medical Practitioners
LQC	Legally Qualified Chair
MA 1983	Medical Act 1983
MHPS	Maintaining high professional standards in the modern NHS
MoU	memorandum of understanding
MPS	Medical Protection Society
MPTS	Medical Practitioners Tribunal Service
NCAS	National Clinical Assessment Service
NCTL	National College for Teaching and Leadership
NMC	Nursing and Midwifery Council
NMO 2001	Nursing and Midwifery Order 2001 SI 2002 No 253
NPSA	National Patient Safety Agency
OA 1958	Opticians Act 1958
OA 1989	Opticians Act 1989
OCCS	Optical Consumer Complaints Service
OHPA	Office of the Health Professions Adjudicator
PACE	Police and Criminal Evidence Act 1984
PALS	Patient Advisory Liaison Service
PD	Practice Direction
PDP	personal development plan
PFA 2012	Protection of Freedoms Act 2012
PO 2010	Pharmacy Order 2010
POCA 1999	Protection of Children Act 1999
POCA list	Protection of Children Act list
POVA list	Protection of Vulnerable Adults list
PSA	Professional Standards Authority for Health and Social Care
PSNI	Pharmaceutical Society of Northern Ireland
ROA 1974	Rehabilitation of Offenders Act 1974
RPS	Royal Pharmaceutical Society of Great Britain
SGC	Sentencing Guidelines Council
SJP	structured judgment process
SMART	specific, measurable, achievable, relevant, time based
SOR	Sex Offenders Register
SRA	Solicitors Regulation Authority
SVGA 2006	Safeguarding Vulnerable Groups Act 2006
UKCP	United Kingdom Council for Psychotherapy
UPC	unprofessional conduct

CHAPTER 1

General legal principles and preliminary matters; human rights, charges and abuse of process

continued

Key points

Key legal issues in fitness to practise proceedings[1]

- *Overarching objective:* The fundamental purpose of all proceedings brought by healthcare regulators is to protect the public. This has three elements to it: a) protecting and promoting the health, safety and wellbeing of the public; b) promoting and maintaining public confidence in the profession; c) promoting and maintaining proper standards and conduct for members of the professions.
- *Fit to practise:* Means being competent, respectable, honest, trustworthy, able to work with patients and others, and in sufficiently good health to practise.
- *Unprofessional conduct (UPC):* Means conduct in a registrant's professional or personal life that falls seriously short of that expected of a professional and is morally blameworthy or deserving of public opprobrium. (See also *Misconduct* below.)
- *The European Convention on Human Rights (ECHR):* Applies to regulatory proceedings, although it may not if there is no prospect of a sanction affecting a registrant's ability to practise. The most important articles are Article 6 (right to a fair trial) and Article 8 (right to privacy).
- *Charges:* A registrant should be informed of the allegation and supporting facts promptly, in plain language, accurately and in sufficient detail to answer them. Serious allegations such as dishonesty, sexual misconduct, etc must be pleaded.
- *Amending charges:* Should be done as soon as practicable but may be done later if no unfairness is caused. A registrant must be given time to assess and re-prepare his or her case.
- *Delay:* A case should be heard within a reasonable time. If there is delay it will not found an abuse of process unless incurable unfairness is caused. No abuse flows from delay caused by a registrant.
- *Disclosure:* A regulator has a continuing duty to review the unused material it holds and disclose material that may undermine its case or may assist the registrant. There is no duty on the regulator to gather evidence that helps the registrant. However, if a registrant is prejudiced by a lack of access to material a regulator can readily obtain, it should assist if it considers it reasonable so to do. Failure by a regulator to provide reasons may found an abuse of process argument.

Interim orders hearing

- *Burden and standard of proof:* The regulator brings the case and, while there is no strict burden and standard as understood in a full fitness to practise (FTP) hearing, an interim orders tribunal may only impose conditions or suspend a registrant when it is *satisfied that there may be impairment* of fitness which poses a *real risk* to the public, the public interest or the profession.

1 Regulators may use slightly different terminology when referring to a registrant's conduct or the stages of a hearing. However most terms are generic or easily understood.

- *Evidence*: Information may be scant. No evidence is called. The registrant is permitted to make representations. The interim orders tribunal makes no findings of fact.
- *Decision*: Any order must be *necessary* to protect the public, *otherwise in the public interest* (which includes upholding confidence in and standing of the profession) or in the registrant's interest.
- *Reasons*: Reasons must be given for any order and the length of the order.

Full fitness to practise hearings

- *Evidence:* Hearsay is admissible even if it is the principal evidence, but there should be safeguards and the overall fairness of proceedings should be carefully assessed.
- *Evidence:* Character is important at *all* stages of an FTP hearing and the tribunal must be carefully advised on the evidential use and weight of good or bad character.
- *Tribunal impartiality:* The tribunal should be, and be seen to be, divorced from any interest in the allegations, the parties or the result. (This also applies to interim orders tribunals.)
- *Legally Qualified Chair (LQC):* Means a barrister or solicitor who chairs the tribunal which may therefore sit without a legal assessor. The LQC will lead and advise the tribunal on issues of law which should, in the main, be done in open session. An LQC has no casting vote. LQCs must be careful that they 'chair' proceedings and do not 'direct' them.
- *Legal assessor:* Is there to advise on law and procedure. The legal assessor plays no part in determining facts. Advice should be given with all parties present. The legal assessor is also there to assist (but not advise) the parties on disputed law or procedure. (This also applies to interim orders tribunals.)
- *Specialist advisers:* Are present to help interpret expert evidence. Advice should be given with all parties present so they may challenge it if they wish.
- *Legal representation:* A registrant is entitled to be represented at FTP or interim order hearings since these may materially affect the right to practise.
- *Absence of registrant:* Provided all reasonable effort has been made to inform the registrant, the interim order or FTP hearing may proceed in his or her absence.
- *Staged process:* The FTP tribunal will: a) consider evidence to make findings of fact; b) determine current impairment based upon such misconduct or deficient performance as is proved on the facts; c) consider what sanction is necessary to meet any identified risk.
- *Burden and standard of proof regarding the facts:* The burden is on the regulator. The standard is the balance of probability.
- *Half-time submissions:* May be made in accordance with the case of *R v Galbraith* (see para 2.384 below).
- *Impairment:* Is a question of *judgment* for the tribunal. There is no burden or standard of proof. It may be based on past facts but impair-

ment must be *current*. The tribunal must consider matters looking forward and assess risk whether in misconduct, performance, etc.

- *Misconduct:* Difficult to define, but it is a *serious failure* to adhere to accepted professional standards. It means more than just negligence. It is likely to be repeat behaviour, but may only be one serious event. (See also *UPC* above.)
- *Deficient professional performance:* Means conduct in practice or, practice-related activities, that has *fallen far short of the standards expected of a reasonably competent practitioner* and done so on more than one occasion. One exceptionally serious event may suffice. A registrant will be required to undergo assessment.
- *Criminal findings:* Are always treated with the utmost seriousness, they may, and frequently do, found a case in misconduct.
- *Adverse health:* Poor health that affects the quality of service to patients or their safety may found a case of impairment. A registrant will be required to undergo assessment.
- *Determination by another professional body:* May also found a case in impairment.
- *Sanctions:* Should be *proportionate and no more than necessary* to meet the risk identified by the tribunal in their finding of current impairment. The interests of the public, patients and profession come before that of the practitioner albeit the public should not be deprived of a competent registrant longer than is necessary to meet the risk. Cases of dishonesty, sexual misconduct and child pornography are always treated very seriously. Addictions may be met by conditions to facilitate the registrant's safe return to practice. Likewise deficient performance, but the emphasis is on safety and if it cannot be secured then suspension or erasure will result.
- *Jurisdiction:* Matters that occurred outside the UK and/or before a registrant was registered may nonetheless found a case because the emphasis is on public protection and the profession.
- *Key documents and rules:* The regulator's published guidance will be carefully considered by a tribunal particularly when considering sanctions based on breaches. Each regulator has its own procedural rules to follow in addition to the matters set out in this chapter.
- *Reasons:* The tribunal should give *sufficient* reasons on the facts for the registrant to understand what has been proved against him or her. The tribunal should give *full and detailed* reasons on impairment and sanction sufficient to be clear to any reviewing tribunal or court.
- *Voluntary erasure/removal:* A process whereby some registrants are able to withdraw from their profession by applying to their regulator for removal from the register. It is only permitted if there are no FTP issues, or no serious FTP issues, and the latter are admitted. The registrant should genuinely be leaving practice and it must be in the public interest to be dealt with in this way (eg, in cases involving serious health problems).
- *Tribunal:* The multitude of healthcare regulators use a wide variety of names including tribunal, panel and committee. Many of these have

subdivisions such as health committee or conduct committee. In chapter 1 the term *tribunal* has been used to include all such names. If a specific type or name of tribunal is important to the point being discussed or stems from a case report, then the proper name is used.

Introduction

1.1 All healthcare regulators that deal with a registrant's[2] fitness to practise (FTP) are concerned with the same broad values – namely, upholding patient safety and maintaining the standards of the professions such that the public may have confidence in healthcare providers. This necessarily involves receiving, investigating and determining matters of complaint. There are a number of fundamental legal principles applicable to these regulatory functions and any proceedings that follow.

1.2 These values have now been re-emphasised and enshrined in statute by some regulators. For example, Medical Act 1983 s1(1A) provides that the fundamental purpose of proceedings is to protect the public. This has three elements to it: protecting and promoting the health, safety and well-being of the public; promoting and maintaining public confidence in the profession; and promoting and maintaining proper standards and conduct for members of the professions.[3] Likewise, articles 3(4) and (4A) of the Nursing and Midwifery Order (NMO) 2001, as amended, refer in almost identical language to the overarching objective of protecting the public and the same three elements.

1.3 However, while the emphasis is and must always be on protecting the public and the public interest, it is worth remembering that these interests may be met by the rehabilitation and retraining of a registrant who has erred as much as by his or her removal from any register. For this reason, there is and always should be a theme of fairness and proportionality running through all proceedings from investigation to sanction.

1.4 While the principles affect all who serve or care for the public, this book deals with healthcare professionals regulated by the General Medical Council (GMC), Nursing and Midwifery Council (NMC), General Dental Council (GDC), General Optical Council (GOC), General Osteopathic Council (GOsC), the Health and Care Professions Council (HCPC) and the General Pharmaceutical Council (GPhC).

1.5 To emphasise the separation between the presenting/prosecuting regulator and the decision-making body, the GMC and HCPC have both established independent tribunals. GMC proceedings are held at the Medical Practitioners Tribunal Service (MPTS), while HCPC proceedings are held at the Health and Care Professionals Tribunal Service (HCPTS). While other regulators have not followed suit, they operate based on the separation of these roles within the regulator's organisation. In October 2017 the

2 The term 'registrant' is used as a generic term to cover healthcare practitioners whose practice and conduct are governed by regulatory bodies.

3 Medical Act 1983 s1(1A) (as amended by the General Medical Council (Fitness to Practice and Over-arching Objective) and the Professional Standards Authority for Health and Social Care (References to Court) Order 2015 SI No 794.

government issued a consultation paper entitled *Promoting professionalism reforming regulation*, the findings of which may impact upon the number, status and function of many of the healthcare regulators.

1.6 Perhaps the most oft-stated principle in legal proceedings is that individuals have a 'right to a fair trial'. Whether this is expressed in terms of European or domestic legislation and/or case-law, it encompasses several issues including delay, disclosure of information, attendance at hearings, admission of evidence, reasons for decisions, the effect of sanctions and so on. Regulatory proceedings, while now recognised as being firmly civil in nature, fall somewhere between criminal and civil in process and effect. As such, guidance on some of the above case-issues and the way they are dealt with may be drawn from both the civil and criminal branches of the law.

1.7 Despite the obvious similarity between regulatory and criminal proceedings in terms of charges, the adversarial nature of hearings and the imposition and effect of sanctions, there is a continued drive towards emphasising the civil nature of regulatory hearings. This has led to a reluctance by some to accept the applicability of settled authorities in the criminal field and the constant re-litigation of points such as the meaning of dishonesty (of which more later). This has created uncertainty in regulatory proceedings, particularly over matters for which there is no civil case guidance such as character evidence. In addition, while hearsay is now regarded as admissible pursuant to civil rules of evidence, the principles from criminal cases are used in assessing whether it is fair to do so.

1.8 There seems little benefit in this continued argument. If an authority is clear, sound and its application results in a fair hearing, tribunals would do well to adopt the principles irrespective of its originating jurisdiction. In this way a useful body of regulatory authorities and principles may emerge.

1.9 Matters are complicated by the fact that each of the regulators has its own set of procedural rules or 'orders of council'. While there are common themes, the wording is often different for each regulator and this can lead to different considerations. Given this, it is important to ensure that a registrant's case has been properly referred to the correct tribunal.

1.10 Each regulator has its own staged process and some apply slightly different tests. It is important to be aware of these differences when considering case-management, since non-compliance with directions may lead to adverse inferences. Furthermore, some regulators control cases by way of a case-manager, while others have management meetings or hearings and some a combination of both. The same caution should be applied to reviews post-hearing. While the basic principles of law may be the same, there are nuances of language, procedure and style that may wrong-foot the unwary.

1.11 Examples of differences are:

- Until recently, some regulators did not allow for service by email or only some documents or notices and not others. This should be checked carefully regarding each document or notice.
- Some tribunals hear submissions, retire and make a decision at each stage of facts, impairment and sanction. Others retire and consider all matters at the same time.
- Some regulators (eg GOsC) decide upon unprofessional conduct (UPC) which is not limited to matters of current impairment and does not include the 'impairment' stage of the process.

- Some regulators have a 'fitness to practise tribunal' (others call this a panel or committee) which hears a variety of cases including matters of conduct and/or health, whereas others have a separate Conduct and Competence Committee (CCC) and a Health Committee (HC).
- As can be seen, regulators have different names for their panels despite fulfilling the same functions.

1.12 In this chapter, the term 'tribunal' is used as a generic term to cover the FTP tribunals, CCCs, interim orders tribunals (IOTs) and the other panels or committees operated by the various regulators. Furthermore, while reference may be made to the GMC, NMC or other rules to introduce or illustrate a point, care should be taken to apply the correct council rules/orders of council when arguing matters pertinent to a case.

1.13 One notable difference in process is that the FTP tribunal of the GOsC does not make findings regarding current impairment. Instead, it considers whether any misconduct found proved amounts to UPC. This means that historical misconduct which might be regarded by other regulators as remediated by age and/or subsequent good behaviour leading to no current impairment, can still be marked by a finding of UPC. The proceedings then move to the issue of sanction at which point the date of the UPC and intervening behaviour is considered alongside the well-known issues of public interest and protection.

1.14 The principles outlined below approximate the timeline of proceedings from charge to sanction.

The meaning of fitness to practise

1.15 The following principles are adapted from a policy statement by the GMC.[4] While they are formulated for doctors, they set out the basic headings under which the fitness to practise of all healthcare professionals are likely to be assessed. Key words are in italics.

1.16 To practise safely, registrants must be *competent* in what they do. Registrants must establish and maintain *effective relationships* with patients, *respect personal boundaries* and a patient's autonomy, and act responsibly and appropriately if the registrant or a colleague fall ill and his or her performance suffers.

1.17 But these attributes, while essential, are not enough. Registrants have a *respected* position in society and their work gives them privileged access to patients, some of whom may be very vulnerable. A registrant whose conduct has shown that he or she cannot *justify the trust* placed in him or her should not continue in unrestricted practice while that remains the case.

1.18 In short, the public is entitled to expect that their healthcare providers are *fit to practise*, and follow principles of *good practice* published by the relevant regulator.[5]

4 Approved in 2001.

5 Examples are: *Good medical practice* (GMC); *Standards for Pharmacy Professionals* (GPhC); *The Code. Professional standards of practice and behaviour for nurses and midwives* (NMC).

1.19 These principles or guidelines are updated and modernised from time to time, albeit that such modernisation does not always lead to greater clarity. While they are referred to as 'guidance', they are regarded by any tribunal as the bedrock of good practice. Breaches are cited by presenting advocates as indicative of misconduct, impairment and the reason for sanctions.

1.20 Because many of the guidelines overlap, it is important to consider carefully which ones really apply to a case. There are occasions when multiple breaches are cited, albeit there is only one matter under consideration. While such citation may be valid in some cases, there are times when one or two guidelines will properly indicate the central concern and/or gravity of a case. With multiple citation there is a real risk that the severity of misconduct is judged by the number of rules breached when they are simply examples of one central breach.

1.21 One citation of negligible benefit to a tribunal is alleging that a registrant has breached the guideline to 'uphold the reputation of the profession' or 'keep to the code'. This is stating the obvious, despite which it is trotted out on a regular basis. Advocates and thereafter tribunals would do well to look critically at which one or two breaches really encompass the misconduct and stop referring to multiple make-weights and technical breaches that add nothing to a case.

1.22 As an example of guidelines, the GPhC in its *Standards for pharmacy professionals handbook* (May 2017) sets out nine clear standards that registrants *must* adhere to:

1) Provide person-centred care
2) Work in partnership with others
3) Communicate effectively
4) Maintain, develop and use their professional knowledge and skill
5) Use professional judgment
6) Behave in a professional manner
7) Respect and maintain the person's confidentiality and privacy
8) Speak up when they have concerns or when things go wrong
9) Demonstrate leadership

The handbook then provides detailed guidance on each of these standards.

1.23 The current NMC equivalent called *The Code. Professional standards of practice and behaviour for nurses and midwives* (effective from 31 March 2015) includes four major headings:

1) Prioritise people
2) Practise effectively
3) Preserve safety
4) Promote professionalism and trust

Each heading is then followed by several rules and sub-rules, some of which understandably complement or overlap each other.

1.24 The GOsC has four such subject areas:

1) Communication and patient partnership
2) Knowledge, skills and performance
3) Safety and quality in practice
4) Professionalism

Again, each area contains various guidelines to adhere to.

1.25 While all the regulators and their handbooks or codes refer to these as guidelines, the terms 'will' or 'must' denotes that some are mandatory, the term 'should' is an indication as to how to meet the standard, the term 'may' denotes a choice to be made using professional judgment. Breaches of these are cited as prima facie evidence of misconduct and/or impairment.

1.26 In respect of doctors, the 2006 (old) version of *Good medical practice* set out similar standards in a concise and affirmative way under the following main headings:[6]

- *Good (clinical) care* – registrants must provide good standards of clinical care, must practise within the limits of their competence, and must ensure that patients are not put at unnecessary risk.
- *Maintaining good (medical) practice* – registrants must keep up to date with developments in their field, maintain their skills and audit their performance.
- *Relationships with patients* – registrants must develop and maintain successful relationships with their patients, by respecting patients' autonomy and other rights.
- *Working with colleagues* – registrants must work effectively with their colleagues.
- *Teaching and training* – where registrants have teaching responsibilities they must develop the skills, attitudes and practices of a competent teacher.
- *Probity* – registrants must be honest and trustworthy.
- *Health* – registrants must not allow their own health condition to endanger patients.

1.27 In April 2013 a new version of *Good medical practice* recast the above in a more discursive way adopting four 'domains' of:

1) Knowledge, skills and performance
2) Safety and quality
3) Communication, partnership and teamwork
4) Maintaining trust

This was further updated in April 2014 to include minimum requirements and standards of the English language.

1.28 The intention behind the 2013 update is said to have been to make the guidelines less directive and more of a partnership, however the terms 'you must' or 'you should' remain frequent. It is perhaps unfortunate that well-known and easily understood phrases such as 'registrants must be honest and trustworthy' and 'probity is at the heart of the profession' have been dispensed with.

1.29 In common with the other guidance, the new version of *Good medical practice* has a bullet-point list at the start of the guidance which neatly encapsulates good practice. They are set out below.

6 Drawn from *Good medical practice 2006* but of general application.

Patients must be able to trust doctors with their lives and health. To justify that trust you must show respect for human life and make sure your practice meets the standards expected of you in four domains.

Knowledge, skills and performance

- Make the care of your patient your first concern.
- Provide a good standard of practice and care.
  - Keep your professional knowledge and skills up to date.
  - Recognise and work within the limits of your competence.

Safety and quality

- Take prompt action if you think that patient safety, dignity or comfort is being compromised.
- Protect and promote the health of patients and the public.

Communication, partnership and teamwork

- Treat patients as individuals and respect their dignity.
  - Treat patients politely and considerately.
  - Respect patients' right to confidentiality.
- Work in partnership with patients.
  - Listen to, and respond to, their concerns and preferences.
  - Give patients the information they want or need in a way they can understand.
  - Respect patients' right to reach decisions with you about their treatment and care.
  - Support patients in caring for themselves to improve and maintain their health.
- Work with colleagues in the ways that best serve patients' interests.

Maintaining trust

- Be honest and open and act with integrity.
- Never discriminate unfairly against patients or colleagues.
- Never abuse your patients' trust in you or the public's trust in the profession

You are personally accountable for your professional practice and must always be prepared to justify your decisions and actions.

There is a clear emphasis on working in partnership with patients, providing detailed explanations enabling them to make informed choices rather than telling them what to do. In addition, respect for the dignity of colleagues, patients and their relatives are emphasised.

1.30 The Introduction of *Good medical practice*, 'Professionalism', sets out what is or should be at the heart of all healthcare practice:

1. Patients need good doctors. Good doctors make the care of their patients their first concern: they are competent, keep their knowledge and skills up to date, establish and maintain good relationships with patients and colleagues, are honest and trustworthy, and act with integrity and within the law.
2. Good doctors work in partnership with patients and respect their rights to privacy and dignity. They treat each patient as an individual. They do their best to make sure all patients receive good care and treatment that will support them to live as well as possible, whatever their illness or disability.
3. *Good medical practice* describes what is expected of all doctors registered with the General Medical Council (GMC). It is your responsibility to be familiar with *Good medical practice* and the explanatory guidance which supports it, and to follow the guidance they contain.

4. You must use your judgement in applying the principles to the various situations you will face as a doctor, whether or not you hold a licence to practise, whatever field of medicine you work in, and whether or not you routinely see patients. You must be prepared to explain and justify your decisions and actions.

There is a clear emphasis on remaining up to date with and using one's own judgment to apply the above principles whatever the situation.

1.31 The healthcare regulators have legal powers to act where it appears that a registrant's fitness to practise may be affected by poor skills or performance, ill-health, misconduct, UPC or a criminal conviction or caution.

The healthcare councils' role in regulation

1.32 All human beings make mistakes from time to time. Healthcare professionals are no different. While occasional one-off mistakes need to be thoroughly investigated and any harm put right by those involved, they are unlikely in themselves to indicate a fitness to practise problem. *Good medical practice* (2013) put it this way:

> . . . you must demonstrate . . . that you work in line with the principles and values set out in this guidance. Serious or persistent failure to follow this guidance will put your registration at risk.[7]

1.33 A question of fitness to practise is likely to arise if:

- *A registrant's performance has harmed patients or put patients at risk of harm.* A risk of harm will usually be demonstrated by a series of incidents that cause concern locally. These incidents may indicate persistent technical failings or other repeated departures from good practice which are not being, or cannot be, safely managed locally or local management has been tried and has failed.
- *A registrant has shown a deliberate or reckless disregard of clinical responsibilities towards patients.* An isolated lapse from high standards of conduct – such as an atypical rude outburst – would not in itself suggest that the registrant's fitness to practise is in question. Misconduct, whether criminal or not, which indicates a lack of integrity on the part of the registrant, an unwillingness to practise ethically or responsibly, or a serious lack of insight into obvious problems of poor practice will bring a registrant's registration into question.
- *A registrant's health is compromising patient safety.* The regulator does not need to be involved merely because a registrant is unwell, even if the illness is serious. However, a registrant's fitness to practise is brought into question if it appears that the registrant has a serious medical condition (including an addiction to drugs or alcohol) *and* the registrant does not appear to be following appropriate medical advice about modifying his or her practice as necessary in order to minimise the risk to patients.
- *A registrant has abused a patient's trust or violated a patient's autonomy or other fundamental rights.* Conduct that shows that a registrant has acted

7 *Good medical practice 2013*, p5.

without regard for patients' rights or feelings, or has abused his or her professional position as a registrant, will usually give rise to questions about a registrant's fitness to practise.

- *A registrant has behaved dishonestly, fraudulently or in a way designed to mislead or harm others.* The registrant's behaviour was such that public confidence in doctors generally might be undermined if the GMC did not take action.

1.34 The advice above is only illustrative of the sort of behaviour which could call registration into question. *Good medical practice* and other published guidance provide a more complete picture of behaviour of this kind, but even that is not exhaustive. The outcome of any case will always depend on its own particular facts.

1.35 While the above is adapted from guidance published by the GMC, it encapsulates the issues that should guide all healthcare practitioners. The other professions covered by this work have similar codes of conduct or statements of ethics.

1.36 As the above makes clear, everyone makes mistakes, and the majority are dealt with by means other than fitness to practise procedures. It is only when a practitioner falls 'seriously short' of what is expected and this adversely impacts upon patients or the profession that it is appropriate to instigate proceedings.

The European Convention on Human Rights

> It is undoubtedly the case that the European Convention on Human Rights (ECHR) applies to regulatory proceedings, although there may be argument when there is no prospect of suspension or erasure.
>
> The better approach to case preparation and presentation is to adopt the *spirit* of, in particular, Article 6 (right to a fair trial), the letter of which is frequently reflected in domestic case-law.
>
> The two articles of the ECHR which have most relevance to regulatory proceedings are Articles 6 and 8. They respectively provide for what are colloquially called the 'right to a fair trial' and the 'right to privacy'.

Article 6

1.37 Article 6 of the ECHR guarantees certain minimum rights when facing a trial and provides as follows:

> 1. In the determination of his civil rights and obligations or of any criminal charge against him, everyone is entitled to a fair and public hearing within a reasonable time by an independent and impartial tribunal established by law. Judgment shall be pronounced publicly but the press and public may be excluded from all or part of the trial in the interest of morals, public order or national security in a democratic society, where the interests of juveniles or the protection of the private lives of the parties so require, or to the extent strictly necessary in the opinion of the court in special circumstances where publicity would prejudice the interests of justice.

2. Everyone charged with a criminal offence shall be presumed innocent until proved guilty according to law.

3. Everyone charged with a criminal offence has the following minimum rights:

(a) to be informed promptly, in a language which he understands and in detail, of the nature and cause of the accusation against him;
(b) to have adequate time and facilities for the preparation of his defence;
(c) to defend himself in person or through legal assistance of his own choosing or, if he has not sufficient means to pay for legal assistance, to be given it free when the interests of justice so require;
(d) to examine or have examined witnesses against him and to obtain the attendance and examination of witnesses on his behalf under the same conditions as witnesses against him;
(e) to have the free assistance of an interpreter if he cannot understand or speak the language used in court.

1.38 Therefore:

a) A proper hearing should be:
   - fair;
   - public;
   - reasonably timeous.
b) A proper tribunal should be:
   - legally empowered;
   - impartial;
   - independent.
c) A defendant has the right to:
   - prompt and proper information;
   - time and facility to prepare;
   - choose to represent himself or herself, or appoint a lawyer;
   - funds for a lawyer if necessary;
   - challenge and question his accuser(s);
   - an interpreter if one is needed.

1.39 The above all seem quite straightforward and obvious, but the principles have been applied/misapplied and interpreted/re-interpreted through case-law such that they do not always appear to mean what they say. There is also the issue of whether the ECHR applies to some regulatory proceedings at all.

1.40 Since the majority decision of the European Court of Human Rights (ECtHR) in *Le Compte, Van Leuven and De Meyere v Belgium*[8] it has been accepted that a decision of a professional tribunal affecting the right to practise the profession is a determination of civil rights and obligations.

1.41 In *Wickramsinghe v UK*[9] it was held that disciplinary proceedings before the GMC constituted a civil rather than criminal case. Similarly in *General Medical Council v Michael Pembrey*[10] it was held that Article 6 was applicable to Professional Conduct Committee proceedings since these were civil proceedings within the meaning of the article. This was endorsed by the Privy Council in *Preiss v General Dental Council.*[11]

8 (1982) 4 EHRR 1.
9 [1998] EHRLR 338.
10 [2002] Lloyd's Rep Med 434.
11 [2001] Lloyd's Rep Med 491.

1.42 The first line of Article 6(1) makes it plain that the provisions will apply whenever the outcome of proceedings determines a person's civil rights. This includes a registrant's right to continue to practise in his or her profession. Thus it applies in principle to any disciplinary process where erasure or suspension is possible – see *Ghosh v General Medical Council,*[12] a decision of the Privy Council. There are, however, two lines of approach to this.

1.43 In *R v General Medical Council ex p Kypros Nicolaides*[13] Tucker J said that the question of whether Article 6 applies to the proceedings does not arise at the outset but depends on the outcome of the case. This is because the result may not affect his or her right to practise.

1.44 On the other hand, in *Tehrani v United Kingdom Central Council for Nursing Midwifery and Health Visiting*[14] it was said that:

> . . . if the petitioner can establish that the disciplinary proceedings *could* result in a finding that would constitute a determination of her civil rights and obligations, the decision to initiate those disciplinary proceedings is open to challenge as being incompatible with the petitioner's convention rights.[15] [Emphasis added.]

1.45 In *R (Johnson) v Nursing and Midwifery Council,*[16] a case before the Professional Conduct Committee, Beatson J approached the case from both the domestic and the ECHR viewpoints. In *R (Madan) v General Medical Council*[17] Richards J accepted that Article 6 applied with respect to interim order proceedings where an interim suspension order was made because it substantially affected M's right to practise.

1.46 The distinction in approach based on consequences is also apparent when considering the cases of *Kulkarni v Milton Keynes Hospital NHS Trust*[18] and *R (Puri) v Bradford Teaching Hospitals NHS Foundation Trust.*[19] *Kulkarni* is discussed at para 2.308 under the issue of representation. There it was decided that Article 6 was engaged when K faced grave charges (alleged sexual assault) that, if proved, would have a severe impact on his ability to work. This clearly reflects the discussion on the applicability of the ECHR in *Ghosh v General Medical Council*[20] above (para 1.42).

1.47 In *Puri,* P appealed against his dismissal on grounds of misconduct following an internal disciplinary hearing. Blair J held that the disciplinary proceedings did not prevent P from working in either NHS or private practice unlike those in *Kulkarni* which constituted a criminal offence if proved. Article 6 was thus not engaged.

1.48 In *R (Bonhoeffer) v General Medical Council*[21] Stadlen J approached the issue of admitting hearsay evidence under rule 34 of the GMC (FTP)

12 [2001] 1 WLR 1915.
13 [2001] Lloyd's Rep Med 525.
14 [2001] SC 581.
15 Per Lord Mackay of Drumadoon at para [33].
16 [2008] EWHC 885 (Admin).
17 [2001] EWHC 322 (Admin).
18 [2009] EWCA Civ 789.
19 [2011] EWHC 970 (Admin).
20 [2001] 1 WLR 1915.
21 [2011] EWHC 1585 (Admin).

Rules 2004[22] (which provide for the admission of evidence provided it is relevant, fair and desirable so to do) by reference to Article 6 and both criminal and disciplinary case-law.

1.49 In *Selvarajan v General Medical Council* Blake J observed that: 'It is common ground that disciplinary proceedings that might deprive the Appellant of his livelihood engage the Article 6 obligation . . .'.[23]

1.50 When dealing with the issue of disclosure in *R (McCarthy) v (1) The Visitors to the Inns of Court, (2) The Bar Standards Board*[24] (BSB) Burnett LJ observed that: 'There is no difficulty in accepting the proposition that the civil limb of Article 6 applies to professional disciplinary proceedings including those prosecuted by the BSB.' He continued to observe that 'the question whether a finding of non-disclosure in disciplinary proceedings calls for a rehearing is answered in the same way whether it is approached via the common law or article 6'.[25] The ultimate question is whether the proceedings as a whole were fair.[26]

1.51 The above is a helpful observation in that it reinforces the notion that whether the argument is based on European or domestic law, the question and the answer is and should be the same. The case is discussed more fully at para 1.255 below regarding disclosure. See also *White v Nursing and Midwifery Council; Turner v Nursing and Midwifery Council*[27] and *Thorneycroft v Nursing and Midwifery Council*[28] discussed under hearsay at paras 1.127 below.

1.52 It is perhaps rather artificial and unhelpful to decide whether to apply Article 6 principles depending on the possible outcome of a case, but for the moment that appears to be the position. In any event, there is considerable overlap between the principles of European law, domestic law, natural justice and many of the regulator's own rules of practice. For that reason it is submitted that the better approach is to proceed on the basis that Article 6 does apply both in letter and in spirit unless the contrary is proved. That is certainly the approach adopted in this chapter.

1.53 The author takes comfort in that approach from the case of *Perry v Nursing and Midwifery Council*[29] which deals with interim orders. P sought to argue that his Article 6 and Article 8 rights had been infringed by his being prevented from exploring the substance of the allegations he faced or from giving evidence about them. While the court ultimately rejected P's reasoning, it proceeded on the basis that Articles 6 and 8 were engaged, citing *Micallef v Malta*[30] in so doing.

1.54 In its reasoning, the court adopted the approach in *Micallef* that while some rights and safeguards are inalienable, other rights may apply only to an extent compatible with the nature of interim order proceedings. Both

22 Contained in the Schedule to the General Medical Council (Fitness to Practise) Rules Order of Council 2004 SI No 2608.

23 [2008] EWHC 182 (Admin) at [10].

24 [2015] EWCA Civ 12 at [23].

25 At [24].

26 At [25].

27 [2014] EWHC 520 (Admin).

28 [2014] EWHC 1565 (Admin).

29 [2013] EWCA Civ 145.

30 [2010] 50 EHRR 37.

parties should be permitted to make submissions on the need for an order and the registrant may give evidence as to the impact any such order may have. The tribunal may assess the weight of evidence and reject what is plainly wrong, but they do not make a judgment on the allegation.

Public hearings

1.55 The norm is for interim order hearings to be held in private and FTP hearings to be heard in public. However, if an FTP case concerns or touches upon issues of health, the tribunal will go into private session while those matters are dealt with. There may be circumstances in which a tribunal hears evidence in private session which is unrelated to health matters. However, this is the exception and it is incumbent on the party applying for a private hearing to prove that it is justified.

1.56 All regulatory tribunals now have the power to adopt such measures as they consider appropriate to prevent the quality of a witness' evidence from being adversely affected. Witnesses may be treated as vulnerable witnesses if the quality of their evidence is likely to be adversely affected because of their youth, physical disability, mental disorder, impairment of intellectual or social function, making sexual allegations against a registrant, or complaining of intimidation. These special measures may include the use of video-links, pre-recorded evidence, interpreters, intermediaries, screens, limitation on cross-examination and finally hearing evidence in private. However, the latter is the exception and cannot be insisted upon by a witness.

1.57 In *Miller v General Medical Council*[31] the GMC applied to hear an entire case in private. Witness A indicated that he would only give evidence on those terms. He would not give evidence even with other special measures such as a screen or anonymising his name in the record of proceedings. The tribunal granted the application on the basis that A would probably not give evidence otherwise, and M was not prejudiced since he could cross-examine and present his case in any event. M appealed the decision on the bases that the GMC had not established that A had a settled intention not to give evidence or in the alternative, there was no objectively reasonable foundation for that intention. M argued that he was unlawfully denied the right to a public hearing.

1.58 HHJ Pelling quashed the order on several grounds. The starting point is the registrant's right to a public hearing. This is distinct from the public interest in open justice. The onus is on the GMC to prove that a departure from the default position is both necessary and proportionate. This was an extreme order and there had been no attempt to provide a lesser relief such as screens, video-link, hearing A in private or anonymising A's evidence. The GMC did not call A to give evidence at the application or appeal, so his actual intention had not been fully assessed. The GMC had failed to meet the test of necessity and proportionality.

1.59 HHJ Pelling placed emphasis on *R v Legal Aid Board ex p Kaim Todner*[32] which provides a general rationale as to why hearings should be in public 'unless justice requires it'.[33]

31 [2013] EWHC 1934 (Admin).

32 [1998] EWCA Civ 958, paras 4–5.

33 Para 5.

1.60 The principles include that open justice:

- deters inappropriate behavior by the court;
- maintains public confidence in the administration of justice;
- demonstrates that justice is administered impartially;
- may result in the discovery of evidence that would remain hidden if proceedings were behind closed doors or witnesses were anonymous;
- reduces the likelihood of inaccurate or ill-informed comment;
- allows the restriction of secrecy only to cases where justice would be frustrated without it reduces the risk of contempt proceedings.

The burden is on the party seeking derogation from the principle of the registrant's right to open justice and, second, the public interest in the same. However, none of the above should preclude a registrant from applying, or a tribunal ruling, to hear an appropriate case in private. The principles affecting the quality of a witness's evidence, their ability to participate in proceedings or their or their family's personal safety apply equally to registrants. Appropriate cases may include where there is a real risk of suicide by, or assault upon, the registrant, or retribution by or upon his/her family. Any ruling may be reviewed during proceedings, since findings of fact or misconduct, etc may affect the balancing exercise as between the registrant's interest and the public interest.

Article 8

1.61 Article 8 of the ECHR provides that:

> 1. Everyone has the right to respect for his private and family life, his home and his correspondence.
>
> 2. There shall be no interference by a public authority with the exercise of this right except such as is in accordance with the law and is necessary in a democratic society in the interests of national security, public safety or the economic well-being of the country, for the prevention of disorder or crime, for the protection of health or morals, or for the protection of the rights and freedoms of others.

1.62 While Article 8 is more frequently concerned with the rights of patients infringed by healthcare personnel or regulators through mismanagement or misuse of information, the case of *Bonhoeffer* (above para 1.48 and discussed fully under hearsay evidence at para 2.109 below) demonstrates its applicability to regulatory proceedings.

1.63 The 'right to privacy', as this is frequently called, confers a 'right to respect' for the four areas mentioned (privacy, family, home, correspondence), however the protection is qualified not absolute. The right may be infringed in the circumstances specified under clause 2. In regulatory proceedings the most relevant circumstances are: in accordance with the law and *necessary* for public safety, or the protection of health or the rights of others.

1.64 There are two aspects to the right: first, a right to protection from interference by public authorities; and second, there may be a duty imposed upon authorities to secure respect for those rights from others.

1.65 Regulatory bodies are entitled to investigate allegations and bring proceedings with the intention of protecting the profession, the public or the practitioner. Proceedings brought for these reasons are clearly capable of satisfying the qualification of Article 8 thereby permitting interference with a registrant's rights. However, as with all matters of competing rights such as those between the registrant, the complainant and the public interest, there is a balance to be struck. Three particular criticisms may be levelled at regulatory proceedings: delay, publicity and harsh sanction.

1.66 While these have to date been dealt with as Article 6 matters infringing the right to a fair trial, they may also be raised under Article 8.

Delay and publicity (Articles 6 and 8)

1.67 Regulatory proceedings frequently have a devastating effect upon the registrant and his or her practice, family and private life. This effect is magnified if an interim order is imposed which either suspends the registrant or, seriously curtails his or her ability to practise by way of conditions. The damage is further exacerbated by the fact that regulatory proceedings frequently take many months, sometimes years, to come to a final hearing. In the meantime the registrant is expected to deal with the pressures placed upon his or her family, etc.

1.68 Given that serious and complex criminal allegations are now routinely concluded within a very few months (and rarely beyond a year), lengthy delay in regulatory proceedings may be unjustifiable, particularly where there are few or no witnesses or the facts are hardly disputed. Frequently there appears to be little or no justification for such delay. Part of the problem may be the routine imposition of an 18-month interim order granted on the basis that the Interim Orders Tribunal does not know how long the investigation will take or when the case will come before the FTP Tribunal. Delay – whether caused, contributed to or wholly divorced from an interim order – should be examined in the light of the registrant's Article 8 rights.

1.69 In *R (Johnson and Maggs) v Nursing and Midwifery Council (No 2)*[34] a finding of misconduct (with no sanction) was quashed in a case which took 86 days to hear, was spread over 33 months and concluded over eight years after the registrants were notified of the allegations. By this time the allegations were nine to 13 years in the past. The delay was described as 'disgraceful' and breached Article 6.

1.70 By way of contrast, in *Goodwin v Health and Care Professions Council*[35] a delay of almost two years did not infringe the registrant's right to a hearing within a reasonable time. The case was a complex one with multiple allegations of incompetence across many areas of G's practice and ability.

1.71 The issue of delay as mitigation and in respect of interim orders is discussed more fully at paras 1.180 and 2.71 below. Suffice it to say that in respect of mitigation it may be taken into account, but each case is to be decided on its own facts. As regards interim orders, the administrative court is now more inclined to scrutinise the evidence used to justify a case and the reasons for delay taking account of both the public interest and the registrant's Article 6 and Article 8 rights.

34 [2013] EWHC 2140 (Admin).

35 [2014] EWHC 1897 (Admin).

1.72 Article 8 places a duty on the regulator not to interfere and to prevent interference by others. This must necessarily include others acting upon its behalf namely its investigatory and regulatory arm. Given this, Article 8 may well be engaged when the delay and/or publicity consequent upon proceedings adversely affects the rights protected.

1.73 In *Bonhoeffer* (para 1.62 above) the court took specific note of the fact that serious allegations would adversely affect B's reputation (and thus his private life) if they were proved at first instance even if he were subsequently acquitted on appeal. The damage is already done. The court held that B's right to respect for his reputation and private life are matters to be considered before the case came to trial.

1.74 This healthy dose of reality may be readily imported into an argument regarding the effect that extended delay and publicity has upon a registrant's Article 8 rights even where his or her reputation may not be as eminent as B's.

1.75 See also the case of *Houshian v General Medical Council*[36] at para 2.51 below in which the issue of damage to reputation and to earnings was considered when quashing an interim order to suspend a practitioner.

1.76 Two further cases illustrate the importance of considering Article 8 in regulatory and allied proceedings. Following enhanced Criminal Records Bureau (CRB) checks, the disclosure of allegations that J and A had abused care-home residents was said to breach the registrant's Article 8 rights. In *R (J) v Chief Constable of Devon & Cornwall*[37] the allegations had been investigated by the police who took no action and, the matter was not even referred the NMC. In *R (A) v Chief Constable of Kent*[38] A successfully appealed the dismissal proceedings and, once again neither the NMC, Crown Prosecution Service (CPS) or Independent Safeguarding Authority (ISA) took any action against her.

1.77 *General Dental Council v Rimmer*[39] is a case in which an interference with rights (the privacy of patient records) was ruled to be Article 8 compliant. The GDC wished to obtain R's computerised patient records. Some patients withheld their consent to disclosure. R consented subject to the court ruling that disclosure was appropriate and that reasonable limits and safeguards were in place. Lloyd-Jones J cited comments by Thorpe LJ in *A Health Authority v X and others*,[40] in concluding that, with appropriate safeguards in place, the public interest was best served by the proper investigation of complaints and subsequent administration of disciplinary proceedings. The court balanced the competing interests of patient confidentiality with effective regulatory proceedings and declared that the disclosure was lawful, necessary, proportionate and for a legitimate purpose. It was thus compliant with Article 8.

36 [2012] EWHC 3458 (QB).
37 [2012] EWHC 2996 (Admin).
38 [2013] EWHC 424 (Admin).
39 [2010] EWHC 1049 (Admin).
40 [2001] EWCA Civ 2014.

Sanction

1.78 As regards sanction, much is rightly made of the need to protect the public, professions and uphold standards. Sanctions are imposed which are *necessary* to meet identified risks. However, where there has been delay, publicity, an interim order or other factor that have already adversely affected the registrant's Article 8 rights, there may come a point at which the balance tips in favour of the registrant.

1.79 It is submitted that the adverse effect of sanctions upon a registrant's Article 8 rights *should* be considered in the light of the whole proceedings and the effect they have had to date, not just in isolation. In *Selvarajan v General Medical Council*[41] it was held that delay may be a mitigating factor on sanctions (see para 1.181 below). Given this, and the approach in *Bonhoeffer,* there is no reason why the cumulative effect of proceedings upon a registrant's Article 8 rights should be ignored in mitigation always allowing for deference to the principle of protecting the public.

1.80 This point was reiterated in *Kamberova v Nursing and Midwifery Council,*[42] a case in which K spent many months subject to either an interim suspension or conditions that prevented her from finding work. Following the FTP hearing a 12-month suspension was imposed which K appealed. Dingemans J held that the tribunal should have taken account of the interim order as a matter of fairness and when considering the proportionality of the eventual suspension. In remitting the matter back to the tribunal Dingemans J directed that they take the delay in the appeal procedure into account since to do otherwise would be to disregard the fact that K could end up suspended for longer than 12 months in any event.

1.81 The above was revisited in *Akhtar v General Dental Council,*[43] in which the FTP tribunal's approach of taking an interim suspension order into account was noted with approval.

Charges

Clear, succinct and confined to the evidence

> The particulars of the allegation and the facts upon which they are founded should be clear and settled in advance of any hearing.
>
> If in doubt, clarification and/or further and better particulars should be obtained.
>
> A tribunal may, having heard from both parties, amend either the allegation or the facts provided no injustice is caused but this should be the exception not the rule.

41 [2008] EWHC 182 (Admin).
42 [2016] E WHC 2955 (Admin).
43 [2017] EWHC 1986 (Admin).

1.82 Healthcare regulators are public authorities and, as stated above, the ECHR applies to disciplinary proceedings.[44] An important right in this respect is to have sufficient and proper notice of the allegation.

1.83 Article 6(3) provides that everyone charged with a criminal offence has the following minimum rights:

- to be *informed promptly*, in a language which he or she understands and *in detail*, of the nature and cause of the accusation against him or her;
- to have adequate time and facilities for the preparation of his or her defence.

1.84 While disciplinary proceedings are not criminal in nature (see *Wickramsinghe v UK*[45] above), what follows demonstrates the application of the above rights in disciplinary proceedings.

1.85 Domestic law is clearly supported by the requirements of Article 6. In *Albert and Le Compte v Belgium*[46] the ECtHR indicated that this principle should apply to disciplinary proceedings. Subsequent case-law upheld the requirement to list offences giving the date and place thereof, the relevant articles of the Criminal Code and the name of the victim (see *Brozicek v Italy*[47]).

1.86 In *Gee v General Medical Council*[48] the court held it to be a requirement that the registrant had fair notice of the nature of the evidence to be led in support of the allegations, time to prepare for his defence and, that the tribunal should make plain which of the allegations of fact, if any, they had found proved.

1.87 Healthcare regulators have taken cognisance of the Criminal Procedure Rules (CPR)[49] which require an indictment or charge to contain a statement and description of the offence, the relevant legislation and such particulars of the conduct said to constitute the offence as make it clear what the prosecutor alleges against the defendant.

1.88 In fitness to practise proceedings, a document variously entitled 'notice of proceedings', 'notice of hearing' or similar is used to identify both the case brought against the registrant and the alleged facts upon which it is based. It is one of the most important documents in the case and should be drafted with some care. Although amendments may be made, there are limitations. It is only fair and reasonable that both parties and the tribunal have a firm and settled idea of what the case is about before it is under way.

1.89 Each regulator has its own set of rules,[50] but the central requirements are as follows:

a) Regarding notice:
   - As soon as reasonably practicable after an allegation has been referred to a tribunal, the council's registrar or appointed officer should serve a notice of hearing on the registrant.

44 *Preiss v General Dental Council* [2001] UKPC 36 para [9]; *Ghosh v General Medical Council* [2001] UKPC 29 para [31].

45 [1998] EHRLR 338.

46 (1983) 5 EHRR 533.

47 (1990) 112 EHRR 371.

48 [1987] 1 WLR 564.

49 The rules are regularly updated but the principle of clarity remains.

50 See GMC (FTP) Rules 2004 rr15 and 16 as a good example.

- The notice should particularise the allegation against the practitioner and the facts upon which it is based.

b) Regarding case-management – again the procedures vary. Some regulators employ case managers others use case-management hearings. However, in general either (or their equivalent) may issue directions including such of the following as are appropriate having regard to the nature of the allegation, any representations made by the parties and all other material factors:
   - that each party disclose to or inform the other of:
     - the material they intend to rely upon namely documentary evidence, details of the witnesses (this includes the practitioner if giving evidence), signed witness statements, any expert report and skeleton arguments;
     - time estimates;
     - whether or not the health of the practitioner is to be raised as an issue;
   - that the practitioner indicates, so far as is practicable:
     - whether the allegation is admitted;
     - which facts are admitted and which remain in dispute;
     - which witness evidence is admitted and which witnesses are required for cross-examination; and
     - whether any preliminary legal arguments are to be made;
   - where the allegation is admitted, a direction that the parties produce a statement of agreed facts.

1.90 The above notices and directions post-date the various stages of investigation, case correspondence and/or hearings that occur before referral to the tribunal or, the final hearing. The case is thus already some way (perhaps many months) down the line by the time allegations and notices are drafted. The regulator should be in a position to provide precise particulars of the allegation and the facts. Furthermore, any areas of dispute should be defined and refined in the case-management process. The effect of this is that by the time a case comes before the tribunal the disputed allegations and facts should be clear but, this is not always the case.

1.91 In recent times, the length and detail of notices has increased. This may reflect the requirement to provide sufficient particulars to the registrant so that he or she understands the case against him or her. However, since 'case' has generally been understood to mean the alleged facts as well as how those facts constitute impairment, the consequence has been the inclusion of peripheral or irrelevant details which obscure the real facts relied upon for the issue of impairment. A particularly unhelpful method of drafting is to list multiple charges and sub-charges followed by further charges and sub-charges, relating the latter back to the former. This is often the case with dishonesty and sexual motivation. For example, a registrant may face factual allegations at charges 1–7 (each with sub-charges a/b/c) and at charges 8, 9 or 10 (a,b or c) it is alleged that he or she was dishonest or sexually motivated, as the case may be. If there are one or two alleged incidents and one issue of dishonesty or sexual motivation this is not a problem. However, where there are multiple allegations and multiple states of mind such as dishonesty, lack of integrity, misleading, sexual motivation, inappropriateness, etc, it is a recipe for confusion and causes tribunals real difficulty in their deliberations. In such cases, the drafting of charges by counsel would save both time and expense.

1.92 In *R (Wheeler) v Assistant Commissioner House of the Metropolitan Police*[51] it was alleged that W had failed to carry out duties 'to an acceptable standard', thereby breaching the code of conduct. Stanley Burnton J said:

> Vagueness is a ground for judicial review if it leads to unfairness in the proceedings, and the danger with a vague charge is that the parties, and in particular the respondent, do not know with some precision what is alleged against them, and therefore are not fully able to address those matters in the course of a hearing.[52]

His Lordship commented that while the particulars of a disciplinary charge may be refined following an initial draft, it should be sufficiently particularised well before the hearing for the respondent to know what it is alleged he or she failed to do and, in what respects he or she failed.

1.93 In *Sheill v General Medical Council*[53] Foskett J quashed the tribunal's finding of dishonesty because the head of charge was unspecific regarding the circumstances in which it was alleged that S had made a false claim. His Lordship stated that when it is alleged that a false or dishonest claim had been made in a document it would be usual for the document to be identified by date or description in the charge. This was not done, neither was there any request for further and better particulars before or at the start of the hearing.

1.94 On the face of it, the lack of a request for further and better particulars is a serious failing by the defence team. Equal criticism can be made of the prosecutor who should provide appropriate details without the need to be asked. If in doubt, particulars should be sought and/or given. It is highly unlikely that anyone will be criticised for such an approach whereas a failure may bring censure.

1.95 It is of particular importance that the allegations are clear both to the practitioner and to the tribunal, since the proceedings should remain within the factual limits of the allegations unless they are amended. As Pill LJ observed in *Strouthos v London Underground Ltd*,[54] 'it is a basic proposition, whether in criminal or disciplinary proceedings, that the charge against the defendant or employee facing dismissal should be precisely framed and that the evidence should be confined to the particulars in the charge'.[55]

1.96 This is made clear from the comment by Silber J in *Cohen v General Medical Council*[56] that findings in relation to a charge at stage one of the process 'must be focused solely on the heads of the charges themselves'.[57] This is of particular relevance when scrutinising the reasons given by the

51 [2008] EWHC 439 (Admin).
52 At para [6].
53 [2008] EWHC 2967 (Admin).
54 [2004] EWCA Civ 402.
55 At para [12].
56 [2008] EWHC 581 (Admin).
57 At para [48].

panel. Adverse findings have been quashed in a number of cases where the reasons demonstrate that consideration has been given to extraneous matters.

1.97 In *Roomi v General Medical Council*[58] Collins J allowed R's appeal against a finding of impairment by reason of deficient professional performance (ie lack of competence) on the grounds that the finding by the panel went beyond the allegations contained in the notice of hearing. During the case R called evidence to show that he had taken steps to improve his skills. The tribunal concluded that the deficiencies identified in the notice had been remedied. However, the tribunal still made an adverse finding relying on managerial matters out-with the original allegations. Not surprisingly, His Lordship was critical both of the tribunal for going beyond the matters alleged and of the legal assessor for failing to advise them of their error.

1.98 Similarly, in *Chauhan v General Medical Council*[59] King J allowed C's appeal against findings of dishonesty and impairment because the tribunal failed to confine itself to the proper ambit of the disciplinary charges and considered prejudicial factual matters outwith the notice of hearing. The tribunal made findings of fact adverse to the registrant which could have been the subject of professional misconduct but were not within the charges as formulated. King J ruled that the findings of fact could not be properly or fairly used by the tribunal to support its decision. He further concluded that the tribunal had considered evidence of behaviour not the subject of a charge when determining the issue of dishonesty. He quoted Silber J from *Cohen* (para 1.96 above) that the process must focus solely on the heads of charge and rejected the GMC's submission that the extraneous material, even if strictly outside the ambit of the charges, could nonetheless be introduced as evidence of C's propensity to dishonestly exaggerate his expertise.

1.99 A further example is that of *R (El-Baroudy) v General Medical Council*,[60] in which E – a forensic medical examiner – performed no meaningful examination of AR, a man in custody, and yet certified him fit to be detained. AR was in fact unconscious, in need of urgent medical attention and died three hours later. E was charged with failing to provide proper clinical care to AR but there was no allegation that this caused or failed to prevent AR's death. The tribunal found E impaired referring to AR's death and the 'loss of an opportunity for AR to survive' through E's neglect of care. The court held that had causation been part of the case against E it should have been clearly stated. Since there was no such allegation the evidence on such issues should not have been led.

1.100 The approach outlined above is to be contrasted with criminal cases where the prohibition on bad character has been removed and, previous *or subsequent* misconduct is admitted far more frequently. This may become more important in disciplinary proceedings, since character evidence is now recognised as important for the fact-finding and the impairment stages and not just sanction. (See the section on character below, at

58 [2009] EWHC 2188 (Admin).
59 [2010] EWHC 2093 (Admin).
60 [2013] EWHC 2894 (Admin).

para 2.164. Also note the issue of the registrant's conduct and/or lies in the tribunal at para 2.233.)

1.101 The decision went the other way in *Richards v Law Society*,[61] in which the Divisional Court held that the purpose of a rule 4(2) statement (now a rule 5(2) statement under the Solicitors (Disciplinary Proceedings) Rules 2007[62]) is to inform the solicitor in advance of the case he or she has to meet. The tribunal found the case proved on a basis different from that in the statement. However, since the case was made clear in correspondence well before the hearing, R had received advance notice of the point upon which they found against him.

1.102 In *Hutchinson v General Dental Council*[63] Blair J differentiated between the vagueness of the charges and the specific behaviour clearly alleged. The clearly alleged misconduct was a failure to take adequate care over the sterility of dental instruments but the instances of occurrence described as 'regularly' or 'on occasions' were insufficiently specific to permit a proper response. While the clearly alleged misconduct meant that a fair hearing was possible, he stopped the case on its merits taking account of such matters as the lack of supporting evidence and the possibility of prejudice caused by delay and lack of specificity.

1.103 A final case in point is *R (Johnson) v Nursing and Midwifery Council*[64] in which J and M faced allegations relating to their management of a nursing home. (The facts appear below under 'disclosure' at para 1.271.) They submitted that the charges were so vague as to be unfair and contrary to ECHR Article 6 arguing that the lack of particularity was evident from the number of unknown dates, the breadth of the period covered by the charges and the unknown number and frequency of the alleged events. The court asked itself two questions: 1) did the charges provide sufficient information for them to know with reasonable clarity the case they had to meet; and 2) is a stay the only possible remedy?

1.104 The court found that neither European nor domestic law required the detail of particulars suggested by J and M and referred to criminal cases, especially those involving historic sexual abuse. It is not always possible to provide details of dates and locations but, the public interest requires that such matters be tried. In accordance with criminal cases the court held that the fitness to practise process itself is equipped to deal with many such issues. A stay is an exceptional remedy and it is only to be granted if a fair trial is impossible.

1.105 It is of importance to note that the court took into account the stage at which the application was made, namely at the outset of proceedings. While this was not premature (and in criminal proceedings submissions on the indictment are made at the outset), it did mean that the tribunal was deprived of any evidence which may help them in their decision. J and M had thus created an even greater hurdle for themselves.

61 [2009] EWHC 2087 (Admin) (Sir Anthony May P and Saunders J).

62 SI No 3588.

63 [2008] EWHC 2896 (Admin).

64 [2008] EWHC 885 (Admin).

1.106 The above principles can be drawn together when considering the case of *Thaker v Solicitors Regulation Authority*[65] (SRA), in which T appealed against the decision of the Solicitors Disciplinary Tribunal to strike him off. The court ordered a retrial on the basis that the original hearing was unfair owing to the manner in which the case was pleaded and presented by the SRA. A solicitor, faced with being struck off for dishonesty or gross negligence, is entitled to a coherent and intelligible statement of the allegations and the facts relied upon. This is particularly important in complex cases, or when a registrant is said to have known or ought to have known about alleged facts. During their opening it became clear that the SRA's case was far wider than that alleged in the statement of facts. The tribunal refused T's application to adjourn. The court said that while adjourning was a matter of discretion, the fact that the case went far beyond the original allegations meant that time for consideration was the *least that should have been granted*. In addition, by allowing the proceedings to range far and wide with submissions and evidence beyond the identified relevant transactions, the tribunal had caused injustice to T.

1.107 It is submitted that a reasonable rule of thumb is to consider whether the charge provides sufficient information to allow a full and fair response. If it does not, can this be cured by amendment and a reasonable time to adjust? If amendment and time will make no appreciable difference, and the respondent is at a disadvantage, is there still an overriding public-interest requirement to look into the allegation? If there is such an overriding requirement – for example, in cases of historic sexual abuse – the tribunal must keep the issue of fairness under review. If it is apparent that even with the flexibility available to a tribunal a fair hearing cannot be maintained, then the case should be stayed.

1.108 The interpretation of the above cases has led to rather verbose allegations that have been treated by both sides in an unnecessarily confrontational way. The latter is perhaps a reflection of the quasi-criminal adversarial system but it is of little assistance to the tribunal. As to verbosity, rather than pick a representative sample of important alleged facts there has been a tendency to list everything. Additionally, there has been a tendency to allege that a registrant has *failed* to do something rather than that he or she 'did not' do something. 'Failed' carries overtones of fault which may result in the defence refusing to admit facts which really do not require dispute. While some cases necessarily require a failure to be alleged, where possible, it is better to allege that a registrant 'did not' do something which fact may then be admitted in whole or in part and leave the issue of fault or failure to legal argument and the judgment of the tribunal. (See the general drafting guide at paras 1.137 below.)

1.109 That the concern over particulars had become a problem was clear not just from the cases, but from the comments of Dame Janet Smith in the *Fifth Report of the Shipman Inquiry* where she said:

> . . . it does appear to me that, in some types of case (for example, one that depends to a large extent upon a performance or health assessment), it would be sufficient if the doctor were to be told (adopting the words of the adjudication stage test proposed by the GMC) that it was alleged that

65 [2011] EWHC 660 (Admin) (Jackson LJ and Sweeney J).

> his/her fitness to practise was impaired (to a degree justifying action on registration) by reason of the matters contained in the assessment report. Even in conduct cases, I doubt that the degree of particularity that appears to have been given in the past is necessary for the giving of proper notice to the doctor. Reading some [Professional Complaints Committee] decisions, it appears that the proceedings have been broken down into the consideration of every single element which must be proved in order to support the allegation of [serious professional misconduct]. I do wonder whether this is really necessary; it fosters the impression that these are criminal proceedings, whereas they are not.[66]

1.110 These problems prompted a welcome move towards more succinct formulation and the prioritisation of allegations. However, there has been some backtracking from this and charges frequently contain multiple assertions of unnecessary detail or allegations with very little to differentiate them. Examples include charges that assert something is: not clinically justified, inappropriate, unsafe, not in a patient's best interests or not a recognised technique.

1.111 The touchstone of regulation is whether given the circumstances of the case an act is clinically justified and in the best interest of the patient. Whoever drafts the allegations should look carefully at the need for such multiple-choice charges. It will be rare indeed for anyone to argue that an inappropriate, unsafe or unrecognised technique is clinically justified or good practice or, that to act otherwise than in a patient's best interests is appropriate. Conversely while it may be that *in extremis*, a registrant must employ an unsafe or an unrecognised technique to do so would arguably be good practice and not worthy or opprobrium.

1.112 In cases with shorter heads of charge, the accuracy and completeness of the regulator's opening address is important. As with criminal proceedings it should describe and circumscribe the scope of the case. Ordinarily the regulator should not go outside its case as stated in the opening.

Some specific requirements

1.113 In addition to the general principle of knowing the case, the courts have ruled that certain specific allegations must be included in an allegation. Again, the accuracy and completeness of the opening is important if the heads of charge are in a shortened form.

Dishonesty

1.114 This must be clearly and unambiguously stated.

1.115 In *Salha and Abusheikha v General Medical Council*[67] the Privy Council held that a fundamental principle of fairness requires a charge of dishonesty to be unambiguously formulated and adequately particularised. It found that there was no justification for findings of dishonesty or lack of integrity against the doctors as it was not alleged against them.

1.116 If a regulator considers that a registrant's conduct was dishonest (as opposed to some lesser degree of culpability) it is essential that this is

66 At para 25.273.

67 Privy Council 32/2003 and 35/2003.

specifically pleaded. A failure to include such an allegation if the facts may properly support such an inference can amount to a procedural error or 'under-prosecution' on the part of the regulator (see *R (Council for the Regulation of Healthcare Professionals) v (1) The Nursing and Midwifery Council (2) United Kingdom*[68]).

1.117 See also *Singleton v Law Society*,[69] in which it was said that: 'It is unacceptable for the Tribunal to make findings of dishonesty when there has been no documentary pleading of such an allegation in a clear and *timeous* way' (emphasis added).[70]

1.118 It is not necessary to allege dishonesty if the allegation is already clearly contained in the words used – for example, 'you stole a bag'. If there are other conclusions that a tribunal might be asked to reach regarding a registrant's motives or state of mind (eg deliberate, misleading, etc) these should be clearly pleaded.

1.119 The case of *Brett v Solicitiors Regulation Authority*[71] is of some interest on this point. B was found to have been dishonest in that he *knowingly* allowing inaccurate information to be given in court. On appeal the court quashed the finding of dishonesty and substituted a finding that B had behaved recklessly since he had acted on the mistaken but apparently genuinely held belief that he was obliged to protect client privilege. The court commented that it may not always be appropriate to equate knowingly misleading with dishonesty.

1.120 Cases in which 'knowingly misleading' does not equate to dishonesty will be rare indeed. That said, if the regulator asserts dishonesty it should do so explicitly. It may not be sufficient to simply suggest knowingly is the same as dishonest.

1.121 The test for dishonesty was re-cast in the case of *Ivey v Genting Casinos UK Ltd (t/a Crockfords)*.[72] Interestingly, it would be clear from the new dishonesty test that B would not be guilty of dishonesty since he genuinely held the belief that he had to mislead the court to protect client privilege. (See dishonesty and lack of integrity at paras 3.243 and 3.320 respectively.)

Sexual motivation

1.122 This must be spelled out in all relevant cases.

1.123 In *R (Council for the Regulation of Healthcare Professionals) v General Medical Council and Rajeshwar*[73] the court held that it was a serious procedural irregularity and 'under-prosecution' not to plead sexual motivation.

1.124 It is worth noting that an allegation of 'indecency' may be made even where the registrant has been acquitted of indecent assault. However, the better approach is to charge the actions as 'sexually motivated', not least because there is an element of subjective judgment in what is or is not indecent. On the other side of the coin, the defence and the tribunal are entitled to rely on the fact that a charge does *not* contain allegations

68 [2007] EWHC 1806 (Admin).
69 [2005] EWHC 2915 (QB).
70 At para [13].
71 [2014] EWHC 2974 (Admin).
72 [2017] UKSC 67.
73 [2005] EWHC 2973 (Admin).

of indecency or sexual motivation since this sort of decision must be a properly reasoned and appropriate one.

1.125 The difficulty in assessing sexual motivation was made plain in the cases of *Arunkalaivanan v General Medical Council*[74] and *General Medical Council v Jagjivan.*[75]

1.126 In *Arunkalaivanan*, the distinction was made between a clumsy and inept breast examination which may have left a patient feeling violated or ill-cared for, and one which was sexually motivated. A was certainly guilty of the former, but not the latter. However, the distinction required very careful consideration of the facts, including an assessment of A's character and how it impinged upon any motive he may or may not have.

1.127 In *Jagjivan* the tribunal concluded that J's conduct in telling a patient that she could raise her heart-rate by touching her nipples, touching or stimulating her vagina and then placing his hand over hers was not sexually motivated. That finding was quashed on appeal by the GMC. The High Court concluded that making such comments to a partially dressed patient could not be motivated other than for sexual reasons, irrespective of J's character or his own professed sexuality or lack of sexual interest in the patient.

1.128 The difficulty with sexual motivation is that proof requires the tribunal to draw an inference regarding a registrant's state of mind from the facts which may not be entirely clear. It is not the same as criminal cases of sexual assault, which are often simply a question of touching a person in an intimate area for which there is no excuse. In clinical practice there may well be legitimate reasons for such touching, and the reasons or apparent reasons for this may be clouded by a registrant's clinical abilities, his or her explanation of the process, or by a patient's understandable response to such ineptitude.

Alternatives

1.129 Lesser alternatives must be included where different interpretations and conclusions can be drawn from the reasons for a practitioner's actions. However, care must be taken to limit these to the most serious allegations. By way of example when alleging dishonesty, a clear and appropriate charge may suggest that an alleged statement was: a) misleading; b) intended to mislead; and c) dishonest.

1.130 In *R (Farag) v General Medical Council*[76] the tribunal's finding of dishonesty was quashed. The GMC presented the case for dishonesty on the basis that F was not ill despite submitting sick notes to his employer. This was demonstrated by the fact that he was working elsewhere at the time. The tribunal rejected this, declining to go behind the contents of the sick-note, but found F to be dishonest because he had been selective about the information that he had given to the Trust regarding his alternative employment. This was not the way that the GMC had put the case. The court found that the defence had not had an opportunity to answer this alternative case. There are clear parallels to be drawn with the cases regard-

74 [2014] EWHC 873 (Admin).
75 [2017] EWHC 1247 (Admin).
76 [2009] EWHC 2667 (Admin).

ing consideration of extraneous matters. This illustrates the importance of an accurate opening as discussed at para 1.172 above.

Summary or wrap-up clauses and narrative

1.131 These should be limited to those cases where it is absolutely necessary, for example to indicate the seriousness of alleged events. Narrative that explains the circumstances of events should also be avoided.

1.132 There are two distinct types of summary clause: 'specific aggravating factors' and 'generic summary clauses'. The former are likely to be required when particular factual findings need to be made regarding aggravating features of the alleged misconduct. Examples are when the allegations describe the misconduct as dishonest, misleading or sexually motivated. These are factual issues which must be proved to the required standard. The second type of clause, encompassing terms such as 'not of the standard expected of . . .' or 'inappropriate or inadequate', are not factual matters for stage one. However, they may be relevant to the exercise of the tribunal's judgment when it comes to impairment. Most regulators provide specific guidance on the use of such adjectives in order to be consistent in drafting and presenting cases.

1.133 Catch-all or wrap-up charges should not be included unless there is a specific need in the case. For example, in performance cases it may be necessary to state how far a registrant's fitness to practise has fallen short of an accepted standard.

1.134 In *Williams v General Medical Council*[77] Davis J was critical of what he referred to as a 'summation charge' or 'sweeping-up' charge which added very little to what had gone before. Likewise in *Misra v General Medical Council,*[78] a case concerning professional misconduct, the Privy Council criticised the charges as unnecessary and oppressive when an allegation of dishonesty was seemingly routinely added to each disputed fact.

1.135 The *GMC drafting guide* takes up the points made in *Williams* and *Misra*, and advises that:

> . . . it is important to ensure that the charges identify the core areas of concern, and relate to matters which are serious enough to justify impairment proceedings. Impairment of fitness to practise is judged 'in the round', so it may be necessary to look at the cumulative effect of a series of faults. However, drafters should consider carefully whether each incident relied on should genuinely attract criticism.[79]

1.136 The principle has equal application to all disciplinary proceedings.

Drafting principles

1.137 The following is a summary of general drafting principles:[80]

- The notice needs to be sufficiently particularised regarding the basis of the alleged impairment, but without unnecessary detail. It is not a

77 [2007] EWHC 2603 (Admin).

78 [2003] UKPC 7.

79 *GMC Guidance on charge drafting for notices of hearing,* 3 February 2010.

80 Based on the GMC publication on charging principles but of general application.

narrative of the case, a summary of the evidence, or an opening statement. It should set out the facts which the regulator says indicate impairment.

- Charges should be unambiguously drafted, using succinct plain language, concise and without numerous sub-clauses. They should say what is meant.
- A charge should be chronological.
- A charge should:
  - identify and describe the registrant's practice and location;
  - describe the key factual elements of what is alleged avoiding unnecessary narrative detail;
  - indicate what is being criticised and how it is being criticised. Guidance may be obtained from an expert report or from publications such as *Good medical practice* or other specific guidance; it is not necessary to tie allegations to specific provisions in such guidance.
- It should allege that practice is impaired by reason of misconduct or poor performance etc as the case may be.
- When deciding what facts to allege, only those provable through admissible evidence should be included.
- The 'best evidence' rule provides a good starting point such that direct evidence should be used before hearsay. Supporting evidence from another witness or documentation is also desirable but not essential.
- 'Failed' versus 'did not': The term 'you failed' – eg 'You failed to examine patient A' – means that the regulator must prove two elements: first, that the practitioner did not examine patient A, and second that the practitioner *should* have done so. This approach should only be adopted where the *failure to examine is core* to the allegation otherwise the wording should be: 'You did not examine patient A'.

1.138 In *SRA v Chan*,[81] strong criticism was made of 'unnecessarily convoluted and prolix' allegations. The court commented that allegations should be simply stated followed by short particulars. Furthermore, the number of allegations should be the minimum needed to meet the justice of the case and not the maximum number possible.

1.139 It is extraordinary that such comments are still necessitated given the fact that regulatory proceedings are intended to regulate and protect, not prosecute and punish. Regulators and their tribunals would do well to keep this principle firmly in mind when considering the length and breadth of allegations.

1.140 One continued nuisance is the use of the word 'failed' in the charges. Despite the clear guidance above, the term is still used when it is unnecessary. In all but the most obvious cases, it would be far better to put the allegation in two simple parts: i) 'you did not do X'; and ii) this was a failure. This simple expedient would enable any admissions or agreement upon the facts to be settled without blame. The issue of any blame or failure can then be dealt with separately. See also the comment at para 1.91

81 [2015] EWHC 2659.

above regarding multiple charges, sub-charges and cross-referral between these when dealing with various alternative states of mind.

Amending the charges

> The allegations/charges may be amended provided no injustice is caused.
>
> The later and/or more substantial the change, the more likely it is to cause injustice.
>
> If the risk of injustice can be met then charges may be changed late in the proceedings. Some difficulties may be dealt with by adjourning to allow all parties time to prepare the newly altered case, or to call or recall witnesses.

1.141 The principles on charging and drafting have equal input to amending charges.

1.142 Article 6(3) of the ECHR is engaged when there is a change in the nature of an allegation. Since an accused is entitled to proper notification of a charge he or she is also entitled to proper notification of a change and, adequate time and facility to deal with the change. In *Mattoccia v Italy*[82] the ECtHR found that M had been denied the right to proper notification by vague charges the essential details of which were repeatedly altered during trial with no allowance given to him to deal with 'yet another new version of events' late in the hearing.

1.143 In *O'Reilly v Mackman*[83] Lord Diplock stated that:

> . . . the requirement that a person who is charged with having done something which, if proved to the satisfaction of a statutory tribunal, has consequences that will, or may, affect him adversely, should be given a fair opportunity of hearing what is alleged against him . . . is so fundamental to any civilised legal system that it is to be presumed that Parliament intended a failure to observe it should render null and void any decision reached in breach of this requirement.[84]

1.144 The regulators' rules each provide for amending the particulars of the allegation or the alleged facts provided it can be done without injustice. Before such amendments are made, the tribunal must consult with the legal assessor and hear from both parties. However, the timing of amendment is open to further argument given the staged process of regulatory hearings.

1.145 It follows from the requirement of a fair hearing that the registrant is entitled to proper notice of the allegation. That much is uncontroversial. The authorities are, however, less clear on the issues of when notice has to be provided and when it is too late. In *Singleton v Law Society* (above) the High Court held that: 'It is unacceptable for the Tribunal to make findings of dishonesty when there has been no documentary pleading of such an allegation in a clear and *timeous* way'.[85] This was followed in *R (Council for the Regulation of Healthcare Professionals) v (1) The Nursing and Midwifery*

82 Application no 23969/94, (2003) 36 EHRR 47.

83 [1983] 2 AC 237.

84 At p276B–C.

85 At para 13.

Council (2) Kingdom (above) where the High Court ruled that a failure to cite dishonesty was a 'serious procedural error', but Beatson J '[rejected] the submission that the Committee could not reconsider or amend the charge once the facts were proved'.[86]

1.146 From *Singleton*, notice must be 'timeous', whereas in *Kingdom* the judge envisaged a serious amendment to an allegation (averring dishonesty) even after the tribunal had retired to consider the facts. The two are difficult to reconcile, from which it may be said that each case must be considered on its own facts. The principle consideration is, as ever, fairness.

1.147 Assistance may be gleaned from criminal proceedings in which a defective indictment may also be amended by the judge at any stage before or during trial provided this can be done *without injustice* (Indictments Act 1915 s5). The starting point is that the longer the interval between arraignment and amendment the less likely that it can be done without causing injustice – see *R v Johal and Ram*.[87] However, the courts have given an increasingly liberal interpretation to this section and, amendment may be made if an indictment is bad for duplicity, or it does not accord with the evidence before the committing magistrates, or the evidence given at trial, or when the evidence discloses more than one offence, or when it does not include a defendant who may be properly joined. Finally the court may substitute a different offence or add another – see *R v Radley*[88] and *R v Johal and Ram*.

1.148 The clear notion is that unless there is unfairness that cannot be cured by allowing time, or recalling witnesses, charges may be amended at the latter stages of a trial.

1.149 If there is to be a retrial, amendment can again be made but with the same caveat, namely that there is no injustice – see *R v Swaine*.[89]

1.150 The limits of these points are met in three cases. In *R v Newington*[90] the Court of Appeal commented per curiam that while a judge had the power to amend an indictment during his summing up it was:

> . . . questionable whether it was ever wise to [do so] especially in a long and complex case . . . it must inevitably deprive defence counsel, no matter that he does not object strenuously, or at all . . . of the opportunity to address the jury on the implications of the amendment. Furthermore, there is a risk to the Judge being unequal to the task of properly adjusting his summing-up to accommodate the change brought about by the amendment.[91]

1.151 By way of contrast, in *R v Bonner*[92] (a case of historic indecent assault) the Court of Appeal said that an amendment to the date of the alleged offence *after* the summing up was to be discouraged but, if the interests of justice required it, then it should be made only after the defence has been given time to consider recalling witnesses or calling further evidence. This case should be treated with some caution before reliance is placed upon it since the date was not an essential particular of the allegation.

86 At para 32.
87 (1972) 56 Cr App R 348.
88 (1974) 58 Cr App R 394.
89 [2001] Crim LR 166, CA.
90 (1990) 91 Cr App R 247, CA.
91 At p251.
92 [1974] Crim LR 479.

1.152 In *R v Piggott and Litwin*,[93] following a successful submission of no case to answer, it was held to be inappropriate to permit amendment of the indictment, discharge of the jury and retrial of P and L on a basis withdrawn by the Crown prior to committal. The initial amendments which included the addition of new counts caused injustice and should not have been permitted. The retrial on the amended indictment was consequently an abuse of process and should have been stayed.

1.153 Referring the criminal principles back to *Singleton* and *Kingdom* and the conflict between the 'timeous' change in the former and the late change in the latter, the following lines of reasoning emerge:

- major alterations to charges should be made as soon (timeous) as is reasonably practicable after the issue has arisen;
- late and/or major changes may be made provided there is no injustice *and*, any unfairness can be met by allowing time or opportunity to prepare;
- each case must be decided on its own facts.

1.154 This line of reasoning has recently been approved in *Professional Standards Authority v Health and Care Professions Council and Doree*[94] (see below at paras 3.137 and 3.173) in which the HCPC did not apply to amend the charges after the evidence had been heard nor did the tribunal suggest this. The Professional Standards Authority (PSA) raised this on appeal (along with other matters) as a case of 'undercharging' and serious procedural irregularity. The PSA submitted that amending the charges after they had been considered to ensure they were proved was not unfair, even though they also sought to argue that this 'would or should' have made a difference on sanction and was thus prejudicial to D. At first instance Lang J regarded a retrospective amendment 'to secure a guilty finding' as being a 'gross breach of fair hearing procedure'.

1.155 On appeal, counsel for the PSA argued that the tribunal should have amended the allegations to 'conform to their relevant findings of fact' or invite the HCPC to do so. While it was conceded that a tribunal may amend an allegation to conform with findings of fact, counsel for the HCPC argued that this should only be done if the tribunal was 'satisfied that such amendments could be made without unfairness' and not to do in this case was certainly not a serious procedural error. Lindblom J said 'I accept those submissions . . . There will no doubt be cases where a late amendment of the allegations faced by a registrant will be justified, even after the evidence has been heard and findings of fact have been made'.[95]

1.156 While the case is in the main argued from the perspective of the HCPC, the point is clear that amendments may be made even after the evidence is complete but only if this does not cause prejudice to the registrant. However, it is plainly a case-specific exercise.

1.157 It remains to be seen whether the recently formulated principle of an 'overarching objective' in healthcare regulation to protect the public will lend weight to the acceptability of late amendments as against the unfairness of such changes to the registrant.

93 (1999) 2 Cr App R 320, CA.

94 [2017] EWCA Civ 319.

95 At [56].

Pre-hearing matters

Abuse of process

1.158 Abuse of process is a phrase used to cover a number of alleged wrongs by a party to litigation. In regulatory proceedings, it is most frequently encountered when the registrant alleges that a regulator has caused unreasonable delay, or has acted so unfairly that the case should be stayed. Apart from delay examples of alleged abuse include incomplete or non-disclosure of information, going back on a promise not to proceed and over-charging. It is not limited to these headings and abuse may be argued where the acts or omissions of one party cause injustice or unfairness to the other. However, proving abuse is difficult and a case should only be stayed if it is demonstrated on balance of probabilities that a fair hearing cannot take place or that it would be unfair to proceed for some other equally compelling reason.

1.159 In its broadest sense, an abuse of process is 'something so unfair and wrong that the court should not allow a prosecution to proceed with what is in all other respects a regular proceeding' (*Connelly v DPP*).[96]

1.160 The relief sought by a registrant will normally be to stay proceedings in whole or in part. In *R v Maxwell*[97] the court reiterated the two bases upon which a stay may be granted – first, that a fair trial is impossible; and second, where to proceed offends the court's sense of justice and propriety. The distinction being that the latter involves a consideration of the competing interests of the prosecution and the accused whereas the former does not. The same principles apply in regulatory proceedings behind which stands the overarching objective.

1.161 It should be noted that an abuse of process argument raised before a hearing commences is not to be confused with a submission that there is no case to answer. The latter can only be judged at the close of the prosecution or regulator's case in accordance with *R v Galbraith*[98] (for which see para 2.389 below). The principles set out in *Galbraith* have no bearing on an abuse of process argument.

Delay

> ECHR Article 6 and domestic case-law confer a right to a hearing within a reasonable time however to stay proceedings is an exceptional course and delay is not a ground unless there is material prejudice to the extent that no fair trial is possible.
>
> Where a regulatory body's rules impose a time bar preventing proceedings save in exceptional circumstances, an assessment of those circumstances must be fair, transparent and understandable.

1.162 Both domestic case-law and the ECHR confer a right to the speedy and just resolution of disputes. However, while delay may constitute a breach

96 [1964] AC 1254.
97 [2010] UKSC 48.
98 (1981) 73 Cr App R 124.

of the ECHR or the rules of a regulatory body, mere delay is insufficient to stop proceedings. Where the regulatory body has rules concerning old complaints, this may give rise to further argument concerning the just application of those rules.

1.163 As we have seen, ECHR Article 6(1) provides for 'the determination of [civil rights and criminal charges by] a fair and public hearing within a reasonable time'.

1.164 It has been said that Article 6 is to be given a broad and purposive interpretation: *Moreiva de Azevedo v Portugal*.[99] Much of the case-law concerning the application of Article 6 stems from the criminal jurisdiction and it is instructive to start there.

1.165 In *Porter v Magill; Weeks v Magill*,[100] the House of Lords confirmed that there was no requirement to demonstrate specific prejudice in order to establish a breach of the right to trial within a reasonable time. However, while it may be possible to establish a breach, subsequent case-law makes it clear that this alone is not sufficient to stay proceedings.

1.166 In *Dyer v Watson*,[101] the Privy Council gave the following general guidance:

- Unless the time elapsed, on its face and without more, gave grounds for real concern, it is almost certainly unnecessary to go further.
- If there are grounds for real concern, it is a) necessary for the court to look at the detailed facts and circumstances; and b) necessary for the state to explain and justify the apparently excessive lapse of time.
- Relevant factors include the complexity of the case, the conduct of the defendant, and the manner in which the case had been dealt with by the administrative and judicial authorities.
- The state could not lay the blame on prosecutors, judges, lists, funding etc but neither was the court to shut its eyes to the practicalities of litigation and the organisation of cases.
- A marked lack of expedition, if unjustified, would point towards unreasonable delay.

1.167 The principal issues on delay are to be found in *Attorney-General's Reference (No 2 of 2001)*[102] where it was held that:

i) a stay would only be appropriate if a fair trial is no longer possible or if it is for any compelling reason unfair to try the defendant; and
ii) time runs from the earliest time when the defendant was officially alerted to the likelihood of criminal proceedings being taken against him or her, which would normally be when he or she was charged or served with a summons.

1.168 As to point i), the court held that where there was a breach, there had to be an appropriate remedy which would depend on the nature of the breach and all the circumstances, including particularly the stage at which the breach was established.

99 (1990) 13 EHRR 721.
100 [2002] 2 AC 357.
101 [2004] 1 AC 379.
102 [2004] 2 AC 72, HL.

1.169 Apart from public acknowledgement of the breach, pre-trial remedies could include expediting the hearing and/or granting bail. Neither the prosecutor nor the court would further breach Article 6 by continuing with the prosecution since the breach consisted of the delay which had accrued. Post-trial remedies may include a reduction in sentence or the payment of compensation to an acquitted defendant (see *Selvarajan v General Medical Council*[103] below at para 1.181).

1.170 It was further noted that there could be circumstances which justified a stay even when the fairness of the trial itself was not in question but the delay was such that it would be unfair to try the accused.

1.171 Cases where it might be unfair to try the defendant include cases of bad faith, executive manipulation and abuse of process, or where the delay was of such an order, or a prosecutor's breach of professional duty was such as to make it unfair that the proceedings should continue. Such cases would be 'very exceptional [and] a stay would never be an appropriate remedy if any lesser remedy would adequately vindicate the defendant's Convention right'.[104]

1.172 The circumstances where it might be unfair to continue are of the kind illustrated by *R v Horseferry Road Magistrates' Court ex p Bennett*[105] (in which a government agency acted unlawfully to wrongly detain a man and arrange his return to the UK rather than use lawful means) but as is noted such circumstances are exceptional and a stay would never be appropriate if any lesser remedy would adequately protect the defendant's ECHR rights.

1.173 The following comments of Lightman J in *R v General Medical Council ex p Toth*[106] are also particularly pertinent:

> The Act and Rules set out to provide a just balance between the legitimate expectation of the complainant that a complaint of serious professional misconduct will be fully investigated and the need for legitimate safeguards for the practitioner, who as a professional man may be considered particularly vulnerable to and damaged by unwarranted charges against him.[107]
>
> . . .
>
> The general principles underlying the Act and Rules are that (a) the public have an interest in the maintenance of standards and the investigation of complaints of serious professional misconduct against practitioners; (b) public confidence in the GMC and the medical profession requires, and complainants have a legitimate expectation, that such complaints (in the absence of some special and sufficient reason) will be publicly investigated by the [panel]; and (c) justice should in such cases be seen to be done. This must be most particularly the case where the practitioner continues to be registered and to practise.[108]

103 [2008] EWHC 182 (Admin).
104 *Attorney-General's Reference (No 2 of 2001)* [2004] 2 AC 72 at para 25.
105 [1994] 1 AC 42.
106 [2000] EWHC 361 (Admin).
107 At para [10].
108 At para [14].

1.174 In *R (Gibson) v General Medical Council and another*[109] Elias J relied upon Lightman J's observations in *Toth* (above), summing these up thus:

> . . . both the legitimate expectation of complainants and the public confidence in the regulation of the medical profession require that the complaint should, in the absence of some special and sufficient reason, be publicly investigated. It would undermine that important principle if mere unreasonable delay, absent prejudice, were to require a stay to be granted.[110]

1.175 For the purposes of the ECHR, time runs from when a person is subjected to a 'charge' meaning that he or she is officially notified of or substantially affected by proceedings (*Deweer v Belgium*;[111] *Eckle v Germany*[112]). In regulatory proceedings, this is likely to be the date of the letter notifying the registrant of the allegations.

1.176 While there have been two lines of authority on the application of Article 6 to disciplinary proceedings, the better approach is that Article 6 does in fact apply. See under ECHR above:

- *Ex p Kypros Nicolaides:* whether Article 6 applies to the proceedings does not arise at the outset, but depends on the outcome of the case.
- *Tehrani v UKCC*: 'if the petitioner can establish that the disciplinary proceedings could result in a finding that would constitute a determination of her civil rights and obligations, the decision to initiate those disciplinary proceedings is open to challenge as being incompatible with the petitioner's convention rights'.
- *Preiss v General Dental Council*: 'Since the decision of a majority of the European Court of Human Rights in *Le Compte, Van Leuven and De Meyere v Belgium* (1981) 4 EHRR 1 it has been accepted that a decision of a professional tribunal affecting the right to practise the profession is a determination of civil rights and obligations'.
- In *R (Johnson) v Nursing and Midwifery Council*[113] Beatson J approached the case from both the domestic and the ECHR viewpoints.

1.177 The principles as applied to regulatory proceedings have resulted in much the same conclusion. A registrant must show on a balance of probabilities that he or she will suffer or has suffered serious prejudice to the extent that no fair trial can be held.

1.178 Stays are thus to be granted:

- in exceptional circumstances only;
- it will be even more rare where there is no fault on the part of the regulator or complainant;
- delay caused by the complexity of the case or by the registrant should never be the basis of a stay (see also *Haikel v General Medical Council*[114]).

109 [2004] EWHC 2781 (Admin).
110 At para 36 of his judgment.
111 (1980) 2 EHRR 439.
112 (1983) 5 EHRR 1.
113 [2008] EWHC 885 (Admin).
114 [2002] UKPC 37.

1.179 In *Williams v General Medical Council*[115] W failed in his attempt to set aside a finding of serious professional misconduct on the basis of a 15-month delay between the matter being referred to the GMC and the hearing and, the failure by the GMC to serve a notice of inquiry on him expeditiously as required by the GMC (FTP) Rules 2004. The tribunal finding that delay in service of the notice was 'not unreasonable' for the purposes of ECHR Article 6 was not the same as a finding that the rule requiring service 'as soon as may be' had been met. However, a stay or dismissal of proceedings requires 'exceptional' circumstances and, without material prejudice a breach of the rule was of no practical significance.

Delay as mitigation

1.180 Delay other than that caused by the registrant may give rise to matters in mitigation. This is particularly so if the practitioner has been the subject of an interim order, albeit that the purpose of interim orders and/or sanctions are not to punish the registrant but to protect the public.

1.181 In *Selvarajan v General Medical Council*[116] S was erased from the medical register in 2006 after he admitted defrauding the local authority of £150,000 between March 1994 and November 1996. S argued that unreasonable delay was relevant to mitigation. Blake J accepted the argument as a matter of common sense, practice, fairness and from the GMC's own indicative sanctions guidelines. He stated that:[117]

> It is common sense that the longer the threat of erasure has been hanging over the head of a professional person terminating their ability to practise their vocation, and with it the extinction of their means of earning a living and the deprivation of their practice, the more severe the sanction will be and the more punitive it will appear to be to the recipient, even if in disciplinary proceedings the purpose of the sanction is not intended to be punitive.

1.182 His Lordship noted the differing purpose of regulatory proceedings but nonetheless stated: 'I . . . see no reason in logic, policy or common sense why any delay since the conduct was committed or notified to those in authority let alone unreasonable delay in prosecuting charges, should not be capable of mitigating the penalty.' He went on to confirm that whether delay in fact mitigates the sanction is case-specific and it will clearly not do so in every case.

1.183 The court held that if the delay was such as to breach the registrant's Article 6 right to a fair and timely hearing it would be 'far more contrary to the public interest and the vindication of the reputation of the profession' if disciplinary tribunals did *not* have the capacity to remedy any delay by adjusting the sanction. If this were not the case, the only sanction against delay would be to stay more cases.

1.184 However, delay will not and indeed ought not to mitigate sanction in every case. Despite the delay the sanction of erasure was upheld owing to the 'very serious and sustained' misconduct which was 'totally undermin-

115 [2007] EWHC 2603 (Admin).
116 [2008] EWHC 182 (Admin).
117 At para 28.

ing to the trust and respect' accorded to the profession. In addition, this was not on the borderline of erasure and suspension where mitigation based on delay may well have been compelling as to outcome. Furthermore, while the prospect of erasure had been over S's head for a very long time, he had not been the subject of an interim suspension or restrictions and had continued to earn a living when, given the obvious sanction, if there had been no delay, he would not.

1.185 The issue of delay was central to a reduction of sanction in *Rahman v Bar Standards Board*.[118] In June 2010, R admitted two charges of professional misconduct and was suspended for 18 months. He appealed the sanction but, for reasons that are not clear, the appeal was not heard until February 2013, by which time, had the sanction been effective immediately, he would have been back at work. The suspension was reduced to three months because the delay and the blight of proceedings hanging over him had had such an affect upon his practice that it was unfair to ignore it.

1.186 In *Okeke v Nursing and Midwifery Council*[119] comment to similar effect was made regarding a four-and-a-half-year period between referral and determination. Legatt J held that this was too long and the CCC had not taken this delay into account. In remitting the case for reconsideration on other grounds, his Lordship commented that the new tribunal should pay regard to the unreasonable delay and the effect it had had upon the registrant. See also *R (Madan) v General Medical Council* under interim orders below.

1.187 While it may be possible to allege abuse of process through a breach of Article 6, it will only succeed when a fair hearing is not possible or it would be otherwise unfair to try the registrant. Mere delay, absent prejudice, is not sufficient.[120] The need to maintain public confidence in the regulation of the professions requires that a complaint should, in the absence of some special and sufficient reason be publicly investigated.

1.188 Some regulators place time-limits on the receipt and prosecution of complaints unless to proceed 'is in the public interest, in the exceptional circumstances of the case'[121] or, 'it is necessary for the protection of the public, or otherwise in the public interest'.[122] These rules and any permitted circumvention of the time-bar must be strictly applied.

1.189 The above rules concerning delay were considered in *R (Peacock) v General Medical Council*,[123] *R (Gwynn) v General Medical Council*[124] and *R (Rycroft) v Royal Pharmaceutical Society of Great Britain*[125] (RPS).

1.190 In *Peacock* Gibbs J held that the regulator's decision to permit an allegation that P's fitness is impaired to proceed, despite the lapse of some seven

118 [2013] All ER(D) 156.

119 [2013] EWHC 714.

120 [2004] EWHC 2781 (Admin); see also *Attorney-General's Ref (No 2 of 2001)* [2003] UKHL 68.

121 GMC (FTP) Rules 2004 r4(5).

122 General Pharmaceutical Council (Fitness to Practise and Disqualification etc) Rules 2010 r6(2).

123 [2007] EWHC 585 (Admin).

124 [2007] EWHC 3145 (Admin).

125 [2010] EWHC 2832 (Admin).

years since the most recent events giving rise to the allegation, was unlawful. Prescription of certain drugs to the complainant led to a series of cardiac arrests which had caused neurological brain injury in 1998. The regulator permitted the complaint to proceed because the case 'raise[d] serious allegations' into the prescribing habits of P. The judge held that the judicial review challenge was not premature. There was no need to wait until the substantive finding because there would be no satisfactory remedy later in the proceedings. He went on to hold that on the facts of the case, there were no exceptional circumstances rendering it in the public interest to take the complaint further. At its gravest, the complaint was of serious negligence relating to one patient and one example of prescribing or a series of prescriptions. There was no sensible explanation for the delay.

1.191 In *Gwynn*, the GMC alleged that G's fitness to practise was impaired due to deficient professional performance regarding ten patients, and misconduct in relation to one other patient. Four of the complaints arose from procedures carried out more than five years earlier. G applied for the proceedings to be stayed on the basis that there were no exceptional circumstances as required by GMC (FTP) Rules 2004 r4(5). Not surprisingly, Sullivan J found that the GMC was bound to have regard to rule 4(5) when deciding whether to pursue cases that were over five years old. However, it was plain that it had not, and the subsequent attempt to do so retrospectively did not cure the defect. Indeed the lateness of the attempt compounded the situation since the decisions were made close to or on the eve of proceedings. Sullivan J concluded that it would be very difficult for any decision-maker to exclude the imminent hearing from his mind and without any identification of the required 'exceptional circumstances' or any express application of the rule 4(5) test, there was the very real possibility that undue weight was given to the imminence of the hearing.

1.192 The case against *Gwynn* also raised the spectre of re-opening a case closed four-and-a-half years previously by a caseworker because it disclosed no misconduct or impairment. G argued that the GMC could not re-open a previously rejected complaint, and even if it could, it was unfair and/or unreasonable to do. Sullivan J agreed stating that the only way the GMC could re-open such a case was if the complainant asked the GMC to re-consider its decision.

1.193 In *Rycroft*, R took over the role of superintendent pharmacist for a chain of pharmacies in May 2002. In May 2006 the RPS received an allegation that they were re-using medication returned by clients. In April 2009 the registrar referred the matter to the Investigating Committee. Rule 9(1)(a) and (2)(a) of the Royal Pharmaceutical Society of Great Britain (Fitness to Practise and Disqualification etc) Rules 2007[126] provided that the registrar shall not refer a fitness to practise matter or any other matter respectively if the conduct alleged is more than five years old, unless he or she considers it to be necessary for the protection of the public or otherwise in the public interest.

1.194 R sought to rely on *Gwynn* when arguing that the registrar was under an implied duty to make a referral within a reasonable period, and that in order for proceedings to be quashed and stayed, it was *not* necessary for

126 SI No 442.

the claimant to demonstrate prejudice. In rejecting R's contention, Williams J took account of the earlier decision of *R (Gibson) v General Medical Council*[127] that a stay should not be imposed even when unjustifiable delay was established unless:

> The defendant shows on balance of probabilities that owing to the delay he will suffer serious prejudice to the extent that no fair trial can be held: in other words that the continuance of the prosecution amounts to a misuse of the process of the court.[128]

(See *Attorney-General's Ref (No 1 of 1990)*.[129])

1.195 He concluded that the registrar is under an implicit obligation to make a referral within a reasonable time but a failure to do so did not amount to a reason for quashing the referral and staying proceedings unless the delay caused prejudice to such an extent that no fair disciplinary process is possible or that it is unfair for the process to continue. Despite there being inordinate and unjustified delay, it did not prevent a fair hearing or make it unfair to proceed.

1.196 Finally, in *Rycroft* Williams J stated that while the extent of reasons may depend upon the nature of the decision, in deciding to refer a case where the conduct had occurred more than five years previously, the registrar had to address the statutory criteria and provide sufficient reasons to support his conclusion. The registrar purported to do so by stating that the referral was necessary 'for the protection of the public of otherwise in the public interest . . . because the allegations are of a serious nature and it is necessary . . . to maintain public confidence in the profession'.[130] These reasons were wholly inadequate rendering the decision to refer unlawful. Ordinarily this would have resulted in the decision being quashed but that was unnecessary in the light of pre-trial correspondence.

1.197 The conclusions from the above are:

- The courts and regulatory tribunals are willing to recognise an abuse of process and/or a breach of Article 6 and/or breach of an implied statutory duty but this alone will not give rise to a stay. The circumstances must be exceptional and there must be incurable prejudice.
- In referring cases after time-limits imposed by regulation, there must be clearly defined and exceptional circumstances. These may relate to the lapse of time.
- That the allegation raises serious concern about a practitioner's fitness to practise is *not* an exceptional circumstance, since this is a necessary precursor to any referral to a tribunal. Joinder of similar allegations is not an exceptional circumstance save that similar fact issues may at least be arguable when considering the protections of the public. On this last point it is worth considering the question of the admissibility of bad character (see 'character' at para 2.164 et seq below). Delay may be raised in mitigation of the sanction in appropriate cases. These are likely to be cases where risk to the public (patients) is minimal.

127 [2004] EWHC 2781 (Admin).

128 At para 20.

129 [1992] QB 630 at p644B.

130 At para 48.

Illness and/or retirement of registrant

1.198 In addition to delay, a registrant's inability to prepare for or participate in the hearing may found an abuse argument or be a reason to stay the proceedings. However, once again there is a careful balance to be met. The issue of illness may also arise in cases where voluntary erasure is sought. Whilst there is some cross-over between a stay and voluntary erasure they are distinct issues that require separate consideration.

1.199 In *Brabazon-Drenning v United Kingdom Central Council for Nursing Midwifery and Health Visiting*[131] Elias J voiced the principle that:

> Save in very exceptional circumstances where the public interest points strongly to the contrary, it must be wrong for a committee which has the livelihood and reputation of a professional individual in the palm of its hands to go ahead with the hearing when there is unchallenged evidence that the individual is simply not fit to withstand the rigours of the disciplinary process.

The statement of principle mirrors the situation in criminal proceedings whether looked at from a domestic or a European perspective.

1.200 In *Varma v General Medical Council*[132] V was informed in April 2003 of the GMC's intention to take action over matters that occurred in June 2002. The tribunal hearing did not begin until May 2006. The GMC admitted that there had been unacceptable delay on their part. V claimed that he could not attend through ill-health (caused in part by the delay) and that the case should be stayed at least until he was well. The tribunal concluded his absence was voluntary and declined to stay proceedings because the medical evidence indicated he was able to attend, understand and participate. Forbes J ruled that in the absence of serious prejudice such that no fair trial can be held, a stay should not be granted in cases of delay.

1.201 While V did have health difficulties, Forbes J held that the tribunal had balanced his rights against the public interest in investigating and adjudicating upon serious matters and, since the decision was a matter of judicial assessment rather than a conclusion based on facts the court should be slow to interfere with an exercise of judgment by a specialist tribunal – see *R v S*.[133]

1.202 Forbes J also referred to *R (TP) v West London Youth Court*[134] in which it was said that, 'a trial should not be abandoned before all practical steps to overcome the difficulties have been exhausted'.[135] V received daily transcripts and was even permitted to communicate directly with the tribunal by email. He was also granted a number of adjournments to prepare his case. Collectively these measures were sufficient to guarantee the fairness of the proceedings.

1.203 As stated above, Forbes J made the important distinction between a stay which is a discretionary judicial assessment based on fairness and voluntary erasure which involves an evidential assessment taking account of the

131 [2001] HRLR 6.
132 [2008] EWHC 753 (Admin).
133 [2006] EWCA Crim 756.
134 [2005] EWHC 2583 (Admin).
135 At para [18].

public interest and the interests of the registrant. That distinction was reaffirmed in *R (Al-Zayyat) v General Medical Council*[136] in which applications for voluntary erasure and a stay were made. There was clear psychiatric evidence to the effect that AZ was too ill to participate in the FTP proceedings. Mitting J held that the tribunal's decision that AZ was not genuinely ill was perverse and no reason to refuse a voluntary erasure. *Al-Zayaat* is not authority for the proposition that proof of ill-health necessarily supports an application for voluntary erasure, but it does mean that such applications must be decided on a proper assessment of the evidence.

1.204 In *R (Li) v GMC*[137] HHJ Wood QC commented that it was significant Forbes J had 'emphasised [the] continuing responsibility of the tribunal which could consider the question of effective participation at any stage including during the course of a hearing'. In this case, L was adjudged unfit to practise, unfit to attend or participate in an FTP hearing and that to do so would be profoundly damaging to his mental health. On the basis that L had at some time expressed a wish to work in Australia, the GMC proceeded but declared themselves neutral in that they did not dispute the medical evidence and said they would not appeal any stay of proceedings. The FTP Tribunal first declined voluntary erasure and then declined to stay proceedings. HHJ Wood QC ruled that the refusals were both irrational and were not conclusions any reasonable tribunal could properly reach. The refusal to stay even more so given the GMC had conceded they would not appeal such a decision.

1.205 HHJ Wood QC concluded that the tribunal was in error in placing any weight on L's distant and unrealistic hope that he may practise again one day. The undisputed medical evidence was that L 'could not participate in the hearing without significant consequences to his health'. In addition, proceeding carried with it a risk that L would commit suicide. The learned judge concluded that that risk and/or the GMC's concession that it would not contest a stay was substantial support for the grant of voluntary erasure.

1.206 The case of *R (Jackson) v General Medical Council*[138] illustrates the fine detail with which such cases should be examined and explained. J faced very serious allegations which raised a clear public interest in proceeding. J could not work any longer and had firmly stated that he did not wish to do so. Medical evidence showed that he would not be able to participate effectively in a hearing but he might however be able to provide some instructions. Dingemans J upheld the rationale of the decision since there was a clear assessment of the evidence save for the issue of providing instructions. This latter point was not explored or explained and the decision was therefore quashed.

1.207 The recent case of *Clarke v General Optical Council*[139] (see below at paras 3.127 and 3.385) may provide further weight to an application for voluntary erasure or an argument to stay of proceedings as an abuse of process. The latter could be argued on the basis that any public protection

136 [2010] EWHC 3213 (Admin).
137 [2013] EWHC 522 (Admin).
138 [2013] EWHC 2595 (Admin).
139 [2017] EWHC 521 (Admin).

issues are met by a registrant retiring and thus the public interest in proceeding is substantially reduced. While the argument may not be popular with regulators it should be given proper consideration. What is the point of proceedings if after considerable personal and financial cost they bring little or no practical advantage or protection to the public?

1.208 Following certain admitted failings C sold his practice and sought voluntary erasure but the GOC declined to permit this. He was suspended for 12 months and on review was erased from the register for reasons that were plainly wrong. What is of note is Fraser J's analysis of risk. C had admitted his failings and his responsibilities and, he had sold his business and retired. His retirement meant there was no risk to the public. Fraser J was careful to note that there was no place for sympathy and that it was *not* an issue of 'retiring with dignity' but of looking at the legal criteria.

1.209 In considering current impairment he reviewed various familiar cases including *Council for Healthcare and Regulatory Excellence v NMC and Grant* and *Meadows v GMC*, but also emphasised the three points made by Silber J in *Cohen v GMC* that 'It must be highly relevant in determining if a doctor's fitness to practise is impaired that first his or her conduct which led to the charge is easily remediable, second that it has been remedied and third that it is highly unlikely to be repeated'.[140]

1.210 In respect of the *Cohen* criteria Fraser J observed that the second factor (remediability) was arguably met by C no longer practising and the third criteria (risk of repetition) was nil since C had retired. He was careful to state that his decision was 'not to be interpreted as authority for the proposition that [retirement could be used] to avoid disciplinary proceeding.' However, retirement was a 'highly material and relevant factor' in assessing risk to the public. Since that assessment had not been undertaken the finding of impairment and the sanction were quashed.

1.211 From *Varma, Li* and *Jackson* above, it is clear that a stay is a discretionary judicial decision and voluntary erasure is a decision to be made on the evidence. The regulator may argue that the public interest requires proceedings to continue. However, if there is no risk to the public because the registrant has in fact retired (or is too ill ever to practise), the imperative to proceed is substantially reduced. That may tip the balance in favour of a stay or accepting voluntary erasure since the continuation of proceedings which results in suspending or erasing a registrant whose career has already ended does little to protect the public or public interest and less to enhance the standing of the regulator.

1.212 This latter point (standing of the regulator) may be of importance in weighing the public interest. Pursuing a registrant who is ill, in his or her 60s or 70s and not going to return to practice, is unlikely to be in the public interest other than in cases of serious dishonesty, serious sexual misconduct or where conduct has directly contributed to death or injury. It does not enhance the reputation of the profession or the regulator to pursue everything. There are clearly some cases where, even if misconduct/UPC could be proved, a well-informed member of the public would regard proceedings as wrong.

140 At [65].

1.213 Recent examples known to the author include proceeding against registrants in their 60s and 70s who have retired and left the country; are detained in hospital due to mental health problems; are confined to home on a Zimmer-frame; have suffered strokes or equally serious physical or mental breakdown. Some cases have exacerbated illness and/or caused illness to family members which is wholly contrary to the public interest.

1.214 In such cases, there is a danger that regulators interpret minimal contact from the registrant as indicative of non-cooperation. However, it may well be that the objective examination of this fact reveals they really have indeed retired. For example, it is plain that a registrant has retired when he or she phones and writes to confirm this and moves from London to a village on the west coast of Ireland from where all phone or written contact ensues. Proceeding on the wholly unlikely premise that someone will suddenly gain accreditation and return to work is, frankly, unreasonable if no serious issues of public protection or public interest arise.

1.215 Given the human cost (particularly to registrants) and the monetary cost of proceedings, a greater measure of common sense and pragmatism must be introduced into decisions to proceed or not, or to accept voluntary erasure or an agreed disposal irrespective of whether the registrant admits their guilt, or the regulator may prove its case.

1.216 Regulators are there to regulate, which is to take a reasonable overall approach to arrive at a desired position for the profession and the public. This does not equate to prosecuting cases when little or no public benefit ensues. Conversely, a regulator that acts with compassion and realism is to be respected not reviled.

Charges – unwarranted or oppressive

1.217 Complaint may be made if a charge is unwarranted, unnecessary or oppressive. This would be the case if a serious charge were brought which adds nothing to the case.

1.218 As a first principle, cases such as *Roomi v General Medical Council*[141] and *Chauhan v General Medical Council*[142] make it plain that any serious allegation relied upon by the regulator as proof of misconduct must be charged. If the allegation is not charged, then evidence cannot be called upon it nor can a registrant be accused or cross-examined upon it. (See also *R (El-Baroudy) v General Medical Council.*[143]) This is distinct from a registrant's attitude to the charges as displayed in any tribunal hearing. This latter conduct cannot form part of the case against the registrant (although if a registrant has lied to his or her regulator, this could result in new proceedings).

1.219 The need for care in drafting charges is particularly acute in cases of dishonesty even more so with the change in law as to what constitutes dishonesty. The difficulty is made plain by the distinction between *Misra v*

141 [2009] EWHC 2188 (Admin).
142 [2010] EWHC 2093 (Admin).
143 [2013] EWHC 2894 (Admin).

General Medical Council[144] and *Nicholas-Pillai v General Medical Council*[145] in which both doctors were charged with dishonesty. In *Misra,* M was alleged to have been informed of four phone-calls regarding a patient and not acting upon them. He admitted two calls, but told the patient's son he was not aware of two others, and in his response to the allegations he maintained this. He was charged with dishonesty in respect of what he told the son and the solicitor who drafted his written response to the charges. The Privy Council's opinion was that the charges of dishonesty were unnecessary and oppressive. They added nothing to his culpability regarding the phone-calls and were nothing more than him asserting what he honestly believed to be true. This is distinct from *Nicholas-Pillai* a case in which NP created documents that were inaccurate and intended to mislead. He thus manufactured a defence by creating false documents. NP's conduct clearly added to the seriousness of the case and went way beyond denial of the allegations against him.

1.220 Given the above cases, the following points are clear: Is the allegation more than a bare denial – that is, more than an honest statement of the registrant's case as he or she believed it to be? If it is, then it is potentially chargeable. If not, it should not be charged. Alternatively, is it a separate act that is relied upon to prove misconduct which should be charged, or is it merely the recitation of a registrant's defence which should not?

1.221 If a charge is aimed at an honestly held defence as opposed to a separate act relied upon to prove misconduct, it is in danger of being both unnecessary and oppressive.

1.222 See also *R (Johnson) v Nursing and Midwifery Council*[146] (above) on the particularity of charges – a stay is the exception, granted only if a fair trial is not possible.

Regulator revisiting a decision

1.223 In *Akewushola v Secretary of State for the Home Department*[147] the court stated that tribunals only have a limited power to correct 'accidental errors'. Such corrections must not 'substantially affect the rights of the parties or the decision arrived at'. Once a panel has discharged its function by giving its final decision, it is 'functus officio' and cannot reconsider the matter – see *Baxendale-Walker v Law Society*.[148]

1.224 In *R (B) v Nursing and Midwifery Council*[149] the NMC investigations committee concluded B had no case to answer. The NMC suggested the investigations committee had considered the wrong guidelines and invited it to reconsider the decision together with other allegations. The investigations committee duly did so, rescinded the finding of no case and reinstated proceedings. It purported to act either under the 'slip rule' or on the basis its original decision was an accidental error and *R (Jenkinson) v*

144 [2003] UKPC 7.
145 [2009] EWHC 1048 (Admin).
146 [2008] EWHC 885 (Admin).
147 [2000] 1 WLR 2295.
148 [2006] EWHC 643 (Admin).
149 [2012] EWHC 1264 (Admin).

Nursing & Midwifery Council[150] applied. The court rejected both arguments. On the one hand, a deliberate decision, even a flawed one, made after an assessment of the facts as they were believed to be, could not be corrected as a slip. On the other hand, the NMC had acted unfairly, contrary to its own procedures and had breached B's legitimate expectations of closure. The case could not be reopened simply because the NMC questioned the basis or quality of the earlier decision. *Jenkinson* was distinguished since in that case the parties agreed that a decision could not stand it being based on a conviction that was quashed by the court of appeal and, rescinding the previous decision was of benefit to *J* whereas such a course was detrimental to *B*.

1.225 This subject was revisited in *Fajemisin v The General Dental Council.*[151] F faced disciplinary proceedings and sought voluntary erasure, which was refused. Subsequently it was discovered that F had not completed his required continuing professional development (CPD) and the registrar advised F he would be erased. This was done in error and contrary to the GDC policy of not erasing for CPD reasons when a registrant faced FTP proceedings. The error was discovered and F was not erased. F challenged the FTP proceedings on the basis that he had been notified he would be erased and so was no longer a dentist subject to FTP proceedings. The Professional Conduct Committee rejected this argument on the basis that the decision not to erase on CPD grounds was a revocable administrative one. Keith J considered *Akewushola* (above) and held that the decision to erase F from the register for CPD reasons was intentional and not an accident, even though it had been made in ignorance of the facts. However, he went on to consider the decision of *Porteous v West Dorset District Council*[152] where the court held that a decision made in ignorance of the facts can be revisited if the factual basis 'amounted to a fundamental mistake of fact'. The registrar's decision to erase F had been made in ignorance of the facts, namely the pending FTP proceedings. As such it could be revisited.

1.226 Two more cases illustrate the dividing line. In *Gannon v General Medical Council*[153] the assistant registrar acting pursuant to rule 4(5) of the GMC (FTP) Rules 2004, allowed a case to proceed after five years had elapsed on the basis that there was a public interest in so doing and the circumstances were exceptional. G challenged the decision, one ground being that the assistant registrar had failed to revisit his decision when asked so to do. The court dismissed this on the basis that the assistant registrar was 'functus officio' once the decision was made and had no power to reconsider it.

1.227 However, *R (Chaudhuri) v General Medical Council*[154] suggests a more nuanced and common-sense approach. In this case, the assistant registrar referred complaints to case-examiners on the mistaken belief that they were not more than five years old. When C pointed out her error, the GMC refused to revisit the decision. On appeal, the court adopted a purposive

150 [2009] EWHC 1111 (Admin).
151 [2013] EWHC 3501 (Admin).
152 [2004] EWCA Civ 244.
153 [2015] EWHC 1998 (Admin).
154 [2015] EWHC 6621 (Admin).

approach to the rule which is designed to prevent the prosecution of stale events save in exceptional circumstances. Haddon-Cave J noted that the wording of rule 4(5) provides an objective test with only two outcomes. Had the assistant registrar known of her error, she would not have referred the case onward. He concluded that the assistant registrar had made a 'material error' in her decision and this empowered the court to revisit and quash the decision and remit it for reconsideration.

1.228 C also argued that the GMC had acted unlawfully in not revisiting the assistant registrar's decision. The GMC argued it had no power to do this. Haddon-Cave J followed *Fajemisin* (above) commenting that 'public bodies have the inherent or implied power to revisit and revoke any decision vitiated by a fundamental mistake as to the underlying facts . . . to suggest otherwise would be to allow process to triumph over common sense'.[155] He expressed the view that this inherent power applied to all such errors including those that 'substantially affect the rights of the parties or the decision taken'. *Gannon* was distinguished on the basis that there was no fundamental mistake of fact. There is a second distinguishing feature in that *Chaudhuri* involved the application of a test whose answer is objective and determined by the true facts. *Gannon* and cases cited within the proceedings involved the application of subjective judgement on matters of public interest and exceptional circumstances.

1.229 Finally, Haddon-Cave J rejected the GMC's argument that it did not really matter if the rule 4 decision was wrong since there were additional safeguards further down the line of the process. This was no answer to the 'distinct and free-standing safeguard' of the five-year rule applicable at the rule 4 stage – *D v General Medical Council*.[156]

1.230 The above cases demonstrate that, as a matter of common-sense and fairness, there will be occasions when regulatory bodies can revisit objective decisions made in ignorance of the true facts. This includes decisions that have a fundamental impact on the parties and proceedings. However, subjective decisions which involve an element of judgment on the facts as they are believed to be, are not to be revisited even if that judgment is later shown to be based in error. All the more so if the change of decision is averse to the registrant.

Regulator going back on a promise

1.231 A registrant may argue that he or she has received and relied upon a promise that a case will not proceed – however, to succeed in any such argument requires several hurdles to be crossed. While assistance is to be gained from the practice in criminal proceedings, the overarching objective of protecting the public may have a part to play in such an argument. Although there may be good reason to stop a criminal case where a defendant has acted upon a promise, this may be trumped in regulatory proceedings by the necessity of proceeding in order to protect the public.

1.232 The suggestion that a defendant might have a 'legitimate expectation' that a case will not proceed was firmly rejected as a basis for a stay in *R v*

155 At paras 46 and 46.
156 [2013] EWHC 2839 (Admin).

Abu Hamza.[157] It is now firmly settled that there must, first, be an explicit and unequivocal representation by a person in authority with the conduct of the investigation or the case; and second, the defendant has relied and acted upon that representation to his detriment. However, even this may not suffice if new previously unknown information comes to light which requires the representation to be revisited.

1.233 Examples within the criminal sphere include *R v Croydon JJ ex p Dean,*[158] in which a witness was assured that he would not be prosecuted if he gave evidence for the prosecution in a trial; and *R v Bloomfield,*[159] in which an unequivocal undertaking was given in open court by counsel to offer no evidence and there was no change in circumstances to alter that position. However, *R v Gripton*[160] makes it plain that the witness must be aware of the undertaking. The point is made in *R v Townsend*[161] that the longer someone is left to rely upon a promise the greater the injustice if the prosecution reneges on its word.

1.234 However, while such cases provide examples and some guidance, the principle set out in *Abu Hamza* is clear that there must be a promise by a person in authority which is relied upon and there must be prejudice to the registrant because of this.

Disclosure

> The regulator must disclose unused material in its possession to the registrant. It should do so in sufficient time to allow the registrant time to properly consider and/or use it. There is a continuing obligation of disclosure upon the regulator.
>
> While there is a duty to prevent inequality of arms, there is no positive duty on a disciplinary body to gather evidence to assist the practitioner.
>
> To allege unfairness under ECHR Article 6(3)(b), a complainant must demonstrate that a duty exists, that it has been breached and that this has caused an inequality of arms.
>
> Each case will depend on its own facts.

1.235 Late, partial or non-disclosure of unused material has caused difficulty in both the criminal and the regulatory arenas. It frequently stems from a misunderstanding of what should be disclosed and/or requested. In addition, the adversarial nature of litigation is unhelpful, with the prosecution/regulator interpreting the rules in a strict fashion against the defence and the defence making unfocussed requests for information. It has led on the one hand to miscarriages of justice, and on the other to lengthy but ultimately unsustainable abuse of process arguments. Repeated failure by the

157 [2007] 1 Cr App R 27.
158 (1994) 98 Cr App R 76 DC.
159 [1997] 1 Cr App R 135.
160 [2011] Crim LR 388.
161 [1997] 2 Cr App R 540.

prosecution to even assess, let alone disclose, unused material is very much in the public eye at present.

1.236 In regulatory proceedings, the first difficulty is the lack of definition or law concerning disclosure. While the proceedings are now firmly regarded as civil, there is a tendency to apply the criminal disclosure procedure.

1.237 Unused material is the information and evidence generated by or coming into the possession of the regulator while investigating or prosecuting a case.

1.238 Proper disclosure means that the unused material in the hands of the regulator should be assessed using the appropriate test and, if disclosable, it should be provided in sufficient time to give the defence a reasonable opportunity to assess, investigate and deploy the evidence or information flowing there-from.

1.239 In *Rajan v General Medical Council*[162] it was held that the duty on a regulator is to disclose 'relevant and material [evidence]' and, relying on the principle established in cases such as *R v Maguire*[163] and *R v Ward*,[164] this should be done 'on a date well before the date of the hearing'.

1.240 Relevant and material evidence is not limited to information the regulator does not use but is evidence that might weaken the regulator's case or strengthen the registrant's. While there is no clear parallel with criminal procedures, the regulator must assess material in the light of the registrant's case, and demonstrate that it has done so.

1.241 The Privy Council concluded that the finding against *Rajan* was unsafe 'because that failure denied to the appellant and his advisors a proper opportunity to advance a case which might have succeeded'.[165]

1.242 The complainant alleged that she had been assaulted by R during an appointment. She was uncertain as to the date but had made various entries in her diary. R had no recollection of the relevant consultation and defended himself on the basis of his usual and proper practice in consultations with female patients. Immediately before the hearing, a diary entry by the complainant was disclosed. It is not clear if R saw the diary before the hearing, however what is clear is that disclosure having been delayed until the day of the hearing, the defence were unable to consider it properly and assess its significance. On appeal, a new defence case was mounted to the effect that the consultation had never taken place and the complainant's allegations were a fantasy. This approach was arguable and may have been supported by psychiatric evidence.

1.243 The matter to which the unused material in *Rajan* was relevant was quite tightly defined. That is rarely the case. More frequently, disclosure concerns categories of evidence or larger volumes of material. Notwithstanding the additional work that may be involved, it behoves all parties to remember that 'over-disclosure' is unlikely to cause injustice. It is almost always under-disclosure or non-disclosure that leads to argument or a miscarriage of justice. The political imperatives of the Criminal Procedure Investigations Act (CPIA) 1996 (the belief that defendants

162 [2000] UKPC 1.

163 (1992) 94 Cr App R 133.

164 (1993) 96 Cr App R 1.

165 At para [17].

create a defence through the deployment of unused material) and, the reduction of public funds available to prosecute or defend cases are not so pressing in regulatory proceedings. Furthermore, while the CPIA 1996 has some, albeit inadequate, safeguards built into the process, these are absent in regulatory legislation.

1.244 While there are no absolute parallels with criminal or civil proceedings, most disciplinary proceedings tend to follow the rules of disclosure in the criminal courts. The obvious reason for this is that the regulator is the investigating and/or prosecuting body with access to the relevant witnesses and material and, will frequently have greater resources than the registrant. It is also the custodian of the information obtained in the investigation. In recent years there has been a deliberate drive by government to reduce disclosure in criminal proceedings. Since regulatory proceedings are not criminal, arguably that reduction does not apply. Having said that, the criminal rules of disclosure do provide a framework within which to operate.

1.245 Disclosure in criminal proceedings is a hugely complex topic, hedged around with legislation, codes, rules and the competing views of prosecution, defence and the court acting in its case-management capacity. The main principles are derived from the CPIA 1996; the CPIA codes of conduct; the Police and Criminal Evidence Act (PACE) 1984; the Criminal Justice Act (CJA) 2003; the Criminal Justice and Immigration Act 2008; the Criminal Procedure Rules (CPR) (which are updated regularly); Crown Court Protocols; Attorney General's Guidelines; and more. In the background, there is of course the ECHR Article 6 right to a fair and timely hearing.

1.246 In broad terms, the principles of disclosure are: first, that the prosecution should disclose to the defence any prosecution material which 'might reasonably be considered capable of undermining the case for the prosecution . . . or of assisting the case for the accused',[166] and second, that this should be kept under review up until the point of conviction or acquittal.[167] In particular, disclosure should be reconsidered in the light of the defence case statement and, if the defence feel that material is being withheld they can apply under section 8 of the CPIA 1996 for further disclosure. Finally, disclosure should be made as soon as is reasonably practicable.[168]

1.247 In *R v H*[169] the House of Lords held that: 'The golden rule is that full disclosure of [material that weakens the prosecution or strengthens the defence] should be made'.[170]

1.248 The CPIA codes of practice provide first that:

> . . . material [of any kind] may be relevant to the investigation if it appears . . . that it has some bearing on any offence . . . or any person being investigated, or on the surrounding circumstances of the case, unless it is incapable of having any impact on the case.[171]

166 CPIA 1996 s3.
167 CPIA 1996 s7A.
168 CPIA 1996 s13.
169 [2004] 2 AC 134.
170 At para 14.
171 CPIA 1996 Codes of Practice r2.1.

And second that:

> In conducting an investigation, the investigator should pursue all reasonable lines of inquiry, whether these point towards or away from the suspect. What is reasonable in each case will depend on the particular circumstances.[172]

1.249 From the above it is reasonable to expect, first, that the investigating and prosecuting bodies should look into exculpatory matters just as much as those that support their case; and second, that the exculpatory material is disclosed because it is material relevant to the case for the defendant. Unfortunately, expectation is not always met with fulfilment.

1.250 As cases have become more complex and expensive and disclosure has become more burdensome, so the pressures to restrict disclosure have increased. The now defunct Attorney-General's 1981 *Guidelines on disclosure* envisaged that material 'having some bearing on the offence(s) charged and the surrounding circumstances of the case' would be disclosed. In *Rowe and Davis v UK*[173] the ECtHR emphasised that disclosure should include all material evidence in the possession of the crown whether for or against the accused.

1.251 Disclosure under the CPR and CPIA 1996 does not require the wide disclosure envisioned by *Rowe and Davis* indeed it is designed to do quite the reverse. Disclosure is now expected to focus on what may undermine the prosecution or assist the defence case. A principal way to restrict disclosure is to require the defence to declare its case in a defence statement and thereafter for the prosecution to focus its investigation of unused material on matters impacting upon the defence disclosed therein. The justification seems to be based on the widely-promoted belief that defendants 'ambush' the prosecution and construct a defense by deploying unused material that is not relevant to what would otherwise be their real case. It is also intended to cut costs.

1.252 This process is said to be a focus on what is relevant to the issues that determine guilt or innocence. In *R v M*[174] it was held that this approach does not breach the ECHR. While this case deals with an earlier incarnation of the process, it is equally applicable to date.

1.253 A focused approach is not unreasonable if undertaken properly by professionals who know what they are doing and they undertake the work fairly with an equal eye to guilt and innocence. However, that is an aspiration which is rarely met. Investigators do not look at all lines of inquiry; they naturally concentrate on those that inculpate and they do not always inform prosecutors of material they hold. Furthermore, it is often the case that neither investigators nor prosecutors review the material they have or if they do, they fail to recognise or disclose material helpful to the defence.

1.254 Defence statements are now used as pleadings against a defendant. They may be shown to witnesses to elicit their comments and are used as tools to cross-examine if there is any deviation from the contents of the statement. This is a far cry from their original supposed purpose of disclosure. By

172 CPIA 1996 Codes of Practice r3.5.
173 (2000) 30 EHRR 1.
174 [2003] EWCA Crim 3764.

adopting the approach to disclosure used in criminal proceedings there is a risk that its flows will be imported into regulatory proceedures.

1.255 In *McCarthy v Visitors to the Inns of Court and Bar Standards Board*[175] the BSB, acting in contravention of its own rules, withheld a draft statement on the basis that to do so prevented M from altering his evidence. On appeal following M's disbarment, Moses LJ ruled that the BSB had a duty to serve any draft earlier statement which 'might reasonably be considered *capable* of undermining the [BSB's] case in that it might have an impact upon the witnesses' accuracy and credibility'.[176]

1.256 During the High Court proceedings, the BSB sought to argue that its disclosure obligation was no greater than any other civil litigant. Moses LJ rejected this stating that it was 'beyond question that in disciplinary proceedings with the potential for such grave consequences, draft statements capable of being used to discredit a witness should be disclosed'.[177] He continued that:

> No-one responsible for the prosecution [of a criminal case] would hesitate in disclosing a previous draft of a statement such as that which was finally signed and served [in this case] . . . if there is no inconsistency, the prosecution has nothing to lose and if there is, there is no warrant for concealing it. I can see no basis why the position should be different in relation to disciplinary proceedings . . . The demands of elementary fairness impose such an obligation.[178]

1.257 The comparison with criminal proceedings is notable, as is the acknowledgement that it is 'difficult' for prosecutors to judge how the defence may deploy an inconsistency between statements. However, it is worth emphasising that despite this Moses LJ could see no justification for a different approach in regulatory proceedings.

1.258 Finally, Moses LJ considered whether the unfairness necessarily required that the earlier proceedings be quashed. The case turned upon whether certain letters regarding a direct access case had been sent as M asserted or whether they had been fabricated by him at a later date. The letters plainly had not been sent as M alleged and, Moses LJ refused the appeal on the basis that when all the evidence was looked at there was 'no real possibility of any alternative result' to the finding against M.

1.259 The case went to appeal on the issue of whether Moses LJ should have quashed the findings and remitted the case back to the BSB for a re-hearing. The Appeal Court supported Moses LJ's approach to disclosure both in terms of the need for fairness and the analogy with criminal proceedings particularly in a case which had the 'potential to destroy a professional reputation and bring to an end a professional career'.

1.260 An important principle underlined by the Appeal Court is the question of what happens when the regulator infringes ECHR Article 6 or indulges in procedural impropriety. The court answered this question as follows, noting that the answer is the same whether viewed through domestic or European jurisprudence:

175 [2013] EWHC 3253 (Admin) and [2015] EWCA Civ 12.

176 At para [12].

177 At para [17].

178 At para [18].

> In criminal cases involving article 6 the test was settled by the Supreme Court in *McInnes v Her Majesty's Advocate*[179] [in which] Lord Hope identified two questions that fall to be considered in disclosure cases. The first is whether the material under consideration should have been disclosed. The second is the consequence of any failure to disclose. As to the second he said:
>
>> The test that should be applied is whether, taking all the circumstances of the trial into account, there is a real possibility that the jury would have arrived at a different verdict.

1.261 The court continued that:

> There is no reason to apply a different test in disciplinary proceedings when it is established that there has been material non-disclosure. Is there a real possibility that that the Tribunal would have come to a different conclusion had the disclosure been made? That involves a consideration not only of the content of the undisclosed material but also an evaluation of the various ways in which its disclosure might have affected the course of the proceedings.[180]

1.262 In respect of disclosure and the duties of the regulator, it is clear that Moses LJ's approach is correct. Regulators may not be able to easily determine what the defence will deploy, and as such full disclosure should be made. Regulatory proceedings are intended to protect and serve the public in three ways: policing bad practitioners, supporting good ones and rehabilitating those who have erred but who have the potential to be good.

1.263 On a different point, in subsequent proceedings the Visitors to the Inns of Court held that a fair hearing was not precluded by delay or by the BSB's witnesses knowing what matters may be put to them in cross-examination. The Visitors considered *R v Graham and others*[181] and *R v Bell*[182] on balancing the public interest and the defendant's in the retrial of serious offences. They concluded that the allegations were serious, should be litigated and a fair hearing could take place

1.264 The question of disclosure was central in *Anwar v National College for Teaching and Leadership*,[183] a case of a school pursuing an 'undue amount of religious influence' in its education and approach (the so-called 'Islamic Trojan-Horse' case). The National College for Teaching and Leadership (NCTL) alleged that there was one overall conspiracy, but brought two sets of proceedings – one against five members of the school's Senior Leadership Team (SLT) and the other against two teachers. Information disclosed in the first (SLT) case was withheld in the second two-teacher case. The case against A and A was proved, and they appealed on the basis that the information served in the SLT proceedings should have been disclosed. Phillips J criticised but did not rule upon the separation of proceedings. However, he concluded that the NCTL was 'obliged to disclose material from the SLT proceedings which might assist the Appellants' case or damage its own'.

179 [2010] UKSC 7.
180 See paras 25 and 26.
181 [1997] 1 Cr App R 302.
182 [2010] 1 Cr App R 27 407.
183 [2016] EWHC 2507 (Admin).

1.265 On any view, the statements of the SLT members denying the same matters levelled against the two teachers and expert reports disclosed in the SLT proceedings were disclosable. The failure of the NCTL to disclose these documents was compounded by the tribunal's failure to order disclosure and rendered the proceedings unjust.

1.266 Disclosure does not include an obligation to disclose neutral evidence or evidence adverse to the defence *R v H* (above), nor does it include a duty to assist the defence in investigating its own case *R v Khan*[184] (withholding of a witness statement subsequently used to cross-examine the defendant was upheld). However, a regulator should not use this as a reason to refuse a reasonable request by a registrant to obtain relevant information which she is unable to obtain through no fault of her own (see below at para 1.270).

1.267 Non-disclosure may result in an application to stay proceedings as an abuse of process. This has been argued in cases too numerous to set out but, it is not sufficient just to prove non-disclosure – the defence must demonstrate prejudice. In *R v Hadley*[185] the crown declined to serve video evidence but instead relied upon summaries. In quashing the conviction Moore-Blick LJ said that the appellant had to demonstrate that the undisclosed material was capable of affecting the jury.

1.268 In *Brants v Director of Public Prosecutions*[186] there were 13 adjournments before the Crown provided disclosure that had been ordered by the court. The Divisional Court rejected B's appeal against the magistrates' court refusing to stay proceedings. It held that delay alone will not warrant a stay since the public interest in prosecuting cases transcends the notion of punishing the Crown for causing delay.

1.269 In civil proceedings, a claimant must provide sufficient disclosure to enable a defendant to properly instruct his or her representatives and refute, insofar as he or she can, the case against him or her – see *AF (No 3)*.[187]

Third party disclosure

1.270 In *R v Flook*[188] the court held that the Crown has a duty to pursue reasonable lines of inquiry regarding material held by third-parties and to take reasonable steps to obtain it if it appears capable of meeting the test for primary disclosure set out in CPIA 1996 s3 (undermining or assisting etc). Disciplinary tribunals have tended to follow the criminal rules of disclosure which include the CPIA 1996 code of practice for investigators discussed above. This might appear to place a burden on the regulators to search for and consider all material both inculpatory and exculpatory. However, as with criminal proceedings, it is unlikely that merely asserting a lack of disclosure will avail the defence. The registrant will have to demonstrate that there has been prejudice and unfairness. In addition, the

184 [2007] EWCA Crim 2911.
185 [2006] EWCA Crim 2544.
186 (2011) 175 JP 246.
187 [2009] 3 WLR 74, HL, reference to *A and others v UK* (2009) 49 EHRR 29.
188 [2010] 1 Cr App R 30.

decision in *R (Johnson) v Nursing and Midwifery Council*[189] places limits on the inquiries the regulator may be expected to make.

1.271 In *Johnson*, J applied for judicial review of the Professional Conduct Committee's refusal to stay proceedings on grounds (among others) of a failure to obtain relevant documents and other evidence. The NMC had agreed to do what they considered reasonable to obtain various records but they refused to obtain those they regarded as irrelevant. Beatson J held that the ECHR Article 6 right to adequate facilities to prepare and equality of arms was case/fact-specific. There was a balance to be struck between the parties to ensure fairness. This did *not* include a positive duty on the part of the regulator to gather evidence for the defence, provided the registrant was not at a disadvantage in having to gather the evidence he or she wished to deploy.

1.272 The principle in *Jespers v Belgium*[190] that:

> Article 6(3)(b) recognized the right of the accused to have at his disposal . . . *all* relevant elements that have been or could be collected by the competent authorities [and] if the element in question is a document, access to that document is a necessary 'facility'[191]

is *not* authority for a singular positive duty on regulators to gather evidence for the defence.

1.273 The result is that the registrant must go further than simply assert a breach of ECHR Article 6. The registrant will have to establish that there is inequality or unfairness in his having to obtain documentation before a duty may be placed upon the regulator. Since J had done little or nothing to obtain the documents required, a complaint could not be leveled against the regulator.

1.274 In *R (Phillips) v Nursing and Midwifery Council*[192] the court adopted a similar approach when considering P's appeal based on the NMC's failure to call the patient who was named in the charge and a psychiatrist. Lloyd-Jones J held that P could have taken steps to obtain evidence and call witnesses. There was thus no basis to challenge the NMC's decision.

Double jeopardy and related abuse arguments

> Regulatory proceedings need not be stayed pending the outcome of criminal proceedings unless there are exceptional circumstances, such as an impossible workload from which the defendant can demonstrate serious prejudice or injustice. Arguments regarding double jeopardy, privilege and publicity are otherwise unlikely to succeed.

1.275 The interplay between civil and criminal proceedings has been and remains a contentious area, all the more so as the boundaries between these two strands of process blur through greater regulation, and simultaneous

189 [2008] EWHC 885 (Admin).
190 (1983) 5 EHRR CD 305.
191 At para 55.
192 [2008] EWHC 1698 (Admin).

actions brought by claimants. The argument has usually been that civil proceedings should await the outcome of a criminal trial so that matters disclosed by the defence in civil proceedings do not compromise the defendant in his or her trial. However, criminal trials have changed markedly and the advent of defence disclosure means that the arguments deployed to stay or postpone civil or regulatory proceedings are less likely to prevail. A defendant must now disclose not only his or her defence and the details of witnesses relied upon, but must set out where he or she takes issue with the prosecution case and why. All parties, including defendants and their advocates, are expected to comply with the CPR designed to assist the trial process the effects of which are most keenly felt by the defence.

Is the principle of parallel proceedings acceptable?

1.276 The answer to this fundamental question is – yes. In *Jefferson Ltd v Bhetcha*[193] the plaintiff company J brought a claim to recover monies appropriated by its former employee B, who also faced criminal prosecution in connection with this. The Court of Appeal confirmed that the court had the discretion to stay or adjourn the civil proceedings having regard to the concurrent criminal proceedings, but the defendant would have to persuade the court why this should happen. As Megaw J stated:

> . . . while each case must be judged on its own facts, the burden is on the defendant in the civil action to show that it is just and convenient that the plaintiff's ordinary rights of having his claim processed and heard and decided should be interfered with . . . one factor to be taken into account, and it may well be a very important factor, is whether there is a real danger of the causing of injustice in the criminal proceedings . . .[194]

1.277 The arguments deployed to prevent parallel proceedings are that: information necessarily disclosed in one hearing could be used in the other when it would not otherwise be available; the information may be statements that incriminate the witness/defendant or documents that are probative in the criminal hearing or, it may be that witnesses are rehearsed in their evidence; alternatively, there may be arguments regarding prejudicial publicity or that parallel proceedings place an unfair burden on one party.

1.278 None of the arguments are received with enthusiasm by the higher courts. With the move towards swifter justice and more case management, the emphasis is on continuing proceedings unless the court is persuaded otherwise by the risk of serious prejudice or injustice.

1.279 In *Mote v Secretary of State for Work and Pensions and another*[195] the Court of Appeal reviewed the matter of concurrent proceedings and reaffirmed that the civil court continues to enjoy the discretion to adjourn but that civil proceedings could frequently continue *without* prejudicing the criminal trial. The criminal courts have the power to stay proceedings as an abuse of process and, to control the admission of evidence. The fact that D may have to disclose his or her criminal defence during civil

193 [1979] 1 WLR 898.
194 At p905.
195 [2007] EWCA Civ 1324.

proceedings causes no prejudice since he or she is expected to disclose this in any event.

Privilege against self-incrimination – statements by the defendant

1.280 The privilege against self-incrimination prohibits a witness from being compelled to answer questions or produce documents if the answers or material might incriminate him or her in criminal proceedings. The fact that the exercise of that right means that someone may lose in civil proceedings does not provide a defence, although it may in exceptional circumstances provide grounds for postponement.

1.281 In *V v C*[196] the company V sought £11.3m and damages against C for misappropriation of funds. C said he could not respond to the particulars of claim for fear of self-incrimination. V sought summary judgment against him. The Court of Appeal confirmed that privilege arose when a person was being compelled on 'pain of punishment' to answer questions and held that pleadings in defence of an application for summary judgment did not involve compulsion. C could choose to plead his case or not, although the result might be that judgment is entered against him.

1.282 It is plain from *V v C* that the right to privilege against self-incrimination does not provide a 'right to silence' in civil cases, nor does the threat of criminal proceedings provide a defence. Civil claims are not prevented because the defendant may have to disclose his or her defence to criminal proceedings, not least because it is reasonable to proceed on the basis that a defence is deployed to exculpate. Finally, the introduction of defence case statements in criminal trials means that a defence should now be disclosed and, although the 'right to silence' exists it has been emasculated by adverse inferences being drawn when it is relied upon.

1.283 C could have applied to postpone the civil proceedings pending the outcome of the criminal trial, however following *Jefferson Ltd v Bhetcha*[197] above, the burden would be upon him to persuade the court that the civil proceedings could not be tried fairly, or trying them might affect the fairness of a criminal trial.

1.284 As alternatives, a defendant might try to argue that any civil court order should contain a clause preventing the use of disclosed material in other proceedings, or seek to agree such issues with the Crown Prosecution Service – however, absent exceptional circumstances both are unlikely to succeed.

1.285 On the other side of the coin, there may be merit in a claimant deferring civil proceedings until the outcome of a criminal trial since a conviction will undoubtedly make it more difficult for the defendant's civil case to succeed. This may reduce costs and improve the claimant's prospects, particularly if the defendant's assets are restrained.

1.286 The tension between a professional's duty to disclose and possible self-incrimination was addressed in *R v Institute of Chartered Accountants in England and Wales, ex p Nawaz*.[198] As with most regulators, the Institute of Chartered Accountants in England and Wales (ICAEW) requires its

196 [2001] EWCA Civ 1509.

197 [1979] 1 WLR 898.

198 [1997] EWCA Civ 1530 (CA – Leggat LJ) and [1997] PNLR 433 (High Court – Sedley J).

professional members to assist in the investigation of complaints. Understandably members may be loathe to do so, on the basis of self-incrimination. That was exactly the case for N who was disciplined for refusing to disclose information to his governing body on the basis that the information could be used against him. Sedley J in the High Court held that in becoming a member of the ICAEW he had contracted to abide by its regulations and as such had waived privilege. The ICAEW was obliged to investigate misconduct, and the requirement to provide information was a reasonable part of that public function. It was a duty undertaken by a professional when joining such a body. In addition, the issue of fairness includes fairness to the public which necessitates the detection and prevention of malpractice.

1.287 This approach was endorsed by Leggat LJ in the Court of Appeal, who stated that members of a profession '[accept] its duties and liabilities as well as its rights and powers' and that this acceptance includes waiver of privilege. Furthermore, he stated that it was plainly in the public interest and the interests of the profession that complaints are fully investigated.

1.288 The significance of the regulator's duty to investigate and the public interest in their so doing even if it results in a member being required to disclose material adverse to the member's personal interests, was reaffirmed in *Macpherson v Law Society*.[199] This was revisited in *Iqbal v Solicitors Regulation Authority*[200] where the court commented upon I's failure to give oral evidence. While an individual may remain silent, that may be taken into account in civil and, subject to certain safeguards, in criminal proceedings. The court commented that the public 'would expect' a professional person to account for his actions when facing serious allegations. In response to this the SRA issued a further practice direction (No 5 of 2013) to the effect that adverse inferences may now be drawn if a solicitor does not subject himself or herself to cross-examination. It specifically provides that this is the case even if a written statement is provided.

1.289 Likewise in *Ashiq v Bar Standards Board*[201] the Board of Visitors rejected the argument that to require a barrister to produce bank statements to support his assertion that he had paid a debt reversed the burden of proof. Under the Bar Code of Conduct A had a duty to respond 'positively' to reasonable requests and, his failure to do so was a matter from which the tribunal could draw an adverse inference.

1.290 The overriding conclusion from the above is that a registrant's failure to give evidence may result in an adverse inference being drawn unless it is unfair so to do or there is specific provision to prevent this. However, while there is force in the comment that regulators expect their registrants to account for their actions and the public would be best protected if this were the case, the practicalities are more difficult to determine.

Privilege against self-incrimination – statements by lawyers

1.291 Statements made by a defendant's lawyer, while not strictly *self*-incrimination, may provide admissible evidence in subsequent proceedings since

199 [2005] EWHC 2837 (Admin).
200 [2012] EWHC 3251 (Admin).
201 PC 2010/0185/A, 27 March 2013

they are usually deemed to be made on authority. In *R v Turner*,[202] pre-trial representations by an advocate at an early hearing were deployed. In *R v Hayes*[203] pre-trial negotiations on pleas contained in correspondence were deemed admissible. In *R (Firth) v Epping Magistrates' Court*[204] the pre-trial case-management form produced by F's advocate citing a defence of self-defence was used in committal proceedings to prove his presence at the scene of the crime when the evidence did not otherwise identify him. This caused considerable consternation given that defence representatives are obliged to fill in a form that could be used against their own client. It led to suggestions of simply marking the form 'privileged'. Thankfully, common-sense appears to have prevailed in the subsequent case of *R v Newell*[205] in which the contents of a 'plea and case-management form' were deployed against N when the prosecution perceived a difference between what he said in evidence and what his lawyer had placed on the form.

1.292 On appeal, the court held that a form filled in by an advocate was filled in with implied if not express authority. Alternatively, the advocate had ostensible authority to do so. In addition, the form was spoken to by counsel in court in N's presence so was again admissible but, the principle object of the form is to assist the court in the management of cases. The defence case is more readily to be observed in the defence case statement. For these reasons, the form should have been excluded by the trial judge under PACE 1984 s78 as being unfair in all the circumstances. While each case should be decided on its own facts, an example of the appropriate use of such a form may be where the defence seek to ambush the Crown while they are in breach of their obligations under the CPR by failing to provide a defence case statement.

1.293 From this it may be concluded that statements made by lawyers, whether in writing or orally, are admissible against a defendant, but that they should only be deployed in exceptional circumstances such as correcting unfairness to the prosecution caused by a deliberate and inappropriate conduct of the defence case.

1.294 There is no reason to exclude statements made by a defendant's lawyers in civil or disciplinary proceedings from subsequent criminal proceedings, or vice versa. This would include comments made during cross-examination and/or legal or factual argument.

1.295 Having said the above, with the exception of solicitors' accounts, regulatory bodies cannot generally require the production of documents that are subject to legal professional privilege: *Parry-Jones v The Law Society*.[206]

Privilege against self-incrimination – documents

1.296 In *C plc v P and Attorney-General (Intervenor)*[207] the Court of Appeal held that the privilege against self-incrimination is no basis for withholding incriminating material (child pornography on a computer) found during

202 (1975) 61 Cr App R 67.
203 [2004] EWCA Crim 2844.
204 [2011] EWHC 388 (Admin).
205 [2012] EWCA Crim 650.
206 [1969] 1 Ch 1.
207 [2007] EWCA Civ 493.

the execution of a civil search order. The privilege against self-incrimination does not apply to material that exists independent of answers from compulsory questions. Furthermore, even if material is ruled inadmissible under PACE 1984 s78 (as having an adverse/unfair effect on the proceedings) if that material leads to further evidence, there is no basis to exclude the latter. Subject to section 78 and overriding issues such as the prohibition on the use of evidence tainted by torture, the central principle of admissibility in criminal proceedings is relevance and not how or why the material was obtained. Likewise, relevance and fairness are the touchstones of admissibility in regulatory proceedings.

Adverse publicity

1.297 Adverse publicity as a ground for staying criminal proceedings, while still available in principle, is now all but defunct. Much of the case-law revolves around the freedom of the press to report matters, and the need for justice to be both open and public. The pendulum has swung against the idea that a jury could not ignore prejudicial material and the courts are far more willing to trust jurors and their oath. The deluge of prejudicial comment or other material that surrounds terrorist cases or high-profile murders have not prevented trials.

1.298 Furthermore, regulatory proceedings are intended to be public, albeit with a discretion to exclude the public in certain circumstances. These include considerations of an interim order and/or when the physical or mental health of a registrant may be in question. There is a balance to be met between the interests of the maker of the allegation, any patient(s) concerned, whether a public hearing would adversely affect the health of the practitioner, the public interest. The latter point of public interest is accorded great weight since the primary function of the regulators is to protect public interest and uphold standards. This requires application of the old adage that justice must be seen to be done. However, justice is not achieved 'at any price' and the health or safety of a registrant is an important consideration, particularly if there are concerns regarding a registrant's mental health and, for example, there is a risk of suicide.

1.299 As a ground for staying regulatory proceedings, the position is even more remote than in criminal trials since the tribunals consist of professional people guided by a legal assessor. However, cases such as *Roomi v General Medical Council*[208] (see para 1.278 above under charging protocols) show that mistakes can be made, and if a tribunal has demonstrably taken account of inappropriate material the decision may be open to challenge.

Double jeopardy

1.300 'Double jeopardy' is the term used when a defendant repeatedly faces criminal proceedings for the same offence of which he or she has been acquitted. The principle that 'no-one should be tried twice' finds its origins in the doctrine of abuse of process – see *Connelly v Director of Public Prosecutions*.[209]

208 [2009] EWHC 2188 (Admin).
209 [1964] AC 1254.

1.301 The rule has always been tightly restricted, and on serious cases where fresh compelling evidence is available, it has now been entirely abrogated by Part 10 of the CJA 2003. In any event, it is limited to previous consideration by the criminal courts. Attempts to extend the principle to prevent the criminal trial for matters litigated in a civil court have failed. In *R v L*[210] L's conviction of the manslaughter of his child was upheld despite the previous finding by the judge in care proceedings that he could not determine whether it was the mother or father who was responsible.

1.302 In *R v Statutory Committee of the Pharmaceutical Society of Great Britain*[211] the *omission* of any double-jeopardy rule in regulatory proceedings was specifically noted and, in *R (Redgrave) v Commissioner of Police for the Metropolis*[212] it was held that there was no issue of double jeopardy where misconduct proceedings were brought against a police officer after the High Court had refused to issue a voluntary bill on criminal charges, this refusal being treated as similar to an acquittal.

1.303 In *Bhatt v General Medical Council*[213] the court held that the GMC was entitled to bring a case against B based upon seven allegations of indecent assault of which he had been acquitted in the criminal court. Langstaff J reiterated the position that staying a case as an abuse of process is an exceptional course and should be taken only when a registrant cannot receive a fair hearing or, it would be unfair for a hearing to take place. The principal reasons why the case was not stayed are that the proceedings are of a different nature with a different purpose (upholding professional standards etc) and a different burden of proof. Furthermore, the plea of autrefois acquit did not apply to regulatory proceedings – see also *R (Redgrave) v Commissioner of the Police for the Metropolis.*[214]

1.304 However, that is not the end of the matter, and any issue of double jeopardy should be closely examined with reference to the instant proceedings and previous proceedings.

1.305 Internal disciplinary proceedings were held to be no bar to subsequent proceedings in *Cristou v Haringey LBC*.[215] C and M received written warnings under the council's simplified disciplinary procedure regarding their parts in the 'Baby P' case, which concerned the death of a baby and the inadequacies of the local authority's child-protection procedures. Following the mother pleading guilty to causing or allowing Baby P's death, and the ensuing report on safeguarding children in Haringey, further disciplinary proceedings resulted in their dismissal for gross misconduct.

1.306 The court rejected the submission that the second set of proceedings was an abuse of process, or was barred by the principle of res judicata because of the earlier proceedings. The court held that while an employer's internal disciplinary process may be loosely described as a tribunal, it was far removed from the professional or sporting regulatory/disciplinary bodies set up to oversee professionals.

210 [2006] 1 WLR 3092.
211 [1981] 2 All ER 805.
212 [2003] EWCA Civ 4.
213 [2011] EWHC 783 (Admin).
214 [2003] 1 WLR 1136.
215 [2013] EWCA Civ 178.

1.307 The court held that: 'The critical question is not the formality of the procedures, but rather whether they operate independently of the parties such that it is appropriate to describe their function as an adjudication between the parties.'

1.308 In *Mattu v University Hospitals of Coventry and Warwickshire NHS Trust*[216] the court held that an employer's disciplinary procedures were not 'judicial proceedings' within the meaning of Article 6 of the ECHR because the employer was not by that process determining civil rights, rather he was asserting a right pursuant to a contract. He was not acting as a judge but protecting a contractual interest.

1.309 In *R (Coke-Wallis) v Institute of Chartered Accountants in England and Wales*[217] Lord Clarke giving judgment in the Supreme Court concluded that res judicata *did* apply to a disciplinary committee of the Institute of Chartered Accountants set up by the byelaws of a Charter. The byelaws were akin to statute but added '. . . even if the byelaws created only private rights as between the institute and its members, I see no reason why the principle of cause of action estoppel should not apply'. A complaint against CW was dismissed on the merits because the conviction in Jersey that was relied upon was not indictable in the UK. The attempt by the Institute of Chartered Accountants to bring a second set of proceedings based upon the facts alleged in the Jersey matter was stayed by the Supreme Court. Both complaints relied upon the same conduct and, the first case having been dismissed, the second case breached the principles of res judicata.

1.310 The more recent case of *R (Mandic-Bozic) v British Association for Counselling and Psychotherapies*[218] sheds a little more light on the matter. MB was a member of both the British Association for Counselling and Psychotherapy (BACP) and the United Kingdom Council for Psychotherapy (UKCP). The UKCP heard a complaint by a patient as part of its FTP process. The UKCP found that MB was not currently impaired. Following this, the patient complained in the same terms to the BACP which then sought to bring similar regulatory proceedings arguing that the allegations were worded differently, and its standards were different to those of the UKCP. MB argued that the second set of proceedings was an abuse of process since the complaints had already been fully litigated and a decision had been made on the merits (action estoppel). Furthermore, the proceedings were a collateral attack upon the proceedings of the UKCP.

1.311 Mostyn J found in MB's favour on both grounds. Relying upon Lord Sumption's analysis of res judicata in *Virgin Atlantic Airways Ltd v Zodiac Seats UK Ltd*,[219] he ruled that the allegations were essentially the same, and although one regulator used different language in its proceedings, the standards they covered were essentially the same. The second proceedings were basically the same as the first which had been a judicial process with a public conclusion made by a competent tribunal on the merits. Although the UKBC and BACP were different bodies this did not disallow MB's

216 [2012] EWCA Civ 641.
217 [2011] 2 AC 146.
218 [2016] EWHC 3134.
219 [2013] UKSC 46, [2014] 1 AC 160.

argument since they had the same aims and, the complainant and the complaint were the same in both proceedings

1.312 Mostyn J further ruled that the second BACP proceedings were a collateral attack on the UKCP proceedings and it would be manifestly unfair to subject MB to a such a hearing. In so doing Mostyn J placed reliance upon the principles espoused in *Secretary of State for Business, Innovation and Skills v Weston*[220] in which two attempts were made by two 'organs of the state' to disqualify company directors. The first failed attempt was by the CPS in the Crown Court in criminal proceedings. The High Court rejected a second attempt made by the secretary of state in insolvency proceedings.

1.313 From the above slightly unusual case, it can be seen that where the process, complaint and evidence is the same and, where the aims of the regulatory bodies are essentially the same, there is scope for arguing res judicata. The big difference with this and other cases is of course the fact that in most cases the argument is run regarding criminal proceedings which have a very different emphasis to regulatory proceedings.

1.314 *Gray v Police Appeals Tribunal*[221] is another example of proceedings being quashed by the appellate court. G was convicted of several serious sexual offences and imprisoned. Disciplinary proceedings resulted in his dismissal from the police force. His conviction was quashed and a subsequent retrial resulted in an acquittal. Following this the Police Appeal Tribunal reviewed G's case and he was reinstated by the tribunal which decided his case should not be remitted back for reconsideration. Within two days of his reinstatement G was subjected to disciplinary proceedings on exactly the same matters. Again, the charges were found proved and G was once more dismissed. G argued in the hearing and at the subsequent Police Appeal Tribunal that the matter had been litigated and a final decision reached by the earlier Police Appeal Tribunal when it decided not to remit the case for rehearing. On appeal Coulson J quashed the findings against G stating that the earlier Police Appeal Tribunal decision was clearly a final decision taken on the merits and intended to bring an end to proceedings. In so doing, he referred to the case of *Coke-Wallis* (above) and to Arden LJ's judgment[222] in *JSC Aeroflot-Russian Airlines v Berezovsky and another*[223] of which he said:

> Finality is fundamental to the rule of law. Legal certainty means the element of security that results from legal decisions becoming final and legal rules coming into force. Legal certainty is important because it smoothes the way for social and commercial interaction.

(See also *R (B) v Nursing and Midwifery Council*[224] at para 1.224 regarding regulators revisiting a decision.)

220 [2014] EWHC 2933 (Ch).
221 [2016] EWHC 1239 (Admin).
222 At paras 20–22.
223 [2014] EWCA Civ 20.
224 [2012] EWHC 1264 (Admin).

An acquittal does not bar regulatory proceedings

1.315 While cases will have to be carefully considered, the tide is now clearly running against the registrant when it comes to arguing that regulatory proceedings should be stayed owing to what has occurred in criminal proceedings – see *Bhatt v General Medical Council* (see above at para 1.303).

1.316 In *Redgrave v Commissioner of the Metropolis,*[225] Simon Brown LJ commended the now superseded Home Office guidance which suggested it would normally be unfair to rely upon substantially the same conduct as had been dismissed during criminal proceedings or, if it was not substantially the same but was an essential element of the alleged misconduct and it had been resolved in the officer's favour. That principle was followed in *Sacha v GMC*, but it no longer represents the law.[226]

1.317 In *Ashraf v General Dental Council*[227] the divisional court firmly discouraged arguments suggesting that regulatory proceedings following an acquittal were unfair merely because a sanction may be serious or the conduct relied upon was substantially the same as that dismissed at trial. A was acquitted of fraud against the NHS and sought a stay against the GDC in its subsequent proceedings against him. In so doing, A relied on *Redgrave* (above).

1.318 Leveson LJ dismissed the suggestion that *Redgrave* established any general principle. It was simply that in that case, the evidential basis of the allegations had collapsed. His Lordship referred to *Bhatt v GMC* (para 1.303 above) in which the fact-specific, limited and obiter nature of the comments in *Redgrave* was emphasised in particular that they 'no longer represent the law'. Leveson LJ commented that 'the continued anxious citation of this line of authority ought to be discouraged', observing that the comment in *Redgrave* was merely to the effect that a regulator may wish to take account of Home Office guidance. That guidance has in any event changed such that an acquittal is merely one factor to consider in deciding whether to bring proceedings. Whilst not intending to provide 'definitive guidance', Leveson J commented at para 35 that:

> . . . although it is not inherently unfair to bring misconduct charges against a professional who has already been acquitted in the criminal courts, this does not mean that there will not be circumstances in which it may well be unfair to proceed . . . Without seeking to be determinative, it might be that no further investigation by the regulator is justified because the allegations do not, in any way, touch upon professional responsibilities either to [patients or the NHS]. . . .[Each regulator must decide] how they go about achieving their regulatory objectives and, bearing those objectives in mind, faithfully apply the well-known principles engaged within the concept of abuse of process.

1.319 That the approach to acquittals has been changing for some time is clear from *R (Sinha) v General Medical Council*[228] a case in which poor investigation by police meant that the principal line of defence (contamination of witnesses, collusion between them and with the investigating officer)

225 [2003] 1 WLR 1136.
226 [2009] EWHC 302 (Admin).
227 [2014] EWHC 2618 (Admin).
228 [2008] EWHC 1732 (Admin), [2009] EWCA Civ 80.

could not be properly tested. Following a voir-dire, it was determined that no fair trial could be heard. The prosecution offered no evidence and T was acquitted. The cases of *Bolton v Law Society* (above), *Redgrave* (above) and *Selvarajan v General Medical Council*[229] were distinguished because they did not deal with cases stopped on the basis that no fair trial could be held. Irwin J noted the function of regulatory proceedings and found that the termination of criminal proceedings was a factor to take into account but it was not determinative. In addition, the tribunal and all parties had a duty to ensure that a fair hearing could be held. With those safeguards in place some allegations were proved but some were dismissed.

Rehearsal of evidence

1.320 The fact that civil proceedings provide an opportunity for the rehearsal of witnesses, argument or unfair tailoring of cross-examination in criminal proceedings is no reason to stay the civil case. The argument was soundly rejected by the Court of Appeal in *Mote v Secretary of State for Work and Pensions and another.*[230] It was also rejected in *Bhatt* (above) given that the tribunal was informed of the previous court case and was alert to the issue of contamination and rehearsal. Any such issue could in any event be explored in cross-examination.

Conducting concurrent litigation

1.321 The burden of conducting concurrent litigation may lead to the postponement of civil proceedings but only in exceptional circumstances. In *R v Institute of Chartered Accountants in England ex p Brindle*[231] the Court of Appeal stayed disciplinary proceedings principally on grounds of the volume of work in litigating on separate fronts. The case concerned the collapse of the Bank of Credit and Commerce International (BCCI) and was colossal. Contrast *R v Chance ex p Smith*[232] in which the Divisional Court refused an application by Robert Maxwell's accountants for judicial review of a refusal to stay civil proceedings on the grounds of the volume and number of enquiries (Serious Fraud Office, Department of Trade and Industry, Parliamentary Committee, civil and disciplinary hearings). Henry LJ said that *Ex p Brindle* was 'decided on its own facts', which is frequently taken to mean a judge disagrees with and seeks to limit application of a decision. He concluded that the overlap in preparation was useful to the defence since work in one case could be deployed in another and, if conflicting demands were made the tribunals should sort these out for or among themselves.

1.322 In *R (Land and others) v Executive Counsel of the Joint Disciplinary Scheme*[233] Stanley Burnton J clearly preferred the approach taken in *Ex p Smith*, suggesting that regulatory proceedings were capable of dealing

229 [2008] EWHC 182 (Admin).
230 [2007] EWCA Civ 1324.
231 [1994] BCC 297.
232 [1995] BCC 1095.
233 [2002] EWHC 2086 (Admin).

with such issues and it was in accordance with the Court of Appeal's judgment in *R v Panel on Takeovers and Mergers ex p Al-Fayed*.[234]

1.323 Finally, in *R (Ranson) v Institute of Actuaries*[235] Moses J stayed civil proceedings largely on the basis that the case placed a huge burden on litigants in person. He confirmed that this was a power to be exercised sparingly and that considerable weight was due to the decision of the regulatory body.

1.324 The contrasting cases do provide a glimmer of hope but make it plain that a stay will only be granted in exceptional circumstance where the burden of preparation is intolerable and will lead to injustice. This is only likely to succeed where preparation in one case does not assist preparation in the other.

The jurisdiction of regulatory bodies

> The fact that matters complained of occurred outside the UK and/or before a practitioner was registered with a regulatory body is no bar to proceedings.
>
> The fact that the matters may have already been adjudicated upon in another jurisdiction is also no bar to proceedings.

1.325 The regulators have the power to consider acts that occurred outside the UK whether or not they have been adjudicated upon elsewhere, and they may consider acts that occurred before the registrant became a registered practitioner.

1.326 In *Mohammed v General Medical Council*[236] M was suspended for six months following disciplinary proceedings brought by the Irish Medical Council. Subsequently the GMC brought proceedings relating to the same misconduct and he was suspended for a further three months. In rejecting his appeal, the High Court referred to Medical Act 1983 s35C(2) which permitted a finding of impairment based on the determination of a regulatory body in the UK or elsewhere, and under section 35C(3) was not prevented from doing so on the basis that the acts occurred outside the UK or prior to registration. The court held that since the tribunal could base a finding of impairment on another regulatory body's decision it, by implication, had the power to take such action as it considered appropriate. (See also *R (Hollis) v Association of Chartered Certified Accountants*[237] at para 3.88 below.)

1.327 In *Swanney v General Medical Council*[238] S admitted disciplinary charges relating to misconduct that occurred in Canada in 1999–2000. At that time S was not registered in the UK. By the time he pleaded (in 2003) S had dual registration in the UK and British Columbia, Canada. In 2007 the GMC brought charges in relation to the same misconduct. S argued that the GMC had no jurisdiction since at the time he was not registered or

234 [1992] BCC 524.
235 [2004] EWHC 3087 (Admin).
236 [2007] EWHC 2728 (Admin).
237 [2014] EWHC 2572 (Admin).
238 2008 SLT 646.

practising in the UK, the matter occurred abroad and he was at risk of double jeopardy The Court of Session rejected each of his contentions. It noted that Medical Act 1983 s36(1)(b) authorises the GMC to take action against a registrant 'whether while so registered or not' which made it 'completely clear that the committee was being given authority by Parliament to explore an issue of serious professional misconduct in relation to actions which may have occurred while the subject of the inquiry was not a registered person in the United Kingdom'.

1.328 The court was concerned that the public would be at risk if a registrant found guilty of serious professional misconduct in some other jurisdiction could come to the UK and practise with impunity. The geographical location of the conduct was irrelevant given the legislative purpose of public protection. The court also dismissed the argument on double jeopardy on the basis that the purpose of each set of proceedings was to determine whether S ought to practise without restriction in each specific jurisdiction. The purposes were thus different and there was no prejudice or double jeopardy.

CHAPTER 2

Hearings (interim orders and full hearings), evidence and procedure

continued

Interim orders

> Interim orders may be imposed prior to the substantive hearing on fitness if they are necessary to protect the public, or are in the public interest or in the registrant's interest.
>
> The threshold for an interim order is a high one because a registrant may be temporarily suspended or subject to conditions that limit or prevent his or her practise.
>
> No judgment is made regarding the alleged facts, so evidence is not called but the tribunal must be satisfied that, on a fair analysis, there may be a prima facie case.
>
> A registrant should be given a full opportunity to make representations. However, an Interim Orders Tribunal (IOT) may proceed without the registrant provided all reasonable effort has been made to inform him or her of the hearing.

Overview

2.1 Healthcare regulators have the power to suspend or temporarily restrict the activities of practitioners. Examples are to be found in Medical Act (MA) 1983 s41A and Dentists Act (DA) 1984 s32(4), which were brought into force owing to the fact that the General Medical Council (GMC) was unable to remove Dr Shipman from practice until the conclusion of his trial for murder and the subsequent fitness to practise (FTP) hearing.

2.2 In general terms, interim orders may be made in proceedings brought by a regulator when the Interim Orders Tribunal is *satisfied* that it is:

- necessary for the protection of the public; or
- is otherwise in the public interest; or
- in the interests of the practitioner.

2.3 The public interest includes:

- preserving public confidence in the profession; and
- maintaining and declaring proper standards of conduct and performance.

2.4 As well as the element of protecting the public, it is important to note that when considering risk to the public, the order that is imposed, if any, must be that which is *necessary* to meet the risk. The issue of proportionality is of equal importance here as it is in FTP proceedings. Article 8 of the European Convention on Human Rights (ECHR) may also be engaged (see under sanctions below for more on proportionality).

2.5 An interim order may be up to 18 months in length, however the regulator may apply to the High Court[1] for an extension of up to 12 months. Repeat applications may be made.

1 If the registered address is Scotland or Northern Ireland, the Court of Sessions and High Court of NI respectively.

2.6 To suspend someone from practice or impose conditions is a serious step. Provision is thus made by the GMC to review an interim order every six months. However, following a first or subsequent review a registrant may request an early review of the order. This may occur after three months have elapsed from its imposition. The review should then take place as soon as practicable after the request. The six-monthly review is also reduced to three if:

- an order for conditions is replaced by suspension;
- an order for suspension is replaced by conditions;
- the High Court extends an order.

2.7 Other regulators have similar provisions such as a first review at six months and regular reviews thereafter.

2.8 An Interim Orders Tribunal hearing may proceed in the absence of the registrant and the Interim Orders Tribunal may impose an order provided he or she has been given the opportunity to attend and be heard. To proceed in absence, notice of the hearing must be served 'in such time before the hearing as is reasonable in the circumstances of the case'[2] however, as with FTP hearings, service does not have to be effected on the individual or indeed effective. The rules require only that all reasonable effort is made to effect service. (This topic is dealt with in greater detail under the FTP Tribunal and absence of the registrant.)

2.9 The registrar, appointed officer or, where there is no such person, the Investigating Committee, may refer a case to an Interim Orders Tribunal at any stage if he or she is of the opinion that the Interim Orders Tribunal should consider making an interim order.[3] Case examiners, Investigation Committees or their equivalent also have the power to direct the registrar to refer a case to the Interim Orders Tribunal.[4]

Guidance on referral to an Interim Orders Tribunal

2.10 The regulators provide guidance on the type of cases that suggest referral is appropriate. These include (but are not limited to) three broad categories:

1) *Risk from clinical practise.* If the allegations are substantiated, there is an ongoing risk to patients from the registrant's clinical practise. For example, allegations of a series of failures to provide a proper standard of care, or one particularly serious failure, or allegations that indicate a serious lack of basic medical knowledge or skills. This category includes cases where a registrant has appeared before the FTP Tribunal and been subject to an order but has not been immediately suspended, however new information, not available at the time of the original determination, suggests that the registrant poses an immediate risk to patients.
2) *Risk from non-clinical issues.* If the allegations are substantiated, the registrant poses a risk to patients if allowed to continue in unrestricted

2 General Medical Council (FTP) Rules ('GMC (FTP) Rules') 2004 SI No 2608 r26(1) but of general application.

3 GMC (FTP) Rules 2004 (as amended) r6.

4 GMC (FTP) Rules 2004 r8(6) and MA 1983 s35C(8) (both as amended).

practice. This category deals with cases where public confidence in the profession may be seriously damaged by the registrant concerned holding unrestricted registration. It includes cases where the registrant faces allegations of a nature so serious that it would not be in the public interest for the registrant to hold unrestricted registration pending their resolution even though there may be no evidence of a direct risk to patients. Such cases are likely to be under investigation by the police and include cases of homicide, sexual offences and abuse of children. The point at which registrants who are the subject of criminal investigations should be referred to an Interim Orders Tribunal is flexible and will depend on all the circumstances of the case

3) *Breaches of existing orders.* Where a registrant has breached restrictions imposed on his or her registration, broken undertakings to his or her regulator to limit their practice, refused to co-operate with a performance or health assessment or, prevaricates or falls ill temporarily so that completion of an assessment or medical examination is delayed.

Evidence

2.11 The Interim Orders Tribunal has a duty to act to protect members of the public and the wider public interest. Cases are referred as soon as information made available suggests that a registrant's registration needs to be restricted on an interim basis. Because of this, the information available to an Interim Orders Tribunal may be received rather late in the day and is likely to be less detailed than that available to the FTP Tribunal.

2.12 It is important to note on this issue that the Interim Orders Tribunal makes no findings of fact and does not usually hear evidence although it does receive information and submissions. However, it is also important to note the comments of Collins J in *R (George) v General Medical Council*[5] relating to late service of bulky documentation which meant that G did not have his side of events fully and properly considered, particularly when it came to argue upon the proportionality of the order of suspension sought by the regulator and whether a lesser order of conditions would have met the perceived risk. In this respect, attention should also be paid to the comments in *NMC v Kidd; NMC v De'filippis*[6] in which proper notice of a request for an extension to an interim order was not given. The emphasis is upon the regulator giving *sufficient* notice for the registrant to *properly* respond thereby avoiding unfairness. This should prevent precipitate listing or requests for lengthy delays to gather excessive material.

2.13 The principles regarding a regulator's duty to properly investigate, disclose and accurately articulate matters in FTP hearings have equal application to Interim Orders Tribunal hearings. This is of particular importance since the registrant has no opportunity to call evidence in rebuttal and, interim orders may have far-reaching effects upon his or her ability to practise. The admission of hearsay is a matter of some difficulty, since Interim Orders Tribunal hearings are principally based upon reports and not live evidence. It is very important for the material to be accurately

5 [2003] EWHC 1124 (Admin).

6 [2014] EWHC 847 (Admin).

stated by the regulator and carefully weighed by the tribunal. The registrant must be given a proper opportunity to make representations upon the alleged facts, risks, order and timescale.

2.14 One of the problems facing both a regulator and a registrant is the delay caused by the primacy of criminal proceedings. In *General Medical Council v Srinivas*[7] the point is made that a regulator should not interview witnesses or act in a way that may adversely affect criminal proceedings. However, that is not an excuse for the regulator to do nothing. They should at the very least consider the overall criminal allegations and keep themselves informed as to the likely outcome of proceedings and their seriousness to give some initial and timely consideration to whether this supports a case of misconduct.

2.15 In *Srinivas* HHJ Gilbart QC said that the:

> GMC must continue to act with expedition in a case which affects Dr Srinivas' ability to practise as a doctor. The fact that it is now over 3 years since this matter came to light, and over 2 years since his suspension, adds weight to that point. So does the fact that he was acquitted of all criminal charges, albeit that that cannot prove his innocence.

He observed that the acquittals made expedition 'essential'.

2.16 While the fact of an acquittal may be used to differentiate *Srinivas* it should not be a mantra to argue that doing nothing and then trying to catch up is the way things work. Regulators should be ready to get on with the case as soon as criminal proceedings have concluded.

The test

2.17 The Interim Orders Tribunal will impose an order if it is satisfied that in all the circumstances of the case there *may* be impairment of the registrant's fitness to practise which poses a real risk to members of the public, or may adversely affect the public interest or the interests of the registrant.

2.18 In deciding whether and what order to make, the Interim Orders Tribunal should balance the interests of the registrant and the interests of the public. The appropriate order is that which is *necessary* to guard against the risk or, is otherwise in the public or the practitioner's interest.

2.19 In reaching a decision whether to impose an interim order, an Interim Orders Tribunal should consider the following:

- the seriousness of risk to members of the public and, in assessing this, the tribunal should consider the seriousness of the allegation(s), the weight of the information and the risk of further incidents;
- whether public confidence in the profession is likely to be seriously damaged if the registrant continues to hold unrestricted registration;
- whether it is in the registrant's interests to hold unrestricted registration (eg the registrant may lack insight and need protection from himself or herself).

2.20 It is for the Interim Orders Tribunal to decide what weight to give to these factors, remembering that its first duty is to protect the public and the public interest. It should not assume responsibility for the treatment or

7 [2012] EWHC 670 (Admin).

rehabilitation of a registrant, although it may impose interim conditions relating to ongoing treatment and supervision.

2.21 Whether an Interim Orders Tribunal is satisfied that there may or may not be impairment is a matter of professional judgment. (See under FTP Tribunal for more on 'impairment'.)

2.22 While cases such as *Patel v GMC*[8] (see below at para 2.62) make it clear that a registrant's good character is not simply to be ignored in interim orders tribunal (IOT) proceedings, the weight to be given to it may be limited. In *Kumar v GMC*[9] Underhill J commented that he had no reason to doubt that the authors of various testimonial were voicing their genuine beliefs but pointed out that the fact that a doctor has on many occasions been competent and made a good impression is not inconsistent with a failure to meet standards on other occasions. He also emphasised the nature of the test applicable in an IOT hearing which is to assess risk.

2.23 The balance to such concerns is that a registrant's good character may give weight to an assertion that he or she will abide by undertakings or conditions of practice pending final resolution of the case. This is an important factor, since cases still take months if not years to be heard during which time a registrant's career, ability to earn and family life are or may be severely affected. A tribunal should not assume that there is risk simply because a serious accusation has been made. If it satisfied that there is risk, it must spell out why, what the risk is, and how it can be met only by the order proposed and not by any lesser order.

Interim conditions or interim suspension?

2.24 Having concluded that an order is necessary, the Interim Orders Tribunal must first consider whether conditions are appropriate to meet the risk. If they are not, then the tribunal should consider suspension. The tribunal must balance the need to impose an order with the impact on the registrant, ie the tribunal must consider whether suspension or the imposition of conditions is a proportionate response to the possible risk to members of the public, the public interest or the registrant's own interests.

2.25 An interim suspension must be *necessary for the protection of the public* or is *otherwise in the public interest*, although the latter is likely to be rare. The difference is that the former requires there to be a real risk to patients or the public, whereas the latter is more an issue of desirability and maintaining standards – see *R (Shiekh) v General Dental Council*[10] (see also under 'sanctions'). Where an Interim Orders Tribunal does impose an interim suspension order, while no judgment is made on the facts, it at least carries the implication that suspension or erasure is a real possibility following the full FTP hearing.

2.26 In proceedings brought by the General Osteopathic Council, the only order available to the Interim Orders Tribunal is suspension. While this reduces the options available to the tribunal, it in no way reduces the twin requirements of necessity and public protection before an order can be made.

8 [2012] EWHC 3688 (Admin).
9 [2013] EWHC 452 (Admin).
10 [2007] EWHC 2972 (Admin).

Unlike other regulators, the General Osteopathic Council's Interim Orders Tribunal may take account of undertakings as an alternative to suspension. Such undertakings must meet any identifiable risks and should be capable of independent verification before they can be accepted by a tribunal. They should be proffered in writing by the registrant, the tribunal does not invite undertakings nor draft them nor does it 'negotiate' although it may in general terms voice the concerns which any undertakings should address. If undertakings are offered, the Interim Orders Tribunal must be satisfied that they do not meet the identified risks before it may consider suspension.

2.27 The Interim Orders Tribunal is required to take into account the following factors:

- the seriousness of the allegation;
- the nature and strength of the evidence including any admissions (whether there is a prima facie case);
- the registrant's previous character and conduct including compliance with any previous orders or undertakings;
- the likelihood of repetition of the alleged conduct;
- any evidence of appropriate steps taken to address the concerns.

2.28 Where the registrant has been charged with a criminal offence, the tribunal is entitled to work on the basis that there is sufficient evidence to justify charges being brought by the Crown Prosecution Service (CPS). It is not always necessary to hear evidence or submissions as to the strength or weaknesses of the case, but each case must be decided on its own facts: *Fallon v Horseracing Regulatory Authority*.[11]

2.29 The impact on the registrant's right to practise, finances and reputation must be properly considered, bearing in mind the principles of necessity and proportionality – see *R (Madan) v General Medical Council*.[12]

2.30 *Madan* also provides some guidance on the issue of necessity. M was employed as a medical officer in child health. There were no complaints about her medical practice. She also ran a slimming clinic and prescribed appetite suppressants. It is about this that complaints were made. The Interim Orders Tribunal concluded that there was 'prima-facie evidence of inappropriate and irresponsible prescribing which, if proved, posed a risk to patients'.[13] It rejected conditions, and suspended M for 18 months. On appeal, Richards J held that 'whether one agrees or disagrees with [the judgment] on the merits, [it] cannot be said to have been manifestly wrong'[14] and he declined to substitute conditions. He also stated that the reasons given were adequate, intelligible and sufficient. (See also *Houshian* below on non-clinical risks at para 2.51).

2.31 Difficulty may arise when a registrant has been accused but is neither arrested nor charged. Where there is merely a complaint with little or no supporting information, it may, at times, behove the regulator to wait a short time for reliable information upon which to base (or refuse to make) an application. That is a matter of judgement for the regulator, but it is not

11 [2006] EWHC 2030 (QB).
12 [2001] EWHC 577 (Admin).
13 At para 18.
14 At para 10.

unknown for a serious accusation to be made and then withdrawn or disproved after a short period of reflection. If an arrest has occurred, the tribunal may proceed on the basis that the arrest has some evidential foundation, but it should not simply assume that an arrest will precipitate a charge. If a registrant has not been arrested or charged, the difficulty is more pronounced since the allegation is merely a complaint. In either circumstance the Interim Orders Tribunal will have to carefully assess the reliability of the information provided and weigh this against the effect an interim order may have on the registrant.

2.32 It is incumbent on the regulator not to rush to an Interim Orders Tribunal because a complaint is serious. The regulator should properly assess the available information to see whether it merits an application which has an arguable chance of success based upon the reliability of the information and weigh this against the effect of an order upon the registrant.

2.33 If imposing conditions, the Interim Orders Tribunal must ensure that they are workable, enforceable and will protect the public, the wider public interest or the registrant's own interests. As with FTP proceedings, the regulators provide guidance in various 'conditions banks'.

2.34 When considering whether or not to make an interim order, the tribunal cannot accept any undertakings or assurances given by the registrant.

Period of order

2.35 The maximum period for which an initial order may be imposed is 18 months, although as with any interim order this may be extended. In considering the period, the Interim Orders Tribunal should bear in mind the time that is likely to be needed before the matter is resolved and the impact of the order upon the registrant.

2.36 It is important to note that 18 months is a maximum and not a given or a target. The tribunal should not simply impose an order of 18 months without careful analysis of the information and the reasons why such a lengthy order is sought. While there may be good reason to impose an 18-month order in a complex case with several witnesses, there will be little justification in a case with one witness or minimal documentation.

2.37 Two difficulties are not infrequently encountered. First, the length of time the regulator may take to prepare a case after criminal proceedings have concluded. Second, the regulator widening an enquiry regarding a simple case to include making inquiries at every previous hospital in which a registrant has worked on the pre-text that such a fishing-expedition is warranted for purposes of context or public protection.

2.38 Simple cases are now heard in the criminal courts within a very few months of first complaint. There is no reason why regulatory proceedings should be any less timely since it is in both the public and the registrant's interests.

Reasons for decisions

2.39 The Interim Orders Tribunal must provide reasons for its decisions both upon the imposition (or non-imposition) of an order and the initial period of time for which it is imposed. The courts do not expect a tribunal to give long detailed reasons, but the reasons given must be clear and explain how the decisions were reached, including identifying the interest(s) for which the order is considered necessary. In *R (Walker) v General Medical Council*[15] Stanley Burnton J said that:

> . . . a lack of adequate reasons, or a decision which is disproportionate in its interference with the rights of the doctor in question will encourage the court to examine broadly the decision made by the committee and substitute its own in a way which it might be less willing to do where the decision appeared to be fully reasoned and proportional.
>
> . . . the court will normally give broad credit to the appreciation by a professionally qualified Committee of the conduct of the accused doctor [and where] full and substantial reasons are given . . . the court will give considerable weight to those and will be slow to interfere.[16]

2.40 It is worth noting here that the principle of giving weight to the decisions of a properly appointed tribunal in any profession is a theme running through many decisions in both interim order and fitness to practise cases.

Risk from non-clinical issues (necessity, desirability and public interest)

2.41 As stated above, the regulators provide guidance for the referral of serious cases such as homicide, assaults or sexual offences which fall into the first category of cases, where the issue is the necessity of protecting the public. However, guidance is lacking on matters of integrity or honesty where there is no such necessity and, matters are 'otherwise in the public interest'. This is somewhat surprising given the importance attached to matters of probity and the potential affect suspension may have on the registrant. The previously mentioned comments of Collins J in *R (George) v General Medical Council*[17] relating to late service of bulky documentation resulting in G not presenting his best arguments may well have relevance here.

2.42 Consideration has been given to the meaning of 'in the public interest' in a number of cases. In *R (Shiekh) v General Dental Council*,[18] S who received a suspended prison sentence for fraud posed no direct risk to the safety of the public. The case concerned his character not his clinical ability. Davis J overturned the GDC's suspension, finding that:

> It is a very serious thing indeed for a dentist or a doctor to be suspended. It is serious in many cases just because of the impact on that person's right to earn a living. It is serious in all cases because of the detriment to him in reputational terms. Accordingly, it is . . . likely to be a relatively rare case where a suspension order will be made on an interim basis on the ground that it is in the public interest.[19]

15 [2003] EWHC 2308 (Admin) at paras 9 and 10.
16 At paras [9] and [10].
17 [2003] EWHC 1124 (Admin).
18 [2007] EWHC 2972 (Admin).
19 At para [16].

2.43 On the absence of 'necessity' when considering public interest, Davis J commented that if public interest is to be raised it at least carried 'some implication of necessity and certainly it at least carries the implication of desirability'.[20] He went on to say that 'the bar is set high' and 'in the ordinary case at least, necessity is an appropriate yardstick. That is so because of reasons of proportionality'.[21] There is also an interesting parallel to be drawn with the ECHR Article 8 argument in *Bonhoeffer* at para 1.61 and the damage to a registrant's reputation caused by the commencement of proceedings.

2.44 In *R (Sosanya) v General Medical Council*[22] Davis J again overturned a suspension imposed on grounds of public protection. S's husband had been convicted of fraud and she awaited trial on charges of money laundering. He overturned the first because the charge did not relate to clinical practice, and in respect of the public interest he observed that the charges the doctor was facing were denied and that she had been 'convicted of nothing'.[23] He framed two questions for the tribunal to ask itself – on the one hand, 'will it be acceptable for us not to suspend in a case of this kind [if the charges are eventually proved?' and, on the other hand, 'will it be acceptable for us to suspend an applicant in a case of this kind [if the charges are eventually dismissed]?'[24]

2.45 The 'alternate question' approach was adopted in *Rashid v General Medical Council*[25] another case of alleged fraud. HHJ Gosnell commented that to answer the two questions required careful consideration of both the 'nature of the offence' and the 'cogency of the evidence'. He added that 'the risk of an injustice is all the higher where the evidence is weak'. At the time of the IOT which suspended him, R had not been charged or even interviewed by the police. Given the lack of patient-related issues and the paucity of evidence the suspension was terminated as 'neither necessary, desirable nor proportionate'.

2.46 Importing 'necessity' into the test for public interest has not occurred without criticism. In *Sandler v General Medical Council*[26] and *Bradshaw v General Medical Council*[27] the court refused to overturn suspensions imposed by the Interim Orders Tribunal.

2.47 In *Sandler* the doctor was suspended for allegedly failing to carry out examinations before completing 116 cremation certificates, which is a criminal offence. Nicol J agreed that there should be no suspension unless it was proportional and at least 'desirable' in the public interest, but he declined to go further adding 'the Court must be cautious about superimposing additional tests over and above those which Parliament has set'.[28]

2.48 In *Bradshaw*, a former Civil Aviation Authority medical officer was suspended on grounds of risk to the public, public interest and own

20 At para. [15].
21 At para [16].
22 [2009] EWHC 2814 (Admin).
23 At para [17].
24 At para 29.
25 [2012] EWHC 2862 (Admin).
26 [2010] EWHC 1029 (Admin), Nicol J.
27 [2010] EWHC 1296 (Admin), Judge Kaye QC.
28 *Sandler v General Dental Council* [2010] EWHC 1279 (Admin), Nicol J at para 14.

interest. There was no criticism of his clinical competence, rather the case was one of dishonesty surrounding the investigation of an alleged affair with a colleague. While HHJ Kaye QC commented that absent any clinical or patient issues, suspension for an affair alone might well be disproportionate, here B had lied to an investigation, falsely accused a colleague and fabricated evidence. Despite there being no issues of clinical competence, the GMC was rightly concerned regarding the public perception of doctors and, of the risk that B may be persuaded to lie if he was accused of something by a patient.

2.49 The High Court has emphasised that each case turns on its facts. That a distinction is to be made between what is necessary to protect the public and what is otherwise in the public or individual interest is clear from the relevant statutes and the regulators' own rules. However, the breadth of the distinction is not yet settled when considering public interest. One thing is certain, an interim order must be a proportionate response to the material put before the Interim Orders Tribunal taking account of seriousness, strength of evidence and, the impact of the order upon the registrant who must be given the opportunity to properly argue against the alleged facts and/or risks.

2.50 In *Harry v General Medical Council*[29] Burnett J comments that:

> The test of necessity attaches to the protection of the public, rather than the 'public interest' limb of the test. Nonetheless, there is some implication of necessity or desirability.[30]

He said that 'Suspension is concerned to protect against a real continuing risk'. He considered the information provided by the GMC and found that there was nothing to suggest H would repeat his conduct. There was thus 'no real risk' to members of the public. Burnett J also considered the effect of the suspension which was to prevent H from working at all and concluded that the imposition of an interim suspension was 'heavy handed and disproportionate'.

2.51 The impact of suspension on the registrant as a matter to consider was highlighted in *Houshian v General Medical Council*.[31] Central to the FTP process against H was the allegation that an employment tribunal found he had forged documents in relation to unfair dismissal proceedings and made unreasonable allegations against his employer. H continued to deny these findings although he did not appeal the employment tribunal decision. While the FTP process ground forward, the matter was not placed before the Interim Orders Tribunal for 12 months. When it was, the Interim Orders Tribunal suspended H to 'protect the reputation of the profession and maintain public confidence'. It regarded suspension as 'necessary'. The suspension was terminated on appeal. King J stressed several matters relating to the consequences of the suspension and proportionality. In particular, any damage to public confidence must be *serious*. He remarked that:

29 [2012] EWHC 2762 (QB).

30 At para 2.

31 [2012] EWHC 3458 (QB).

> It is therefore the responsibility of the IOP [Interim Orders Panel] to consider whether, if allegations are later proved, it will damage public confidence to learn the doctor continued working with patients while the matter was investigated.[32]

2.52 The Interim Orders Tribunal did not identify the risk or the degree of risk affecting public confidence in or the reputation of the profession. The seriousness of the allegations is no substitute for the proper assessment of this risk. In addition, the delay in bringing proceedings and the delay before they are determined could not be ignored.

2.53 King J stated that:

> The importance of the principle of proportionality in determining whether an interim order should be made pending the resolution of as yet unproven allegations faced by the practitioner, cannot be overstated. A suspension has potentially three very important consequences for a practitioner. First there is the impact upon the person's right to earn a living . . . Secondly, there is the obvious detriment to him in terms of his reputation. Thirdly it deprives the practitioner of showing that during the relevant period he has conducted himself well and competently.

2.54 In his judgment, King J took a middle ground as between the differing approaches of *Sandler* and *Shiekh*. He agreed with Davis J's comments that the public interest 'carried some implication of necessity and certainly the implication of desirability'. He also accepted Nicol J's word of caution in *Sandler* regarding importing such language into test. He did not express a preference, but ultimately agreed with the view as expressed by Davis J in *Shiekh* that suspension on grounds of public interest would be 'relatively rare'.

2.55 In terminating the suspension, King J accepted all three grounds of unfairness applied to H. He took account of the four-year period of unblemished practice before the matter was reported, the delay in applying for the interim order and the fact that the case was listed to be heard fully by the FTP tribunal in four months. He distinguished *Abdullah v General Medical Council*[33] which concerned allegations of sexual misconduct in a clinical setting.

2.56 However, even in *Abdullah,* Lindblom J is careful to assert that not every case of sexual misconduct necessitates an interim order of suspension.[34] The Interim Orders Tribunal must consider the distinct features and facts of each case and weigh up the material taking account of any flaws or inconsistencies and the impact on the practitioner. The opinion of the regulator is a matter to be given such weight as the tribunal considers appropriate – it should not simply defer to that opinion. Likewise the opinion of the Primary Care Trust in prior proceedings should be considered and, the Interim Orders Tribunal may take a more or less serious view.

2.57 Lindblom J describes the careful process undertaken by the IOP and comments:[35]

32 At [20].

33 [2012] EWHC 2506 (Admin).

34 See para 96.

35 At paras 98–99.

> The allegations faced by the claimant are not, I believe, so vague and inconsistent that his suspension from practice while they are investigated cannot be justified. Although, after their enquiry, the police had concluded that the evidence they had was not enough to support a prosecution . . . they did not dismiss [the] allegations as fanciful.
>
> Whether or not the assertions made by [the complainant] are truthful will emerge when they are put to the test. They may prove to be; they may not. However, the IOP did not ignore the imperfections in the case . . .

2.58 This was also the approach in *General Medical Council v E*[36] a case in which the registrant faced the serious allegation of multiple rape against one patient. An Interim Orders Tribunal imposed conditions upon E for 18 months, which were so onerous that it had the same effect as a suspension, all but preventing practise. The GMC sought a 12-month extension of these conditions. HHJ Pelling QC allowed a six-month extension but only on modified conditions. He took account of E's 20 years of blameless practice as against the complainant, whose accusations he judged to be 'manifestly unreliable' and 'sufficiently unreliable that it must be discounted [in the absence of independent supporting evidence]'. He emphasised that the complainant's vulnerability and mental ill-health, while contributing to the long delay, should not be used as a reason to disadvantage her and leave her without a voice. However, he accepted the view that if the complainant cannot or will not provide a statement to support her allegation then there will come a point at which the case must be discontinued. In imposing altered conditions, HHJ Pelling commented:

> Conditions that are proportionate when they are first imposed can become disproportionate with the passage of time and thus delay is a material consideration in deciding whether it would be proportionate to continue the interim order or relax it in whole or part.

2.59 The issue of proportionality was also raised in *Malik v General Medical Council*[37] a case in which M was suspended for submitting numerous assessments as part of his continuing e-portfolio. The basis of the suspension was that his probity was in question, which led to issues of public protection and trust in the profession. HHJ Raynor held that on clear evidence from colleagues there was no concern regarding M's clinical competence, as such suspension could not be justified on the ground of public protection. As to the issue of public interest, he ruled that in the absence of continued dishonest conduct confidence in the profession would not be undermined if M were not suspended. HHJ Raynor thus ruled that suspension was disproportionate and a 'particularly draconian step' in a case that prevented M from practising and meant he lost his training position and his ability to support his family.

2.60 Importantly, HHJ Raynor observed that he had to look at the position as it was before him taking account of any facts, circumstances or changes since the Interim Orders Tribunal decided the matter. This line of reasoning was followed in *Kashif v General Medical Council*[38] in which a narrow-

36 [2013] EWHC 3425 (Admin).

37 [2013] EWHC 2902 (Admin).

38 [2013] EWHC 4185 (Admin).

ing of the allegations against K meant that circumstances had changed since the original order was imposed.

2.61 The issue of reputation and 27 years of good service was central to the balancing exercise and assessment of risk in *R (Rhodes) v Police and Crime Commissioner for Lincolnshire*[39]. In concluding that a decision to suspend R was 'Wednesbury unreasonable', the court regarded it as 'remarkable and disturbing' that the seriousness of the allegation was not set against R's unblemished career.

2.62 In *Patel v GMC*[40] P, a 73-year-old GP faced allegations of misusing £1.8m of public funds when acting as a school governor. This was said to have occurred over six years. P had an unblemished career as a GP for 40 years; he denied the charge and there was no suggestion he had been motivated by personal gain. Eady J reviewed various authorities and concluded that: 'If it is genuinely the case that the public interest [or public confidence] requires to be protected then it seems likely that the individual reputation will have to yield.' However, he went on to quash the interim suspension order on the basis that no reasonable and properly informed member of the public would be offended by his being allowed to practise pending trial. He placed weight on there being no threat to patient welfare and added that the public are quite able to understand that a person is innocent until proved guilty and the practical consequences of this.

2.63 *Bhatnagar v General Medical Council*[41] provides a good contrast. Some four years prior to this case, B was suspended from practice for misconduct which included findings of dishonesty. He now faced further allegations of dishonesty including in relation to the previous investigation. While Edward-Stewart J regarded the fact that B had practised for many years without causing any concern in respect of patient safety as a 'powerful point', the breadth of the alleged dishonesty including in connection with his practice and his regulator meant suspension was properly justified. He distinguished cases such as that of *Patel* above where the dishonesty did not go to the heart of the activities of a doctor.

2.64 The issues of proportionality, necessity and impact were all revisited recently in *General Medical Council v Chopra*[42] – see below under extension of interim orders.

2.65 In *Davey v General Dental Council*[43] the court distinguished between an interim order and an immediate order following an adverse finding and sanction by the FTP tribunal. Following the FTP process, which resulted in a sanction of suspension, D was made the subject of an interim order on public interest grounds alone.

2.66 Master Bard ruled that an adverse finding meant that any issue of reputational damage was no longer arguable. The issue became one of the financial impact on the registrant but when the ratio of *Shiekh* was considered, in particular the rarity of suspension on grounds of public

39 [2013] EWHC 1009 (Admin).
40 [2012] EWHC 3688 (Admin).
41 [2013] EWHC 3412 (Admin).
42 [2017] EWHC 819 (Admin).
43 [2015] EWHC 1632 (Admin).

interest, he concluded that an immediate order was wrong whether from the perspective of necessity or desirability.

Review of interim orders

2.67 Reviews must take place at regular intervals, not least because the information first provided is likely to be incomplete, and because of the serious effect an interim order may have upon a registrant. The evidence, risk(s) identified and the order must all be reassessed.

2.68 The GMC has introduced a system of reviews on the papers whereby a registrant can agree to the continuation of an interim order whether on the same terms or varied terms. The facts and reasons behind the agreement are settled on paper as is the order itself. The process is overseen and sanctioned by a Legally Qualified Chair (LQC) on the papers. If the LQC has any doubts about the matter, it is referred to an interim orders tribunal hearing.

2.69 A review hearing provides an opportunity to revisit the initial information and reconsider the matter in the light of any fresh material. New material should be given significant weight. In particular, a registrant may be able to argue that recent material more accurately reflects his or her current skills as opposed to mere allegations of shortcomings and, demonstrate that concerns raised at an earlier hearing have been understood and are being or have been addressed. Through this, the registrant may be able to argue that an order for suspension should be replaced by conditions or, that conditions may be relaxed, or that there be no order.

2.70 *General Medical Council v Khan*[44] is an example of how the assessment should refer to tangible and current risks. The GMC applied to extend an interim order of conditions. This was opposed on the basis that if K remained in his current post there was no risk to the public or public interest. HHJ Davis accepted this proposition but, could not exclude the risk of K moving to general practice and so could not exclude the risk to the public. The order was maintained but the conditions were reduced to ones he regarded as 'reasonably and demonstrably necessary'. (See also *Malik* and *Kashif* at paras 2.59 and 2.60 above.)

Extension of interim orders

2.71 Interim orders are intended to be of limited, though not necessarily short, duration. However, they can be extended following an application to the High Court. Since the regulator makes the application to extend, it is the regulator that bears the burden of proving the case for an extension (on the balance of probabilities), although a registrant may consent to such an extension. The latter course may well be in the registrant's own interests if a final hearing is imminent.

2.72 In considering whether to extend an interim order, the judge should consider the same factors as when the order was first imposed taking account of any change in circumstances since that time. These factors include the gravity of the allegation(s), the risk of harm to patients and the

44 [2013] EWHC 823 (Admin).

seriousness of that risk, the wider public interest, the reasons why a case has not been concluded and, the prejudice to the registrant caused by a continuation of the order. The judge does not make findings of fact – rather, it is a case of whether the allegations as a whole justify continuation of the interim order because it is necessary for the protection of the public or practitioner, or is otherwise in the public interest: *General Medical Council v Hiew.*[45]

2.73 That approach has been consistently followed (see, for example, *Perry v Nursing and Midwifery Council*[46]) although in *Houshian* (above) the point is made that each case turns on its own facts.

2.74 In *Perry*, P sought to argue that fairness meant he should have the opportunity to give evidence as to the substance of the allegation. The court rejected this argument. It proceeded on the basis that ECHR Article 6 (and Article 8) was engaged to the extent compatible with the instant proceedings relying upon *Micallef v Malta*[47] in so doing. It concluded that both sides must have the opportunity to address the need for and type or interim order. The registrant may give evidence concerning the effect of an interim order upon his practice. Stanley Burnton LJ also noted that since an Interim Order Committee or a judge faced with an application to extend an order has to consider the nature of the evidence, and may 'discount evidence that is inconsistent with objective or undisputed evidence or which is manifestly unreliable', they may hear from the registrant as to why the material may be unreliable. However, their function is not to decide the ultimate issue of whether the allegation is well-founded or true which is for the FTP Committee to determine. P was therefore not entitled to address that issue in evidence.

2.75 This position was repeated in *General Medical Council v Qureshi*,[48] where the High Court said it was not there to decide upon the merits of the competing medical opinions regarding Q's alleged mental condition and any risks arising there-from. If the GMC's expert was correct, the potential risk to the public was established. However, since there was a dispute about risk between experts and the prospect of unfairness if a lengthy extension were made, the court only granted a short extension to expedite a final hearing.

2.76 In the first edition of this book, two cases were cited to demonstrate the application of the balancing exercise, albeit that both resulted in extension. First, in *General Medical Council v Razoq*[49] the GMC applied for an extension pending the outcome of criminal proceedings. They wished to place all matters before the FTP Tribunal rather than deal with some before and some after the criminal trial. The criminal case was moving very slowly, however the allegations concerned probity and honesty, and were thus serious. The High Court expressed concern about the significant delay and the effect this would have in de-skilling R who may thereby only return to work with conditions. The court sought to protect R from

45 [2007] 1 WLR 2007, CA.
46 [2013] EWCA Civ 145.
47 [2010] 50 EHRR 37.
48 [2014] EWHC 775 (Admin).
49 [2010] EWHC 2258 (Admin).

such prejudice and only granted an extension of eight months during which time the criminal trial ought to conclude. Any further delay would require a fresh application to extend the interim order.

2.77 Second, in *R (Nursing and Midwifery Council) v Fofanah*[50] the High Court granted an eight-month extension to an interim order of suspension. There had already been considerable delay and two previous extensions but, the allegations were serious and had now been proved. The risk of harm to patients was thus considered to be serious, the delay was not entirely caused by the NMC and, the extension caused no additional prejudice to F.

2.78 Matters have moved on since the above, following a plethora of hearings wherein concern was expressed about lengthy delay to cases and further applications to extend interim orders. In *R (Nursing and Midwifery Council) v Chua*[51] Parker J expressed anxiety and regret when granting a 12-month extension to an 18-month interim order. Such comment was repeated in several cases, such as *Nursing and Midwifery Council v Bass*[52] and *R (Nursing and Midwifery Council) v Pitts.*[53]

2.79 In *Nursing and Midwifery Council v Adina*[54] Burnett J granted only half the extension sought and stressed that 'extensions of suspension orders do not follow as a matter of course'; and in *R (Nursing and Midwifery Council) v McKenzie*[55] he advised the NMC to deal with matters swiftly since this was to everyone's benefit. In *General Medical Council v Gill*[56] HHJ Judge Pelling QC criticised the GMC for routinely seeking the maximum (18-month) interim order and then seeking to extend it. On the evidence provided to justify the application, he concluded that the extension sought was 'wholly inappropriate'. In *Wisson v Health Professions Council*[57] Edwards-Stuart J indicated that pressure needed to be placed on the Health Professions Council to conclude proceedings more quickly.

2.80 The message from the above cases is that the evidence justifying the proposed extension and any reasons for delay should be closely scrutinised. However, progress in the reduction of extensions remained slow and the matter was taken a stage further in the following.

2.81 In *Nursing and Midwifery Council v David Miller*[58] M faced serious allegations of dishonesty and aggressive conduct, however the issues were not complex. An 18-month suspension order was extended by the Administrative Court for nine months, and then again for a short period owing to an error in the original extension pending a full review – by which time, M had been suspended for almost two and a half years. Blake J declined to extend the order, citing in particular M's inability to practise his profession and his ECHR Article 6 right to have the matter dealt with in a reasonable timescale. While recognising that the NMC has limited

50 [2011] EWHC 1346 (Admin).
51 [2011] EWHC 3162 (Admin).
52 [2011] EWHC 3346 (Admin).
53 [2011] EWHC 2466 (Admin).
54 [2011] EWHC 2159 (Admin).
55 [2011] EWHC 3361 (Admin).
56 [2011] EWHC 2645 (Admin).
57 [2011] EWHC 3579 (Admin).
58 [2011] EWHC 2601 (Admin).

resources, Blake J regarded the investigation as 'leisurely', and this continued despite Mitting J's reluctance to allow the first extension which should have goaded the NMC to complete the case within that nine-month extension.

2.82 In *Nursing and Midwifery Council v Maceda*[59] M was made the subject of an interim suspension order in February 2010. In September 2010 the external investigating solicitor advised there was insufficient evidence to charge M but the NMC continued to investigate. Case progression was slow, but a three-month extension granted despite which, by November 2011, no charges had been drawn up. Instead the NMC proposed further investigations. Bean J refused to extend the interim order stating that the decision to grant the original order to protect the public was not 'decisive for all time', nor was it conclusive in an application to renew. The delay was for the most part unexplained, and it was not appropriate to extend the order any further. While M could no longer work due to health issues, removing any potential risk to the public, the important factor is that the court took account of the delay in refusing to extend the interim order.

2.83 In *Nursing and Midwifery Council v Kidd and De' filippis*[60] the court sought to 'lay down the marker' for all regulators that applying for extensions is not to be taken lightly. The court criticised the NMC for leaving routine applications to the last minute thereby rendering them 'artificially' urgent whilst at the same time presenting the registrant with a suggested consent order. While the latter is not improper, it is potentially unfair. The lateness of the applications meant that the registrants had insufficient time to consider matters. The court stated that ordinarily a registrant should be given at least seven days' notice to enable him or her to respond properly. The court commented that 'serious and elementary issues of fairness' arise. In these cases, short extensions were granted, but the registrants were given liberty to apply to vary the orders.

2.84 That extension is not a 'box-ticking exercise' is made clear by *General Medical Council v Makki*,[61] a case involving alleged sexual misconduct in which an extension was granted regarding some conditions but the condition requiring a chaperone to be present when dealing with a female patient was refused. The conditions had been extended once already. A chaperone was an intrusive condition and it was not appropriate to extend the requirement beyond the time needed to properly investigate the case.

2.85 The position shifted one stage further in the cases of *General Medical Council v E*[62] and *General Medical Council v Agrawal*.[63] In both cases, the High Court took account of the long delays and inactivity of the regulator, but also assessed the weight of the evidence against the registrant. In *General Medical Council v E* the investigation of serious allegations, including rape suffered 'inactivity for prolonged periods' at the hands of the regulator. The decision of HHJ Pelling on the first extension is dealt with above at para 2.79, particularly in relation to the weight of the evidence.

59 [2011] EWHC 3004 (Admin).

60 [2014] EWHC 847 (Admin).

61 [2014] EWHC 769 (Admin).

62 [2014] EWHC 1620 (Admin) (and [2013] EWHC 3425 (Admin), HHJ Pelling).

63 [2014] EWHC 1669 (Admin).

His comment on delay is also noteworthy. Despite these comments, the case did not progress. A further extension was sought and refused by Stuart-Smith J. The litany of delay and inactivity recited at para 22 of his judgment is remarkable. All the more so given that it continued even after the principal complaint of rape was discontinued. Stuart-Smith J refused the extension owing to the GMC's failure to properly address in evidence the factors laid down in *Hiew* (above). In so doing, he looked in detail at: i) the seriousness of the remaining charges; ii) the nature of the remaining evidence available to the GMC; iii) the risk or lack of risk of harm to patients; iv) why there had been such delay; v) the prejudice to E; and vi) the public interest.

2.86 The same critical analysis of the factors set out in *Hiew* (above) and an emphasis on the weakness of the case resulted in refusal of the extension in *Agrawal*. A faced serious allegations regarding his competence, but the case had not been investigated or prosecuted with due expedition. Had it been, it would have been referred to the FTP Tribunal or otherwise concluded 12 months previously. HHJ Raynor QC took account of the following: i) the weakness of the case; ii) A had answered the allegations fully; iii) A's case was supported by witnesses of repute; iv) and the Interim Orders Tribunal had previously commented on the weakness of the case and reduced the conditions.

2.87 This welcome line of cases urging careful analysis was continued in *Avracmucz v Nursing and Midwifery Council*,[64] in which the court emphasised that each case and each registrant must be considered individually. They should not be treated as one of many or one of a class of individuals.

2.88 In *Houshian v GMC*[65] referred to above, the point was well made that the importance of proportionality 'cannot be overstated' since an interim order of suspension adversely affects the registrant's 'right to earn a living . . . his reputation [and deprives the practitioner the opportunity to show] he has conducted himself well and competently'.

2.89 Despite all the above, there is still room for improvement. In *General Medical Council v Chopra*[66] C was subject to an interim order of conditions due to be reviewed by the High Court. Prior to the High Court hearing, the GMC sought an early review of the existing order and raised additional concerns. The GMC sought and obtained an interim order of suspension. The reasoning provided by the interim orders tribunal was brief and it included the comment that the performance issues could be dealt with by conditions but the probity issues could not. The tribunal failed to clearly articulate the balancing exercise, taking account of the impact upon C and his many patients in a rural area and the weight to be attached to the evidence some of which was questionable since other allegations had been dropped as being unfounded.

2.90 Owing to the lack of clarity, Andrews J reviewed both the extension and the justification for the order itself. She referred to *Harry v General Medical*

64 [2014] EWHC 2913 (Admin).

65 [2012] EWHC 3458 (Admin).

66 [2017] EWHC 819 (Admin).

Council[67] (above at para 2.50) and held that the failures were contrary to the above stated principles and guidance. The risk-assessment was inadequate and there was no explanation as to why conditions could not meet some of the alleged risks. She refused to extend the interim order thus allowing it to lapse. A new interim orders tribunal could then reconsider the case.

2.91 From the above it is clear that routine applications to extend interim orders are no longer appropriate. Any request to extend must be supported by cogent evidence as to the allegations and the supposed risks taking account of any changes in the evidence, and cogent evidence as to what has caused the case to be delayed. Delay caused by the regulator will be critically examined. Extensions may not be granted, even in serious cases, when the delay cannot be justified. This is particularly so where there is a serious adverse effect upon the registrant. The court is no longer prepared to accept the bald assertion that the public, or the public interest, require protection to excuse months if not years of delay. The interim orders tribunal and ultimately the regulator should be of a similar mind.

Fitness to practise hearings

Evidence

Hearsay and absent witnesses

> The FTP Tribunal has the discretion to proceed in the absence of a witness and to admit hearsay evidence, but the decision to proceed must be taken with 'the utmost care and caution' and only after full consideration of the competing interests with emphasis on those of the registrant.
>
> There must be compelling reasons to deprive a registrant of the opportunity to cross-examine a witness – more so if the case or its consequences are serious.

2.92 Hearsay evidence is, by its very nature, not the best evidence, being second-hand or reported – however, it is admissible in civil proceedings pursuant to the Civil Evidence Act (CEA) 1995 and in criminal proceedings pursuant to the Criminal Justice Act (CJA) 2003. While regulatory proceedings are now recognised to be civil in nature, the admission of evidence in regulatory proceedings is generally governed by the twin issues of relevance and fairness – the latter being decided in part through the consideration of criminal authorities.

2.93 Relevance is usually reasonably easy to determine the question being whether the evidence is probative of a fact in issue or, supports or contradicts an argument or proposition that enables a party to prove its own case or disprove the opposing case. Of course not every fact argument or proposition requires proving or disproving and the tribunal should not be drawn into 'satellite litigation'. What is important is to admit evidence on those matters that enable a tribunal to decide the charges before it.

67 [2012] EWHC 2762.

Ultimately, evidence is only relevant if it helps to prove or disprove a charge (or at the later stages of a hearing, if it is relevant to impairment or sanction).

2.94 As to the issue of fairness, despite the civil nature of the proceedings tribunals are usually guided by criminal authorities on hearsay and the CJA 2003. This section deals with how these are applied to regulatory proceedings.

2.95 The principal guide to admissibility is 'fairness', balancing the interests of the prosecution and the defence. This approach has led to the increased use of hearsay but it is by no means routine and, each case and each application to admit hearsay must be carefully considered on its own facts.

2.96 In the Appeal Court judgment in *Horncastle*[68] Thomas LJ stated that it is 'ordinarily essential that evidence of the truth of a matter be given in person by a witness who speaks from his own observation or knowledge'.[69]

2.97 However, in some cases it may be the only evidence on an issue or of particular importance. The admission of hearsay is thus capable of being prejudicial to the fairness of proceedings but, its exclusion may also cause prejudice. Since tribunals should not consider prejudicial matters the admission of hearsay evidence must be carefully scrutinised.[70]

2.98 Rules for regulatory proceedings generally provide a wider remit to receive evidence that a tribunal considers to be relevant and fair bearing in mind its' purpose of protecting the public and upholding standards. By way of example, the GMC (FTP) Rules 2004 allow for the admission of evidence that the tribunal considers to be:

> (1) . . . fair and relevant to the case before them whether or not such evidence would be admissible in a court of law.
>
> (2) Where evidence would not be admissible in criminal proceedings in England . . . the Panel shall not admit such evidence unless . . . satisfied that their duty of making due inquiry into the case before them makes its admission desirable.[71]

2.99 The NMC tribunals have a similar remit to receive evidence that it considers to be 'relevant and fair'.[72]

2.100 While the above rules permit the admission of evidence that might not be admitted in criminal cases, they should not be regarded as an easy route to the admission of hearsay. The central requirement is 'fairness'. This was emphasised in *Ogbonna v Nursing and Midwifery Council*[73] in which Rimer LJ rejected the notion promoted by the Nursing and Midwifery Council (NMC) that the rule admitting evidence 'subject only to the requirements of relevance and fairness' establishes a general principle to admit hearsay evidence as a matter of course and then address the issue of fairness by determining the weight to attach to that evidence.

68 [2009] EWCA Crim 964 – a judgment said to complement the Supreme Court's own.

69 At para [7].

70 See, for example, *Chauhan v General Medical Council* [2010] EWHC 2093 (Admin); *Roomi v General Medical Council* [2009] EWHC 2188 (Admin).

71 GMC (FTP) Rules 2004 r34(1) and (2) but of general application.

72 Nursing and Midwifery Council (Fitness to Practise) Rules Order of Council (NMC (FTP) Rules) 2004 SI No 1761 r31(1).

73 [2010] EWCA Civ 1216.

2.101 The determination of fairness is fact-sensitive and will depend on the nature of the evidence, the reason for the non-attendance of a witness, what steps were taken to secure the attendance of that witness and the problems admission may cause to the registrant. Where such evidence is admitted, it is likely to carry less weight by virtue of the fact that it has not been tested in cross-examination. However, the principle of attaching less weight should not be seen as a mantra or an excuse to admit hearsay. How weight is assessed must be carefully explained by the tribunal in any decision. (See further para 2.134 below.)

2.102 In *Ogbonna*, O faced three serious charges all of which were found proved and she was struck off the register. On count one, the NMC placed sole reliance upon the statement of O's line manager P, with whom she was not on good terms. P did not give evidence rather her statement was adduced as hearsay despite O's wish to cross-examine her. P had moved to the Caribbean. The NMC said that P was not available even though they had made no inquiry regarding her availability and said that no video-link was available at the tribunal hearing. On appeal Davies J found that the tribunal had misdirected itself in finding that P was not available since no inquiry had been made. The NMC (FTP) Rules 2004 required the tribunal to consider the overall fairness of the hearing before admitting hearsay and, given the misdirection the test had not been met.

2.103 In her judgment on the first appeal, Davies J stated that:

> The evidence of the sole witness of fact was critical. That fact together with the evidence of bad feeling between the two women meant that every effort should have been made to secure Ms Pilgrim's attendance. Fairness required that the appellant was entitled to test the evidence of Ms Pilgrim by way of cross-examination unless good and cogent reasons could be given for non-attendance.[74]

2.104 The NMC challenged her judgment on the basis that it curtailed the admissibility of hearsay statements. However, the Court of Appeal upheld Davies J's decision 'in the particular circumstances' of the case. Her judgment was 'focused on the particular facts of the case and did not purport to lay down any more general principle than the need for a proper consideration to be given to the criterion of fairness when the question of [admitting hearsay arises]'.[75]

2.105 Rimer LJ stated that:

> . . . decisions as to the admission or exclusion of a hearsay statement [are] to be governed by considerations, *inter alia*, of fairness . . . [Here the NMC was seeking to adduce P's] statement as the sole evidence supporting the material parts of Charge 1 when it knew that that evidence was roundly disputed and could not be tested by cross-examination. It was [doing so in support of a case whose outcome could be and in the event was] the wrecking of [O's] career as a midwife, a career which had lasted over 20 years. I should have thought it was obvious that, in the circumstances, fairness to [O] demanded that in principle the statement ought only to be admitted if she had the opportunity of cross-examining [P] upon it.
>
> . . . it should have been obvious to the NMC that it could and should have sought to make arrangements to enable such cross-examination to take

74 At p154.
75 At para 25.

> place . . . either by flying [P] to the UK at its expense, or else by setting up a video link.[76]

2.106 As for balancing fairness to the NMC he said:

> If . . . despite reasonable efforts the NMC could not [arrange for P] to be available for cross examination then the case for admitting her hearsay statement might well have been strong. But the NMC made no such efforts at all.[77]

2.107 The latter comment accords with the general principal that fairness means fairness to both sides. The danger when annunciating this principle is that fairness to the prosecution is frequently deployed as a reason to admit matters that plainly should not be admitted. This is precisely what happened in *Ogbonna*.

2.108 While no general principle was established other than to re-affirm the need to consider fairness before admitting hearsay, the circumstance bear repeating since they may be persuasive in any given case:

- the witness was the sole and critical witness;
- there was a history of animosity between the registrant and the witness;
- there was a factual conflict between the registrant and the witness;
- the consequence to the registrant could be (and was) the destruction of her career.

2.109 Although there is no absolute right to cross-examine a witness, there must be compelling reasons to deprive a registrant of this opportunity. This is all the more important if the case is serious and would have serious consequences if proved. Until recently, consequence has ordinarily meant sanction but, following *R (Bonhoeffer) v General Medical Council*[78] serious damage to reputation or standing should now be considered. Furthermore, it may no longer be sufficient to argue that an adverse finding based on hearsay can simply be challenged on appeal. The fact that the damage to the registrant will already have been done by then must be considered *before* the case proceeds further.

2.110 Professor Bonhoeffer faced several allegations of sexual misconduct while practising in Kenya. The GMC's case relied principally upon evidence from X who was willing to travel to London to give evidence. However, the police advised the GMC that he risked reprisals if he did so (not from B) and the GMC applied to admit X's evidence as hearsay. The tribunal found that the police assessment of risk was wrong and that the evidence would not have been admissible in a criminal trial, but nonetheless admitted the evidence on the basis that it was appropriate given their remit of making 'due enquiry'[79] and, it was not unfair to B to do so. B challenged the decision (by way of judicial review) as irrational, unlawful, a misapplication of the rules and in breach of ECHR Article 6 (right to a fair trial). The GMC argued that B had misconstrued the rules, the decision was reasonable and it was in the public interest to enquire into such serious

76 At paras 23 and 24 of the judgment.
77 At para 24.
78 [2011] EWHC 1585 (Admin).
79 GMC (FTP) Rules 2004 r34.

allegations. The GMC also argued that B's challenge was premature, should only succeed if he could demonstrate that a fair hearing was not possible and, his rights were guaranteed by the tribunal's duty to properly assess evidence and his ability to appeal if convicted.

2.111 The court (Laws LJ, Stadlen J) upheld B's challenge concluding that:

- The admission of hearsay was not necessarily unfair. Evidence that would not be admitted in a criminal trial may be fairly and properly admitted under the tribunal's own rules of practice. The key issue was whether admitting important evidence with no opportunity to cross-examine a witness was fair at common law and/or under Article 6 given the seriousness of the case and any safeguards.
- There is no absolute rule that a registrant must be afforded the opportunity to cross-examine a witness, even where the witness provides the sole or decisive evidence. However, B's case was not argued upon whether such a rule existed but, was based on the facts. A key point was the serious (criminal) nature of the allegations and the very serious consequences if proved. As a general rule, the more serious the charges or consequences the greater the need for procedural safeguards to ensure a fair hearing. Labelling the proceedings as quasi-criminal or civil was not helpful. The main issues were seriousness and consequences. B's right to cross-examine a critical witness with whom his case conflicted could only be countered by *compelling* factors.
- The tribunal did not find that X would be at any greater risk by giving live evidence than from reading his statement, nor had it considered the absence of the safeguards provided in criminal trials. The CJA 2003 curtails the routes and reasons by which hearsay is admitted. The court concluded that there were no compelling factors outweighing B's right to cross-examine X. The case was very serious, both in terms of the allegation and any consequences. Finally, X had repeatedly said he was prepared to give live evidence and the tribunal's decision was, on the facts, irrational.

2.112 Interestingly, the challenge occurred before the substantive hearing rather than the usual process of alleging unfairness 'post conviction'. The court took specific account of B's reputation and the damage to it if he were convicted, even if he later succeeded on appeal. This is an interesting extension/importation of what are normally regarded as ECHR Article 8 rights (to respect for a private and family life) into matters usually falling to be decided under Article 6, namely procedural and trial fairness.

2.113 It is also important to consider the position in criminal proceedings, since there has been a considerable amount of to-and-fro between the domestic courts and the European Court of Human Rights (ECtHR).

2.114 In its initial decision on *Al-Khawaja and Tahery*[80] the ECtHR concluded that a conviction based 'solely or decisively' on the statement of a witness whom the defendant had no opportunity to contradict was incompatible with Article 6. This was rejected by the Supreme Court in *Horncastle*,[81] setting the Supreme Court and the ECtHR at odds. The Supreme Court concluded that

80 (2009) 49 EHRR 1.

81 [2009] UKSC 14, [2010] UKHRR 1.

the safeguards in the CJA 2003, H's ability to challenge the credibility of the principal witness, other evidence of his presence at the scene and, a full and clear judicial direction were sufficient safeguards and, evidence of a proper balance. Following this, the UK government referred the initial judgment in *Al-Khawaja and Tahery* to the Grand Chamber of the ECtHR.

2.115 The Grand Chamber decision in *Al-Khawaja and Tahery v UK*[82] effectively reversed the earlier decision. It concluded that an inability to cross-examine did not automatically result in unfairness or mean that Article 6 was breached, however there must be strong procedural safeguards to alleviate the difficulties caused to the defence.

2.116 The facts of each case are quite instructive and demonstrate the balance between fairness and unfairness. Al-Khawaja, a consultant physician, faced two counts of indecent assault on female patients under hypnosis. One patient (S) committed suicide before the trial, but a statement given to the police was admitted. The second complainant gave evidence and was cross-examined, as were two of S's friends in whom S had confided soon after the alleged incident. The trial judge cautioned the jury regarding S's untested evidence. Tahery allegedly stabbed someone during a fight. The only direct witness was too frightened to give evidence. The jury were likewise cautioned regarding the dangers of relying upon his untested statement.

2.117 The ECtHR reaffirmed the principles that: a) evidence must ordinarily be presented live at a hearing to enable the defendant to challenge it; b) there must be a good reason for non-attendance of a witness; and c) a conviction based solely or decisively on the statement of an absent witness was likely to be incompatible with the requirements of fairness under ECHR Article 6. However, the court went on to say that the last principle was not absolute and inflexible. Account should be taken of the safeguards in the particular legal system and, the court should weigh the competing interests of the defendant, the complainant and the public interest in the proper administration of justice. Applying these rules, regarding *Al-Khawaja* although S was the only witness, her story could only be told through her statement. There was strong evidence to corroborate her account (both a 'recent complaint' and another similar incident) and, the jury had been properly directed. These provided sufficient safeguards or counterbalancing factors. In *Tahery*, the fact that T could challenge the prosecution case by giving evidence himself and the judge could and did give a strong warning to the jury were insufficient to counter the unfairness caused by reading the statement of the only witness against him.

2.118 In conclusion, hearsay is admissible in regulatory proceedings subject to the safeguards provided by the regulator's own rules (if any) and provided there has been:

- appropriate and proportionate enquiry into the reasons why a witness is absent together with any supporting evidence;
- appropriate and proportionate enquiry into alternatives means of facilitating live evidence (video-link, recorded interviews, alternative premises for hearings etc);
- proper consideration of the competing interests of the parties;

82 [2011] ECHR 2127 (Grand Chamber).

- proper consideration of whether it is the sole or decisive evidence or there is any supporting material;
- a proper appraisal of the overall fairness of proceedings in the light of all the above.

2.119 Two further cases demonstrating the above process in action are *R (Thompson) v General Chiropractic Council*[83] and *Khan v General Teaching Council for England*.[84]

2.120 In *Thompson*, T wished to call an expert witness but the tribunal took the view that his evidence was not relevant and set a hearing date when he was unavailable. The tribunal further considered that the hearing date was appropriate considering the interests of all parties and the need to avoid unnecessary delay. Lloyd Jones J concluded that while the court would normally be reluctant to interfere with the judgment of a professional tribunal it had a supervisory jurisdiction to ensure that parties are given a fair hearing. A short adjournment would cause no substantial prejudice. The expert evidence was crucial to the defence and, having concluded it was relevant, T should have been permitted to argue the point (irrespective of its merits on which his Lordship made no comment).

2.121 In *Khan* two matters were in issue. The first was the tribunal's decision to proceed in K's absence rather than to adjourn. The second was that the tribunal relied upon transcripts of the students' complaints. Ouseley J dismissed K's appeal on both grounds. As to the adjournment his Lordship held that K had to show that the tribunal had acted outside its proper discretion, was wrong in principle, unfair or unreasonable or, that they had ignored relevant facts or considered irrelevant ones. K could not do so and the tribunal was right to proceed. As to the facts, again K had to show that the factual decision was wrong. Given that there was no reason to doubt the transcripts (K's representatives had the opportunity to check their accuracy) sight of the originals would not disclose collusion, manipulation, or other such matters which could be addressed by cross-examination on when, how and by whom statements were taken.

2.122 The issue of anonymous hearsay was revisited in *White v Nursing and Midwifery Council; Turner v Nursing and Midwifery Council*[85] in which Mitting J held that:

> . . . it is difficult to conceive of circumstances in which the admission of potentially significant evidence which is both anonymous and hearsay will not infringe the requirement of fairness.

2.123 W and T faced allegations of falsifying discharge times to meet departmental targets. The NMC relied upon six live witnesses and three anonymous letters. Mitting J adopted a staged assessment of the evidence. He considered the ECHR Article 6(1) right to a fair, public and timely hearing applied to proceedings which materially affect a professional's practice, but concluded that Article 6(3) does not apply since there is no express right to cross-examine witnesses.

83 [2008] EWHC 2499 (Admin).
84 [2010] EWHC 3404 (Admin).
85 [2014] EWHC 520 (Admin).

2.124 The NMC rules (which mirror that of other regulators) permit the admission of evidence subject only to the limitation that it must be *relevant and fair* to do so. However, this is subject to the above cases of *Bonhoeffer* regarding fairness and *Ogbonna* regarding the opportunity to test significant witnesses. Mitting J held that the anonymous letters were inadmissible and 'should not have been relied on'.

2.125 Hearsay itself is not expressly excluded by domestic or ECHR rulings – see *Al-Khawaja* (above). The general rule preventing anonymous hearsay provided for in *R v Ford*[86] is itself subject to the admission of business documents pursuant to CJA 2003 s117. Mitting J concluded that patient records were analogous to business record but then differentiated such records from the evidence in this case which dealt directly with W and T's actions and attitude. It was potentially significant regarding W and T's conduct and attitude. He concluded that the evidence should not have been admitted. It was doubly unfair. Anonymity prevented W and T from advancing reasons why the authors of the letters might be critical of them and, since it was hearsay, they could not test it in cross-examination.

2.126 This evidence was different to simple hearsay which may be tested or contradicted by other enquiry or evidence. This could not be done and as such the requirement of fairness could not be met. However, he was careful to limit his ruling to the facts in hand and did not suggest that anonymous hearsay was prohibited in every case. Evidence such as hospital or business records could still be admitted.

2.127 The case of *Thorneycroft v Nursing and Midwifery Council*[87] is an object lesson in what should *not* be done. T a nurse with 25 years' experience was accused of using derogatory language about patients. The allegations were between four and nine years old. They were set against a background of colleagues who provided glowing testimonials of his professionalism and, his counter-allegations that the complainants were engaged in spreading lies and senior executives were engaged in a witch-hunt. T informed the Conduct and Competence Committee (CCC) that he could neither attend nor instruct anyone to defend himself owing to lack of funds. He was suspended following a finding of impairment through misconduct.

2.128 The CCC admitted and relied upon three witnesses of fact, two of whom refused to attend, citing alleged reasons of ill-health. The fact of their non-attendance was not communicated to T. Despite T disputing their evidence and it being sole and decisive in respect of certain matters, the CCC admitted the witness statements. In so doing the tribunal did not consider T's written representations regarding the possible ill-will held by the complainants or his good character but instead relied on the NMC case presenter's erroneous assertion that these important facts were not relevant. The single live witness did not save the day for the NMC since that witness' evidence was bound up with the untried and untested absent witnesses.

2.129 In allowing the appeal, HHJ Thomas QC reaffirmed the principles in *Ogbonna* and *Bonhoeffer*. A review of the reasons shows that the CCC failed to take any proper steps to assess whether admitting the evidence was fair. It failed to consider: the sole and decisive nature of the evidence

86 [2010] EWCA Crim 2250.
87 [2014[EWHC 1565 (Admin).

or T's written challenges thereto; whether the reasons asserted for absence were in fact valid; what the NMC had done to facilitate attendance of witnessed or the provision of evidence by other means; the veracity, credibility or reliability of the witness statements; and the seriousness of the allegations and the impact of an adverse finding to T.

2.130 In addition, T was not informed of the witnesses' absence. The NMC's failure to provide T's testimonial witness statements to the CCC deprived the CCC of material relevant to the credibility of the witnesses. Permitting the case presenter to review material that the CCC should itself have reviewed was a serious error. The CCC had in effect allowed the NMC's case-presenter to usurp its function. This was a case in which character went to the heart of the credibility of the allegation. As such the character evidence was important material to consider at the fact-finding stage – see also *Donkin v Law Society*.[88]

2.131 While hearsay may bring its own difficulties in terms of admission and probative value, it must nevertheless be properly assessed. in *R (H) v Nursing and Midwifery Council*[89] alongside other failings the CCC was criticised for dismissing defence witness evidence as 'predominantly hearsay' and failing to assess the weight to give to such evidence.

2.132 Despite clear guidance in the above authorities, cases such as *Smith v Bar Standards Board*[90] show that regulators still get this wrong. S faced a complaint of negligence in the drafting of documents. The complaint was made by his instructing solicitor on behalf of their client Mr A. The Bar Standards Board (BSB) took the somewhat extraordinary action of asking the solicitor to take the statement of complaint from Mr A despite the solicitor having a clear interest in blaming S. During the proceedings Mr A declined to attend because, apparently, he did not wish to and felt he could not give any useful evidence. This was communicated by the instructing solicitor following which Mr A confirmed that, although he stood by his feelings of being 'let down' by S, he had moved on with his life and would not attend to give evidence. Nothing was done by the BSB to secure Mr A's attendance. Despite this, the tribunal admitted Mr A's statement.

2.133 The reasons for this were described by Collins J as 'truly extraordinary', since it would seem that although the BSB had taken *no* steps to secure Mr A's attendance, the tribunal did not find they had failed to take reasonable steps. That is plainly perverse, as Collins J described it. Closer reading suggests a thought process that is no better. It would appear that the tribunal concluded that even if the BSB had written to Mr A 'inviting him to attend' he would not. It rather suggests their reasoning was along the lines of 'we know the BSB have done nothing but trying would have achieved nothing, so we will admit the evidence'.

2.134 The tribunal sought to justify and explain its decision on the basis that they could adjust the weight they would give to the hearsay statement of Mr A at the end of the proceedings. Collins J regarded the suggestion:

> . . . that the weight of [Mr A's] evidence was in effect all that mattered was equally perverse in that it ignored the obvious unfairness which would

88 [2007] EWHC 414 (Admin).
89 [2013] EWHC 4258 (Admin).
90 [2016] EWHC 3015 (Admin).

result and equally ignored the fact that [the solicitors] had an interest in procuring a statement which exonerated them and blamed [S].[91]

2.135 It is plain from the above that while adjusting the weight applicable to evidence is something a tribunal may do *as part of* deciding whether to admit evidence it is not a substitute for fairness and it is most certainly not the deciding factor in admitting hearsay.

2.136 *Belal v General Medical Council*[92] is a useful reminder of two points. The case involved admission of a document under rule 34(2) of the GMC (FTP) Rules 2004 which sets out the FTP Tribunal's general duty to make due inquiry. B signed a document declaring his status as 'active' when he was suspended. The first point is to examine whether the evidence in question is in fact hearsay (is it tendered for the truth of its contents?). In this case the issue was whether he had signed the document and not whether the declaration was true. As such it was not hearsay. The second point is that the FTP tribunal may admit evidence under its duty of due inquiry which may not be admissible in criminal proceedings. Here the document was highly relevant and, since B agreed he had signed it, admitting it caused no unfairness.

2.137 Drawing the above strands together, the principle question of admissibility is determined by the requirements of relevance and fairness. As to relevance, if the evidence goes to a peripheral matter or is not challenged, then it is far less controversial to admit it. If the evidence is important or central to the case advanced by either party the decision to admit is very much an issue of fairness.

2.138 The decision on fairness is likely to be informed by an assessment of the following matters (and see *Razzaq v Financial Services Authority*[93]):

- fairness and relevance is the litmus test of admissibility;
- fairness is fact and case-sensitive;
- what is fair in one case may be unfair in another;
- there is no absolute right to cross-examine a witness, but that is *not* an excuse to start from a point that hearsay is probably admissible;
- good and cogent reasons for a witness' absence is an important factor to weigh in favour of admission;
- the reasons must be *compelling* if the evidence is critical in establishing a serious allegation against a registrant;
- sole and decisive evidence should not be admitted unless the circumstances are exceptional;
- anonymous hearsay evidence should not ordinarily be admitted;
- the tribunal may give less weight to hearsay evidence it has admitted;
- the tribunal must assess the impact on the registrant's case;
- the tribunal must assess these matters even if the registrant does not attend or makes no representations since R may be unrepresented a/or have little understanding of these matters.

91 At [43].
92 [2011] EWHC 2859.
93 [2014] EWCA Civ 770.

2.139 *Ward v Nursing and Midwifery Council*[94] is a case where the NMC got it right (almost) and the decision to admit hearsay was upheld. The Committee recognised the fact-sensitive nature of relevance and fairness. It noted that W had been provided with copy statements and they did not form the only or decisive evidence. Furthermore, W could have provided a written response. The 'scant' effort made by the NMC was criticised when balancing the issue of fairness but since W failed to attend the hearing she was not deprived of the opportunity to cross-examine the witnesses by their absence – rather, she damaged her case by her own absence. Finally, the Committee noted that the issue of what weight to give to the statements was to be carefully assessed at the close of all the evidence.

Witnesses attending but becoming ill

2.140 The evidence of an absent witness may be admitted with caution as stated above, however there are some cases in which a witness starts his or her evidence but becomes unwell or unavailable for some other reason. The issue for the tribunal is what to do with the evidence that it has heard?

2.141 In *R v Stretton and McCallion*[95] S and M faced allegations of attempted rape. Both said the complainant V had consented to their actions. They were represented by the same counsel. V was cross-examined for three and a half hours on behalf of M, but had not been questioned on behalf of S. She was unable to continue. HHJ Gower's decision to allow the case to continue with a strong warning to the jury regarding the reliance they should place on V's evidence was upheld. The Appeal Court considered this to be a matter of judicial discretion. The learned judge's direction was as follows:

> What you have got to think about is this: whether you are satisfied in your own minds and sure that the cross-examination which Mr Hopkins (defence counsel) was able to do sufficiently probed and tested the evidence of V so as to enable you to judge fairly her credibility. If you feel that [S and M were deprived of the opportunity] of testing and probing her evidence, why then my advice to you would be that you should acquit [them] because unless you feel sure that you as the jury are in a position to make a proper assessment of her credibility, this case does not get off the ground . . . It is a matter of common sense and fairness.

2.142 The defence argued that having made some ground in cross-examination they were deprived of the opportunity of gaining further concessions from the witness. The Court of Appeal concluded that the judge was in a good position to assess whether there was 'any real prospect' of that happening.

2.143 In *R v Lawless and Basford*[96] the position was different in that a co-accused 'D' gave 'damning' evidence against the defendants. D then suffered a heart-attack and his evidence which was the 'only direct evidence' was 'wholly unchallenged and untested'. The judge sought to direct the jury that they should assume cross-examination would have 'weakened or destroyed' D's evidence, but he neither explained how this might happen

94 [2014] EWHC 1158 (Admin).
95 (1988) 86 Cr App R 7.
96 (1994) 98 Cr App R 342.

nor who might do this nor how they might decide this point. Given the centrality of the evidence, the complete lack of challenge and the fact that no direction could cure the prejudice their convictions were quashed.

2.144 The matter was next visited in *PM v The Queen*.[97] Here there was some limited cross-examination of a witness who was 'integral' to the prosecution case. The court of appeal commented that:

> The essential principle is that a defendant must be given an adequate and proper opportunity to challenge and contest the evidence . . . In *Lawless & Basford* the defence were deprived of the that opportunity because [the cross-examination of D and their own evidence was the only means of challenging the prosecution's case]. By way of contrast in *Stretton & McCallion* the defendants did have a fair opportunity to challenge the complainant's evidence, despite the fact that the cross-examination was curtailed when considered in the context of the directions given to the jury.[98]

2.145 Without adopting it as a model, the court commented[99] that the direction in *Stretton & McCallion* had virtue to it but that in many cases it ought to be clear whether the defendant had been deprived of a fair opportunity to challenge a witness' evidence. If they have been so deprived the jury should be directed to ignore it or be discharged. The court further commented that the judge would be able to properly assess what difference cross-examination would make.

2.146 The final case is that of *R v Andrew Michael Lawless*.[100] In the domestic court it was held that the overriding question is whether it is still possible to have a fair trial. The witness was cross-examined for two hours. The trial judge's decision to continue with a strong direction to the jury was upheld. The judge's directions included a warning that the jury should 'examine [the] evidence with particular care' and be 'very aware' they had only seen partial cross-examination and 'did not have the opportunity of seeing how he might react to [other possible challenges]'.

2.147 The appeal court also commented that L had at least had some chance to test the witness L was at least in a better position that he would have been if the witness statement had been read and not challenged at all. This latter comment was criticised as being an abstract exercise and depended on how long the cross-examination took. It was further criticised in that the complaint was of an inadequate opportunity to cross-examine the witness as distinct from no opportunity to do so and therefore the proper approach was set out in *Al-Khawaja and Tahery v UK*.[101]

2.148 The ECtHR commented that the court should:

> . . . consider whether there was good reason for the curtailment [of cross-examination]; whether [the witness gave sole or decisive evidence] for the applicant's conviction; whether there were counterbalancing safeguards, which permitted a fair and proper assessment of the reliability of that evidence to take place.[102]

97 [2008] EWCA Crim 2787.

98 At [15].

99 At [24].

100 [2011] EWCA Crim 59 and in the ECtHR, *Lawless v UK* Application no 44324/11 (16 October 2012).

101 [2011] ECHR 2127 [GC].

102 At [25].

The court upheld the conviction on the basis that there had been robust cross-examination that had gained no concessions from the witness, there were procedural safeguards in that the judge could have discharged the jury, the judge correctly identified the issue as one of the reliability of the witness, he was entitled to form the view that cross-examination had not damaged the reliability of the witness and, finally, the jury had been properly warned:

> . . . as to the limitations in evidence which had not been subjected to full cross-examination and as to the dangers in accepting that evidence.[103]

2.149 Drawing the above strands together, it is important to note that each case is decided on its own facts and, whilst length of cross-examination may give some indication, the key is not how long it took but whether the cross-examination had been sufficient to test the reliability of the witness. The tribunal is a professional body and, having seen the witness may be able to assess whether additional cross-examination could have extracted further evidence beneficial to the defence. However, the comment from the ECtHR is compelling – if the tribunal 'cannot conduct a fair and proper assessment of the reliability of the witness' evidence, they should disregard that evidence'.[104]

2.150 It is respectfully suggested that the appropriate course is for the tribunal to first consider whether there is good reason for the witness' non-availability. If there is not, the evidence should be excluded from their deliberations. If there is, the tribunal should consider whether it can 'conduct a fair and proper assessment of the reliability of the witness', taking account of the length, breadth and depth of cross-examination. If it can, then the evidence should be admitted. Conversely, if the tribunal is satisfied that the registrant was unable to sufficiently probe and test the evidence for the panel to properly assess the credibility of the witness then the evidence should be ignored. The tribunal is a professional body in a similar position to a trial-judge. It has the assistance of a legal assessor or will be chaired by an LQC. It should be able to exclude the evidence from its deliberations. If it cannot do so, it should recuse itself and order a new hearing.

Vulnerable witnesses and special measures

2.151 All the regulators have provisions to assist vulnerable witnesses when giving evidence. As an example, rule 36 of the GMC (Fitness to Practise) Rules 2004 provides that the following witnesses may be treated as vulnerable 'if the quality of their evidence is likely to be adversely affected as a result'. A witness:

- aged under 17 at the time of the hearing;
- with a mental disorder as defined by Mental Health Act 1983;
- significantly impaired in relation to intelligence and social functioning;

103 At [35].
104 At [35].

- with physical disabilities who requires assistance to give evidence;
- where the allegation is of a sexual nature and the witness was the alleged victim;
- who complains of intimidation.

2.152 The tribunal must hear from both parties and the legal assessor following which it may 'adopt such measures as it considers desirable to enable it to receive evidence from a vulnerable witness'.[105]

2.153 Measures include but are not limited to using video links, pre-recorded evidence-in-chief (but only if the witness is available for cross-examination) interpreters, signers, translators and intermediaries; screens or other measures the tribunal considers necessary to prevent the identity of a witness being revealed or access to the witness by the registrant.[106]

2.154 In cases involving sexual allegations the complainant 'shall not' be cross-examined by the registrant acting in person without the prior written consent of the complainant. If the absence of such written consent, the registrant must appoint an advocate to cross-examine, failing which the GMC will appoint one on the registrant's behalf.[107]

2.155 In *Virdee v General Pharmaceutical Council*[108] V faced charges of sexual harassment and/or assault. The complainant A adopted her witness statement as her evidence in chief and, gave evidence from behind a screen. Andrews J dismissed V's appeal commenting that there was no unfairness in the procedure, quite the reverse. Vulnerable witnesses such as A are not expected to relive such events and a professional tribunal assisted by counsel for the GPhC and for the defence are well placed to judge the credibility and reliability of a complainant.

2.156 However, *Miller v General Medical Council*[109] demonstrates that there is a limit to what a witness can 'demand' and a balance must be struck between the interests of the witness and the registrant. In *Miller* the witness declined to give evidence unless the entire proceedings were held in private. M objected on the basis that he had a right to a fair and public hearing. The tribunal's decision to hold the case in private was quashed on the basis that the regulator had failed to demonstrate that it was both necessary and proportionate to derogate from the norm of a public hearing. (See above under public hearing for a fuller discussion.)

2.157 As with so much in regulatory proceedings, each case will require careful analysis and a decision on its own facts balancing the vulnerabilities of a witness against the rights of a registrant. However, through all this runs the thread of the overarching objective of protecting the public (see para 1.2). This objective is best met by a professional tribunal giving full and fair consideration to all the facts. This in turn is achieved if both sides are, within reason, given the opportunity to present their best evidence free from fear or favour. It is important to remember that this last principle of giving their best evidence applies just as much to a registrant, and a

105 Rule 36(2).
106 Rule 36(3).
107 Rule 36(4) and (5).
108 [2015] EWHC 169 (Admin).
109 [2013] EWHC 1934 (Admin).

tribunal is entitled to manage its own hearing in terms of publicity, timing, support, etc, to ensure that a registrant does not suffer prejudice.

Opinion evidence regarding misconduct

2.158 This issue was considered in *Enemuwe v Nursing and Midwifery Council.*[110] During a hearing before the CCC, the report and findings of an investigation by a Supervisor of Midwives was admitted in evidence. The CCC purported to admit the document pursuant to NMC (Fitness to Practise) Rules 2004 rule 31(1) on the basis that it was relevant and fair. In its reasons, the CCC clearly took some account of the report's findings. The exact form of the document admitted by the CCC was not clear from either the transcript or the comments of counsel, which is itself a concern.

2.159 Holman J ruled that to allow such evidence was a 'serious irregularity' pursuant to rule 52.11(3) of the Civil Procedure Rules 1998.[111] He adopted comment by counsel that 'normally the findings of fact made at some earlier investigation by another tribunal or another person are not admissible'. Indeed, Holman J said they were 'completely irrelevant'.

2.160 The CCC fell into a basic error in taking account of another tribunal's findings. As with any FTP tribunal, it was the CCC's task to consider the case on the evidence it heard and ignore the views anyone else may have on evidence it had not heard. Even if the witnesses were the same the CCC could not assess the way the evidence was delivered nor the impact of cross-examination.

2.161 *Enemuwe* is quite different to the case of *R (Squier) v General Medical Council*[112] where redacted decisions were admitted but for a different reason. In *Enemuwe* the report and findings concerned the very matters that the CCC had to make a judgment upon. In *Squier* the admission of redacted High Court judgments concerning cases in which Dr Squier's evidence had been rejected or criticised, was permissible as important background information for understanding the basis of her evidence. It was not admitted as proof that her evidence was rejected in those proceedings.

2.162 There is an important distinction between admitting information to place matters in context and relying on the information as probative of the case in issue before the FTP tribunal. That point was emphasised by Ouseley J in reaffirming that the FTP tribunal is the decision-maker on facts and evidence and it should not simply adopt the findings of another body as its own.

2.163 It is difficult to understand how the CCC in *Enemuwe* concluded that to admit this evidence was relevant and fair. The fact that there has been a previous investigation may at times be admitted to place matters in context but the admission of someone else's opinion on the guilt/innocence of a registrant is not admissible. Witnesses are not generally permitted to provide evidence on the 'ultimate issue' to be decided and the tribunal should be careful to ensure this does not happen.

110 [2015] EWHC 2081 (Admin).
111 SI No 3132.
112 [2015] EWHC 299 (Admin).

Character evidence

> Character is an integral part of the FTP process. It is equally important when considering credibility and propensity, whether at the fact-finding stage, when judging the issue of impairment or when considering sanction.

Overview

2.164 In regulatory proceedings as in criminal proceedings, the character of the registrant is an important factor to be considered. In the past, regulators argued that character is irrelevant in the fact-finding stage. Some still seek to argue that all registrants are supposed to have a good character and thus it is of little importance. No authority has been provided to support this approach, which is contrary to common practice and appears to be both unfair and biased. A registrant accused of serious misconduct is entitled to rely on the fact that they have not transgressed in the past and should be believed on oath. To do otherwise leaves a professional whose career may be at stake in a worse position than a rogue facing criminal proceedings. There are in effect three levels of character to consider – good, intermediate and bad.

2.165 Although good character does not provide a defence to or excuse for any forms of misconduct, it has always been recognised as an important factor in criminal cases. Despite the above concerns, the change in regulatory proceedings from an isolative consideration of a registrant's alleged misconduct and impairment, to consideration of these matters in the context of his or her character (past, present *and likely future conduct*) brings regulatory proceedings in line with the established model in criminal trials. It accords with common sense and is fairer for reasons which become obvious when one considers the familiar 'forward-looking' approach to impairment (see the discussion on impairment at para 3.1 et seq, in particular 3.54 et seq). Character should be considered by the tribunal at *all* stages of the FTP process – facts, impairment, sanction and even immediacy of order.

2.166 This principle was revisited in *Wisson v Health Professions Council*[113] by Collins J who reaffirmed that while good character may clearly go to mitigation it is also relevant when credibility is an issue. Where there is an evidential dispute between a witness and a registrant, the registrant's credibility is important, and good character is a factor to be considered. How much weight to give to character in assessing a registrant is of course a matter for the tribunal.

2.167 As stated above, some regulators or advocates continue to wrongly assert that character evidence is of limited relevance at the fact-finding stage. The case of *Arunkalaivanan v General Medical Council*,[114] a case of alleged sexual motivation, highlights the importance of assessing what inferences can be properly drawn in the light of character evidence.

113 [2013] EWHC 1036 (Admin).
114 [2014] EWHC 873 (Admin).

2.168 A was accused of conducting a breast examination inappropriately. His conduct was said to be sexually motivated. The finding that A's handling of the patient's breasts was inappropriate (inept) flowed from the determination of a straightforward factual dispute which required the comparison of witnesses taking account of A's good character and credibility.

2.169 However, the issue of sexual motivation is an inference to be drawn or rejected following the determination of the facts. The tribunal appeared to elide their finding of fact with the issue of sexual motivation. It did not take account of A's character in deciding whether the facts found proved were sexually motivated or were the result of an insensitive, clumsy and poorly executed examination. The latter may well leave the patient feeling ill-treated or even violated, but it is not a sexually motivated act. On appeal, the facts remained as proved, but the finding of sexual motivation was quashed.

2.170 In addition to the above, it is to be noted that character may equally go to the issue of propensity. Where either credibility or propensity is in dispute, a tribunal should follow the lead taken in criminal cases. It is not appropriate for a regulator to suggest that all registrants should have a good character and then invite the tribunal to ignore the importance of that fact.

How should character be considered?

Good character

2.171 The following is adapted from the type of direction given in criminal proceedings. There are two distinct parts, known as 'first limb' and 'second limb' – they deal with credibility and propensity, respectively. This or advice in similar terms adapted to the facts of the case must be given by the legal assessor or the LQC. A failure properly to consider character may be fatal to a finding adverse to the registrant.

2.172 In criminal proceedings, good character means the defendant has no previous convictions or cautions. Reference might also be made to the registrant not being the subject of any other court order such as a bind-over or an anti-social behaviour order (ASBO) if relevant. For regulatory proceedings this would also mean an absence of previous penalties such as erasure or suspension, findings of impairment, misconduct, deficient professional performance, warnings, undertakings that recognise failures in conduct or performance short of misconduct and internal disciplinary proceedings as the case may be.

2.173 In short, good character may a) support a registrant's credibility – when the registrant says that he or she did or did not do something the registrant is entitled to expect weight to be given to his or her word; and b) it may impact upon the issue of propensity and support the argument that the registrant is less likely to act in the way alleged than a person who is not of good character. The legal assessor or LQC's advice should be as follows:[115]

115 Adapted from the Judicial Studies Board, *Crown Court Bench Book 2017* (Chapter 11).

- The registrant is a person aged X years and is of good character. He has no previous convictions/disciplinary matters or other reprehensible conduct proved against him. Good character is not a defence to the charges, but it is relevant to your consideration of the case in two ways.
  - First, the registrant has given evidence (or as the case may be he has made pre-hearing comments). His good character supports his credibility. It is a positive feature which you should take into account when considering whether you accept what he told you or what he said in his pre-hearing comments.
  - Second, the fact that the registrant has no previous convictions/ disciplinary/reprehensible matters to his name may mean that he is less likely to have committed the act/omission alleged against him.
- It is said that for the first time in his life he is accused of [misconduct / unprofessional conduct (UPC) etc] and he is not the sort of person who would be likely to cast his good character aside in this way. That is a matter to which you should pay close attention.
- What weight you give to the registrant's good character and the extent to which it assists on the facts of this case is a matter for you to decide. In making that assessment, the tribunal is entitled to take account of everything it has heard about him.
- In considering an 'out of court statement' the tribunal should bear in mind that the statement was not given under oath or affirmation and was not tested in cross-examination.

2.174 A registrant is entitled to a *full* character direction if he has not given evidence but relies on an 'out of court statement' such as a formal interview with the above caveat as to the lack of oath or testing. He is entitled to a second-limb (propensity) direction if he has not made a statement or given evidence.

2.175 As with all matters of weighing evidence, how important it is and how much it assists on any topic is a matter for the tribunal.

2.176 An important fact to take into consideration is that many tribunals may now draw an adverse inference against a registrant who does not give evidence. This does not remove the need for a good character direction, nor does it nullify the fact that due consideration should be given to a registrant's good character. However, in practical terms if the tribunal is at the point of drawing an adverse inference, which it may only do if there is already strong evidence against a registrant, good character is unlikely to save him or her. (See para 12.402 et seq regarding adverse inferences.)

2.177 As outlined above, when a registrant gives evidence, he or she is entitled to a 'first-limb' character-direction regarding his or her credibility. Failure to do so may be fatal to the eventual decision of the tribunal – see *R v Berrada*.[116] If the registrant does not give evidence but relies on other exculpatory statements by him or her as recounted by others (eg in police interviews), the registrant is entitled to a direction but modified in regard to the weight to be given to such comments because they are not made on

116 (1990) 91 Cr App R 131.

oath – see *R v Vye*.[117] If the registrant has made no comments and does not give evidence, then a first-limb direction is not required.

2.178 In *Vye* the court of appeal held that the second limb direction should always be given regardless of whether an accused gives evidence. Such a policy decision was approved by the House of Lords in *R v Aziz*.[118]

2.179 Where matters occurred many years ago, the good character of the registrant in the intervening years may have particular significance – see *R v Small*.[119] In *GJB v R*[120] reference was made to this intervening time being a 'third limb' of the direction. The Court of Appeal rejected this, saying it is merely an appropriate adaptation of the propensity limb but, it illustrates how the legal assessor or LQC's advice should be properly crafted. This may be of particular significance given the lengthy delay before cases are heard by regulatory tribunals. A careful assessment of character and its impact on a decision may be of particular importance.

2.180 Consideration should be given to the length and breadth of experience any witnesses (written or oral) have of the registrant and their knowledge of the case. These are factors that the tribunal should consider when determining weight. Clearly if experienced reliable professionals have known a registrant for many years, then he or she is entitled to expect considerable weight to be attached to their evidence (always remembering that character is not in itself a defence). A reference provided by a professional person with knowledge of the case is likely to be accorded far more weight than a general reference by a friend or pastoral figure or one provided in ignorance of the case.

2.181 It behooves registrants to provide tribunals with the letter and/or the information given to character witnesses when they are asked to provide their opinions. This allows a tribunal to assess the weight to give to the opinion and is fair to both registrant and regulator.

'Intermediate' character

2.182 In criminal proceedings it is often argued that a person who has old, spent or irrelevant convictions should benefit from a good character direction. It may be that the convictions are not mentioned in evidence or, they are mentioned to give a full picture and the jury is told to ignore them because they are old or spent, etc. Examples might be an old incident of speeding, a minor matter of public disorder or similar – these would probably be irrelevant on a charge of dishonesty and vice versa. The principal rule is that the jury must not be misled – likewise the tribunal should not be misled, nor should it mislead itself.[121]

2.183 Cautions involve an admission of guilt and may be evidence of bad character. Fixed penalty notices (even those for disorder) do not and are not. While convictions may, after a period of time become spent under the Rehabilitation of Offenders Act (ROA) 1974, this is relevant to civil matters and does not necessarily affect their relevance in criminal or regulatory

117 [1993] 1 WLR 471.

118 [1996] AC 41.

119 [2008] EWCA Crim 2788.

120 [2011] EWCA Crim 867.

121 *R v Gray* [2004] 2 Cr App R 498 and *R v Martin* [2000] 2 Cr App R 42.

proceedings. The ROA 1974 does not apply to disciplinary proceedings against any registrants working in healthcare. Age is only one factor to consider in deciding whether a registrant may have regained his or her character.

2.184 As for incidents of previous misconduct or deficient performance, different considerations apply. If a registrant has a previous 'incident' on either his professional or personal record, it is a matter for the tribunal to consider its age, nature and intervening events before deciding whether having balanced the interests of both parties and the interests of justice, it is fair and reasonable to treat the registrant as someone who has regained his or her good character. This is a matter of discretion for the tribunal.[122] Of course if the previous incident is relevant to an issue the tribunal has to decide then it may be impossible to disregard despite the passage of time – see *R v Rackham*[123] in which a sexual preference for young girls was in issue. An old conviction for unlawful (ie under-age) sexual intercourse was clearly relevant to character.

2.185 In regulatory proceedings, offences or previous misconduct involving dishonesty, sexual matters or pornographic material will almost always be relevant since these have a direct impact upon the safety of patients and the interests of the profession and, in particular, how the public (and the profession) must be able to place absolute trust in registrants. However, once again the tribunal should consider matters of the time elapsed, conduct since the previous incident and the similarity or otherwise it has to the current allegation when deciding what weight to apply to this evidence.

2.186 The advice for someone with old, irrelevant or otherwise spent convictions or similarly historical matters of misconduct, UPC or reprehensible conduct proved should be akin to the following:

> The registrant has [X previous matters which are relatively minor and were committed Y years ago]. Because of their nature and age, he is to be regarded as if he were a person of previous good character. This does not mean that he could not have committed the allegations with which he is charged but it should be taken into account in his favour in two ways:
>
> First, the registrant gave evidence and the fact that he is to be treated as someone of good character is something that you should take into account when you are deciding whether you believe his evidence.
>
> Second, the fact that the registrant is now [X] years old and has not had any [offence/misconduct/UPC etc] proved against him for over Y years may mean that it is less likely that he would have acted as alleged.
>
> You should take the fact that R is to be regarded as a person of good character into account in his favour in the two ways I have just explained. It is for you to decide what importance you attach to it.

2.187 Notwithstanding the above, it is important to reiterate that the ROA 1974 does not apply to healthcare proceedings which have protection of the public as their overarching objective. Because of this, previous conduct which might be disregarded in criminal proceedings may still have an importance and an impact in regulatory proceedings.

122 *R v S* [2008] All ER (D) 295 (Nov).

123 [1997] 2 Cr App R 222.

2.188 If a registrant has a previous more recent or unspent matter to his or her name which is dissimilar to the charge he or she faces, the registrant may yet introduce this in evidence to demonstrate that difference. In these circumstances, the tribunal should be reminded that the registrant has no previous offences or misconduct of the type charged, and although this is not a defence, it may make it less likely that the registrant has committed the alleged act(s) he or she now faces.

Bad character

The principles of the Criminal Justice Act 2003

2.189 The time-honoured approach of excluding bad character in criminal proceedings was swept away by the CJA 2003. The general exclusion was replaced by a complex set of rules, the interpretation and application of which is still evolving. Whether this was a political decision or one based on evidence is moot, but the effect of the CJA 2003 is to bring bad character to centre-stage in criminal trials. Despite being civil in nature, regulatory proceedings still take an evidential lead from criminal proceedings as to how bad character is to be considered. Having said that, the over-riding principles in respect of admitting any evidence remain relevance and fairness. This should be considered at all stages of a regulatory case since matters of character are relevant to all such stages.

2.190 Bad character may be defined as 'evidence of or a disposition towards misconduct which is not to do with the alleged facts before the tribunal or in connection with the investigation or prosecution thereof'.[124] 'Misconduct' is defined as an offence or other 'reprehensible behaviour'[125] which must itself have an element of culpability or blameworthiness as distinct from conduct that is irritating, inconvenient or merely upsetting to others.[126]

2.191 Given the wide ambit of the definition, even allegations of which a defendant has been acquitted are admissible to establish past misconduct if the prosecution can show it is relevant to an important issue and the defence do not succeed in excluding it (see CJA 2003 s101 below). This accords with the House of Lords decision in *R v Z*[127] in which multiple allegations of rape successfully defended on the basis of consent, were deployed by the prosecution to prove a further alleged offence where again the defence was consent. The relevance was that the previous matters demonstrated the improbability of his being so unlucky as to mistakenly believe a woman was consenting and be accused of rape for the fifth or sixth time.

2.192 While one talks in terms of 'previous convictions', matters occurring after the incident with which the tribunal is concerned may be admissible and, may be of particular relevance – see *R v Adenusi*[128] (and see the above discussion on good character post the alleged misconduct).

124 Adapted from CJA 2003 s98.
125 CJA 2003 s112.
126 *R v Renda* [2006] 1 WLR 2948.
127 [2000] 2 AC 483.
128 (2007) 171 JP 169.

2.193 In regulatory proceedings the tribunal may be asked to consider the admissibility of criminal misconduct (convictions, cautions etc) or previous regulatory misconduct, UPC or deficient performance. As with any matter of evidence, it is important for the tribunal (or indeed the parties in pre-hearing negotiation) to analyse the previous conduct and assess whether it is probative in the current case or merely prejudicial. As outlined under intermediate character above and even with the overarching objective firmly in mind, not every misdemeanor or previous incident of deficient performance will be relevant to prove the regulator's case.

2.194 Bad character is now admissible in criminal proceedings under seven 'gateways' pursuant to CJA 2003 s101. In short these are as follows:

a) all parties agree to its admission;
b) the evidence is given by the defendant;
c) it is important explanatory evidence;
d) it is relevant to an important matter in issue between the defendant and the prosecution;
e) it has substantial probative value in relation to an important matter in issue between one defendant and another;
f) it corrects a false impression given by the defendant;
g) the defendant has attacked the character of another person.

2.195 It is important that the tribunal consider evidence of bad character in a proper staged process. The stages are (adapted from criminal procedure):

1) the tribunal determines admissibility;
2) the tribunal determines any application to exclude;
3) the weight to be given to the admitted evidence is a matter for the tribunal subject to appropriate advice as to the use(s) to which the evidence may be put;
4) the reasons for admission must be kept under review. If the ground of the hearing has shifted, the significance of the evidence may also have changed.

The tribunal should apply its mind to matters in this way and deal with these issues in its reasons.

2.196 The tribunal should also be warned a) not to place undue reliance on previous matters; b) that bad character cannot bolster a weak case; and c) that current misconduct should not be inferred from past misdemeanors – see *R v Hanson*.[129]

2.197 Because the tribunal is judge of both law and fact, there is always the danger that it will hear an application that discloses bad character material but then, following advice, it decides to disregard it. While it is always to be remembered that a tribunal comprises of professionals whose ability to sit upon tribunals has been assessed and affirmed by the regulatory body, to expect it to ignore irrelevant or marginally relevant previous misconduct may be a tall order. This is particularly so given that once character evidence is adduced its' application is not limited to the matters pertinent to the gateway by which it was admitted. It is in evidence generally and

129 [2005] 1 WLR 3169.

may be applied as the tribunal thinks appropriate.[130] This is subject only to a requirement for caution if evidence admissible and intended as background evidence might also go to propensity.[131]

2.198 Given the above, if possible and without misleading the tribunal, it is preferable for the parties to arrive at an agreed position to preserve both fairness and the appearance of fairness in FTP proceedings. Issues of character should always be discussed with the legal assessor beforehand.

2.199 Gateways a) and b) require no elaboration save to say that it is preferable for counsel to obtain the registrant's agreement in writing before admitting previous matters or eliciting them voluntarily.

2.200 Evidence admissible under gateways d) and g) must be excluded on a defence application if its admission would have 'such an adverse effect on proceedings that the court ought not to admit it – see CJA 2003 s101(3). (See also Police and Criminal Evidence Act 1984 s78 which gives the court power to exclude evidence that has such an adverse effect on proceedings. It applies to all gateways.)

2.201 Important explanatory evidence in c) means essential background evidence without which it would be 'impossible or difficult to properly understand other evidence in the case and its value for understanding the case as a whole is substantial'.[132] As stated above, this gateway should not be used slide in propensity evidence that would not otherwise be admitted. Where explanatory evidence is admitted the better practice is to deal with it by way of agreement thus avoiding distraction and prejudice.[133]

In respect of d), important matters in issue are defined in the rather clumsy language of section 103. In essence they encompass whether the defendant has i) a propensity to commit the offences of the kind charged or ii) a propensity to be untruthful. Offences are of the same kind if they are of the same description, type or category. The only caveats to admission are that evidence of propensity under i) which is loosely akin to similar-fact evidence as opposed to untruthfulness, should not be admitted if the fact of the propensity makes it no more likely that he is guilty of the offence or, that the lapse of time since the earlier incident would make its admission unjust. 'Important matters' are yet further defined in section 112 as being 'of substantial importance in the context of the case as a whole'.

2.202 Gateway d) is not qualified by the old rule regarding similar fact evidence that its probative value is outweighed by its prejudicial effect. It need only be 'relevant'.[134] This is of particular importance as regards propensity since this is now a matter specifically in issue between prosecution and defence.[135]

130 *R v Highton* [2005] 1 WLR 3472 (and several subsequent cases dealing with each of the gateways).

131 *R v Davis* (2008) 172 JP 358.

132 CJA 2003 s102(a) and (b).

133 *R v Cundell* [2009] EWCA Crim 2072 (a case on gateway a) but where the evidence would otherwise have been admitted under c)).

134 *R v Weir and others* [2006] 1 WLR 1885 (see the judgment in the case of the appellant *Somanathan*).

135 CJA 2003 s103.

2.203 The tribunal ought to apply its mind to propensity evidence in the following manner:

- Does the history establish a propensity to commit offences of the kind charged?
- Does that propensity make it more likely that he or she committed the offence?
- If the offence is of the same category or description (as opposed to type), is it just to rely upon it?
- Is it otherwise unfair to admit the evidence?

2.204 Propensity can be established by one previous event if it is of sufficient probative value – see *Hanson* (above). Whether the evidence is relevant, probative or ought to be excluded involves consideration of matters such as similarity of fact, the gravity and age of the previous conduct. The age of the conduct is particularly important since old events may simply be prejudicial without establishing any propensity.

2.205 In *R v Ngyuen*[136] and *R v O'Dowd*[137] there were one and three previous incidents respectively. In *Ngyuen* the Court of Appeal ruled that a jury must be sure the incident took place before considering whether it showed propensity. In *O'Dowd* it ruled that the jury should scrutinise the disputed incidents with the same care as the allegation on the indictment before considering propensity. However, where there are multiple allegations the Supreme Court has taken a different approach.

2.206 In *R v Mitchell*[138] the court endorsed the *Ngyuen* approach where there is one previous alleged incident but where there were several incidents (in *Mitchell* there were seven) it was more appropriate to take a 'holistic' approach. It was not necessary for each incident to be considered in isolation indeed there may be good reason not to do so since one allegation may corroborate another or render a denial improbable (similar to the reasoning in *R v Z* (above)). A jury need not be satisfied beyond reasonable doubt about each specific allegation, what was important was to be satisfied to the required standard that the incidents collectively prove that a propensity exists.

2.207 The principle to be derived from the above is that where there is a single allegation of misconduct said to demonstrate propensity a tribunal should be satisfied on balance of probabilities that the incident occurred before it may go on to consider whether it demonstrates propensity. Where there are multiple allegations the tribunal members do not have to agree on every incident, but each member must be satisfied on balance of probability that the incidents collectively demonstrate the propensity complained of.

2.208 In assessing all such matters, the tribunal should bear in mind that propensity is not the central issue to a case and it should not allow itself to become sidetracked or prejudiced by peripheral matters.

2.209 Propensity to untruthfulness is distinct from mere dishonesty, which may or may not involve lying.

136 [2008] EWCA Crim 585.
137 [2009] EWCA Crim 905.
138 [2016] UKSC 55.

2.210 Gateway e) is concerned with cut-throat defences. If the matter in issue is propensity to commit the type of offence then there is no limitation as between defendants save that it must be of substantial probative value. However, if the matter concerns a propensity to untruthfulness then under section 104, evidence as to a co-defendant's propensity to be untruthful is admissible only if one defendant has undermined the case for the other.

2.211 Gateway f) is essentially concerned with calling evidence in rebuttal of good character evidence led by the defence where such evidence is apt to mislead the jury.

2.212 Gateway g) is concerned with the position where an 'imputation' has been cast upon another meaning that the other has committed an offence or is otherwise of bad character as defined by CJA 2003 s98.

Cross-admissibility in cases involving multiple charges

2.213 Section 112 provides that where a defendant faces multiple charges in the same case, the bad-character provisions apply as if the charges were in separate proceedings. Thus each count is cross-admissible against the other(s) pursuant to a gateway of admissibility. The intention is that if D faces several similar charges or, several similar accusations are brought in support of one charge, one accuser may support evidence from another. The rational, absent collusion between witnesses, is that there may be probative value in a multiplicity of similar allegations or, in the unlikelihood of multiple false allegations by independent witnesses.

2.214 In *R v Chopra*[139] it was considered more likely that a dentist had assaulted three complainants who made individual and independent complaint rather than if it was just one complainant. The court clearly took a holistic approach considering the evidence in the round when looking at cross-admissibility. However, in *R v Norris*[140] it was necessary for the jury to be sure that N had deliberately killed one patient by fatal injection before using that as evidence when considering other patient deaths.

2.215 The risk of collusion goes to the weight to be applied to evidence and not to its cross-admissibility since admissibility is approached on the basis that evidence is true unless it is patently obvious no jury could find it so – see *R v H*,[141] a pre-CJA case but which was followed in *Weir and others* (see para 2.202 above). The caveat to admissibility is now in CJA 2003 s109, from which a tribunal need not assume evidence is true if 'no reasonable court or jury could reasonably find it to be true'. In addition, under section 107 if it becomes clear that evidence admitted as genuine is in fact contaminated by collusion or otherwise, the judge should direct an acquittal or a retrial if, bearing in mind the importance of the contaminated evidence, a conviction would be unsafe. In *Bhatt v GMC*[142] Langstaff J commented that section 107 applies only to criminal proceedings and 'not obviously' to disciplinary hearings. However, if collusion or the risk of collusion is established then a conviction may well be regarded as unsafe.[143]

139 [2007] 1 Cr App R 16.
140 [2009] EWCA Crim 2697.
141 [1995] 2 AC 596, HL.
142 [2011] EWHC 783 (Admin).
143 *R v Pepperrell* [2009] EWCA Crim 1209.

2.216 A tribunal should be alive to the issue of contamination and deal with it as a matter of fairness and the weight to be applied to the evidence generally. If there is clear evidence of contamination, or the risk thereof, then doubtless the tribunal will apply less or even no weight to the particular evidence.

2.217 In considering cross-admissibility of allegations and/or other alleged misconduct, it is important to remember the message from *Chauhan v General Medical Council*[144] referred to previously (at para 2.97) that the panel should confine itself to the proper ambit of the disciplinary charges and should not consider prejudicial factual matters out-with the notice of hearing. The tribunal made findings of fact adverse to the registrant which could have been the subject of professional misconduct but were not within the charges as formulated. King J ruled that the findings of fact could not be properly or fairly used by the tribunal to support its decision. He further concluded that the tribunal had considered evidence of behaviour not the subject of a charge when determining the issue of dishonesty. He quoted Silber J from *Cohen v General Medical Council* (see para 1.96 above) that the process must focus solely on the heads of charge and rejected the GMC's submission that the extraneous material, even if strictly outside the ambit of the charges, could nonetheless be introduced as evidence of C's propensity to dishonestly exaggerate his expertise.

The character of a witness

2.218 In *R (H) v Nursing and Midwifery Council*[145] HHJ Pelling QC restated the principles concerning the admission of a witness' bad character. H, a mental healthcare nurse, was accused of entering a sexual relationship with A while he was under her care during 2005. H's case was that any such relationship (which eventually led to their marrying) only occurred in late 2006 after she had referred A to the care of another practitioner and she and A met again by chance. During the factual dispute regarding when the sexual relationship started, H sought to rely upon the evidence of P regarding the chance meeting, and upon A's convictions including one for dishonesty dating from 1989. The Committee declined to admit the conviction on the basis that it was now old, not relevant to the case, had little probative value and its admission was unfair.

2.219 HHJ Pelling highlighted that when the case is based on one person's word against another it was important to first compare the accounts with any documentary records. He reaffirmed that a conviction for dishonesty, or a conviction following a not guilty plea is potentially relevant to credibility and that fairness was irrelevant to the issue of admissibility of a conviction. He commented that 'the only basis on which it could be [excluded] was on the grounds of relevancy or inadmissibility by operation of statute [such as] the rehabilitation of offenders legislation'.

144 [2010] EWHC 2093 (Admin).
145 [2013] EWHC 4258 (Admin).

When should character be considered?

2.220 For some time, the view was wrongly held that character was only relevant to issues of sanction and, to a lesser extent impairment. Thankfully this error has now been laid bare and it is recognised that character is relevant to *all* stages of a hearing. How much weight to attach to character remains a matter for the tribunal.

2.221 There remains a concern that some regulators are of the view that good character is expected of all registrants and thus it is of little or no value. No justification has been advanced for this other than the suggestion that it is in some way unfair to place extra weight upon good character. There is no evidence that tribunals do place undue weight on character, and it is submitted that it would be unfair simply to ditch an element of a case that is beneficial to a registrant. The concern may be more founded in the fact that some regulators are beginning to forget that they regulate to protect the public, they do not prosecute with a view to obtaining a conviction.

Facts

2.222 At the fact-finding stage, character is likely to be relevant to veracity and propensity (truthfulness and the likelihood of committing an offence).

2.223 If some or all of the alleged conduct is disputed by a registrant, character is relevant to the weight to be applied to his or her evidence and to the cogency of his or her denials. It is also relevant when assessing the likelihood or other-wise of the registrant doing a specific act given that he or she has or has not previously committed the act complained of or anything else. How much weight is applied to character under each limb is a matter for the tribunal, but each limb must be considered.

Impairment

2.224 Character is of considerable importance at the impairment stage. The cases of *Cohen, Zygmunt* and *Cheatle* (see under impairment at paras 3.50 and 3.51 in particular) all require consideration of impairment in the light of all the facts and not just the misconduct admitted or found proved. A tribunal is to judge whether, given the facts admitted or proved, a registrant's fitness *is* impaired. In doing so the tribunal must judge matters now and look forward to consider how the registrant will behave in the future. The tribunal is making a judgment on risk to the profession, the public and the practitioner. These decisions can in part be explained as an assessment of the facts and risks in light of the registrant's character.

2.225 As stated above, good character is not a defence, conversely bad character is not always a signpost to future misconduct or risk. These should be weighed in the balance and may play an important role albeit subordinate to the risks implicit in the facts found proved.

2.226 Good character may play an important role when considering undertakings offered by a registrant or, when he or she asserts that a lesson has been learned following an admission of misconduct (a guilty plea). Clearly if the registrant has been disbelieved on oath that is not the case. The second limb of character (propensity) is likely to be of considerable importance, the more so because of the approach required by *Cohen, Zygmunt* and *Cheatle.*

Sanctions

2.227 While impairment involves a risk-assessment, the sanction stage involves the assessment of a *proportionate* response. Emphasis is rightly placed upon public protection and the public interest in declaring and upholding standards but, this does not preclude the consideration of character in appropriate cases.

2.228 If impairment stems from such gross misconduct that it is necessary to impose an immediate and lengthy order of suspension or order erasure to protect the profession or the public (eg sexual misconduct, dishonesty etc), then good character will play a much lesser role in determining sanction.

2.229 However, if the interests of the profession are less prominent and there is a greater public interest in returning the registrant to safe practice, character may play an important role in assessing the type or length of sanction. This is applicable in two instances:

a) where a short period of suspension is required to 'send a message' or uphold standards the tribunal will have to consider whether a shorter period is appropriate for a registrant with an otherwise unblemished record. A long order may not be necessary and may be disproportionate in the circumstances of such a case;
b) where the seriousness of the misconduct places the registrant on the cusp of one sanction or another, his or her good character may again play an important role in deciding whether to apply a greater sanction or, to mitigate the sanction from potential erasure to suspension or from suspension to conditions etc.

2.230 The above are all part and parcel of balancing the public and registrant's interests, protecting the profession but, allowing an otherwise good registrant to return to safe practice. To what extent character affects the type or length of sanction is a matter for the tribunal's professional judgment.

Immediate orders

2.231 Finally, the tribunal should consider whether a registrant's good character affects the decision to impose an immediate order of conditions or of suspension. There may be occasions when an immediate order is not necessary to protect the public or in the practitioner's own interests but a short suspension is otherwise required to uphold and declare standards.

2.232 The imposition of an immediate order, pending the expiry of the 28-day period during which a registrant may appeal, has the effect of lengthening the term of a suspension. If a suspension is short (eg two to three months) the effect of an immediate order is a 30–50 per cent increase in the suspension beyond that deemed appropriate. Despite the tenet that sanctions are not intended to be punitive, this may clearly have a punitive effect and be unfair and/or disproportionate. A registrant may ask for time to arrange his or her professional affairs before the sanction is invoked. While such applications are not to be encouraged, it is not necessarily an unreasonable request to make. A registrant's previous good character and clinical ability may be relevant in determining whether it is in the public interest to permit him or her to remain in unrestricted practice for a short period before the sanction bites so that they are not deprived of an otherwise competent practitioner longer than is necessary.

Conduct during the hearing and lies

2.233 A registrant's conduct during a hearing is clearly capable of influencing the tribunal. At its most basic, a calm and polite witness is likely to be given more credence over an excitable or rude one. (This subject is covered in more detail below at para 3.176 on the issue of insight and sanction.)

2.234 It is important to ensure that a tribunal does not fall into the trap of using discreditable or even dishonest behaviour in the tribunal setting as direct evidence of guilt regarding the conduct complained of. That is impermissible, since the tribunal would be considering facts (poor behaviour) that are not the subject of the charge. However, if some or all the facts charged are found proved, and if they amount to misconduct, a registrant's behaviour and demeanour in the hearing may be highly relevant to the issues of insight and current impairment.

2.235 Dishonest or discreditable behaviour is relevant when the tribunal looks at the question of whether a registrant has gained insight into any alleged misconduct. That said it is one factor to consider among many and is not conclusive. There may be several reasons why a registrant is rude or excitable in a hearing not least because the stress he or she may be under. It is important that a tribunal considers this evidence with care and caution before relying upon it.

2.236 A tribunal may accept or reject all or part of a witness's evidence, including the registrant. It may reject evidence it finds to be unreliable, inaccurate or untrue – however, if a tribunal rejects part of a witness's or registrant's evidence it does not automatically follow that all of the evidence must be rejected. A tribunal is entitled to accept part and reject part of any witness's evidence, provided it is satisfied it is correct to do so and it provides reasons for its decision.

2.237 When considering the registrant, if the tribunal finds that he or she is unreliable, inaccurate or lying, that finding may be considered as part of the case as a whole – but the tribunal should not simply reject all of a registrant's case because he or she is disbelieved on one part. In addition, that finding cannot be used as a reason to increase sanction. Lies or similar discreditable conduct in a hearing may well be relevant to insight and the risk of repetition, which are central to the question of current impairment and the need for a sanction – but the appropriate sanction can only be determined by and imposed upon the facts charged and found proved. Such conduct may in effect negate any mitigation, but it cannot amplify the seriousness of the case charged and proved.

2.238 In *Rehman v Bar Standards Board*[146] the tribunal found that R had lied in his evidence to the disciplinary tribunal. However, on appeal the Board of Visitors 'had no hesitation' in concluding that the tribunal had been wrong to take this into account when deciding whether the conduct

146 PC2008/0235/A and PC2010/0012/A, 19 July 2013.

originally complained of was discreditable since it was not part of the circumstances relating to the charge and did not relate to the offence.

Review hearings

2.239 Review hearings involve many of the matters germane to an FTP hearing, however they do not re-assess the initial misconduct or performance allegations. The decision has already been reached that there has in the past been misconduct, UPC, or deficient performance etc. The review tribunal is convened to reassess a registrant's case after a period has elapsed with a view to ascertaining what progress, if any, has been made by the registrant towards rehabilitation and safe practice.

2.240 The facts and seriousness of the original allegation is an important context to the review, but the assessment of progress and rehabilitation is done by considering if or how a registrant has met learning goals set by a previous tribunal, changed his or her practice or whether he or she has demonstrated insight into previously identified failings.

2.241 While the legal burden of proving the case has not shifted from the regulator, a registrant has a persuasive or evidential burden to show that he or she has addressed the concerns identified in the earlier FTP hearing. If the registrant has not addressed *all* the concerns, he or she should explain why. It is certainly in the registrant's interests to make positive suggestions as to how any unmet concerns may be addressed, either by extending the existing sanction or by imposing a different one. If the registrant does not discharge this evidential burden, then the reviewing tribunal has all the sanctioning powers available to it including imposing a more serious sanction than the original.

2.242 Any registrant who has been subject to a 'conditions of practice' order will have their adherence to those conditions analysed. Suggestions by the original tribunal regarding information that the reviewing tribunal may find of assistance (eg a reflective statement and/or certificates of training) should be carefully considered by the registrant. While the suggestions are not binding, they are made with a view to highlighting what the FTP tribunal considers would assist the review process. Again these are not determinative, but reviewing tribunals do set considerable store by these suggestions and if they are not met the registrant should be in a position to explain why.

2.243 A registrant who has been suspended is in the difficult position of having a more limited opportunity either to demonstrate rehabilitation or to keep their skills up to date. However, this can be achieved in part by a careful choice of study and compliance with continuing professional development (CPD) training and/or employment in a complimentary field. All of these may assist in preventing or reducing de-skilling, broaden the registrant's scope and understanding or good practice and demonstrate commitment to good practice. For example, a nurse might work as a healthcare assistant, an osteopath might work as a sports therapist. However, in taking up such alternatives, a registrant must be careful not to continue to hold himself or herself out as being a practitioner in the field from which they are suspended. Nor must the interim job be seen as a means to circumvent the sanction.

2.244 Much of the above was spelled out by Blake J in *Abrahaem v General Medical Council*:[147]

> . . . the review has to consider whether *all* the concerns raised in the original finding of impairment through misconduct have been sufficiently addressed to the Panel's satisfaction. In practical terms there is a persuasive burden on the practitioner at a review to demonstrate that he or she has fully acknowledged why past professional performance was deficient and through insight, application, education, supervision or other achievement sufficiently addressed the past impairments.

2.245 The NMC list of matters to consider on review include the following:

- Since the sanction was imposed has the registrant:
- complied with any conditions? (What evidence is there to demonstrate this and what is the quality of the evidence?)
- show insight into their failings? (Has this improved or worsened since the sanction was imposed?)
- maintained their skills & knowledge?
- practised safely in the interim
- demonstrated that they are safe to practise?

Ultimately the above go to the question of whether the registrant is fit to return to practice without restriction or, whether it remains *necessary* (or otherwise in the public interest) to impose a sanction. If the necessity remains, the tribunal must decide what sanction is required to meet that necessity.

2.246 The cases of *Arora v General Medical Council*[148] and *R (Adeyemi) v General Medical Council*[149] make it clear that that the above principles apply equally to cases of deficient performance. In *Arora* serious long-term deficiencies were not remediated despite extensive training and supervision. Lang J upheld the decision to erase since there was 'no prospect of remediation or of a return to practice'. Similarly, in *Adeyami*, A's failure to comply with all conditions led a reviewing tribunal to conclude that conditions did not protect the public. She was thus suspended and, on further review, was erased from the register. Bean J followed the view expressed in *Abrahaem*. He acknowledged that the fact the burden is on the registrant may place him or her at a disadvantage but stressed the GMC's duty to protect the public as the basis for such decisions.

2.247 In *Bamgbelu v General Dental Council*[150] B was placed on a 12-month conditions of practise order. Contrary to one of the conditions, B continued to practise for some time without a supervisor. B also failed to meet several other conditions. A nine-month extension to the conditions was upheld by HHJ Gore QC because B had failed to demonstrate that he had addressed the original concerns upon which his impairment was founded and there was limited evidence of rehabilitation.

147 [2008] EWHC 183 (Admin) (at para 23).
148 [2012] EWHC 1560 (Admin).
149 [2012] EWHC 425 (Admin).
150 [2013] EWHC 1169 (Admin).

2.248 In the similar case of *Mould v General Dental Council*[151] M was placed under conditions to appoint a mentor with whom he was to meet regularly and, create a personal development plan (PDP) to address his misconduct. M failed to draw up the PDP, appointed the mentor seven weeks late and, after a year had only met the mentor three times. HHJ Gore QC upheld the reviewing committee's suspension of M based on his continued lack of insight and, given his failures to date, there was no guarantee he would abide by the conditions. The committee was entitled to conclude that the maintenance of standards, public protection and public confidence outweighed any effect on M.

2.249 *Hosny v General Medical Council*[152] provides another example. H was suspended for misconduct in the dishonest use of false references and failure to disclose restrictions to her practice in various application forms. While suspended, she repeated her misconduct. On review and at appeal she challenged the findings against her. Her lack of insight and remediation was evident and she was erased from the register.

2.250 A failure to comply with undertakings may have similar consequences as shown by *Depner v General Medical Council*[153] in which D was found guilty of misconduct for failing to abide by his undertaking to undergo a performance assessment.

2.251 The case of *Molubi v NMC*[154] is another example of a review resulting in a striking-off order. In 2011 M was suspended following proof of misconduct based on her failings at a care home which included poor observation and monitoring of patients as well as poor record keeping. The case was reviewed several times over the years, and a conditions of practice order was imposed in early 2015. A final review in 2016 resulted in M being struck off since, although she had made some progress, she maintained her position of blaming the home and others who worked there. The tribunal concluded that M was highly unlikely to remediate her misconduct or alter her stance, and imposed a striking-off order on ground of patient safety. This was upheld on appeal, the court commenting that if M had been able to demonstrate compliance with the conditions the matter may have ended differently, but the decision was neither disproportionate nor wrong in law.

2.252 A recent example is *McDermott v HCPC*[155] in which a finding of continued impairment was upheld owing to clearly identified continuing concerns, but an order of suspension was quashed and remitted to another FTP tribunal to consider appropriate conditions of practice. Yip J's reasons for quashing the order were that M had demonstrated a clear commitment to practice, had complied with interim conditions and received positive references. She concluded that M had progressed while the conditions in place had protected the public. To suspend M was disproportionate.

2.253 Because a review hearing involves reconsideration of the case in the light of progress and may result in a more serious sanction, the registrant

151 [2012] EWHC 3114 (Admin).
152 [2012] EWHC 2665 (Admin).
153 [2012] EWHC 1705 (Admin).
154 [2016] CSIH 95.
155 [2017] EWHC 2899 (Admin).

must receive proper notice of the hearing to include the possible consequences of non-attendance. This was made clear in *LM v Nursing and Midwifery Council*[156] in which LM, who was not represented, failed to attend the review through ill-health. She had been told at the original hearings that a striking-off would be disproportionate. Following her non-attendance, she was struck-off, however this was quashed on appeal, the court observing that the letter of notice did not make clear that M was at risk of a strike-off on a review hearing since sanction was at large.

2.254 From the above case it is important that the notice of hearing contains not just the date and location of the hearing but also a clear warning that sanction is at large including more severe sanctions than were previously imposed. While it is a registrant's choice whether he or she attends or not, non-attendance can make it very difficult for a tribunal to assess progress since the sanction was imposed. While the tribunal will strive to do so, the registrant who does not attend a review places himself or herself at a disadvantage, particularly since the registrant bears the evidential burden of proving that he or she is fit to return to practice without restriction or with a less restrictive sanction.

Non-compliance hearings

2.255 A difficulty with cases of deficient performance may arise when a registrant fails or refuses to comply with an assessment of their practice. In some cases, this has led to an impasse with repeated requests or directions not being complied with and cases being delayed. To cater for this situation, the GMC has now introduced non-compliance hearings through GMC (Fitness to Practise) Rules 2004 rule 17(ZA), as amended.

2.256 Under this new rule, if a registrant has failed to submit to or comply with a reasonable direction for an assessment of their health, performance or English language proficiency, or has failed a language assessment, or has failed to provide information or documents requested in respect of their fitness to practise, then non-compliance proceedings may be commenced.

2.257 Non-compliance proceedings do not assess the registrant's fitness to practise – they only deal with compliance as regards the assessment. The hearing proceeds in a very similar fashion to a FTP hearing, with the GMC presenting its case, the registrant presenting his or her case and the tribunal making its decision on whether there has been compliance or not.

2.258 The tribunal must be satisfied that the request for an assessment was reasonable; that there has been a failure to comply; and that there is no reasonable excuse for that failure (ie reasons outside the control of the registrant). If there has been such a failure, it may, after hearing from the parties, impose an order of conditions for up to three years, or it may suspend the registrant. This suspension will be reviewed, but if following two years of suspension the registrant has still not complied, then the suspension may be made indefinite. When imposing a sanction, the tribunal must be satisfied that a sanction is necessary in order to protect

156 [2016] CSIH 86.

the public. As with conditions in the FTP arena, they must be measurable, workable and sufficient to protect the public. If a registrant has simply refused or unreasonably failed to comply with an assessment, then conditions are unlikely to be appropriate.

The tribunal and the hearing

Membership of the tribunal

2.259 Membership of a regulatory tribunal is a matter for the regulator whose decisions in this respect have been approved either by Parliament or the Privy Council. Suggestions that a tribunal with two lay-members should be afforded less deference were firmly rejected by Lang J in *Martin v General Medical Council.*[157] Furthermore, unless specifically required by its rules of practice, a tribunal does not have to contain a member with the same expertise as the registrant – see *Southall v General Medical Council.*[158]

2.260 The Medical Practitioners Tribunal Service (MPTS) has introduced LQCs into both interim orders tribunal and medical practitioner tribunal hearings, initially as a 'pilot scheme' however it quickly became clear that the MPTS intends to use LQCs in most if not all their hearings. The MPTS has recently dispensed with the services of Legal Assessors who are not also LQCs.

2.261 A great deal of time and effort was wasted on challenging the use of LQCs in principle, and/or how an LQC would rule on or advise his or her colleagues of the applicable law. In practice they will, or at the least should, do the same as in any other jurisdiction – namely, set out the principles applicable to the case. If the regulator and registrant are represented, this does not need to be a detailed review, but should simply highlight the applicable principles. If a registrant is not represented, the review will need to be more detailed. It may assist the process and the registrant if this is done at the outset of the hearing to provide a framework for the hearing, rather than doing it after the evidence has been heard.

2.262 A more thorny issue is whether an LQC should repeat any advice given to colleagues when deliberating 'in camera' which is *additional* to that given in open session. If it is straightforward, clear and not open to debate, there may be little reason to do so. However, if there is any complexity to the issue or it is a matter open to debate, the safer course would be to reconvene the hearing and listen to any submission. While this may take a short while, it is better to act openly and fairly than face a challenge to the proceedings in the appellate courts.

2.263 The advent and roll-out of LQCs will undoubtedly have received a boost following criticism of the tribunal in the case of *Squier v General Medical Council.*[159] Many of the tribunal's findings were criticised, and Mitting J observed that it was desirable for complex cases such as this to be chaired by a lawyer with judicial experience. While this may include a

157 [2011] EWHC 3204 (Admin).
158 [2010] EWCA Civ 407.
159 [2016] EWHC 2739 (Admin).

layperson and need not specifically be an LQC, it is clear that in future LQCs will be employed in complex or contentious cases.

Impartiality and independence of the tribunal

> The question is whether the fair-minded and informed observer, having considered the facts, would conclude that there was a real possibility that the tribunal was biased.

2.264 Alongside Lord Hope's admirably short statement of principle in *Porter v Magill*[160] it is useful to remember his description of a fair-minded and informed observer given in *Helow v Secretary of State for the Home Department and another*:[161]

> The observer who is fair-minded is the sort of person who reserves judgment on every point until she has seen and fully understood both sides of the argument. She is not unduly sensitive or suspicious as Kirby J observed in *Johnson v Johnson* (2000) 2001 CLR 488, 509, para 53. Her approach must not be confused with that of the person who has brought the complaint. The 'real possibility' test, ensures that there is this measure of detachment. The assumptions that the complainer makes are not to be attributed to the observer unless they can be justified objectively. But she is not complacent either. She knows that fairness requires that a judge must be, and must be seen to be, unbiased. She knows that judges, like anybody else, have their weaknesses. She will not shrink from the conclusion, if it can be justified objectively, that things that they have said or done or associations they have formed may make it difficult for them to judge the case before them impartially.
>
> Then there is the attribute that the observer is 'informed'. It makes the point that, before she takes a balanced approach to any information she is given, she will take the trouble to inform herself on all matters that are relevant. She is the sort of person who takes the trouble to read the text of an article as well as the headlines. She is able to put whatever she has read or seen into its overall social, political or geographical context. She is fair minded, so she will appreciate the context forms an important part of the material which she must consider before passing judgment.

2.265 ECHR Article 6 provides for the right to adjudication by an independent and impartial tribunal. Independence means separated from the executive and from the parties. Impartial means lacking in both bias and/or the appearance of bias.

2.266 To emphasise the separation of the executive from the adjudicating tribunal the GMC and the Health and Care Professions Council (HCPC) have each created the independent tribunals of the MPTS and the Health and Care Professionals Tribunal Service (HCPCTS) respectively. Other regulators draw up the rules, and appoint both the prosecutors and the adjudicating tribunals to judge cases – which remains unsatisfactory.

2.267 The mere fact that disciplinary proceedings against registrants are determined by a body which includes members of the same profession does not itself offend the requirement of independence and it accords with

160 [2001] UKHL 67, [2002] 2 AC 357, at para 103, per Lord Hope.

161 [2008] 1 WLR 2416 at paras 2 and 3.

the principle that a governing body is best placed to judge what is right for its profession – see *Stefan v UK*.[162]

2.268 The Office of the Health Professions Adjudicator (OHPA) was established by the Health and Social Care Act (HSCA) 2008 to take over proceedings at the GMC and then roll out the idea of the MPTS to other regulators, however this withered on the vine and the OHPA was abolished. As stated above, the MPTS, an 'operationally separate' arm of the GMC, now adjudicates in proceedings brought by the GMC and the HCPC have taken a similar course. Interestingly, the question of an over-riding healthcare regulatory tribunal service has reared its head once more.

2.269 In October 2017 the government issued a consultation paper entitled *Promoting professionalism reforming regulation*, the findings of which may impact upon the number, status and function of many of the healthcare regulators, including separation of the investigatory, prosecutorial and adjudication functions of the regulatory process. If or how this affects healthcare regulation remains to be seen, but there is clear reference to transparency and independence within the paper.

2.270 *Porter v Magill* provides the definitive statement on apparent bias as set out in the head-note. In addition, *R v Bow Street Metropolitan Stipendiary Magistrate ex p Pinochet Ugarte (No 2)*[163] makes clear the doctrine of automatic disqualification – namely, that no one should be a judge in his or her own cause. The case revolved around the appearance of bias through Lord Hoffmann being a member of the House of Lords panel that gave judgment against Senator Pinochet in *Pinochet No 1*. Lord Hoffmann was at the time a director of, and raised funds for, Amnesty International Charity Ltd. This company is part of Amnesty International whose antipathetic views of Pinochet and the human rights abuses in Chile were well known. Amnesty International was a party to the proceedings and supported the deportation and prosecution of Pinochet

2.271 It was not suggested that Lord Hoffmann had any pecuniary interest in the decision – rather, it was an interest in a cause supported by a party. This led Lord Browne-Wilkinson to conclude that Lord Hoffmann should have automatically disqualified himself. His Lordship stated that there was no reason to limit the ambit of interests to pecuniary, proprietary or economic ones. Here the decision impacted upon a cause the judge promoted with others. While there was no suggestion of financial gain, his Lordship said 'there is no room for fine distinctions [if justice is done and seen to be done]'.[164] His Lordship emphasised the very unusual nature of the case, including the fact that Amnesty International was a party to the proceedings and argued for a specific result.

2.272 Lord Nolan's admirably short comment at page 14 sums up the matter nicely – 'where the impartiality of a judge is in question the appearance of the matter is just as important as the reality'.

2.273 In *Langborger v Sweden*[165] it was stated that in assessing independence and impartiality, regard must be had to:

162 (1998) 25 EHRR CD130.
163 [2000] 1 AC 119 – *Pinochet No 2*.
164 At p11.
165 (1990) 12 EHRR 416.

- the way panel members are appointed;
- their term of office;
- the existence of guarantees against outside pressure;
- whether the regulator has the appearance of independence.

2.274 There must also be a modicum of common-sense and practicality in appointing tribunal members. In *R (Michalak) v General Medical Council*[166] the medical member of the tribunal became ill after 34 days and 28 witnesses. The registrar appointed a substitute member, a decision the Tribunal approved in the interests of justice. Parker J reviewed the relevant GMC Rules (the GMC (Constitution of Panels & Investigation Committee) Rules 2004, now superseded by the GMC (Constitution of Panels, Tribunals & Investigation Committee) Rules 2015) and concluded that provided the decision was in the interests of justice, for a proper purpose and the parties had been given sufficient time to make appropriate representations, it was reasonable course to take within the rules.

2.275 In *Tehrani v United Kingdom Central Council for Nursing, Midwifery and Health Visiting*[167] approved in *Preiss v General Dental Council*,[168] it was held that the fact that a member of the General Council could move between tribunals was sufficient to raise a real risk that the tribunals did not meet the requirements of independence and impartiality. There was also the added difficulty of the lack of an appeal.

2.276 The Bar Council's own Disciplinary Tribunal failed to satisfy ECHR Article 6 in *P (a barrister) v General Council of the Bar*.[169] The tribunal comprised members nominated by the President of the Council of the Inns of Court, some of whom came from a pool of names put forward by the Bar Council. One such member was also a member of the Bar Council's own Professional Conduct and Complaints Committee. The court held that i) there was a breach of Article 6; ii) there was apparent bias satisfying the test in *Porter v Magill*; and iii) the committee and the Bar Council had a common interest in convictions. The member should have been disqualified at common law, under the *Pinochet* principle. Contrast *Holder v Law Society*[170] in which the Divisional Court held the Solicitors Disciplinary Tribunal to be an independent and impartial tribunal that complied with Article 6.

2.277 Similarly, in *Holmes v Royal College of Veterinary Surgeons*[171] the fact that prosecutors and tribunal members may be drawn from the same governing body did not create the appearance of bias since the governing body had, ensured effective separation of prosecutors from tribunal members.

2.278 Evidence as to what happens generally and what happened in a specific instance may satisfy a criticism raised, but this is not a course to be recommended. In *Flaherty v National Greyhound Racing Club Ltd*[172] the Court of Appeal rejected an allegation of apparent bias against a steward. While the

166 [2011] EWHC 2307 (Admin).
167 [2001] IRLR 208.
168 [2001] UKPC 36, [2001] 1 WLR 1926.
169 [2005] 1 WLR 3019.
170 [2005] EWHC 2023 (Admin).
171 [2011] UKPC 48.
172 [2005] EWCA Civ 1117.

court was critical of the fact that the chief executive retired with the stewards on the tribunal, their clear evidence was that he did not take part in deliberations. The court commented that sporting bodies should be permitted to deal with disciplinary matters without the courts intervening, provided their proceedings were consistent with the fundamental requirement of fairness. With respect to the National Greyhound Racing Club, when it comes to public safety, there is a distinction to be made between procedures that govern professional sporting complaints and professional healthcare complaints.

2.279 In *R (Kaur) v ILEX*[173] K, a student member of the Institute of Legal Executives (ILEX), was accused of cheating in two examinations. One charge was found proved by a tribunal consisting of two lay members and a serving ILEX council member. Her appeal was dismissed by a tribunal consisting of two lay members and the vice-president of ILEX. She appealed on grounds of both apparent bias and automatic disqualification. Rix LJ allowed the appeal, concluding that the two doctrines were really part of 'a single overarching requirement: that judges should not sit [on cases] . . . where there is a real possibility on the objective appearance of things, assessed by the fair-minded and informed observer . . . that the tribunal could be biased'.[174] He reiterated that any personal interest upon which this may be argued had to be more than negligible, and concluded that by either test the vice-president was disqualified because of her senior role in ILEX and her consequent interest in its disciplinary policy.

2.280 In coming to his conclusion, Rix LJ reviewed several of the principal authorities on apparent bias including *Ex Parte Pinochet (No 2)* and *Porter v Magill*, above. This case is therefore a useful authority on the issue of bias.

2.281 *Russell v Bar Standards Board*[175] adds a note of reason to challenges against the constitution of tribunals. Complaint was made that a panellist had not been appointed in accordance with the rules. The court held that the panelist was 'clothed' with authority despite an irregularity in the nomination procedure. There needed to be a substantive defect in the process for the court to strike-down a tribunal's decision. However, the position is not entirely settled since R and sought leave to appeal and Jackson LJ in delivering the judgment of the court observed that this was arguable and leave to appeal would have been granted if the point was 'critical' but it was not and thus leave was refused.[176]

2.282 In the case of *Rasool v General Pharmaceutical Council*[177] Carr J provides a useful overview of the test for bias and apparent bias in the following terms: 'would a fair-minded observer, having considered the relevant facts, conclude that there was a real possibility that the tribunal was (consciously or subconsciously) biased'.

2.283 From the above it can be concluded that tribunals should be, and be seen to be, divorced from any interest in the allegations, proceedings or

173 [2011] EWCA Civ 1168.

174 At para 45.

175 PC2008/0263/D5, 23 May 2013.

176 *R (Russell and others) v BSB* [2014] EWCA Civ 1630.

177 [2015] EWHC 217 (Admin) at para 25.

result. Interest includes an intellectual or social concern or any other concern that is more than just passing.

2.284 In addition, tribunals have a duty to conduct hearings in accordance with the rules of natural justice. In *R (Hill) v Institute of Chartered Accountants in England and Wales*[178] a disciplinary tribunal member left the hearing early, thereby missing a crucial part of the evidence. Despite his absence being agreed by both sides and the crucial evidence being supplied in a transcript, the High Court disapproved, stating that it was contrary to the rules of natural justice to continue without the tribunal member. The court distinguished cases where procedures had been breached but that breach may be waived and, cases where the procedure was freely and knowingly consented to before any breach. Since H had consented to the tribunal member's absence, there was in this case no breach of natural justice. See also *Millar v Dickson*[179] making the point that such consent or agreement must be informed, unequivocal and voluntary.

2.285 In *Lawrence v General Medical Council*[180] the FTP tribunal found that L had disclosed his own sexual fantasies to a patient and had attempted to engage in a relationship with her. In coming to its conclusions, the tribunal relied upon the purported expertise of one of its members on the issue of erotic transference, a subject not disclosed to L, who thus had no opportunity to address it. The findings were quashed as being in breach of natural justice. The court stated that tribunal members cannot give evidence to each other, nor may they rely upon material that the parties have had no opportunity to address or challenge.

2.286 Bias is not to be confused with a regulatory tribunal's function which is to hold an inquisitorial hearing. In *R (Banerjee) v General Medical Council*[181] it was submitted that the tribunal was either biased or appeared biased, and had intervened to the extent of usurping counsel's role. It was argued this was plain from the number and style of questions, an apparent closed mind (as evidenced by the words used), the questions were formulated as cross-examination and the tribunal had usurped GMC counsel's role when compared to the questions she had asked. The questions were described as persistent and hostile. It was submitted that this led to an appearance of unfairness and a real danger that the hearing was unfair.

2.287 Walker J roundly dismissed the multiplicity of complaints, stating that:

> . . . members of a tribunal, if they are concerned about whether a witness is being truthful on a particular matter, are entitled to probe that witness about that matter and consider whether it affects their assessment of the witness' evidence on other matters.[182]

2.288 It is plain from the judgment that the tribunal were deeply concerned over B's conduct and explanation for that conduct. B had difficulty answering the questions posed which merely heightened the concerns of the tribunal. The real complaint appears to be founded in the fact that the questions hit the mark.

178 [2013] EWCA Civ 555.
179 [2002] 1 WLR 1615 (at para 31).
180 [2012] EWHC 464 (Admin).
181 [2015] EWHC 2263 (Admin), [2017] EWCA Civ 78.
182 Para A 1.25 of the annex to judgment.

2.289 Dr Bannerjee took her case to the Appeal Court which also rejected her assertions. The court reiterated the matters it had to consider as follows:

i) whether excessive questioning or adverse comment has created a 'real danger' that the hearing was unfair;
ii) whether such questions indicate denial of a fair hearing by a tribunal that has closed its mind to argument and indulged in the 'perils of self-persuasion';
iii) the number, length, circumstances and terms used in any question must be looked at in the context of the whole case;
iv) the timing and tone of the questions. Early interruption may be less appropriate than subsequent requests for clarity. Forceful interruption may adversely affect cross-examination;
v) any such review requires flexibility since there are many issues that may render a hearing unfair.

2.290 The court concluded that the tribunal was entitled to robustly explore matters upon which it was entitled to expect clear consistent answers.

Legal assessors

2.291 The role of the legal assessor is to advise the tribunal on matters of law, evidence, procedure and on its powers. The legal assessor has no part to play in respect of fact-finding, decisions or on the weight or cogency to be attached to evidence.

2.292 The legal assessor may only advise upon its admissibility and, outline such factors as may impact upon matters of weight and cogency (eg time-lapse may affect memory, an honest witness may be mistaken etc) but he or she should be careful not to express or be seen to express an opinion on the evidence and what impact those factors have, if any – see *Walker v General Medical Council.*[183]

2.293 Likewise, the legal assessor has no part to play in the decisions on impairment or sanction other than to advise upon the legal parameters and/or upon the legal accuracy of arguments deployed without giving a personal opinion on their veracity:

> The legal assessor is not a judge and his advice . . . is not a summing up . . . The legal assessor simply advises the [panel] on points of law . . . The [panel is master] of both law and fact . . .[184]

2.294 It is an advisory role, not a decision-making one. Any advice by a legal assessor should be given in open session with the parties afforded the opportunity to comment upon it – see *Nwabueze v General Medical Council.*[185] The tribunal is not bound to accept the legal advice given but, if it does not, it must clearly state this and, give full reasons. These principles were restated when Parker J reviewed several authorities in *Yaacoub v General Medical Council.*[186]

183 [2002] UKPC 57.
184 *Libman v General Medical Council* [1972] AC 214 (per Lord Hailsham at p3, numbered point 4).
185 [2000] 1 WLR 1760, PC.
186 [2012] EWHC 2779 (Admin).

2.295 If a registrant is represented, then the legal assessor may be invited to discuss matters with counsel for the registrant and the regulator in order to clarify or reduce areas of conflict or, to determine disputes on admissibility of evidence to prevent a tribunal from becoming contaminated by inadmissible evidence. In the case of *Fish v General Medical Council*[187] Foskett J commented that discussions such as the above and discussions regarding any legal advice the assessor intends to give are to be encouraged.

2.296 If a registrant is not represented, then the legal assessor may do the above, but he or she should only do so with counsel for the regulator present to prevent a possible perception of bias and/or allegations of erroneous or biased advice. The legal assessor should never see the registrant alone. In the hearing, the legal assessor may assist by explaining procedure and/or rules of practice and evidence to the registrant, and explain what areas of evidence should be focused upon bearing in mind the decision(s) that the tribunal has to make. The legal assessor may not represent the registrant by putting questions or making submissions on his or her behalf. However, if a registrant is struggling to express him/herself such that they cannot put their case or it is not comprehensible to the witness or tribunal, the legal assessor may invite the registrant to explain the point they wish to make and thereafter advise how that point may be put to the witness as a question. Before taking this course, the legal assessor should inform the tribunal that this is what he or she proposes to do in order to assist the registrant and the witness and ensure fairness to all parties.

Specialist advisers

> Specialist advisers are present to assist in the interpretation and/or significance of expert evidence. They should not give an opinion or comment upon the issue of fitness to practise. An adviser is not part of the tribunal, and as such he or she should not retire with the panel.
>
> Any advice must be given publicly, affording the parties an opportunity to challenge it including calling evidence if necessary.

2.297 If a registrant's fitness to practise is allegedly impaired by reason of adverse physical or mental health, a tribunal may direct that a specialist health or performance adviser be appointed to assist the tribunal, or that a health or performance assessment be carried out and a report provided. These assessors are distinct from legal assessors in that they are there to comment upon the evidence whereas legal assessors are not.

2.298 The case of *Watson v General Medical Council*[188] provides assistance on the role of such assessors. Stanley Burnton J reviewed both domestic and

187 [2012] EWHC 1269 (Admin).
188 [2005] EWHC 1896 (Admin).

European cases when making his decisions. These included *Richardson v Redpath Brown & Co Ltd*[189] in which Viscount Simon LC said:

> [T]o treat a medical assessor, or indeed any assessor, as though he were an unsworn witness in the special confidence of the judge, whose testimony cannot be challenged by cross-examination and perhaps cannot even be fully appreciated by the parties until judgment is given, is to misunderstand what the true functions of an assessor are. He is an expert available for the judge to consult if the judge requires assistance in understanding the effect and meaning of technical evidence. He may in proper cases suggest to the judge questions which the judge himself might put to an expert witness with a view to testing the witness's view or to making plain his meaning. The judge may consult him in cases if need as to the proper technical inferences to be drawn from the proved facts, or as to the extent of the difference between apparently contradictory conclusions in the expert field . . . but I cannot agree that [giving evidence] is within the scope of an assessor's legitimate contribution.[190]

2.299 His Lordship also considered the position of similar independent advisers in European jurisdictions, the magistrates' clerk in the UK and a legal assessor in *Nwabueze v General Medical Council.*[191]

2.300 His Lordship concluded that:

> The role of a medical assessor is not the same as a legal assessor to a tribunal . . . legal advisors do not in general give their personal views on the facts . . .[192]
>
> . . . those who advise a tribunal on issues of fact, whether as its experts or as assessors, should do so openly, in the presence of the parties [giving them an opportunity] to make submissions on that advise before the tribunal makes its decision [and to call experts in response if the advice is 'controversial'].[193]
>
> The medical assessors' special relationship with a tribunal makes it the more important that all their advice is given in the presence of the parties. The assessors are not parties to the case. Nor are they members of the panel. Where their advice may be adverse to the practitioner's case, it is particularly important that it is given in the presence of the parties [and that they be given] an opportunity to address that advice. Otherwise, the suspicion may be created that the advice given in private [is different] or that the assessors have exercised influence on the decision of the tribunal]. A perception of unfairness and of bias on the part of the tribunal is liable to be created.[194]

2.301 Specialist advisers should thus give advice in the presence of the parties, this being limited to the significance of the information before the tribunal. They are not entitled to express an opinion on the registrant's fitness to practise.

189 [1944] AC 62.
190 At pp770–771.
191 [2000] 1 WLR 1760.
192 At [56].
193 At [60].
194 At [61].

Legal representation

> A registrant is entitled and best advised to be represented by counsel in *regulatory* proceedings before a tribunal determining fitness to practise (including interim orders tribunals) since they have the potential substantially to affect his or her right to practise.
>
> A registrant *may* be entitled to representation in *disciplinary* proceedings if these have the potential substantially to affect his or her right to practise, or are likely to influence other proceedings that may themselves have such an impact. The risk should be closely considered since it may be indirect and not immediately apparent. If in doubt, it would be wise for the registrant to seek, and the regulator to permit, legal representation.

2.302 As noted previously, ECHR Article 6 guarantees certain minimum rights when facing a trial upon civil and/or criminal matters. These rights include:

- a fair and public hearing in the determination of civil or criminal matters and, when charged with a criminal offence;
- to have adequate time and facility to prepare; and
- to defend himself or herself in person or through legal assistance of his or her own choosing or, if he or she has not sufficient means to pay for legal assistance, to be given it free when the interests of justice so require.

2.303 However, as we have seen from the section on the ECHR above, it is not always clear that the convention applies to regulatory proceedings. On the one hand they may determine the right to practise a profession, and the ECHR is then engaged; on the other, if proceedings are unlikely to affect the right to practise then arguably the ECHR will not apply. The uncertainty is an unfortunate state of affairs. It remains a bone of contention in disciplinary proceedings.

2.304 On the one hand, there is some merit to keeping proceedings simple and less formal. However, informality is sometimes achieved by the denial of support or representation to registrants. Such a stance risks unfairness to the registrant and witnesses, and it taints the process from the start. From the registrant's perspective, it may well give the appearance of conscious or unconscious bias.

2.305 In criminal proceedings, a defendant is entitled to be represented by a properly qualified representative of his or her choice, however in publicly funded (legally aided) cases this does not mean quite what it says. There are two aspects – first, in choosing a representative; and second, hearing dates being fixed so that a chosen representative can attend. If a representation order is held by one firm, transferring to another is extremely difficult and may only occur in limited circumstances with the leave of the court. Despite the fact that counsel's availability should be considered, it is rarely a determining factor. In civil proceedings, public funding for representation is severely curtailed if not entirely extinguished.

2.306 In disciplinary proceedings, the registrant is frequently represented or seeks to be represented by someone chosen, appointed or paid for through a professional or union defence fund. It is important for the registrant to understand that, subject to the availability of funding, he or she has the right to choose an advocate for the hearing. The union or defence fund cannot dictate who this is. However, the author has noticed an increase in the withdrawal of funding immediately before proceedings commence or part way through, leaving the registrant to fend for himself or herself or pay for continued representation. While there may be a reason for such withdrawal, it can place both the registrant and any tribunal in a difficult position. It is a timely reminder that funds are not unlimited. Early, independent and realistic expert advice is a safeguard to the registrant, the funding authority and to the fairness of proceedings.

2.307 Whether a registrant is entitled to be represented depends on the type of proceedings and the affect they may have on the registrant's career. Interim order hearings and FTP hearings before regulatory tribunals require access to representation at the very least. Internal disciplinary proceedings are less likely to merit representation, particularly if the proceedings are not determinative of a registrant's right to practise. The fact that both High and Appeal Court rulings have been reversed suggests this is and will remain a thorny issue.

2.308 In *Kulkarni v Milton Keynes Hospital NHS Trust*[195] the purported contractual restrictions upon the right to representation were examined. K, a trainee doctor, was accused of misconduct (a sexual assault) and a Medical Protection Society (MPS) representative was assigned to his case. The representative was not legally qualified. The trust argued that based on Department of Health policy, K could be accompanied by a representative *not* acting in a legal capacity during the disciplinary proceedings. The MPS suggested that the trust had the discretion to allow legal representation and, since the case was complex and serious it should be exercised in favour of proper representation. The trust refused arguing that there were no exceptional circumstances to deviate from normal procedure. K sought a declaration that the trust had acted unlawfully and in breach of contract in their refusal to allow legal representation. The High Court dismissed K's application on the basis that the express contractual term did not permit legal representation so one could not be implied. Even if there was discretion to do so, the case was not exceptional. The court held that the refusal of legal representation was not a denial of natural justice and, queried whether ECHR Article 6 applied to disciplinary proceedings. K appealed and the Court of Appeal held that, given the terms of K's employment contract, he was entitled to be represented at his disciplinary hearing by a lawyer instructed by the MPS.

2.309 In his judgment Smith LJ states that:

> . . . the distinction which the [ECtHR made in *Le Compte v Belgium*] was that in ordinary disciplinary proceedings, where all that could be at stake was the loss of a specific job, Article 6 would not be engaged. However, where the effect of the proceedings could be far more serious and could, as in this case, deprive the employee of the right to practise his or her profession, the article would be engaged.[196]

195 [2008] EWHC 1861 (QB).
196 At para 65.

Since this was a sexual allegation there would undoubtedly be alert-letters warning others not to employ K if the matters were found proved. This would effectively end K's NHS practice.

2.310 From *Kulkarni*, Article 6 appears to be engaged when a registrant faces grave and/or quasi-criminal charges that, if proved, will have a severe impact on his or her ability to work. This clearly reflects the discussion on the applicability of the ECHR (see *Ghosh v General Medical Council*[197]). The decision was doubtless welcome to those accused of misconduct, but was met with less enthusiasm by NHS bodies.

2.311 In *Hameed v Central Manchester University Hospitals NHS Foundation Trust*[198] H argued that disciplinary proceedings which resulted in her dismissal for gross misconduct were not Article 6 compliant. H used surgical scissors in an operation when they were no longer sterile having been used previously, and sought to persuade others to lie in a subsequent investigation. Swift J distinguished *Kulkarni* on the facts since although H's dismissal would make employment difficult, it was not impossible. Nor were there exceptional circumstances justifying departure from the normal procedures of the disciplinary process.

2.312 Swift J accepted the submission that it is:

> . . . unsatisfactory for the decision as to whether article 6 applies to disciplinary proceedings against hospital practitioners to be taken on a case by case basis, depending on the gravity of the charge, the prospect of proceedings resulting in dismissal and/or the evidence about the . . . chances of obtaining alternative employment in the event of dismissal.[199]

2.313 Not surprisingly Her Ladyship agreed such an approach caused uncertainty in the application of Article 6, but opined that given the wide range of circumstances in which disciplinary proceedings may be brought pursuant to the *Maintaining high professional standards in the modern NHS framework*[200] it was arguable that Article 6 did not apply.

2.314 Although it is a case on the impartiality of a tribunal, it is worth reiterating that in *R (Puri) v Bradford Teaching Hospitals NHS Foundation Trust*[201] the registrant was dismissed following internal disciplinary proceedings before a tribunal of trust employees. On appeal Blair J found that, since the proceedings did not deprive P of his right to practise, as such Article 6 was not engaged.

2.315 In *R (G) v Governors of X School and Y City Council*[202] G faced the school's disciplinary procedures for allegedly kissing a pupil and was dismissed for abuse of trust and misconduct. This meant he would be reported to the Secretary of State for Children, Schools and Families as possibly unsuited to work with children and could be placed on the

197 [2000] 1 WLR 1915.

198 [2010] EWHC 2009 (QB).

199 At para 89.

200 *Maintaining high professional standards in the modern NHS* – a Department of Health publication from 2003 reflecting the procedures agreed between the Department of Health, NHS, British Medical Association and British Dental Association regarding the resolution of conduct issues.

201 [2011] EWHC 970 (Admin).

202 [2011] UKSC 30.

'children's barred list' by the Independent Safeguarding Authority (ISA). G sought a declaration that the denial of a lawyer was in breach of his Article 6 right to representation. The High Court and the Appeal Court agreed. The latter reasoned that G's right to practise his profession was at stake in the barring procedure before the ISA and this was likely to be 'profoundly' affected by the disciplinary proceedings. These in turn might well be affected by a professional advocate. Article 6 was engaged and G should have been afforded the opportunity to have a legal representatives present.

2.316 The Supreme Court disagreed (4:1) and held that the facts of each case must be considered on its merits taking account of: whether or not the first proceedings are determinative of the second; how closely linked the proceedings really are; whether the proceedings have the same object; and any policy reasons for dis-applying Article 6. The majority judgment given by Lord Dyson was that Article 6 undoubtedly applied to the ISA proceedings because these directly affected G's right to practise his profession as a teaching assistant and to continue to work with children. However, the disciplinary proceedings did not determine this but were merely concerned with whether G should be employed by the school. The disciplinary proceedings did not directly determine or substantially influence the ISA proceedings which were entirely independent. A judgment by the ISA would only be made after a full and independent assessment of the facts and merits of the case. Article 6 was thus not engaged at the stage of the disciplinary process.

2.317 Lord Kerr dissented, suggesting that the different stages could not be looked at in isolation. He thought the ISA would be substantially influenced by the school's disciplinary proceedings because this was where the evidence had been tested and was where G's rights should be protected.

2.318 With respect to the majority, while it may be correct to assert that the ISA should not be affected by the disciplinary proceedings, the idea that the views of the school governors will have 'receded far into the background' risks overstating the point. Lord Kerr's view that the ISA is likely to pay 'close attention' to what was said, done, proved or disproved in live evidence before the governors is far more realistic.

2.319 The regulators have their own rules, investigations, fact-finding tribunals and appeals. They ought to be independent of and not influenced by internal disciplinary proceedings. However, a number of residual concerns remain. Disciplinary proceedings differ as between workplaces, and the reliability and fairness of some may be in question. What is clear is that when disciplinary proceedings have the potential substantially to affect a registrant's right to practise, or are likely to influence other proceedings that may themselves have such an impact, it is important that the registrant is properly represented in those disciplinary proceedings. This will protect the integrity of those proceedings and may affect the admissibility of any matters found proved.

2.320 The above concerns relate to the question of whether a regulator seeks to refer to disciplinary proceedings or findings at any subsequent regulatory hearing. They could only do so on the basis that the information is relevant and probative. If the registrant was not represented at the earlier disciplinary proceedings and matters went against him or her, it may well be argued that to introduce the material is unfair and/or prejudicial, particularly if it is capable of being described as of profound importance. The propriety and fairness of the earlier proceedings may then require examination. This risk is avoided if registrants are afforded access to appropriate assistance and representation from the outset. A little flexibility at the early stages may prevent a whole raft of problems later on.

2.321 A final matter relating to healthcare professionals is the system of alert letters regarding patient, public or staff safety, or other publicity within the health service itself. These may broadcast decisions or allegations leading to damage to reputation and make work within the public sector and/or the private sector impossible. If that happens or if there is a risk of this, then it remains arguable that a registrant should be represented (see *Bonhoeffer* discussed above under hearsay and under Article 8 at para 1.61).

2.322 The above issues were revisited in *Stevens v University of Birmingham*[203] where S faced serious allegations with serious consequences to both his professional and personal standing. The university was responsible for investigating the complaints. It had employed an external HR consultant and provided the services of a senior staff member to assist the appointed investigator. The allegations were both extensive and technical. S wished to attend the investigatory meeting with the support of an experienced representative from the MPS who had assisted him from the outset. The university refused, saying that that S had no contractual right to an MPS representative and his request would mark a departure from the procedure the university had agreed with the union. S was only entitled to have a staff member or union representative present despite his being neither a union or staff member.

2.323 Andrews J ruled that S's contract did not permit a representative from the MPS but that the university's behaviour seriously damaged the implied term in any contract of employment that the employer must not act in a manner likely to seriously damage or destroy the relationship of mutual trust and confidence with the employee. S's request was for someone to be present who had sufficient knowledge and understanding to be render 'meaningful assistance'. The choice suggested by the university was said to be 'no choice at all', since such persons 'would not have the technical know-how . . . necessary [in this case]'. The position could not be rectified by the suggestion that the representative could sit outside with S leaving the hearing to consult and then returning. Nor could it be cured later by his having legal representation should the matter go to a full disciplinary process.

2.324 Andrews J made two important observations. First that:

> The presence of an appropriate assistant at the investigatory meeting could make all the difference between [a report that led to no further action or one that led to disciplinary proceedings].[204]

Second:

203 [2015] EWHC 2300 (QB).

204 At para 91.

> *Both parties* must be assumed to be aiming to get to the truth and to put the investigator in the best possible position to provide a comprehensive and balanced report to the decision maker.[205]

2.325 This second point is of particular importance, since a prosecuting regulator cannot help but start or appear to start from the stance that the registrant is guilty. In this case there was an 'objective perception of an inequality of arms' because the university had enlisted help for itself and denied it to S. Its stance was 'patently unfair' and 'objectively unfair'. The suggestion that allowing for proper representation would in some way upset the union was regarded as 'astonishing' and given short shrift indeed. It suggested that the university started from the viewpoint that the registrant was guilty or had something to hide.

2.326 The emphasis on each case being decided on its own facts is of course the reason why this problem will not go away, particularly when decisions may turn on very fine distinctions of fact and degree. What is important to note from the above case is that reliance on a contractual clause limiting the attendance of advisors may not be straightforward.

2.327 Instead of standing on principle, it would be better to proceed on the assumption that everyone wishes to get to the truth. If there is any doubt, it would behoove the registrant to be represented and the regulator to permit representation whether the proceedings are internal disciplinary proceedings or not. The alternative is the risk of further lengthy, expensive and stressful litigation which benefits no one.

Absence of the practitioner

> The tribunal has the discretion to proceed in the absence of the practitioner but:
>
> a) there must be strict adherence to the requirement that all reasonable effort to effect service has been made; and
> b) the decision to proceed must be taken with 'the utmost care and caution' and only after full consideration of the competing interests with emphasis on those of the practitioner.

2.328 In broad terms, proceedings may continue in the absence of a practitioner however this is subject to compliance with the appropriate rules of process and the general rule that all participants – complainant, accused and witnesses should normally be present.

2.329 When a registrant is neither present nor represented before the FTP Tribunal, it may nevertheless proceed to consider and determine the allegation or adjourn and issue directions if they are satisfied that 'all reasonable efforts' have been made to serve the practitioner with notice of the hearing.[206]

2.330 The equivalent of this rule applies to interim order cases before most regulators. In GMC proceedings notice (whether effective or not) must be

205 At para 93.
206 GMC (FTP) Rules 2004 r31; NMC (FTP) Rules 2004 r21.

served in 'such time as is reasonable in the circumstances of the case'. Ordinarily this will be at least seven days, but it may be shorter in exceptional circumstances.[207]

2.331 It is incumbent upon all practitioners to maintain a professional or other address for service of documentation. If they change this address it is their responsibility to notify their regulator. Because the onus is on the practitioner to maintain lines of communication, it is not unusual for proceedings to go ahead in his or her absence if the safeguards provided by the rules have been met.

2.332 The rules do *not* require actual service to be made upon the registrant. The tribunal may proceed if satisfied that 'all reasonable effort/steps have been made to serve [in accordance with the rules]'. This is because it is the practitioner's duty to be contactable, and when the regulator has done all it reasonably can, the paramount principles of protecting the public and the public interest come into play. Neither is served by delay.

2.333 To be satisfied that all reasonable effort or steps have been made or taken, the tribunal must receive evidence. This is either explicit in the rules or implicit but settled in law. It is not sufficient for the tribunal simply to be told that service has been attempted. However, meeting the above criterion is not particularly difficult and in practice it is usually settled by the regulator proving service by way of reference to recorded delivery documentation, email receipts or both.

Service of notices and documents

2.334 Each regulator's rules of practice provide that once a matter has been referred to a tribunal, a notice giving details of the allegation and the date of any tribunal hearing should be served upon the registrant as soon as reasonably practicable. Generally there will be at least 28 days' notice.[208] The notice should include reference to the fact that a tribunal may proceed in the absence of the registrant provided 'all reasonable effort' has been used to effect service.[209] Some regulators require more than one notice with a general 28-day notice giving details of the allegation and hearing and, a further notice with precise details of time and place seven days before the hearing. Notice may be shortened by consent; or if the registrar, case-manager or investigating committee, as the case may be, considers it reasonable, in the public interest and in the exceptional circumstances of the case.

2.335 Each regulator has its own rules on service. They should be rigorously adhered to and will be strictly construed, both to prove service and in deciding whether to continue in the registrant's absence or adjourn. In general, service may be by post to a registrant's professional address; or the address of the registrant's solicitor, trade union or defence organisation; or email to the registrant's previously notified email address or that of registrant's representative. Service may be proved by evidence of confirmation of registered posting or recorded delivery, receipt of email or a signed statement of delivery to the registrant's proper address/email

207 GMC (FTP) Rules 2004 r26.
208 GMC (FTP) Rules 2004 r15; NMC (FTP) Rules 2004 r11.
209 GMC (FTP) Rules 2004 r31.

address or that of his or her representative. Notice does not actually have to reach the registrant – it is enough to ensure that the rules have been adhered to.[210]

2.336 While a tribunal may proceed in absence, it should carefully consider whether it is fair and in the interests of justice so to do.

2.337 In *R v Hayward*[211] the Court of Appeal summarised the principles to be applied when dealing with an absent defendant as follows:

(a) An accused has, in general, a right to be present and represented at his trial.
(b) The above rights can be waived by the accused:
  (i) they may be wholly waived if, knowing or having the means of knowledge of his trial he deliberately and voluntarily absents himself and/or withdraws instructions from those representing him;
  (ii) they may be partly waived if, being present and represented at the outset, the accused behaves in such a way as to obstruct the proceedings and/or withdraws his instructions from those representing him.
(c) The trial judge has a discretion to permit a trial to take place or continue in the absence of an accused and/or his legal representatives.
(d) That discretion must be exercised with great care and it is only in rare and exceptional cases that it should be exercised in favour of a trial taking place or continuing, particularly if the accused is unrepresented.
(e) In exercising that discretion, fairness to the defence is of prime importance but fairness to the prosecution must also be taken into account. The judge must have regard to all the circumstances of the case including, in particular:
  (i) the nature and circumstances of the accused's behaviour in absenting himself from or disrupting the trial and, in particular, whether his behaviour was deliberate, voluntary and such as plainly waives his right to appear;
  (ii) whether an adjournment might result in his attending voluntarily and/or not disrupting proceedings;
  (iii) the likely length of such an adjournment;
  (iv) whether though absent, he is, or wishes to be, legally represented at the trial or has waived his right to representation;
  (v) the extent to which his legal representatives are able to present his defence;
  (vi) the extent of the disadvantage to him in not being able to give his account of events, having regard to the nature of the evidence against him;
  (vii) the risk of the jury reaching an improper conclusion about his absence (but see (f) below);
  (viii) the seriousness of the offence to the accused, victim and public;
  (ix) the general public interest and the particular interest of victims and witnesses that a trial should take place within a reasonable time of the alleged events;
  (x) the effect of delay on the memories of witnesses;

210 See as an example, GMC (FTP) Rules 2004 r40 as amended to allow service by email; and MA 1983 Sch 4 para 8.

211 [2001] 2 Cr App R 11.

(xi) where there are co-defendants, the undesirability of separate trials, and the prospects of a fair trial for those who are present.

(f) If the judge decides that a trial should take place or continue in the absence of an unrepresented accused, he must ensure that the trial is as fair as the circumstances permit. He must, take reasonable steps, both during the giving of evidence and in the summing up, to expose weaknesses in the prosecution case and to make such points on behalf of the accused as the evidence permits. In summing up he must warn the jury that absence is not an admission of guilt and adds nothing to the prosecution case.[212]

2.338 *Hayward* was considered and approved by the House of Lords in *R v Jones*,[213] Lord Bingham making the following important observations:

> . . . the discretion to commence a trial in the absence of a defendant should be exercised with the utmost care and caution . . . If the absence of the defendant is attributable to involuntary illness or incapacity it would very rarely, if ever, be right to exercise the discretion in favour of commencing the trial, at any rate unless the defendant is represented and asks that the trial should begin.[214]
>
> . . . the European Court of Human Rights has never found a breach of the Convention where a defendant, fully informed of a forthcoming trial, has voluntarily chosen not to attend and the trial has continued.[215]

2.339 Lord Hoffmann pointed out the principle repeatedly emphasised in the Strasbourg jurisprudence, that:

> The question . . . is not whether the defendants waived the right to a fair trial but whether in all the circumstances they got one. It is whether on the particular facts of the case the proceedings, taken as a whole and including the appellate process, satisfied the requirements of the Convention.[216]

2.340 Lord Bingham added two caveats to the *Hayward* principles. First, the seriousness of the offence should not be considered, the principles would be the same whether the offence was serious or minor. Second, even if the accused absconded voluntarily, it would generally be desirable that he or she be represented.

2.341 Mr Jones took the matter to the ECtHR, arguing that the case had been a breach of his Article 6 right to a fair trial. However, the ECtHR declined to admit his complaint, ruling that the proceedings were fair since he had deliberately absented himself and, when he subsequently appealed, he could have called fresh evidence. His complaint was thus 'manifestly ill founded'.[217]

2.342 While the above principles emanate from the criminal jurisdiction, the judgment of the Privy Council in *Tait v Royal College of Veterinary Surgeons*[218] makes it clear they have equal application to professional disciplinary hearings.

212 At para 22.
213 [2002] UKHL 5.
214 At para [6].
215 At para [9].
216 At para [20].
217 App no 30900/02, [2003] ECHR 713.
218 [2003] UKPC 34.

2.343 The clear message is that absence is not a bar to proceeding, but great caution should be exercised. In view of the need to ensure compliance with Article 6 rights, that caution is entirely appropriate as is the focus on the practitioner's rights albeit taking account of other competing interests. However, if a tribunal proceeds with due care and diligence, voluntary absence will not avail the registrant on appeal.

2.344 In the criminal jurisdiction, if a defendant is absent from court for reasons beyond his or her control, such as illness, the trial may not continue in the defendant's absence unless he or she consents.[219] If the defendant becomes ill during his or her trial, the judge must either adjourn the case until the defendant recovers or discharge the jury.[220] Again these criminal principles have equal application in regulatory proceedings.

2.345 A number of cases illustrate the rather slavish application of the above principles of service, but also the caution with which the discretion to proceed must be exercised.

2.346 In *Jatta v Nursing and Midwifery Council*[221] the tribunal continued with disciplinary proceedings in the absence of the practitioner. Notice had been properly served at his registered address although the council was aware that he was travelling abroad and no longer lived there. While the tribunal could have adjourned for a message to be sent to J's email address (which was known and would probably have resulted in contact and attendance), the rules only required all reasonable efforts be made to comply with the rules. Since they provided for postal service not email service, the Court of Appeal held that there had been no procedural irregularity in proceeding in absence.

2.347 The above rather mechanical adherence to procedure proves the point that absence is no bar to proceedings once the rules have been complied with. It is strange that in this age of electronic communication the NMC rules require notice of a hearing to be served by post if the registrant is not represented but may be by email to his representative if he has one. However, the NMC rules do allow for email service of documents and notices other than the notice of hearing. Unlike the NMC, the GMC (FTP) (Amendment) Rules 2009,[222] which came into force on 7 August 2009, amended rule 40(2) of the 2004 Rules to allow for service of notices and documents on the registrant to be by email. It is important that the specific requirements of the regulator are met.

2.348 In *R (Raheem) v Nursing and Midwifery Council*[223] Holman J held that the NMC's Conduct and Competence Committee had not exercised its discretion properly when proceeding on an allegation of misconduct in the absence of the practitioner. Notice had been properly served even though R had not received the recorded delivery envelope and was unaware of the hearing. However, the legal assessor did not give any or any sufficient advice to the tribunal as to the separate exercise of the discretion to

219 *Jones (No 2)* [1972] 1 WLR 887 Roskill LJ adopting dicta of Williams J in *R v Abrahams* (1895) 21 VLR 343.

220 *R v Howson* (1982) 74 Cr App R 172.

221 [2009] EWCA Civ 824.

222 Schedule to the General Medical Council (Fitness to Practise) (Amendment) Rules Order of Council 2009 SI No 1913.

223 [2010] EWHC 2549 (Admin).

proceed in absence, nor did it give any detailed consideration of the matter rather it went straight to its ruling. Holman J concluded that since the decision to continue in absence must be taken with the utmost care and caution, the legal assessor's advice was significantly flawed. Furthermore, it was important for the tribunal to demonstrate its application of the care and caution required.

2.349 While *Raheem* may arguably be an appeal allowed in part upon defective reasons, the message is clear: there must be a demonstrably careful and reasoned approach to the issue. Despite the ruling in *Jatta* and, in light of *Raheem*, it is submitted that the increased reliance upon email now means that it would be unwise to proceed without clear evidence covering both traditional and electronic methods of service. The optional methods of service provided by the GMC (FTP) Rules 2004 make this a necessity. While the NMC rules may only require service by letter, it is not unreasonable to expect communication by email and failure to do so may lead to further challenge and wasted costs if it later transpires that an injustice has occurred.

2.350 The case of *Norton v Bar Standards Board*[224] reinforced the applicability of the principles in *Jones*. The tribunal failed to address the issue of whether N's absence was voluntary or not, or whether an adjournment may secure his attendance; and failed to take account of the fact that although proceedings should be heard timeously, no witnesses would be affected by a delay. An important point made by Fulford LJ is that the tribunal must 'apply those parts of the criteria that are relevant'.[225] The 'checklist' of matters to consider as set out in *Jones* is thus to be adapted to the facts of each case.

2.351 In providing advice to the Tribunal, counsel and particularly the Legal Assessor must ensure they adhere to the wording of the rules namely to consider whether '*all* reasonable efforts' have been expended. In *Kumar v General Medical Council*[226] use of the phrase 'reasonable efforts' was said to be 'literally wrong'.

2.352 Two more recent cases – *General Medical Council v Adeogba* and *General Medical Council v Visvardis*[227] – shed further light on this issue.

2.353 In *Adeogba,* A who practised mainly in Germany but also worked occasionally in the UK, moved to Nigeria following the imposition of an interim order of suspension. A had engaged in the interim orders tribunal process, however he did not tell the GMC that he had moved, nor did he provide a forwarding address. The GMC provided written notice of impending FTP proceedings to A at what was his last known address, but they were returned undelivered. Notice by email also raised no response. Unsurprisingly, the FTP tribunal proceeded in absence and A was eventually erased from the register. A appealed on the basis that the tribunal should not have proceeded in absence. Somewhat surprisingly HHJ Wood QC allowed the appeal, stating that the GMC should have done more to try to contact A (eg contact ex-colleagues and contact overseas institutions)

224 [2014] EWHC 2681 (Admin).
225 At [55].
226 [2013] EWHC 452 (Admin).
227 [2016] EWCA Civ 162.

and had wrongly equated non-engagement with voluntary absence. That decision was firmly overturned by the Appeal Court which re-affirmed that the GMC was entitled to rely upon the address provided by a registrant. While the FTP tribunal was deprived of A's input, it had been careful to ensure that the hearing was as fair as circumstances would allow, and the process could not be subverted by a registrant adopting an 'ostrich-like' attitude or failing to engage. Allowing adjournments in such circumstances would mean the system grinding to a halt and 'any culture of adjournment is to be deprecated'.

2.354 Sir Brian Leveson observed that the principles in *Jones* 'provide a useful starting point', but he also drew a distinction between criminal and disciplinary proceedings, the latter having the statutory objective to protect, promote and maintain the health and safety of the public. In this respect he said 'the fair, economical, expeditious and efficient disposal of allegations made against medical practitioners is of very real importance'.[228]

2.355 *Visvardis* also makes it plain that there is an expectation that a registrant will engage positively. Rather than engage in that way, V sought to challenge the legality of the FTP process. He applied to cancel proceedings, during which he asserted he had neither the time nor funds to engage representation. His application was refused but he was not informed until the day of the hearing. The FTP tribunal found that V had neither chased the decision nor indicated a desire to attend, and concluded that an adjournment would not secure V's attendance. On appeal, HHJ Bird stated that a registrant had a right to attend and the fact that he had not expressly stated that desire was irrelevant. In addition, the tribunal had not properly considered the disadvantage to the registrant of proceeding in his absence. The Appeal Court reversed that decision and upheld the tribunal's determination. It commented that V had failed to engage in the case-management process but had embarked on a 'collateral attack' with a view to disrupting the case. The court took note of the fact that V had provided a written response to the case at an earlier stage, and said that his non-attendance and the lack of a full account from him did not prevail over other considerations. If that could happen 'cases would never be heard'.

2.356 Further examples of good practice are *Yusuf v Royal Pharmaceutical Society of Great Britain*[229] and *Varma v General Medical Council*.[230] In *Yusuf*, Munby J approved the council's staged approach of identifying the key issue in the case (in this instance, whether Y had voluntarily absented himself) then assessing the evidence in a fair and measured way before concluding that he had. It then separately considered whether to proceed doing so with the 'utmost caution'. This approach was said to be unassailable. In *Varma*, the practitioner had been granted short stays on medical grounds but, the evidence did not justify a complete stay since he was capable of participating in the proceedings. The tribunal proceeded having properly balanced the competing interests of the practitioner against the

228 At [17].
229 [2009] EWHC 867 (Admin).
230 [2008] EWHC 753 (Admin).

public interest of dealing with serious allegations. In fact, V was able to attend some parts of the hearing. Forbes J approved the separation of the decision to refuse an application to stay from the decision whether to proceed in absence.

2.357 In contrast, the case of *R (Al-Zayyat) v General Medical Council*[231] is an example of poor practice. AZ had been involved in a high-profile criminal trial at which she had given evidence for the prosecution. She was later subjected to FTP proceedings, however medical evidence confirmed that she was too ill to attend and likely to suffer a mental breakdown if she did. The tribunal concluded that it had to decide whether the illness was genuine or fake, and not being satisfied that the illness was genuine, it determined to proceed in absence. Mitting J reiterated that to proceed when a registrant was absent involuntarily was unusual and potentially unfair. He concluded that the decision to proceed was perverse in the absence of evidence showing the illness was not genuine and involuntary. It would also seem that the tribunal reversed the burden of proof (in not being satisfied the illness was genuine).

2.358 A word of caution for practitioners is added by *Abdalla v Health Professions Council*[232] in which A sought to argue that proceeding in her absence was in breach of her ECHR Article 6(1) rights and/or it was a breach of natural justice. Sullivan J rejected this argument. Having failed to produce medical evidence to support her claim that she could not attend, he stated that A:

> . . . was certainly entitled – whether under Article 6(1) or as a matter of fairness or natural justice – to an opportunity to attend the hearing. But if she chose not to avail herself of that opportunity then the committee was entitled to proceed in her absence.[233]

2.359 The word of caution stems from the court concluding that the lack of funds to pay for legal representation which resulted in solicitors declining to act would not justify further adjournment when there was no realistic prospect of that situation changing in the reasonably near future. Ms A could have appeared and explained the position to the panel herself, although whether this would have made any difference is debateable given the public (and personal) interest in resolving allegations which were by then at least two-and-a-half years old.

2.360 The importance of providing medical evidence to support an application to adjourn on health grounds was demonstrated in *Faulkner v Nursing and Midwifery Council*.[234] The decision to proceed in the absence of the registrant who failed to provide such evidence was upheld. Although F later gave evidence via a telephone link, he was restricted to addressing sanctions, since the decisions on misconduct and impairment had already been made in his absence. Similarly, in *R (Tinsa) v General Medical Council*[235] T had been convicted of public order offences and failing to surrender to bail. On appeal following disciplinary proceedings he

231 [2010] EWHC 3213 (Admin).
232 [2009] EWHC 3498 (Admin).
233 At para [6].
234 [2009] EWHC 3349 (Admin).
235 [2008] EWHC 1284 (Admin).

submitted that he was unable to represent himself through mental illness, and the tribunal should have adjourned to obtain psychiatric evidence to assist on sanction. Underhill J concluded that there was no evidence before the tribunal to support T's claim that he was suffering from mental illness at the time or in difficulty defending himself or that he wanted an adjournment.

2.361 The court acknowledged that an appeal may be allowed if subsequent new or fresh evidence (ie not before the tribunal) demonstrates that an appellant was not in a fit state to defend himself at the time. However, the fresh evidence provided did not establish that T was unfit to defend himself. Finally, he stated that there was no basis to suggest that the tribunal had erred in law by failing to adjourn and obtain medical evidence of its own motion.

2.362 *R (Gatawa) v Nursing and Midwifery Council*[236] demonstrates that if an adjournment is sought on medical grounds, the evidence relied upon must be cogent and deal with the essential issue of whether the registrant is fit to stand trial. G's representative applied for an adjournment based on a doctor's letter stating that G was suffering from depression and anxiety and, her ability to give coherent answers when cross-examined could be affected. The tribunal's refusal to adjourn was upheld by Andrews J because the letter did not indicate that G was unfit to instruct her representative or unfit to attend or otherwise lacked capacity.

2.363 In *Guest v General Medical Council*[237] G faced serious charges of dishonesty. Proceedings commenced in her absence, but she made contact on the second day saying that she was ill and would not attend. She did not indicate a wish to have the proceedings adjourned and it proceeded. The case was proved and she was erased. HHJ Davies upheld the decision to proceed observing that there was nothing to suggest G did not make a rational informed decision and, she knew the importance of being present and/or being represented. (Contrast the approach in *Brabazon-Drenning* at para 1.199 above in respect of a registrant absent through illness.)

2.364 Similar considerations applied in *Rehman v Bar Standards Board*[238] in which it was emphasised that adjournments on medical grounds were fact-specific. R had to produce independent medical evidence from a doctor with expertise in the condition who had examined R. It should identify the condition relied upon, how it prevented participation and provide a prognosis. The tribunal could then assess the weight to give to the evidence and what adjustment may be made to accommodate R so he could participate effectively. This would include taking account of the nature of the hearing and the merits of his case.

2.365 The recent case of *Hayat v General Medical Council*[239] has injected a note of caution into the interpretation of sick certificates against the registrant. H was certified fit to attend proceedings on a Friday however, on the Monday a GP's certificate was produced stating that H was not fit

236 [2013] EWHC 3455 (Admin).
237 [2013] EWHC 3121 (Admin).
238 [2016] EWHC 1229 (Admin).
239 [2017] EWHC 1899 (Admin).

to *work*. The tribunal proceeded in H's absence because the statement '[did not] suggest that he is not fit to attend and fully participate in these proceedings'. The tribunal concluded that H had voluntarily absented himself and proceeded in his absence. While there was every reason to be suspicious about H's alleged medical condition, Lang J held that the tribunal could not simply disregard the new medical evidence which post-dated the previous opinion. She continued that:

> Whilst there may be occasions where a registrant is fit enough to attend a court hearing, even though he is certified unfit for work, that will depend upon an evaluation of the individual circumstances of the case . . . the Tribunal ought to have given careful consideration to the question whether and to what extent the Appellant's condition would affect his ability to take part in the proceedings. The fact that his GP had certified him as unfit for work should have prompted them to consider whether that could also mean that he was not well enough to conduct a lengthy [and demanding disciplinary hearing in which he would need to be well enough to do himself justice].[240]

2.366 *Held v General Dental Council*[241] is an example of a registrant leaving matters to the last minute. H did not attend the PCC hearing but sought an adjournment the day before it was due to start, ostensibly to obtain or provide new evidence. The PCC concluded that he had in fact decided not to attend and had put such matters as he wished to argue in writing. The court upheld the decision of the PCC to continue in H's absence. Davies J referred to *McDaid v Nursing and Midwifery Council*[242] in which Elder J commented that the duty on the PCC is to ensure that the hearing is as fair as circumstances permit. This includes a duty to 'take reasonable steps to expose weaknesses in the [regulator's] case and make such points on behalf of the absent defendant as evidence permits', but this did not amount to cross-examining in the same way as a defendant may. He also held that H had failed to show that the fresh evidence he sought could not have been obtained before the PCC hearing.

2.367 Contrast, *Thiruvengadam v General Medical Council*[243] where the court quashed the decision to proceed in absence. The case was complex and involved allegations that, if proved, would inevitably prevent T from practising. T sought an adjournment because his solicitors withdrew when the Medical Defence Union stopped funds. T did not attend, the adjournment was refused and, the case was proved in his absence resulting in his erasure. Gillen J observed that the tribunal had properly balanced the public interest in a timely determination against T's interests and, criticised T's non-attendance as 'manifestly ill-advised'. However, he also took account of the fact that T may have despaired at the seemingly impossible task of representing himself. This, together with the inevitable consequences that flowed from an adverse finding, meant this was a rare case where an adjournment to obtain representation should have been granted.

240 At [54].
241 [2015] EWHC 669 (Admin).
242 [2013] EWHC 586 (Admin).
243 [2010] NIQB 123.

2.368 Finally, in the case of *Ward v Nursing and Midwifery Council*[244] Hickinbottom J dealt with an appeal in the absence of W on the basis that there was no unfairness to W and it was in the interests of justice to do so. He took account of the following: W knew about the hearing, did not apply for an adjournment or contact the court until the last moment, her solicitors had lodged grounds of appeal before they came off the record, costs would be incurred and there was no guarantee she would attend any adjourned hearing. The events underlying the appeal were three years back and the NMC are entitled to finality indeed that was in everyone's interests.

2.369 See also *Rich v General Medical Council*[245] in which Males J took account of the weakness of R's case, which would not be improved by the adjournment R sought. He concluded that the public interest and the 'over-riding objective' required the matter to be concluded before him.

2.370 Clearly, as with so many issues, each decision is likely to be fact-/case-specific but, unless there is evidence before the tribunal to raise a concern, there is no requirement to adjourn on grounds of health. There may of course be rare cases where subsequent evidence comes to light, and doubtless these can be considered on their merits when they arise.

The burden and standard of proof

> The burden of proving disputed facts is on the prosecuting authority.
>
> The standard required is 'on the balance of probabilities'.
>
> The standard does not change with the seriousness of the allegation.
>
> Serious allegations do not require better evidence.
>
> It is common-sense that to prove that an unlikely event occurred may require persuasive evidence.
>
> Similarly the consequences of a finding do not alter the standard.

2.371 In all healthcare disciplinary proceedings the burden of proving allegations against a practitioner rests with the prosecuting council. This relates only to the facts to be proved and the statutory ground, ie misconduct, UPC, lack of competence or health. Any issue of whether the facts that are found proved amount to grounds for impairment is a separate matter of 'judgment' by the tribunal. It does not involve burdens or standards of proof. (See below under 'impairment'.)

2.372 The standard required to prove factual allegations is now settled in healthcare fitness to practise proceedings as being to the civil standard, or the 'balance of probabilities'.

2.373 Despite the apparent simplicity in meaning of 'on the balance of probabilities', there has been debate on whether the seriousness of an allegation affects the threshold of the test. The starting point of this is *Re H*

244 [2014] EWHC 1158 (Admin).
245 [2013] EWHC 1673 (Admin).

(minors)[246] in which Lord Nicholls of Birkenhead expressed the opinion that the balance of probabilities test is satisfied if 'the court considers that, on the evidence, the occurrence of the event was more likely than not'.[247] His Lordship continued:

> When assessing the probabilities the court will have in mind as a factor, to whatever extent is appropriate in the particular case, that the more serious the allegation the less likely it is that the event occurred and, hence, the stronger should be the evidence before the court concludes that the allegation is established on the balance of probability. Fraud is usually less likely than negligence. Deliberate physical injury is usually less likely than accidental physical injury. A stepfather is usually less likely to have repeatedly raped and had non-consensual oral sex with his under-age stepdaughter than on some occasion to have lost his temper and slapped her. Built into the preponderance of probability standard is a generous degree of flexibility in respect of the seriousness of the allegation.
>
> Although the result is much the same, this does not mean that where a serious allegation is in issue the standard of proof required is higher. It means only that the inherent probability or improbability of an event is itself a matter to be taken into account when weighing the probabilities and deciding whether, on balance, the event occurred. The more improbable the event, the stronger must be the evidence that it did occur before, on the balance of probability, its occurrence will be established. Ungoed-Thomas J. expressed this neatly in *In re Dellow's Will Trusts*[248] 'The more serious the allegation the more cogent is the evidence required to overcome the unlikelihood of what is alleged and thus to prove it.'[249]

2.374 Some of the above was seized upon as suggesting that a higher threshold needs to be attained when matters are serious and/or have serious consequences. However, in *Re B (children)*[250] and *Re D (Secretary of State for Northern Ireland intervening)*[251] the House of Lords made clear that while the seriousness of an allegation or its consequences may necessitate more careful consideration of the evidence, it did *not* affect the test to be applied.

2.375 In *Re D* the court stated that the civil standard of proof on the balance of probabilities was 'finite and unvarying'. The speeches reflected comments in *R (N) v Mental Health Review Tribunal*[252] that while a court or tribunal might have to look at facts more critically or more anxiously because of the inherent unlikelihood of an occurrence, the seriousness of an allegation, or, in some cases, the consequences which could follow, those were all matters of ordinary experience, requiring the application of good sense by the court or tribunal. They did *not* require a different standard of proof or an especially cogent standard of evidence.

2.376 In *Re B (children)* Lord Hoffmann commented that:

246 [1995] UKHL 16.
247 At para 73.
248 *In re Dellow's Will Trusts* [1964] 1 WLR 451.
249 At paras 73–74.
250 [2008] UKHL 35.
251 [2008] UKHL 33.
252 [2005] EWCA Civ 1605.

> There is only one rule of law, namely that the occurrence of the fact in issue must be proved to have been more probable than not. Common sense, not law, requires that in deciding this question, regard should be had, to whatever extent appropriate, to inherent probabilities . . . it is common sense to start with the assumption that most parents do not abuse their children. But this assumption may be swiftly dispelled by other compelling evidence . . . It would be absurd to suggest that the tribunal must in all cases assume that serious conduct is unlikely to have occurred. In many cases, the other evidence will show that it was all too likely.[253]

And Baroness Hale of Richmond:

> . . . [announced loud and clear that there is one test]. The inherent probabilities were simply something to be taken into account, where relevant, in deciding where the truth lay . . . there is no logical or necessary connection between seriousness and probability.[254]

2.377 Thus *Re B (children)* and *Re D* endorse the general approach that a serious allegation will require careful analysis of the evidence taking account of inherent probabilities and other matters requiring the application of good sense, but neither the probability, seriousness nor its consequences require a different standard of proof or an especially cogent type of evidence. *Re B* and *Re H* are quoted in the judgment of Judge Behrens in *Hosny v General Medical Council*.[255]

2.378 Foskett J added further comment in *Fish v General Medical Council*,[256] a case involving dishonesty in which he said:

> What, however, seems to be a proposition of common sense and common fairness is this: an allegation of dishonesty should not be found to be established against anyone, particularly someone who has not been dishonest previously, except on solid grounds. Given the consequences of such a finding for an otherwise responsible and competent [registrant], any Tribunal will almost certainly (without express reminder) approach such an allegation in that way.

It is worth noting that the tribunal's finding of dishonesty in this case was criticised since the actions ascribed to the doctor served no clear purpose without a 'strained analysis' of the facts and possible motives for acting as alleged.

2.379 This line of reasoning was also ventilated by Green J in *Moseka v Nursing and Midwifery Council*[257] in his comments concerning the variable nature of the standard of proof as applied to cases of alleged dishonesty:

> The consequences for an Appellant of being struck off are particularly severe. They entail the loss of livelihood. This can be a much more severe sanction than many a low level criminal punishment. The severity of the consequences is a factor that a regulatory authority will need to bear in mind when applying the civil standard of proof. It is trite that the standard of proof can adjust to the context. In a regulatory case where dishonesty is the issue even on the civil standard the CCC should apply particular care.

253 Para 15.

254 Paras 70 and 73.

255 [2011] EWHC 1355 (Admin).

256 [2012] EWHC 1269 (Admin) (para 66).

257 [2014] EWHC 846 (Admin).

If dishonesty is found then the likelihood of a severe sanction being imposed (including striking off) is quite high.[258]

2.380 A lack of motive to lie was an important factor in *Radeke v General Dental Council*.[259] R had given one version of events to a colleague and another to the coroner at an inquest many months later. The GDC asserted that he had lied to either the colleague or the coroner. The FTP tribunal found he had acted dishonestly and lied to the coroner. Turner J quashed these findings, asserting that honest witnesses can be mistaken and give inconsistent accounts over time. With no clear motive to lie, he considered dishonesty to be improbable, even more so since lying to the coroner would make R, a man of good character, a perjurer as well. The case illustrates that serious findings should be based on cogent evidence with clear consideration given to the inherent probability of events.

2.381 Similarly, the motive of S was something that Mitting J commented upon in the case of *Squier v General Medical Council*.[260] S was accused of dishonesty in giving expert evidence in numerous cases. Mitting J observed that the real accusation was that S had breached her duties as an expert and in so doing had attempted to mislead tribunals. A finding of dishonesty added nothing to such a serious allegation unless there were some ulterior motive for giving evidence such as for profit. No such ulterior motive was suggested it always being accepted that S's views were genuinely held.

2.382 The matter was revisited to a limited extent in *Sharma v General Medical Council*[261] in which the legal assessor was criticised for not reminding the tribunal of the dictum in *Re H*. While the appeal was dismissed, a short reminder of the above principles by the legal assessor is clearly the best approach.

2.383 It is submitted that the essence of all the above cases remains clear. Serious allegations require cogent evidence and careful analysis but this does not change the standard of proof. It is to be hoped that this apparently simple but seemingly vexed issue can finally be put to bed.

Is there a case to answer? Half-time submissions

> Submissions of no case to answer may be made in respect of a case or a specific allegation.
>
> They may be made where: a) there is no evidence; or b) there is some evidence but it is weak, vague or inconsistent and, looked at 'in the round', a panel could not properly find the case (or fact) proved.

2.384 The rules of the healthcare regulators make different provision regarding the approach to submissions at the close of the prosecution case. Some regulators, such as the GMC, limit submissions to whether there is a case

258 At para 25.
259 [2015] EWHC 778 (Admin).
260 [2016] EWHC 2739 (Admin).
261 [2014] EWHC 1471 (Admin).

to answer on the facts. Others, such as the General Osteopathic Council (GOsC) and the HCPC, permit submissions on both the facts and whether any facts found proved may give rise to impairment. The HCPC rules make no express provision for half-time submissions but their 2017 practice note[262] makes it plain that a submission of no case to answer may be made on both the facts and on impairment. It does so in the following terms:

> No useful purpose is served by a Panel continuing proceedings if, based upon the case which it has been put before the Panel there is no real prospect of the HCPC proving the facts alleged or of the Panel concluding that the facts amount to the statutory ground of the allegation (e.g. misconduct) and, in turn, that fitness to practise is impaired.

While there is a reference to 'no real prospect' the document makes it clear that the test to be applied is that set out in *R v Galbraith*.[263]

2.385 Submissions are made only on the evidence and information furnished by the prosecution. It is worth noting that the rules generally provide for submissions regarding whether there is *sufficient* evidence. This highlights the issues set out in *R v Galbraith* below that a submission may still be made when there is some evidence on a matter as opposed to none. It is therefore very important to analyse the quality of the evidence at the close of the regulator's case to see whether it merits the epithet of sufficient or not.

2.386 That the test is 'sufficiency' of evidence was reiterated in *R (Sharaf) v General Medical Council*.[264] The test is whether a tribunal *could* on balance of probability find facts proved not whether they would do so.

2.387 Half-time submissions may be made in relation to the entire case or against discrete allegations. The latter is particularly important in complex cases with lengthy particulars where there may be some evidence regarding various allegations but little or none regarding others. This is a key opportunity to challenge the case as a whole, or to reduce its scope and/or gravity. To this end, the advocate should make separate submissions where appropriate, as well as any global one(s), and the tribunal should look at them separately. Not only does this provide clarity and the opportunity for each submission to be given the attention it deserves, it also reflects the staged approach set out in *Cohen v General Medical Council*[265] to first make findings of fact, then consider impairment and finally decide sanctions.

2.388 Some regulators make express provision for submissions on the sufficiency of the evidence to a) find a fact or facts proved or b) support a finding of impairment. They are worded slightly differently (eg the GMC rules refer to whether submissions should be upheld, while the NMC rule refers to determining whether there is a case to answer) but the meaning is the same.[266]

2.389 Half-time submissions are based upon the test laid down by Lord Lane LCJ in the case of *R v Galbraith* as follows:

262 HCPTS Practice Note: 'Half Time' Submissions.
263 (1981) 73 Cr App R 124.
264 [2013] EWHC 3332 (Admin).
265 [2008] EWHC 581 (Admin).
266 GMC (FTP) Rules 2004 r17(2)(g); NMC (FTP) Rules 2004 r24(7) and (8).

(1) If there is no evidence that the crime alleged has been committed by the defendant, there is no difficulty. The judge will of course stop the case.

(2) The difficulty arises where there is some evidence but it is of a tenuous character, for example because of inherent weakness or vagueness or because it is inconsistent with other evidence:

(a) where the judge comes to the conclusion that the prosecution evidence, taken at its highest, is such that a jury properly directed could not properly convict upon it, it is his duty, upon submission being made, to stop the case,

(b) where however the prosecution evidence is such that its strength or weakness depends on the view to be taken of a witness's reliability or other matters which are generally speaking within the province of the jury and where on one possible view of the facts there is evidence upon which a jury could properly come to the conclusion that the defendant is guilty, then the judge should allow the matter to be tried by the jury . . . There will of course, as always in this branch of the law, be borderline cases. They can safely be left to the discretion of the judge.[267]

2.390 As His Lordship states, the first part of the test (where there is no evidence) is straightforward – it is the second part, and particularly the caveat regarding borderline cases, that causes the most difficulty. Various re-statements or commentaries have provided some assistance, but the question remains to some extent a matter of art rather than science.

2.391 As to the second limb, the problem in criminal cases is that the trial judge should not usurp the function of the jury. While His Lordship states that a case may also be stopped where there is some evidence but it is of a tenuous character because of inherent weakness, vagueness or inconsistency, those are matters usually left to a jury.

2.392 In regulatory proceedings the same effect is obtained by the tribunal asking itself the question, 'is there any evidence upon which *a properly directed panel could* find the alleged facts proved?'. If the answer is 'yes it could' (not that it would), then the tribunal should proceed to hear the defence case receiving evidence from the registrant and any supporting witnesses or material.

2.393 Assistance, often referred to as a 'gloss', was provided by Turner J in *R v Shippey*[268] who said that the requirement to take the prosecution evidence at its highest did not mean 'picking out all the plums and leaving the duff behind'. Just because some parts of the evidence supported the prosecution case did not mean that a case should inevitably go to the jury. The judge should assess the evidence and, if it is self-contradictory and out of reason or common sense then it was tenuous and suffered from inherent weakness. In *R v Pryor, Sparkes and Walker*[269] a case from the Northern Ireland Court of Appeal it was said that *R v Shippey* was a case on its own facts that did not establish any new principles. This was further explained in *R v Alobaydi*[270] in which it was said that the inconsistencies between the witnesses in *Shippey* were so substantial as to render the

267 Per Lord Lane at p127.

268 [1988] Crim LR 767, QBD.

269 [2004] EWCA Crim 1163.

270 [2007] EWCA Crim 145.

complainant's whole evidence incredible. It was thus no more than an application of the principles in *Galbraith*.

2.394 Three further cases in point are:

- *R v P*,[271] a case involving circumstantial evidence where the court stated that the correct approach is to look at the evidence in the round, treat it with appropriate care and scrutiny and ask whether there is evidence upon which a properly directed jury could convict;
- *R v Jabber*[272] – where a case rested upon the drawing of an inference it does not have to be an inference that only an unreasonable person would fail to draw;
- *R v Gian and Mohd-Yusoff*,[273] in which it was said that the fact that a proposition consistent with innocence could not be scientifically excluded did not justify stopping the case. Juries assess all evidence, including expert evidence to make realistic judgments, not ones based on fanciful possibilities.

The same may be said of regulatory tribunals.

2.395 The application of the principle is well stated in *R v Hassan*,[274] where Lord Lowry LCJ said:

> I entirely accept the principles as stated by Lord Lane, always remembering that no evidence does not mean literally no evidence, but rather no evidence on which a reasonable jury properly directed *could* (and I emphasise that word) return a verdict of guilty.

2.396 The principles to be drawn from the above are:

- If there is no evidence, a half-time submission should be made and the tribunal should stop the case or dismiss a particular allegation.
- Where there is some evidence, a registrant will need to assess the *quality* of the evidence to see whether a submission can be made or not. To succeed a registrant must persuade the tribunal that the council has failed to present evidence capable of supporting the particular(s), or that such fact(s) about which there is evidence are themselves incapable of supporting a case of impairment.
- The quality of the evidence must be tested *holistically* looking at its strengths (eg clarity, any supporting evidence, what reasonable inferences may be drawn etc) *and* at its weakness (eg lack of reliability, inconsistency with other evidence, vagueness, lacking common-sense, unable to meet a reasoned as opposed to fanciful argument etc).
- If the registrant is not represented, the legal assessor or the LQC should consider whether there is a case to answer. A lack of representation should not deprive a registrant of the important safeguard provided by the regulator's rules. Assistance from the regulator's presenting advocate should be sought in determining this issue.

2.397 If following this exercise, the tribunal finds no evidence to support the case or the relevant particular(s), it has an obligation to stop the case.

271 [2008] 2 Cr App R 6, CA.

272 [2006] 10 *Archbold News* 3.

273 [2010] Crim LR 409, CA.

274 [1981] 9 NIJB.

However, if on one possible view of the fact(s) there is evidence on which the tribunal could properly come to the conclusion that the allegation is well-founded (ie there is evidence capable of founding a case), then the proceedings should continue. This does not mean that there will necessarily be sufficient information to find the facts proved to the required standard at the close of the evidence, only that there is a case to answer.

2.398 *R v F (S)*[275] reaffirmed that *Galbraith* is the benchmark case for submissions of no case to answer as distinct from arguments regarding the cogency of evidence in abuse of process applications.

2.399 Attempts have been made to suggest that *Galbraith* only applies where the burden of proof is to the criminal standard and not the civil and that the approach of the civil courts propounded in *Benham Ltd v Kythira Investments Ltd*[276] should be followed namely that the regulator need only produce a 'scintilla' of evidence. However, there has been little support for this, and cases such as *R (Sharaf) v General Medical Council* (above) strongly suggest that the *Galbraith* test remains the correct one in regulatory proceedings.

2.400 It is of note that the comment in *Benham* was in the context of the Civil Procedure Rules and the question was 'what is the test for a submission of no case when the defendant has *not* been "put to his election" before making submissions?' That is if, contrary to the general rule, he or she has not been asked to indicate whether or not he or she will give evidence if he or she loses the submission. In those circumstances alone the question should be:

> Have the claimants advanced a prima facie case, a case to answer, a scintilla of evidence, to support the inference for which they contend, sufficient to call for an explanation from the defendants? That it may be a weak case and unlikely to succeed unless assisted, rather than contradicted, by the defendant's evidence, or by adverse inferences to be drawn from the defendant's not calling any evidence, would not allow it to be dismissed on a no case submission.[277]

2.401 There is no such election before submissions in regulatory proceedings triggering an altered test. Regulatory proceedings are on all fours with criminal trials at this point where evidence and witnesses are being assessed, rather than issues of contract or tort. It is noteworthy that although Simon Brown LJ used three phrases all required the evidence called to be 'sufficient to call for an explanation'. In any event there would be little benefit to a new approach since if there is only a scintilla of evidence, there is the clear prospect of the case falling foul of the principles of proportionality and public interest in continuing a weak prosecution. In this respect, it is useful to recall the approach of the HCPC, referred to at para 2.384 above. No useful purpose is served by striving to prove a weak case at all costs to the regulator or the registrant.

275 [2011] EWCA Crim 1844.
276 [2003] EWCA Civ 1794.
277 At para 39.

The defence case

Adverse inference from silence

2.402 Following any half-time submissions, the registrant may give evidence, call witnesses and tender documentation relied upon. The process and criteria for admission (fairness and relevance) are the same as those that bind the regulator and do not need repeating. However what if the registrant declines to give evidence? In common with criminal proceedings, an adverse inference may be drawn from a registrant's failure either to answer questions during the investigatory process or, a failure to give evidence.

2.403 One particular concern is that in criminal proceedings there are safeguards built in to how and when such inferences can be drawn. Regulatory proceedings are less explicit and tend to refer to stock phrases such as 'if in all the circumstances it is fair to do so'. To make matters clear, the FTP rules of several regulators now specify that an adverse inference may be drawn.

2.404 Given the adversarial nature of regulatory proceedings and the adoption of this concept from criminal proceedings, it is to the criminal law that one may turn for guidance. Before doing so, the GMC guidance is a good example of how most regulators deal with this topic.

2.405 Paragraph 30 of *Good medical practice* states that a registrant:

> . . . must cooperate fully with any formal inquiry into the treatment of a patient and with any complaints procedure which applies to your work. You must give, to those who are entitled to ask for it, any relevant information in connection with an investigation into your own, or another health care professional's conduct, performance or health.

2.406 Thereafter, rule16(8)[278] provides that:

> A FTP Panel may draw such inferences as it considers appropriate in respect of the failure by a party to comply with directions issued by the Case Manager.

Other regulators provide for adverse inferences in a similar fashion.

2.407 Rule 17(8) provides that where a registrant against whom there is 'credible evidence' that his or her fitness to practise is impaired has failed to comply with a reasonable request for an assessment, the FTP tribunal may take that failure into account in deciding whether his or her fitness to practise is impaired.

2.408 In *Harford v Nursing and Midwifery Council*[279] a finding of misconduct against H was upheld on the basis that H had failed to co-operate with an investigation by her employers in respect of a colleague. The then NMC Code required co-operation with internal or external investigations. The current code is more explicit, stating that a registrant must:

> Cooperate with all investigations and audits . . . [including] either against you or relating to others, whether individuals or organisations. It also includes cooperating with requests to act as a witness . . .[280]

278 GMC (FTP) Rules 2004.
279 [2013] EWHC 696 (Admin).
280 At para 23.

2.409 The issue of the conflict between a professional's duty to disclose and possible self-incrimination is dealt with above, at para 1.286, under abuse of process arguments regarding parallel criminal and civil proceedings. However, in brief cases such as *R v Institute of Chartered Accountants in England and Wales, ex p Nawaz*[281] and *Macpherson v Law Society*[282] make it plain that arguments based on self-incrimination are not well received. The courts have re-affirmed the overriding principle of public-protection within which the professional registrant has a duty to assist his or her regulator in the investigation of a complaint by disclosing information.

2.410 This was revisited in *Iqbal v Solicitors Regulation Authority*[283] where the court commented that the public 'would expect' a professional person to account for his or her actions when facing serious allegations. In response to this, the Solicitors Regulation Authority (SRA) issued a further practice direction (No 5 of 2013) to the effect that adverse inferences may now be drawn if a solicitor does not subject himself or herself to cross-examination. It specifically provides that this is the case even if a written statement is provided.

2.411 Likewise, in *Ashiq v Bar Standards Board*[284] the Board of Visitors rejected the argument that to require a barrister to produce bank statements to support his assertion that he had paid a debt reversed the burden of proof. Under the Bar Code of Conduct he had a duty to respond 'positively' to reasonable requests, and his failure to do so was a matter from which the tribunal could draw an adverse inference. The Board accepted that it should only do so 'if it was the only inference to be drawn'. By simply providing his bank statement A could have proved he had paid the debt. Even one line would have done so, but he declined. It was patently reasonable to infer that his refusal was because the documents would not support his case – indeed, it was the only inference that could be drawn.

2.412 The above cases clearly indicate that a registrant's failure to give evidence may and frequently will result in an adverse inference being drawn unless it is unfair so to do or there is specific provision to prevent this. While the principle is easily stated, as ever, the practicalities are more difficult to determine.

2.413 In criminal proceedings, adverse inferences from silence are governed by Criminal Justice and Public Order Act (CJPOA) 1994 ss35 and 38. Section 35:

1) provides that unless a) guilt is not in issue or b) the physical or mental condition of the accused makes it undesirable for him to give evidence;
2) provides that if D a) declines to give evidence or b) during evidence declines to answer questions without good cause, the court or jury may 'draw such inferences as appear proper';
3) provides that in determining guilt, the court or jury may 'draw such inferences as appear proper';
4) makes it clear that an accused cannot be compelled to give evidence;

281 [1997] CLY 1 (CA – Leggat LJ) and [1997] PNLR 433 (High Court – Sedley J).
282 [2005] 2837 (Admin).
283 [2012] EWHC 3251 (Admin).
284 (27 March 2013) PC 2010/0185/A.

5) makes a distinction between refusing to give evidence at all and, failing to answer some questions having been sworn. It provides that: if having been sworn D refuses to answer questions he 'shall be taken to do so without good cause unless (a) he is entitled to rely on any enactment . . . or on . . . privilege'; or (b) the court exercising its 'general discretion excuses him from answering'.

2.414 Section 38(3) provides a specific limit to adverse inferences in that:

> A person shall not have proceedings against him transferred to the Crown Court for trial, have a case to answer or be convicted of an offence solely on an inference drawn from such a failure or refusal . . .

2.415 If the defence wish to rely upon the section 35(1)(b) exception of adverse physical or mental health, they must call evidence on the issue. The court is entitled to take account of D's conduct both before and after the alleged offence, but not of the offence itself: *R v Friend*.[285] This exception has been extended beyond simple impact upon the defendant's health to include such circumstances as appear the court to justify this course: *R v Cowan; R v Gayle; R v Ricciardi*.[286]

2.416 A more refined approach to include other circumstances that make the giving of evidence 'undesirable' is indicated by *R v Dixon (Jordan)*.[287] The fact that giving evidence may cause some difficulty did not justify a failure to give evidence but may be considered is assessing the weight to be given to a defendant's evidence. In *R v Tabbakh*[288] the court said that a defendant's inability to control himself or to sufficiently remember his evidence may be considered. The significance of the defendant's evidence was also a matter to consider. The more significant the evidence, the more severe the condition would have to be to render his giving evidence undesirable.

2.417 The court in *R v Cowan and others* set down five prerequisites before an adverse inference may be drawn. Adapted to regulatory proceedings these provide:

> The Tribunal must remember (ie the Legal Assessor should advise) that
> (i) The burden of proof remains upon the regulator throughout.
> (ii) The registrant has the right to remain silent.
> (iii) An inference from failure cannot on its own prove guilt.
> (iv) The tribunal must be satisfied that the regulator has established a case 'sufficiently compelling' to call for an answer before drawing any inferences from silence.
> (v) If, having considered any defence evidence to explain silence (if any), the tribunal concludes that silence can *only* sensibly be attributed to the registrant having no answer or none that would stand up to cross-examination, they may draw an adverse inference.

The term 'sufficiently compelling' was added by the court of appeal in *R v Birchall*.[289]

285 [1997] 2 Cr App R 231.
286 [1996] 1 Cr App R 1.
287 [2014] 1 WLR 525.
288 [2009] EWCA Crim 464.
289 [1999] Crim LR 311.

2.418 It should be noted that *evidence* is required to excuse silence not an explanation provided by an advocate.

2.419 In *R v Napper*[290] the Court of Appeal rejected the argument that a failure by the police to question N about certain matters deprived him of the opportunity to give an account when matters were fresh in his mind. The simple point was made that he could have made a statement to his solicitor and subsequently refreshed his memory from that.

2.420 From the above it is plain that the appellate courts place considerable weight upon public protection, the regulator's duty to investigate matters in the public interest and the registrant's duty to provide an explanation where required. In view of this, where adverse inferences might be drawn it is important to ensure that proceedings remain fair. The tribunal should go through the five-point process set out above before drawing an adverse inference from silence.

2.421 The case of *Radeke v General Dental Council*[291] adds a further layer of complexity. In this case R was unfit to attend the hearing so did not give evidence. Neither did he provide a formal witness statement. While no adverse inference was drawn in this case, Turner J commented that he could envisage circumstances in which a registrant is not fit to attend a hearing but could provide a statement. Failure to provide such a statement could result in an adverse inference being drawn in accordance with *Wiszniewski v Central Manchester HA*.[292] *Radeke* is therefore a warning shot to a registrant who says nothing, does not attend and provides no statement.

2.422 An additional consideration for any registrant and for those advising registrants is the duty of candour applicable to all healthcare workers. In 2015, the GMC and NMC published a joint guidance document entitled *Openness and honesty when things go wrong: the professional duty of candour.* Whilst much of the document is concerned with being candid to patients and work colleagues in order to foster a culture of personal and institutional responsibility and improvement, the front page makes it clear that:

> Healthcare professionals must also be open and honest with their colleagues, employers and relevant organisations, and take part in reviews and investigations when requested. They must also be open and honest with their regulators, raising concerns where appropriate. They must support and encourage each other to be open and honest, and not stop someone from raising concerns.

Within the above, there is a clear imperative to co-operate with investigations. The guidance specifically warns that a tribunal will regard a failure to report a concern or covering-up an incident as an aggravating feature in any case. Whilst a lack of candour cannot be viewed as aggravating any facts (unless it is specifically charged), where a registrant has not been candid, this is likely to be viewed as indicating a lack of insight and relevant to the issue of risk and repetition when it comes to impairment or sanction.

290 (1997) 161 JP 16.
291 [2015] EWHC 778 (Admin).
292 [1998] Lloyd's Rep Med 223.

CHAPTER 3

Outcomes, findings and sanctions

continued

Findings

Impairment

> There is no burden or standard of proof – it is a question of 'judgment' by the tribunal.
>
> Impairment may be based upon historical matters or a continuing state of affairs but it is to be judged at the time of the hearing. To do this, the tribunal must look forward taking account of any reparation, changes in practice, conduct or attitude since the matter(s) found proved actually occurred.
>
> Personal mitigation is less relevant, but effort to accept and correct remediable errors should be taken into account.

3.1 All regulators take action when a registrant's fitness to practise (FTP) is called into question. Each will inquire into whether a registrant's fitness is 'impaired', save for the GOSc which considers Unprofessional Conduct (UPC). The term impaired is an ordinary word in common usage. It is not defined in the Medical Act (MA) 1983 or its equivalents, and there has been argument on its meaning and effect in matters of professional discipline. Regarding the GOsC, if there is a finding of UPC then the matters that are considered regarding impairment are considered at the sanction stage.

3.2 The Health and Care Professions Council (HCPC) publication *Managing fitness to practise*[1] states:

> When we say that someone is fit to practise, we mean that they have the skills, knowledge, character and health to practise their profession safely and effectively. We also mean that we trust them to act legally.

Although this publication has been superseded, this definition neatly encapsulates the entirety of fitness to practise and registrants, representatives and tribunals would do well to consider it a universal statement.

3.3 The definition has been replicated by the HCPC in their online information, save that the reference to health has been removed. This must simply be an oversight, since being well enough to practise is undoubtedly part of the test. The reference to 'trust them legally' has also been removed, however the online definition goes on to make the point that:

> . . . fitness to practise is not just about professional performance. It also includes acts by a registrant which may affect public protection or confidence in the profession. This may include matters not directly related to professional practice.

3.4 All the regulators publish guidance – *Good medical practice* (General Medical Council (GMC)); *Standards for pharmacy professionals* (General Pharmaceutical Council (GPhC)); *The Code. Professional standards of practice and behaviour for nurses and midwives* (Nursing and Midwifery Council (NMC)) being but three examples. The GPhC publication is particularly clear, comprehensive and easy to follow.

1 HCPC, *Managing fitness to practise. A guide for employers and registrants* (July 2007), p2.

3.5 In *Council for Healthcare Regulatory Excellence v Nursing and Midwifery Council and Grant*[2] Cox J referred to the *Shipman Inquiry fifth report*[3] in which Smith LJ set out the following questions as an appropriate test for an FTP tribunal considering the issue of impairment. It is now almost universally relied upon:

> Do our findings of fact, in respect of the [registrant's misconduct] show that his fitness to practise is impaired in . . . that he has:
> (a) in the past acted and/or is liable in the future to act so as to put a patient or patients at unwarranted risk of harm.
> (b) has in the past brought and/or is liable in the future to bring the profession into disrepute.
> (c) has in the past breached and/or is liable in the future to breach one of the fundamental tenets of the profession.
> (d) Has in the past acted dishonestly and/or is liable in the future to act dishonestly.

3.6 In her judgment, Cox J describes the above in the following terms:

> The value of this test, in my view, is threefold: it identifies the various types of activity which will arise for consideration in any case where fitness to practise is in issue; it requires an examination of both the past and the future; and it distils and reflects, for ease of application, the principles of interpretation which appear in the authorities.[4]

3.7 The four central limbs of impairment in respect of misconduct are thus identified to be: risk to patients; disrepute to the profession; breaching a fundamental principle; and dishonesty. It is important to note that the questions are asked in both the past and present/future tenses, reaffirming that current impairment is a judgment combining a consideration of previous acts/omissions and the risk of similar conduct in the future. This risk-assessment informs the entire process of protecting the public and the public interest.

3.8 It is important to recall the staged process that the tribunal *must* follow in regulatory hearings: first to make findings of fact; then to consider misconduct; then impairment; and finally to decide sanctions. This is made clear by cases such as *Cohen v General Medical Council*[5] and *Cheatle v General Medical Council*[6] with which the tribunal will be familiar. The stages give the practitioner several chances to challenge the case – first on the facts; second on what conclusions can be drawn from the facts found proved; and finally what sanctions may be imposed thereafter. Even if misconduct or poor performance is proved, that does not mean that impairment necessarily follows, or if it does, that sanctions are necessarily burdensome to the individual.

3.9 The case of *Saha v General Medical Council*[7] is not authority for an alternative proposition. In that case, one issue to be determined was the

2 [2011] EWHC 927 (Admin) at para 116.

3 *The Shipman Inquiry 2004, fifth report – Safeguarding patients: lessons from the past – proposals for the future* (9 December 2004).

4 Para [76].

5 [2008] EWHC 581 (Admin).

6 [2009] EWHC 645 (Admin).

7 [2009] EWHC 1907 (Admin).

separate consideration of misconduct and impairment. Stephen Morris QC sitting as a Deputy High Court Judge held that while it would be better if the tribunal clearly indicated distinct consideration of the two issues, it was not fatal in *all* cases if it did not. The rules require two steps, but where misconduct inevitably or necessarily leads to a finding of impairment it may be that the reasoning for misconduct and impairment cannot be distinguished. While this may be correct as a matter of logic, it is submitted that the staged process should be adopted, with the tribunal giving clear and separate judgment upon each issue.

3.10 Unlike matters of fact which are to be decided on balance of probabilities, whether or not proven facts amount to impairment are matters of judgment not proof – *Council for the Regulation of Healthcare Professionals v General Medical Council and Biswas*.[8]

3.11 Where a tribunal finds some charges proved but others not, it may still reach the view that a registrant's fitness to practise is impaired. In *Ndisang v Nursing and Midwifery Council*[9] N faced four charges. The first charge was not proved; the second was proved; and the third and fourth were admitted. N appealed and was successful in respect of the third charge only on a technical matter. The court held that this had no effect on the tribunal's finding of fitness to practise or the sanction imposed.

3.12 The GMC's authority to take action regarding a practitioner stems from section 35C of the MA 1983. Other regulators act upon similar authority so it is set out below as of general application.

- Section 35C(1) says that the section applies when an allegation is made that a practitioner's 'fitness to practise *is* impaired' (emphasis added).
- Section 35C(2) provides that a person's fitness to practise *shall be regarded as impaired* by reason only of the following five factors:
  - misconduct;
  - deficient professional performance;
  - a criminal conviction or caution in the British Islands for a criminal offence, or a conviction elsewhere for an offence which, if committed in England and Wales, would constitute a criminal offence;
  - adverse physical or mental health;
  - a determination by a body in the UK responsible under any enactment for the regulation of a health or social care profession to the effect that his fitness to practise as a member of that profession is impaired, or a determination by a regulatory body elsewhere to the same effect.
- Section 35C(3) makes it clear that the section applies even if the matter(s) complained of occurred abroad, or before the practitioner was in fact registered.

3.13 While there is no definition, the above categories of misconduct, poor performance, health, conviction or other censure provide a broad idea of what is likely to be regarded as impairment; whether it is, of course, is fact-specific. Further help is gleaned from *The meaning of fitness to practise*[10]

8 [2006] EWHC 464 (Admin).

9 [2009] EWHC 2487 (Admin).

10 GMC, *The meaning of fitness to practise*. A GMC policy statement approved in 2001.

provided by the GMC and summarised below. This illustrates the sort of behaviour that could call registration into question. It should be read in conjunction with the GMC's *Good medical practice*[11] but is a sensible starting point. Similar publications by other regulators give equally clear guidance (see, for example, the 2017 GPhC publication *Standards for pharmacy professionals*).

3.14 As a general principle, it is accepted and acceptable that everyone sometimes makes a mistake. One-off incidents will need to be investigated and any harm put right but, unless very serious or with very serious consequences, they are unlikely in themselves to indicate a fitness to practise problem. *Good medical practice* 2006 put it this way: 'Serious or persistent failures to meet the standards in this booklet will put your registration at risk.' The 2013 edition advises that:

> To maintain your licence to practise, you must demonstrate, through the revalidation process, that you work in line with the principles and values set out in this guidance. Serious or persistent failure to follow this guidance will put your registration at risk.[12]

3.15 A good example of one serious incident not being sufficient to prove impairment is that of *R (Vali) v General Optical Council*[13] in which a failure by V to follow up and repeat pressure-tests on a patient's eyes was held on appeal not to be sufficient to find impairment. The incident complained of occurred several years before the hearing during which time there had been no other complaints about V indeed there was clear evidence of an improving practice. (See the discussion under 'Insight' below.)

3.16 However, queries regarding fitness to practise are likely to arise if a registrant has acted or failed to act with the following result(s):

- *The registrant's performance has harmed patients or put patients at risk of harm.* This might be indicated by a series of incidents, persistent technical failures or repeated departures from good practice.
- *The registrant shows a deliberate or reckless disregard of clinical responsibility towards patients.* This may manifest itself in an unwillingness to practise ethically or responsibly or a serious lack of insight into obvious problems of poor practice; it need not be criminal, but may indicate a lack of integrity.
- *The registrant's health is compromising patient safety.* A serious medical condition (including an addiction to drugs or alcohol) and a failure (or inability) to follow appropriate medical advice about modifying practice to minimise the risk to patients would meet this test.
- *The registrant has abused a patient's trust, violated a patient's autonomy or other fundamental right.* Acting without regard for patients' rights or feelings, or abusing his professional position as a doctor, will usually give rise to questions about a doctor's fitness to practise.
- *The registrant has behaved dishonestly, fraudulently or in a way designed to mislead or harm others.* This behaviour is such that public confidence in

11 GMC, *Good medical practice*. (Current edition is 2013.)

12 *Good medical practice* (2013) at p5.

13 [2011] EWHC 310 (Admin).

the profession generally might be undermined if the regulator did not take action.

3.17 Guidance published by the HCPC entitled *The fitness to practise process* (information for employers and managers)[14] sets the matter out as follows:

> . . . a registrant's fitness to practise is likely to be impaired if the evidence shows that they:
>
> were dishonest, committed fraud or abused someone's trust
> exploited a vulnerable person
> failed to respect service users' rights to make choices about their own care
> have health problems which they have not dealt with, and which may affect the safety of service users
> hid mistakes or tried to block our investigation
> had an improper relationship with a service user
> carried out reckless or deliberately harmful acts
> seriously or persistently failed to meet standards
> were involved in sexual misconduct or indecency (including any involvement in child pornography)
> have a substance abuse or misuse problem
> have been violent or displayed threatening behaviour
> carried out other, equally serious, activities which affect public confidence in their profession

3.18 The above advice is illustrative of the behaviour or circumstances which could call registration into question. Guidance published by the individual regulators and referred to above provides a more complete picture but it is not exhaustive. It is always most important to remember that, while other cases are illustrative, the outcome of any case depends on its own facts.

Misconduct (and unprofessional conduct)

Overview

3.19 Until relatively recently a finding of misconduct on the facts was likely to result in a judgment of impairment. However, consistent with the words '*is* impaired' and with the oft-stated intent to regulate rather than punish, tribunals must look forward and not just look back over past events. Cases of misconduct, particularly ones concerning errors in professional judgment, should be considered in the light of surrounding events including those that have occurred since the incident(s) complained of and any subsequent efforts at rectification. This is important because registrants may find themselves before a tribunal for one or two errors of judgment in patient management or professional conduct that fall short of deficient professional performance which covers a range of errors over a range of patients.

3.20 If a tribunal has made a judgment of misconduct based upon the facts found proved, it must now receive evidence on matters that might previously be regarded as mitigation – eg other competent work, pressures on the hospital, overwork, understaffing etc – and, crucially, evidence on whether the misconduct is capable of remedy and whether it has been remediated by the registrant. The tribunal must thus consider what has

14 2015 edn.

occurred in the light of the registrant's professional record and both personal and professional character, before and after the event.

3.21 While each case is dealt with on its own facts, it may be that the above is unlikely to assist a registrant accused of gross misconduct such as serious dishonesty, sexual impropriety or other similarly reprehensible acts. It can and may make all the difference where the misconduct is relatively minor, or the care of or attitude toward an individual patient has been poor but it has been acknowledged and practice or attitudes have been modified appropriately.

3.22 It may be suggested that this makes it more difficult for the regulator to sustain allegations of impairment due to misconduct when a registrant has made a serious mistake. However, this is in accordance with the fundamental principle of enabling an otherwise competent registrant to return to safe practice as opposed to merely dolling out punishment. It was also not the intention of the legislature, As Silber J stated in *Cohen v General Medical Council* 'the fact that stage 2 is separate from stage 1 shows that it was not intended that every case of misconduct found at stage 1 must automatically mean that the practitioner's fitness to practise is impaired'.[15]

3.23 Having outlined the principles, it is helpful to consider some of the cases in which this line of reasoning has now been made clear.

What is misconduct?

3.24 Misconduct and/or lack of competence are not defined by the regulators. They are potentially wide concepts, and may include some though not all departures from good practice. Additionally, not all misconduct will be so serious or beyond remedy to impair current fitness to practise. Whether there is reference to 'serious' or 'gross' misconduct or not, a degree of gravity is required since matters must be reasonably serious to go to the Interim Orders Tribunal or FTP Tribunals. There is also a distinction to be made between misconduct and lack of competence. This may have an important effect on sanction and the public or professional perception or stigma attached to proceedings – see *R (Remedy UK Ltd) v General Medical Council*.[16] On the facts of a case, it may be beneficial and possible to argue that neither misconduct nor lack of competence are made out, or that it is only the latter.

3.25 Misconduct has been described and defined in several cases, the following being the most important.

3.26 In *Nandi v General Medical Council*[17] Collins J adopted the observation of Lord Clyde in *Rylands v General Medical Council*[18] that:

> . . . professional misconduct is 'a falling short by omission or commission of the standards of conduct expected among medical practitioners, and such falling short must be serious'. The adjective 'serious' must be given its proper weight, and in other contexts there has been reference to conduct which would be regarded as deplorable by fellow practitioners. It is of

15 [2008] EWHC 581 (Admin) para 63.

16 [2010] EWHC 1245 (Admin).

17 [2004] EWHC 2317 (Admin) per Collins J, paras 31–33.

18 [1999] Lloyd's Rep Med 139.

course possible for negligent conduct to amount to serious professional misconduct, but the negligence must be to a high degree.[19]

3.27 His lordship stated that it is not restricted to conduct which is morally blameworthy. It could include seriously negligent treatment or a failure to provide treatment measured by objective professional standards. Obviously, dishonest conduct can very easily be regarded as serious professional misconduct, but conduct which does not amount in any way to dishonesty can constitute serious professional misconduct if it falls far short of the standard that is considered appropriate by the profession.

3.28 Lord Cooke of Thorndon in the Privy Council case of *Preiss v General Dental Council*[20] (GDC) said:

> It is settled that serious professional misconduct does not require moral turpitude. Gross professional negligence can fall within it. Something more is required than a degree of professional negligence enough to give rise to civil liability but not calling for the opprobrium that inevitably attaches to the disciplinary offence.[21]

3.29 In *R (Calhaem) v General Medical Council*[22] Jackson J stated that:

> The word 'misconduct' in [MA 1983] section 35C(2)(a) does not mean any breach of the duty owed by a doctor to his patient: it connotes a serious breach which indicates that the doctor's fitness to practise is impaired.

3.30 Following a review of the authorities, His Lordship derived five principles relevant to that case, which involved failures by a consultant anaesthetist and departure from *Good medical practice* in the context of a serious operation. These are:[23]

a) Mere negligence does not constitute 'misconduct' within the meaning of section 35C(2)(a) of the MA 1983. Nevertheless, and depending upon the circumstances, negligent acts or omissions which are particularly serious may amount to 'misconduct'.
b) A single negligent act or omission is less likely to cross the threshold of 'misconduct' than multiple acts or omissions. Nevertheless, and depending upon the circumstances, a single negligent act or omission, if particularly grave, could be characterised as 'misconduct'.
c) 'Deficient professional performance' within the meaning of section 35C(2)(b) is conceptually separate both from negligence and from misconduct. It does not mean any instance of sub-standard work. It connotes a level of professional performance which indicates that the doctor's fitness to practise is impaired. It is unacceptably low which (save in exceptional circumstances) has been demonstrated by reference to a fair sample of the doctor's work.
d) A single instance of negligent treatment, unless very serious indeed, would be unlikely to constitute 'deficient professional performance'.

19 At 149.
20 [2001] UKPC 36.
21 At para 28.
22 [2007] EWHC 2606 (Admin) at para 26.
23 See para 39 of the judgment.

e) It is neither necessary nor appropriate to extend the interpretation of 'deficient professional performance' in order to encompass matters which constitute 'misconduct'.

3.31 In *Mallon v General Medical Council*[24] Clarke LJ poured a little cold water on attempts to refine the meaning of misconduct or serious professional misconduct. He described misconduct as a 'wrongful or inadequate mode of performance of professional duty'. However, he regarded descriptions of 'serious' or 'would be regarded as deplorable by fellow practitioners' (per Collins J in *Nandi*) as 'tending to obscure rather than assist'. He said that it was better to leave such matters to the skilled judgment of the tribunal rather than pursue a 'definitional chimera'.

3.32 The above outline the limits of misconduct. This is important since a registrant may face a hearing not because of personal impropriety but because he or she has mismanaged or been negligent in a specific case. Previously, little account was taken of other positive factors. Now, it is important to set the matters complained of in the context of his or her whole practice. This is further apparent from a review of the facts and outcome of *Calhaem* (paras 3.29–3.20 above).

3.33 C, an anesthetist, made a number of mistakes while treating one patient. These resulted in the patient being taken to intensive care, although she eventually made a full recovery. The tribunal found that C's actions did amount to misconduct and deficient professional performance such that his fitness to practise was impaired. C was suspended for three months. Jackson J held that although all C's mistakes related to just one patient they did cross the line between negligence and misconduct. However, he quashed the finding of deficient professional performance because the legal assessor failed to advise the tribunal that this could only result from one episode of treatment in 'exceptional circumstances'. As a result, the sanction was downgraded, although the finding of impairment itself remained.

3.34 In *Williams v General Medical Council*[25] disciplinary action was taken on the basis of W's allegedly negligent conduct. He failed to disclose material based on an honest belief that it had no forensic value. W argued he had not acted in bad faith and a finding of serious professional misconduct was not justified. Davies J dismissed the appeal, citing *Preiss* (above) stating that gross or culpable negligence can constitute serious professional misconduct. Davies J concluded that the panel was entitled to take account of the fact that W had the highest responsibility, his evidence could be pivotal in criminal trials and the serious consequences of his actions. A finding of serious professional misconduct was justified given W's 'uncorrected' and 'formidable' errors over a three-year period.

3.35 In *R (Remedy UK Ltd) v General Medical Council* (see para 3.24 above) the court reviewed several authorities in relation to the meaning of misconduct, including *Roylance v General Medical Council (No 2)*[26] *Allinson v General Council of Medical Education and Registration,*[27] *Marten v Royal*

24 [2007] CSIH 17, 2007 SC 426.
25 [2007] EWHC 2603 (Admin).
26 [2000] 1 AC 311.
27 [1894] 1 QB 750.

College of Veterinary Surgeons Disciplinary Committee[28] and *Meadow v General Medical Council*[29] and derived the following principles regarding misconduct and fitness to practise:

(1) Misconduct is of two principal kinds. First, it may involve sufficiently serious misconduct in the exercise of professional practice such that it can properly be described as misconduct going to fitness to practise. Second, it can involve conduct of a morally culpable or otherwise disgraceful kind which may and often will occur out-with the course of professional practice itself, but which brings disgrace upon the doctor and thereby prejudices the reputation of the profession.

(2) Misconduct falling within the first limb need not arise in the context of a doctor exercising his clinical practice, but it must be in the exercise of the doctor's medical calling. There is no single or simple test for defining when that condition is satisfied.

(3) Conduct can properly be described as linked to the practice of medicine, even though it involves the exercise of administrative or managerial functions, where they are part of the day to day practice of a professional doctor. These functions include the matters identified in *Sadler v General Medical Council*, such as proper record-keeping, adequate patient communication, proper courtesy shown to patients and so forth. Usually a failure adequately to perform these functions will fall within the scope of deficient performance rather than misconduct, but in a sufficiently grave case, where the negligence is gross, there is no reason in principle why a misconduct charge should not be sustained.

(4) Misconduct may also fall within the scope of a medical calling where it has no direct link with clinical practice at all. *Meadow* -provides an example, where the activity in question was acting as an expert witness. It was an unusual case in the sense that Professor Meadow's error was to fail to recognise the limit of his skill and expertise. But he failed to do so in a context where he was being asked for his professional opinion as an expert paediatrician. Other examples may be someone who is involved in medical education or research when medical skills are directly engaged.

(5) *Roylance* demonstrates that the obligation to take responsibility for the care of patients does not cease simply because a doctor is exercising managerial or administrative functions one step removed from direct patient care. Depending upon the nature of the duties being exercised, a continuing obligation to focus on patient care may co-exist with a range of distinct administrative duties, even where other doctors with a different specialty have primary responsibility for the patients concerned.

(6) Conduct falls into the second limb if it is dishonourable or disgraceful or attracts some kind of opprobrium; that fact may be sufficient to bring the profession of medicine into disrepute. It matters not whether such conduct is directly related to the exercise of professional skills.

(7) Deficient performance or incompetence, like misconduct falling within the first limb, it may in principle arise from the inadequate performance of any function which is part of a medical calling. Which charge is appropriate depends on the gravity of the alleged incompetence. Incompetence falling short of gross negligence but which is still

28 [1966] 1 QB 1.

29 [2007] 1 QB 462.

seriously deficient will fall under [MA 1983] section 35C(2)(b) [deficient professional performance] rather than (a) [misconduct].

(8) Poor judgment could not of itself constitute gross negligence or negligence of a high degree but it may in an appropriate case, and particularly if exercised over a period of time, constitute seriously deficient performance.

(9) Unlike the concept of misconduct, conduct unrelated to the profession of medicine could not amount to deficient performance putting fitness to practise in question. Even where deficient performance leads to a lack of confidence and trust in the medical profession, as it well might – not least in the eyes of those patients adversely affected by the incompetent doctor's treatment – this will not of itself suffice to justify a finding of gross misconduct. The conduct must be at least disreputable before it can fall into the second misconduct limb.

(10) Accordingly, action taken in good faith and for legitimate reasons, however inefficient or ill-judged, is not capable of constituting misconduct within the meaning of section 35C(2)(a) [misconduct] merely because it might damage the reputation of the profession. Were that not the position then Professor Meadow would have been guilty of misconduct on this basis alone. But that was never how the case was treated.[30]

3.36 The court commented that there was no clear boundary between conduct capable of rendering a doctor unfit to practise and conduct which is not. Fitness to practise is not solely limited to clinical practice alone. It may include other aspects of a doctor's calling 'sufficiently closely linked to the practise of medicine' (eg deficient research, incompetent teaching).

3.37 *Kumar v General Medical Council*[31] provides an example of misconduct based upon K acting as an expert witness in a murder trial. K had never done so before and was reckless in several ways. K's report was 'seriously deficient' not only for the criminal case but as a report in itself. K appealed against an order of suspension and Ousely J, upholding the suspension stated that *Meadow v General Medical Council* (above) was not authority for the proposition that misconduct requires recklessness or bad faith.

3.38 His Lordship reaffirmed the test in *Preiss v General Dental Council*[32] that the conduct (preparing a report, giving evidence etc) 'may be of such a nature or degree of incompetence or negligence, that it amounts to misconduct without bad faith or recklessness'.[33] He further adopted the reasoning of Sales J in *Yeong v General Medical Council*[34] that remediability or the unlikelihood of repetition do not preclude impairment. There are cases where:

> The need to uphold public confidence in the profession, and declaring and upholding standards of behaviour, may mean that a doctor's fitness to practise is impaired by reason of certain acts of misconduct of themselves: the public simply would not have confidence in him or in the profession's standards if the Panel regarded that sort of conduct as leaving fitness unimpaired. Such a finding is necessary to re-affirm to the public and practitioners the standards of conduct expected of them.

30 At para 37.
31 [2012] EWHC 2688 (Admin).
32 [2001] 1 WLR 1926.
33 At [59].
34 [2009] EWHC 1923 (Admin).

3.39 While the facts in *Kumar* are unusual in that they involve incompetence as a purported expert in court proceedings, the principle that serious incompetence or negligence may amount to misconduct is applicable across a registrant's practice.

3.40 Clearly risk plays a part in determining how much care and attention a registrant needs to apply to any act, but the fact that that there has been a failure, and this has caused harm, does not automatically mean there is misconduct.

3.41 In *Hindmarch v Nursing and Midwifery Council*[35] H checked a delivery of medication in a bedroom rather than in the storage room, since the latter was too small for that purpose. At some point a patient managed to obtain and take several tablets, becoming seriously unwell. Although the patient was taken to hospital, no lasting harm was done. The Conduct and Competence Committee (CCC) found that the events were particularly grave because the care home in which H worked catered for elderly and dementing patients. H was found to be impaired and was suspended. On appeal, Hindmarch J held that insufficient weight had been given to the nature of what had occurred. H had not given the wrong medication or an overdose to the patient – instead she had lost control of a bottle when under pressure acting alone on a difficult shift. He concluded that while the loss of the medication was a failure, it was unlikely that fellow professionals would consider it to be deplorable or gross misconduct. His following comment is a timely reminder to regulators and tribunals that registrants are only human:[36]

> ... when looking at the gravity of the omission they should have been considering all the surrounding circumstances and asking how grave the omission was. It is often the case in a medical setting that a minor mistake can have serious consequences sadly, but that does not convert negligence into gross negligence by itself.

3.42 The case may be explained as an example of a tribunal placing too much emphasis on the consequences of an incident rather than the incident itself. In today's 'blame culture' and the quest to apportion fault, regulators must guard against the argument that 'something serious happened – someone must be to blame' as a reason to bring proceedings. While consequences may be a very good reason to bring proceedings, that is not always the case.

3.43 In *Schodlock v General Medical Council*[37] the issue of whether a series of six findings of 'misconduct' could collectively amount to 'serious misconduct' was discussed. While not entirely excluding this, Vos and Moore-Bick LJJ were sceptical of this concept. Vos LJ considered this would not be possible in the normal case but would need 'a very unusual case on very unusual facts'. Beatson LJ expressed the view that: 'A small number of allegations of misconduct that individually are held not to be serious misconduct should normally not be regarded collectively as serious misconduct.' However, he continued to say that provided it is made clear in the charges, if there were a '*large* number of findings of misconduct, particularly where they are the same or similar misconduct ... it should in principle be open [to an

35 [2016] EWHC 2233 (Admin).

36 At para 39.

37 [2015] EWCA Civ 769.

FTP Panel to find that] cumulatively they are to be regarded as serious misconduct capable of impairing a doctor's fitness to practise'.

3.44 The judgments in *Schodlock* make it plain that while the door was not closed to the suggestion that serial misconduct can amount to serious misconduct, it was only wedged ajar to allow for that possibility in rare or unusual cases. It is unlikely to succeed in run-of-the-mill ones.

Unprofessional conduct

3.45 The principles in respect misconduct apply equally to the question of what amounts to unprofessional conduct (UPC) albeit that this is defined in a slightly different way namely conduct that attracts 'moral blameworthiness' or public 'opprobrium'.

3.46 In *Spencer v General Osteopathic Council*,[38] a case concerning three incidents of alleged inadequate note-taking regarding a patient history and examination, Irwin LJ set the matter out as follows:[39]

> . . . the starting point for interpreting the Osteopaths Act 1993 must be the language of the Act itself. Although one notes that 'unacceptable professional conduct' has the definition in Section 20(2): 'conduct which falls short of the standard required of a registered osteopath"' . . . The critical term is. conduct' . . . [The sense if which is] behaviour, or the manner of conducting oneself. It seems to me that at first blush this simply does imply, at least to some degree, moral blameworthiness. Whether the finding is 'misconduct' or 'unacceptable professional conduct', there is in my view an implication of moral blameworthiness, and a degree of opprobrium is likely to be conveyed to the ordinary intelligent citizen. That is an observation not merely about the natural meaning of the language, but about the likely effect of the finding in such a case as this, given the obligatory reporting of the finding under the Act.

3.47 His Lordship noted that a breach of the relevant code of practice may be relevant to a finding of professional incompetence or UPC, albeit that:

> No single instance of negligence or unacceptable care would be sufficient to found a conclusion of 'professional incompetence'. A breach was thus a 'starting point and is relevant, but cannot be definitive or indeed even raise a presumption that 'professional incompetence' or 'unacceptable professional conduct' is made out.[40]

3.48 Irwin J rejected the suggestion that a UPC required a lesser threshold than misconduct noting that the Osteopaths Act 1993:

> . . . stipulates that if unacceptable professional conduct is made out, there has to be at least a formal admonition and publicity which is bound to affect the Registrant's professional reputation. Those are considerable sanctions. In my view, they support the natural meaning of the language contained in the statute and point to a threshold for a finding of 'unacceptable professional conduct' which there is no reason to distinguish from 'misconduct' in the medical and dental legislation.[41]

38 [2012] EWHC 3147 (Admin), [2013] 1 WLR 1307.

39 At [23].

40 At [24].

41 At [25].

3.49 From the above it is plain that UPC and misconduct are interchangeable concepts of equal gravity and, where principles of misconduct are explored such as remediability (see below) they apply to UPC as much as to misconduct.

Is the misconduct capable of remedy?

3.50 This was outlined in *Cohen v General Medical Council*,[42] in which Silber J said:

> Any approach to the issue of whether a doctor's fitness to practise should be regarded as 'impaired' must take account of 'the need to protect the individual patient, and the collective need to maintain confidence [in the] profession as well as declaring and upholding proper standards of conduct and behaviour of the public in their doctors and that public interest includes amongst other things the protection of patients, maintenance of public confidence in the' (sic). In my view, at stage 2 when fitness to practise is being considered, the task of the Panel is to take account of the misconduct of the practitioner and then to consider it in the light of all the other relevant factors known to them in answering whether by reason of the doctor's misconduct, his or her fitness to practise has been impaired. It must not be forgotten that a finding in respect of fitness to practise determines whether sanctions can be imposed: s 35D of the [MA 1983].[43]
>
> There must always be situations in which a Panel can properly conclude that the act of misconduct was an isolated error on the part of a medical practitioner and that the chance of it being repeated in the future is so remote that his or her fitness to practise has not been impaired. Indeed the Rules have been drafted on the basis that the once the Panel has found misconduct, it has to consider as a separate and discreet (sic) exercise whether the practitioner's fitness to practise has been impaired . . .[44]
>
> . . . It must be highly relevant in determining if a doctor's fitness to practise is impaired that first his or her conduct which led to the charge is easily remediable, second that it has been remedied and third that it is highly unlikely to be repeated.[45]

3.51 In *R (Zygmunt) v General Medical Council*[46] Mitting J ruled that evidence that Z was a safe doctor, given by many colleagues, should have been adduced at the second (impairment) stage rather than when deciding on sanction as had hitherto been the case. He noted that even if a tribunal found that a practitioner was guilty of misconduct it may yet conclude that his fitness to practise is not impaired. It is an issue to be addressed separately. He noted that Dame Janet Smith in the *Fifth Shipman Inquiry report* (2004) recognised that present impairment must be gauged partly by his or her past conduct or performance but also by reference to how he or she is likely to behave or perform in the future. He said:

> In a misconduct or deficient performance case . . . It may well be, especially in circumstances in which the practitioner does acknowledge his deficiencies and takes prompt and sufficient steps to remedy them, that there will

42 [2008] EWHC 581 (Admin) paras 62–63.

43 At para 62.

44 At para 64.

45 At para 65.

46 [2008] EWHC 2643 (Admin).

be cases in which a practitioner is no longer any less fit to practise than colleagues with an unblemished record.[47]

3.52 Mitting J adopted the approach of Silber J in *Cohen* that when fitness to practise is being considered, the task of the tribunal is to take account of the misconduct of the registrant and then to consider in the light of all the other relevant factors known to them whether his or her fitness to practise *is* (rather than *has been*) impaired.

3.53 The correct approach is to focus on the registrant's fitness to practise as at the date of the hearing. In *Sarkodie-Gyan v Nursing and Midwifery Council*,[48] a health case, the issue of present impairment and looking forward (see the next section) was considered. Unfortunately, looking forward turned into speculation. S had a history of addiction and depression. She had recently recovered but this had not been tested in stressful situations at work. HHJ Grenfell held that the tribunal had been wrong to speculate on whether S was susceptible to depression in the future. In the absence of evidence that there was a real risk of relapse in S's case which could amount to present impairment, there was nothing to suggest that she was more susceptible to further episodes than any other nurse in a similar situation. By speculating that she might be susceptible to future impairment, the tribunal had effectively reversed the burden of proof.

Looking forward

3.54 The fact that the panel must look to the future (but not speculate) was made plain in *Meadow v General Medical Council*[49] in which it was said that:

> . . . the purpose of FTP proceedings is not to punish the practitioner for past misdoings but to protect the public against the acts and omissions of those who are not fit to practise. The FTP thus looks forward not back. However, in order to form a view as to the fitness of a person to practise today, it is evident that it will have to take account of the way in which the person concerned has acted or failed to act in the past.[50]

3.55 This was reiterated in *Azzam v General Medical Council*:[51]

> [The FTP Panel should] . . . consider facts material to the practitioner's fitness to practise looking forward and for that purpose to take into account evidence as to his present skills or lack of them and any steps taken, since the conduct criticised, to remedy any defects in skill . . . [S]ome elements of reputation and character may well be matters of pure mitigation, not to be taken into account at the 'impairment' stage . . . However, the line is a fine one and it is clear to me that evidence of a doctor's overall ability is relevant to the question of fitness to practise . . . The panel must consider that evidence (in the same manner as any other evidence received) and weigh it up, decide whether to accept it and then to determine whether, in the light of the further evidence that it does accept and the facts found proved at stage 1, the practitioner's fitness to practise is impaired.

47 At [31].
48 [2009] EWHC 2131 (Admin).
49 [2006] EWCA Civ 1390, per Sir Anthony Clarke, MR.
50 At para 32.
51 [2008] EWHC 2711 (Admin) para 44, per McCombe J.

3.56 Finally, Cranston J provided guidance in *Cheatle v General Medical Council*:[52]

> . . . a panel must engage in a two-step process. First, it must decide whether there has been misconduct, deficient professional performance or whether the other circumstances set out in the section are present. Then it must go on to determine whether, as a result, fitness to practise is impaired. Thus it may be that despite a doctor having been guilty of misconduct, for example, a Fitness to Practise Panel may decide that his or her fitness to practise is not impaired.
>
> . . . the issue becomes whether that misconduct, in the context of the doctor's behaviour both before the misconduct and to the present time is such as to mean that his or her fitness to practise is impaired . . . Seen within the context of an otherwise unblemished record a Panel could conclude that, looking forward, his or her FTP is not impaired, despite the misconduct.

3.57 In *Cheatle*, the tribunal was criticised for declining to hear evidence of C's heavy workload, the pressure created by the absence of a colleague or other evidence regarding C's ability. It was further criticised for not considering the effect of MA 1983 s47 which meant that suspending C ended his NHS contract which may have been disproportionate.

Deficient professional performance

3.58 In essence, this encompasses conduct that has fallen far short of the standards expected of a reasonably competent practitioner on more than one occasion. It need not be a repeat of the same conduct. One exceptionally serious event may also amount to deficient professional performance. Conduct occurring outside the UK and/or before the registrant was in fact registered may still found a case on deficient professional performance, the reason of course being risk to the public and profession.

3.59 In *Holton v General Medical Council*[53] the point was clarified that performance is to be measured as against that expected of a reasonably competent practitioner of the same grade (nurse against nurse, surgeon against surgeon, specialist against specialist) in the job the registrant is actually doing. Deficient professional performance may also stem from one aspect of the registrant's work, provided it is a significant aspect, notwithstanding that his or her other work is of an acceptable standard.

3.60 While there may be some overlap between misconduct and deficient professional performance it is important to note that they are different and are intended to be so. In *R (Vali) v General Optical Council*[54] Ouseley J emphasised that the distinction should be maintained both in charging and in the FTP process since the concepts were aimed at different concerns and, in respect of deficient performance one may expect to be dealing with an underlying pattern of conduct in a registrant's practice.

3.61 Performance issues may be worded slightly differently – for the nurse, impairment may be evident through a 'lack of competence'; for the pharmacist deficient professional performance specifically includes

52 [2009] EWHC 645 (Admin) paras 19 and 22.

53 [2006] EWHC 2960 (Admin).

54 [2011] EWHC 310 (Admin).

incompetence. What is plain is that the standard required for both conduct and performance cases is the same and that is a standard falling *well below* the expected norm. It should be a 'serious lapse' – see *Vranicki v Architects Registration Board*[55] (a case on the parallel issue of serious professional incompetence and unacceptable professional conduct in architects). As Jackson J put it in *R (Calhaem) v General Medical Council* (see para 3.65 below) it must be 'unacceptably low' and demonstrated across a range of work albeit that one incident that is 'very serious indeed' may suffice.

3.62 In *Krippendorf v General Medical Council*[56] the Privy Council quashed a finding of seriously deficient professional performance on the basis that the right approach, at least in this case, was to assess the appellant's past performance over a significant period of time.

3.63 In *Sadler v General Medical Council*[57] the Privy Council approved the following definition provided by the GMC while emphasising that it was not exhaustive:

> Seriously deficient performance is . . . 'a departure from good professional practice, whether or not it is covered by specific GMC guidance, sufficiently serious to call into question a doctor's registration.' This means that we will question your registration if we believe that you have been, repeatedly or persistently, not meeting the professional standards appropriate to the work you have been doing – especially if you might be putting patients at risk.[58]

3.64 The Privy Council dealt with a finding of seriously deficient professional misconduct based upon a detailed assessment of S's work as a surgeon over a lengthy period. This included a detailed review of six separate operations four of which were found to be unsatisfactory. Lord Walker said that:

> [62] Although in *Krippendorf* the Board did not criticise the phrase 'repeatedly or persistently' in the GMC's guidance, it is important to bear in mind that that guidance is a generalisation seeking to cover a very wide range of professional performance. The professional demands made on a general practitioner are very different from those made on a consultant surgeon. A continuing failure to organise the efficient management of a general practice may (in a sufficiently bad case) amount to seriously deficient performance, but in the nature of things it must be assessed on very different evidence from that relating to shortcomings of technique in major surgery. It would plainly be contrary to the public interest if a sub-standard surgeon could not be dealt with by the CPP unless and until he had repeatedly made the same error in the course of similar operations. But as a general rule the GMC should not (and their Lordships have no reason to suppose they would) seek to aggregate a number of totally dissimilar incidents and alleged shortcomings in order to make out a case of seriously deficient performance against any practitioner.
>
> [63] . . . Their Lordships do not consider negligence to be a relevant or useful concept at a performance hearing before the CPP. Negligence is

55 [2007] EWHC 506 (Admin), Collins J.

56 [2001] 1 WLR 1054.

57 [2003] UKPC 59.

58 GMC publication *When your professional performance is questioned* (1997 edn).

concerned with compensating loss . . . Seriously deficient performance is a much wider concept since (as already mentioned) it can extend to such matters as poor record-keeping, poor maintenance of professional obligations of confidentiality, or even deficiencies (if serious and persistent) in consideration and courtesy towards patients. It does not depend on proof of causation of actionable loss. (On the other hand one isolated error of judgment by a surgeon might give rise to liability in negligence but would be unlikely, unless very serious indeed, to amount by itself to seriously deficient performance.)

3.65 Jackson J in *R (Calhaem) v General Medical Council*[59] further defined deficient professional performance, having conducted a review of several cases:

From this review of the authorities, I derive five principles which are relevant to the present case:

(1) & (2) see under misconduct (Mere negligence is not misconduct unless 'particularly serious'; multiple acts/omissions are more likely to be misconduct; a single particularly grave act could be misconduct)

(3) 'Deficient professional performance' within the meaning of 35C(2)(b) is conceptually separate both from negligence and from misconduct. It connotes a standard of professional performance which is unacceptably low and which (save in exceptional circumstances) has been demonstrated by reference to a fair sample of the doctor's work.

(4) A single instance of negligent treatment, unless very serious indeed, would be unlikely to constitute 'deficient professional performance'.

(5) It is neither necessary nor appropriate to extend the interpretation of 'deficient professional performance' in order to encompass matters which constitute 'misconduct'.

3.66 C made a number of negligent errors regarding one patient. The finding of misconduct was upheld. The finding of deficient professional performance was quashed since the tribunal had not properly considered the issue of exceptionality when there was only one incident.

3.67 In *Rao v General Medical Council*[60] the Privy Council quashed a finding of serious professional misconduct noting that only one instance of clinical failure was alleged. That incident undoubtedly amounted to negligence, but it was only a 'borderline case' of serious professional misconduct.

3.68 From the above it is clear that deficient professional performance may involve one very serious clinical error but is more frequently associated with poor treatment or other conduct associated with practice measured over a lengthy period or a number of instances. Terms such as negligence do not assist in judging the issue. The conduct must itself relate directly to the registrant's work or, be closely connected to his or her practice. The latter includes important ancillary matters such as practice management, deficiency in records and paperwork and deficiency in patient-relations.

3.69 At an FTP hearing, performance related issues clinical or otherwise will almost certainly be addressed by experts. The regulator will call an expert in the appropriate area of practice to provide evidence upon what is the accepted norm and to advise upon whether the conduct complained of falls below or falls well below that expected of a competent practitioner. The registrant may either accept his or her opinion in whole or in part or,

59 [2007] EWHC 2606 (Admin) para 39.

60 [2002] UKPC 65.

contest the opinion in which case an expert is likely to be needed to provide an alternative opinion. In *Uruakpa v General Medical Council*[61] the point was reiterated that it is for the regulator to set the standard of medical competence and the assessment thereof. If a registrant fails to submit to an assessment set by the regulator then a tribunal is quite entitled to find the registrant impaired by reason of having insufficient up-to-date information to meet the tribunal's duty to protect the public.

3.70 As with misconduct, matters addressing the issues of insight, remedy and future performance will all be of vital importance in addressing the issue of current impairment and sanction. (See above under 'misconduct'.)

3.71 Where the registrant has not acted in the patient's best interests, and has failed to provide an adequate level of care, falling well below the professional standards expected of a registrant and where a persistent failure to provide clinical care is apparent, erasure may be considered to be the only appropriate sanction. An important factor in such cases is whether the registrant has, or has the potential to develop, insight into these failures. Where there is no evidence of this, other forms of sanction may be insufficient – see *Garfoot v General Medical Council.*[62]

3.72 The distinction to be made between misconduct and lack of competence is important because lack of competence may invoke a lesser range of sanction, and to some, a remediable lack of competence carries less stigma. It may be possible to argue that facts found proved amount to lack of competence but not misconduct. The professional and/or personal circumstances of a registrant may provide mitigation upon the level of culpability and thus be relevant to the issue of whether the facts amount to misconduct and/or lack of competence.[63] However, issues such as a high caseload or personal trauma should be reported, discussed with a superior or result in requests for help. They may explain, but do not excuse, poor performance or conduct, since registrants are expected to take personal responsibility for their actions or omissions. Evidence of past or subsequent good practice is important, although more general character evidence is unlikely to be relevant. Somewhat perversely, emphasising mitigating factors could undermine a registrant's ability to demonstrate insight (see below), and a case-by-case approach should be adopted.

Criminal convictions, discharges and cautions (in the UK or elsewhere)

3.73 Most regulators have specific rules for dealing with conviction or caution cases, which provide that the production of a certified copy of a notice of conviction is conclusive evidence of the offence committed and the facts thereof. The only challenge a registrant may make is that he or she is not

61 [2010] EWHC 1302 (Admin), Saunders J.

62 [2002] UKPC 35.

63 *Campbell v General Medical Council* [2005] EWCA Civ 250; *Cohen v General Medical Council* [2008] EWHC 581 (Admin).

the person who is referred to in the notice,[64] the registrant may not re-open and contest the facts behind the conviction – see *R (Trivedi) v General Medical Council*[65] and *Shepherd v Law Society*.[66]

3.74 In cases of criminal conduct, the interests of the profession always come first and impairment is a frequent result.

3.75 A distinction is sometimes argued between a conviction that attracts a sentence and one that attracts a conditional or absolute discharge. This argument was rejected in *R v Patel*, a case involving employment by the police but equally applicable to healthcare registrants.[67] Hughes LJ noted that while section 14 of the Powers of Criminal Courts (Sentencing) Act 2000 prevents the discharge from ranking as a conviction,

> . . . it does not enable any person to assert that they have never committed the offence or for that matter that they have never been found guilty of it. [One must look to the Rehabilitation of Offenders Act 1974 for that.][68]
>
> [in sensitive employment the employer is] entitled to be interested not only in a conviction as defined by section 14 but in the antecedent offence . . . [There is] nothing to prevent employers who are exempt from the ROA 1974 and have a legitimate interest in asking questions about criminal conduct, in asking properly framed questions . . . such as 'Have you ever been found guilty of a criminal offence?' . . . 'Have you ever committed a criminal offence?' . . . 'Have you ever appeared in court and been sentenced, including an absolute or conditional discharge, for an offence?'

The Rehabilitation of Offenders Act (ROA) 1974 does not apply to healthcare registrants. Thus convictions do not become spent as regards registrants regardless of the time elapsed and, although a conviction from which a discharge resulted may not be deployed as a basis for impairment, a registrant may not deny commission of the offence and that can be a basis for impairment. The elapse of time since a conviction will be a factor the tribunal takes into account in deciding whether a registrant's fitness is *currently* impaired but it is not determinative.

3.76 A caution is administered only when there is an admission of guilt, the fact of the caution and the underlying events may well be a basis for impairment.

3.77 As regards a case upon which a registrant was acquitted, acquittal is not the same as never having done the act. Acquittal merely means that a jury could not be sure (beyond reasonable doubt) that the registrant committed the act/omission alleged. In *Bhatt v General Medical Council*[69] the court held that the GMC was entitled to bring a case against B based upon seven allegations of indecent assault of which he had been acquitted. The principal reasons were that the proceedings are of a different nature with a different purpose (upholding professional standards etc) and a different burden of proof. Furthermore, the plea of autrefois acquit (meaning 'previously acquitted of the same offence') does not apply to

64 See, eg GMC (FTP) Rules 2004 r34(3); NMC (FTP) Rules 2004 r31(3).

65 [1996] EWCA Civ 503 (PC).

66 [1996] EWCA Civ 977.

67 [2006] EWCA Crim 2689.

68 At paras 7 and 17.

69 [2011] EWHC 783 (Admin).

regulatory proceedings. (See also *R (Redgrave) v Commissioner of the Police of the Metropolis*[70] and *Ashraf v General Dental Council*,[71] discussed at para 1.317 which makes it abundantly clear that an acquittal is no bar to regulatory proceedings.)

3.78 The position is different in respect of civil proceedings against a registrant. The findings of a civil court provide prima facie evidence of the facts alleged and may found a case of misconduct etc but, the registrant may challenge the correctness of that prima facie case – see *General Medical Council v Spackman*.[72]

3.79 In cases involving convictions or cautions for offences involving dishonesty, sexual offences, child pornography, drug misuse or other serious criminal offences, the wider public interest issues of upholding the reputation of the profession and maintaining confidence in the regulatory process will be of the greatest significance. It is highly likely to outweigh any argument concerning the registrant's risk or lack of risk to potential service users.

Adverse physical or mental health issues

3.80 While registrants do not necessarily have to be in the best health to practise safely, regulators will investigate a registrant's physical and/or mental health status in circumstances where it may affect his or her ability to practise safely. Frequent problems include mental health issues, depression and alcohol or substance dependency. Recurrent illness is also an issue.

3.81 Registrants may be required to undergo physical or psychiatric assessment, including substance dependence, to assess their ability to continue in practice, whether restricted or otherwise. A report will be provided to the tribunal and the expert assessor will usually be called to give evidence. Refusal to undergo such an assessment will almost certainly result in suspension or erasure. Health matters are dealt with in private session.

3.82 An important point is again whether the health issues are adversely affecting the registrant's ability to practise safely or are otherwise adversely impacting upon the profession (or the registrant):

> If a doctor is suffering from ill health (for example, severe depression), one might say that s/he is not fit to practise because his/her concentration is so affected that s/he cannot make effective decisions on diagnosis and treatment; s/he presents a risk to patients.[73]

3.83 Some regulators do not consider erasure as appropriate if impairment results *only* through adverse health issues. However, where those or coincident issues also amount to misconduct no such limitation applies. In *Crabbie v General Medical Council*[74] (a case decided under the old GMC regime) the Privy Council held that the Conduct Committee should not

70 [2003] 1 WLR 1136.
71 [2014] EWHC 2618 (Admin).
72 [1943] AC 627.
73 *Fifth Shipman Report* at 25.44 (on issues of what amounts to impairment).
74 [2002] UKPC 45.

refer a case to the Health Committee (which cannot strike off) unless and until it is satisfied that striking off would not be the right order to make. These committees have now been replaced by the single FTP Tribunal but the principle remains the same, such that if there are other concerns that contribute to the registrant's unfitness (ie unless health is the only relevant issue) all sanctions remain available including erasure.

3.84 In *Sarkodie-Gyan v Nursing and Midwifery Council*[75] (discussed at para 3.54 above) the issue of *present* impairment and looking forward was not properly considered. SG's history of addiction and depression (now in remission) was quite capable of amounting to impairment but, in the light of her remission it was wrong to speculate on her susceptibility to depression in the future. In the absence of evidence of a risk of relapse which could amount to present impairment there was nothing to suggest that she was more susceptible to further episodes than any other nurse in a similar situation.

3.85 Contrast the case of *Goodchild-Simpson v General Medical Council*[76] in which GS had been the subject of both suspensions and conditions over many years owing to mental health issues. Latterly he had practised under conditions but in 2011 concerns were raised regarding his clinical competence. GS undertook a performance assessment during which multiple concerns were raised. The issues of performance and health were interlinked but what is important is that the FTP tribunal found that GS 'suffered from a serious condition that was at risk of relapse' which, among other matters, affected his ability to exercise good medical judgment. The tribunal's conclusion that GS was impaired on both performance and health grounds was upheld with emphasis being placed on the fact that the evidence suggested patients were at risk.

A determination by another healthcare body

3.86 This heading needs no elaboration. The criterion is self-explanatory, and the issues of public protection and public interest etc are the same as cases involving convictions or other misconduct or deficient performance.

3.87 In *R (Alhy) v General Medical Council*[77] A was convicted of two offences in France relating to the deaths of two patients. He was fined and given a suspended sentence, but not banned from general practice. A failed to disclose this to the GMC, and he was subsequently erased from practice for misconduct in that non-disclosure and for a lack of insight into his original errors. He challenged the erasure as being a harsher penalty than the original sentence. This was dismissed by HHJ Belcher who said it was not the regulator's role to investigate decisions in another jurisdiction. The FTP Tribunal was there simply to decide on the facts, whether these amounted to impairment and if so to decide the appropriate sanction, if any, bearing in mind the central issue of protecting the public.

75 [2009] EWHC 2131 (Admin).
76 [2014] EWHC 1343 (Admin).
77 [2011] EWHC 2277 (Admin).

3.88 This principle was reiterated and arguably extended in *R (Hollis) v Association of Chartered Certified Accountants*[78] (ACCA). H's conduct was criticised in a High Court judgment, and in subsequent disciplinary proceedings the Committee relied upon these criticisms as 'findings of fact in civil proceedings' as permitted by the ACCA's disciplinary rules. H appealed on the basis that the criticisms were not findings since they were not material to the judgment of the court. Sales J dismissed the appeal commenting that the term 'finding of fact' is an ordinary phrase intended to include all such matters as could properly be described as a decision on the facts made by a court when giving its judgment.

3.89 However, some care needs to be taken in admitting this information. The rule of admitting the finding of another healthcare body as proof of misconduct thereby preventing the re-litigation of a proven case is quite distinct from the admission of hearsay or opinion evidence during proceedings. As set out in *Enemuwe v Nursing and Midwifery Council*[79] (see above para 2.158 et seq), hearsay opinion evidence may be admitted to place matters in context or as explanatory or background information, but it is not admissible for the purposes of proving a fact in issue against a registrant.

3.90 In *Peckitt v GDC*[80] P, a dentist and maxillo-facial surgeon, was erased as a surgeon by the Medical Practitioners Tribunal Service (MPTS) following charges of assault and dishonesty being proved against him. P sought to challenge the subsequent decision of the GDC in respect of his registration as a dentist on several grounds, including its reliance on the decision of the MPTS. Kerr J noted that section 27(2) of the Dentists Act 1984 (as amended) provides that '[a] person's fitness to practise *shall* be regarded as impaired' (emphasis added) by, among other things, the decision of another healthcare regulator. His Lordship noted that section 27(2):

> . . . [provides] for a finding of impairment by reason of the determination of another regulatory body and not the truth of the facts underlying that determination. So to that extent I think [counsel] is right that it is not, at least other than in exceptional cases, for the second disciplinary panel to revisit the factual territory of the first. That seems to me to be the position, other than in rare and exceptional cases.[81]

He continued that:

> There could, at least in theory, be a case in which the first body's decision was so manifestly flawed or perverse that it would be wrong for the second body to blind itself to that fact [or to uncritically adopt] a determination [where there is] stark evidence that the decision [is] plainly wrong.[82]

3.91 The position is thus quite clear that the finding of a healthcare regulator may and should be relied upon without inquiry into the evidence and background, unless there is unequivocal evidence that the decision was wrong.

78 [2014] EWHC 2572 (Admin).
79 [2015] EWHC 2081 (Admin).
80 [2016] EWHC 1803 (Admin).
81 At [37].
82 At [38].

Decisions of the tribunal

> Reasons do not have to cover every aspect of the case, but should be sufficient in breadth and detail to ensure that a party is able fully to understand the decision, why it has been made and on what evidence.
>
> The tribunal must clearly set out how the law or rules have been applied to the evidence and, what evidence is accepted and what rejected with reasons.

Reasons for decisions – interim orders tribunal

3.92 The interim orders tribunal must provide reasons for its decisions both upon the imposition (or non-imposition) of an order and the period for which it is imposed. The courts do not expect an interim orders tribunal to give long detailed reasons, but the reasons given must be clear and explain how the decisions were reached, including identifying the interest(s) for which the order is considered necessary.

3.93 In *R (Walker) v General Medical Council*[83] Stanley Burnton J said that:

> . . . a lack of adequate reasons, or a decision which is disproportionate in its interference with the rights of the doctor in question will encourage the court to examine broadly the decision made by the committee and substitute its own in a way which it might be less willing to do where the decision appeared to be fully reasoned and proportional.
>
> . . . the court will normally give broad credit to the appreciation by a professionally qualified Committee of the conduct of the accused doctor [and where] full and substantial reasons are given . . . the court will give considerable weight to those and will be slow to interfere.

3.94 The following comments regarding FTP hearings also apply.

Reasons for decisions – fitness to practise tribunal

3.95 In *English v Emery Reimbold & Strich Ltd*[84] the comment was made that 'justice will not be done if it is not apparent to the parties why one has won and the other has lost'. Tribunals must provide sufficient reasons for their decisions to be clear and understandable. This is important both from the public perspective and from the registrant's. The *Fifth Shipman Inquiry Report* recommended that FTP Tribunals should give reasons for their main findings of fact.[85]

3.96 As to the facts, in *Gupta v General Medical Council*[86] the Privy Council stated that, save in exceptional cases, there is no general duty on the tribunal to give reasons for its decisions on matters of fact, particularly when the central issue is the credibility or reliability of a witness or evidence. However, the tribunal may give reasons if it considers it appropriate.

83 [2003] EWHC 2308 (Admin) (at paras 9 and 10).

84 [2002] 1 WLR 2409.

85 *The Shipman Inquiry 2004, Fifth Report – Safeguarding patients: lessons from the past – proposals for the future*, Cm 6394, published 9 December 2004.

86 [2001] UKPC 61.

This would be so when without reasons, the losing party will not know why it has lost. If the reasons for winning or losing are obvious, then reasons do not need to be given.

3.97 In *Phipps v General Medical Council*[87] this area of law including *Gupta* and *English v Reimbold* (above) was re-analysed by Wall LJ who observed that 'what was exceptional in 2001 may well have become commonplace in 2006'.

3.98 Finally on facts, in *Southall v General Medical Council*[88] Leveson LJ expressing the view that:

> . . . in straightforward cases, setting out the facts to be proved (as is the present practice of the GMC) and finding them proved or not proved will generally be sufficient both to demonstrate to the parties why they won or lost and to explain to any appellate tribunal the facts found. In most cases, particularly those concerned with comparatively simple conflicts of factual evidence, it will be obvious whose evidence has been rejected and why.[89]

3.99 Unfortunately the case was not straightforward and the tribunal's reasons were inadequate because they failed to explain why S's evidence was rejected on a key point.

3.100 Leveson LJ queried the idea propounded in *Gupta* based upon the decision of *Wickramsinghe v UK*[90] that a registrant can study a transcript of the hearing, to see what evidence was accepted/rejected and why since this assumes that the tribunal will deal with and give full reasons on all issues. That assumption cannot be safely made as it might be in a criminal trial where a judge's summing is expected to provide an impartial analysis of fact and argument.

3.101 The need to deal with the aspects of the defence case as much as that of the regulator was made plain in *Brennan v Health Professions Council*[91] (HPC) the so-called 'blood-gate' case of the physiotherapist fabricating a blood injury in a rugby match and giving false evidence to an inquiry. The case was clearly serious, but Ouseley J quashed the sanction of a strike-off order since the tribunal had not adequately dealt with B's case in its reasons on sanction.

3.102 While not every issue needs to be decided and written up in lengthy judgment, the better approach to reasons on all aspects of a regulatory case is to be found in the cases of *Selvanathan v General Medical Council*[92] and *Needham v Nursing and Midwifery Council.*[93]

3.103 In *Selvanathan* the purely factual allegations were not in dispute, and S accepted that he had been clumsy but he denied dishonesty. He gave evidence and called two character witnesses. Lord Hope said that reasons should always be given by the tribunal on the issue of misconduct and penalty so that the registrant can make an informed decision to accept or appeal the decision. On the issue of facts, where the dispute was a relat-

87 [2006] EWCA Civ 397.
88 [2010] EWCA Civ 407.
89 At [55].
90 Application no 31503/96, [1998] EHRLR 338.
91 [2011] EWHC 41 (Admin).
92 (2000) 59 BMRL 95.
93 [2003] EWHC 1141 (Admin).

ively simple one, the registrant only needed to know whether the decision was for or against him or her.

3.104 In *Council for the Regulation of Healthcare Professionals v General Dental Council and Marshall*[94] the court held that tribunals must give reasons for imposing particular sanctions and why in the opinion of the tribunal the chosen sanction protects the public. In addition, while the indicative sanction guidelines referred to previously are guidelines and not tariffs, the panel's reasons must demonstrate that it has paid due regard to the guidelines. This is particularly important since it will inform any appellate court or review panel that account has been taken of the regulator's opinion on sanction and what is or may be necessary to protect the public and the profession – see *Salha and another v General Medical Council.*[95]

3.105 In *Needham v Nursing and Midwifery Council* the additional point was made that reasons should be sufficiently clear for any appellate court or review tribunal to understand exactly why a particular decision has been made. Thus tribunals should formulate their reasons by 'reference to the degree of illumination which a subsequent Committee might require'.[96]

3.106 When conflicting expert evidence is received, the tribunal should give cogent reasons for its decision – see *English v Reimbold* (para 3.95 above).

3.107 The rule to be drawn from the above is that if a case is straightforward, then reasons on the facts need not be given if what is accepted or rejected and the reasons why are clear. When the case is not straightforward and can properly be described as exceptional, the position is different – in such cases, sufficient reasons should be given to inform the parties what findings have been made, what evidence has been accepted or rejected and why. At all other stages of the hearing, the tribunal should give reasons in accordance with the judgments of *Selvanathan* and *Needham.*

3.108 Much of the above was reiterated in *R (Kaftan) v General Medical Council*[97] in which Hickinbottom J said that the parties must simply be able to understand why one party won and the other lost on any issue and/or on the case. Despite the guidance and the apparent simplicity with which it is stated, the steady flow of complaints regarding reasons demonstrates just how difficult the exercise can be.

Sanctions

> The principal aims of sanctions are to protect the public, uphold the standards and reputation of the profession and maintain public confidence therein.
>
> The punitive effect of sanctions is only one (and not the most important) factor to be borne in mind when assessing whether a sanction is proportional to the matters found proved against a practitioner.

94 [2006] EWHC 1870 (Admin).
95 [2003] UKPC 80.
96 At [14].
97 [2009] EWHC 3585 (Admin).

General principles

Objectives and proportionality

3.109 A good starting point for sanctions is the *Report of the Committee of Inquiry into the Regulation of the Medical Profession* (1975), known as the *Merrison report*, in which it was said that 'the GMC should be able to take action in relation to the registration of a doctor . . . in the interests of the public' which had 'two closely woven strands', the need to protect the individual patient and the need to maintain the confidence of the public in their doctors.

3.110 All healthcare regulators state their main objectives to be protecting patients and the public, declaring and upholding standards of conduct, promoting good practice and maintaining public confidence in their respective professions. These are expressed as follows:

- The GMC:

  . . . to protect, promote and maintain the health and safety of the public[98]
- The NMC:

  . . . to establish from time to time standards of education and training, conduct and performance for nurses and midwives and to ensure the maintenance of those standards

  . . . safeguard the health and well-being of persons using or needing the services of practitioners[99]

Sanctions guidance

3.111 Each body produces a code of practice and/or guidance, such as the GMC's *Good medical practice*, setting out the principles and values on which good practice is founded and the standards which society and the individual profession expects of its registrants (irrespective of their area of practice) throughout their careers. These standards and objectives include behaviour and governance, as well as patient care and similar matters fundamental to healthcare professionals. The NMC's document, *The Code. Standards of conduct, performance and ethics for nurses and midwives*, similarly deals with all aspects of patient care, dignity, confidentiality, consent, boundaries, working with others maintaining standards, integrity and the reputation of the profession.

3.112 The most recent versions of each of these publications make it plain that the regulators expect registrants to uphold appropriate standards outside their spheres of practice. The 2017 document *Standards for Pharmacy Professionals* states that:

> The standards need to be met at all times, not only during working hours. This is because the attitudes and behaviours of professionals outside of work can affect the trust and confidence of patients and the public in pharmacy professionals.

3.113 This principle is applicable to all healthcare professionals with cases being brought in respect of disreputable conduct from inappropriate comments

98 MA 1983 s1A.

99 Nursing and Midwifery Order 2001 SI 2002 No 253 Part 2 article 3(2) and (4) respectively.

online to criminal behaviour encompassing misuse of computers and phones whether it be downloading pornography or sending threatening/sexualised/inappropriate texts, to public incidents such as drink-driving or public disorder or private incidents such as assaults within the context of a marriage or family difficulty.

3.114 In passing, it is again important to note that cases may well be brought if a registrant accepts a caution for low-level criminal behaviour, since a caution necessarily involves an admission of guilt.

3.115 A failure to follow published guidance such as *Good medical practice* or the NMC code may well found a case against a practitioner, although it does not by itself necessarily establish impairment.

3.116 Where the misconduct is grave or there has been a serious departure from professional standards, erasure from the register may be the only means of protecting patients and/or maintaining public confidence in the profession. If possible, a balance may be struck between the individual interest and the public interest, but this cannot always be achieved.

The overarching objective and proportionality

3.117 The importance of the above objectives and guidance is that the public interests and standing of the profession comes before the interests or rehabilitation of the practitioner appearing before the tribunal. As Lord Millett said in *Ghosh v General Medical Council*:[100]

> . . . the primary considerations on the question of penalty are the maintenance of professional standards and the public interest, which includes not only the protection of the public but also the preservation of public confidence in the medical profession.

3.118 *Raschid and Fatnani v General Medical Council*[101] makes it plain that the tribunal 'is centrally concerned with the reputation or standing of the profession rather than the punishment of the doctor', this is despite the fact that sanctions may have a punitive, even a devastating effect. While a balance is to be struck between the necessity of imposing a sanction and the effect that sanction has on the individual, in *Bolton v Law Society*[102] (a case concerning a solicitor, but of general importance) Sir Thomas Bingham MR remarked that:

> . . . A profession's most valuable asset is its collective reputation and the confidence which that inspires.
>
> . . . the reputation of the profession is more important than the fortunes of an individual member. Membership of a profession brings many benefits but that is part of the price.

3.119 Further comment upon the primary importance of the profession rather than the individual is to be found in the judgment of Sir Anthony Clarke MR in *Meadow v General Medical Council*:[103]

100 [2000] 1 WLR 1915 at para 34.

101 [2007] 1 WLR 1460 at para 16.

102 [1993] EWCA Civ 32 per Lord Bingham MR at paras 15 and 16 (also *Gupta v General Medical Council* [2002] 1 WLR 1691).

103 [2006] EWCA Civ 1390 at para 32.

> . . . the purpose of [fitness to practise] proceedings is not to punish the practitioner for past misdoings but to protect the public against the acts and omissions of those who are not fit to practise.

3.120 By way of contrast, in *Bijl v General Medical Council*[104] it was said that:

> [A panel should not feel obliged to erase] an otherwise competent and useful doctor who presents no danger to the public in order to satisfy [public] demand for blame and punishment.

3.121 However, in this context it is to be noted that *Bijl* was a case concerning clinical errors of judgment during an operation and did not involve allegations such as dishonesty or inappropriate sexual behaviour which are in themselves serious and are most damaging to the profession. Comments by Ouseley J in *General Medical Council v Bawa-Garba*[105] (see para 3.210 below) may limit the reliance to be placed on *Bijl* which he said simply restates:

> . . . that sanctions are not punitive and that the issue is not to be determined by expressions of opinion by the public . . . or by members of the medical profession . . . [He said that comments by the public or by doctors did not assist decisions concerning upholding standards and public confidence.] The relevant tests with cautionary words in relation to public confidence and the impact on a professional are now to be found in the cases [of]: *Jagjivan, Fatnami and Raschid and Bolton*. Those cases effectively supersede *Bijl*, which is an incomplete statement of the law now to be found in sections 1 and 40A of MA 1983, with the requirement to consider public confidence and maintenance of proper standards separately from patient safety. [39]

This comment is somewhat unfortunate given that *Bilj* provides one of the few restraining notes on issues of sanction.

3.122 Having said that, the comments by Charles J in *Hayat v General Medical Council*[106] are important to note. He placed emphasis on a regulator identifying what will happen after a sanction such as suspension is imposed. H was suspended for 18 months following significant and widespread deficits in his practice. In reducing the suspension to 13 months Charles J said:

> . . . [if you] stop to think of what you are doing to a doctor who is suspended, and when you identify what is being done to H; given the mortgage that he has taken out to buy the premises for his practice and the expenditure he has, the considerable significance of depriving somebody of being able to make his living by exercising his professional qualifications as a doctor is very apparent. It follows that there is a real need to identify what the next steps are, and how long they are going to take and thereby to seek to minimise the period of any suspension.

3.123 The effect of suspension can be catastrophic. His Lordship's comments make it plain that any sanction must be the minimum required to meet identified risks and analysis of that issue must include some assessment of how the registrant will be managed back into practice. If this is not

104 [2001] UKPC 42.
105 [2018[EWHC 76 (Admin).
106 [2014] EWHC 1477 (Admin) (para 32).

done, there is a risk that a sanction becomes punitive by destroying the registrant's livelihood and/or any chance of a return to safe practice.

3.124 Some support for these concerns may be garnered from the case of *Robinson v Solicitors Regulation Authority*[107] in which it was said that although the *Bolton* principle remains good law, a disciplinary tribunal in imposing a sanction must take account of the registrant's European Convention on Human Rights (ECHR) Article 6 and Article 8 rights.

3.125 There is growing support for a more reasoned, targeted and proportional approach in respect of dishonesty cases. Dishonesty is rightly considered to be very serious – indeed, it is the fourth ground outlined in the *Shipman report* and adopted in *CHRE v NMC and Grant* (see para 3.5 onwards) as being a basis for impairment. Until recently, any finding of dishonesty placed a registrant at risk of erasure/a strike-off order. However, cases such as *Lusinga v Nursing and Midwifery Council*[108] and *Watters v Nursing and Midwifery Council*[109] discussed under sanctions for dishonesty (see para 3.315 below) advocate a more nuanced approach. In short, not all cases of dishonesty will merit the most severe sanction.

3.126 A further interesting question will be what effect the new definition of dishonesty has. In *Ivey v Genting Casinos UK Ltd (t/a Crockfords Club)*[110] the court swept away the familiar two-part objective/subjective test for dishonesty asserting that *Ghosh* did not represent the law. Although *Ivey* does not exclude subjective consideration of the facts, the objective measure of dishonesty may result in a finding of dishonesty where one would not currently be made. If that is right, the degree of dishonesty will have to be carefully considered when it comes to sanction since it may not be in the public interest to strike-off or suspend registrants in every such case.

3.127 The case of *Clarke v General Optical Council*[111] (GOC) considers the issue of proportionality from an angle that is sometimes overlooked – namely, the risk to the public when a registrant retires or is about to do so. Following certain admitted failings, C faced both civil and disciplinary proceedings. C sold his practice and sought voluntary erasure, but the GOC declined to permit this. He was suspended for 12 months to allow for a period of reflection or to cease practise. If he continued to practise, he should complete the relevant compulsory education and training (CET). The tribunal found that erasure was disproportionate. C opted to retire. He undertook not to practise and to remove himself from the register within 14 days. A review tribunal erased C for reasons that included his not completing his CET. This latter point was clearly an error, since C had been offered the options of continuing in practice and completing the CET, or of retiring, in which case he would of course not complete his CET.

3.128 What is of note is Fraser J's analysis of risk. C had always admitted his failings and his responsibilities. He had not practised since an interim

107 [2012] EWHC 3054 (Admin).
108 [2017] EWHC 1458 (Admin).
109 [2017] EWHC 1888 (Admin).
110 [2017] UKSC 67.
111 [2017] EWHC 521 (Admin).

suspension order (ISO) was imposed, and had set out in clear terms that he intended to retire from the profession and from healthcare entirely. C submitted that his undertakings and his retirement meant that no sanction was necessary. The tribunal held that it had no power to accept undertakings and observed that it did not think that no order would be logical given the finding of impairment. His Lordship queried this latter observation because, since C had retired there was no risk to the public. He was careful to note that there was no place for sympathy and that it was *not* an issue of 'retiring with dignity' but of looking at the legal criteria.

3.129 In considering current impairment he reviewed various familiar cases including *CHRE v NMC and Grant, Meadow v GMC* and *Cohen v GMC*. He emphasised the three points made by Silber J in Cohen observing that:

> It must be highly relevant in determining if a doctor's fitness to practise is impaired that first his or her conduct which led to the charge is easily remediable, second that it has been remedied and third that it is highly unlikely to be repeated.[112]

3.130 In respect of the *Cohen* criteria Fraser J observed that the second factor (remediability) was arguably met by C no longer practising and the third criteria (risk of repetition) was nil since C had retired, sold his practice and wished to remove himself from the register. Francis J said this latter point had not been considered at all. He was careful to state that his decision was 'not to be interpreted as authority for the proposition that [retirement could be used] to avoid disciplinary proceedings'. However, retirement was a 'highly material and relevant factor' in assessing risk to the public. Since that assessment had not been undertaken the finding of impairment and the sanction were quashed.

3.131 This case is important when considering errors by a registrant at the end of his or her career. Unlike other regulators, the GOC provides no process for voluntary erasure, but this did not mean that the end of a registrant's practice was irrelevant. There are some cases where the continuation of proceedings and/or seeking erasure does little to protect the public and less to enhance the standing of the regulator.

3.132 The regulators each produce guidelines on sanctions. The purpose is not to set out what a tribunal must do, but to advise the tribunal what, in the opinion of the regulator, may be appropriate or should at least be considered. The regulators regard their sanctions guidance as providing a crucial link between the two key regulatory roles of setting standards for the profession and of taking action when a registrant's fitness to practise is called into question because those standards have not been met.

3.133 The aim of the guidance is to promote consistency and transparency in decisions. All parties are aware from the outset of the approach that may be expected of the tribunal. As Mr Justice Collins said in *Council for the Regulation of Healthcare Professionals v (1) General Medical Council (2) Leeper*[113] in relation to the GMC's guidance:

> It helps to achieve a consistent approach to the imposition of penalties where serious professional misconduct is established. The [panel] must

112 At [65].
113 [2004] EWHC 1850 (Admin).

have regard to it although obviously each case will depend on its own facts and guidance is what it says and must not be regarded as laying down a rigid tariff.

3.134 In *R (Abrahaem) v General Medical Council*[114] Mr Justice Newman, described the sanctions guidance as:

> . . . very useful guidelines and they form a framework which enables any tribunal, including this court, to focus its attention on the relevant issues. But one has to come back to the essential exercise which the law now requires in what lies behind the purpose of sanctions, which, as I have already pointed out, is not to be punitive but to protect the public interest; public interest is a label which gives rise to separate areas of consideration.

3.135 See also *Hazelhurst v Solicitors Regulation Authority*[115] (SRA) a case in which Davies J quashed a financial penalty against four partners in a firm who, upon discovering wholesale dishonesty by a hitherto trustworthy employee, immediately referred the matter to the SRA, admitted their failure to supervise the staff member and repaid all sums so that no client suffered loss, costing the partners c£80,000–90,000. The decision was made on the basis that the solicitors' failure, such as it was, had to be balanced against the fact that others failed to spot the misconduct, and there had been no reason to suspect the staff-member. In truth, the sanction was punitive and served no purpose in protecting the public or upholding standards.

3.136 The tribunal's decision on sanction is a matter of discretion and judgment, but it should take into consideration the standards of good practice established by the regulator and the sanctions guidance. Departure from the guidance must be explained. This was revisited in *Professional Standards Authority v Health and Care Professions Council and Doree*[116] a case in which the Professional Standards Authority (PSA) appealed against the imposition of a caution order following findings of bullying and sexual harassment. At first instance, Lang J dismissed the appeal and commented that the PSA was simply being 'wise after the event' and looking at the transcript to see how the case might have been dealt with differently. Leave was granted on several grounds including on the tribunal's departure from the HCPC's Indicative Sanctions Policy (ISP). In dismissing the appeal, Lindblom J said that there is:

> . . . no basis in the relevant jurisprudence for the contention that it was incumbent on the Panel to 'adhere' to the guidance in the [ISP] . . . [beyond] having proper regard to the guidance and applying it as its own terms suggest, unless the Panel had sound reasons for departing from it – in which case they had to state those reasons clearly in their decision.[117]

His Lordship continues that the fact the tribunal had 'proper regard' to the ISP was clear. He also noted that the ISP is intended to be flexible and is couched in terms that a particular order 'may' be appropriate if certain criteria are met but 'it did not seek to be comprehensive or specific in

114 [2004] EWHC 279 (Admin) para [36].

115 [2011] EWHC 462 (Admin).

116 [2017] EWCA Civ 319.

117 At [29].

describing all the circumstances in [a particular order] may be a suitable sanction'.[118]

3.137 The above is a timely reminder that any regulator's sanction guidance or policy is simply an expression of opinion as to what may be appropriate. It is not proscriptive and does not prevent a panel from departing from imposing what it considers to be the appropriate sanction. What remains clear is that if there is a departure from the guidance that departure should be explained. There are of course valid policy reasons for such a requirement namely to ensure the public and public interest remain protected and to ensure a level of consistency and fairness between cases.

3.138 If a departure from the guidance is in the regulator's opinion not sufficiently well explained, not justified or does not protect the public, the regulator may well challenge the sanction. The GMC has proved itself to be very proactive in this respect. In *General Medical Council v Narayan*[119] the tribunal appeared to depart from *Sanctions Guidance* and give too much weight to one limb of the overarching objective rather than considering all three limbs equally. N indulged in repeated inappropriate sexualised contact with medical students. There were some 'low-level' acts such as sending texts, inviting a student home, asking personal questions, brushing hair or lightly kissing a student on the cheek however there was more serious conduct including the suggestion that spending time with him would improve results. The tribunal found this constituted a pattern of misconduct and an abuse of authority. N gave evidence regarding reparation, seeking psychological treatment and the effect any suspension may have on the students. The tribunal imposed conditions. On appeal Jay J noted that the guidance on abuse of position (paras 141 and 144) principally deal with abuse of the doctor/patient relationship however, the guidance on more serious outcomes (para 132) includes sexual harassment. He observed that N's conduct was 'entirely reprehensible' but was not of the 'utmost seriousness' although it was serious and as such the guidance suggested suspension or erasure would usually apply. The tribunal's decision on sanction did not deal with para 132 and did not explain why a more serious sanction was not imposed. The case was remitted to the tribunal for reconsideration.

Mitigation

3.139 The fact that the public and the profession are of primary importance, and not the registrant, may well influence the validity of some mitigation. In *Gupta v General Medical Council*[120] the Privy Council declared that:

> . . . the relevant committee is not concerned exclusively, or even primarily, with the punishment of the practitioner concerned. Their Lordships refer, for example, to the judgment of Sir Thomas Bingham MR in *Bolton v Law Society* [1994] 1 WLR 512, 517–519 where his Lordship set out the general approach that has to be adopted. In particular he pointed out that, since the professional body is not primarily concerned with matters of punishment, considerations which would normally weigh in mitigation of punishment

118 At [31].
119 [2017] EWHC 2695 (Admin).
120 [2002] 1 WLR 1691 para [18].

> have less effect on the exercise of this kind of jurisdiction. And he observed that it can never be an objection to an order for suspension that the practitioner may be unable to re-establish his practice when the period has passed.

This means that a careful assessment is required as to what mitigation is available to the registrant and how it is to be presented.

3.140 The importance of a full assessment of available mitigation is clear from *Wisniewska v Nursing and Midwifery Council*[121] in which Hayden J emphasised the fact that mitigation may affect not just the length of a sanction but it may affect the type of sanction that is appropriate. In W, there were only two sanctions under consideration namely strike-off and suspension. His Lordship commented that:

> . . . where there are only two options for sanction, as here, i.e. striking off or suspension, it is critical that the available mitigation is not only applied when considering 'striking off' but also when evaluating the proportionality of a suspension. The danger is that the committee rejects suspension and comes only fully to evaluate the mitigation when considering striking off.[122]

3.141 This case follows comments made by Kerr J *in O v Nursing and Midwifery Council*[123] that any assessment of mitigation must be carefully set out in the reasons but also, more importantly, it is almost a direct lift of comments by Ouseley J in *Brennan v Health Professions Council*[124] that:

> . . . where there are only two possible candidates for the appropriate sanction, namely suspension or striking-off, it is critical that all the available mitigation is considered at the stage of considering suspension, as well as when considering striking-off.[125]

3.142 From the above it is plain that although mitigation may reduce a term of suspension, it may also pull a case back from the brink of strike-off and mean that a suspension is proportionate. Mitigation must be assessed by the tribunal when looking at both these issues.

3.143 In deciding what sanction to impose, if any, the tribunal should have regard to the principle of proportionality, weighing the interests of the public against those of the practitioner. Any sanction and the period for which it is imposed must be *necessary* to protect the public interest. The tribunal should consider the sanctions available starting with the least restrictive.

3.144 The sanctions guidance sets out the criteria to take into account when considering which sanction to impose. These include: the seriousness of the conduct found proved; early admissions; evidence of insight and reparation or retraining; references and testimonials. If the tribunal deals with matters in this way, and provided the sanction is not unreasonable or disproportionate, the higher courts are unlikely to interfere having repeatedly held that the regulator is best placed to decide what level of sanction is necessary and proportionate in its own professional field – see

121 [2016] EWHC 2672 (Admin).
122 At [20].
123 [2015] EWHC 2949 (Admin).
124 [2011] EWHC 41 (Admin).
125 At [77].

Fouche v Nursing and Midwifery Council[126] and *Raschid and Fatnani v General Medical Council.*[127]

3.145 While there may be a public interest in enabling a registrant's return to *safe* practice and the tribunal should facilitate this where appropriate, the protection of patients and the wider public interest remain the primary concern. The fact that a registrant has been subjected to an interim order for conditions or suspension carries little weight since the interim order tribunal makes no findings of fact. It also applies a different test when considering whether to impose an interim order to the test applied by the FTP tribunal considering final sanctions.

The effect of an interim order

3.146 How much weight to give to the existence and impact of an interim order is dependent on the rules of each regulator. For example, the GMC sanctions guidance[128] advises that tribunals should 'not give undue weight' to it. With respect, that is perhaps obvious, as is the comment that an interim order is imposed pursuant to a different test. What is important is that regulatory sanctions are imposed primarily to protect the public and/or the public interest. They have a different purpose to criminal sanctions, the punitive effect of which is measured having taken account of any pre-trial remand or bail conditions.

3.147 However, it is now plain that an interim order *may* have an impact upon sanction. In *Ujam v General Medical Council*[129] Eady J observed that it 'should be borne in mind as part of the background circumstances', but he said it is 'inappropriate' to draw any further analogy with criminal cases. This appears to run contrary to *Selvarajan v General Medical Council*[130] in which the court observed that the passage of time and the fact that there has been unreasonable delay may be mitigation (see the discussion on delay at para 1.181 above).

3.148 The effect of an interim order was reconsidered in *Kamberova v NMC*[131] in which Dingemans J allowed K's appeal against a 12-month suspension order the tribunal having taken no account of the fact that K had been placed on an interim suspension order (ISO). He observed that:

> If proceedings are long delayed and a person is subject to suspension in the interim period, that period of suspension may affect the proportionality of the length of the subsequent period of suspension. Whether it has that effect is for the Committee to determine. If the appropriate sanction is one of striking off, then the fact that there has been an ISO may be of no relevant effect. However if the appropriate sanction is a short period of suspension, the fact that there has been an interim period of suspension may be relevant. This is particularly the case given the number of cases before this court in which ISOs of considerable length have, because of delays in arranging hearings, had to be extended.[132]

126 [2011] EWHC 133 (Admin).
127 [2007] EWCA Civ 46.
128 GMC *Sanctions guidance* 2016, para 22.
129 [2012] EWHC 683 (Admin).
130 [2008] EWHC 182 (Admin).
131 [2016] EWHC 2955 (Admin).
132 At [35].

3.149 Thus, Dingemans J held that the tribunal should have taken account of the interim order as a matter of fairness and when considering the proportionality of the eventual suspension. In remitting the matter back to the tribunal he directed that they take the delay in the appeal procedure into account since to do otherwise would be to disregard the fact that K could end up suspended for longer than 12 months in any event.

3.150 The above was revisited in *Akhtar v General Dental Council*[133] in which the FTP tribunal's approach of taking an interim suspension order into account was noted with approval.

3.151 Clearly, being suspended will not save a registrant from being struck off if that is the appropriate sanction. That principle is clear from *Okeke v Nursing and Midwifery Council*.[134] However, it is no longer tenable for a regulator to suggest that an interim suspension order is simply to be ignored if a suspension is appropriate. Whether this affects the eventual length of the sanction is a matter for the tribunal. What is important is that the interim order and its effect on the registrant is at least considered.

3.152 The tribunal should be alive to the issue of unintended consequences and seek appropriate guidance from the legal assessor. In *Cheatle* (above) the tribunal was criticised for not considering the effect of MA 1983 s47 which meant that suspending C ended his NHS contract which may have been disproportionate.

3.153 This point was revisited in *Jasinarachchi v General Medical Council*[135] in which J's appeal against a suspension was allowed and the case remitted to the FTP tribunal for further consideration of sanction. When imposing a sanction of suspension J argued that this was intended to have a corrective but temporary impact upon his ability to practise. In fact it brought his training contract to an end with little certainty of his being able to find an alternative.

3.154 The case is also interesting since the information J relied upon (a letter from the Deanery) *could* have been obtained before the FTP imposed the sanction and so was not in accordance with the principles of admitting fresh evidence as set down in *Ladd v Marshall*[136] (that the information was not previously available, may have an important influence on the result and is credible). However, exceptionally the evidence was admitted since it was credible and could very well have an impact upon an issue of which the FTP tribunal had been unaware.

3.155 The tribunal should not confuse suspension and the imposition of conditions. The latter must be reasonable and workable. In *Udom v General Medical Council*[137] the tribunal found U's fitness to practise impaired by reason of health and competence. It imposed a sanction which purported to be conditions that he was not to practise unsupervised for a period of nine months and was, during that period, to undergo a series of clinical attachments. The effect of the order was to suspend U from practice. Suspension and conditions of practice are separate mutually exclusive

133 [2017] EWHC 1986 (Admin).
134 [2013] EWHC 714 (Admin).
135 [2014] EWHC 3570 (Admin).
136 [1954] 1 WLR 489.
137 [2009] EWHC 3242 (Admin).

sanctions. Accordingly, the tribunal had been wrong to impose conditions which had the effect of suspending the registrant.

3.156 In *S v General Medical Council*[138] S was erased from the register following proof of charges relating to performance and misconduct including harassment of a former patient. Both were linked to S's alcoholism. Sullivan J upheld erasure largely because S had persistently failed to make any attempt to address his alcoholism and attendant problems. He was thus largely responsible for them. A health issue might otherwise be dealt with by suspension.

3.157 Sullivan J summarised the issues regarding sanction as follows:

> [13] Sanctions are not a punishment. They are imposed in order to protect patients and to ensure that doctors who are not properly capable of acting as such, and treating patients competently, should not be able to do so. If a doctor has been guilty of misconduct, whether or not directly connected with his activities as a doctor (for example, he has been convicted of a criminal offence, which is not directly related to his practice as a doctor) that can inevitably reduce public confidence in the profession. It is also a breach of the proper standards of conduct and behaviour to be expected of a doctor, thus a sanction of lesser or greater seriousness, depending on the nature of the misconduct, can be imposed.
>
> [14] In imposing sanctions the Panel must apply the principle of proportionality weighing the public interest against the interest of the practitioner. If a practitioner can, through treatment or training, or the imposition of conditions of one sort or another, be brought back to be trusted as a competent doctor, or if guilty of a form of misconduct, but a highly competent practitioner, the public interest may indicate that in such a case it would be wrong to deprive the public of his services for any longer than is strictly necessary.
>
> [15] Suspension is intended to send out a signal that the behaviour is regarded as unacceptable, but is not so serious as to justify erasure. That may arise not only because of the nature of the conduct in question, but also where there has been an acknowledgment of fault and where the Panel is satisfied that there is unlikely to be any repetition.
>
> [16] So far as erasure is concerned, it is to be noted that there is a distinction drawn, which has always been drawn, albeit now they are dealt with by the same Fitness to Practise Panel, between cases which are regarded as health cases and cases regarded as conduct cases. There used, until recently, to be a division between the two, but it must be borne in mind that the division cannot necessarily be strictly applied because health issues may be material where there has been misconduct. However, the misconduct may be so serious that notwithstanding that it was caused by what might be regarded as health problems, it has to result in erasure, particularly if it appears to the Panel that there is a lack of insight and so a real risk of repetition of such sort of conduct.
>
> [17 In setting out the factors which are material in deciding upon suspension, as opposed to erasure, the guidance notes that no evidence of repetition is a factor. The Panel may be satisfied that the doctor has insight and does not pose a significant risk of repeating and, in cases where the only issue relates to the doctor's health, there is a risk to the patient's safety if the doctor is allowed to continue to practise even under conditions. That means

138 [2007] EWHC 3257 (Admin) at para 13ff.

> that in a pure health case it may well be appropriate to impose suspension rather than merely conditions.
>
> [18] Erasure is likely to be appropriate where there is a serious departure from professional standards, where serious harm is done to others, where there is a continuing risk and where there is a persistent lack of insight into the seriousness of actions or their consequences. It is noted that erasure is not available in cases where the only issue relates to the doctor's health. That then is the guidance that the Panel has to apply and in this case they clearly considered the guidance and took it properly into account.

3.158 *Brennan v Health Professions Council*[139] provides useful guidance in cases where a penalty is imposed solely on grounds of the reputation of the profession. Ouseley J suggested that maintenance of public confidence in the profession was achieved by the finding that the registrant's fitness to practise was impaired. When imposing sanction, the starting point and the fundamental factor was public safety. If a sanction is imposed to uphold the reputation of the profession, careful consideration would be needed as to whether the most severe sanction of striking off is necessary and proportionate, particularly where the registrant had demonstrated insight and such conduct was unlikely to be repeated. This suggests that there would have to be some evidence that the reputation of the profession would be harmed if a lesser sanction than strike off was imposed.

3.159 In *Brennan*, a physiotherapist employed by a rugby team, on instruction from his coach, provided a player with a blood capsule in order for him to fake an injury during a match so that he could be substituted. B then assisted his employer in covering up the incident by provided false evidence at the subsequent investigation. B's conduct was dishonest, premeditated and continued over a period of time. However, it involved no deception of his employer and no patient harm. There was evidence that B was an 'excellent physiotherapist' and he made full admissions before the HPC. The High Court quashed the striking-off order imposed by the HPC and remitted the case back to the regulator to re-determine, with a direction to reach a fully and properly reasoned decision on sanction taking account of the concerns set out in its judgment. The court indicated that a suspension order would have been sufficient but declined to substitute such an order since it was accepted that a striking off order may be appropriate if the registrant lacked insight, or it was necessary as a deterrent to address a real problem in the profession concerning this type of conduct.

3.160 Dishonesty is of course one of the most serious adverse findings that can be made against a registrant, and although it may not always result in erasure or striking-off a register, that is frequently the case. In addition, a distinction is to be drawn between healthcare cases and those involving lawyers.

3.161 In *Siddiqui v General Medical Council*[140] HHJ Pelling QC referred to the case of *Solicitors Regulation Authority v Sharma*[141] in which the court held that dishonesty by a solicitor is harmful to the public who must be able to

139 [2011] EWHC 41 (Admin).

140 [2013] EWHC 1083 (Admin).

141 [2010] EWHC 2022 (Admin).

trust their lawyers. This maxim was applied to nurses in *Ajala v Nursing and Midwifery Council*.[142] HHJ Pelling QC regarded this principle to be applicable to doctors; however, the case of *R (Hassan) v General Optical Council*[143] brings a note of caution to this line of thought. *Sharma* suggests a solicitor should be struck off for dishonesty 'save in exceptional circumstances'. It therefore creates a presumption of striking-off. That presumption has not been written into the guidance of the GOC or other healthcare regulators, and tribunals should not assume it is applicable in healthcare cases merely because it applies in one field of professional regulation.

Insight

Overview

3.162 Insight is the ability of a registrant to step outside the confines of his or her own self-interest in the FTP process and consider the allegations dispassionately. It involves consideration and/or recognition of whether the registrant is in the wrong, and if so to what extent. It may involve apologising or making reparation; it certainly includes demonstrating that the registrant has learned from his or her mistakes and moved forward, or that he or she has the capacity to learn and progress. An important question for the tribunal is: does the registrant demonstrate that he or she has insight or the capacity to gain or improve it?

3.163 The GMC's 2016 *Sanctions guidance* makes the following points:

> 41 Expressing insight involves demonstrating reflection and remediation
> 42 . . . doctor is likely to have insight if they:
> (a) accept they should have behaved differently (showing empathy and understanding)
> (b) take timely steps to remediate . . . and apologise at an early stage before the hearing c demonstrate the timely development of insight during the investigation and hearing
>
> . . .
>
> 48 A doctor is likely to lack insight if they:
> (a) refuse to apologise or accept their mistakes
> (b) promise to remediate, but fail to take appropriate steps, or only do so when prompted immediately before or during the hearing
> (c) do not demonstrate the timely development of insight d fail to tell the truth (including being dishonest or misleading) during the hearing

3.164 The guidance makes the point that the tribunal should be aware that cultural and language issues may affect whether a registrant appears to demonstrate insight or not. The effect of language, intonation, non-verbal cues such as eye-contact, expressions and body language must all be carefully considered. There are wide variations as between cultures and people expressing themselves in their second language, and the tribunal should not simply jump to conclusions.

3.165 Examining the extent of the registrant's insight is as essential to the tribunal's task in assessing sanction as it is to the issue of current

142 [2012] EWHC 2976 (Admin).
143 [2013] EWHC 1887 (Admin).

impairment. In *Council for Healthcare Regulatory Excellence v Nursing and Midwifery Council and Grant*[144] the point was made that: 'When considering whether fitness to practise is currently impaired, the level of insight shown by the practitioner is central to a proper determination . . .'.

3.166 Establishing insight is relevant when assessing risk. The tribunal will look for evidence of remorse, apology, understanding impact and remediation of conduct. This includes looking for such evidence during the hearing itself. The level of a registrant's insight may be critical to the question of current impairment and thus to sanction.

3.167 However, insight is not the only factor and, whilst it is important it is not determinative. This was made clear by Ouseley J in *R (Vali) v General Optical Council*.[145] V failed to perform various tests and to refer a patient for further investigation. This was regarded as misconduct however she was found to be impaired principally on the basis that the FTP Tribunal rejected her evidence and thus concluded that she lacked insight into her misconduct. This latter finding of impairment was quashed. The incident complained of occurred in 2005, four and half years before the FTP hearing. There were no other complaints in that period and no adverse information from the regulator. In the interim V had improved her skill base and her career trajectory was good such that she was now supervising and teaching others. The court concluded that V's career would not have progressed in the way that it had if she remained a risk to the public or to the profession.

3.168 The important point was made that the tribunal cannot simply equate rejection of the registrant's version of events with a lack of insight. It is a factor and an important one at that, but it is not necessarily determinative.

3.169 The case of *Ashton v GMC*[146] deals with both a lack of insight and a failure to give evidence. A failed to refer a patient for urgent examination and, following protracted proceedings, he was found guilty of misconduct and suspended. A did not call or give evidence to challenge the case against him nor did he acknowledge or explain his inadequate care of the patient. Despite a long and otherwise unblemished career, his failure to acknowledge his deficiencies left the FTP Tribunal, and eventually the court, with no evidence of insight or remediation and, most importantly, no evidence that his deficiencies were capable of remediation. These were described as '[matters] of significant concern and weight in considering the issue of impairment'.

3.170 Interestingly, despite these difficulties, the imposition of an immediate order was quashed on the basis that A currently worked satisfactorily in a 'remote field of medicine' and was unlikely to be able to find work outside that field in the 28 days before the order for suspension came into effect. Any risk to the public was thus negligible, and an immediate order was not necessary.

144 [2011] EWHC 927 (Admin) at para 116.

145 [2011] EWHC 310 (Admin).

146 [2013] EWHC 943 (Admin).

3.171 *Karwal v General Medical Council*[147] further refines the issue of insight. In 2008 K was found to have made false representations regarding an investment scheme involving £188,000. She was suspended for 12 months. She was further suspended in 2010 when the review tribunal concluded that she continued to demonstrate a lack of insight and a lack of real acceptance of the finding of dishonesty. Rafferty J upheld the further sanction. She held that the review tribunal was obliged to consider the dishonesty and the issue of insight namely whether a registrant had appreciated the gravity of the matter. While she stated that maintaining one's innocence was not simply to be equated with a lack of insight, the reviewing tribunal had been careful to justify its view that K had not fully appreciated the gravity of the matter as opposed to trying to minimise it.

Insight and contesting a case

3.172 In *R (Alhy) v General Medical Council*[148] when considering insight, HHJ Belcher commented that there is a significant distinction between maintaining innocence during criminal proceedings and continuing to do so once they had concluded. She stated that A was entitled to maintain his innocence in criminal proceedings, indeed he was entitled to do so once the criminal proceedings had finished – but by doing so 'it is inevitable that it will follow that he is not prepared to accept the matters found against him or take appropriate action in relations to them or to consider the risk that might arise from them'. She regarded it as perfectly proper for the FTP tribunal to take such concerns into account.

3.173 The issue of insight and how a tribunal may assess and give weight to it was revisited in *Professional Standards Authority v Health and Care Professions Council and Doree*[149] a case involving allegations of bullying and sexual harassment. Following an appeal by the PSA against a caution order Lindblom J observed:

> I do not accept that, in principle, a professional disciplinary committee may only reasonably find that a registrant has shown insight or remorse after he has himself given oral evidence to demonstrate it, and has made himself available for cross-examination or other questioning on that evidence – even if it has rejected his evidence on some or all of the allegations he faced. Whether a registrant has shown insight into his misconduct, and how much insight he has shown, are classically matters of fact and judgment for the professional disciplinary committee in the light of the evidence before it. . . . In assessing a registrant's insight, a professional disciplinary committee will need to weigh all the relevant evidence, both oral and written, which provides a picture of it. This may include evidence given by other witnesses about the registrant's conduct as an employee or as a professional colleague, and, where this is also relevant, the quality of his work with patients, as well as any objective evidence, such as specific work he has done in an effort to address his failings.[150]

147 [2011] EWHC 826 (Admin).
148 [2011] EWHC 2277 (Admin).
149 [2017] EWCA Civ 319.
150 At [38].

3.174 From *Doree* it is clear that the simplistic notion that contesting a case proves a lack of insight is wrong. A registrant may accept one allegation but believe that he or she has good reason to contest another. It may be that the registrant is proved right; alternatively that even if the registrant contests matters, during his or her evidence he or she demonstrates an acceptance and understanding of the allegation and its impact on patients, the public or the profession as the case may be.

3.175 However, the fact that the registrant is insightful and remorseful is not of itself always sufficient. This was the case in *Onyeaso v General Medical Council*.[151] O had stolen prescription forms and used another doctor's name to obtain medicine for a genuine but embarrassing condition. She admitted the offence, and was cautioned by the police. During FTP proceedings she admitted the facts and agreed that she had then been impaired but submitted she had reflected upon her misconduct and remediated her impairment. Despite this, O was erased from the register. The FTP tribunal took account of a suspension five years beforehand which related to dishonestly withholding information in an application form. Parker J upheld the erasure commenting that recognising a wrong-doing as O had done is 'essential' in assessing insight, but even this may not be enough. All relevant matters must be considered when assessing insight risk and sanction, including the seriousness of the allegations, previous dishonesty and a registrant's conduct in the proceedings.

Conduct during the hearing

3.176 The issue of a registrant's conduct during the hearing may cause some difficulty, not least because there are conflicting decisions. However, it is perhaps possible to reconcile these cases by disregarding conduct until the issue of insight is to be considered, and that is most properly done at the impairment and/or the sanction stages.

3.177 At stage one, the tribunal must focus solely on the allegations in the heads of charge. This is made clear from the comment of Silber J in *Cohen* that findings in relation to a charge at stage one 'must be focused solely on the heads of the charges themselves'.[152] Since the registrant's conduct is not part of the charge, it is not relevant to the facts stage. Current poor conduct cannot be treated as an aggravating fact since present conduct post-dates the events that form the basis of charge.

3.178 In *Cheatle*[153] when dealing with the issue of current impairment, Cranston J observed that it is important to look at any misconduct 'in the context of the doctor's behaviour both before the misconduct and to the present time'. That suggests current conduct is relevant to impairment which is stage two.

3.179 In *Nicholas-Pillai v General Medical Council*,[154] a case in which NP contested critical allegations of dishonest note-keeping, Mitting J made the important point that:

151 [2013] EWHC 4787 (Admin).
152 [2008] EWHC 581 (Admin) para [48].
153 [2009] EWHC 645 (Admin) para [22].
154 [2009] EWHC 1048 (Admin).

> In the ordinary case such as this, the attitude of the practitioner to the events which give rise to the specific allegations against him is, in principle, something which can be taken into account either in his favour or against him by the panel, both at the stage when it considers whether his fitness to practise is impaired, and at the stage of determining what sanction should be imposed upon him.[155]

(See also *Misra v General Medical Council.*[156])

3.180 Conversely, in *Nagiub v General Medical Council*,[157] Foskett J observed that the behaviour of a registrant – even the gratuitously rude, offensive and racist behaviour said to have been indulged in by N throughout the FTP hearing – is not relevant to the issue of impairment. The determination on impairment should only relate to matters which have been found proved against the doctor. In *Nagiub* as in other cases, the point is made that the registrant is under the greatest pressure and may behave in a way that is out of character. However, the way a registrant conducts himself or herself during proceedings is arguably still part of their profession since they have a duty to uphold standards and assist their regulator in so doing and it is difficult to reconcile the comments in *Nagiub* with cases such as *Nicholas-Pillai* and *Cheatle*.

3.181 The subsequent case of *Vaghela v General Medical Council*[158] emphasised the link between insight and a registrant's conduct in the hearing. Sales J upheld the decision to erase V stating that the FTP tribunal had been 'fully entitled' to take account of how V had conducted himself when assessing his insight and the 'seriousness and currency of the impairment'. While a tribunal should give some allowance to an unrepresented registrant, he commented that 'a person representing himself can do so in a moderate and restrained way without resorting to lies and unjustified attacks on other individuals'. He added that 'in relation to assessing matters such as his insight . . . it would have been extraordinary if the tribunal had not had regard to material of this kind'.[159]

3.182 Unsurprisingly, the approach of taking a registrant's conduct into account when considering his or her current insight and attitude towards the allegation(s) has gained traction. Provided proper allowance is made for a registrant's stress, distress and any cultural or language difficulties, it is a matter of common-sense to take the registrant's attitude into account. As stated in *R (Alhy) v General Medical Council* (above) HHJ Belcher drew a significant distinction between maintaining innocence during criminal proceedings and continuing to do so once they had concluded. While poor conduct was not the issue in that case, maintaining his innocence in the face of an adverse finding was relevant to his failure to recognise the wrongdoing found proved and the risks that flow there-from.

3.183 In *Giwa-Osagie v General Medical Council*[160] at the impairment stage of its proceedings the FTP tribunal made particular reference to O's continued

155 At para 19.
156 [2003] UKPC 7.
157 [2011] EWHC 366 (Admin).
158 [2013] EWHC 1594 (Admin).
159 At para 49.
160 [2013] EWHC 1514 (Admin).

denial of events including his stating that the findings of fact were wrong and 'not based on the truth' and witnesses had lied or conspired against him. The tribunal concluded that O's misconduct was 'the product of attitudinal deficiencies which you have repeatedly failed to acknowledge . . . [and your evidence] . . . demonstrated your continuing lack of insight into the nature of your misconduct'. Having made that finding, the tribunal concluded there was a real risk of repetition putting both patients and the public interest at risk. It thus concluded that O was currently impaired. Thereafter the tribunal took the same matters into account in determining sanction.

3.184 Cranston J found that the tribunal:

> . . . took into account the appellant's record and accepted that misconduct can in principle be remedied. However, it was clearly influenced by the fact that the appellant continued to assert that he was a victim of a conspiracy, that there was false evidence against him, and that he had not done anything wrong. [It] was obviously impressed by what it regarded as the attitudinal deficiencies and lack of insight the appellant demonstrated. That was a matter that the Panel returned to in its finding on sanction. That being the case, the Panel's findings on both misconduct and impairment cannot be challenged.[161]

3.185 In *Hussain v General Medical Council*[162] H accused witnesses of lies, racism and indulging in a conspiracy to pervert the FTP process. In so doing, he completely failed to recognise his own shortcomings, and showed no insight into the findings of professionals involved in disciplinary proceedings prior to the FTP process or of the FTP tribunal itself. On appeal Bean J said that:

> An aggressively run defence is not 'misconduct'. But the presence or absence of insight into one's failings is often relevant to whether a doctor's fitness to practise remains impaired. If Dr Hussain had immediately admitted his wrongdoing in 2010 his case might have been presented on the basis that it was a long time ago, that he had learned the error of his ways and that his fitness to practise was therefore no longer impaired. But that was not what happened. On the contrary: his case to the Panel was that he had done no wrong, that Dr [H] and his colleagues were racists and that Mrs [W] was lying as part of a 'joint venture' with Dr [H] which had brought about his removal from the practice. This showed, in the words of Judge Bird [who dealt with the initial appeal], a 'complete and total lack of insight' into his conduct. In those circumstances, like the judge, I consider that the Panel were entitled to find that the Appellant's fitness to practise remained impaired by reason of the misconduct which they had found proved against him.

3.186 The issue was revisited In *Professional Standards Authority v General Pharmaceutical Council and Onwughalu*,[163] a case in which after some prevarication O pleaded guilty to two counts of child cruelty and received a custodial sentence. Her fitness to practise was found to be impaired because of the convictions. Despite minimising her conduct, contradicting her guilty pleas and asserting that her conduct was an error of judgment

161 At [29] and [30].
162 [2014] EWCA Civ 2246.
163 [2014] EWHC 2521 (Admin).

rather than deliberate concealment of a child's injuries, the FTP tribunal only imposed a 12-month order of suspension 'to give her time to demonstrate insight'. This approach was roundly criticised. The sanction was quashed and replaced with erasure. Cox J held that the FTP's original sanction was inconsistent with the fact that O had failed to show any insight during the hearing and, the tribunal had not considered V's lack of integrity at the impairment stage.

3.187 The danger of placing an over-reliance on demeanour was made plain in *Suddock v Nursing and Midwifery Council*[164] in which Andrews J criticised the tribunal for placing too much reliance on S's demeanour when assessing her credibility rather than looking at her account in the context of the other evidence. While her ladyship commented that demeanour is not irrelevant, 'Experience has taught us that the way in which someone behaves while giving evidence is not a reliable indicator of whether he/she is telling the truth'.[165] Furthermore, that:

> . . . the way in which the witness's evidence fits with any non-contentious evidence or agreed facts and with contemporaneous documents and the inherent probabilities and improbabilities of his or her account of events, as well as consistencies and inconsistencies (both internally and with the evidence of others) are likely to be far more reliable indicators of where the truth lies. The decision maker should therefore test the evidence against those yardsticks . . . before adding demeanour into the equation.[166]

Notably this was, unlike many such cases, a case in which there was some evidence to support S's allegation of a conspiracy against her. It is highly likely that the tribunal dismissed this not because of the merits but because it focused too much on her demeanour. In that respect, it is an object lesson in any registrant being represented.

3.188 Drawing the above together, the author suggests that the following staged process is appropriate:

- The FTP tribunal will avoid controversy at the fact-finding stage by focusing only on the charges and the registrant's conduct at the time of the alleged misconduct or deficiency. Poor conduct in the hearing should be ignored for the purposes of fact-finding. However, the situation changes at the next stage.
- When it comes to impairment, this should be taken in two stages.
  - The FTP tribunal should first look at impairment, considering the facts found proved and the registrant's subsequent professional conduct *out-with* the proceedings. The tribunal should ask itself 'are these facts capable *in principle* of founding impairment'? If they are not, the case falls away.
  - If they are, the tribunal should then consider whether that impairment remains current. It is here where a registrant's conduct during the proceedings bites, since current impairment is to some extent (but not exclusively) determined by insight, and that may in part be measured by a registrant's conduct and demeanour.

164 [2015] EWHC 3612 (Admin).
165 At [59].
166 At [59].

- While a tribunal should give such leeway as it considers fair to a registrant facing FTP proceedings, if his or her conduct goes beyond a robust defence and is gratuitously rude, involves lies, unjustified attacks upon witnesses or is otherwise indicative of a failure to acknowledge proven misconduct then it may well indicate a lack of insight into the misconduct alleged. A tribunal would be entitled to take account of such behaviour in moving from the question of 'impairment in principle' to the question of whether such impairment is current.
- The same may be said in respect of risk and appropriate sanction. If the registrant's conduct indicates that he or she does not recognise the risks that flow from his or her proven misconduct and impairment and/or that he or she cannot or will not change his or her ways to meet those risks, then it may be indicative of a need for one sanction rather than another to protect patients, the public interest or the registrant's interests.

3.189 Throughout the above suggested staged process, care must be taken to ensure that the registrant's conduct is not used as an 'aggravating feature' to justify a harsher sanction. That would be wrong. The reason why a registrant may continue to deny matters proved against him or her and what this discloses regarding his or her appreciation of the gravity and effect of any proven misconduct should only be looked at in respect of insight regarding the alleged facts found proved and the impairment found as a result of those facts.

Non-attendance of registrant: effect on sanction

3.190 Many of the issues discussed above relate to measuring the conduct of the registrant both at the time of events found proved and subsequently. While the legal burden of proving a case always remains with the regulator, there are times at which the registrant has an evidential burden. That is, the burden of supporting a particular assertion or argument. If a registrant declines to attend, the registrant's absence will materially affect his or her chances of arguing his or her case.

3.191 This point was made plain in *Burrows v General Pharmaceutical Council*,[167] a case in which B was erased from practice having failed to attend proceedings when facing charges of dishonesty. B swapped the label from a new dress to an old one which she returned to a store, and by so doing obtained £45 by deception. This was dealt with by way of a caution which involves acceptance of guilt. The acceptance of dishonesty and of guilt was challenged in the regulatory proceedings and, unsurprisingly it was rejected. The tribunal concluded that B had no insight and expressed no remorse and concluded that suspension would not result in either. B was therefore erased from the register.

3.192 Although B had been present in the earlier parts of the hearing, she was absent on a pre-booked holiday when the issues of impairment and sanction were decided. She was represented and did not seek an adjournment. B appealed regarding the issues of insight and sanction. Kerr J dismissed her arguments commenting that 'The main difficulty with [her] arguments is that [she] did not attend to answer questions as to her state

167 [2016] EWHC 1050 (Admin).

of mind'. He acknowledged that B undoubtedly found the proceedings stressful but non-attendance 'carried with it the high risk that she would lose the prospect of a benign interpretation of her conduct and a lenient sanction, having deprived the Committee, by her absence, of the opportunity to test the level of her insight'.[168]

3.193 As to the issue of sanction, his comments were even more robust: 'In a case of obvious dishonesty, not attending the hearing amounts virtually to courting removal.' His Lordship went on to suggest that regulators should spell out in any notice of hearing that 'the consequences of non-attendance are likely to be severely prejudicial',[169] but concluded that there was nothing wrong or unfair in the procedure or decisions in this case.

3.194 Kerr J continued with the above approach in *Kimmance v General Medical Council*[170] in two pithy and incisive comments:

> There was indeed no evidence of insight and remediation in this case. I do not much like those jargon words. They do not do much to illuminate the reality, which is that a doctor or other professional who has done wrong has to look at his or her conduct with a self-critical eye, acknowledge fault, say sorry and convince a panel that there is real reason to believe he or she has learned a lesson from the experience. Nine times out of ten, you cannot do that if you do not turn up to the hearing.[171]
>
> . . .
>
> I fear that in many cases registered professionals are not made fully aware of the dangers of not attending. In a regulatory jurisdiction, where issues of insight and remediation are very important, and where the conduct complained of is clearly very serious, non-attendance of the hearing can come close to professional suicide.[172]

3.195 Importantly, this case, while it involved allegations of dishonesty, centred around K's inability to conduct himself in a reasoned and reasonable fashion in family proceedings following the breakdown of his marriage. His behaviour was offensive and threatening to individuals and institutions and not behaviour 'befitting a doctor' and it continued during the regulatory proceedings. The risk in non-attendance is thus not limited to cases of dishonesty.

3.196 *Kimmance* makes it clear that in any serious case, non-attendance may have catastrophic consequences and almost certainly will have such consequences if the evidential burden rests with the registrant to demonstrate insight and remediation. The consequences of non-attendance are such that if a registrant *truly* cannot attend they *must* provide conclusive evidence to that effect. Conversely, if a tribunal is to proceed in absence when a registrant's career is in the balance it must be satisfied on *cogent evidence* that it is fair to do so. A certificate that someone is unfit to work may not be enough. A couple of failed attempts by a regulator to make contact leading to the regulator's assumption and assertion of non-engagement may not be enough if there has been prior engagement. In any event attendance may be

168 At [53] and [54].

169 At [58].

170 [2016] EWHC 1808 (Admin).

171 At [66].

172 At [71].

facilitated by phone or video link and a tribunal should explore whether these have been explained, offered and rejected before coming to a conclusion adverse to a registrant. (See also *Parkinson v Nursing and Midwifery Council*[173] and *Kearsey v Nursing and Midwifery Council*.[174])

Examples and guidance on sanction in particular categories of cases

Introduction

3.197 Decisions of healthcare regulators tend to be fact-specific and are therefore not regarded as forming a coherent body of jurisprudence. It is not possible to rely on any one case as a *firm* indicator of the appropriate outcome in another. However particular features are regarded as significant by regulators and tribunals alike, and will be of assistance in advising a registrant as to the range of likely sanctions and in deciding how to pitch submissions on mitigation.

3.198 In *Shah v General Pharmaceutical Council*,[175] S sought to argue that previous decisions to reprimand practitioners who had committed dispensing errors, retained out of date medication and thereby breached fundamental principles of good practice and/or otherwise brought the profession into disrepute created a norm in limiting sanction to reprimands. Wynn-Williams J dismissed the argument on the basis that the decisions were fact specific and created no such expectation.

3.199 The appellate courts may accord special respect to the judgment of the professional decision-making body in the shape of the tribunal recognising that such tribunals are in the best position to judge what is best for the profession – see *Ghosh v General Medical Council*.[176] They will frequently uphold a tribunal decision on sanction even if the court itself considers the decision to be lenient or harsh. However, the degree of respect from the appellate courts is not set in stone. The GMC is proving to be quite bullish in challenges sanctions under MA 1983 s40A with notable success in some high profile cases (see para 3.121).

3.200 In *Professional Standards Authority v Health and Care Professions Council and Gaffar*[177] the PSA appealed the decision of the HCPC's Competence and Conduct Committee. G was convicted of dishonestly making false representations that he had an MSc, for gain, namely to secure employment. The CCC concluded he had been punished enough, was an excellent employee and that public confidence did not require a finding of impairment. Carr J roundly disagreed. She concluded that G's repeated and quite sophisticated dishonesty breached the fundamental tenet of honesty. Without the very powerful testament of colleagues and G's clear remorse she would have struck him off. Instead G was suspended for six months. When considering the case, Carr J commented that tribunals

173 [2010] EWHC 1898 (Admin).
174 [2016] EWHC 1603 (Admin).
175 [2011] EWHC 73 (Admin).
176 [2001] UKPC 29, [2001] 1 WLR 1915.
177 [2014] EWHC 2723 (Admin).

may be afforded less respect or deference in cases of dishonesty than of clinical error.

3.201 All tribunals will first consider the regulator's sanctions guidance. Mitigation is frequently a case of arguing why a panel should follow or may depart from the guidance. The guidance is of considerable importance designed to promote consistency in similar cases but, it is guidance and not intended to be a rigid tariff (see *Council for the Regulation of Healthcare Professionals v (1) General Medical Council (2) Leeper* at para 3.133 above).

Recent cases demonstrate that the GMC will challenge sanctions that it considers are outside the ambit of the guidance and are insufficient to protect the public or maintain standards or trust in the profession. The High Court has upheld several such challenges.

Drug and alcohol misuse

3.202 Many cases where the registrant's fitness to practise is said to be impaired by reason of drug or alcohol dependency but which do not involve other criminal misconduct (eg drink-driving, assault or possession offences) will be dealt with as a health issue. Some regulators have specific Health Committees for such cases. Being treated as a health issue will affect the range of sanctions available. While the panel is not responsible for the care or rehabilitation of any registrant, the continued or return to *safe* practice of an otherwise competent registrant is in the public interest. A panel may endeavour to facilitate the registrant's safe practice if this outweighs the public and professional interest of upholding standards etc (see the chapters dealing with specific regulators for details of the powers of sanction).

3.203 Referral to a Health Committee will not be appropriate in all cases. A convictions case will almost certainly be dealt with as a conduct matter or mixed conduct and health. In *Crabbie v General Medical Council*[178] there was medical evidence that C suffered from alcohol dependency at the time of the matters that brought her before the tribunal. She had been convicted of causing death by dangerous driving and driving with excess alcohol and sentenced to five years' imprisonment and disqualified from driving for ten years. The matter was reported to the GMC as a conviction case. The Professional Conduct Committee refused C's application to transfer the case to the Health Committee. On appeal, the court upheld the principle that if the case is one where erasure is a serious possibility, it should not be referred to the Health Committee.

3.204 In other, less serious, cases, conditions of practice may be an appropriate disposal. This is where a requirement to co-operate with a treatment regime and provide reports periodically from a supervising medical practitioner (or, for example, a counsellor) arguably provides the requisite level of protection to the public. Representatives of registrants will need to ensure in such cases that there is supporting documentation from the medical practitioner or counsellor indicating a willingness to co-operate with the conditions and provide the information specified in any order. It will frequently be appropriate to call the existing or proposed supervisor to

178 [2002] UKPC 45.

advise the tribunal as to his or her attitude to public protection and registrant rehabilitation.

3.205 It is open to a Health Committee to conclude that a registrant is suffering from alcohol dependency in cases where there is evidence from medical assessors, whether the specific diagnosis has been canvassed with the registrant or not. In *Boodoo v General Medical Council*[179] the court noted that the evidence contained clear reference to the attributes of the condition, accordingly the conclusion was neither wrong nor unjust.

3.206 The important features to consider are the attitude of the registrant to rehabilitation, and whether the public interest (risk to patients and professional standards etc) outweighs or is itself outweighed by the prospect of a registrant's return to practice.

Convictions and cautions

3.207 Most regulators have specific rules for dealing with conviction or caution cases, which provide that the fact of conviction or caution is taken as proof of the facts of the offence (see chapters dealing with specific regulators for the applicable rule). It is not the function of a tribunal considering such a case to go behind the facts of the conviction or caution, or re-try the criminal case. Having decided that the registrant's fitness to practise is impaired by the conviction or caution, the tribunal then adopts the same approach to sanction as in other cases.

3.208 The interests of the profession will necessarily be treated as of paramount importance in any case involving criminal misconduct. Because of this, conviction cases are frequently met with suspension or erasure. Where a case does not involve dishonesty, sexual or pornographic offences, and/or any risk to patients or the profession can be properly addressed, erasure or suspension do not always result. Alternatively, if suspension is the result, in deciding the term of the suspension, the tribunal may take account of the registrant's possible return to safe practice in the future.

3.209 Convictions or cautions for offences involving dishonesty are likely to be regarded as particularly serious, especially if the offence was committed in the course of a registrant's professional practice. In *R (Rogers) v General Medical Council*[180] R received a suspended sentence having pleaded guilty to many offences of obtaining prescription drugs by deception and possession of controlled drugs. The conviction was reported to the GMC and R was erased from the register. On appeal, the court held that the sanction was appropriate in the light of various aggravating factors which included the repetition of the offence and the use of prescription forms to obtain the drugs.

3.210 In conviction cases, particularly for serious criminal offences, the wider public interest issues of upholding the reputation of the profession and maintaining confidence in the regulatory process will be of the greatest significance. It is highly likely to outweigh any argument concerning the registrant's risk or lack of risk to potential service users. This principle was

179 [2004] EWHC 2712 (Admin).
180 [2004] EWHC 424 (Admin).

highlighted in *General Medical Council v Bawa-Garba*[181] who, along with another, was convicted of gross-negligence manslaughter of a child in hospital. She pleaded guilty and was given a two-year sentence suspended for two years. The child attended hospital with multiple symptoms which BG failed to properly assess, diagnose or alert colleagues to. BG was the junior doctor on duty working a double shift having returned to work following maternity leave. She did not realise how de-skilled she had become, nor did the hospital provide appropriate levels of support. She was of good character and by all accounts a skilled and dedicated doctor held in high regard. Her failings were described as 'truly exceptionally bad' and contributed to the child dying earlier than would otherwise have been the case, albeit there were wider contributory failings in the hospital. The events happened two years prior to the regulatory proceedings during which time she had remained in employment without concern and it was accepted that she had remediated her failings and was not a risk to the public. The GMC appealed the suspension asserting that BG should be erased from the register. Following reiteration of the familiar issues in the sanction guidance regarding serious cases, mitigating and aggravating factors, etc the court erased her from the register. The court rejected the GMC's contention that in a conviction of gross negligence manslaughter raised he presumption of erasure but held that suspension did not reflect the full force of the jury's verdict or the need to maintain public confidence in the profession and uphold standards. Personal mitigation and remediation were of limited weight in such a case. (see also the comments re *Bijl* v GMC at para 3.121 above). (See also *Professional Standards Authority v Health and Care Professions Council and Gaffar* at para 3.200 above.)

3.211 In *Chandrasekera v Nursing and Midwifery Council*[182] the registrant pleaded guilty to manslaughter of her husband on grounds of diminished responsibility. She suffered from depression and anxiety at the time. There was no suggestion of any criticism of her professional performance. C was initially suspended from practice by the Interim Orders Tribunal. On review this was replaced with interim conditions, and subsequently even this was revoked, allowing her to return to unrestricted practice pending conclusion of her case. She was later struck-off by the CCC and appealed. The court upheld the decision to strike her off, notwithstanding the earlier decision to allow her to return to unrestricted practice. The committee's view that the conviction (or the behaviour that led to it) was fundamentally incompatible with remaining on the register was one that it was entitled to reach.

3.212 Cases involving conviction or caution for the possession of or other involvement with indecent images of children will focus on the wider public interest in determining sanction. They are almost inevitably dealt with by suspension or erasure (see below).

3.213 Perhaps obviously, a decision of a regulatory body based upon a conviction that is subsequently overturned, may also be quashed. In *R (Jenkinson) v Nursing and Midwifery Council*[183] the registrant had been convicted of causing grievous bodily harm to a patient in her care who had died. At

181 [2018] EWHC 76 (Admin).
182 [2009] EWHC 144 (Admin).
183 [2009] EWHC 1111 (Admin).

trial, evidence was given by an expert as to the functioning of a ventilator that had been operative in the patient's death. The expert's evidence was subsequently discredited, and the criminal conviction overturned. The court held that once the conviction had been quashed, the finding of misconduct and the decision on sanction 'fell away'.

3.214 In *Council for the Regulation of Healthcare Professionals v General Dental Council and Fleischmann*[184] the court observed that if a registrant has been convicted of a serious criminal offence and is still serving his or her sentence at the time the matter comes before a tribunal (F was undergoing a Sex-Offenders Treatment Programme), they should not normally be permitted to resume practice until the criminal sentence has been satisfactorily completed. In such cases, therefore, representatives may need to consider requesting postponement of the hearing until after completion of the sentence. F pleaded guilty to 12 counts of downloading child pornography, and was sentenced to a community rehabilitation order. The FTP tribunal suspended F for 12 months, however this was replaced with erasure on the basis that only this would uphold the standing of the profession.

3.215 The issue was revisited in *Obukofe v General Medical Council.*[185] In 2011 O received a suspended sentence for three sexual assaults, and ordered to sign the Sex Offenders Register (SOR) for seven years. In 2013 an FTP tribunal suspended O from practice for 12 months. O's appeal was dismissed by Popplewell J, who highlighted the distinction between a Sex-Offenders Treatment Programme and the Sex Offenders Register. In *Fleischman* the court was concerned that the treatment programme be completed satisfactorily before any consideration is given to resuming practice. In O's case, the tribunal disregarded the issue of the Sex Offenders Register and exercised its own judgment as to the appropriate sanction. As such, it had acted appropriately and in accordance with the *Fleischmann* principle.

Sexual offences and pornography

Introduction

3.216 Cases involving sexual offences and/or sexual impropriety with a patient, and/or cases involving pornography, particularly child pornography, are treated with the utmost seriousness. They will almost inevitably be met with an order of suspension, or more likely of erasure, this being necessary to protect patients, promote trust in the professions and uphold standards.

3.217 While it may be that in some cases a distinction is possible in respect of some adult pornography, that is by no means certain given that there may be issues of misusing a trust's/employer's IT equipment, as well as concerns over the objectification of women or men.

Sexual offences involving children and child pornography

3.218 Conduct involving sexual assault and/or sexual abuse of children and/or child pornography is an abuse of trust and fundamentally incompatible

184 [2005] EWHC 87 (QB).
185 [2014] EWHC 408 (Admin).

with the role of a health professional. An example of the approach adopted by the courts to such conduct is provided in the Privy Council case of *Haikel v General Medical Council.*[186] This concerned a GP who conducted intimate examinations of female patients which were not clinically appropriate and without offering chaperones to those patients. Upholding the sanction of erasure, their Lordships stated that:

> The public, and in particular female patients, must have confidence in the medical profession whatever their state of health might be. The conduct as found proved against Dr Haikel undoubtedly undermines such confidence and a severe sanction was inevitable. Their Lordships are satisfied that erasure was neither unreasonable, excessive nor disproportionate but necessary in the public interest.[187]

3.219 Two scales have been used to measure the seriousness of images. The ten-point Copine scale ('Combating Paedophile Information Networks in Europe') was originally developed for therapeutic purposes. This was adapted to a five-point scale in *R v Oliver.*[188] The Sentencing Council has now produced guidelines on cases involving indecent photographs, pseudo photographs and similar material. The latter guidelines are now of most importance. The most serious offences are in Category A. Seriousness increases as one moves from possession to distribution to production. The table gives a brief description, the starting point for sentences and, the range within which sentence would normally sit bearing in mind any aggravating or mitigating features.

	Possession	Sharing	Creating
Category A Images involve penetrative sexual activity Images involve sexual activity with an animal or sadism	1yr custody Range: 6m–3yrs	3yrs custody Range: 2–5yrs	6yrs custody Range: 4–9yrs
Category B images involving non-penetrative sexual activity	6m custody Range: High level community sentence to 18m custody	12m custody Range: 6m–2yrs	2yrs custody Range: 1–4yrs
Category C Indecent images not falling within categories A or B	High level community order Range: medium community order to 6m custody	3m custody Range: high level community order to 6m	18m custody Range: 1–3yrs

Distribution includes possession with a view to distributing or sharing images. Production includes the taking or making of any image at source, for instance the original image. Making an image by simple downloading should be treated as possession for the purposes of sentencing. To move

186 [2002] UKPC 37.
187 At para 29.
188 [2003] 1 Cr App R 28.

from a short or even a moderate prison term to a community order would require clear evidence of rehabilitation or the prospect thereof.

For further guidelines see the Sentencing Council's website: www.sentencingcouncil.org.uk.

3.220 Child pornography is illegal, and even when accessed outside the workplace it will usually result in erasure – there being no other way of maintaining public confidence in the profession.

3.221 In *Council for the Regulation of Healthcare Professionals v General Dental Council and Fleischmann* (above) the CRHP challenged as 'unduly lenient' one year's suspension of a dentist convicted of several counts of possession of indecent photographs of children. The images included some level 5 images, the most serious level on the scale used at the time which included images of sadism and bestiality. The registrant pleaded guilty and was sentenced to a community rehabilitation order for three years and banned from unsupervised access to children under 16. The court upheld the CRHP's challenge, describing it as 'manifest' that a 12-month suspension in such a case could not protect the reputation of the profession or maintain standards. The court issued some guidance on cases of internet child pornography.

3.222 In essence, *any* involvement with child pornography is illegal and morally unacceptable. While the criminal courts distinguish between degrees of seriousness, they do so for sentencing purposes. All regulators regard any conviction for child pornography as grave, being a fundamental breach of trust, and inevitably brings the profession into disrepute. Erasure will almost certainly result. In *R (Low) v General Osteopathic Council*[189] L was removed from the register, having pleaded guilty to ten specimen counts of possessing child pornography. The charges were indicative of possessing over 800 level 1 images and six level 2 images. Whilst these are at the lower end of seriousness according to the system used at the time, the quantity adds to the seriousness of the case.

3.223 If an exceptional course is taken and erasure does not result, the tribunal must provide particularly careful and clear reasons to protect public confidence in the profession. Anything less will reflect badly upon the profession, and will doubtless result in further litigation at appellate level.

Adult pornography

3.224 The position in relation to lawful adult pornography is more complex. The issue is likely to arise where pornographic material has been accessed at work. In *Council for the Regulation of Healthcare Professionals v Nursing and Midwifery Council and Truscott*[190] the High Court declined to overturn a 'lenient' five-year caution order imposed by the NMC on a nurse for accessing adult pornographic material while working in an adolescent hospital. The court deferred to the NMC tribunal's view that his conduct was not incompatible with his role as a nurse.

3.225 On the other hand, in *R (Harry) v General Medical Council*,[191] a six-month suspension order imposed by the GMC on a doctor who accessed

189 [2007] EWHC 2839 (Admin).

190 [2004] EWCA Civ 1356.

191 *R (Omboye Pax Harry) v General Medical Council* [2006] EWCA Crim 3050.

adult pornographic material while working in a single-handed practice, when no patients were present, was not considered to be too severe, despite full admissions, no repetition and good testimonials.

Sexual conduct with patients

3.226 Registrants who enter a consensual sexual relationship with a patient risk being struck off the register, since it is viewed as a breach of one of the fundamental tenets of the relationship of a health professional with his or her patients. This is particularly the case where the registrant is a psychiatrist or the patient is vulnerable. (Arguably all patients are vulnerable to some extent.)

3.227 Examples are *Dare v General Medical Council*[192] and *Wentzel v General Medical Council*.[193] In *Dare*, D, a psychiatrist, was struck off following use of 'his position of trust to establish an improper relationship'. In *Wentzel* the court reiterated the tenet that the reputation of the profession was more important than the fortunes of any individual member. W was erased from the medical register despite being an able practitioner, having been found guilty of sexually exploiting a vulnerable patient and then lying to his superiors.

3.228 A slightly more lenient approach was adopted by Collins J in *R (Bevan) v General Medical Council*,[194] commenting on the sanction of erasure imposed on a GP for having a 14-month sexual relationship with a patient whose marriage was breaking up:

> Every medical practitioner must know that a sexual relationship with a patient will almost inevitably be regarded as serious professional misconduct and will court erasure. There is always the element of a breach of trust and a concern that advantage is being taken of a vulnerable individual. This is particularly the case where a patient has any psychiatric problems and it is not in those circumstances surprising that erasure has been upheld, however harsh the penalty might seem, where a psychiatrist has entered into such a relationship with one of his patients.[195]

3.229 However, striking-off is not inevitable:

> ... sexual relations with a patient do not in my judgment automatically mean that there must be erasure, albeit they may mean that erasure will be considered as an option, and indeed perhaps even as the most probable option in most cases. But it is also in the public interest that good doctors should be able to continue in practice if that can be done consistently with the sending out of the message that particular forms of conduct will not be tolerated and the public can be satisfied that serious penalties will result.[196]

3.230 In *Bevan*, Collins J considered that testimonials, particularly from patients, were both material and important considerations in determining sanction, and indicated that a suspension order could have been imposed, although he declined to allow the appeal on this basis. By way of contrast, in *Council for the Regulation of Healthcare Professionals v General Medical*

192 [2002] UKPC 54.
193 [2004] EWHC 381 (Admin).
194 [2005] EWHC 174 (Admin).
195 At [19].
196 At [49].

Council and Leeper,[197] a case involving similar facts, an order of conditions on L's practice was considered to be too lenient.

3.231 Although in both cases the patients were considered to be vulnerable because they were going through marital breakdowns, the registrants were GPs not psychiatrists. The distinction drawn from the relative positions of power and vulnerability is a fine one and needs careful consideration by the tribunal.

3.232 In *Giele v General Medical Council*[198] Collins J replaced erasure with suspension of a surgeon who had entered into a sexual relationship with a patient, whom he later became aware was vulnerable. Once the relationship had started, the patient received no further treatment from G, although he remained on the record as her consultant. Collins J reiterated the need to maintain public confidence by:

> . . . imposing such sanction as is in all the circumstances appropriate [which included] not ending the career of a competent doctor . . . the fact that many patients and colleagues have, in the knowledge of the misconduct found, clearly indicated their views that erasure was not needed is a matter which can carry some weight in deciding how confidence can properly be maintained.[199]

3.233 In *Raschid and Fatnani v General Medical Council*[200] Laws LJ reiterated that the two principles that are especially important in cases of this kind were the preservation of public confidence in the profession and the need to give special place to the judgment of regulatory bodies. The impact on the individual can only ever be of secondary importance.

3.234 In *Yeong v General Medical Council*[201] Y challenged his 12-month suspension for impairment by way of misconduct following a sexual relationship with a former patient. He sought to rely on psychiatric evidence to suggest he was a low risk not having any disposition to engage in such relationships. Sales J dismissed the psychiatric evidence, stating that:

> The question of the possibility of a recurrence of such misconduct . . . was a matter of the ordinary assessment of likely human behaviour . . . [and] . . . is the sort of task which courts and tribunals regularly perform without needing to refer to expert psychiatric evidence.[202]

3.235 He distinguished *Cohen, Meadow* and *Azzam* because they concerned misconduct by way of clinical errors, and stated that:

> . . . the general public interest in clearly marking proper standards of behaviour for doctors in respect of relationships with their patients so as to uphold public confidence in the medical profession was by far the weightiest factor pointing in favour of the finding of impairment of fitness to practise and the sanction which was imposed.[203]

197 [2004] EWHC 1850 (Admin).
198 [2005] EWHC 2143 (Admin).
199 At para 29.
200 [2007] EWCA Civ 46, [2007] 1 WLR 1460.
201 [2009] EWHC 1923 (Admin).
202 At [38].
203 At [40].

3.236 Y's conduct had breached the fundamental rule of the doctor–patient relationship and had undermined confidence in the profession as a whole. This required a firm mark of disapproval and a declaration of the proper standards to be adhered to in order to promote public confidence.

3.237 Sales J made the point that this type of conduct is not easily remediable and the weight to be attached to remedial effort is less in this type of case:

> . . . where the conduct consists of violating such a fundamental rule of the professional relationship between medical practitioner and patient and thereby undermining public confidence in the medical profession, a finding of impairment of fitness to practise may be justified on the grounds that it is necessary to reaffirm clear standards of professional conduct so as to maintain public confidence in the practitioner and in the profession. In such a case, the efforts made by the medical practitioner in question to address his behaviour for the future may carry very much less weight than in a case where the misconduct consists of clinical errors or incompetence.[204]
>
> . . .
>
> The [FTP Panel] was entitled to conclude that Dr Yeong's case was one in which the question of remedial steps and compliance with improved practising standards for the future was of less importance than the imposition of a sanction which would convey a clear public statement of the importance with which the fundamental standard of professional conduct in relation to relationships between medical practitioners and patients is to be regarded.[205]

3.238 Contrast *Raza v General Medical Council*[206] in which R was suspended for 12 months for impairment by way of misconduct. R allegedly conducted himself inappropriately in a consultation, behaving in a sexually motivated way and abusing his position. It was submitted that the incident was in fact entirely innocent, he was of good character and there was no suggestion of predatory behaviour. The tribunal found that he had an 'underlying attitude' but did not expand upon this. HHJ Pelling QC concluded that the tribunal had not taken proper account of R's good character and record, this being a single isolated event, and the tribunal had misjudged his remedial action (ensuring that a chaperone is always present when examining female patients) in concluding it was for his benefit and not that of patients. He concluded that the tribunal had not approached its task of considering current impairment because of past misconduct in a proper fashion, nor had it provided adequate reasons.

3.239 The conclusion to draw is that cases of sexual misconduct will always attract the prospect of suspension or erasure. If there is a relationship of *particular* trust, such as that between a psychiatrist and a vulnerable patient, erasure will almost certainly result. Erasure or lengthy suspension is only likely to be prevented where there is no such relationship and, there is very strong evidence that the public interest is better served by keeping an otherwise excellent registrant in practice. Such cases are likely to be rare, and evidence from colleagues and from patients will assist the panel on a matter of such close judgment.

204 At [48].
205 At [58].
206 [2011] EWHC 790 (Admin).

Sexual motivation

3.240 A point of considerable significance is the care with which advocates must address and a tribunal must assess and explain whether any potentially sexual incident was in fact sexually motivated. While it may be that the latter appears to flow from the former, that is not always the case. Care must be taken not to elide the concept of sexual motivation with sexual assault, or to assume sexual motivation flows from conduct such as the inappropriate touching of an intimate part of the body.

3.241 The case of *Angamuthu Arunkalaivanan v General Medical Council*[207] highlights this, and the importance of properly assessing the probative value of character evidence. AA was accused of conducting a breast examination inappropriately. His conduct was said to be sexually motivated. The finding that AA's handling of the patient's breasts was inappropriate flowed from the determination of a straightforward factual dispute which required the comparison of witnesses taking account of AA's good character and credibility.

3.242 However, the issue of sexual motivation is an inference to be drawn (or not) following determination of the facts. The tribunal appeared to elide their finding of fact with the issue of sexual motivation. It did not take account of AA's character in deciding whether the facts found proved were sexually motivated, or were the result of an insensitive, clumsy and poorly executed examination. The latter may well leave the patent feeling ill-treated or even violated, but it is not a sexually motivated act. On appeal, the facts remained as proved, but the finding of sexual motivation was quashed.

Dishonesty

3.243 All the regulators covered in this book require registrants to be honest and trustworthy. Any matter of dishonesty is regarded as particularly serious, since it is seen to undermine trust in the profession concerned, regardless of whether it leads to direct patient harm. This was made clear in *Dey v General Medical Council*:[208]

> . . . health authorities must be able to place complete reliance on the integrity of practitioners; and the Committee is entitled to regard conduct which undermines that confidence as calculated to reflect on the standards and reputation of the profession.

See also *R (Rogers) v General Medical Council*[209] above.

3.244 Despite the importance of honesty in all healthcare practice and/or the seriousness with which dishonesty is viewed, it is a topic over which there has been uncertainty for several years. For example – Which test defines dishonesty? Who should we measure any conduct against? Should dishonesty always be visited with sanctions at the upper end of the scale?

207 [2014] EWHC 873 (Admin).
208 [2001] UKPC 44 at para 13.
209 [2004] EWHC 424 (Admin).

3.245 The question of sanction is dealt with below (see para 3.275 onwards). Suffice to say that there is a growing line of authority to support the notion of a scale of dishonesty, and a far more nuanced approach to sanction.

3.246 The test for dishonesty and by whose conduct and ideals this is measured is a more complicated issue. The recent case of *Ivey v Genting Casinos (UK) Ltd t/a Crockfords*[210] has had a profound impact on both, and may finally have brought some clarity.

3.247 Although the Supreme Court was not invited to redefine dishonesty and its pronouncement is arguably obiter there is no doubt that it will be adopted (see comments by Sir Brian Leveson in *DPP v Patterson*[211]). It is in effect a response to Mostyn J's ruling in *Kirschner v General Dental Council*[212] that:

> In my opinion there should be but one test for dishonesty in all civil proceedings, whatever their nature. That test should be as propounded by the Privy Council in Barlow Clowes . . .[213]

3.248 Most recently in *General Medical Council v Krishnan*[214] HHJ Sycamore held that the test as set out in *Ivey* applied to regulatory proceedings.

A short history

3.249 For many years a debate existed over which test applied in regulatory proceedings – the test from *Twinsectra Ltd v Yardley and others*[215] or that from *R v Ghosh.*[216] The *Twinsectra* test changed over time to an objective test. Although it was said that this change did not apply to regulatory proceedings (see *Bryant v Law Society*[217] and *Bultitude v Law Society*[218]), this view was rejected by Mostyn J in *Kirschner* (above).

Twinsectra and Royal Brunei Airlines Sdn Bhd v Tan[219]

3.250 *Twinsectra* involved the liability of a trustee for the wrongful acts of a third party (accessory liability) a central issue being whether the trustee had been dishonest in 'shutting his eyes' to what was occurring. At first instance, Carnworth J held that the trustee was misguided but not dishonest. That decision was finally upheld by the House of Lords, whose members analysed the meaning of dishonesty as explained by Lord Nicholls in *Royal Brunei Airlines.* Lords Steyn Hoffmann and Hutton concluded that dishonesty required a subjective element. Lord Slynn was less clear, but also appeared to accept elements of a subjective test. Lord Millett concluded that the test for dishonesty was objective.

3.251 In his reasons Lord Hoffmann said:

210 [2017] UKSC 67.
211 [2017] EWHC 2820 (Admin).
212 [2015] EWHC 1377 (Admin).
213 At [19].
214 [2017] EWHC 2892 (Admin).
215 [2002] UKHL 12.
216 [1982] QB 1053.
217 [2007] EWHC 3043 (Admin).
218 [2004] EWCA Civ 1853.
219 [1995] 2 AC 378, PC.

> I consider that [the principles laid down in Royal Brunei Airlines] require a dishonest state of mind, that is to say, consciousness that one is transgressing ordinary standards of honest behaviour.[220]

3.252 Lord Hutton observed that that *Royal Brunei Airlines* did not impose a purely objective test since Lord Nicholl stated that honesty has a 'strong subjective element to it and it [refers to conduct] assessed in the light of what a person actually knew at the time [as opposed to what the reasonable man may know]'. Lord Hutton said that 'carelessness is not dishonesty'; furthermore, he considered that the objective/subjective two-stage test was appropriate. In contrast, Lord Millett concluded that accessory liability was strict albeit he said ' account must be taken of subjective considerations such as the defendant's experience and intelligence and his actual state of knowledge'. Lord Steyn and Lord Slynn's judgment add little, save that both appear to confirm a subjective element.

3.253 The clear majority decision in *Twinsectra* appears to be that proof of dishonesty required proof of both an objective and a subjective element.

Ghosh

3.254 Despite the existence of *Twinsectra,* determining whether a registrant acted dishonestly, has more often entailed tribunals adopting the test of dishonesty from *R v Ghosh*. The test being adapted for use in regulatory proceedings thus:

> If the tribunal is satisfied on the balance of probabilities that the registrant acted as alleged, the next question is whether the registrant was acting dishonestly. To resolve that issue it will need to consider two questions:
>
> Q1) Is the tribunal satisfied on the balance of probability that what the registrant did was dishonest by the ordinary standards of reasonable and honest people? It is for the tribunal to decide what those standards are and to apply them to this question.
>
> If the tribunal is not so satisfied, that is an end to the issue. If, it is satisfied it should move to the second question.
>
> Q2) Is the tribunal satisfied on the balance of probability that the registrant realised what he was doing was dishonest by those standards?
>
> If the tribunal is so satisfied it will find that he was dishonest, whether the registrant personally regarded it as dishonest or not.

3.255 For several years there was much debate as to whether the *Ghosh* test should be used in regulatory proceedings at all. The debate was started by Singh J in *Uddin v General Medical Council*[221] and continued with Patterson J in *Mills v GDC,*[222] both of whom suggested that a more 'nuanced' approach should be adopted. Unfortunately, neither explained what the nuances may be, other than the obvious point that a full direction for dishonesty is not needed in all cases. It is irrelevant when the issue is whether a defendant is responsible for an obviously dishonest act (eg stealing a handbag). The same may be said of regulatory proceedings. No one would argue that stealing medicine from a hospital or entering

220 At [20].
221 [2012] EWHC 2669 (Admin).
222 [2014] EWHC 89 (Admin).

misleading data in a clinical record is 'wrong'. The issue is not dishonesty but, in the first case 'did the registrant take it?' and in the second, did he deliberately enter the information with the intention to mislead or was he simply mistaken?' Neither example requires a dishonesty direction. The turmoil continued in cases that followed, such as *Fabiyi v NMC*[223] and *Sharma v GMC*.[224]

Barlow Clowes

3.256 The next important case in this short history is *Barlow Clowes International Ltd v Eurotrust International Ltd*[225] in which C operated various fraudulent investment schemes through his company BCI Ltd. The case involved the issue of whether companies and individuals through whom C and BCI Ltd operated their fraudulent transactions knew or closed their minds to the obvious fact that the transactions were dishonest and were thus dishonest themselves.

3.257 In the advice from the Board, Lord Hoffmann observed that:

> The judge stated the law in terms largely derived from . . . *Royal Brunei Airlines* . . .. [namely] that liability for dishonest assistance requires a dishonest state of mind . . . [which] may consist in knowledge that the transaction is [dishonest, eg misappropriation of other people's money], or it may consist in suspicion combined with a conscious decision not to make inquiries which might result in knowledge: see *Manifest Shipping Co Ltd v Uni-Polaris Insurance Co Ltd*.[226] Although a dishonest state of mind is a subjective mental state, the standard by which the law determines whether it is dishonest is objective. If by ordinary standards a defendant's mental state would be characterised as dishonest, it is irrelevant that the defendant judges by different standards. The Court of Appeal held this to be a correct state of the law and their Lordships agree[227] [emphasis added].

3.258 Lord Hoffmann referred to the above quotes from *Royal Brunei* and strongly affirmed that, despite what they appear to say, they did not support the two-stage dishonesty test. They simply meant that *a person only had to know they were participating in an act that was contrary to normal acceptable standards, not whether he agreed with those standards.*

3.259 As Mostyn J put it in *Kirschner*:

> Under the *Barlow Clowes* test the only relevant mental state of a defendant accused of dishonesty in civil proceedings is his or her knowledge. Once the knowledge of the defendant has been established it is then for the tribunal to act as the 'spokesman of the fair and reasonable man . . .' and to determine if the defendant, possessed of that knowledge, and having engaged in the transactions in question, was dishonest by ordinary standards.[228]

223 [2012] EWHC 1441 (Admin).

224 [2014] EWHC 1471 (Admin).

225 [2005] UKPC 37.

226 [2003] 1 AC 469.

227 At [10].

228 At [20].

Ivey v Genting Casinos

3.260 *Ivey v Genting Casinos*[229] involved an allegation of cheating at cards. I employed two methods to operate his 'sting'. First, with the help of an accomplice he persuaded the casino's croupier to rotate cards depending on whether they were 'good' or 'bad' on the pretext that this was a superstition. In fact, it referred to the card-number, and was thus relevant to the odds of winning or losing the game. Once rotated, I could keep track of the good and bad cards by skilled observation of the miniscule differences in the pattern on the back of the cards. This is called 'edge-sorting'. The employee had no idea that the rotation actually enabled I to identify the cards and so swing the odds in his favour. He 'won' £7.7 million, but the casino refused to pay and accused him of cheating. I firmly asserted that he did not think he had cheated, that he had merely used a known legitimate technique.

3.261 At first instance, on appeal and finally in the Supreme Court I was found to have cheated. In its judgment, the Supreme Court said 'the question which matters is not whether [I] thought of it as cheating but whether in fact and in law it was'.[230] The court then set about debating the ingredients of cheating and whether this included an element of dishonesty.

3.262 Lord Hughes, who gave the judgment of the court, observed that: 'Although the majority of cheating will involve something the ordinary person (or juror) would describe as dishonest, this is not invariably so.'[231] While His Lordship's examples were not entirely convincing, having made the assertion he then went on to consider the deception played on the croupier. Persuading her to do something for the apparently innocuous reason of satisfying I's superstition when it was in fact integral to his sting was in his view dishonest, unless it did not satisfy the second limb of the *Ghosh* test. However, rather than settle this question, the court set about dismantling the validity of the *Ghosh* test. Again, some of the reasoning is rather theoretical. For example, it was suggested that the more dubious and 'warped' the defendant's beliefs are the less likely a jury is to find him dishonest. If through his own warped ideas a defendant does not recognise what others view as dishonest, he could not be dishonest under the second limb of *Ghosh*. His Lordship described it thus:

> The principal objection to the second leg of the *Ghosh* test is that the less the defendant's standards conform to what society in general expects, the less likely he is to be held criminally responsible for his behaviour.[232]

It has to be said that it has little if anything to do with the reality of the modern criminal court.

3.263 His Lordship observed that in *Ghosh* the two-part test was used 'to preserve the principle that criminal responsibility for dishonesty must depend on the actual state of mind of the defendant', however this was entirely unnecessary. The example used in *Ghosh* was of the foreign man believing public transport was free and thus not paying his fare. However,

229 [2017] UKSC 67.

230 At [27].

231 At [45].

232 At [58].

such a person would be innocent under the first limb, let alone the second, because:

> . . . in order to determine the honesty or otherwise of a person's conduct, one must ask what he knew or believed about the facts affecting the area of activity in which he was engaging. [To decide whether the traveller] was dishonest by the standards of ordinary people, it would be necessary to establish his own actual state of knowledge . . . Because he genuinely believes that public transport is free, there is nothing objectively dishonest about his not paying . . .

He continued:

> . . . . [dishonestly is intended] to characterise what the defendant did, but in characterising it one must first ascertain his actual state of mind as to the facts in which he did it. It was not correct to postulate that the conventional objective test of dishonesty involves judging only the actions and not the state of knowledge or belief as to the facts in which they were performed. What is objectively judged is the standard of behaviour, given any known actual state of mind of the actor as to the facts.[233]

3.264 *Ivey v Genting* thus settles two points. One, the second limb of *Ghosh* is no longer applicable. Two, the measure of *dishonesty* is objective and involves assessing what the defendant/registrant did in the light of his or her genuine state of mind. The traveller is not guilty of evading his fare because, although he did not pay, he genuinely believed he did not have to. Objectively, he was innocent of any dishonesty.

3.265 Far from removing subjective considerations from dishonesty, *Ivey v Genting* confirms them, but establishes them as applicable to the defendant/registrant's knowledge of the facts and not his or her knowledge of what others may think.

3.266 The battleground in dishonesty is thus likely to be whether the defendant/registrant genuinely held the belief. This places it alongside mistake of fact and/or self-defence. A genuine mistake of fact is in many cases a defence. In the latter, a jury routinely applies a two-stage test namely what are the facts as the defendant believed them to be and, assuming such facts, was his response objectively reasonable.

3.267 As Mostyn J put it in *Kirschner:*

> Under the *Barlow Clowes* test the only relevant mental state of a defendant accused of dishonesty in civil proceedings is his or her knowledge. Once the knowledge of the defendant has been established it is then for the tribunal to act as the 'spokesman of the fair and reasonable man . . .' and to determine if the defendant, possessed of that knowledge, and having engaged in the transactions in question, was dishonest by ordinary standards.[234]

Whose dishonesty is it anyway?

3.268 This area of controversy has also been swept aside by *Ivey v Genting*. It arose from the case of *Hussain v General Medical Council*[235] in which

233 At [60].
234 At [20].
235 [2014] EWCA Civ 2246.

Longmore LJ suggested obiter that the objective part of the *Ghosh* test should be altered to be an assessment of the standards of 'reasonable and honest doctors' as opposed to people. He gave little explanation for this, and it opened the way for argument and confusion over whether the standard varied as between registrants and who would be the measure thereof. That said, it cannot seriously be suggested that the standards of honest registrants are or ought to be different to that of honest people. Nor would it be right to suggest that the test is applied by tribunals without consideration of any professional context.

3.269 Unfortunately, Longmore J's obiter suggestion gained some traction in comments such as those of Popplewell J in *Professional Standards Authority v Health and Care Professions Council and David*[236] who mentioned 'a more limited cohort of professionals from whom the [registrant] comes'. It was, however, rejected in *Dowson v GMC*[237] and again in *R v Hayes.*[238] In *Hayes* the Court of Appeal said the measure of *objective* dishonesty is that of the reasonable honest person observing that:

> Not only is there is no authority for the proposition that objective standards of honesty are to be set by a market, but such a principle would gravely affect the proper conduct of business . . . [From] time to time, markets adopt patterns of behaviour which are dishonest by the standards of honest and reasonable people . . . [abandoning ordinary standards of honesty and damaging the market] . . . Therefore, to depart from the view that standards of honesty are determined by the standards of ordinary reasonable and honest people is not only unsupported by authority, but would undermine the maintenance of ordinary standards of honesty and integrity that are essential to the conduct of business and markets.

3.270 While the above comments were made in the criminal jurisdiction and refer to the financial markets, where the public may well feel that brokers have behaved and continue to behave dishonestly, they are of direct relevance to regulatory proceedings and the objective dishonesty test.

3.271 While the supposed modification may be thought to apply to the regulatory version of *Twinsectra,* Mostyn J firmly trounced that idea in *Kirschner* thus:

> Ordinary standards mean general ordinary standards and not the standards of the class or cohort from which the defendant happens to come, although it is hard to see that they would or could be different. In neither of *Twinsectra* nor *Barlow Clowes* was this tweak to the objective test suggested and neither could it be inferred. In the former case the defendant was a solicitor but he was judged by general ordinary standards.[239]

3.272 The comments in *Kirschner* are important since they forewarn of the point made by Lord Hughes in *Ivey v Genting* that 'the question whether his conduct was honest or dishonest is to be determined by the fact-finder by applying the (objective) standards of ordinary decent people'.[240]

236 [2014] EWHC 4657 (Admin).
237 [2015] EWHC 3379 (Admin).
238 [2015] EWCA Crim 1944.
239 At [20].
240 At [74].

3.273 There can be no doubt that the suggestion first floated in *Hussain* does not apply to the new test and has also been consigned to history by *Ivey v Geuting* where it should remain.

The new dishonesty test

3.274 The test in dishonesty is thus now:

1) What is the defendant/registrant's *genuine state of mind* regarding his or her act?
   This is a subjective test and will be determined by an analysis of whether the belief is held not an analysis of whether the belief is reasonable. However, the reasonableness of the belief will affect whether the tribunal or a jury find it was genuinely held or not.
2) Was the defendant/registrant's act *in the light of that state of mind* dishonest according to the standards of *ordinary decent people?*
   This is the objective assessment of the act done with the above state of mind.

Both questions are to be answered on the balance of probability.

Sanctions in dishonesty cases

3.275 Notwithstanding the concern with which dishonesty is examined, research by Policis for the Professional Standards Authority – *Dishonest behaviour by health and care professionals* (2016) – suggests that there may be a mismatch between the view of regulators compared to registrants and the public. This may require a more nuanced approach to the way dishonesty cases are presented and disposed of.

3.276 As may be expected, where there is premeditated, systemic or long-term dishonesty, or a fundamental betrayal of patient trust, regulators, registrants and the public expect the guilty party to be excluded from the relevant profession to maintain public confidence therein. This is particularly the case where there is an identifiable victim of misconduct, or a vulnerable patient. However, in contrast to regulators, where there is no identifiable or immediate victim, the public and registrants are more likely to focus on rehabilitation, improving insight and the managed continuation of practice. In addition, where there is a culture of inappropriate tolerance, neither the public nor registrants wished to see individuals being targeted of scapegoated.

3.277 The report tentatively suggests that a more nuanced approach may be appropriate in cases of dishonesty. This might focus on issues such as whether the dishonest conduct was in the registrant's professional or private life, whether it involves a risk to the standing of the profession, the degree of that risk and whether it can be managed. This latter point would involve the familiar ground of the registrant demonstrating insight or the capacity for insight and thus whether they can be rehabilitated.

3.278 The issue of whether someone is a scapegoat is perhaps more difficult to deal with, since regulatory proceedings, once they are set in motion, are a blunt instrument. Nonetheless, proportionality in sanction is a well-known principle and a sanction should not be increased to pander to public demand or to make an example of a registrant or for a regulator to prove it is 'doing something'. Support for this may be found in *Royal College of Veterinary Surgeons v Samuel*[241] in which the Privy Council considered the question whether 'behaviour remote from . . . professional practice may be sufficiently disgraceful to constitute serious professional misconduct'.

3.279 S was convicted of assault and theft as part of a dispute with a neighbour and was thereafter removed from the register on the basis of protecting the reputation of the profession. The Privy Council clearly distinguished between 'the public' as being measured by ill-informed tabloid/online opinion or reaction and the *fully* informed, open-minded individual. The Privy Council concluded that the latter would not lose confidence in the profession since S's conduct had little material impact on S's fitness to practise.

3.280 The above was revisited in *R (Pitt and Tyas) v General Pharmaceutical Council*[242] in which a challenge was raised to the 2017 GPhC *Standards for pharmacy professionals* which are said to apply 'at all times, not just in working hours [because] the attitudes and behaviours or professionals outside of work can affect [public trust and confidence'. The standards require 'appropriate' behaviour, including being polite and considerate, honest, empathetic, respectful and so on. The standards were challenged as intrusive and uncertain.

3.281 Singh J rejected the challenge observing that the standards were 'intended to guide' in a practical sense, and provided examples of appropriate conduct. They did not enlarge the meaning of misconduct. He commented:

> . . . there may be occasions which occur outside normal working hours and perhaps in a context which is completely unrelated to the professional work of a pharmacist which may be relevant to the safe and effective care which will be provided to patients. For example, if a pharmacy professional engages in a racist tirade on Twitter, that may well shed light on how he or she might provide professional services to a person from an ethnic minority.

3.282 The conduct of registrants in their private lives is clearly within the scope of the interim order tribunal or FTP tribunal. However, it is incumbent on any tribunal to carefully consider and equally carefully articulate if, how and why any such conduct impacts upon patient safety or the wider public interest.

3.283 The impact of *Ivey v Genting Casinos* (above) is also a factor to consider. The familiar authorities on sanction in cases of dishonesty emerged during the life of the two-stage (*Ghosh*) dishonesty test. It is arguable that the altered test may catch registrants who would not have been regarded as dishonest when those authorities emerged. Furthermore, some have argued that the single stage objective test is less of a hurdle and as such may catch less-serious behaviour. If that is right, is it fair for the sanctions drawn under the rigours of the old test to be applied to less-serious misconduct? The contrary simplistic argument is 'dishonesty is dishonesty' and a registrant found guilty of dishonesty should receive a severe sanction.

241 [2014] UKPC 13.
242 [2017] EWHC 809 (Admin).

Such a blunt approach may cause unfair damage to a registrant and/or deprive the public of someone who is capable of reform and upon whom such a sanction would not until very recently be passed. How this pans out remains to be seen but there will doubtless be arguments raised on this very topic.

3.284 That there may well be an impact is made plain by Mostyn J in *Kerschner* above, where he refers to the test for dishonesty in *Barlow Clowes* which *Ivey v Genting* confirms is the correct test:

> . . . if the *Barlow Clowes* test were adopted for disciplinary proceedings, as I think it ought to be, the tribunal may conclude on the evidence that a defendant accused of dishonesty was actually aware that he was doing wrong; but such a finding would not be necessary to establish dishonesty. The presence or absence of such awareness would however be highly relevant in the sanctions phase of the proceedings.[243]

His Lordship plainly envisages a distinction between those who are caught under the new regime but might have escaped censure under the old test.

3.285 Dishonesty cases are wide-ranging and include conduct both inside and outside the workplace, such as:

- conviction for an offence of dishonesty such as theft;
- defrauding a regulator, employer, colleague, patient or other person. Examples include working in two jobs without declaring this; working while on sick leave; or seeing patients privately without informing the employer / service provider;
- submitting a false reference or including false information on a CV or application form;
- plagiarism or cheating in order to obtain a qualification;
- research misconduct such as presenting misleading information in publications and dishonesty in clinical drug trials;
- failure to disclose to the regulatory body or an employer criminal convictions or cautions; and
- improperly amending or changing the details on patient records.

3.286 *Bolton v Law Society*[244] is the starting-point in any case of dishonesty. B, a newly qualified solicitor, mishandled money in a client account. He admitted his misconduct and the money was repaid. The Solicitors Disciplinary Tribunal found that B was 'an honest man' and that his conduct was naïve and foolish rather than premeditated or deliberate. Although such conduct would normally be regarded as so very serious as to merit being struck off, in the circumstances the appropriate penalty was the more lenient order of suspension. In the leading judgment, Lord Bingham stated that:

> Any solicitor who is shown to have discharged his professional duties with anything less than complete integrity, probity and trustworthiness must expect severe sanctions to be imposed upon him . . . Lapses from the required high standard may of course take different forms and be of varying degrees. The most serious involves proven dishonesty, whether or not leading to criminal proceedings or penalties. In such cases the Tribunal has almost invariably, no matter how strong the mitigation advanced by the solicitor,

243 At [21].

244 [1994] 1 WLR 512, [1993] EWCA Civ 32.

> order that he be struck off the role of solicitors . . . If a solicitor is not shown to have acted dishonestly, but is shown to have fallen below the required standards of integrity, probity and trustworthiness, his lapse is less serious but it remains very serious indeed in a member of a profession whose reputation depends upon trust. A striking off order will not necessarily follow in such a case, but it may well. The decision whether to strike off or to suspend will often involve a fine and difficult exercise of judgment, to be made by the tribunal as an informed and expert body on all the facts of the case. Only in a very unusual and venial case of this kind would the tribunal be likely to regard as appropriate any order less severe than one of suspension.[245]

3.287 As is stated elsewhere, the comment is made in *Bolton* that the profession is more important than the individual. The approach in *Bolton* means that insight, mitigating evidence, testimonials, evidence that the registrant has learned his or her lesson and the consequences of a sanction on the registrant, are considered to be of limited weight in cases involving integrity. (The same reasoning applies to cases of sexual misconduct.)

3.288 This was affirmed in *Law Society v Salsbury*,[246] albeit with the qualification that the human rights of the registrant under Articles 6 and 8 of the ECHR must also be taken into account. See also the Court of Appeal case of *Solicitors Regulation Authority v Dennison*.[247]

3.289 The Law Society cases have been repeatedly applied to health professionals – see, for example, *Gupta v General Medical Council*[248] in which the Privy Council upheld the GMC's decision to strike off G who had permitted her husband to continue to practise despite his being struck off at an earlier date. There was no concern about G's clinical practise and it was accepted that she was doing important work in her community and had support from her patients. Referring to *Bolton*, the Privy Council considered that upholding the reputation of the profession was more important than the consequences for the individual.

3.290 While erasure is not necessary and/or inevitable in every case of dishonesty, a lesser sanction is only likely to be imposed where there is compelling evidence of insight, that the dishonesty in question was out of character or isolated in its duration or range and that permitting the registrant to return to practice would not damage the reputation of the profession: see *Atkinson v General Medical Council*.[249] In *General Medical Council v Theodoropoulos*[250] it was reiterated that a tribunal should carefully assess issues of foresight, planning and seriousness in assessing whether dishonest events are truly isolated and whether insight and remediation are possible let alone whether they are likely. To gain employment T changed his entry on the medical register to falsely show that he had a licence to practise when he did not. He did not attend the tribunal hearing but in written submissions he denied any wrongdoing asserting that the change was an error by GMC staff. The tribunal found this to be a serious act of dishonesty breaching a fundamental tenet of the profession but

245 At p518B–E.
246 [2008] EWCA Civ 1285, [2009] 1 WLR 1286.
247 [2012] EWCA Civ 421.
248 [2001] UKPC 61, [2002] 1 WLR 1691.
249 [2009] EWHC 3636 (Admin), at [13].
250 [2017] EWHC 1984 (Admin).

described it as an isolated incident in a non-clinical setting. It commented that it had no evidence of remediation or insight but neither did it have any evidence to suggest T was incapable of developing the same. He was thus suspended. On appeal, T was erased from the register. Lewis J commented that T's conduct did indeed breach a fundamental tenet and adversely affected the integrity of the system for job applications designed to protect the public. He rejected the reasons given for not erasing (isolated incident, non-clinical setting, no evidence to show T could not gain insight) and concluded that T's conduct was fundamentally incompatible with registration. It was not an isolated incident but a course of conduct requiring forethought and planning. It was calculated, deliberate and undermined the trust in the profession. It did not need to be in a clinical setting to merit erasure. He concluded that since the tribunal had failed to recognise the gravity of the misconduct and in the absence of any insight or remediation erasure was the proper sanction. In addition, there is merit in not depriving the public of an otherwise honest and competent practitioner – an argument highlighted previously and below.

3.291 If a registrant fails to attend the hearing or demonstrate insight and remorse or assure the tribunal that there will be no repetition, then he or she forfeits the small chance of persuading the tribunal to adopt a more lenient sanction: *Parkinson v Nursing and Midwifery Council*.[251] (See also the discussion on 'Insight' above at para 3.163 and cases such as *Kimmance v General Medical Council* above at para 3.196.[252])

3.292 That should be balanced with the following comments by Collins J in *Council for the Regulation of Healthcare Professionals v General Medical Council and Southall*:[253]

> Absence of remorse and contrition is likely to be indicative of a lack of insight or of maintenance of unreasonable views. In either event, it may show that a risk of repetition exists. This is clearly relevant in deciding on the appropriate sanction. But lack of remorse should not result in a higher sanction as punishment. Punishment may be an inevitable effect of whatever sanction is imposed but it must not be an element in deciding what is the appropriate sanction.

3.293 In non-dishonesty cases, different considerations may apply between health professionals and solicitors. The loss to the profession of a competent and well-respected professional who presents no danger to the public is a factor that can be taken into account – see *Bijl v General Medical Council*.[254] However, following comments by Ousely J in *General Medical Council v Bawa-Garba*[255] care must be exercised in placing reliance on the familiar comment from *Bijl*. The principle from *Bijl* is undoubtedly correct but in essence it is really a re-statement of the need for proportionality in sanction (see para 3.121 above). In *Southall*[256] it was stated that:

251 [2010] EWHC 1898 (Admin), per Mitting J at [18].

252 [2016] EWHC 1808 (Admin).

253 [2005] EWHC 579 (Admin) at [30].

254 [2001] UKPC 42.

255 [2018] EWHC 76 (Admin).

256 [2005] EWHC 579 (Admin) at para 13.

> It is clearly in the public interest that doctors who are competent and for whose skills many patients and colleagues have nothing but praise should not be precluded from practice altogether if that can be achieved with no danger to the public and with no damage to the reputation of the profession. So much was made clear by the Privy Council in *Bijl v General Medical Council* . . .
>
> It follows that in my view testimonials can in the case of doctors be accorded greater weight than in the case of solicitors. The requirement of absolute honesty so that there can be absolute trust in a solicitor is obviously of paramount importance. That he may be a good solicitor is obviously something to be taken into account, but the -public interest in him being able to continue to practise is not so important. Thus testimonials which establish that a doctor is, in the view of eminent colleagues and of nursing staff who have worked with him, one who is not only competent but whose loss to the profession and to his potential patients would be serious indeed can, in my opinion, be accorded substantial weight.

3.294 The *Southall* case arguably included elements of dishonesty since S, an eminent paediatrician, provided a misleading and incomplete report, including statistical evidence upon sudden cot-deaths, in a murder trial based on inadequate material and without himself being a statistician. He was found to have been guilty of serious professional misconduct, including irresponsible and misleading conduct. The tribunal found that although he had not intended to mislead, his misguided insistence as to the correctness of his statistical evidence was 'disturbing and serious'.

3.295 See also similar comments by Collins J in *Giele v General Medical Council* (at para 3.232 above), a case involving an inappropriate sexual relationship. Notably the court was able to take account of the many patients and colleagues who, with knowledge of the misconduct, indicated that erasure was not needed. While this is more the exception than the rule, the case demonstrates the balance between upholding standards and not depriving the public of competent registrants unnecessarily.

3.296 In *Brennan v Health Professions Council* (at para 3.158 above) Ouseley J provided useful guidance on cases where the principal reason for sanction is the reputation of the profession. A very careful balancing exercise is required, and careful consideration would be needed regarding necessity and proportionality.

3.297 From the above it is clear that in appropriate cases a lesser sanction may be imposed. *R (James) v Nursing and Midwifery Council*[257] is a rare example of the courts accepting that cautioning a registrant can be an appropriate sanction in some dishonesty cases. J pleaded guilty to possession of criminal property obtained by her husband (a non-work related dishonesty offence). Despite evidence that J had excellent nursing qualities and capabilities, the NMC struck her off. The High Court granted her appeal and remitted the case back to the NMC due to inadequate reasoning. In so doing, the High Court noted that the NMC appeared not to have taken into account character and mitigation evidence. In relation to sanction Holman J stated that while there were considerable arguments both for and against striking off, 'it seems to me that this is a case that required very definite step by step consideration of the sanction of caution and

257 [2008] EWHC 365 (Admin).

suspension', and furthermore that there were 'considerable arguments in favour of each of the alternative lesser penalties of caution or suspension'.

3.298 In *Nicholas-Pillai v General Medical Council*,[258] a case in which NP contested critical allegations of dishonest note-keeping, Mitting J made the important point that:

> In the ordinary case such as this, the attitude of the practitioner to the events which give rise to the specific allegations against him is, in principle, something which can be taken into account either in his favour or against him by the panel, both at the stage when it considers whether his fitness to practise is impaired, and at the stage of determining what sanction should be imposed upon him.[259]

3.299 From this it is plain that an early plea and acceptance of a case may precipitate a reduced sanction. Contesting a matter throughout may result in a higher sanction, since the tribunal may conclude that there is no insight, no remorse and no room for leniency.

3.300 The sanctions guidelines do not set specific tariffs to be imposed in dishonesty cases. Tribunals have the full range of sanctions available to them. The need to distinguish between serious and less serious cases, the emphasis on early admissions and insight, the public interest in retaining good and competent health professionals where there is no likelihood of repetition suggests that erasure should not just become the norm for dishonesty.

3.301 Each case must be very carefully considered, and tribunals may, and in appropriate cases should, consider and impose lesser sanctions. That such a course may be exceptional is no reason to do otherwise when the case requires it.

3.302 *Jerry v Nursing and Midwifery Council*[260] is a salutary reminder of the consequence of dishonestly covering up an error such as failing to properly record information which of itself might not merit proceedings let alone sanction. J was struck off for exactly such dishonesty it being 'fundamentally incompatible' with registration.

3.303 There is also the spectre of the Professional Standards Authority acting when a sanction is considered to be unduly lenient. In *Professional Standards Authority v Health and Care Professionals Council and Ajeneye*[261] a caution order was regarded as such where A provided false references for two acquaintances enabling them to obtain paid employment for which they were unqualified. This caused harm to one patient and risked harm to others. The seriousness was compounded by A's attempt to blame others in the contested tribunal hearing. Following the ruling of undue leniency, the PSA, HCPC and A agreed to his being suspended for three months. This was reviewed and resulted in a further three-month suspension. Many would consider him lucky to remain on the register at all.

258 [2009] EWHC 1048 (Admin).

259 At para 19.

260 [2016] EWHC 681 (Admin).

261 [2016] EWHC 1237 (Admin).

3.304 *PSA v Silva and The Nursing and Midwifery Council*[262] involves undue leniency from the perspective of a deficiency in the charges. S failed to report instances of abuse alleged by elderly patients. This was found to be misconduct but did not result in a finding of current impairment. The PSA challenged that finding on the basis of a serious procedural irregularity, namely the failure to bring charges concerning S's reasons and motivation for failing to report the abuse which would allow the tribunal to consider these matters.

3.305 In contrast to the above, in *Professional Standards Authority for Health and Social Care v Nursing and Midwifery Council and SM*[263] the court upheld a finding of no impairment in circumstances not unlike that of *Jerry v Nursing and Midwifery Council* above. SM dishonestly attempted to cover up a medication error by failing to report her error, destroying two vials of morphine, making an incorrect entry in the controlled drug book and forging a colleague's signature. When interviewed, S admitted the above. She was demoted and given a written warning by her employer who nonetheless supported her continued practice as a good and competent nurse. The NMC's CCC noted this was a single incident in a long and unblemished career; it found that she had full insight and had undertaken appropriate remediation. The CCC placed considerable weight upon two reflective statements and SM's 'honest and candid oral evidence'. It also noted that she had suffered relevant health issues (depression) at the time. As a result of all the above, the CCC concluded that SM was not impaired.

3.306 The PSA appealed on the basis that the finding did not meet the public interest objective, either in protecting the public or in maintaining confidence in the profession.

3.307 The court reaffirmed the principle that not every finding of misconduct will result in a finding of current impairment. An isolated incident, unlikely to recur, where there is full admission or reparation and full insight may in appropriate cases mean that a registrant is not current impaired. The court observed that:

> We do not agree with the submission that a perceived need for a penalty means that a finding of current impairment must be made. Whether to make such a finding is a discrete exercise to be addressed on its merits. In any event, in the circumstances of the present case, we would echo the comments of the learned judge in *Uppal* to the effect that professional standards and public confidence have been upheld by a rigorous regulatory process which resulted in a finding of misconduct.[264]

3.308 The reference to *Uppal* is important, since in that case the court rejected the suggestion that a finding of dishonesty necessitated a finding of impairment: 'even in cases of dishonesty, a separate assessment of impairment is required, and not every act of dishonesty results in impairment' (*Professional Standards Authority for Health and Social Care v GMC and Uppal*).[265] A finding of no current impairment was upheld in circumstances of an 'isolated lapse' in a blameless career with little chance of

262 [2016] EWHC 754 (Admin).
263 [2017] CSIH 29.
264 At [30].
265 [2015] EWHC 1304 (Admin).

repetition. The important point was made that there had been a 'rigorous disciplinary assessment of [U's] fitness to practise, resulting in a finding of misconduct on her record, with the option of a warning by way of sanction'.

3.309 While warnings may not always be available without a finding of impairment the fact of proceedings and the fact of a judicial finding on the facts should both to be regarded as protective measures to both the public and the public interest in appropriate cases. The comments by Cox J in *Council for Healthcare Regulatory Excellence v Nursing and Midwifery Council and another*[266] are important namely, that when assessing current impairment, a committee should consider the future risk to patients and whether standards or public confidence would be undermined if a finding of impairment were not made. However, this should not be read as meaning an adverse finding in the facts that a finding of impairment necessarily follows.

3.310 The need for some regulators to adjust their approach to dishonesty cases is made plain in *Lusinga v Nursing and Midwifery Council*[267] in which Kerr J expressed the hope that:

> . . . the Indicative Sanctions Guidance will be looked at again in the light of this judgment. The guidance does not differentiate between different forms of dishonesty, and takes one of the most serious forms of dishonesty (fraudulent financial gain) as the paradigm, without alluding to the possibility that dishonest conduct can take various forms; some criminal, some not; some destroying trust instantly, others merely undermining it to a greater or lesser extent . . .[268]
>
> The guidance, in my respectful opinion, needs to be more nuanced in that respect. It should not lump the thief and the fraudster together with the mere contract-breaker.[269]

3.311 L faced an allegation that he i) did not inform his employer that he was undertaking additional work and ii) this was 'dishonest in that he sought to conceal' his additional work from his employer. L, who was represented, admitted the above, but when asked to explain his dishonesty, it was clear he denied it. The tribunal vacated his plea on the basis of confusion, but then seemed to blame him for the error. They subsequently found the case proved and struck him off.

3.312 Kerr J criticised the charge as being entirely uncertain. He noted that it may be plain in straightforward cases of theft, forging prescriptions or working while claiming sick pay but here the dishonesty was said to be 'not seeking permission to do [lawful work permission for which] could not be unreasonably withheld'. Kerr J noted that the fault for the confusion was not L's, he had maintained his version of events. The fault was in the poorly drafted charge.

3.313 In addition, he observed that:

> . . . on the scale of dishonesty, this was at the very bottom end. There was concealment but not active deception. There was no ill-gotten financial gain nor an attempt at one. Mr Lusinga was merely 'moonlighting' [furthermore]

266 [2011] EWHC 927 (Admin).
267 [2017] EWHC 1458 (Admin).
268 At [103].
269 At [104].

> As Mr Lusinga neither made any fraudulent gain, nor told any lie, nor committed any crime, he should not have been treated as [a criminal] . . .[270]

3.314 Such comments provide a sense of proportion and are welcome. A finding of dishonesty usually has very serious consequences, and there are times when a tribunal will bend over backwards not to make such a finding because of this. Alternatively, a plea will be entered to try and mitigate sanction when the plea is itself not merited.

3.315 This line of taking an individual nuanced approach to sanction in dishonesty cases is supported by *Watters v Nursing and Midwifery Council*[271] in which a striking-off order was replaced by a short period of suspension for one incident of low-level dishonesty in a 26-year career. The case involved falsifying the date in a year-old training certificate to make it look like W's training was current. No patients were put at risk, and she subsequently brought her training up to date.

3.316 While the court drew attention to *Parkinson v Nursing and Midwifery Council*[272] and the principle that a finding of dishonesty coupled with a lack of regret or insight brings with it a risk of severe sanction that risk does not *necessitate* such a sanction in all cases. The distinction was drawn between cases where a registrant fails to cooperate with an investigation or a tribunal or persists in misconduct and cases where there is engagement and insight even if allegations are denied as they were in *Watters.*

3.317 The case of *General Medical Council v Nwachuku*[273] (aka *R (Nwachuku) v GMC*) provides some assistance on the limit to this principle. N booked three 12-hour locum shifts at hospital, one of which was counter-signed early at his request. On one shift, N sought to leave hospital three-and-a-half hours early, without arranging cover and contrary to his booking. Subsequently, he submitted his timesheet. N's actions were found to be deliberate and dishonest, but notwithstanding this his fitness to practise was not found to be currently impaired. The High Court upheld the GMC's appeal against this finding. O'Farrell J found that the dishonesty was serious, since had falsified a record for gain. In addition, obtained a countersignature knowing he would not complete his shift, and failed to correct his agency invoice when the hospital challenged him. She noted that the testimonials did not speak to N's honesty and were thus of limited relevance, and he had made no admissions prior to the facts being proved against him. She concluded that the FTP tribunal had placed undue weight on N's reflective statement made after the case had been proved. While N had stopped doing locum work, there was little to suggest N had accepted responsibility for his misconduct or addressed the risk of repetition. O'Farrell J quashed the finding of no impairment and remitted the case back to the tribunal for sanction.

3.318 While dishonesty is always to be regarded as serious, both *Lusinga* and *Watters* show there is a need for regulators and tribunals to recognise that they are to be considered on a scale of seriousness. This is relevant to the starting point for sanction. *Nwachuku* reminds us that the end-point of

270 At [83] and [84].
271 [2017] EWHC 1888 (Admin).
272 [2010] EWHC 1898 (Admin).
273 [2017] EWHC 2085 (Admin).

sanction is informed by the familiar issues of a timely admission, reflection, remorse, reparation and, through all this, insight. This is also reflected in the comments of Mostyn J in *Kirschner* above.

3.319 Contrast the approach in *General Medical Council v Jagjivan and Professional Standards Authority*,[274] a case involving sexually motivated misconduct. During an examination J suggested a patient touch her own nipples and vagina to increase her own heart-rate. He then went further and placed his hand on top of hers when near her vagina. The FTP tribunal found this conduct was not sexually motivated and that J was not impaired. The GMC appealed the decisions pursuant to section 40A of the MA 1983. The court found that such conduct could not be anything other than sexually motivated, and remitted the case back to the tribunal to reconsider impairment. This case sets out the principles applicable to an appeal under section 40A.

Lack of integrity / fit and proper person

3.320 A registrant may face a charge of acting 'without integrity' either alone or as part of a graded series of alternative allegations in the form '(a) X was dishonest (b) X lacked integrity (c) X was misleading'. The rationale for this gradation appears to be based on the view that a 'lack of integrity' is synonymous with objective dishonesty only, and not subjective dishonesty This approach brings with it the dangers of a regulator over-charging a case; a registrant being tempted to plea-bargain away a charge of dishonesty; and a tribunal taking an easy middle-route. None of this is satisfactory, if one takes a moment to consider what lack of integrity means and what the consequences of an adverse finding may be. Whether the case of *Ivey v Genting Casinos* (above) has put paid to the distinction between lack of integrity and dishonesty remains to be seen.

3.321 The case of *Hoodless and Blackwell v Financial Services Authority*[275] (FSA) is usually cited as providing the definition for a lack of integrity. The case involved consideration of whether H and B were 'fit and proper persons' to perform the controlled function of investment advisers. The FSA considered they were not, and withdrew its approval. They appealed. The tribunal first concluded that:

> [The] Fit and Proper test for Approved Persons is not judged in the abstract, but in relation to the particular controlled functions to be performed in a particular firm.

Furthermore that:

> The most important considerations include, 'honesty, integrity and reputation' and 'competence and capability.[276]

3.322 The tribunal considered the 'fit and proper' test to be both fact and function specific and, it involves a number of familiar considerations. Having dealt with the familiar two-stage *Ghosh* approach regarding dishonesty, the tribunal next looked at integrity, stating that:

274 [2017] EWHC 1247 (Admin).
275 [2003] FSMT 0007.
276 At [11] and [12].

> . . . we were required, as an additional matter, to consider the applicants' integrity, which both sides accepted involved the application of objective ethical standards. In our view 'integrity' connotes moral soundness, rectitude and steady adherence to an ethical code. A person lacks integrity if [he is] unable to appreciate the distinction between what is honest or dishonest by ordinary standards. (This presupposes, of course, circumstances where ordinary standards are clear. Where there are genuinely grey areas, a finding of lack of integrity would not be appropriate.)[277]

3.323 The following points emerge. First, a lack of integrity is taken to mean a lack of moral soundness or rectitude and an inability to adhere to an objective moral code. Second, the tribunal does not limit the ethical code to that of honesty. Rather it uses honesty and the objective limb of honesty as an example of an ethical code. The inability to distinguish between and thus adhere to what is regarded by ordinary standards as honest conduct is simply an example of a lack of integrity. It is clear from this that the court viewed a lack of integrity as being wider than just objective dishonesty.

3.324 In *Vukelic v FSA*[278] and in *Atlantic Law LLP and Greystoke v Financial Services Authority*[279] the Upper Tribunal cautioned against trying to formulate a comprehensive test for lack of integrity observing that it is 'elusive to define in a vacuum but still readily recognisable by those with specialist knowledge and/or experience in a particular market'. Such caution was reinforced in *Solicitors Regulation Authority v Chan*[280] in which Davis LJ said:

> . . . it serves no purpose to expatiate on its meaning. Want of integrity is capable of being identified as present or not, as the case may be, by an informed tribunal or court by reference to the facts of a particular case.

3.325 That a lack of integrity is not the same as dishonesty is clear from the familiar case of *Bolton v Law Society*[281] in which the distinction is made for the purposes of sanction between a solicitor who is 'not shown to have acted dishonestly, but is shown to have fallen below the required standards of integrity, probity and trustworthiness'.

3.326 In *Batra v Financial Conduct Authority*[282] B was found to lack integrity because he was reckless as to the accuracy of financial information put in mortgage application forms. It was not clear that he knew the amounts were wrong, it was clear that he did not bother to check. As such his 'disregard for whether the contents of mortgage application forms, bearing declarations as to their truth and accuracy, are correct [demonstrated] a clear lack of integrity'.[283]

3.327 *Batra* is authority for the submission that recklessness may itself demonstrate a lack of integrity. Likewise, in *Vukelic* the tribunal concluded

277 At [19].
278 (2009) FIN.0002/2008.
279 [2010] UKUT B30 (TCC) para [96].
280 [2015] EWHC 2659 (Admin).
281 [1994] 1 WLR 512.
282 [2014] UKUT 0214 (TCC).
283 At [30].

that V had not acted deliberately (and was therefore not dishonest) but, he 'turned a blind eye to what was obvious' and thus lacked integrity.

In addition, in *First Financial Advisors Limited v Financial Services Authority*[284] the tribunal observed that:

> Even though a person might not have been dishonest, if they either lack an ethical compass, or their ethical compass to a material extent points them in the wrong direction, that person will lack integrity.

As to the issue of sanction, the distinction between dishonesty and a lack of integrity is made plain in *Bolton v Law Society* above (para 3.286) and was cited with approval in *Ballard v Solicitors Regulation Authority*.[285]

3.328 From the above it appears plain that the concept of integrity or the lack thereof is for the tribunal to decide on the facts of the case. It is not the same as dishonesty. The deliberate or reckless breach of a professional code or, an ordinarily recognised ethical or moral code will suffice. This approach was followed in four recent cases.

3.329 In *Solicitors Regulation Authority v Wingate and another*[286] Holman J observed that:

> . . . dishonesty and lack of integrity are not the same. While all dishonesty involves a lack of integrity, not all lack of integrity involves dishonesty. The law requires a subjective element to any finding or conclusion of dishonesty, but the question whether a person lacked integrity is objective.[287]

3.330 Again, in *Scott v Solicitors Regulation Authority*[288] Holroyde J expressly approved the *Hoodless and Blackwell* definition. He cited the hypothetical example of a solicitor using money from the client account for his own purposes but then replacing it. When challenged, the solicitor says he knows it is wrong but he always intended to repay it and did repay it. He thought people would conclude that it didn't matter and was not dishonest. The solicitor might be acquitted of subjective dishonesty, but he certainly lacks integrity. Finally, this approach was approved by Morris J in *Newell-Austin v Solicitors Regulation Authority*[289] who observed that:

> Lack of integrity and dishonesty are not synonymous. A person may lack integrity even though not established as being dishonest . . . it is clear that, by contrast with the test of dishonesty, the test of 'lack of integrity' is an objective test alone.

3.331 Into what by now appears to be a reasonably settled world falls the case of *Malins v Solicitors Regulation Authority*[290] in which Mostyn J concluded that lack of integrity is synonymous with dishonesty. As with many of the above cases, he reviewed the authorities, but he also looked at the Oxford English Dictionary (OED) which, in his view, suggested that integrity and honesty are synonyms. In so doing, he referred to *Bar Standards Board v*

284 [2012] UKUT B16 (TCC).
285 [2017] EWHC 164 (Admin).
286 [2016] EWHC 3455 (Admin).
287 At [37].
288 [2016] EWHC 1256 (Admin).
289 [2017] EWHC 411 (Admin).
290 [2017] EWHC 835 (Admin).

Howd[291] in which Lang J undertook the same exercise, and came to the same conclusion, when considering the meaning of the phrase 'honesty and integrity' in the Bar Code of Conduct. Lang J thought they meant the same thing in much the same way as 'terms and conditions' are taken as referring to the same thing namely the 'details'.

3.332 The facts in *Malins* are not particularly complex. M created backdated documents and having deployed them, dishonestly relied on them or permitted others to be misled by them in litigation. What is bizarre is that the SRA did not allege dishonesty in the *creation* of the documents minutes before they were dishonestly deployed and relied upon. Only lack of integrity was alleged in their creation. When M faced disciplinary proceedings, it was plain, despite assertions to the contrary, the SRA's case was that making the documents was itself dishonest. It is equally plain that despite it not being charged the tribunal found M to be dishonest in making the documents and used that finding as support for dishonesty in the final count.

3.333 In his judgment Mostyn J rejects the suggestion that dishonesty and lack of integrity are different. In so doing, he suggests that if they were different, a regulator 'could side-step the requirement of proving the subjective element of dishonesty in any case by the simple expedient of charging the same facts as want of integrity'.[292] He then asserts that the SRA have done just that. He supports his reasoning by reference to the SRA's principles, which do not require a solicitor to act honestly, only to act with integrity. He concludes that the inclusion of one and the absence of the other suggests they are the same thing. Finally, he asked counsel to provide examples of acts that were without integrity but not dishonest. When in his view counsel could not do this, he concluded that dishonesty and lack of integrity are indeed the same.

3.334 With respect to Mostyn J, as can be seen from the previous cases there are cases where integrity and honesty and their antonyms are seen and repeatedly held to be different. It is less than convincing to aver that the terms 'honesty and integrity' mean the same thing, as an explanation for the absence of honesty in the SRA's rules and use the same reasoning to explain the presence of both in the Bar Standards Board's (BSB's) rules. In addition, the OED provides several descriptors for integrity beside that of honesty.

3.335 The simple explanation for the problems encountered in *Malins* is that the charges were poorly drafted and proceedings equally poorly conducted. The SRA's case was clearly one of dishonesty from start to finish. To suggest otherwise was a nonsense. Where Mostyn J is correct is his concern that 'lack of integrity' may be alleged by a regulator in order to 'side-step' the high bar required to prove dishonesty. It is submitted that rather than eliding the two separate concepts of honesty and integrity, the better course is to ensure that a case is properly charged. The regulator should nail its colours to the mast and the tribunal should ensure it deals only with what is charged. Those principles are as old as the hills, albeit they may need repeating on occasion.

291 [2017] EWHC 210 (Admin).
292 At [29].

3.336 The above was visited yet again in *Williams v Solicitors Regulatory Authority*[293] in which both Sir Brian Leveson and Carr J reject Mostyn J's conflation of honesty and integrity. Leveson commented thus:

> I would reject Mostyn J's description of . . . want of integrity as second-degree dishonesty. Honesty . . . is a base standard which society requires everyone to meet. Professional standard, however, rightly impose on those who aspire to them a higher obligation to demonstrate integrity in all of their work. There is a real difference between them.[294]

3.337 Carr J notes that:

> Dishonesty and want of integrity have long been treated as different (if overlapping) regulatory concepts. One can lack integrity without being dishonest ...

And later that:

> . . . on the authorities and as a matter of principle, that, in the field of solicitors' regulation, the concepts of dishonesty and want of integrity are indeed separate and distinct. Want of integrity arises when, objectively judged, a solicitor fails to meet the high professional standards to be expected of a solicitor. It does not require the subjective element of conscious wrongdoing.[295]

3.338 From the above it is clear that there is authority for the proposition that lack of integrity is a wider concept than dishonesty. However, the suggestion in *Newell-Austin v Solicitors Regulation Authority* that the two are differentiated by the subjective second limb of *Ghosh* as defining dishonesty now looks doubtful. *Ivey v Genting* has done away with that second limb of *Ghosh*, thereby raising the spectre of 'lack of integrity' being swept away as well. It may provide traction for the reasoning in *Malins* and *Howd* that lack of integrity is synonymous albeit those cases were still dealing with the old two-stage test.

3.339 It would indeed be a pity if lack of integrity were subsumed into the now objective definition of dishonesty, since the earlier cases demonstrate that it has a real part to play in regulatory proceedings dealing with disreputable behaviour that falls short of or is distinguishable from dishonesty. Its demise would remove a weapon in the regulator's armoury and may force a registrant to either fight or plead to a charge that does not reflect his misconduct.

3.340 It would be a wiser course to take note of the comments in the three cases of *Vukelic, Atlantic Law* and *Chan* (above) and not over-define the concept into oblivion.

3.341 One final issue is, assuming the charge remains, whether the defence may be content to face or plead to charges that allege lack of integrity on the basis that the latter may result in a lesser penalty.

293 [2017] EWHC 1478 (Admin).

294 At [120].

295 At [50] and [54].

Deficient professional performance and/or lack of competence

3.342 Most regulators use the term 'deficient professional performance', however the NMC uses the term 'lack of competence' to mean the same thing. Cases fall into this category where a registrant has failed to act in the best interests of a patient, or provided inadequate care falling *well* below the expected standard of a competent practitioner. (See, for example, *Calhaem* and the discussion of deficient performance above at para 3.58 onwards and 3.61) It is usually marked by either a repeated failure to undertake a procedure or treatment in a competent fashion, or it may cover a wider range of issues indicative of more general failings. What is important is that it is distinct from misconduct. Where issues of deficient performance arise, there will almost certainly be a comprehensive performance assessment. These can be very detailed wide-ranging and are necessarily both expensive for the regulator and intrusive to the registrant.

3.343 It is important to note that any assessment is concerned with the performance of the registrant in the part of their practice over which concern has been raised and in closely allied areas. It is not a general assessment of their overall competence, albeit that a tribunal may conclude that a registrant is not fit to practise through specific or more general concerns. Performance assessments form part of a process that includes supervision and retraining in order to improve a registrant's performance thereby protecting and serving the public. As such, there is past assessment, but there is also a process of looking forward to see if and how a registrant has improved. That is in the public interest and in the registrant's interests – *Sadler v General Medical Council*.[296]

3.344 The range of cases in this category is necessarily wide, however of particular importance is the issue of patient protection. This is best served by considering whether the registrant has developed, or has the potential to develop, insight into his or her failures. Has the registrant altered his or her practices as a result of matters, sought assistance from a mentor or senior practitioner? Has the registrant sought to improve his or her knowledge base – be it clinical, practical, social, business etc – to prevent such occurrences? If the registrant has done none of the above, then is he or she open to suggestion, or is the failure indicative of an inability to gain insight?

3.345 In *Ghosh v General Medical Council*[297] the Privy Council provided guidance on such cases. G was found guilty of two matters of serious professional misconduct. One concerned the inaccurate and false completion of a cremation form. The second concerned a failure to visit a patient but nonetheless providing a prescription without assessing the condition of the patient or his treatment needs. G prescribed antibiotics to the second patient who was in fact suffering from life-threatening illnesses. G was placed under conditions, including that she undertake supervised re-training to remedy her clinical deficiencies; at the next hearing provide evidence that she had done so; not engage in locum posts; not engage in any unsupervised or single-handed practice; and to advise any prospective

296 [2003] UKPC 59.
297 [2001] UKPC 29.

employer and any agency of the conditions. G singularly failed to meet the above conditions, indeed her conduct worsened with further complaints and a period of unexplained absence when seconded to a practice. She also failed to give adequate reasons for any these failings. She was subsequently erased from the register.

3.346 In its decision to uphold erasure their Lordships commented that:

> . . . conditional registration, while in itself a lesser penalty than suspension in that the practitioner is permitted to continue in practice for the time being, is potentially more severe in that failure to comply with the conditions is likely to lead to erasure. The nature of the conditions imposed on Dr Ghosh indicated that she was regarded as unfit to practise unless she successfully completed a programme of supervised retraining. The original Committee did not decide that conditional registration was a sufficient penalty, but that Dr Ghosh needed to undergo retraining if the public was to be adequately protected. The logical response to her failure to complete such a programme was erasure, not suspension.
>
> Their Lordships have themselves reviewed the evidence, and are satisfied that this was a bad case. Dr Ghosh never acknowledged the seriousness of her original misconduct, and patently failed to attend, let alone successfully complete, the programme that had been arranged for her. Her conduct in leaving the country for 2½ months without prior warning or subsequent explanation was unprofessional and in the highest degree irresponsible. On the evidence before it and without seeing Dr Ghosh and hearing her in person the Committee had no material on which it could be satisfied that Dr Ghosh would be any more likely to comply with the terms of a further period of conditional registration than she had in the past. Their Lordships recognise, as the Committee must have done, that erasure will effectively bring Dr Ghosh's career as a doctor to an end. But they consider that, in all the circumstances, the Committee had no real alternative but to order her name to be erased from the register.[298]

3.347 It is quite plain that the Privy Council regarded conditions as potentially burdensome but that they provide the registrant with the opportunity to prove that he or she has rectified the errors complained of. If a registrant does demonstrate insight, then he or she may well save his or her career, but if there is no evidence of rectification there is in their Lordships' words 'no material . . . [and thus] . . . no alternative but [erasure]'.

3.348 In measuring the performance of a registrant, he or she is to be measured against the standards reasonably expected of a competent practitioner in the position that they occupy. In *Holton v General Medical Council*[299] the court regarded the test as an objective one and said that matters such as the registrant's lack of training, their personality and concerns 'personal to the doctor' are irrelevant. What is relevant is the circumstances under which the registrant was working, factors external to the registrant, such as pressure of work, lack of resources, isolation due to lack of colleagues and other such circumstances operative at the time. This delineation between internal/personal and external factors is an important one, since the former affect a registrant's own ability to perform whereas the latter do not. It is clearly no excuse for incompetence for a

298 At paras 39–40.
299 [2006] EWHC 2960 (Admin).

registrant to say that he or she hasn't been trained for the post, cannot communicate with colleagues or there has been a crisis at home and he or she cannot cope. Conversely, circumstances such as a major emergency may mean that a registrant will have to adjust the way he or she works that does not mean the registrant is not competent, but it may mean that the registrant cannot spend as much time on one aspect of his or her practice as he or she normally would.

3.349 In *Garfoot v General Medical Council*[300] G was erased from the medical register for the repeated 'irresponsible and/or inappropriate prescribing' of controlled drugs to addicts. G had little or no learning in this field and the tribunal found that G essentially provided addicts/patients what they requested. Some patients became addicted to the drugs with which they were being treated.

3.350 The tribunal found that numerous standards of practice were breached in the important area of creating a therapeutic relationship with the patient, thus:

> The Committee had to conclude that, by and large, patients dictated their own prescriptions. The Committee were reinforced in this view by your dismissive attitude to written agreements and to sanctions. The Committee concluded that the battle for medical intervention for change was lost before it had begun.[301]

3.351 Negotiation and agreement is key to treating addiction. The important point is thus G's 'dismissive attitude' toward the therapeutic norms.

3.352 The tribunal also found that despite some two-and-a-half years elapsing between the first letter from the GMC and the tribunal hearing, there was little evidence of concrete change in attitude or practice, concluding that G still has 'difficulty in accepting the need for radical change in your prescribing and doubt that you are capable of achieving such change'. The Privy Council upheld the order of erasure on the basis of the seriousness of the conduct and the fact that no conditions could be devised in order to enable G to continue to practise.

3.353 In *Jalloh v Nursing and Midwifery Council*[302] J was found to have committed a series of mistakes, repeatedly failing to follow procedures and disregarding the interests of a vulnerable patient. The mistakes were serious, and despite her experience and mitigation including her excellent character and record, the risk of repetition remained. She was thus impaired and placed under conditions for 18 months. Silber J endorsed the oft-stated approach that the judgment and sanction of the committee, comprising members of the profession, deserved respect, it being the body best qualified to judge what the profession expects of its members and the measures necessary to maintain appropriate standards. J's appeal against the finding of impairment and the sanction were dismissed.

3.354 From the above it is clear that in some very serious cases no amount of mitigation will prevent erasure of suspension from practice. However, where there is insight and a will to change or the potential for both to

300 [2002] UKPC 35.

301 Quoting the findings of the Professional Conduct Committee at para 7 which are adopted as accurate and requiring the sanction of erasure – see paras 14–16.

302 [2009] EWHC 1697 (Admin).

develop, the public may be better served by the registrant's return to practice if and when it is safe so to do.

3.355 While an assessment may be daunting for a registrant it is intended to ascertain the support or training needed improve their practice and thereby protect and serve the public. However, it does require the co-operation of the practitioner. In *Uruakpa v General Medical Council*[303] the registrant was asked to undertake an assessment but despite his assurances he subsequently refused. He was suspended from practice on grounds of public protection because without the assessment his alleged failings and any risks could not be assessed.

3.356 The position in *Uruakpa* has now been superceded to some extent by the introduction of non-compliance hearings which deal specifically with a registrant who fails or refuses to comply with an assessment of their health, performance or language ability. If a registrant consistently or explicitly refuses to comply, then he or she may be placed on conditions for up to three years or suspended for 12 months. If following review the registrant has been suspended for two years, the tribunal may thereafter suspend indefinitely. The non-compliance process does not assess a registrant's fitness to practise, only the registrant's compliance with a direction to be assessed. As such there is no power to erase a registrant. (See 'Non-Compliance Hearings' at para 2.255 above.)

Voluntary erasure/removal

> A process permitting registrants to withdraw from their profession, provided it is in the public interest for this to be permitted. It is only likely to be permitted if there are no FTP issues or no serious FTP issues. The registrant should genuinely be leaving practice. There must be no question of sweeping matters under the carpet.

Introduction

3.357 Some regulators permit the removal of a registrant's name from the register by consent, however the process is by no means uniform. Broadly speaking, voluntary erasure requires the public interest to be best served by this process. That includes both the protection of patients and upholding the good standing of the profession. The latter is particularly important. There should be no question of sweeping a difficult case under the carpet. However, that does not mean that voluntary erasure should be denied in appropriate cases.

3.358 Despite some variation in each regulator's stance or processes, the principles governing erasure and restoration are the same. In essence it involves balancing the interests of a registrant who is genuinely unwell or has truly retired from practice against the public interest in the investigation and assessments of complaints. This can cause real difficulty since

303 [2010] EWHC 1302 (Admin).

there may be very strong competing interests. The concern is that, with so much emphasis placed on the overarching objective, this translates into a presumption of, or 'need', to prosecute in cases where there is little risk to the public and there is real pain and difficulty caused to registrants.

3.359 Regulators are rightly anxious to ensure that they are seen as independent scrutineers and champions of professionalism and, no one wants to return to the 'bad old days' of complaints swept under the carpet. However, there are times when cases are driven more by a perceived public interest or too much weight being placed on public opinion of the regulator as against the interests of a sick or retired registrant. There is frequently a presumption that the registrant is retiring to avoid public scrutiny, however that is not always the case. Where it becomes obvious that a registrant has retired or is unwell, there may be little point in continuing proceedings, save in the most serious cases.

3.360 Withdrawal from practice, managed and sanctioned by the regulator is, in appropriate cases, just as protective and reassuring to the public as spending a year or more taking a case to an inevitable suspension or erasure. The latter is meaningless if the registrant has retired and has no chance of revalidation or practising again, and it carries with it huge emotional, time and cost implications for all involved. Perhaps the biggest sticking-point in all the procedures is the regulator's requirement that the registrant 'admits everything' – that is, all facts and impairment – before the registrant will be considered for voluntary erasure. Placing such a barrier in the way of a fair consideration of the case out-with the interests of the regulator or the registrant may deprive both of a sensible solution in some cases. In so doing it damages the public interest, in particular its view of the regulator as a just and reasonable entity.

3.361 While the discussion below focusses on the GMC, the principles apply to all regulators.

General Medical Council registrants

3.362 The GMC process is dealt with under regulation 3(1) of the GMC (Voluntary Erasure and Restoration following Voluntary Erasure) Regulations 2004.[304] A doctor may apply to the registrar for voluntary erasure at any point in the fitness to practise process. The application must include:

- details of any current person, body or organisation to whom he or she supplies or has an agreement to provide medical services; if none is current, this should be the most recent person/body/organisation in that position;
- a statement by the practitioner and the person/body/organisation that he/she/it is not aware of any fitness to practise proceedings or of any reason why he or she could be subject to such proceedings; or
- a statement that he or she has not been employed or had an arrangement to provide medical services in the five years prior to the application.

304 SI No 2609.

The registrar may grant the application or, refer it to a medical and lay case examiner, refer the application to an FTP tribunal or reject it.

3.363 An application will be referred to case examiners where an allegation is being investigated, the doctor is liable to investigation, or a case has been referred to an FTP tribunal but has *not yet commenced*. Case examiners may also consider an application if the doctor is currently suspended or subject to conditions or undertakings. If they cannot agree upon the application, it is referred to an Investigation Committee. If an application is received and a hearing before a FTP tribunal *has commenced*, the application will be determined by that tribunal.

3.364 To protect the public interest (patient protection, public confidence in the profession etc), decisions on voluntary erasure are normally only made once current or pending investigations have concluded. Nonetheless, voluntary erasure may be appropriate if it is considered right in all the circumstances, including the public interest, the doctor's health and the likelihood of return to practice. A genuine desire to be removed from the register, demonstrated by, for example, steps taken to retire or stop practice, is a significant factor in favour of voluntary erasure. An application apparently triggered by FTP proceedings will be treated with some scepticism in which case the doctor's insight into issues and his or her record with the regulator will affect how his alleged desire to leave practice is viewed.

3.365 While it may be argued that voluntary erasure best protects the public because a doctor will not be entitled to practise, this may not be the case since he or she may apply for restoration to the register, albeit that restoration is not automatic where FTP concerns were raised during the original voluntary erasure process. There may also be evidential problems if an application for restoration is made some time later. From the GMC's perspective it is preferable for all FTP concerns to be dealt with by admission (or dismissal) such that possible evidential concerns fall away. However, insisting on this in some cases may be disproportionate and do nothing to protect the public or enhance the standing of the regulator.

3.366 Matters to consider in any application for voluntary erasure include the doctor's health, the time elapsed since he or she last practised, the genuineness of the desire to be erased from the register, the likelihood of a future application for restoration and, any evidence that he or she really has no intention to practise in the UK *or elsewhere*. Given the GMC's general duty to protect the public, no distinction is made between an intention to practise in the UK, abroad, privately or in public practice. An intention to practise in another allied field of practice may be of equal relevance. A genuine desire to stop practice altogether is a strong factor in favour of voluntary erasure. Conversely, the likelihood of return is a factor against the process. The stage of the doctor's career may be significant since someone in the latter stages of their career is less likely to return to practice than someone at the start. However, there is no hard and fast rule and each case must be decided on its own merits.

3.367 Although there will always be exceptions, voluntary erasure is unlikely to be appropriate if there are concerns regarding probity, sexual misconduct, harm to patients through deficient performance or cases involving convictions. Confidence in the profession may to be harmed if the regulator is not seen to deal with these issues. Voluntary erasure would only be appropriate in exceptional circumstance such as a doctor who is seriously ill and/or unfit to participate in FTP proceedings.

3.368 Voluntary erasure is more likely to be appropriate if the allegations and evidence relate to a doctor's health even if he or she has indicated that improved health may result in an application to restore. Where health has impacted upon performance, voluntary erasure may depend upon the doctor's ability to participate in any FTP process. A doctor with a chronic condition and remote prospect of return to practice may well be granted voluntary erasure whereas an acute or episodic condition from which recovery may well occur is unlikely to result in voluntary erasure, particularly if it has impacted upon performance.

3.369 A registrant may apply for restoration following voluntary erasure, but the burden lies with him or her to demonstrate that he or she is fit to practise. Any new or outstanding FTP concerns will be referred to the case examiners. Health concerns and/or performance concerns whether arising from historic complaints, referrals, concerns from another jurisdiction or by reason of an extended break from practice, must be met with proof that he or she is fit to practise. Such cases may well require an assessment as part of the restoration process. Cases with multiple concerns, including new or outstanding allegations, are likely be refused by case examiners or referred to the tribunal particularly if a finding of impairment is likely.

3.370 If a doctor has been convicted of a criminal offence, particularly an offence of serious violence, sexual misconduct, or offences involving children and/or pornography such that he or she presents a risk to public confidence in the profession, an application to restore will almost certainly be referred to the FTP Tribunal.

3.371 A registrant may re-apply for restoration at any time after he or she has been refused restoration by a case-examiner. However, repeated applications may to be referred to the FTP Tribunal. If restoration is refused by the FTP Tribunal, he or she may reapply but only if at least 12 months has elapsed since refusal.

3.372 It is plain that the restoration process has safeguards built into it and, a registrant who has been granted voluntary erasure thereby terminating proceedings cannot and will not simply be readmitted to the register. Such a risk is fanciful. His or her application would be scrutinised in light of the voluntary erasure and of the conduct previously complained of.

3.373 In *R (Li) v GMC*[305] L was adjudged unfit to practise, unfit to attend or participate in an FTP hearing and that to do so would be profoundly damaging to his mental health. On the basis that he had at some time expressed a wish to work in Australia, the GMC proceeded, but declared themselves neutral in that they did not dispute the medical evidence and said they would not appeal any stay of proceedings. In so doing, it is arguable that the GMC were ducking their responsibilities. Notwithstanding this 'concession' by the GMC, the tribunal declined voluntary erasure and

305 [2013] EWHC 522 (Admin).

refused to stay proceedings. On appeal both decisions were said to be irrational and unreasonable.

3.374 HHJ Wood QC concluded that the tribunal was in error in placing any weight on L's distant and unrealistic hope that he may practise again one day. The undisputed medical evidence was that L 'could not participate in the hearing without significant consequences to his health'. In addition, proceeding carried with it a risk that L would commit suicide. The learned judge concluded that that risk and/or the GMC's concession that it would not contest a stay was substantial support for the grant of voluntary erasure. One final matter was that although the interests of complainants and their families should be taken into account, this is not a determinative factor.

Health and Care Professions Council registrants

3.375 The HCPC permits disposal of a case by consent provided they are satisfied that 'the appropriate level of public protection is being secured and, doing so would not be detrimental to the wider public interest'.[306]

3.376 The process is staged, and requires:

a) An investigating panel to find that there is a case to answer in order to ensure the allegation has been fully considered.
b) A full and insight-full admission of the case (although minor details should not be a bar to agreement) and of impairment and a willingness to address failures.
c) Any agreed remedial action should be consistent with the likely/expected outcome were the case to be contested.
d) The agreed position is then placed before a tribunal which has the full range of sanctions available to it.
e) The tribunal will then consider whether on the evidence presented it is appropriate to deal with the matter by way of consent or, to reject the proposal and adjourn the case for a full hearing.
f) Since a full hearing is always a possibility, any admissions made for the purpose of the voluntary approach are treated as being 'without prejudice'.

General Dental Council registrants

3.377 Voluntary removal is available to a registrant who has ceased to practise. A registrant may apply to the registrar, which includes making a solemn declaration that he or she has no intention to practise in the future. If there are no ongoing FTP proceedings, then the application is dealt with administratively. If there are ongoing FTP proceedings, the application will be assigned to the 'case-owner' at the GDC who will ask the registrant if they admit both the allegation(s) and impairment. The case owner will also ask for any comments from any complainant(s). This information is then put before the registrar who will decides on the papers. The registrar must provide written reasons for any decision.

306 Health Professions Council Practice Note on Disposal of Cases by Consent (March 2017).

3.378 If the registrant's application is granted this will terminate any ongoing FTP proceedings. If the registrant changes his or her mind and applies to re-join the register, the FTP proceedings terminated by his or her previous voluntary erasure can be taken into account in the decision to readmit or not. If the registrar refuses voluntary erasure the matter will continue to FTP proceedings in the normal way. A registrant can reapply to the FTP tribunal but only if there is a material change in circumstances.

3.379 In deciding whether to grant or refuse voluntary erasure the Registrar must be 'satisfied in all the circumstances that it is right to do so . . . [balancing] the interests of the public and the interests of the registrant'.[307]

3.380 The GDC guidance on this balancing exercise is detailed, informative and very useful since it sets out the competing interests and matters to consider. It is downloadable from the GDC website (www.gdc-org.uk). Essentially, it covers the familiar areas of public protection, public interest (confidence in the profession, upholding standards) and the registrant's interests including his or her health and the likelihood of his or her return to practice. The registrant's health includes the seriousness of any illness, prognosis, impact of proceedings, likelihood of recovery and/or return to work and, the ability of the registrant to participate in proceedings.

3.381 The guidance makes the point that voluntary erasure may be a quick and simple way of protecting the public, but it should not be used to 'escape prosecution'. The fact that a registrant can apply to re-register and the risk of that is a matter to consider. A younger registrant has more time to apply an older registrant less time, and there may be clear evidence of a settled intention to retire. Full admissions and acceptance of impairment may lend weight to erasure, denial of wrongdoing or a fundamental disagreement on seriousness militates against voluntary erasure.

Nursing and Midwifery Council registrants

3.382 Following consultation, the NMC now permits voluntary removal from the register, however there are limitations on the process. NMC guidance emphasises that, where there are FTP proceedings, voluntary removal is only appropriate 'when it is not in the public interest to hold such a hearing and the public and patients will be best protected by the nurse or midwife's immediate removal from the register'. Any application for voluntary removal must include full acceptance of the allegations and impairment and a solemn declaration that the registrant does not intend to practise any more.

3.383 The balancing exercise outlined in respect of other regulators also applies to the NMC process. The case-examiners will consider whether there is a case to answer and the extent of any complaints; following this the competing interests of public scrutiny and protection will be considered against the interests of the registrant. Once again, the regulator has provided detailed guidance on the web (www.nmc-org.uk) that is well worth scrutiny. The NMC emphasises the need to uphold public confidence in the profession and the process requires full admissions before it

307 GDC, *Guidance on the considerations for voluntary removal applications* (November 2016) para 11.

will start. This barrier to 'consensual disposal' is unfortunate since it appears to preclude voluntary removal in cases where the balancing exercise would suggest it would otherwise be appropriate.

3.384 The FTP process and voluntary removal in particular should not be concerned with whether a registrant is seen to be 'getting away with it' or a regulator must be seen to prosecute all complaints. Voluntary removal is a necessary adjunct to the FTP process and it should be available in those cases that, after objective consideration merit closure by means other than the full FTP process which can take years and cause immense difficulty for all sides.

GOC registrants

3.385 Voluntary erasure is not available at GOC proceedings, however the case of *Clarke v General Optical Council*[308] (see variously above) has emphasised that in instituting and continuing proceedings and when considering sanction the question of proportionality and balancing the public interest and the registrant's interests must be rooted in reality. As outlined above, C had fully admitted responsibility for his error and had fully and finally retired from practice. This was clearly relevant to all stages of the process, which did nothing to protect the public or enhance the standing of the regulator.

Costs

3.386 The various healthcare regulators bring proceedings in the public interest, to protect the public or to uphold standards etc, they are not in the position of an ordinary litigant prosecuting a claim. In *Baxendale-Walker v Law Society*[309] Moses LJ held that:

> Absent dishonesty or a lack of good faith, a costs order should not be made against such a regulator unless there is good reason to do so. That reason must be more than that the other party has succeeded. In considering an award of costs against a public regulator the court must weigh on the one hand the financial prejudice to the particular complainant, against the need to encourage public bodies to exercise their public function of making reasonable and sound decisions without fear of exposure to undue financial prejudice, if the decision is successfully challenged.

3.387 That reasoning was expressly adopted in the Court of Appeal thus:

> One crucial feature which should inform the Tribunal's costs decision is that the proceedings were brought by the Law Society in exercise of its regulatory responsibility, in the public interest and the maintenance of proper professional standards. For the Law Society to be exposed to the risk of an adverse costs order simply because properly brought proceedings were unsuccessful might have a chilling effect on the exercise of its regulatory obligations, to the public disadvantage.

308 [2017] EWHC 521 (Admin).
309 [2007] EWCA Civ 233.

There was additional comment that the proceedings were in part justified by W bringing matters on his own head and that he had admitted some of the allegations.

3.388 In *R (Perinpanathan) v City of Westminster Magistrates Court*[310] the court expressed the view that there is no presumption that regulatory bodies carrying out their functions in a reasonable fashion should pay the registrant's costs if the regulator loses the case.

3.389 However, the case of *Smith v Bar Standards Board*[311] makes it plain that where a regulator has acted in an extraordinary, perverse or naïve fashion the registrant may recover his or her costs and, they may be very substantial indeed.

3.390 The reverse point has been made in several cases that regulatory proceedings while civil in nature are not the same as civil proceedings and thus a regulator cannot expect an order for costs to be made if it wins – *Solicitors Regulation Authority v Davis and McGlinchey*.[312]

3.391 If an order is to be made the tribunal should consider whether the regulator has proved all or only part of its case and the means of the registrant. The latter must include consideration of his ability to pay taking account of any other order the tribunal has made such as to suspend or erase a registrant from practice. See, for example, *Merrick v Law Society*[313] and *D'Souza v Law Society*.[314]

310 [2010] 1 WLR 1508.
311 [2016] EWHC 3015 (Admin).
312 [2011] EWHC 232 (Admin).
313 [2007] EWHC 2997 (Admin).
314 [2009] EWHC 2193 (Admin).

CHAPTER 4

The General Medical Council

continued

Key points

- *Regulator:* General Medical Council (GMC)
- *Tribunal service:* Medical Practitioners Tribunal Service (MPTS)
- *Professions regulated:* Doctors
- *Common sources of referral:* Patients, employers, police, other health professionals
- *Type of proceedings:* Fitness to practise
- *Relevant statute:* Medical Act (MA) 1983 (Part V and Sch 4)
- *Fitness to Practise Rules:* General Medical Council (Fitness to Practise) Rules (GMC (FTP) Rules) 2004 SI No 2608
- *Key document: Good medical practice*, current edition published March 2013 (updated April 2014)
- *Two-stage process:* 1) Investigation (GMC (FTP) Rules 2004 Part 2); and 2) adjudication (Procedure of a medical practitioners tribunal (GMC (FTP) Rules 2004 Part 4))
- *Case examiners:* Yes (GMC (FTP) Rules 2004 r8)
- *Adjudication Committee:* medical practitioners tribunal – run by MPTS
- *Location:* Main hearing centre: Manchester
- *Notice of hearing provision:* GMC (FTP) Rules 2004 r15
- *Case management provisions:* GMC (FTP) Rules 2004 r16 and powers of MPTS in respect of failure to comply with Rules or directions (r16A)
- *Procedure before a medical practitioners tribunal:* GMC (FTP) Rules 2004 r17
- *Test:* Whether fitness to practise is impaired by reason of (in summary): a) misconduct; b) deficient professional performance; c) a criminal conviction or caution; d) adverse physical or mental health; e) not having the necessary knowledge of English, f) a determination by another regulator (MA 1983 s35(2))
- *Power to require a doctor to undergo health or performance assessment?* Yes – MA 1983 Sch 4 para 5A(1); GMC (FTP) Rules 2004 r17ZA – power to suspend if fails to comply with assessment
- *Interim order power:* Yes, interim conditions of practice or interim suspension (MA 1983 s41A, GMC (FTP) Rules 2004 Part 7 rr25–27) heard by interim orders tribunal
- *Interim order guidance: Imposing interim orders – guidance for the interim orders tribunal, tribunal chair and medical practitioners tribunal*
- *Limited protection for historic complaints:* GMC (FTP) Rules 2004 r4(5)
- *General composition for final hearings:* Usually three medical practitioners tribunal members – which can include a legally qualified chair
- *Addressing the panel:* Generally seated and 'Sir'/'Madam'
- *Independent legal assessor:* If legally qualified chair, no legal assessor
- *Evidence:* GMC (FTP) Rules 2004 r34(1) – 'may admit any evidence they consider fair and relevant to the case before them, whether or not such evidence would be admissible in a court of law'

- *Half-time submission provision:* GMC (FTP) Rules 2004 r17(2)(g) – 'whether sufficient evidence has been adduced to find the facts proved'
- *Sanction provisions:* MA 1983 s35D
- *Sanction documents:* MPTS/GMC *Sanctions guidance*
- *Review hearings:* MA 1983 s35D, GMC (FTP) Rules 2004 r22
- *Restoration hearings:* GMC (FTP) Rules 2004 Part 6 rr23 and 24
- *Appeal rule:* MA 1983 s40 – appeal provision for Doctors. MA 1983 s40A appeal provision for General Council
- *Costs:* Power to make a costs award where conduct by a party is unreasonable GMC (FTP) Rules 2004 r16B

Introduction

Overview

4.1 This chapter outlines the fitness to practise (FTP) procedures in relation to doctors as investigated by the General Medical Council (GMC) and as heard by the Medical Practitioners Tribunal Service (MPTS). In this chapter, the terms 'doctor' and 'registrant' are used interchangeably to refer to an individual practitioner facing proceedings before the GMC.

4.2 There are two main stages to GMC FTP proceedings – investigation undertaken by the GMC; and adjudication undertaken by the MPTS. The adjudication stage (the hearing) is, a three-stage process of 1) fact-finding, 2) statutory ground and impairment and 3) sanction.

4.3 The over-arching objective of the GMC in exercising their functions is the protection of the public.[1] Seeking to achieve this over-arching objective involves the pursuit of these objectives: a) to protect, promote and maintain the health, safety and well-being of the public; b) to promote and maintain public confidence in the medical profession; and c) to promote and maintain proper professional standards and conduct for members of that profession.[2]

4.4 To meet these objectives, the GMC, through its independent medical practitioners tribunals,[3] has the power to erase or suspend a doctor from the register, place restrictions on his or her practice (conditions of practice) or put a note on the register for a period of time (warning). The GMC, through its interim order tribunals and the medical practitioners tribunals, has the power to impose an interim order until such time as proceedings have been determined.

1 Medical Act (MA) 1983 s1A.
2 MA 1983 s1B.
3 MA 1983 s1(3)(h).

The General Medical Council

4.5 The GMC is the regulatory body governing registered medical practitioners. Doctors can be registered with a licence to practise or registered without a licence to practise.

4.6 Registration with a licence to practise:

- enables doctors to legally practise any activities in the UK which are restricted by law to those holding a licence (such as signing death certificates and writing prescriptions for prescription-only medicines);
- applies only to UK medical practice and has no legal standing outside of the UK;
- means a doctor has to participate in revalidation.

4.7 Registration without a licence:

- allows doctors to show to employers, overseas regulators and others that they remain in good standing with the GMC;
- is an acknowledgement that the doctor's primary medical qualification allowed them to gain entry to the medical register in the UK.[4]

4.8 The licence to practise which is issued by the GMC applies to all doctors in the UK regardless of whether they are working in the NHS or private sector, either on a full- or part-time, permanent or locum basis. It also applies to all levels of registration, whether provisional, full or on the specialist or general registrant register. In the year 2015/16 the GMC had 273,761 registrants.[5] A 'List of registered medical registrants' is maintained on the GMC website and this allows any member of the public to check the registration status of a doctor and see whether they have been or are currently subject to any restrictions.[6]

4.9 The GMC's powers derive from the Medical Act (MA) 1983, as amended.

The meaning of 'fitness to practise'

4.10 The GMC has adopted the following as a statement of policy – set out in relevant part as follows:[7]

> 1. To practise safely, doctors must be competent in what they do. They must establish and maintain effective relationships with patients, respect patients' autonomy and act responsibly and appropriately if they or a colleague fall ill and their performance suffers.

4 See www.gmc-uk.org/doctors/licensing/faq_licence_to_practise.asp.

5 *Promoting Professionalism, reforming regulation a paper for consultation*, Department of Health (October 2017) p10 (available at https://consultations.dh.gov.uk/professional-regulation/regulatory-reform/supporting_documents/Promoting%20professionalism%20reforming%20regulation.pdf).

6 See http://webcache.gmc-uk.org/gmclrmp_enu/start.swe?SWECmd=GotoView&SWEBHWND=&_sn=FpYMhjKlTsJKSzokZRe7rkeEpxFH.bc4p.DP2Jxp7ZuxRHdM3sNTe9-ReBHJgYErYzlLE6DKFG8naVfgsWE.HosOIzFd9dgxon-NBCwYaoGjq98x-g5H.BV3RDF-U-uhQDcqibYYfEUOuz24LFffzfH8bbgRx09MY8P15o7px85bchXwK2Qkl7OPzOLWe2vatmf–1qGfQXU_&SWEView=GMC+WEB+Doctor+Search&SRN=&SWEHo=webcache.gmc-uk.org&SWETS=1511278741&SWEApplet=GMC+WEB+Health+Provider+Search+AppletSee.

7 At www.gmc-uk.org/guidance/21721.asp (2013).

2. But these attributes, while essential, are not enough. Doctors have a respected position in society and their work gives them privileged access to patients, some of whom may be very vulnerable. A doctor whose conduct has shown that he cannot justify the trust placed in him should not continue in unrestricted practice while that remains the case.

3. In short, the public is entitled to expect that their doctor is fit to practise, and follows the GMC's principles of good practice described in *Good medical practice*. This guidance sets out the standards of competence, care and conduct expected of doctors, under the following four domains.

- **Knowledge, skills and performance**: doctors must provide good standards of clinical care, must practise within the limits of their competence, and must keep up to date with developments in their field, maintain their skills and audit their performance
- **Safety and quality**: doctors must ensure that patients are not put at unnecessary risk, by contributing and complying with systems to protect patients. This includes raising concerns about risks to patient safety including those risks posed by the doctors own health.
- **Communication, partnership and teamwork**: doctors must communicate effectively with patients and those close to them, to establish and maintain partnerships with patients. They must work collaboratively with colleagues to maintain or improve patient care and this includes being prepared to contribute to the teaching and training of doctors and students.
- **Maintaining trust**: doctors must be honest and trustworthy towards patients and colleagues in all aspects of their practice, including financial and commercial arrangements and legal or disciplinary proceedings. They must treat patients and colleagues fairly and without discrimination.

4. Most doctors measure up to these standards but a small number fall seriously short and as a result put patients at risk, cause them serious harm or distress or undermine public confidence and trust in doctors generally . . .

The GMC's role in regulation

4.11 Fitness to practise proceedings are concerned with stepping in when there are concerns that the requirements of *Good medical practice* are not being met by a doctor. A question of fitness to practise may arise if, for example:[8]

- a doctor's performance has harmed patients or put patients at risk of harm;
- a doctor has shown a deliberate or reckless disregard of clinical responsibilities towards patients;
- a doctor's health is compromising patient safety;
- a doctor has abused a patient's trust or violated a patient's autonomy or other fundamental rights;
- a doctor has behaved dishonestly, fraudulently or in a way designed to mislead or harm others.

4.12 The advice above is only illustrative of the sort of behaviour which could call registration into question. *Good medical practice* and other published GMC guidance provide a more complete picture of behaviour that may

8 See chapter 1 for further details; list and detail taken from www.gmc-uk.org/guidance/21721.asp.

result in action by the GMC but is not exhaustive. The outcome in any case will depend on its particular facts and any mitigating and aggravating facts.

Key fitness to practise procedure documents[9]

4.13 The key fitness to practise documents include the following:

- MA 1983
- GMC (FTP) Rules 2004[10]
- *Good medical practice* (2013 – updated 2014)[11]
- *Imposing interim orders – guidance for the interim order tribunal, tribunal chairs and medical practitioners tribunals*
- MPTS/GMC *Sanctions guidance*
- *Guidance on earnings* (2017)[12]
- *Guidance to the GMC's Fitness to Practise Rules 2004 (as amended)*[13]
- *Making decisions on cases at the end of the investigation stage: Guidance for the Investigating Committee and Case Examiners*[14]
- *Guidance for the Investigating Committee and Case Examiners when considering allegations about a doctor's involvement in encouraging or assisting suicide*[15]
- *Guidance on convictions, cautions, determinations and other methods of police disposal*[16]
- *Guidance for case examiners and the Investigation Committee on single clinical incidents*[17]
- *Guidance on making decisions on voluntary erasure applications*[18]
- *Appeals by the GMC pursuant to s40A of the Medical Act 1983 ('s40A appeals') guidance for decision-makers*[19]

Relevant legislation and rules

4.14 The MA 1983 provides the fitness to practise procedural framework (Part V and Sch 4). Specific and detailed rules are provided by the GMC (FTP) Rules 2004 as amended. These procedural rules cover the GMC's Investigation Committee, interim order tribunals and medical

9 This is a non-exhaustive list of current guidance. All guidance is currently available at www.gmc-uk.org or www.mpts-uk.org – readers should always check for updated, revised or additional guidance.

10 SI 2004 No 2608.

11 See www.gmc-uk.org/guidance/good-medical-practice.asp.

12 See www.gmc-uk.org/DC4319_Guidance_on_Warnings_25416870.pdf.

13 See www.gmc-uk.org/DC4483_Guidance_to_the_FTP_Rules_28626691.pdf.

14 See www.gmc-uk.org/DC4599_CE_Decision_Guidance___Making_decisions_on_cases_at_the_end_of_the_investigation_stage.pdf_58070536.pdf.

15 See www.mpts-uk.org/DC4317_Guidance_for_FTP_decision_makers_on_assisting_suicide_51026940.pdf.

16 See www.gmc-uk.org/DC4594_CE_Decision_Guidance___Annex_D___Convictions_Guidance.pdf_58067974.pdf.

17 See www.gmc-uk.org/guidance_on_single_clinical_incidents.pdf_25416561.pdf.

18 See www.gmc-uk.org/DC4316_CE_Decision_Guidance___Annex_I___Guidance_on_voluntary_erasure_25416412.pdf.

19 See www.mpts-uk.org/DC8221_Guidance_for_decision_makers___s40A_appeals.pdf_64121775.pdf.

practitioners tribunals. These rules are made under MA 1983 s43 and Sch 4 para 1(1).

Relevant guidance

General Medical Council

4.15 The GMC is empowered by MA 1983 s35 to provide advice for members of the medical profession on i) standards of professional conduct, ii) standards of professional performance and iii) medical ethics.

4.16 The GMC has published guidance pursuant to section 35. This can be useful for understanding the GMC's expectations of doctors, where relevant to fitness to practise concerns. This guidance includes the seminal *Good medical practice* (see below) and the following current guidance:[20]

- *Consent: patients and doctors making decisions together*
- *0–18 years: guidance for all doctors*
- *Protecting children and young people*
- *Leadership and management for all doctors*
- *Raising and acting on concerns about patient safety*
- *Treatment and care towards the end of life*
- *Accountability in mental health teams*
- *Acting as a witness in legal proceedings*
- *Consent to research*
- Confidentiality:
  - *Confidentiality: good practice in handling patient information*
  - *Confidentiality: disclosing information for education and training purposes*
  - *Confidentiality: disclosing information for insurance, employment and similar purposes*
  - *Confidentiality: disclosing information about serious communicable diseases*
  - *Confidentiality: reporting concerns about patients to the DVLA or DVA*
  - *Confidentiality: reporting gunshot or knife wounds*
  - *Confidentiality: responding to criticism in the media*
- *Guidance for doctors who offer cosmetic interventions*
- *Delegation and referral*
- *Doctors' use of social media*
- *Ending your professional relationship with a patient*
- *Financial and commercial arrangements and conflicts of interest*
- *Good practice in research*
- Maintaining boundaries:
  - *Maintaining boundaries: Intimate examinations and chaperones*
  - *Maintaining boundaries: Maintaining a professional boundary between you and your patient*
  - *Maintaining boundaries: Sexual behavior and your duty to report colleagues*
- *Openness and honesty when things go wrong*
- *Personal beliefs and medical practice*

20 Guidance available at www.gmc-uk.org/guidance/ethical_guidance.asp.

- *Prescribing and managing medicines and devices*
- *Reporting criminal and regulatory proceedings within and outside the UK*
- *Responsible consultants or clinicians*
- *Making and using visual and audio recordings of patients*
- *When a patient seeks advice or information about assistance to die*
- *Writing references*

Medical Practitioners Tribunal Service

4.17 The MPTS also publishes factsheets (to assist doctors without legal representation) and guidance for lawyers and others more familiar with the processes of the MPTS.

4.18 Current MPTS factsheets include:[21]

- Case management procedure
- A tribunal's power to draw adverse inferences and refuse to admit evidence
- A tribunal's power to make a costs award
- Representation and legal advice
- Non-legal support
- Disclosing written evidence
- Expert evidence
- Making admissions
- Postponing your hearing
- Making a submission to the tribunal
- Creating a skeleton argument
- Cross examination
- Adjourning your hearing
- Reviews on the papers
- Publishing hearing decisions

4.19 Current MPTS guidance includes:[22]

- *Sanctions guidance* (various versions currently in place depending on when a hearing takes place) and guidance on the relevance of whether a doctor holds a licence to practise
- Listings, case management and costs:
  - *Case management procedures – guidance for parties and representatives*
  - *Holding hearings outside Manchester on an exceptional basis*
  - *The postponement of an interim orders tribunal or a medical practitioners tribunal hearing under Rule 29*
  - *Guidance for medical practitioners tribunals on case management and exercising powers under Rule 16(A)*
  - *Guidance for case managers on the assessment of costs (including annexe 1)*
  - *Schedule of costs*
  - *Costs: ability to pay self-assessment*
- Medical practitioners tribunals:
  - *Guidance for medical practitioners tribunals on dealing with concerns about a doctor's knowledge of English*

21 MPTS factsheets available at www.mpts-uk.org/hearing/7432.asp.

22 MPTS guidance available at www.mpts-uk.org/decisions/1655.asp.

  - *Guidance for tribunals on adjourning to direct an assessment or for further information or reports*
  - *Managing medical practitioners tribunal hearings: guidance for chairs*
  - *Non-compliance hearings: guidance for medical practitioners tribunals*
  - *Substitution of tribunal members at medical practitioners tribunal hearings*
  - *Use of video, telephone evidence and special measures at medical practitioners tribunal hearings*
  - *Undertakings at medical practitioners tribunal hearings*
  - *Taking interim orders into account*
- Interim orders tribunals:
  - *Imposing interim orders: guidance for the interim orders tribunal and medical practitioners tribunal*
  - *Imposing interim orders – supplementary guidance on the licence to practise*
- Conditions and undertakings banks:
  - *Imposing conditions on a doctor's registration (Conditions bank)*
  - *Imposing interim conditions on a doctor's registration (Interim conditions bank)*
  - *Agreeing a doctor's undertakings (Undertakings bank)*
  - *Non-compliance conditions (Non-compliance conditions bank)*
  - *Glossary of terms used in the conditions and undertaking banks*
- Additional MPTS guidance:
  - *Guidance on fit and proper persons to provide representation at medical practitioners tribunals, interim order tribunals and investigation committee hearings*
  - *Guidance for interpreters attending a hearing at the MPTS*
  - *MPTS recording of hearings guidance*
  - *MPTS expert witness protocol*
  - *MPTS witness statement guidance and template*
  - *Policy guidance for medical practitioners tribunals and chairs: conducting reviews on the papers*

Good medical practice

4.20 *Good medical practice* was first published in 1995 (replacing the Blue Book) and sought to set out standards rather than examples of misconduct. It has now been through several iterations. The current version was published in March 2013 and updated in April 2014.[23]

4.21 *Good medical practice* 'describes what is expected of all doctors registered with the General Medical Council (GMC)' with the indication that '[s]erious or persistence failure to follow this guidance will put . . . registration at risk'.[24] *Good medical practice* and other guidance is frequently referred to in fitness to practise proceedings to illustrate which principles and values are alleged to have been breached. There are currently four 'Domains': 1) Knowledge, skills and performance; 2) Safety and quality; 3) Communication, partnership and teamwork; and 4) Maintaining trust.

23 See www.gmc-uk.org/Good_medical_practice___English_1215.pdf_51527435.pdf.

24 *Good medical practice* pp4–5.

Fitness to practise procedures

4.22 The most significant change in recent years is that the GMC have now established the MPTS. The MPTS began the management of FTP hearings on 11 June 2012. In addition, the use of independent legal assessors has been dispensed with in most cases. The overwhelming majority of IOT and FTP hearings will be chaired by an LQC. Unrepresented doctors will no longer have the assistance of an independent lawyer in the proceedings.

Fitness to practise – overview

4.23 There are two distinct stages to the GMC fitness to practise procedures:

1) *Investigation* – cases are investigated as to whether they need to be referred for adjudication.
2) *Adjudication* – hearing the cases that have been referred to the medical practitioners tribunal.

Investigation – overview

Initial assessment

4.24 All complaints and queries are considered by GMC staff who have three options available: 1) close the case, 2) refer the case to the doctor's employer or 3) begin an investigation.

4.25 A matter might be closed in cases where, even if the facts are found proved, no regulatory action would be required. A doctor's responsible officer might be notified in cases where the issues complained of would not, in and of themselves, require action but might if they formed part of a wider pattern of behaviour. Where the complaint arose in a work context, it is likely that the employer/responsible officer is already aware of the issue (and may already have undertaken their own investigation or disciplinary proceedings at the employer level) but previous or additional employers may also be contacted.

Investigation stage

4.26 The investigation stage involves evidence-gathering, which could include the GMC obtaining information from employers, an independent assessment of the doctor's health or clinical performance (which can include as part of the performance an assessment of the standard of a person's knowledge of English), obtaining an expert opinion on a particular issue or gathering witness statements. There is also an opportunity for a registrant to engage with the investigation. It is important that legal advice is sought at this stage, as any response given by a doctor to a complaint can potentially be used by the GMC against a registrant at a full hearing if what is later stated in any eventual hearing is inconsistent. *Good medical practice* places an obligation on registrants to co-operate with such formal inquiries,[25] however co-operation does not need to equate with full disclosure at

25 *Good medical practice* para 73: 'You must co-operate with formal inquiries and complaints procedures and must offer all relevant information while following the guidance in *Confidentiality*.'

such an early stage in proceedings, particularly when a registrant may not know exactly what allegations he or she is responding to. The principle of protection against self-incrimination is also relevant here. However, the level of detailed response a registrant chooses to provide should be carefully considered, with the assistance of legal advice, if possible. Great care must be exercised in suggesting that an allegation is minor or trivial. Even if correct, until the accuracy of such a comment can be ascertained objectively, and independent of the GMC, there is a real danger the GMC will suggest such comments demonstrate a lack of insight. Whilst there is a duty to co-operate the registrant should be aware he or she is co-operating with an investigating and prosecuting regulator not a friend.

4.27 Once sufficient information has been obtained, two case examiners (one of whom is medically qualified) consider the information available and determine the next step. If the evidence does not suggest a serious or persistent breach of the standards expected of a doctor as contained in *Good medical practice* and the doctor's fitness to practise could not be considered to be impaired, then the case examiners may:

- conclude the case with no further action;
- issue a warning;
- agree undertakings to address a problem; or
- refer the case to the MPTS for a medical practitioners tribunal.[26]

4.28 A referral to the MPTS can only occur with the agreement of both a medical and non-medical case examiner. If the two case examiners cannot agree, then the matter will be referred to the Investigation Committee of the GMC.

4.29 A case can be referred to an interim orders tribunal at any time – the interim orders tribunal can place restrictions on a doctor's practice, if required, to, among other things, protect patients while an investigation is being carried out or a case is being prepared for a hearing.

Adjudication stage – overview

4.30 This stage involves a case before a medical practitioners tribunal. The tribunal is usually made up of three people – a chair and two members, one of whom must be medical and one non-medical. In some cases the chair may be legally qualified; if not, then a legal assessor advises the panel.[27] The legal power to use Legally Qualified Chairs (LQCs) came into effect at the end of 2015 and a pilot begain in 2016 initially for less complex hearings. The MPTS *Policy on the use of Legally Qualified Chairs in tribunal hearings* states as follows:[28]

> Tribunals must be a quorum of three constituted of a chair, a medical member and a lay member. A chair may be medically qualified or lay, which includes legally qualified chairs. In all cases the chair is responsible for

26 GMC, *A guide to doctors referred to the GMC*, available at www.gmc-uk.org/concerns/doctors_under_investigation/a_guide_for_referred_doctors.asp.

27 General Medical Council (Legal Assessors) Rules 2004 SI No 2625 – see para 4.118 below.

28 Available at www.mpts-uk.org/DC10491__MPTS_Policy_on_the_use_of_LQCs.pdf_72038353.pdf.

ensuring; the hearing follows the processes set out in the Rules, hearing time is used effectively and that people appearing at the hearing are treated with courtesy and consideration. Where the chair is appointed to sit as a LQC they are additionally required to advise their fellow tribunal members on any questions of law as to evidence or procedure. In all other cases, the tribunal will be advised by a legal assessor.

Following the pilot scheme, it is now clear that the MPTS intends to use LQCs in almost all hearings since this reduces hearing lengths and costs. Legal Assessors will only be used in rare cases considered too onerous to be dealt with by an LQC alone.

4.31 The doctor may be represented by a solicitor, barrister, a representative from a professional organisation or, at the discretion of the tribunal, a member of his or her family or other person. The MPTS has issued *Guidance on fit and proper persons to provide representation at medical practitioners tribunals, interim order tribunals and investigation committee hearings.*[29] The GMC will likely be represented by a solicitor or barrister ('the GMC presenting officer').

4.32 There are three stages to a hearing: 1) fact-finding, 2) statutory ground and impairment and 3) sanction. If no facts are found proved the matter concludes at stage 1. If no impairment is found at the end of stage two, then the tribunal may close the case with or without advice or issue a warning. If impairment is found at stage 2, then the case moves to stage 3 for consideration what if any sanction to impose on the registrant.

4.33 There is the potential for an appeal by the doctor or the GMC under MA 1983 s40A or by the Professional Standards Authority (PSA).

Statutory grounds

4.34 The section below provides basic details relating to each of the statutory grounds. A fuller exposition can be found in chapter 1.

4.35 The MPTS is entitled to restrict or remove the registration of a registrant whose fitness to practise is found to be impaired. Under MA 1983 s35C(2), a registrant's fitness to practise may be found to be impaired by reason of any or all of the following (known as the 'statutory grounds'):

1) misconduct;
2) deficient professional performance;
3) a criminal conviction or caution in the UK (or elsewhere for an offence which would be a criminal offence if committed in the UK);
4) physical or mental ill-health;
5) lack of the necessary knowledge of English language to be able to practise medicine safely in the UK;
6) a determination (decision) by a regulatory body either in the UK or overseas.

29 GMC (FTP) Rules 2004 r33.

'Misconduct'

4.36 In *Nandi v General Medical Council*[30] Collins J adopted the observation of Lord Clyde in *Rylands v General Medical Council*[31] that:

> . . . professional misconduct is 'a falling short by omission or commission of the standards of conduct expected among medical -practitioners, and such falling short must be serious'. The adjective 'serious' must be given its proper weight, and in other contexts there has been reference to conduct which would be regarded as deplorable by fellow practitioners. It is of course possible for negligent conduct to amount to serious professional misconduct, but the negligence must be to a high degree.[32]

4.37 His Lordship stated that it is not restricted to conduct that is morally blameworthy. It could include seriously negligent treatment or a failure to provide treatment measured by objective professional standards. Obviously, dishonest conduct can very easily (although not always) be regarded as serious professional misconduct, but conduct that does not amount in any way to dishonesty can constitute serious professional misconduct if it falls far short of the standard that is considered appropriate by the profession.

4.38 Lord Cooke of Thorndon in the Privy Council case of *Preiss v General Dental Council*[33] said:

> It is settled that serious professional misconduct does not require moral turpitude. Gross professional negligence can fall within it. Something more is required than a degree of professional negligence enough to give rise to civil liability but not calling for the opprobrium that inevitably attaches to the disciplinary offence.[34]

4.39 In *R (Calhaem) v General Medical Council*[35] Jackson J stated that:

> The word 'misconduct' in section 35C(2)(a) does not mean any breach of the duty owed by a doctor to his patient: it connotes a serious breach which indicates that the doctor's fitness to practise is impaired.[36]

4.40 Following a review of the authorities, His Lordship derived five principles relevant to that case which involved failures by a consultant anesthetist and departure from *Good medical practice* in the context of a serious operation. These are:

a) Mere negligence does not constitute 'misconduct' within the meaning of MA 1983 s35C(2)(a). Nevertheless, and depending upon the circumstances, negligent acts or omissions which are particularly serious may amount to 'misconduct'.
b) A single negligent act or omission is less likely to cross the threshold of 'misconduct' than multiple acts or omissions. Nevertheless, and

30 [2004] EWHC 2317 (Admin).
31 [1999] Lloyd's Rep Med 139 at 149.
32 *Nandi v General Medical Council* [2004] EWHC 2317 (Admin) per Collins J at paras 31–33.
33 [2001] UKPC 36.
34 At para 28.
35 [2007] EWHC 2606 (Admin), [2008] LS Law Medical 96.
36 At para 26.

depending upon the circumstances, a single negligent act or omission, if particularly grave, could be characterised as 'misconduct'.

c) 'Deficient professional performance' within the meaning of section 35C(2)(b) is conceptually separate both from negligence and from misconduct. It does not mean any instance of substandard work. It connotes a level of professional performance that indicates that the doctor's fitness to practise is impaired. It is unacceptably low which (save in exceptional circumstances) has been demonstrated by reference to a fair sample of the doctor's work.
d) A single instance of negligent treatment, unless very serious indeed, would be unlikely to constitute 'deficient professional performance'.
e) It is neither necessary nor appropriate to extend the interpretation of 'deficient professional performance' in order to encompass matters that constitute 'misconduct'.[37]

Deficient professional performance[38]

4.41 In essence, this encompasses conduct that has fallen far short of the standards expected of a reasonably competent practitioner and done so on more than one occasion and usually by reference to a fair sample of the registrant's work. It need not be a repeat of the same conduct. One exceptionally serious event may also amount to deficient professional performance.

4.42 Conduct occurring outside the UK and/or before the registrant was in fact registered may still found a case on deficient professional performance, the reason of course being risk to the public and profession. (See also chapter 3 at paras 3.58–3.72.)

Conviction cases

4.43 MA 1983 s35C(2)(c) provides that the GMC has jurisdiction to consider cases where it is alleged that a registrant's fitness to practise is impaired by reason of a conviction or caution in the British Islands for a criminal offence, or a conviction elsewhere for an offence, which, if committed in England and Wales, would constitute a criminal offence. The procedure for dealing with such cases is broadly the same as for those on the other statutory grounds.

4.44 The GMC (FTP) Rules provide[39] that a certified copy of the certificate of conviction (or in Scotland an extract conviction) is proof of the conviction and of the fact upon which it was based. Accordingly, in such cases it will not be open to registrants to suggest that they did not commit the offence in question, and representations will need to focus on any mitigating circumstances, insight, remorse and reparation. The only permissible route for rebutting evidence would be in the rare circumstances where a registrant was able to adduce evidence for the purposes of proving that he

37 At para 39.
38 Other regulators refer to this as 'lack of competence'.
39 GMC (FTP) Rules 2004 r34(3).

or she is not the person referred to in the certificate or extract.[40] There is only a discretion to admit this evidence.

Ill-health

4.45 Where the allegation that fitness to practise is impaired due to physical or mental ill-health, the factual background will be relevant but is likely to be largely admitted. Therefore the main focus will be on the particular health condition in question, and whether it caused or contributed to the alleged facts. If the opinion of an expert is required and the registrant has been assessed by a GMC medical assessor, it is likely that he or she will be called to give evidence. The registrant may need to call his or her own medical expert if the GMC assessor's report is disputed.

4.46 If a medical expert is to be called, then the following evidence should be adduced:

- the expert's professional qualifications and area of specialisation;
- what documentation the expert has considered, whether the expert has personally assessed the registrant, and whether the expert has had any prior involvement with the registrant;
- diagnosis and prognosis, and whether the medical condition in question caused or contributed to the factual allegations; and
- whether a registrant's current fitness to practise is impaired by reason of ill-health, and the likelihood and extent of recurrence of the medical condition, steps that the registrant has already taken to reduce recurrence, and any further steps that can be taken.

Lack of the necessary knowledge of English language

4.47 'The necessary knowledge of English' is defined in the MA 1983 as 'the knowledge of English which, in the interests of himself and his patients, is necessary for the practice of medicine in the United Kingdom' (MA 1983 s55(1)).

4.48 Note that by MA 1983 s2(4), the requirement for necessary knowledge of English shall not apply in determining whether a person's fitness to practise is impaired for the purposes of registration under the MA 1983.

Determination by another regulator

4.49 The fact that matters complained of occurred outside the UK and/or before a practitioner was registered with a regulatory body is no bar to proceedings. The fact that the matters may have already been adjudicated upon in another jurisdiction is also no bar to proceedings.

4.50 The GMC also has jurisdiction to consider allegations on the ground of a determination by a body responsible for the regulation of a health or social care profession that his or her fitness to practise is impaired.

40 GMC (FTP) Rules 2004 r34(5).

Key terms

What is 'impairment'?

4.51 'Impairment' is not defined by legislation, however there is considerable case-law on this issue (see paras 3.1–3.18). Crucially, it is well-established that it is a present-day test. Therefore the purpose of fitness to practise proceedings is not to punish the registrant for past wrongdoings but to protect the public or profession where a registrant's current fitness to practise is impaired. In reaching this decision the tribunal can take into account the past wrongdoing, but it is also required to take into account other relevant factors such as whether the conduct in question is easily remediable, whether it has been remedied and the likelihood of repetition.[41] It is a forward-looking test.[42] Some conduct may be incapable of being easily remedied. In other cases, even if the conduct in question is capable of remedy, and has been remedied, the nature of the conduct may be such that these steps carry little weight. This is where the conduct involved a fundamental breach of professional standards, such that a finding of impairment is required to uphold public confidence in the profession or the regulator amongst other considerations.

4.52 Impairment is a vital concept to understand within this jurisdiction, because the issue of impairment is, arguably, the most crucial determination the medical practitioners tribunal will have to make. While a finding of impairment does not automatically lead to the imposition of a sanction, it makes one much more likely. It is also a difficult determination for a registrant to have made against him or her (regardless of whether any sanction is eventually imposed): it is stating that an individual's fitness to practise *is* impaired – a difficult blow for any professional who has undertaken substantial training to get to that position (whether a junior doctor or consultant) and one that ultimately has to be declared to current and prospective employers for a considerable time period. The issue of impairment must necessarily be a key focus of preparation for any eventual hearing – the way the facts are presented and challenged, and the decisions made upon them will likely have a significant impact on what determinations are made at both the impairment, and if required, the sanction stage.

What is 'insight'?

4.53 'Insight' is the expectation that a registrant will be able to stand back and accept that with hindsight, he or she should have behaved differently, and that it is expected that he or she will take steps to prevent a recurrence and learn from their mistakes. Factors which may assist a committee when considering whether a registrant has the insight necessary to avoid or mitigate sanctions, and to accept and comply with proposed undertakings, include:

41 *Cohen v General Medical Council* [2008] EWHC 581 (Admin). See also *R (Zygmunt) v General Medical Council* [2008] EWHC 2643 (Admin) and *Sarkodie-Gyan v Nursing and Midwifery Council* [2009] EWHC 2131 (Admin).

42 *Meadow v General Medical Council* [2007] EWCA Civ 1390, [2006] QB 462; *Cheatle v General Medical Council* [2009] EWHC 645 (Admin).

- demonstrating an understanding of the gravity of the conduct in question;
- being open and honest when things go wrong;
- showing a willingness to act differently in the future;
- offering an apology;
- the conduct and demeanour of the registrant at the hearing.

The investigation stage in detail

Investigation

4.54 Once the registrar of the GMC receives information about a registrant which falls into any of the categories above, he or she may make appropriate enquiries. The investigation may include:

- obtaining medical records;
- obtaining documentary evidence from third parties;
- taking statements from witnesses;
- obtaining expert reports on clinical or other matters;
- directing the registrant to undergo an assessment of his or her health or performance (which may include as part of a performance assessment an assessment of the standard of the person's knowledge of English). Assessors will produce a report, which will be disclosed.[43]

4.55 At the outcome of the investigation stage, the registrar may decide to conclude the case, issue a warning, or, if an issue is raised that the doctor's fitness is or may be impaired, refer the case forward to a medical practitioners tribunal for adjudication.

Referral of allegations and investigations – overview

4.56 This section outlines the key rules that apply when a complaint is first received. Complaints are usually received from employers, patients, police or other health professionals.

Initial referrals (rule 4)

4.57 The key rules are as follows:

a) Initial referral:
   - Rule 4: Initial consideration by registrar and referral of allegations if any of categories of impairment in MA 1983 s35C(2) may apply.

b) Registrar decision:
   - Case concluded if no question of impairment.
   - Conclude case if vexatious.
   - Advise maker of allegation of other means of resolution (eg NHS complaints procedure) or refer to another body.

43 GMC (FTP) Rules 2004 r7(4) and (5).

c) If the allegation is more than five years old, refer only if in the public interest, in exceptional circumstances to do so[44] (see para 4.122 below and chapter 1 at para 1.191).
d) Refer on for investigation or direct for adjudication.

Convictions, cautions and determinations (rule 5)

4.58 The key rules are as follows:

a) There is a presumption that if a doctor has been the subject of a criminal conviction or caution or a determination by another regulatory body, the matter will proceed directly to adjudication.
b) There is an irrebuttable presumption if an immediate or suspended sentence was imposed following criminal conviction that the matter will proceed directly to adjudication.
c) In other cases further investigation may occur before referral.
d) There is no requirement for the GMC to re-prove matters proved in other proceedings.[45]

Investigation (rule 7)

4.59 Investigative steps may include:

- obtaining medical records;
- obtaining other documentary evidence from third parties;
- taking witness statements;
- obtaining expert reports on clinical or other matters;
- directing the registrant to undergo an assessment of his or her health or performance.[46]

Case examiner decision or Investigation Committee (rules 8 and 9)

4.60 A decision is taken by two case examiners (one medical and one non-medical) as to the next step in the process. Before referral for adjudication or the issuing of a warning, the registrant will be informed of allegations and evidence and given at least 28 days to provide written comments.

4.61 Case examiners may decide to:

a) conclude a case;
b) issue a warning;
c) refer for adjudication only if there is realistic prospect of establishing that the practitioner's fitness to practise is impaired to a degree justifying action on registration, can adjourn for further information if required;
d) if both case examiners agree, invite doctor to accept undertakings restricting relevant practice; if no agreement, referred to Investigation Committee.

44 GMC (FTP) Rules 2004 r4(5).

45 GMC (FTP) Rules 2004 r34(3)–(5).

46 Any decision for health/performance assessment must be agreed by medical case examiner.

Undertakings (rule 10)

4.62 Where fitness to practise is found to be impaired (or may become so on recurrence of a medical condition) the registrar may invite a registrant to make undertakings (eg to restrict his or her practice, undergo treatment or retraining). Undertakings can only be sought where to do so would provide sufficient protection to the public. (See *Crabbie v General Medical Council.*[47])

4.63 Where case examiners agree that a registrant's fitness to practise is impaired, they may invite a doctor to agree to undertakings, subject to the following caveats:

a) only if sufficient public protection is achieved through under-takings;
b) undertakings must be accepted, otherwise referred for adjudication;
c) undertakings are reviewed by the GMC Case Review Team.

A doctor ought to take advice when considering undertakings since case examiners may seek unduly onerous undertakings through adopting an overly severe or risk-averse stance. Undertakings should be no more than are necessary to meet the risk identified by any admitted facts or impairment.

Warnings (rule 11)

4.64 The GMC has produced *Guidance on warnings.*[48] As noted above, a warning is available at both the investigation and adjudication stage of fitness to practise proceedings, as para 4 of the guidance indicates:

> At the investigation stage, the case examiners or the Investigation Committee must first apply the investigation stage test and satisfy themselves that there is no realistic prospect of establishing that the doctor's fitness to practise is impaired to a degree requiring action on his or her registration. When a case is referred to the MPTS for a hearing, the tribunal should only consider whether a warning is appropriate, once it has found that the doctor's fitness to practise is not impaired.

4.65 A warning will be issued where the evidence suggests that the registrant's behaviour or performance has fallen below acceptable standards to a degree warranting formal censure by the GMC, but which does not make referral to a medical practitioners tribunal or action on registration necessary. The registrant will be asked to make comments, and he or she can require an oral hearing.

4.66 There is no difference in the 'significance attached to warnings issued at the investigation stage and warnings issued at the adjudication stage'.[49] Warnings are not available where allegations relate solely to a doctor's health – they are available where health is one factor of the case.

4.67 Warnings must be disclosed as per para 8 of the guidance:

> Warnings are disclosed to any person or body who brought the allegation to the attention of the GMC, the practitioner's employer, and any other enquirer. They are published via the GMC's website on the List of Registered Medical Practitioners (LRMP) for a five-year period. After five years,

47 [2002] All ER (D) 153 (Sep).
48 See www.gmc-uk.org/DC4319_Guidance_on_Warnings_25416870.pdf.
49 *Guidance on warnings* para 6.

warnings cease to be published on the LRMP and are no longer disclosed to general enquirers. However they are kept on record and disclosed to employers on request, indefinitely.

4.68 Perhaps most importantly, for the registrant, a 'warning does not prevent a doctor from holding a licence to practise and does not place any restrictions on their registration'.[50] However, that may be too simplistic an approach to the matter because while registration is unrestricted, current and future employability may be significantly affected by the imposition of the warning and the requirement to disclose it.

4.69 Decision-makers are provided with factors to take into account when determining whether a warning would be an appropriate action.[51] These include:

- a clear and specific breach of guidance;
- the conduct approaches but falls short of the relevant test for impairment;
- concerns are sufficiently serious that repetition of them would likely result in an impairment finding;
- the need to formally record the particular concerns.

4.70 The guidance then provides specific advice in types of cases: treatment (para 21), convictions and cautions (para 22) and dishonesty (para 23). The need for a tribunal to take a proportionate approach is highlighted (para 25) as is the relevance (or otherwise) of mitigation (para 31). Personal mitigation cannot be used to reduce a sanction to a warning if fitness to practise has been found to be impaired. At para 33 a non-exhaustive list of aggravating or mitigating factors that might be relevant is provided:

a) insight;
b) apology;
c) previous good history;
d) risk of repetition;
e) remedial steps taken;
f) relevant and appropriate testimonials.

4.71 Reasons are required for a decision (para 34) and Annex A provides a warnings template, but in summary a warning will need to:

a) highlight the concerns requiring the warning;
b) make clear why the concerns impact on patient safety/public confidence in/reputation of the profession;
c) make clear what conduct led to warning, and why it should not be repeated; and
d) refer to any relevant GMC guidance or relevant sections of *Good medical practice*.

4.72 Where a registrant's conduct raises a minor cause for concern, but does not merit a formal warning, a letter of advice may be issued. (See GMC's guidance *Good medical practice*.)

50 *Guidance on warnings* para 9.

51 *Guidance on warnings* para 20.

Review of decisions (rule 12)

4.73 If the GMC conclude a case, issue a warning or accept undertakings, the registrar may review the decision on application of the registrant, complainant or of his or her own initiative if:

a) the decision in question may be materially flawed or there is new information which may have led to a different decision; and
b) the registrar considers a review is necessary for the protection of the public, the prevention of injustice to the registrant, or is otherwise necessary in the public interest.

4.74 There is a two-year limitation on such a review being undertaken unless there are exceptional circumstances.

4.75 The following options are available to the registrar on conclusion of the review:

a) uphold the previous decision;
b) quash the previous decision and substitute a fresh decision;
c) refer for reconsideration by case examiners.

4.76 Reasons for the decision must be provided to all parties.

Health or performance assessments

4.77 A recommendation for a health or performance assessment can be made by a medical case examiner, but in any event must be agreed by a medical case examiner. The power to require a doctor to undergo such an assessment derives from MA 1983 Sch 4 para 5A(1):

> 5A(1) The General Council may make rules –
> (a) authorising the giving of directions by any of –
> (i) the Investigation Committee,
> (ii) a Medical Practitioners Tribunal,
> (iii) such other persons as may be specified in the rules, requiring an assessment of the standard of a registered person's professional performance to be carried out;
> (b) specifying circumstances in which such an assessment may be carried out otherwise than in accordance with a direction.

4.78 GMC (FTP) Rules 2004 r7(3) indicates, together with Sch 1 (for performance assessment) and Sch 2 (for health assessment), further details on this process.

4.79 These assessments can be onerous – the elements of the assessment include a) peer review and b) a test of competence to assess knowledge and skills.[52] The peer review may include any of the following:

- a visit to the doctor's place of work;
- interviews with the doctor;
- interviews with third parties, including the complainant or complainants in the case;
- a review of a sample of the doctor's records and practice documents;

52 For more information see www.gmc-uk.org/concerns/doctors_under_investigation/undergoing_a_test_of_competence.asp.

- a case based discussion using a selection of the above cases to explore the doctor's reasoning;
- observation of the doctor's interaction with patients (where this is practical and the doctor is working).

4.80 Any written advice or information the assessment team choose to obtain is shared with the registrant for comment. A report is then produced and disclosed. The scope and depth of a performance assessment is not to be underestimated and it is in the doctor's interests to take the test seriously and ensure that there is a medically qualified individual with experience within the particular area of practice under investigation. A performance assessment can sometimes result in further areas of concern (unrelated to the initial concerns that triggered the assessment) and therefore further allegations being potentially referred for adjudication – but areas of concern can only form part of formal consideration at a hearing if they are included in the notice of allegation (see *Roomi v General Medical Council*[53]). Any concerns with the performance assessment process (for example, any potential concern about conflict of interest of an assessor or concerns over fairness) should be raised at the time of assessment or recorded in writing directly after. Another consideration may be seeking confirmation of how patient records were selected for any audit undertaken to ensure a fair sample of work over a fair period of time. For a health assessment, the registrant's mental and/or physical health is examined by two separate doctors selected by the GMC. Each examiner then prepares a report.

4.81 Where a doctor refuses to undergo a health or performance assessment, as required, or fails to co-operate with the assessment process, the case will be referred to a medical practitioners tribunal to consider whether the doctor's fitness to practise is impaired and if any action is required on his or her registration. A failure to co-operate could, in and of itself, be deemed a breach of *Good medical practice* para 73:

> You must co-operate fully with any formal inquiry into the treatment of a patient and with any complaints procedure that applies to your work.

The procedure for addressing such a non-compliance are specifically catered for within GMC (FTP) Rules 2004 r17ZA – Procedure at a non-compliance hearing; in MPTS guidance: *Non-compliance hearings: guidance for medical practitioners tribunals*;[54] and in the MPTS factsheet for non-represented doctors.[55]

Interim orders and interim orders tribunals (rules 25–27)

4.82 Interim orders may be made prior to the substantive hearing on fitness if they are necessary to protect the public or in the public interest or in the registrant's interest.

53 [2009] EWHC 2188 (Admin), per Collins J.

54 See www.mpts-uk.org/DC8271_Non_compliance_hearings_guidance_for_medical_practitioners_tribunals.pdf_63980352.pdf.

55 See www.mpts-uk.org/DC8489_How_the_non_compliance_hearing_process_works_64228593.pdf.

4.83 The threshold for an interim order is a low one even though a registrant may be temporarily suspended or be subject to temporary conditions that limit or prevent his or her practice.

4.84 No judgment is made regarding the facts of the allegation, but the tribunal must be satisfied that, on a fair analysis, there *may* be a prima facie case.

4.85 The tribunal may suspend or impose conditions on a registrant's registration on an interim basis, pending investigation/adjudication of the case. The registrar may refer a case to an interim orders tribunal to consider whether such an order should be made for the protection of patients, or in the interests of the public or the registrant. A decision to impose an interim order, particularly interim suspension, can have a devastating impact on a registrant and make it much harder for a doctor to show how (if applicable) he or she has remedied any issues that may eventually be found proved at a full hearing because – particularly if the concerns are clinical in nature – if the interim suspension order remains in place, a registrant will not be able to work as a doctor at all for the duration of the interim suspension order. Referral can occur at any time following initial complaint and hearings can be listed quickly.

4.86 MA 1983 s41A on interim orders provides as follows (emphasis added):

> (A1) Where the matter is referred under section 35C(8) to the MPTS, the MPTS must arrange an Interim Orders Tribunal or a Medical Practitioners Tribunal to decide whether to make an order as mentioned in that provision.
>
> (1) Where an Interim Orders Tribunal or a Medical Practitioners Tribunal in arrangements made under subsection (A1), or a Medical Practitioners Tribunal in their consideration of a matter are satisfied that it is necessary *for the protection of members of the public or is otherwise in the public interest, or is in the interests of a fully registered person,* for the registration of that person to be suspended or to be made subject to conditions, the Tribunal may make an order –
>
> (a) that his registration in the register shall be suspended (that is to say, shall not have effect) during such period *not exceeding eighteen months* as may be specified in the order (an 'interim suspension order'); or
>
> (b) that his registration shall be conditional on his compliance, during such period not exceeding eighteen months as may be specified in the order, with such requirements so specified as the Panel think fit to impose (an 'order for interim conditional registration').

4.87 The procedure governing referrals to an interim orders tribunal and consideration of cases by such a tribunal is governed by Part 7 (rules 25–27).

4.88 The tribunal will comprise three decision makers – a chair (who may or may not be a legally qualified chair), a lay member and a medical member. If the chair is not legally qualified then the tribunal will instead be assisted by a Legal Assessor but this will now be very rare.

4.89 The registrant will be given reasonable notice of the hearing (rule 26), and provided with a reasonable opportunity to make representations. The hearings will normally be held in private (rule 41(3)(a)).

4.90 This is likely to be the first hearing a doctor will be invited to attend and it can be at short notice and somewhat daunting (see below at paras 4.151–4.156 for practical information concerning venues). Again, as much evidence as possible should be gathered to make submissions against an order as persuasive as possible, or if, on advice, an order is likely, consideration should be given to making suggestions for conditions that are realistic, achievable and meet concerns raised and are manageable/the best outcome for the doctor to try and prevent an interim suspension order. It is important to be realistic about conditions and there is absolutely no point in a registrant agreeing to conditions which cannot be met, as it is likely not only to add more stress but also to lead to more onerous conditions or even interim suspension if compliance with conditions cannot be shown at any subsequent review. The MPTS guidance *Imposing interim orders: guidance for the interim orders tribunal and medical practitioners tribunal* and where appropriate *Imposing interim orders – supplementary guidance on the licence to practise*[56] are a helpful starting point for advisers.

4.91 At the first hearing, the tribunal may impose an interim order for a period of up to 18 months. It must be reviewed within six months of being made, and thereafter every six months.[57] A registrant can request an earlier review – which shall be heard as soon as practicable after three months from the date of the immediately preceding order. A review can also take place when new and relevant evidence emerges which could affect the order.

4.92 A medical practitioners tribunal will generally revoke any interim order which is in place prior to its determination at the conclusion of a hearing, or it may decide to impose one where, eg it has decided to adjourn the case.

4.93 For an interim order to be extended beyond 18 months the GMC must apply to the High Court. At review hearings, interim orders can be revoked, modified or replaced, or remain as before.

4.94 Before an interim order is imposed there must be a *real risk to patients, colleagues or other members of the public* – it is not enough to be merely desirable. Relevant considerations include the seriousness of the allegation, the nature of the evidence and the likelihood of repetition.

4.95 Interim orders should rarely be imposed merely to maintain public confidence in the profession/proper standards of conduct and performance (*R (Shiekh) v General Dental Council*[58]). Care must be taken to avoid, as far as possible, any disproportionate consequences such as the loss of a training contract. The tribunal must take into account the impact on the doctor's right to practise, their finances and reputation (*R (Madan) v General Medical Council*[59]). An allegation that is trivial should not be given

56 See www.mpts-uk.org/DC4792_Imposing_Interim_Orders___Guidance_for_the_IOT_and_MPT_28443349.pdf.

57 A review must take place within three months of the first or any subsequent order where a) interim conditions have been replaced with interim suspension, b) interim suspension has been relaced with interim conditions or c) the High Court has extended an order beyond the period initially set.

58 [2007] EWHC 2972 (Admin).

59 [2001] EWHC 577 (Admin).

weight (*General Medical Council v Sheill*[60]) – see chapter 1, para 1.93 for a fuller discussion.

4.96 The doctor has the opportunity to attend and be represented. The process at the hearing, (which will be held in private in accordance with rule 41(3)(a), is that the GMC will make representations as to the need for an interim order, followed by the doctor's opportunity to make representations. Generally the tribunal does not receive oral evidence and are not required to adjudicate on the facts. This is difficult to understand for practitioners who may end up under an interim suspension order without having had the opportunity to challenge the allegations or facts behind them. Indeed, at the point of an interim hearing the allegations may not yet have even been formulated or particularised. The considerations at para 4.26 are equally applicable to interim order tribunal hearings. The legal assessor (if one is present) gives advice to the tribunal and then the tribunal retires to consider their decision, returning to announce their decision and give reasons – it is likely that the doctor will be provided with a written decision there and then. It is important to take the time to consider this decision and ensure that the doctor fully understands what is required of him or her in order to comply with the order.

4.97 Review hearings will follow a similar format, but it will be expected that evidence can be provided to show compliance with the previously imposed order (more relevant where there is a conditions order). Particularly with interim conditions, at review hearings if non-repetition of a less serious issue can be shown it may be sufficient to persuade a tribunal to remove or vary conditions.

Fraud or error in relation to registration

4.98 Where the registrar is satisfied that any entry in the register has been fraudulently procured or incorrectly made, he or she may erase the entry from the register. MA 1983 s39 is the relevant provision, in relation to registration fraud. The appeal mechanism is contained within MA 1983 Sch 3A.

Following a referral to a Fitness to Practise Tribunal

Service of notices and other documents

4.99 Rule 15(2) of the GMC (FTP) Rules 2004 provides that:

> Unless the practitioner consents to a lesser period of notice being given or the Registrar or MPTS considers it in the public interest for there to be such a lesser period, a notice [of the hearing] shall be given by the Registrar or MPTS (as the case may be) at least 28 days before the hearing.
>
> The notice of hearing, shall amongst other matters, specify the date, time and venue of the hearing and 'particularise the allegation against the registrant and the facts upon which it is based . . .' (rule 15(1)(a)(i)).

4.100 Rule 16 deals with case management issues and provides that when a case is referred to a case manager. Rule 16(6) provides a non-exhaustive list of

60 [2006] EWHC 3025 (Admin).

matters that the case manager may make directions on. Case managers can be legally qualified case managers appointed by the MPTS (rule 16(1)). However, the power to make directions under rule 16 can also be exercised by the chair of a medical practitioners tribunal, where the chair is appointed as a case manager for proceedings before that tribunal, or the medical practitioners tribunal itself (rule 16(1A)). Directions may include but are not limited to the following: each party shall disclose to or inform the other of:

(a) the material they intend to rely upon namely documentary evidence, details of the witnesses (this includes the registrant if giving evidence), signed witness statements, any expert report and skeleton arguments;
(b) time estimates;
(c) whether or not the health of the registrant is to be raised as an issue;
(d) that the registrant indicates, so far as is practicable-
  (i) whether the allegation is admitted,
  (ii) which facts are admitted and which remain in dispute,
  (iii) which witness evidence is admitted and which witnesses are required for cross examination, and
  (iv) whether any preliminary legal arguments are to be made;
(e) where the allegation is admitted, a direction that the parties produce a statement of agreed facts ...

Allegations

> The particulars of the allegation and the facts upon which they are founded should be clear and settled in advance of any hearing.
>
> If in doubt, clarification and/or further and better particulars should be obtained.
>
> The tribunal may, having heard from both parties, amend either the allegation or the facts provided no injustice is caused but this should be the exception not the rule.

4.101 In fitness to practise cases the GMC's 'notice of proceedings' identifies both the case brought against a registrant and the alleged facts upon which it is based. It is one of the most important documents in the case and should be drafted with some care. Although amendments may be made, there are limitations. It is only fair and reasonable that both parties and the tribunal have a firm and settled idea of what the case is about before it is under way.

4.102 The particulars of the allegation and the facts upon which they are founded should be made clear in advance of any hearing. In *Gee v General Medical Council*[61] the court held it to be a requirement that the registrant had fair notice of the nature of the evidence to be led in support of the allegations, time to prepare for his or her defence and, that the tribunal should make plain which of the allegations of fact, if any, they had found proved. It is an aspect of European Convention on Human Rights (ECHR) Article 6 (right to a fair trial) that an applicant should be made aware of the charges against him or her. Allegations should not be drafted in a vague or

61 [1987] 1 WLR 564.

ambiguous manner. The case-law relating to the drafting of allegations is discussed in more detail in chapter 1 at para 1.137 onwards.

The following is a summary of the GMC's general principles on drafting:

- The notice needs to be sufficiently particularised as to the basis of the alleged impairment, but without unnecessary detail. It is not a narrative of the case, a summary of the evidence, or an opening statement of case. It should set out the facts which the GMC says indicate impairment.
- Charges should be unambiguously drafted, using succinct plain language, concise and, sub-clauses should be avoided. They should say what is meant.
- A charge should be chronological.
- It should i) identify and describe the doctor's practice and location; ii) describe the key factual elements of what is alleged avoiding unnecessary narrative detail; iii) indicate what is being criticised and how it is being criticised. Guidance may be obtained from an expert report or from publications such as *Good medical practice* or other specific guidance. It is not, however, necessary for allegations to be tied to specific provisions in such guidance.
- It should allege that practice is impaired by reason of misconduct etc, as the case may be.
- Facts should only be alleged where they are provable through admissible evidence (GMC (Fitness to Practise) Rules 2004 r34(1) and (2)) – this should include consideration of the 'best evidence' rule – that is, where possible, the use direct evidence rather than hearsay and, reliance on evidence that is supported by another witness or by documentation.
- The use of 'failed' versus 'did not'. The term 'you failed' (eg 'you failed to examine Patient A') means that the GMC must prove two elements. First that the registrant did not examine Patient A and second that the registrant should have done so. This approach should only be adopted where the failure to examine is core to the allegation, otherwise the wording should be 'you did not examine Patient A'.

4.103 In most cases the drafting is sufficiently clear for the registrant to understand the allegation and be able to respond, but if not, this should be raised at the earliest opportunity with the case manager. Sometimes the matter can be easily rectified (for example, by providing the identity of particular patients/service users) but if not it should be pursued well in advance of the final hearing. One recurrent problem with GMC allegations is their use of multiple alternatives either in the alleged act/omission or the accompanying state of mind or both. It appears to stem from a desire to include every possible alternative as opposed to proceeding with the most serious or most appropriate allegation(s). In addition, rather than use precise language or repeating the same phrase for the same point different words or phrases are used. This causes confusion and uncertainty in hearings, it may weaken or detract from the central thrust of the GMC case.

4.104 In *R (Wheeler) v Assistant Commissioner House of the Metropolitan Police*[62] it was alleged that W had failed to carry out duties 'to an acceptable standard' thereby breaching the code of conduct. Stanley Burnton J said:

62 [2008] EWHC 439 (Admin) at [6].

Vagueness is a ground for judicial review if it leads to unfairness in the proceedings, and the danger with a vague charge is that the parties, and in particular the respondent, do not know with some precision what is alleged against them, and therefore are not fully able to address those matters in the course of a hearing.

4.105 His Lordship commented that while the particulars of a charge may be refined following an initial draft, it should be sufficiently particularised well before the hearing for the respondent to disciplinary charges to know what it is alleged he failed to do and, in what respects he failed.

4.106 The application of Article 6 may be relied upon if necessary to achieve the appropriate level of particularisation. Certain matters are required to be explicitly stated in the allegation, including dishonesty and sexual motivation. For a fuller discussion of the law relating to the drafting of allegations, see chapter 1.

Absence of the registrant

4.107 Rule 15 of the GMC (FTP) Rules 2004 provides that a notice giving details of any hearing should be served upon the registrant. The notice must include reference to rule 31 which empowers the FTP Tribunal to proceed in the absence of the registrant provided 'all reasonable efforts' have been made to effect service. The tribunal has the discretion to proceed in the absence of the registrant but:

- (i) there must be strict adherence to the requirement that all reasonable effort at service has been met; and
- (ii) the decision to proceed must be taken with 'the utmost care and caution' and only after full consideration of the competing interests with emphasis on those of the registrant.

4.108 GMC (FTP) Rules 2004 r40[63] provides that:

(1) Any notice of any hearing required shall be served in accordance with Schedule 4 Para 8 to the Medical Act 1983.

(2) Notice may be served by (a) post or (b) email at an address that the registrant has notified to the Registrar as an address for communications.

(3) If the registrant is represented by a solicitor, trade union or defence organisation it may be served by post or email (at an email address notified as above).

(4) Service of any notice or document may be proved by –
- (a) a confirmation of posting (by Post Office or other delivery service);
- (b) a confirmation of receipt of the relevant electronic mail; or
- (c) a signed statement from any person serving the notice or document confirming that the notice or document was delivered to, sent to or left at –
  - (i) the registrant's proper address;
  - (ii) the solicitor's address or email; or
  - (iii) the trade union or defence organisation's address or email.

4.109 MA 1983 Sch 4 para 8 provides that service of notification shall be made by:

63 As amended to allow service by email.

a) delivering it to the registrant;
b) leaving it at the registrant's proper address;
c) sending it by registered post;
d) sending it by recorded delivery;
e) sending it to an email address which the person provides for the purpose of fitness to practise proceedings

Further investigation of allegations (rule 13A)

4.110 Once a case has been referred to the MPTS, the GMC will continue, with the assistance of its lawyers, to investigate in order to prepare the evidence to be presented at the hearing. This may include:

- obtaining further documentary evidence;
- taking statements from witnesses;
- obtaining expert reports on clinical and other matters;
- directing the registrant to undergo an assessment of his or her health, knowledge of English, or performance.

GMC pre-adjudication case management procedure

Case management (rule 16)

4.111 The rules provide for a case management mechanism intended to reduce delays, narrow the issues before the medical practitioners tribunal and minimise stress to witnesses and the registrant at the hearing. The MPTS may list a pre-hearing meeting before a case manager (rule 16(2)(c)), unless otherwise agreed a practitioner shall be given no less than 14 days notice of any pre-hearing meeting.

4.112 A pre-hearing meeting may be conducted by telephone or other agreed/decided method (rule 16(4)). The case manager will, as necessary, issue directions. See rule 16(6) for a non-exhaustive list. Particularly important is rule 16(6)(d)(i) and (ii) requiring the registrant to indicate, so far as is practicable, whether the allegation is admitted, or which facts are admitted and which remain in dispute. The term 'allegation' means the entirety of the sub-facts and particulars that cumulatively amount to the single global allegation that fitness to practise is impaired. Therefore, indications will be required to each particular not just the global allegation.

4.113 It is important to comply with directions, or if they can not be complied with, to explain why. Rule 16A provides that where a party fails to comply with the FTP Rules or a direction issued by the tribunal or the case manager, the medical practitioners tribunal may draw adverse inferences, refuse to admit evidence where the failure relates to the admissibility of that evidence and award costs in accordance with rule 16B (a costs award). Rule 16B provides a discretion for the medical practitioners tribunal to make a costs award following an application from either party or of its own initiative. A costs award is an order that one party or their representative pay the costs of the other party where the paying party's conduct of the proceedings has been unreasonable. Before making any such award, the medical practitioners tribunal shall receive any evidence and hear submissions from the parties about the alleged failure to comply and the conduct which is claimed is unreasonable. If a costs award is made the medical practitioners tribunal shall announce its decision and give its reasons for making the award. Where an award is made, the amount of costs payabale shall be assessed by a case manager after consideration of a schedule of costs and ability to pay. Various guidance has been provided by the MPTS in relation to this power, including:

- *Guidance for medical practitioners tribunals on case management and exercising powers under rule 16A*[64]
- *Guidance for case managers on the assessment of costs*[65]
- *Schedule of costs* (template document)
- *Costs: Ability to pay self-assessment* (template document)

Amending the allegation(s)

> The allegations/charges may be amended provided no injustice is caused.
>
> The later and/or more substantial the change the more likely it is to cause injustice.
>
> If the risk of injustice can be met then charges may be changed late in the proceedings. Some difficulties may be dealt with by adjourning to allow all parties time to prepare the newly altered case or, call or recall witnesses.

4.114 It is important to note that there is discretion for the tribunal to hear an application to amend particulars during the hearing. Rule 17(6) provides as follows:

> 17(6) Where 'at any time' it appears to the Medical Practitioners Tribunal that –
>
> (a) the allegation or the facts upon which it is based and of which the practitioner has been notifed under rule 15, should be amended; and
>
> (b) the amendment can be made without injustice,
>
> it may, after hearing the parties, amend the allegation in appropriate terms.

4.115 Rule 17(2)(b) also provides that at the hearing the chair of the medical practitioners tribunal shall enquire whether the representative for the GMC wishes to amend the particulars of the allegation, and if that representative so wishes, the medical practitioners tribunal shall consider whether to amend the particulars under rule 17(6). For a consideration of the case-law on charging, see chapter 1. When seeking late amendments, the GMC may place some emphasis on the overarching objective of protecting the public. Whilst this may result in an increased number of applications to amend the allegation to fit the facts as they emerge, it should not become the norm. The principle remains that the allegation should be settled before a hearing and late applications, which are most likely to adversely affect the registrant, are to be avoided. Applications made by the GMC for the purpose of avoiding a half-time submission or to avoid losing a count should not be entertained.

64 See www.mpts-uk.org/DC8272_Guidance_for_medical_practitioners_tribunals_on_case_management_and_exercising_powers_under_Rule_16_A_.pdf_64046476.pdf.

65 See www.mpts-uk.org/DC8443_Guidance_for_case_managers_on_assessing_costs.pdf_64047185.pdf.

Full hearings by the medical practitioners tribunal

Procedure

Order of proceedings

4.116 GMC (FTP) Rules 2004 r17(2) sets out the full and detailed procedure before a medical practitioners tribunal, the order of proceedings is as follows (not all stages will be applicable to all hearings):

1) Preliminary legal arguments (rule 17(2)(a)).
2) Registrant, if present (or GMC presenting officer, if not present), confirms doctor's name and GMC reference number (rule 17(2)(b)(i) and (ii)).
3) The chair of the medical practitioners tribunal shall enquire whether the representative for the GMC wishes to amend the particulars of the allegation, and if that representative so wishes, the medical practitioners tribunal shall consider whether to amend the particulars under rule 17(6).
4) The chair of the medical practitioners tribunal invites any admissions and where admissions are made these facts are announced as proved (rule 17(2)(d) and (e)).
5) For those facts in dispute, the presenting officer will open the case and call witnesses in support of their case (rule 17(2)(f)).
6) At the close of the GMC case the registrant may make submissions regarding whether sufficient evidence has been adduced to find the facts proved and the medical practitioners tribunal shall consider and announce its decision as to whether any such submissions should be upheld (rule 17(2)(g) – see para 4.174 below).
7) The registrant may open his or her case and adduce evidence and call witnesses in support (rule 17(2)(h)).
8) Each party can make submissions as to the facts to be found proven on the basis of the evidence (rule 17(2)(i)).
9) The medical practitioners tribunal deliberate and then announce their findings of fact (rule 17(2)(j)).
10) Further evidence and any further submissions can then be provided as to whether, on the basis of any facts found proved, the registrant's fitness to practise is impaired (rule 17(2)(k)).
11) The medical practitioners tribunal deliberate and then announce any findings in relation to impairment, giving reasons (rule 17(2)(l)).
12) Further evidence and submissions from both parties as to the appropriate sanction, if any, are then heard, or if no impairment is found submissions are heard on the question of whether a warning should be imposed. When considering sanctions the tribunal may take account of any undertakings offered by the registrant (rule 17(2)(m)). Thereafter the tribunal will announce its decision on sanction, giving reasons for the decision (rule 17(2)(n)).
13) Any application for interim suspension or interim conditions should be made and responded to, if required. The medical practitioners tribunal will consider the application and announce its decision with reasons (rule 17(2)(n) and (o)).

14) The tribunal will then deal with any interim order in place against the registrant (rule 17(2)(p)).

General provisions applicable throughout the proceedings

4.117 The remainder of rule 17 addresses issues that may arise at any stage during the proceedings, as follows:

(a) *Amendment applications:* At any time, the medical practitioners tribunal can amend the allegation after hearing from the parties and if the amendment can be made without injustice.
(b) *Adjourning proceedings for a performance, health or knowledge of English assessment:* At any time in the proceedings before a determination is made that the registrant's fitness to practise is impaired, the medical practitioners tribunal, having regard to the nature of the allegation, may adjourn proceedings and direct that an assessment of the practitioner's performance or health or an assessment of the practitioner's knowledge of English occur.
c) *Steps after an assessment has been obtained:* Once an assessment report has been obtained, the medical practitioners tribunal may proceed to consider the allegation in accordance with usual procedure (rule 17(2), above) or refer the allegation to the registrar for consideration by the case examiners in accordance with rule 10(2) (which provides for the circumstances in which certain health issues may be dealt with by way of undertakings (rule 17(3)–(5)).
d) At any stage before making its decision as to sanction or warning, the FTP Tribunal may adjourn for further information or reports to be obtained in order to assist it in exercising its functions (rule 17(9)).

Role of legally qualified chair/legal assessor

4.118 As noted above, a recent change is the move to the MPTS sitting with Legally Qualified Chairs (LQCs). The MPTS *Policy on the use of Legally Qualified Chairs in tribunal hearings*[66] makes clear that the MPTS 'can use LQCs in all types of hearings, such as: Interim order tribunal hearings, including reviews on the papers; New medical practitioner tribunal hearings; Review hearings, including reviews on the papers'.

4.119 The policy statement of the MPTS states as follows:

> Our experience so far has been that using LQCs assists the effective running of hearings. However, we recognize exceptionally, there may be case specific circumstances that indicate a hearing would benefit from the appointment of a legal assessor. This is limited to where a doctor is self-represented and exceptional circumstances are identified or where the length of the hearing is more than 20 days. In such cases, the decision to appoint a legal assessor will be made by the MPTS, on the recommendation of a case manager.

4.120 The criteria for the use of LQCs is set out as follows:

> A hearing will be chaired by a LQC, unless:
> - A doctor is self-represented and during case management exceptional circumstances are identified by the case manager that

66 See www.mpts-uk.org/DC10491__MPTS_Policy_on_the_use_of_LQCs.pdf_72038353.pdf.

indicate the hearing would benefit from a legal assessor. This could include;

- Where the particular vulnerability of a doctor would be best served by the chair and legal advisor to the tribunal being distinct;
- Where it is known that extraordinary or complex legal isues will arise and no preliminary hearing is scheduled to resolve these prior to the substantive hearing.

- The case manager determines that due to the length of a hearing, the tribunal should be supported by a separate legal assessor. This would only be considered in cases longer than 20 days.

Where a legal assessor is appointed, the chair in these cases may be medical, lay or legally qualified sitting as a lay chair.

4.121 For a fuller discussion of the role of the legal assessor/LQC, see chapter 2 at para 2.292. It is clear from the criteria and the pilot that almost all tribunals will now sit with an LQC and without a legal assessor. A legal assessor will only be appointed in truly exceptional circumstances. The MPTS will determine whether a case is exceptional. This change effectively marks the end of legal assessors assisting unrepresented doctors or tribunals dealing with such registrants.

Preliminary legal arguments (rule 30)

4.122 This section addresses some (non-exhaustive) potential preliminary legal arguments which may be relevant to a doctor's case and may need to be raised as a preliminary matter prior to the substantive hearing. Usually preliminary legal arguments that need to be heard by a tribunal are heard at the start of the hearing and time estimates should take into account any time required for such arguments.

Historic complaints (rule 4(5))

> ECHR Article 6 and domestic case-law confer a right to a hearing within a reasonable time, however to stay proceedings is an exceptional course and delay is not a ground unless there is material prejudice to the extent that no fair trial is possible.
>
> Where a regulatory body's rules impose a time bar preventing proceedings save in exceptional circumstances, an assessment of those circumstances must be fair, transparent and understandable – see GMC (FTP) Rules 2004 r4(5).

4.123 This rule recognises the potential difficulty of historic complaints, in the following terms:

> (5) No allegation shall proceed further if, at the time it is first made or first comes to the attention of the General Council, more than five years have elapsed since the most recent events giving rise to the allegation, unless the Registrar considers that is in the public interest for it to proceed.

While delay may in some circumstances constitute a breach of Article 6 rights, mere delay in the absence of serious unfairness will not be sufficient to stop a case from proceeding. In referring cases after the time-limit imposed by rule 4(5), the GMC must clearly define the exceptional circumstances it is relying upon. The fact that an allegation is serious is not of itself an exceptional circumstance since it is a necessary precursor to any referral. Joinder is also not an exceptional circumstance save that it may be if there are important and probative 'similar fact' arguments.[67]

Media and public/private hearings

4.124 GMC (FTP) Rules 2004 r41 provides as to when a committee or medical practitioners tribunal may sit in public or in private. The starting point is that all hearings will be held in public (rule 41(1)), however there is a discretion for a medical practitioners tribunal to 'determine that the public shall be excluded from the proceedings or any part of the proceedings, where they consider that the particular circumstances of the case outweigh the public interest in holding the hearing in public' (rule 41(2)).

4.125 There is a presumption that hearings will be private when considering whether to make or review an interim order (rule 41(3)(a)), unless the registrant requests it to sit in public (rule 41(5)). Where a tribunal is considering an allegation or a non-compliance maters, they may revoke an interim order in public. There is also a presumption that hearings will be held in private when considering the 'physical or mental health of the registrant' (rule 41(3)(b)). However, the tribunal do have a discretion to hold a hearing relating to either interim orders or health issues in public 'where they consider that to do so would be appropriate' having regard to the following factors:

- the interests of the maker of the allegation (if any);
- the interests of any patient concerned;
- whether a public hearing would adversely affect the health of the registrant;
- all the circumstances, including the public interest.

4.126 Clearly, consideration will need to be given to either making or defending an application in relation to the public or private nature of the proceedings.

Preparing for the hearing

> While there is a duty to prevent inequality of arms, there is no positive duty on a disciplinary body to gather evidence to assist the registrant.
>
> To allege unfairness under ECHR Article 6(3)(b) a complainant must demonstrate that a duty exists, that it has been breached and this has caused an inequality of arms.
>
> Each case will depend on its own facts.

67 See *R (Peacock) v General Medical Council* [2007] EWHC 585 (Admin) and *R (Gwynn) v General Medical Council* [2007] EWHC 3145 (Admin) as examples of cases that deal with the relatively rare issue of historical complaints.

Disclosure

4.127 Careful consideration should be given to all disclosure provided by the GMC. If it appears that there are any documents missing, then consideration should be given to raising this with the GMC at the earliest opportunity to ensure the doctor has the benefit of the fullest disclosure. It is important to monitor carefully the content of all witness statements. It is imperative that a doctor, prior to the hearing, has, so far as possible, all the witness statements that the GMC have obtained. Equally, it is important to ensure that the doctor has been provided with all the supporting documents exhibited by each witness through their statement.

4.128 Confirmation should be sought as to what documents the GMC intend to rely on to prove the allegations and which are served as unused. As soon as reasonably possible following complete disclosure (including witness statements), a view should be sought from the GMC as to what documents they may intend to place before the tribunal at the hearing. From the doctor's perspective, careful consideration needs to be given to these documents to ensure that they do not raise any potential concerns that are not the subject of the particulars the tribunal will be asked to adjudicate on (regardless of whether charges are accepted or not). Scrutiny should be given to potential issues of bad character (which may include suggestions of clinical incompetence when the particulars are only concerned with, for example, an alleged dishonest declaration on a form) and hearsay that may be raised within the documentation. A clear decision should be made as to what may need to be removed or redacted. It is important to ensure that any redactions that can be agreed are as fair and balanced as possible but that also they don't render documentation unintelligible for the tribunal or witnesses who will be referred to them. GMC witnesses will be warned, once there is agreement on redactions that they are not to give evidence on these issues.

Witness statements

Live vs read witnesses

4.129 If agreement on redactions of GMC witness statements can be reached such that the whole statement can be agreed, then that means that the statement can simply be read without the witness being called to give live evidence. It is important to understand that if a doctor agrees to a witness statement being read (with or without redactions) that the totality of that witness statement is taken to have been agreed and has as much weight as oral evidence that the tribunal may hear from live witnesses. If there are only minor areas of disagreement in a witness statement and they are peripheral to the allegation then it may be possible to redact them so as to avoid a witness being called for insignificant factual discrepancies. Consideration will need to be given as to which witnesses are required for cross-examination and what if anything the doctor hopes to obtain/challenge from that questioning. Some witnesses will come across better than others and the doctor is likely to have the advantage of having some firsthand knowledge of that individual and how they might come across to the medical practitioners tribunal. While it will be a matter of advice and judgment as to which witnesses are required, consideration must be given as to which charge they go to and how their evidence may assist or hinder the doctor's or GMC's case.

4.130 It must be remembered at all times that these hearings are determined on the civil standard – the balance of probabilities and it is for the GMC to prove their case, not for the doctor to disprove it. Equally, the test of insight is important if every minute detail of every witnesses factual account is challenged (without cause) then this may impact upon issues relating to insight (see chapter 3 at para 3.162).

Doctor's evidence

4.131 A doctor will also need to be advised upon, and at the relevant time, make a final decision about whether he or she will give evidence in his or her case and in so doing be subject to cross-examination and questioning by the tribunal. A key consideration here is that while agreement can be reached between the GMC representative and the doctor's representative(s) outside the hearing room as to which if any issues will or will not be addressed during cross-examination, such agreement cannot be reached with the Tribunal who regulate their own proceedings and can ask the most direct and probing questions of a doctor or indeed any other witness. The doctor must also be carefully advised that there is now an expectation that a registrant will give evidence. Tribunals will readily draw an adverse inference from a failure to give evidence where an explanation is warranted and not forthcoming: see chapter 2 at para 2.402 onwards

4.132 It is usually helpful if a doctor's witness statement addresses the following:

a) introductory paragraphs setting out experience/expertise;
b) paragraphs addressing the specific allegations, identifying which, if any, facts are admitted and which are denied;
c) all mitigating features.

Witness unable to attend in person

4.133 If witnesses are unable to attend in person (for particular reasons – such as surgical commitments etc) then an application can be made for their evidence to be given either via video-link or by phone. As a last resort an application can be made to admit statements to be read as hearsay, however it is likely that the weight given to such statements will be reduced.

Evidence

4.134 The rule relevant to evidence is rule 34, which states:

> (1) The Committee or a Tribunal may admit any evidence they consider fair and relevant to the case before them, whether or not such evidence would be admissible in a court of law.

Hearsay

> The tribunal has the discretion to proceed in the absence of a witness and to admit hearsay evidence but the decision to proceed must be taken with 'the utmost care and caution' and only after full consideration of the competing interests with emphasis on those of the registrant.
>
> There must be compelling reasons to deprive a registrant of the opportunity to cross-examine a witness – this all the more so if the case or its consequences are serious.

4.135 It is outside the scope of this book to provide a full account of hearsay evidence, however chapter 2 provides a fuller discussion of hearsay in the regulatory context. Suffice to say, it important to be alert to hearsay, identify it and determine whether its redaction can be agreed or whether its admissibility and the weight to be placed on it will need to be adjudicated on and at what stage.

4.136 The rules of evidence in these proceedings do not require the exclusion of evidence merely on the ground that it is hearsay. In considering hearsay evidence, allowance needs to be made to the fact that the person who is the source of that evidence is not before the medical practitioners tribunal and therefore the parties have not had the opportunity to question or assess their credibility. Equally, the evidence has not been tested by cross-examination and thus there is no opportunity to see how it withstood that form of challenge. Neither party can know how the person might have responded to cross-examination and it is inappropriate to speculate about such matters. Regard must be had to the circumstances in which the statement was made and the extent to which the hearsay is supported by, or is consistent with, other evidence, and the scope for error or the existence of a reason to be untruthful.

4.137 Although hearsay evidence must be treated with circumspection, there is no rule of law that prevents a prosecuting authority from relying upon hearsay solely or to a decisive degree to support a case where otherwise it would have none.

4.138 A significant case on this issue as it relates to the GMC is *R (Bonhoeffer) v General Medical Council*[68] – see chapter 2 at paras 2.109–2.118 for a full discussion of this case and the recent European Court of Human Rights cases on hearsay evidence.

The burden and standard of proof

The burden of proving disputed facts is on the prosecuting authority.

The standard required is 'on the balance of probabilities'.

The standard does not change with the seriousness of the allegation.

Serious allegations do not require better evidence.

It is just common sense that to prove an unlikely event occurred may require persuasive evidence.

The consequences of a finding are irrelevant.

Preparing a defence

4.139 Careful consideration needs to be given to how a doctor intends, if at all, to meet the case against him or her – although a registrant has no burden to discharge in these proceedings, the burden is on the GMC to prove the allegations on the civil standard of the balance of probabilities.

68 [2010] EWHC 1585 (Admin), [2011] ACD 104.

4.140 Detailed consideration will need to be given to what are often complex and interrelated charges (even in relatively simple cases). Charges need to be understandable and capable of answer.

4.141 The doctor will need to be clear on which charges, if any, admissions will be made and which, if any, will be denied. This will require careful consideration, legal advice and an understanding of the proceedings, evidence and documentation as well as concepts of insight and impairment.

4.142 Consideration should be given to preparing a signed schedule of admissions (a table or list indicating whether a charge, sub-part or stem are admitted or denied in whole or in part) prior to the hearing, which can be provided to the GMC presenting officer and the tribunal on day one of the hearing, or before if so agreed. If served prior to the hearing, or even on day one, it would be sensible to note carefully within that document that any admissions or otherwise are on the basis of the information/evidence served to date. There is no requirement for such a schedule, but as the process of charging and answering charges can become somewhat complex, it is often the most straightforward way.[69]

4.143 The responses to the allegations will need to be made orally to the tribunal at the start of the hearing, in any event, and so can simply be communicated purely orally if this is more convenient to the doctor (as per rule 17(2)(d)).

Defence documents and defence witnesses

4.144 Careful consideration will need to be given to what documents the doctor provides to the tribunal in defending the case against him or her. Depending on the charges, this may include the need for expert evidence to rebut (or in the absence of) GMC expert evidence.

4.145 This clearly needs to be obtained sufficiently early (and in compliance with any case management directions) to enable the report to be served on all parties to see whether the content can be agreed (with or without amendment/redaction) or to see whether the GMC will require the expert for cross-examination – in which case the expert's availability will need to be known at the time the hearing date is set. An educated guess will need to be made as to what day/time of day the expert will need to attend on and this is likely to be subject to change so if possible it is best to have an expert available for several sessions of the hearing. If the expert can only attend at a specific time and this would put their evidence out of turn, provided the doctor would be content for this evidence to be heard out of turn (and where it was unlikely to impact other evidence that might need to be given) then the possibility of taking the expert (or indeed any other time-limited witness) out of turn can be canvassed with those acting for the GMC and if agreement can be reached, leave of the tribunal can be sought. If agreement cannot be reached, the matter can be raised with the

69 The GMC's continued use of multiple alternative allegations makes it very important to pin down what is admitted what is denied and what evidence is to be called. Admissions may affect the relevance and thus the admissibility of some evidence. It is also usually the case that even if an alternative is admitted (eg recklessness or lack of integrity) the GMC will proceed on another (eg intentional or dishonesty). They are thus not alternatives at all but are multiple versions of the event(s) under scrutiny. The GMC will almost always seek to prove the most serious.

tribunal – but clearly reasons will need to be given for the interposing of a witness out of turn and any objections to it met as far as possible. Such an application can be argued, and may be acceded to, provided it does not significantly inconvenience the proceedings, because it is likely to be in the interest of justice and fairness for the doctor to be able to present his or her expert evidence if that is the only time that the expert can attend.

4.146 If a registrant decides to disclose documents at any stage in the proceedings as part of his or her defence, then he or she is advised to ensure that any references to third parties are redacted, in particular references to patients. Particular caution should be exercised when disclosing, for example patient notes, supervision records and practice development reviews. Further registrants are advised to obtain their employer's permission in writing to use such records.

Testimonials and character references

4.147 A doctor will also need to gather relevant and positive testimonials from (if possible and depending on the type of allegation) both before the time of the alleged concerns, during, and after. This is one advantage of how long proceedings can take to come to a full hearing, it gives a proactive registrant (and one who is not limited through the restrictions of an interim orders) the opportunity to ensure that by the date of the tribunal hearing he or she is in the best position possible to show that any concerns (that may or may not be found proved) have been remedied/addressed and demonstrate the steps he or she has taken to address them (if applicable/appropriate).

4.148 Testimonials should be as full as possible, come from individuals who have firsthand knowledge of the doctor and be provided in writing and signed. The writer will need to make it clear in their testimonial that they are fully aware of the charges the doctor faces (it is often simplest to send the charges to a potential referee to avoid any concerns that they are not fully aware of all the details of the charges). These will need to be obtained sufficiently early in the process so that an informed decision can be made about which if any referees might be willing to attend the hearing to give oral evidence.

4.149 Often it can be difficult for doctors to obtain such testimonials from other doctors, for a number of reasons – eg lack of time, lack of firsthand knowledge or a reluctance to become involved in GMC proceedings, particularly if they are still in the employ of the body where the alleged misconduct took place. Every effort should be made to gather as many positive testimonials as possible (although this can be more problematic for junior doctors). However, quality can often be better than pure quantity. It is very helpful if at least one individual can attend to speak to the doctor's ability/credibility/clinical competence (whichever is relevant to the charges faced), because oral evidence can have a much more powerful impact than a written testimonial. However, an individual who does attend to give evidence as a character witness will, in the usual way, be subject to questioning by the GMC representatives and the tribunal and will be under oath. Therefore if an individual also has negative comments on the doctor concerned, these may be elicited through such questioning.

4.150 It is important to note that, with the exception of the doctor, witnesses are not permitted to sit in the hearing prior to their giving of evidence.

Day one of the hearing

Arrival and venue

General

4.151 The main hearing centre is in central Manchester. Hearings may be held in London if there are truly exceptional circumstances (eg very serious health-related issues). The GMC does not regard a lack of funds to travel or pay for accommodation as exceptional and will resist an application based on finances.

4.152 On the (first) day of the hearing, it is advisable to arrive at the relevant venue at least one hour before the hearing is scheduled to start. If there is sufficient space, each doctor will be allocated a private waiting room which can usually be used for the duration of the hearing, depending on demand. Rooms are normally allocated in advance, so when you sign in the reception should be able to provide this information. Many legal teams/doctors attending for longer hearings will consider bringing other essential office equipment with them – such as a laptop (there is wifi access), printer, hole-punch, stapler and other stationery.

4.153 It should be noted that at least nine additional copies of each document intended for distribution will be required: three for the tribunal; two for the GMC if both solicitor and advocate are present; one for the legal assessor (if applicable); one for the tribunal secretary; one for the transcriber (if applicable); and one for the witness table. It is much better to have too many, than too few. Remember that all patient identifying information will need to be fully redacted or anonymised in a way that is clear, consistent and meaningful.

The hearing

4.154 It is advisable on arrival to make contact with the presenting officer for the GMC, the legal assessor (if applicable) and the tribunal secretary in the case, and also locate the hearing room. If there is agreement between the parties that some time is required for final discussions/redactions/narrowing of issues, then this can either be communicated prior to the hearing start time to the tribunal via the tribunal secretary (fairness requires that no party speaks with any of the tribunal members during any part of a hearing without the presence of both parties). The tribunal may agree or, more usually, they will wish to formally convene to be appraised of the situation and time frames and make a decision as to how much time, if any to provide. If a short adjournment (to commence the hearing later that same day) is likely to shorten proceedings or has the potential to, or at least to make them more efficient then the adjournment application may be granted. Such an application can often be shortly and simply put (see para 4.157 below).

4.155 When the hearing is to commence, all parties will be invited to enter the hearing room, name plates will indicate where parties and individuals should sit. There are usually additional chairs for members of the public, interested individuals or journalists to observe the proceedings. No individual (with the exception of the doctor) who is an intended witness in the proceedings is entitled to sit in the hearing room as a member of the public until after they have given their evidence.

4.156 On a practical note, there is no need to stand when a tribunal come into the hearing room, in fact, frequently, they will already be seated when the parties enter. Panellists are currently addressed as either 'Sir/Madam'.

Postponements and adjournments

4.157 GMC (FTP) Rules 2004 r29 provides a discretion for a committee to postpone 'any hearing of which notice has been served on the practitioner' in accordance with the GMC (FTP) Rules 2004, on application or of a committee's, or in the case of a tribunal hearing, the case manager's own motion. This is called a postponement application if the application is made before the opening of the hearing (rule 29(1)) and an adjournment application if made at any stage in the proceedings (rule 29(2)). Each party must be given a reasonable opportunity to make representations on the matter (rule 29(3B)).

Stage 1: findings of fact

Overview

4.158 Having dealt with any preliminary arguments and other matters, such as admissions by the doctor, the tribunal hears evidence and submissions as to whether the facts are proved or whether they are capable of supporting a finding of impairment.

4.159 Evidence, as noted above, can also be received as permitted via videolink, and evidence can be given over the telephone – see further below at para 4.169. Submissions can be made to the tribunal to exclude and disregard inadmissible or unduly prejudicial material.

4.160 The 'presenting officer', ie counsel instructed by the GMC, will open the case, and then present the evidence through read or live witnesses and any relevant supporting documentation. It is good practice to keep a full note of the opening because it is this case the GMC need to meet and it can be important if a half-time submission is being considered. GMC witnesses are called and then can be subject to cross-examination by the doctor's representative, followed by re-examination by the GMC, then questions by the tribunal, followed by any matters arising out of the tribunal's questioning being clarified by first the doctor's representative and then the GMC. Careful consideration needs to be given to what type of cross-examination is required. Clearly, sensitive but relevant and robust cross-examination will be required, if necessary, of a patient complainant. As with any hearing, preparation is the key to determining what if anything needs to be challenged, if possible, through questioning that witness. It is important that cross-examination achieves something. If it is a doctor's case that someone else (for example, another GMC witness) is to blame wholly or partly for the conduct he or she is charged with, then this must be explored with care and with an evidence base because otherwise there is a risk that unsupported aspersions or suggestions could have a detrimental impact on any tribunal's later determination as to the doctor's insight into the issues he or she faces if they are subsequently found proved.

4.161 Once the GMC's evidence has been presented, the doctor may make submissions that insufficient evidence has been adduced to find the disputed facts proved. If this fails, the doctor may give and call evidence on his or her behalf.

4.162 The tribunal then consider 'in camera' (in private) whether the facts have been proved. This process can take quite some time, and parties wait for the decision – although often parties will be released for a period of time (an hour, an afternoon, a day) once the tribunal have an idea of how long they might need to deliberate. This is often a lengthy process as the decision has to be reached and then typed up, read, agreed in written form and then finalised and printed. This can be an anxious wait for the registrant, and while it is often difficult to think in terms of the next stage, it can be a useful distraction to complete preparations for stage 2, in case they are required. If some admissions have been made, then it will be clearer that stage 2 is likely to be reached, and therefore this preparation time is even more important.

4.163 The tribunal apply the civil standard of proof. It is now abundantly clear that there is only one civil standard of proof regardless of the seriousness of the allegations.[70] The tribunal's decision is announced in open session, and a written judgment is distributed.

Witnesses

4.164 Witnesses attending the hearing will be required to take an oath or affirm before giving evidence.[71] Until the point when a witness is required to give evidence in the hearing, a witness of fact cannot be present in the hearing room, without leave of the tribunal[72] (this does not apply to the registrant). It can apply to a representative if they are a friend or colleague who intends to give evidence (character evidence would be permissible as this would not necessarily be a witness of fact), so thought needs to be given to this when deciding upon representation. Once a witness has given their evidence they are then permitted, if they so choose, to remain for the duration of the hearing in their capacity as a member of the public.

4.165 If a witness does not finish his or her evidence in one sitting and there are breaks or overnight adjournments during their evidence, then they remain under oath for the duration of their evidence and are not permitted to discuss the case with anyone else while they are under oath. A reminder is usually given to each witness every time there is a break in their evidence. This is an important consideration for advisers in terms of the timing of cases, because this applies equally to a registrant who gives evidence. Care needs to be taken that a registrant does not go part-heard in their evidence at the point when proceedings need to be adjourned,

70 *Re B (Children)* [2008] UKHL 35.

71 GMC (FTP) Rules 2004 r35(1).

72 GMC (FTP) Rules 2004 r35(6).

because the adviser and registrant will not be able to discuss the case until the registrant completes their evidence.

4.166 All witnesses (unless they are vulnerable witnesses) are first examined by the party calling them, and may then be cross-examined by the opposing party. The witness may then be re-examined. The witness may be questioned by the committee or tribunal at any time.[73] Any further questioning of the witness by the parties shall be at the discretion of the tribunal.[74]

Vulnerable witnesses

4.167 Witnesses, the quality of whose evidence is likely to be adversely affected by the proceedings, may be treated as vulnerable witnesses.[75] They are likely to include any witness under 18 years of age at the time of the hearing, witnesses with a mental disorder within the meaning of the Mental Health Act 1983, those with mental impairment, or physical disabilities that require assistance at the hearing. Also included is any witness making an allegation against a registrant of a sexual nature, where the witness was the alleged victim, and any witness who complains of intimidation.[76] In such instances, the committee may decide to adopt special measures to help them give evidence.[77]

Video-links and other measures

4.168 In certain cases, particularly cases involving vulnerable witnesses, the use of video-links may be permitted. Sometimes the use of pre-recorded evidence will be approved, provided that the witness is available at the hearing to be cross-examined. Screens will be used where it is considered necessary to prevent the witness's identity being revealed to the press or the general public, or to prevent access to the witness by the registrant.

4.169 Hearings may also, if necessary, be held in private. The committee or tribunal may also on the application of a party agree that the identify of a witness should not be revealed in public.[78]

Proceedings in the absence of a witness

4.170 The tribunal has a discretion to proceed in the absence of a witness, and to admit hearsay evidence, but the decision to do so must be taken with great care, and only after full consideration of the competing interests, with an emphasis on those of the registrant.

4.171 There must be compelling reasons to deprive a registrant of the opportunity to cross-examine a witness, particularly if the case or its consequences are serious. See further chapter 2 at para 2.92.

4.172 The tribunal may admit any evidence they consider fair and relevant to the case before them, whether or not such evidence would be admissible in a court of law.[79] Subject to one proviso: where evidence would not be

73 GMC (FTP) Rules 2004 r35(2).
74 GMC (FTP) Rules 2004 r35(3).
75 GMC (FTP) Rules 2004 r36(1).
76 GMC (FTP) Rules 2004 r36(1).
77 GMC (FTP) Rules 2004 r36(3).
78 GMC (FTP) Rules 2004 r35(4).
79 GMC (FTP) Rules 2004 r34(1).

admissible in criminal proceedings, the committee or tribunal shall not admit such evidence unless, they are satisfied that their duty of making due inquiry into the case before them make its admission desirable.

Proceeding in the absence of the registrant[80]

4.173 As discussed at para 4.107, where the registrant is neither present nor represented at a hearing, the committee or tribunal may nevertheless proceed if they are satisfied that all reasonable efforts have been made to notify the registrant of the hearing. For a fuller exposition on when it may be appropriate to exercise the discretion to proceed in the absence of a practitioner see chapter 2 at para 2.328.

Is there a case to answer? Half-time submissions

> Submissions of no case to answer may be made in respect of a case or a specific allegation. They may be made where a) there is no evidence or, b) there is some evidence but it is weak, vague or inconsistent and, looked at 'in the round', a tribunal *could* not properly find the case (or fact) proved (rule 17(2)(g)).

4.174 GMC (FTP) Rules 2004 r17(2)(g) provides the mechanism for a half-time submission to be made:

> . . . the practitioner may make submissions regarding *whether sufficient evidence has been adduced to find some or all of the facts proved,* and the Medical Practitioners Tribunal shall consider and announce its decision as to whether any such submissions should be upheld. [Emphasis added.]

4.175 Such submissions need to be made at the end of the GMC's case on stage 1. At this stage the only information the tribunal can take into account in reaching a decision, if asked to do so, under rule 17(2)(g) is the evidence adduced by the GMC.

4.176 While it is likely to be acceptable to ask for a short amount of time after the GMC have closed their case to decide whether such a submission is required, the reality is that unless the evidence has come out in an entirely different way than expected in the hearing, a preliminary view will have been taken either prior to or during that evidence that such an application may be warranted and therefore can be prepared prior to the end of the GMC case, if possible.

4.177 An application will usually set out the test relied upon and then explain why the GMC's evidence as presented and tested by cross-examination does not meet that test. The GMC will then respond to the application.

4.178 The half-time submission test effectively stems from the well-known criminal case of *R v Galbraith*[81] in which, the test was laid down by Lord Lane, the Chief Justice as follows:

80 GMC (FTP) Rules 2004 r31.
81 [1981] 1 WLR 1039.

(1) If there is no evidence that the crime alleged has been committed by the defendant, there is no difficulty. The judge will of course stop the case.

(2) The difficulty arises where there is some evidence but it is of a tenuous character, for example because of inherent weakness or vagueness or because it is inconsistent with other evidence –

(a) where the judge comes to the conclusion that the prosecution evidence, taken at its highest, is such that a jury properly directed could not properly convict upon it, it is his duty, upon submission being made, to stop the case;

(b) where however the prosecution evidence is such that its strength or weakness depends on the view to be taken of a witness's reliability or other matters which are generally speaking within the province of the jury and where on one possible view of the facts there is evidence upon which a jury could properly come to the conclusion that the defendant is guilty, then the judge should allow the matter to be tried by the jury . . . There will of course, as always in this branch of the law, be borderline cases. They can safely be left to the discretion of the judge.

4.179 In essence, his Lordship held that, first, if there is no evidence the case should be stopped. That is the first limb of the test. The second limb is set out in these terms, that the case should also be stopped where there is some evidence but it is of a tenuous character, for example because of inherent weakness or vagueness or because it is inconsistent with other evidence, and where that evidence, taken at its highest, is such that the tribunal could not properly conclude that a relevant fact is made out.

4.180 A further gloss was put on that test in *R v Shippey*[82] where Turner J said that the requirement to take the prosecution evidence at its highest did not mean 'picking out all the plums and leaving the duff behind'.

4.181 Therefore a doctor will need to persuade the tribunal that the GMC has failed to present any evidence to support the particulars, or evidence which is so tenuous, for example because it is inherently, vague, weak or inconsistent with other evidence, that taken at its highest the tribunal could not on the basis of it properly find the relevant particulars to be well founded, in which case the tribunal would have an obligation to stop the case.

4.182 However, if the tribunal are satisfied, following submissions, that on one possible view of the facts there is evidence on which they could properly come to the conclusion that the allegation is well founded, then the proceedings should continue. Ultimately, if there is some evidence, it is not difficult for a tribunal to determine that the case should continue, this does not, however, mean that there will necessarily be sufficient information to find the facts proved to the civil standard at the end of stage 1.

4.183 An application can be made in relation to all the allegations – globally; however, what is more likely is that an application will be made in relation to particular, discrete allegations. Particularly in complex cases with extensive charges, it is very important for those representing the doctor to monitor and analyse whether any or sufficient evidence has been adduced

82 [1998] Crim LR 767.

in relation to each particular, so that the opportunity to make a submission in relation to a particular is not missed.

4.184 This is a key opportunity, in appropriate cases, to properly challenge whether the case should continue and therefore if there is a need for such an application, it can and should be made.

Stage 2: Findings of impairment

> There is no burden or standard of proof it is a question of 'judgment' by the tribunal.
>
> Impairment may be based upon historical matters or a continuing state of affairs but, it is to be judged at the time of the hearing. To do this the tribunal must look forward taking account of any reparation, changes in practice conduct or attitude since the matter(s) found proved actually occurred.
>
> Personal mitigation is less relevant but effort to accept and correct remediable errors should be taken into account.

4.185 If some or all facts are found proved, then the tribunal will need to go on to consider the issue of impairment (stage 2). Once a decision has been read in relation to facts, it is often sensible to ask for a period of time to fully absorb the decision and then to consider/re-consider the approach to stage 2, in the light of the findings of fact in stage 1 and what the tribunal have concluded to be important/material and what they have not, and any comments they have made on the evidence of various witnesses.

4.186 It is perfectly permissible to ask for some time to consider the decision, even though the expectation may seem to be to move immediately to stage 2. Clearly, stage 2 must always be anticipated and prepared for, submissions and evidence should be ready prior to the determination of stage 1, however time should be taken, if necessary, to adapt the planned approach. For example, if a tribunal find a doctor who did give evidence in his or her defence to lack credibility or have been evasive in answering questions, then this may have a significant impact on what might need to be said in stage 2 submissions and whether a doctor will need to be called again at stage 2. Such a finding at stage 1 could, arguably, for example, be used by the GMC as an illustration of a) lack of insight and b) why fitness to practise is still impaired at today's date.

4.187 The process for this stage, in terms of the hearing, is similar. The GMC will make submissions, followed by those acting for the doctor a) calling any further evidence in relation to impairment not adduced at stage 1 – including testimonials, documentary evidence and live witnesses (which may include recalling the doctor, if advisable – remember the doctor will once again be subjected to the possibility of cross-examination by the GMC and questioning by the tribunal); and b) making submissions in relation to impairment. The tribunal will then retire to deliberate (receiving legal advice from a legal assessor before they do if a legal assessor is present), before announcing their decision in the reconvened hearing. Again the process of deliberations can take quite some time at the impairment stage, and there may be further significant periods of nervous waiting.

4.188 As described above, the term 'impairment' is somewhat elusive (see para 4.51) – it has not been defined, and this is both a positive and a negative for registrants. It is a matter of judgment for the tribunal (with no burden or standard of proof attached to it) and therefore it is important that this issue is at the forefront, as noted above, of a doctor's defence preparation. How a doctor comes across (if he or she does or doesn't give evidence) can have a significant impact on views the tribunal will form when reaching a determination on impairment. The most important issue to grasp is that while the term is undefined, the tribunal, will, as a result of the extensive authorities (all of which add a particular consideration, nuance or gloss to the approach that can/should be taken by the tribunal) be guided as to how to approach this stage of the proceedings, both by GMC counsel and if present, the legal assessor. Submissions on behalf of the doctor are likely to be of most assistance to the tribunal where they are presented under headings/themes that foreshadow the approach that will be commended to the tribunal. Of particular importance are addressing: a) whether the misconduct alleged can be appropriately categorised as serious and if not why not; b) whether, on a forward-looking basis that still takes into account past conduct, public interest or patient safety (etc) are still at risk; c) what steps if any have been taken to address the concerns raised and meet them as far as possible; and d) what aspects, if any, of *Good medical practice* are said to be engaged and is this a fair categorisation of them on the basis of the findings of fact at stage 1.

Importance of testimonials about current performance at stage 2

4.189 In *Meadow v General Medical Council*,[83] Sir Anthony Clarke MR emphasised that the role of the then FTP Tribunal was not to punish the registrant for past wrongdoing, but to protect the public: to look forward, not back. Sir Anthony Clarke acknowledged, however, that the tribunal's view of a registrant's fitness to practise today would inevitably be influenced by how they had acted or failed to act in the past. In this connection, both judges in the Administrative Court held that the then FTP Tribunal's practice of not hearing evidence from testimonials about current performance until the stage of sanction was wrong. Such evidence may be highly relevant to the question of current impairment and should be considered before the tribunal reaches its conclusion on impairment.

4.190 It is important to consider carefully at what stage documentation, testimonials and character witnesses should be provided. Positive general testimonials in a clinical competence case, that don't deal with the facts as alleged, are likely to have no place in proceedings until stage 2 or even 3. However, testimonials attesting to the credibility of the doctor are likely to be admissible at stage 1 if the allegations include dishonesty and therefore an assessment of the doctor's credibility is central to a determination of the facts.

83 [2007] QB 462 at para 32.

Insight

4.191 'Insight' is 'the expectation that a doctor will be able to stand back and accept that, with hindsight, he or she should have behaved differently, and that it is expected that a doctor will take steps to prevent a recurrence' and learn from his or her mistakes (see relevant version of *Sanctions guidance*). See para 4.53 above.

4.192 Factors that may assist a tribunal when considering whether a doctor has demonstrated the insight necessary to avoid or mitigate sanctions and to accept and comply with proposed undertakings include:

- being open and honest when things go wrong offering an apology, although not a prerequisite for insight;
- offering an apology, although not a prerequisite for insight. The *Sanctions guidance* recognises that while the duty to 'offer an apology' where appropriate, reflects that, in our society, it almost always expected that a person will apologise when things go wrong, there can be different cultural factors which influence somebody's willingness to do so;
- conduct and demeanour at the hearing.

Stage 3: Sanctions

Objectives and proportionality: an overview

> The principal aims of sanctions are to protect the public, uphold the standards and reputation of the profession and maintain public confidence therein.
>
> The punitive effect of sanctions is only one (and not the most important) factor to be borne in mind when assessing whether a sanction is proportional to the matters found proved against a registrant.

4.193 The key provisions are:

- MA 1983 s35D;
- MPTS/GMC's *Sanctions guidance*;
- *Good medical practice*.

4.194 Once a decision has been announced in relation to stage 2 (impairment), a registrant will know whether stage 3 (sanction) is necessary. If no impairment is found then the GMC may still invite the tribunal to consider imposing a warning – in which case both the GMC and the doctor's representatives would make submissions to the tribunal, followed by advice from the legal assessor (if one is present) and the tribunal retiring once more to deliberate before announcing their decision.[84]

4.195 If impairment is found, then the approach to stage 3 is similar. The GMC will make any submissions in relation to sanction – usually this will not invite a particular sanction, but simply draw relevant aspects of the case to the tribunal and make observations which may assist the tribunal in their consideration of sanction, if any. Sometimes the GMC will take a

84 See the section above on warnings and the GMC guidance on warnings.

robust view on sanction and have instructions, for example, to seek erasure. It is important to have this conversation with the GMC presenting officer in advance so that the GMC position is known (although often no final instructions are given until the decision on impairment has been considered). It is important to know in advance exactly what suggestions have to be rebutted in submissions on behalf of the doctor. Further evidence and submissions may then be made on the doctor's behalf in relation to sanction. It is important, at this stage, to focus on issues particularly relevant to sanction. By stage 3 much of what can be said will have already been said, and while it is important not to miss key submissions at any stage, repeating previous submissions is unlikely to engage the tribunal fully at this stage. The advantage at this stage is that a doctor has the tribunal's determination on facts and impairment – the concerns of the tribunal are often made plain and it is important to, where possible, take the time to address these concerns and be realistic about what sanction may, if required, sufficiently address the concerns raised.

Mitigation

Personal mitigation

4.196 At this stage, personal mitigation also becomes very important and information as to this can and should be provided to the tribunal with other relevant documentation. However, because disciplinary sanctions are not punitive in nature, personal considerations that would ordinarily weigh in mitigation of punishment have less effect than they would on sentencing in the criminal context. The guidance provides that the risk of harm to the public or the need to protect the public may properly override persuasive mitigation. In performance cases, evidence that failure to meet the expected standards was associated with particular circumstances which no longer exist may give some degree of reassurance. However, the chance of those circumstances recurring may be relevant to the evaluation of risk and to the disposal of the case.

4.197 It is important to remember, that while it may not seem that way for a doctor facing stage 3 proceedings, the purpose of sanctions is not to punish, but to protect the public and maintain confidence in the profession.

Sanctions guidance

4.198 The MPTS/GMC's *Sanctions guidance*, along with *Good medical practice*, are the key documents to consider for this stage of the proceedings. The *Sanctions guidance* aims to promote consistency and transparency in decision-making. In *Council for the Regulation of Healthcare Professionals v (1) General Medical Council (2) Leeper*[85] Collins J stated:

> It helps to achieve a consistent approach to the imposition of penalties where serious professional misconduct is established. The [tribunal] must have regard to it, although obviously each case will depend on its own facts and guidance is what it says and must not be regarded as laying down a rigid tariff.[86]

85 [2004] EWHC 1850 (Admin).
86 [2004] EWHC 1850 (Admin) at para 24.

4.199 Newman J, in *R (Abrahaem) v General Medical Council*[87] described the guidance thus:

> Those are very useful guidelines and they form a framework which enables any tribunal, including this court, to focus its attention on the relevant issues. But one has to come back to the essential exercise which the law now requires in what lies behind the purpose of sanctions, which is not to be punitive but to protect the public interest; public interest is a label which gives rise to separate areas of consideration.

4.200 The observation above reflects the fact that the purpose of sanctions is not punishment, but the protection of patients, the maintenance of public confidence in the profession and declaring and upholding proper standards of conduct and behaviour.

Sanctions should be proportionate

4.201 In *Cohen v General Medical Council* there were four significant factors that led individually and cumulatively to the conclusion that the tribunal had erred in finding C's fitness to practise had been impaired:

a) the tribunal was obliged to explain why it did not accept the expert anaesthetist's opinion in respect of C's misconduct;
b) having found misconduct proved against C the tribunal automatically concluded that his fitness to practise had been impaired without looking at all the other relevant factors, such as C's long and unblemished career record;
c) the tribunal had wrongly disregarded the expert anaesthetist's opinion that C's misconduct would have been easily remediable;
d) the very grave consequences of C's misconduct finding served as a salutary lesson which served to prevent recurrence.

4.202 The court found that C's fitness to practise should not have been regarded as impaired and the sanction imposed by the tribunal was substituted for a warning.

Nature of sanctions

4.203 Where no impairment is found, the tribunal may:

- take no action; or
- issue warnings or order the doctor.

4.204 Where impairment is found, the tribunal may:

- take no action;
- agree, as an alternative to sanctions, to written undertakings;
- impose conditional registration: maximum three years;
- order suspension;
- erase a doctor from the register (save in cases relating solely to a doctor's health) where this is the only means of protecting patients and the wider public interest, which includes maintaining public trust and confidence in the profession.

87 [2004] EWHC 279 (Admin) at para 36.

4.205 For general guidance, see the judgment of Lord Bingham (MR) in *Bolton v The Law Society*.[88]

4.206 Voluntary erasure is also a possibility but only if the registrant applies for it. A doctor may apply in writing to the Registrar for voluntary erasure – that is to have his or her name removed from the register. Regulations provide information on the process for applying for voluntary erasure, including what must be included with and in the written application and the decision-making process.[89] If there are any active proceedings against the doctor at the time of the application then the application will be referred either to case examiners – one lay and one medical (if no tribunal has commenced) for a determination as to whether to reject or grant the application for voluntary erasure. If it is granted no tribunal will follow. See chapter 3 at para 3.357 for further information. There is GMC guidance on voluntary erasure.[90]

4.207 A warning may be considered appropriate in circumstances where there is no risk to the public or to patients. It cannot be given in conjunction with another determination.

4.208 Conditions should be clear, relevant, addressed to the registrant (not to third parties), necessary in order to protect patients, the public or in the interests of the registrant, proportionate to the allegations, formulated so that the conditions are not in effect a suspension, and written in such a way that compliance can be easily verified.

4.209 The guidance provides that conditions can only be adequate when there is reasonable confidence in the registrant's capacity to comply with them. If there is an issue between imposing conditions and suspension, suspension may be necessary to give the public the protection expected.

4.210 Where appropriate, representatives may wish to propose suitable conditions (on instructions from the doctor). The GMC maintains a conditions bank which can be used as a source.

4.211 Suspension may be appropriate and proportionate where a tribunal finds that the withdrawal of registration is necessary for public protection but such withdrawal does not need to last the five-year term that would be a minimum for erasure. Suspension will be for a given period of time not exceeding 12 months. The determination must make clear whether the suspension will be automatically lifted at the end of the stated period or whether it will be reviewed towards the end of the period of suspension.

4.212 Erasure is obviously the most serious sanction. Following erasure a person cannot practise as a doctor. The person can, however, apply for the restoration of his or her name to the register after a minimum of five years. The guidance states that erasure is imposed in order to protect the public and maintain its confidence in the profession as a whole.

4.213 No tribunal may erase purely on health grounds.

88 [1994] 1 WLR 512.

89 General Medical Council (Voluntary Erasure and Restoration following Voluntary Erasure) Regulations Order of Council 2004 SI No 2609.

90 See www.gmc-uk.org/DC4316_CE_Decision_Guidance___Annex_I___Guidance_on_voluntary_erasure_25416412.pdf.

Relevant case-law on suspension and erasure

4.214 In *John v Rees*,[91] Megarry J said of suspension in disciplinary proceedings:

> . . . suspension is merely expulsion pro tanto. Each is penal and each deprives the member concerned of the enjoyment of his rights of membership or office. Accordingly, in my judgment, the rules of natural justice prima facie apply to any such process in the same way that they apply to expulsion.[92]

4.215 Suspension from practice equates in seriousness with permanent exclusion. In the case of *Dad v General Dental Council*,[93] the Privy Council stated in relation to suspension that:

> Such consequences can properly be regarded as inevitable where the nature or gravity of the offence indicated that a dentist was unfit to practise, that rehabilitation was unlikely and that he had to be suspended or have his name erased from the register . . . But, in the present case, where there is a real possibility of rehabilitation and there are no other grounds for doubting the appellant's fitness to practise as a dentist, the consequences were so far out of keeping with what was needed that it could be reasonably be said that the penalty of suspension from the register for 12 months was wrong and unjustified.[94]

4.216 In *Bijl v General Medical Council*[95] where a surgeon had committed serious errors of judgment which, however, did not involve his practical skills as a doctor and were unlikely to be repeated, it was held to be inappropriate that his name should be removed from the medical register.

4.217 Further, per Collins J in *Giele v General Medical Council*:[96]

> I do not doubt that the maintenance of public confidence in the profession must outweigh the interests of the individual doctor. But that confidence will surely be maintained by imposing such sanction as is in all the circumstances appropriate. Thus, in considering the maintenance of confidence, the existence of a public interest in not ending the career of a competent doctor will play a part. Furthermore, the fact that many patients and colleagues have, in the knowledge of the misconduct found, clearly indicated their views that erasure was not needed is a matter which can carry some weight in deciding how confidence can properly be maintained.[97]

Interim orders following determination

4.218 Where a sanction has been imposed, that sanction will not take effect until after the end of the appeal period and therefore it may be that the GMC will make an application to the tribunal for an interim order to be imposed to cover the appeal period (interim suspension or interim conditions). An appeal should be made to the High Court within 28 days 'beginning with the date on which notification of the decision was served'.[98] Therefore no

91 [1969] 2 All ER 274.
92 [1969] 2 All ER 274 at 305E.
93 [2000] UKPC 17.
94 [2000] UKPC 17 at para 13.
95 [2000] UKPC 41.
96 [2006] 1 WLR 942.
97 At para 29.
98 MA 1983 s40(4).

sanction order will have effect until the end of the 28-day period, and if an appeal is lodged within that period, until the appeal has been finally disposed of.

4.219 To cover the appeal period, the tribunal has the power to impose an interim order which will take effect during the 28 days and during any further appeal period (as appeals can take some time to be heard by the High Court). It is for this reason that an interim order is usually imposed at this stage for a period of 18 months. In practice, if no appeal is made then once the appeal period has passed the interim order will cease and be replaced immediately with the full order imposed at the sanction stage by the tribunal.

4.220 Any interim order made is likely to be on the same terms as the substantive order, eg if conditions are imposed they will be be interim conditions. The test is the same as that which applies to interim orders generally (see para 4.82) and an interim order may only be imposed where it is considered by the tribunal to be necessary for the protection of the public or is otherwise in the public interest or the interests of the person concerned.

4.221 An interim order application by the GMC at the end of a tribunal can be a particularly difficult application for registrants to endure, who by this stage often simply want to leave the hearing to process the decisions made against them in the proceedings. Consideration will need to be given as to how, if at all, the application will be responded to. It should not be assumed to be automatic that simply because a sanction has been imposed that an interim order should be. See chapter 2 for further information relation to orders following substantive hearings.

4.222 When a tribunal is considering imposing an interim order, then it is required to invite representations from the parties and take such representations into account. The tribunal should be informed if there are any particular reasons why an interim order should not be imposed, for example, if the registrant has patients booked or needs a period of time to arrange cover for his or her practice. The tribunal will adjourn to deliberate in private and then announce its decision and the reasons for that decision.

Reviews and challenges

Review hearings (rule 22)

4.223 GMC (FTP) Rules 2004 r22 sets out the procedure that a tribunal must follow at a review hearing. It will need to decide whether a doctor's fitness to practise is impaired or if the doctor has failed to comply with any conditions imposed at a previous hearing before determining whether to make a further order. The tribunal's powers are set out in MA 1983 s35D.

4.224 Where a tribunal, having ordered suspension or a period of conditional registration, directs a review hearing pursuant to section 35D, it will assist the registrant if it makes clear what it expects the doctor to do in the interim.

4.225 Under section 35D(12)(d), the tribunal may revoke or vary any of the conditions it has previously imposed, for the remainder of the current period of conditional registration, but shall not extend any period of conditional registration for more than three years at a time. Rule 21B provides a power for review on the papers in appropriate cases. Rules 22A provides for the procedure at a non-compliance review hearing.

Restoration hearings (rules 23 and 24)

4.226 A restoration hearing will be held to consider an application to restore a registrant onto the register.[99] The procedure for such a hearing is set out at rule 24.

Judicial review

4.227 In appropriate circumstances consideration may be given to mounting a challenge to a decision (or omission) of the GMC/MPTS by way of judicial review. Further consideration of when a judicial review may be appropriate in this context and the procedural and substantive requirements of making such an application are considered in chapter 10.

Appeals

Doctor's right of appeal

4.228 The usual route for challenging a decision of a medical practitioners tribunal decision is through the statutory appeal mechanism provided for by the MA 1983. Appeals by the doctor are governed by section 40 of the MA 1983. Appeals should be made to the High Court within 28 days 'beginning with the date on which notification of the decision was served' (section 40(4)) and extend, among other things, to decisions in relation to:

- erasure, suspension, conditional registration or varying conditions;
- directions that the right to make applications for restoration of the doctor's name to the register if previously unsuccessful, be suspended indefinitely (section 41(9));
- refusal to restore a doctor's name to the register.

4.229 There is no statutory appeal available where a doctor has accepted undertakings. In accepting undertakings in response to the findings of the tribunal, a doctor forfeits any right to appeal, because there is no order made against the doctor that could be subject to an appeal (MA 1983 s40(1)).

4.230 It has been recognised by the High Court that judgment exercised by the High Court in such appeals is 'distinctly and firmly a secondary judgment' (per Laws LJ in *Raschid and Fatnani v General Medical Council*).[100]

4.231 For this reason, the High Court will be reluctant to interfere with findings of fact made by the specialist tribunal of the GMC, as enunciated in the case of *Nandi v General Medical Council*:[101]

99 GMC (FTP) Rules 2004 r23.

100 [2007] 1 WLR 1460 at para 20.

101 [2004] EWHC 2317 (Admin) per Collins J at [27].

27. So far as this court's approach is concerned, there is very little, if anything, between counsel. The Committee deals with the matter in stages. First of all, it finds the facts. It then goes on to consider whether, on those facts, it is appropriate to make a finding of serious professional misconduct, and then it considers also the question as to what penalties should be imposed if such a finding is made. So far as findings of fact are concerned, this is an appeal which is not limited but, in accordance with the general approach of the Court of Appeal, there will not be interference with findings of fact unless the court takes the view that they are clearly wrong. The Committee have heard the evidence, have seen the witnesses give that evidence and will be in the best position to judge what evidence they accept and what they reject. Of course, if this court is persuaded that a particular finding was one which was not appropriate, should not have been made and was clearly wrong, then it will interfere, but not otherwise.

4.232 This was also considered in *Council for Healthcare Regulatory Excellence v Nursing and Midwifery Council and Grant*:[102]

Courts considering challenges to decisions of this kind will therefore acknowledge the deference due to the specialist tribunal seized with the task of determining the nature or gravity of the misconduct, and the extent to which it is likely to undermine public confidence in the profession.

Cases in this jurisdiction are, however, particularly fact-sensitive. The degree of deference is likely to be higher where issues of technical competence or clinical practice arise, in assessing how best the needs of the public and of the profession should be protected. It is likely to be lower, where the case concerns behavioural issues such as dishonesty or sexual misconduct; see for example the observations to this effect in *The Council for the Regulation of Health Care Professionals v General Dental Council and Fleischmann* [2005] EWHC 87 (Admin).[103]

Appeals by the General Medical Council

4.233 The GMC have a power to appeal against MPTS decisions pursuant to section 40A of the MA 1983 if they consider that the decision is not sufficient for the protection of the public. This involves consideration of whether it is sufficient a) to protect the health, safety and well-being of the public; b) to maintain public confidence in the medical profession; and c) to maintain proper professional standards and conduct for members of that profession (section 40A(4)). The GMC have the same time-period as a doctor in which to appeal – their window to appeal expires when the doctor's period in which to lodge an appeal expires. The GMC has proved to be both active and robust in pursuing appeals under this new provision.

Professional Standards Authority for Health and Social Care

4.234 The Professional Standards Authority has an oversight function in relation to reviewing all decisions of healthcare regulators fitness to practise decisions, including those of the GMC/MPTS.

102 [2011] EWHC 927 (Admin).

103 [2011] EWHC 927 (Admin), Mrs Justice Cox DBE at paras 62–63.

4.235 This remit involves reporting annually on each regulator; initiating investigations if required; and making a referral to the High Court in cases where decisions appear to be unduly lenient or where a decision should not have been made. Undue leniency may apply to both findings of fact and to sanction. The case of *Council for the Regulation of Healthcare Professionals v General Medical Council and Ruscillo*[104] gives a detailed overview of purpose behind the 2002 Act and the matters the court will take into consideration.

4.236 This power derives from section 29(4) of the NHS Reform and Health Professions Act 2002.[105]

The European Convention on Human Rights

> It is undoubtedly the case that the ECHR applies to regulatory proceedings, although there may be argument when there is no prospect of suspension or erasure.
>
> The better approach to case preparation and presentation is to adopt the *spirit* of, in particular, Article 6 (right to a fair trial), the letter of which is frequently reflected in domestic case-law.

4.237 See chapter 1 at para 1.37 for more detail on Article 6 as it pertains to disciplinary proceedings.

104 [2005] 1 WLR 717.

105 Section 29 provides, so far as is material, as follows (the reference to 'relevant court' being a reference to the High Court): '(4) If the Council considers that – a relevant decision falling within subsection (1) has been unduly lenient, whether as to any finding of professional misconduct or fitness to practise on the part of the registrant concerned (or lack of such a finding), or as to any penalty imposed, or both, or a relevant decision falling within subsection (2) should not have been made, and that it would be desirable for the protection of members of the public for the Council to take action under this section, the Council may refer the case to the relevant court . . . (8) The court may – dismiss the appeal, allow the appeal and quash the relevant decision, substitute for the relevant decision any other decision which could have been made by the committee or other person concerned, or remit the case to the committee or other person concerned to dispose of the case in accordance with the directions of the court, and make such order as to costs . . . as it thinks fit.'

CHAPTER 5

The Nursing and Midwifery Council

continued

Key points

- *Regulator:* Nursing and Midwifery Council (NMC)
- *Professions regulated:* Nurses and midwives
- *Type of proceedings:* Fitness to practise; fraudulent or incorrect entry onto the register; and registration appeals
- *Common sources of referral:* Patients, employers, police
- *Relevant statute:* Nursing and Midwifery Order (NMO) 2001 SI 2002 No 253
- *Fitness to Practise Rules:* Nursing and Midwifery Council (Fitness to Practise) Rules (NMC (FTP) Rules) 2004 (Schedule to SI 2004 No 1761), as amended
- *Key document: The Code: Professional standards of practice and behaviour for nurses and midwives* (NMC Code)
- *Function:* To establish and keep under review standards of conduct, performance and ethics expected of registrants and prospective registrants and to give such guidance as it sees fit, and to make arrangements to protect the public from persons whose fitness to practise is impaired (NMO 2001 art 21)
- *Four-stage process:* Referral, investigation, adjudication and review
- *Two practice committees:* Investigating Committee and Fitness to Practise Committee
- *Location:* The main hearing centres are in London, Cardiff, Edinburgh and Belfast
- *Fitness to practise test:* Whether fitness to practise is impaired by reason of (in summary): a) misconduct; b) lack of competence; c) a criminal conviction or caution; d) physical or mental health; e) not having necessary knowledge of English; or f) a determination by another regulator
- *Notice of hearing provision:* Yes, usually 28 days
- *Case management provisions:* Yes, including power to hold preliminary meetings (NMC (FTP) Rules 2004 r18), power to postpone and adjourn (rule 32) and power to continue in absence of the registrant (rule 21)
- *Case examiners:* Yes (comprising a lay and professional examiner appointed by the Registrar) to determine whether there is a case to answer, where there is an allegation of fitness to practise. Registrar has right of review
- *Investigating Committee:* Yes, to determine an allegation of fraudulent or incorrect entry onto the register, to determine interim orders in fitness to practise cases, and consider whether there is a case to answer in fitness to practise cases where the case examiners cannot agree
- *Interim order power:* Yes, the practice committees have the power to impose interim conditions of practice or interim suspension orders (NMO 2001 art 31; NMC (FTP) Rules 2004 Part 3)
- *Interim order guidance:* Yes.
- *Power to require a registrant to undergo health, competence or language assessment?* Yes

- *Composition of practice committee panels:* Three persons, at least one will be a lay member and at least one will be from the relevant profession. Address the panel as 'Sir'/'Madam'
- *Independent legal assessor:* Yes
- *Fitness to practise hearing procedure:* Four stages – 1) preliminary stage; 2) factual stage; 3) impairment stage; and 4) sanction stage (NMC (FTP) Rules 2004 r24)
- *Burden of proof:* Balance of probabilities (civil standard). Burden on NMC to prove the facts (NMC (FTP) Rules 2004 r30)
- *Submission of no case to answer:* Yes, test is whether 'sufficient evidence' has been presented to find the facts proved or to support a finding of impairment (NMC (FTP) Rules 2004 r24(8) and (9))
- *Sanction provisions:* Power to take no further action or make a caution order of not less than one year and not more than five years; conditions of practice order of not more than three years; suspension order of up to one year; or striking off order (NMO 2001 art 29)
- *Sanction documents: Sanctions guidance*
- *Consensual panel determination and voluntary removal:* Yes
- *Warnings, undertakings and advice:* Yes, can be offered by case examiners and the Investigating Committee
- *Review hearings:* Yes, to review a conditions of practice order or suspension order prior to expiry or otherwise (NMO 2001 art 30)
- *Restoration hearings:* Yes, to consider an application by a person who has been struck off to be restored to the register (NMO 2001 art 33)
- *Registration appeals:* Yes, separate but parallel proceedings
- *Appeal:* Yes, to the High Court (NMO 2001 art 38)
- *Costs:* No general provision

Introduction

5.1 In the UK, nursing and midwifery is a regulated profession[1] – that means, in order to work a nurse or midwife must be on the register maintained by the Nursing and Midwifery Council (NMC). This is regardless of whether the work is temporary or permanent, paid or voluntary, within the NHS or private sector. It is a criminal offence for someone to falsely represent themselves as being on the register, or on a part of it; to use a title of nurse or midwife to which they are not entitled; or to falsely represent himself or herself as having qualifications in nursing or midwifery.[2] It is also an offence for a non-registered midwife or medical practitioner to attend a woman in childbirth, except in emergencies or when undergoing recognised training.[3]

5.2 In order to be on the register a nurse or midwife must:

- comply with NMC standards of education and training;
- pay an annual fee;
- be covered by an appropriate indemnity arrangement;

1 Health Act 1999 s60.

2 Nursing and Midwifery Order (NMO) 2001 SI 2002 No 253 art 44.

3 NMO 2001 art 45.

- certify that he or she is fit to practise (including declaring any police cautions or convictions).

5.3 A nurse or midwife is required to renew his or her registration every three years (called revalidation). In order to maintain registration, the nurse or midwife is required to:

- undertake 450 hours of registered practice over the three-year period (or 900 hours if both a nurse and a midwife);
- undertake 35 specified hours of learning activity, called continuing professional development (CPD), over the three-year period;
- obtain five pieces of practice-related feedback (for example, from patients, carers, peers);
- provide five pieces of written reflective accounts;
- have a reflective discussion with another registered nurse or midwife;
- provide a health and character declaration which includes declaring any conviction or caution or adverse determination by another professional or regulatory body; and
- provide confirmation from a third party (for example, a manager, another registrant or supervisor) that the revalidation requirements have been met.

5.4 The NMC's principal function is to set standards of education and training, conduct and performance for nurses and midwives, and to ensure that the profession maintains those standards.[4] The NMC's overarching objective in exercising its functions is 'the protection of the public'.[5] This involves protecting, promoting and maintaining the health, safety and well-being of the public, promoting and maintaining public confidence in the professions, and promoting and maintaining proper standards of conduct and performance. In furtherance of this objective, the NMC has the power to strike off or suspend a nurse or midwife (called a registrant) from the register, place restrictions on his or her practice (conditions of practice), or put a note on the register for a period of time (caution). The NMC also has the power to impose an interim order until such time as an allegation has been determined. These proceedings are known as 'fitness to practise (FTP) proceedings' and are the subject matter of this chapter. While the fitness to practise proceedings are ongoing, or a sanction has been imposed, a nurse or midwife's registration will not be allowed to lapse.[6]

5.5 The NMC separately has the power to refuse an application for admission to the register. There is a right of appeal, and these proceedings are known as 'registration appeals'; this is dealt with at para 5.386.

Background to regulation

5.6 Nurses and midwives have been subject to statutory regulation for approximately 100 years. The two professions were brought together in 1983 under the auspices of the UK Central Council which maintained the register and which primarily had a disciplinary role, and four National

4 NMO 2001 art 3(2).
5 NMO 2001 art 3(4).
6 NMO 2001 art 12(3).

Boards which primarily dealt with education and training. These functions were brought together with the creation of the NMC in 2002. The NMC is independent of government, and is largely paid for by the profession. Over the years, in order to maintain public confidence, there has been an increase in the number of non-professional (lay) persons involved in regulating the profession. Lay persons now make up 50 per cent of the NMC Board. The work of the NMC is overseen by the Professional Standards Authority for Health and Social Care (PSA) and the NMC is accountable to the parliamentary Health Select Committee and the Charity Commission.

5.7 At the time of writing, the Department of Health is currently consulting over a radical overhaul of the health regulatory system.[7] The proposals include reducing the number of regulators from nine to four, allowing regulators to amend their own procedures, and hints at introducing a single adjudicator and a more inquisitorial as opposed to adversarial system for resolving complaints.

5.8 The NMC currently conducts fitness to practise hearings as prosecutor, judge and jury. The NMC brings a case which is determined by an NMC committee, although NMC committee panels make it clear that they are independent of the NMC. This may give rise to a potential conflict of interest and a number of regulators have recently established separate tribunals to hear cases. It is anticipated the NMC may do likewise at some point in the future.

5.9 The NMC rules were changed in 2004, when the burden of proof was changed from the criminal standard of beyond reasonable doubt, to the civil standard of balance of probabilities. This rule change came into force on 3 November 2008. Despite the rule change, the burden of proof remains with the NMC to prove the allegations – there is no requirement on the registrant to disprove the allegations. The NMC sometimes cite the change in the burden of proof as an indication that the NMC are moving from a criminal towards a civil system. However, the adoption of a civil burden of proof does not require the NMC to adopt other civil tests and procedures. The disciplinary function of the NMC often means that guidance from criminal cases may be more appropriate.

Remit

5.10 The NMC regulates around 690,000 nurses and midwives, across England, Wales, Scotland, Northern Ireland and the Islands.[8] It also regulates health visitors, who are viewed as specialist nurses. It does not regulate healthcare assistants (HCAs), who are increasingly taking on some of the traditional nursing roles. There is an ongoing debate as to whether HCAs should be regulated, but the government decided not to include them in the Health and Social Care Act 2012. At the time of writing, the NMC is considering the results of a consultation on applying the aspects and regulatory functions of its legislation to the newly formed role of Nursing Associate.[9]

7 Department of Health, Promoting professionalism, reforming regulation (31 October 2017).

8 NMC *Annual fitness to practise report 2016–2017.*

9 'Regulation of Nursing Associates in England', Department of Health, 16 October 2017.

5.11 The NMC has power to consider allegations against a registrant where either an entry onto the register has been fraudulently or incorrectly made,[10] or their fitness to practise is impaired for a specific reason namely misconduct,[11] lack of competence,[12] a conviction or caution,[13] physical or mental health,[14] not having the necessary knowledge of English,[15] or where there has been a finding of impairment by any other health or social care regulator[16] (referred to as the 'statutory grounds').

5.12 'Misconduct' is widely defined and includes not just clinical conduct but also managerial and administrative conduct, and can also include conduct unrelated to the performance of a professional role but which brings the profession into disrepute. Any breach of the standards expected of a registrant may constitute misconduct, it is therefore a vague and imprecise concept.

Sources of law

Legislation, standards and guidance

5.13 The NMC derives its regulatory powers from the NMO 2001.[17] Article 21 requires the NMC to establish and keep under review standards of conduct, performance and ethics expected of registrants and prospective registrants and to give such guidance on these matters as it sees fit.[18] It also requires the NMC to make arrangements to protect the public from persons whose fitness to practise is impaired.[19]

5.14 The standards expected of nurses and midwives are set out in *The Code: Professional standards of practice and behaviour for nurses and midwives* ('NMC Code').[20] Adherence to the professional standards set out in the NMC Code is mandatory, and a breach of one or more of the provisions may bring a registrant's fitness to practise into question. The NMC Code requires nurses and midwives to prioritise people, practise effectively, preserve safety and promote professionalism and trust. In particular, they are required to:

- treat people as individuals and uphold their dignity;
- listen to people and respond to their preferences and concerns;
- make sure that people's physical, social and psychological needs are assessed and responded to;
- act in the best interest of people at all times;
- respect people's right to privacy and confidentiality;
- always practice in line with the best available evidence;

10 NMO 2001 art 22(1)(b).
11 NMO 2001 art 22(1)(a)(i).
12 NMO 2001 art 22(1)(a)(ii).
13 NMO 2001 art 22(1)(a)(iii).
14 NMO 2001 art 22(1)(a)(iv).
15 NMO 2001 art 22(1)(a)(iva).
16 NMO 2001 art 22(1)(a)(v).
17 The power to issue Orders in Council derives from the Health Act 1999 ss60 and 62.
18 NMO 2001 art 21(1)(a).
19 NMO 2001 art 21(1)(b).
20 NMC, 31 March 2015, available at www.nmc-uk.org/publications/standards. In relation to pre-31 March 2015 conduct, the provisions of the 2008 Code will still apply.

- communicate clearly;
- work co-operatively;
- share their skill, knowledge and experience for the benefit of people receiving care and their colleagues;
- keep clear and accurate records relevant to their practice;
- be accountable for their decisions to delegate tasks and duties to other people;
- have in place an indemnity arrangement which provides appropriate cover for any practice they take on as a nurse or midwife in the United Kingdom;
- recognise and work within the limits of their competence;
- be open and candid with all service users about all aspects of care and treatment, including when any mistakes or harm have taken place;
- always offer to help if an emergency arises in their practice setting or anywhere else;
- act without delay if they believe that there is a risk to patient safety or public protection;
- raise concerns immediately if they believe a person is vulnerable or at risk and needs extra support and protection;
- advise on, prescribe, supply, dispense or administer medicines within the limits of their training and competence, the law, NMC guidance and other relevant policies, guidance and regulations;
- be aware of, and reduce as far as possible, any potential for harm associated with their practice;
- uphold the reputation of the profession at all times;
- uphold their position as a registered nurse or midwife;
- fulfil all registration requirements;
- co-operate with all investigations and audits;
- respond to any complaints made against them professionally;[21] and
- provide leadership to make sure people's wellbeing is protected and to improve their experiences of the healthcare system.

5.15 In addition, the NMC has produced the following standards:

- *Revalidation. How to revalidate with the NMC*
- *Standards for pre-registration education* (one for nursing and one for midwives)
- *Standards for competence* (one for registered nurses and one for registered midwives
- *Standards of proficiency for specialist community public health nurses*
- *Standards to support learning and assessment in practice*
- *Standards for specialist education and practice*
- *Standards of proficiency for nurse and midwife prescribers*
- *Standards for medicines management*
- *Standards for adaptation to midwifery in the UK*

And the following guidance:

- *Raising concerns: Guidance for nurses and midwives*
- *Social media guidance*
- *The professional duty of candour*

21 The NMC has taken cases against registrants who have failed to cooperate with an investigation, see *Harford v Nursing and Midwifery Council* [2013] EWHC 696 (Admin).

5.16 A failure to comply with the NMC Code or other standards, guidance or advice produced by the NMC can be taken into account in any fitness to practise proceedings, although it does not of itself establish that a registrant's fitness to practise is impaired.[22] However, during a fitness to practise hearing a registrant will be judged against the standards and values set out in the Code. Further, the Code contains a specific requirement that registrants uphold its provisions.[23]

5.17 In addition, registrants are expected to adhere to Professional Standards Authority standards on *Clear sexual boundaries*; national guidelines from professional bodies on best practice; and local policies and guidelines. A failure to do so may be considered to be a breach of one or more of the provisions of the NMC Code.

5.18 Fitness to practise proceedings are governed both by the NMO 2001 and the Nursing and Midwifery Council (Fitness to Practise) Rules Order of Council ('NMC (FTP) Rules') 2004.[24] In accordance with NMO 2001 article 47(1), the NMC (FTP) Rules 2004 have been approved by order of the Privy Council. These rules are explained in more detail below. In addition, the NMC provides guidance to Committees on a range of issues, and these are regularly referred to in hearings.

5.19 The NMO 2001, NMC (FTP) Rules 2004 and NMC Code and other standards can be obtained from the NMC website: www.nmc-uk.org. Both the NMO 2001 and NMC (FTP) Rules 2004 have been amended since their original enactment and the website provides a consolidated version – although it has no official statutory status, it is a useful working document. The website also provides guidance to panels (referred to as 'guides') on interpretation of the statutory provisions. It also provides general advice to registrants, witnesses and members of the public who attend a hearing.

Case-law

5.20 There is a body of regulatory case-law that is developing through High Court, Court of Appeal and Supreme Court decisions. For older cases there are also Privy Council decisions. Regulatory cases relating to the NMC are binding and those relating to other health professions are highly persuasive and generally followed, particularly where they relate to identically worded provisions. In addition, other regulatory decisions and relevant decisions from the civil and criminal courts are also relied upon. This chapter covers key cases used by the NMC or involving the NMC, but for a fuller discussion of the case-law see chapters 1–3.

5.21 The NMC is a public authority and it is reasonably well established that the European Convention on Human Rights (ECHR) applies, especially Article 6 (right to a fair trial). Therefore, decisions of the domestic and European Court of Human Rights (ECtHR) on, for example, the right to a fair hearing, the right to a hearing within a reasonable period of time and the right to a public hearing are also relevant. Potentially Article 8

22 NMO 2001 art 22(4).

23 NMC Code para 20.1.

24 SI No 1761, as amended.

(right to a private and family life) also applies. For a fuller discussion of the applicability of Article 6 and 8 rights see chapter 1 at paras 1.37–1.81.

NMC decisions

5.22 NMC decisions are published on the NMC website. The decisions are not binding on any subsequent FTP committee/panel, and are generally not relied upon in hearings. This is because they are based on different facts and different arguments. However, they can provide a useful indication of how panels views certain conduct.

Fitness to practise – overview

NMC

5.23 In order to carry out its functions the NMC has:

- *Screeners:* who conduct an initial assessment of the referral to establish whether it falls within the NMC's remit and should be investigated.
- *Case examiners:* who consider whether there is a 'case to answer' following an investigation.
- *Investigating Committees:* to determine allegations about fraudulent / incorrect entries onto the register, determine interim orders in fitness to practise cases, and to consider fitness to practise allegations if the case examiners fail to agree.
- *Fitness to Practise Committees:* to determine fitness to practise allegations, including consensual panel determination and voluntary removal. The Committee is also responsible for reviewing sanctions and determine applications for re-registration.

5.24 The constitution of the case examiners and the practice committees is determined by statute.[25] Case examiners will comprise one lay person and one member from the relevant profession. The panels of practice committees are usually made up of three persons and will always comprise at least one lay member and one member from the relevant profession. The chair will be a member of the NMC Board and could be either a lay or professional representative. The committee panellists should be addressed as 'Sir'/'Madam'.

5.25 Seventy-eight per cent of cases are resolved within 15 months,[26] however it can take much longer. If possible, registrants should take steps during this period to address any concerns and gather evidence in support of their case, so that they are fully prepared by the time any hearing takes place.

25 Nursing and Midwifery Council (Midwifery and Practice Committees) (Constitution) Rules 2008 SI No 3148.

26 NMC *Annual fitness to practise report 2016–2017*, chart 2.

Location of hearing centres

5.26 NMC hearing centres are located in London, Cardiff, Edinburgh and Belfast, and other locations throughout the UK. The addresses can be obtained from the NMC website. If a registrant has a particular reason for wanting a different hearing centre to that proposed by the NMC, then this should be raised with the NMC at the earliest opportunity, providing full reasons. However, any amendment to the venue is the exception to the rule. The NMC position is that NMC hearings occur in the hearing centre applicable to the registrant's address on the NMC register.

Assistance

5.27 NMC hearings have potentially serious consequences for a registrant since they can prevent him or her from practising as a nurse or midwife, and can more widely damage the registrant's reputation and affect his or her livelihood. It is therefore vital that a registrant takes such hearings seriously and seeks assistance at the earliest possible opportunity; preferably upon being advised by the referring party of a referral to the NMC or upon receiving the initial NMC Notice of Referral letter. If the registrant is a member of a trade union or professional association, he or she should seek assistance from his or her representative. If the registrant is not a member of such body, then he or she should contact his or her local Citizens Advice Bureau, Legal Advice Centre, a solicitor or a public access barrister specialising in regulatory work.

5.28 Some registrants represent themselves. If so, they are strongly advised to attend other NMC hearings to familiarise themselves with the process.[27] If the registrant has a query relating to his or her case, then the registrant or his or her representative can contact the NMC case officer identified on the correspondence.

Referral

5.29 Anyone can make an allegation about the fitness to practise of a nurse or midwife. There is no need for the conduct in question to have occurred in the UK or relate to a time when the nurse or midwife was registered.[28]

5.30 Between 1 April 2016 and 31 March 2017 there were 5,476 referrals, representing 0.8 per cent of registered nurses and midwives.[29] There has been a steady increase in the number of referrals being made. In 2016/17, 39 per cent of referrals were made by an employer or service provider. This will usually be following an internal disciplinary procedure, however a referral may be made prior to such proceedings being completed in serious cases where the public is at risk, or where a registrant has resigned. The second largest source of referrals is from members of the public and patients, who comprise 29 per cent of referrals.

27 The NMC publishes on its website a schedule of upcoming hearings.

28 NMO 2001 art 22(3).

29 NMC *Annual fitness to practise report 2016–2017* (July 2017).

5.31 Sometimes the nurse or midwife will self-refer. Registrants are required to inform the NMC (and any employer) if he or she has been cautioned, charged or found guilty of a criminal offence (other than a protected caution or conviction).[30] A caution or conviction may be protected where a specified period of time has elapsed since the date of the caution or conviction. The rules in relation to protected cautions and convictions differ depending on location. The NMC provides guidance on what constitutes a protected conviction or caution that is available on their website.[31] Registrants should seek legal advice if they intend not to declare a historic conviction or caution, since in most cases the conviction or caution will need to be declared. Failure to do so within a reasonable period of time may result in a charge of dishonesty.

5.32 Other sources of referral include the police or other regulators. Further, the NMC is permitted to make a referral where it appears to it that there should be a fitness to practise investigation.[32] Registrants should also be aware that the vast majority of, if not all, cautions and convictions will be disclosed on their Enhanced Disclosure and Barring Services Certificates.

5.33 There is no time limit for a complaint to be made. If there has been a long delay, then it may be possible to challenge the delay as an abuse of process or breach of the ECHR. However, the need to maintain public confidence in the regulation of the health profession requires that a complaint should usually be publically investigated unless the delay has caused significant prejudice to the registrant – see para 5.143.

Screening

5.34 Upon receipt of a referral, an allegation will be referred to the screening team (acting on behalf of the Registrar) for initial consideration prior to the NMC conducting its own investigation. Sixty per cent of referrals are closed at this stage.[33] The screeners will consider:

- *Whether a case is serious enough to impair a registrant's fitness to practise.*
- *Whether the referral meets the formal requirements.* The referral must be in writing, identify a nurse or midwife who is on the NMC register, be from an identifiable person or organisation, and be sufficiently detailed. The NMC have a standard referral form that can be used. The NMC can however investigate anonymous allegations where it feels that it is necessary to do so using its powers to conduct its own investigation;
- *Whether there is credible evidence about the concerns.* The NMC will generally not conduct an investigation whilst an employer's disciplinary investigation is ongoing;
- *Whether the registrant in question has already remediated any failure such that there are no outstanding fitness to practise concerns.* However, a referral may still be made where the past incident is considered so serious that further investigation is required.[34]

30 NMC Code para 23.2.

31 NMC Guide ref GUI-2c.

32 NMO 2001 art 22(6).

33 NMC *Annual fitness to practise report 2016–2017* (July 2017).

34 NMC Guide ref SCR-2.

The screening team will send the registrant a notice confirming that an allegation has been made, enclosing documentation and asking the registrant to complete a form confirming his or her contact and employment details. The screening team will also notify the referrer.[35]

5.35 If the screeners decide not to refer the case for a full investigation, the case will be closed. However, if new information is subsequently received this will be considered alongside information already gathered. If the case is closed, the screening team will notify the registrant and the referrer.

Concurrent proceedings including criminal proceedings and double jeopardy

> Regulatory proceedings need not be stayed pending the outcome of criminal or other proceedings unless there are exceptional circumstances such as an impossible workload from which the defendant can demonstrate serious prejudice or injustice.
>
> Arguments regarding double jeopardy, privilege and publicity are otherwise unlikely to succeed.

5.36 Often investigation of an allegation that is subject to a criminal investigation will be suspended pending the outcome of that criminal investigation and any trial. However, there is no requirement on regulators to adjourn. For a fuller discussion see chapter 1, paras 1.278–1.324.

5.37 The NMC guidance makes it clear that their starting point is to investigate without delay and that there must be clear and compelling reasons for an investigation to be put on hold.[36] However, an investigation may be put on hold where:

- there is a real and significant risk that the NMC investigation will prejudice the other investigation;
- it impractical for the NMC investigation to continue at the same time as the other investigation; or
- the NMC will save significant time or costs because it can rely on the information that the other organisation has gathered.

5.38 This guidance does not differentiate between criminal proceedings and other proceedings, although it does acknowledge that prejudice is most likely to occur where there is a police investigation.[37] Where an investigation is put on hold, that decision will be kept under review.[38] The guidance also suggests that there will be occasions when the NMC will conduct an investigation by taking witness statements and gathering evidence, and then put the case on hold at the point that it is ready to be considered by the case examiners. This is because new evidence may come to light from that external investigation. The nature and timescale of the external

35 NMC (FTP) Rules 2004 r2A(3).

36 NMC Guide ref INV-5a.

37 NMC Guide ref INV-5b.

38 NMC Guide ref INV-5f.

investigation is likely to be an important factor.[39] If the NMC closes the case whilst an external investigation is ongoing, the registrant is likely to be warned that the matter can be reopened if new information surfaces.

5.39 Regulators may continue to investigate an allegation that is criminal in nature even where criminal proceedings have not been pursued due to insufficient evidence or there has been an acquittal at trial. This is because the burden of proof in criminal proceedings is 'beyond reasonable doubt', as opposed to a 'balance of probabilities' used in regulatory proceedings (see para 5.261). However, where a police investigations has not resulted in a conviction, and the matter in question is unrelated to a registrant's professional practice, then it is unlikely that the NMC will seek to re-investigate the facts.[40]

Investigation

Generally

5.40 If the screeners conclude that the referral falls within the NMC's remit then the case will be referred to either:

- the case examiners to determine whether there is a case to answer, if the allegation is one of fitness to practise;[41]
- the FTP Committee to determine without consideration by the case examiners.[42] The NMC guidance suggests that this would be exceptional but may occur where a registrant has a criminal conviction which has resulted in immediate imprisonment, is considered to be a 'serious arrestable offence' or involves hate crimes or child pornography;[43] or
- the Investigating Committee to determine if the allegation is one of fraudulent or incorrect entry onto the register.[44]

5.41 If the NMC receives an allegation comprising both fraudulent or incorrect entry and impairment of fitness to practise, the NMC will prioritise the fraudulent or incorrect entry allegation and will only investigate the fitness to practise allegation if the fraudulent or incorrect entry is not pursued. This is because a fraudulent or incorrect entry is viewed as particularly serious since it undermines the integrity of the register.[45] In assessing whether to refer a fraudulent or incorrect entry allegation to the Investigating Committee the investigating registrar will consider whether the information at the time of the application was deliberately misleading or otherwise wrong, false or inaccurate, or whether the entry was made by mistake. A registrar may decide against a referral where there is no suggestion that the entry was fraudulently obtained and the error or inaccuracy is trivial, has been remedied, and it is unlikely that the Investigating Committee would take any action against the registrant.

39 NMC Guide ref INV-5e.
40 NMC Guide ref GUI-2a.
41 NMC (FTP) Rules 2004 r2A(2)(a).
42 NMO 2001 art 22(5)(b); NMC (FTP) Rules 2004 r2A(2)(b).
43 NMC Guide ref GUI-2c.
44 NMO 2001 art 22(5)(a); NMC (FTP) Rules 2004 r2A(1).
45 NMC Guide ref SCR-4.

5.42 Prior to any referral, the case may be referred to the investigations team for further investigation.[46] An investigation can take some time, and will usually involve gathering further information from referrers, employers and witnesses including gathering of documentary evidence, such as patient notes, local policies and procedures, evidence gathered during internal disciplinary investigations including records of any meetings.

Health cases

5.43 A case will only be classified as a health case if there is evidence of a link between what the registrant did and the health condition that they have.[47] In such circumstances the focus of the investigation and proceedings will be on the health condition rather than personal culpability. This is likely to require medical evidence. The NMC states that it will only investigate heath cases where there is a risk of harm to patients and a related risk to public confidence in the profession. A registrant who has a health condition but is currently safe to practise would not generally be considered to be impaired purely because of public confidence. The NMC accept that a registrant who is disabled or has a long-term health condition may nevertheless be able to work with or without adjustments by their employer. Further, a registrant who is signed off sick does not necessarily give rise to fitness to practise concerns.[48] The tension tends to arise where an employer fails to put in place reasonable adjustments to enable a registrant to work safely. In such circumstances a disabled person may find himself or herself subject to a referral. Disability discrimination is outside the scope of this chapter, but is a factor that registrants and their representatives may wish to consider when dealing with health referrals.

5.44 Factors that the NMC will take into account when considering whether or not to refer a health case for investigation include whether:

- the registrant has demonstrated good insight into the extent and effect of his or her condition;
- the registrant is taking appropriate steps to access treatment and is following any advice from the health professionals treating him or her;
- occupational health (where available) is providing support through the employer;
- the registrant is managing his or her practice appropriately, for example by taking sickness absence.

5.45 The NMC in investigating a health referral may require information from the registrant's GP or occupational health department.[49] It is anticipated that the NMC will usually seek to gain the registrant's consent, however a failure to provide consent may be construed as a failure to engage. It is also likely that the NMC will ask the registrant to consent to an independent medical examination.[50] This may include medical testing where the concern is drug or alcohol-related.

46 NMC (FTP) Rules 2004 rr2A(4) and 6B.

47 NMC Guide ref SCR-3b.

48 NMC Guide ref GUI-2d.

49 NMC Guide ref SCR-2e and GUI-2d.

50 NMC (FTP) Rules 2004 r6B(3).

Knowledge of English cases

5.46 If the concern in question relates to knowledge of English, then whether the case will be referred depends on if it places the public at risk of harm, due to, for example: poor handover of essential information; serious record-keeping errors; serious failures to give appropriate care due to poor communication with other health professionals or the patients themselves; and drug errors caused by failure to understand or inability to read prescriptions. However, concerns about spelling or difficulty in understanding regional accents are unlikely to give rise to a fitness to practise concern.[51]

5.47 The NMC can require the registrant to submit to a language assessment.[52] The NMC will make this request in writing and will provide directions as to what is required.[53]

Criminal convictions and caution cases

5.48 The NMC acknowledges that not all criminal convictions and cautions give rise to a fitness to practise concerns. For example, minor driving offences are unlikely to be investigated or referred. However convictions and cautions that damage the reputation of the profession will be referred even if unrelated to the registrant's practice.[54]

Determination by another regulator cases

5.49 Most cases involving determinations by another health or social care regulator will be referred unless there is no current risk of harm to patients, and involves no potential impact on public confidence in the profession, there is no need to take action in order to maintain proper professional standards and conduct.[55]

Lack of competence cases

5.50 In lack of competence cases the NMC also has the power to invite a registrant to submit to a competence assessment,[56] but this power is rarely exercised, if at all. Failure to submit to an assessment is likely to be considered by the NMC to be a lack of engagement on the part of the registrant, and the NMC may seek to charge this as misconduct. Where there is a reason for non-engagement, registrants and their representatives are advised to put the explanation in writing to the NMC; with relevant supporting evidence, where available.

Responding to an allegation

5.51 The registrant is not obliged to provide a response to the allegations at the investigation stage or at all. However, an early response can result in a case being dismissed so written representations are advised if there is

51 NMC Guide ref GUI-2e.
52 NMC (FTP) Rules 2004 r6B(3A).
53 NMC (FTP) Rules 2004 r6B(3A).
54 NMC Guide ref GUI-2c.
55 NMC Guide ref GUI-2f.
56 NMC (FTP) Rules 2004 r6B(2).

uncontested or overwhelming evidence to rebut the allegation, or where the allegation is obviously minor or trivial in nature to such an extent that even if proven on the facts it would not support a finding of impairment at the hearing stage. Where a case involves a conflict of fact the registrant will need to provide clear corroborative evidence to support his or her account, such as contemporaneous nursing records or a statement from a witness.

5.52 Registrants should, however, exercise caution and seek legal advice where possible. If written representations are made at this stage, care must be taken to ensure they are factually accurate and consistent with the registrant's case, since any inconsistencies may be adduced at any subsequent hearing. Further, an ill-considered response could demonstrate lack of insight or understanding of the seriousness of the allegation.

Case to answer

Case examiners

5.53 At the completion of the investigation the case will be referred to two case examiners appointed by the Registrar to consider whether there is a case to answer – ie a realistic prospect that a panel will both find the facts of the allegation proved *and* find that the registrant's practice is currently impaired. The case to answer tests means that only the most serious cases should be referred to the FTP Committee for adjudication. The case examiners will be a lay examiner who is not and has never been a registered nurse, midwife or medical practitioner, and a professional examiner who is a registered nurse or midwife. In 2016/17, the case examiners referred 57 per cent of cases for a hearing, and decided that 43 per cent had no case to answer.[57]

5.54 Before any decision can be made by the case examiners, the NMC is required to send the registrant a 'notice of referral' enclosing all documentation gathered during the investigation.[58] This will include a report containing draft 'Regulatory Concerns'. The registrant will be informed that he or she may provide an initial response to the allegations within 28 days.[59] Registrants are still under no obligation to respond to the allegations at this stage. The notice may be accompanied by notice of hearing for an interim order.

Investigating Committee

5.55 If the case examiners fail to agree whether there is a case to answer, the NMC will refer the allegation to the Investigating Committee to determine the matter.[60] Where this occurs, the Investigating Committee may carry out further investigations, and must again notify the registrant of any additional information or documents and provide the opportunity for

57 NMC *Annual fitness to practise report 2016–2017* (July 2017).
58 NMC (FTP) Rules 2004 r6A.
59 NMC (FTP) Rules 2004 r6B(4).
60 NMC (FTP) Rules 2004 r6C(4).

the registrant to make written representations.[61] The Investigating Committee panel will meet in private to determine whether there is a case to answer.

5.56 Prior to 2015, whether there was a case to answer in all cases was determined by the Investigating Committee who had power to take such steps as are reasonably practicable to obtain as much information about the case prior to making its decision.[62] Following the creation of case examiners, Investigating Committees have retained this power but will rarely have an allegation referred to it. In contrast, case examiners are required to make a decision based on the information that the NMC investigators have obtained and any additional information provided by the Registrant.

Case to answer and undertakings

5.57 Where the case examiners or Investigating Committee agrees that there is a case to answer, they must either refer the matter to the FTP Committee or recommend undertakings to be agreed with the registrant.[63] Undertakings may only be proposed where there is no realistic prospect of the registrant being struck off the register.[64]

5.58 The NMO 2001 provides the Investigating Committee with the option to undertake mediation where there is a case to answer, as an alternative to a referral to the FTP Committee. This power is not currently used by the NMC. Greater use of mediation is one of the recommendations in the Home Office consultation.[65]

5.59 Undertakings are a new concept for the NMC, but have existed for some time for other regulators. An undertaking is a measure agreed with the registrant to address any concerns in their practice that pose a current risk to patients. It may include a specific step that the registrant is expected to take within a specified period of time (see the measures suggested in the NMC Undertakings Bank published on the website). Undertakings are similar to the concept of conditions of practice, but are steps which are agreed by the registrant rather than imposed by a panel and subject to review.

5.60 The NMC suggests that undertakings may be appropriate in relation to allegations of:

- lack of competence;
- misconduct (particularly where the conduct related to clinical practice);
- not having the necessary knowledge of English; or
- health.

5.61 Undertakings are unlikely to be suitable where the allegation concerns:

- misconduct not involving clinical practice;
- criminal convictions or cautions; or

61 NMC (FTP) Rules 2004 r6D(1).

62 NMO 2001 art 26(2)(c).

63 NMC (FTP) Rules 2004 r6C(2)(a) or r6D(2)(a).

64 NMC (FTP) Rules 2004 r6C(2A) or r6D(2A).

65 Department of Health, *Promoting professionalism, reforming regulation* (31 October 2017).

- determinations of impaired fitness to practise by another health or social care regulator.[66]

5.62 Before an undertaking can be imposed, the registrant concerned must admit that the incident took place and accept the need for the proposed measure in order to address areas of their practice which actually or potentially cause patient risk. Further, like a condition of practice, the undertaking must be proportionate, measurable, workable and sufficient to protect patients. If a more restrictive outcome is required, then the matter should be referred to the FTP Committee.

5.63 Where an undertaking is proposed, the wording of the undertaking should be put in writing and sent to the registrant concerned.[67] If the registrant agrees to comply with the undertaking, then he or she must confirm this in writing within 28 days,[68] or such longer period as the NMC agrees. An extension is only likely to be agreed where an initial positive response is received within the 28 days.[69] The NMC does accept that the wording of an undertaking and the accompanying 'statement of regulatory concern', may be subject to a process of negotiation and therefore take longer than 28 days to be agreed.[70] If the undertaking is agreed, the registrant and the complainant will be notified in writing of the undertakings and the date from which it has effect.[71] The case will then be stayed and any interim order will cease.[72]

5.64 If the registrant fails to respond or agree to the undertaking, then the allegation is referred to the FTP Committee to determine.[73] Again, the registrant and complainant will be notified.

During the period of an undertaking, compliance will be monitored by the NMC.

5.65 If an undertaking has been agreed and the Registrar considers that the undertaking should be varied or cease, the case examiners will be informed and may direct that the undertaking continues, be varied (subject to agreement by the registrant) or cease. If the registrant refuses to agree to the varied undertaking, then the matter may be referred to review (see para 5.73), during which period the undertaking will remain in effect. An undertaking may be ceased once the registrant has completed the steps identified in the undertaking. An undertaking may be varied where the original undertaking is no longer workable, or to deal with situations short of a breach (for example where further time for compliance is required).[74]

5.66 If a registrant is in breach of an undertaking, then the Registrar will refer the matter back to the case examiners who may revoke the undertaking and refer the matter to the FTP Committee, or may direct that the

66 NMC Guide ref CAS-2a.
67 NMC (FTP) Rules 2004 r6E(1).
68 NMC (FTP) Rules 2004 r6E(1)(a).
69 NMC Guide ref CAS-2a.
70 NMC Guide ref CAS-2a.
71 NMC (FTP) Rules 2004 r6E(3).
72 NMC (FTP) Rules 2004 r6E(2).
73 NMC (FTP) Rules 2004 r6E(4).
74 NMC Guide ref CAS-2a.

undertaking continues, be varied or ceases.[75] Where a matter is referred to the FTP Committee, the breach of an undertaking will form one of the charges.[76]

No case to answer and warnings or advice

5.67 If the case examiners or Investigating Committee agree that there is no case to answer, they may simply close the case, or may give advice to the registrant or issue the registrant with a warning.[77] This is also a new concept in NMC proceedings.

5.68 'Advice' is defined by the NMC as 'private' guidance to assist a registrant keep his or her practice safe following an acknowledged minor breach of the Code.[78] Therefore it would not be appropriate if the breach is serious or disputed.

5.69 A 'warning' is defined by the NMC as a public recording that the registrant's past conduct was unacceptable without the need to hold a hearing. Warnings are appropriate where there is a real prospect of a finding of impairment in relation to past conduct but there is no current impairment because the registrant has shown insight and remediated any concern. The NMC guidance suggests that warnings can be used for allegations involving:

- serious clinical errors or failings, where problems have been addressed;
- incidents which might affect the public confidence in nurses or midwives which are not directly related to clinical practice; and
- minor offending resulting in criminal convictions or cautions.[79]

5.70 A warning is unlikely to be considered appropriate where the registrant poses a current risk to patients; has insufficient insight; or the allegation is so serious that it impacts on the reputation of the profession. In such circumstances, a warning is considered inappropriate because the registrant may need to be removed from the register, either temporarily or permanently.[80]

5.71 It would also not be appropriate for a warning to be issued in cases where the regulatory concern related to the registrant's health.[81]

Notice of decision

5.72 The registrant and the complainant will be notified of the decision of the case examiners or Investigating Committee as to whether there is or is not a case to answer, together with their reasons.[82] The registrant will also be informed that the allegation may be taken into account if a fresh allegation is received within three years of the date of the notice of decision[83] (see para 5.80). Where a registrant has been given a warning or advice, the

75 NMC (FTP) Rules 2004 r6E(5) and (7).
76 NMC Guide ref CAS-2a.
77 NMC (FTP) Rules 2004 r6C(2B) or r6D(2B).
78 NMC Guide ref CAS-2c.
79 NMC Guide ref CAS-2b.
80 NMC Guide ref CAS-2b.
81 NMC Guide ref CAS-2b.
82 NMC (FTP) Rules 2004 rr6C(2)(b), (3)(a) and (3)(b)(i) or r6D(2)(b), (3)(a) and (3)(b)(i).
83 NMC (FTP) Rules 2004 r6C(3)(b)(iv) or r6D(3)(b)(iv).

notice will also include details of that warning or advice, and the period that a warning will appear on the register.[84] The warning will be published on the NMC website and remain on the registrant's register entry for 12 months.[85]

Review of decisions

5.73 The NMC, in the form of the Registrar, has the right to review all or part of a decision by the case examiners or the Investigating Committee as to whether there is or is not a case to answer.[86] A 'reviewable decision' is defined as:

- a decision by the case examiners or Investigating Committee that there is no case to answer in respect to the fitness to practise allegation;[87]
- a decision by the case examiners or Investigating Committee to recommend undertakings; or
- a direction by the case examiner that an undertaking should no longer apply and the allegation should not be considered further.[88]

5.74 Anyone can request a review, however the NMC will only conduct a review if the Registrar has reason to believe that either the decision in whole or in part is materially flawed, or there is reason to believe that there is new information which may have lead in whole or in part to a different decision. In both cases there is a further requirement that a review should only be conducted if it is in the public interest or is necessary to prevent injustice to the registrant.[89] The NMC guidance suggests that a 'materially flawed' decision is one that applied the wrong legal test, reached a conclusion unsupported by the evidence, failed to understand the investigation, or failed to comply with certain procedural requirements.[90] If a decision is flawed the Registrar will still consider whether that flaw is a material one, ie whether it would have led to a different decision.[91] The NMC guidance suggests that 'new information' is information not in its possession at the time of the decision which would have made a difference to the decision.[92]

5.75 The NMC suggests that there may be a 'public interest' in re-opening a decision where there is a 'real risk' of harm to the public, or a review is required to enable the NMC to uphold standards or maintain confidence in the profession. An attempt to reopen a decision may give rise to fair trial and abuse of process arguments and registrants are strongly urged to seek legal advice were this to be proposed. A review would only be necessary to prevent injustice to the registrant where it is necessary to remove advice or warning imposed on a registrant.

84 NMC (FTP) Rules 2004 r6C(3)(b)(ii)and (iii) or r6D(3)(b)(ii) and (iii).

85 NMC Guide ref CAS-2b.

86 According to NMC (FTP) Rules 2004 r7A(1), 'reviewable decisions' are those reached on or after 9 March 2015.

87 NMC (FTP) Rules 2004 r7A(1).

88 NMC (FTP) Rules 2004 r7A(1A)(a)–(c).

89 NMC (FTP) Rules 2004 r7A(2).

90 NMC Guide ref REV-1a.

91 NMC Guide ref REV-1a.

92 NMC Guide ref REV-1a.

5.76 The registrant, complainant and other interested parties will be informed of the decision to carry out a review and invited to make representations.[93] Where the decision is considered to be materially flawed, they will be provided with reasons.[94] Where there is new evidence, they will be provided with that new evidence (if appropriate).[95] The NMC may conduct further investigations,[96] and take into account any representations made. The Registrar will then conduct a review taking into account any information or representations received. If the Registrar considers that a fresh decision is required in the public interest (or necessary to prevent injustice to the registrant) then the Registrar may:

- refer the matter back to the case examiners for reconsideration; or
- substitute the original decision for any decision that the case examiners or Investigating Committee could have made.

5.77 In deciding whether to refer the original decision back to the case examiners or substitute for a new decision, the NMC guidance suggests that the Registrar may take into account:

- whether the matter requires a total re-examination of the evidence, or relates to a narrower issue of interpretation which the Registrar can make;
- whether the allegation itself, and in particular the specialist clinical knowledge of a registered case examiner, is required to assess the case; and / or
- the delay to the progress of the case, and the interest of both the registrant and the wider public in concluding cases expeditiously.[97]

5.78 If the Registrar considers that a fresh decision is not required, the Registrar must confirm the original decision.[98]

5.79 The registrant, complainant and other interested parties will be notified of the decision and the reasons.[99] Unless there are exceptional circumstances, no review should commence more than one year after the date of the decision.[100]

Reconsideration of allegation

5.80 If there has been a finding of no case to answer by either the case examiners or the Investigating Committee, and the NMC receives a fresh allegation within three years of the notice of the decision, the case examiners or Investigating Committee may take the previous allegation into account when considering the fresh allegation and may refer both allegations to the FTP Committee.[101]

5.81 It should be noted that this rule does not prevent the NMC from referring to panels allegations which are more than three years old, specifically

93 NMC (FTP) Rules 2004 r7A(3)(a) and (c).
94 NMC (FTP) Rules 2004 r7A(4).
95 NMC (FTP) Rules 2004 r7A(3)(b) and (c).
96 NMC (FTP) Rules 2004 r7A(5).
97 NMC Guide ref REV-1b.
98 NMC (FTP) Rules 2004 r7A(8).
99 NMC (FTP) Rules 2004 r7A(9).
100 NMC (FTP) Rules 2004 r7A(10).
101 NMC (FTP) Rules 2004 r7.

in situations where the referral related to matters found proved at a local level or matters which occurred over a period of time. A registrant in such circumstances should exercise caution in claiming an unblemished career or the absence of any previous concerns relating to misconduct or competence.

Interim orders and hearings

> Interim orders may be made if they are necessary to protect the public or in the public interest or in the registrant's interest prior to the substantive hearing on fitness to practise.
>
> The threshold for an interim order is a high one because a registrant may be temporarily suspended or be subject to temporary conditions that limit or prevent his or her practice.
>
> No judgment is made regarding the facts of the allegation but the panel must be satisfied that, on a fair analysis, there may be a prima facie case. The registrant should be given the opportunity to make representations and may adduce evidence.

Interim orders

5.82 Both the Investigating Committee and the FTP Committee have the power to impose an interim suspension or conditions of practice order under NMO 2001 article 31, at any stage during the proceedings. Committee panels have the power to impose an interim suspension order, preventing a registrant from practising, or an interim conditions of practice order permitting a registrant to continue to practise but only under certain conditions. An interim order does not prevent a registrant working in an alternative non-regulated role such as a health care assistant.

5.83 An interim order may be imposed following the referral of an allegation to a Practice Committee while the case is still under investigation but no final decision has been reached.[102] So, for example, the Investigating Committee can receive a referral from the case examiners before they have determined whether there is a case to answer.[103] The Investigating Committee may also impose an interim order where it has determined that an entry to the register was fraudulently procured or incorrectly made and should be amended or removed,[104] or any time before or after it has referred a case to the FTP Committee.[105] Further, the FTP Committee may impose an interim order any time prior to a hearing, during a hearing

102 NMO 2001 art 31(1).
103 NMC (FTP) Rules 2004 r6C(5).
104 NMO 2001 art 26(11).
105 NMO 2001 art 31(1)(a) and (b).

if it is adjourned part-heard for any reason, or after reaching a final decision in order to cover an appeal period.[106]

5.84 Interim orders can have serious consequences for a registrant's livelihood and career and should only be imposed where the relevant committee is satisfied that it is necessary for the protection of members of the public, or is otherwise in the public interest, or is in the interests of the registrant.[107] An order may be imposed in the registrant's own interest where, for example, there is evidence that the registrant's work is adversely affecting his or her health.

5.85 An order on public protection grounds requires that there is a real risk to patients, colleagues or other members of the public. The test is whether an order is *necessary*, not merely that an order may be desirable. The NMC guidance suggests that panels should consider three factors:

a) the seriousness of the regulatory concern, ie how much harm was caused or could have been caused to the public. Cases involving dishonesty, sexual misconduct or involving the death of a patient being considered more serious;
b) the likelihood of the alleged conduct being repeated if an interim order was not imposed;
c) to consider each case on its own facts.[108]

5.86 The courts have held that the wider public interest – such as maintaining public confidence in the profession and upholding standards – is only a sufficient reason for imposing an order in rare circumstances,[109] and that the bar is set high.[110] Therefore, in many cases an interim order can be resisted on the grounds that it is not necessary in all the circumstances. However, registrants and their representatives should note that a strict reading of the case-law suggests that the requirement of necessity only applies to interim orders made solely on public protection grounds and not those made on wider public interest grounds or in the interest of the registrant. In fact, the legal position is not currently clear[111] (see chapter 2 at paras 2.41–2.66). In any event, there is still a requirement that any order imposed on the basis of an undetermined allegation must be proportionate. The NMC guidance accepts that it should be relatively 'rare' for an interim order to be imposed on the wider public interest grounds, and that the threshold 'is high'.[112] Thus a dishonesty, sexual misconduct or criminal caution or conviction case, where the matter involved no risk to patients, an interim order may not be necessary.[113]

106 NMO 2001 art 31(1)(a) and (c).
107 NMO 2001 art 31(2).
108 NMC Guide ref INT-2b; also see *R (Nowak) v Nursing and Midwifery Council* [2013] EWHC 4341 (Admin).
109 *R (Shiekh) v General Dental Council* [2007] EWHC 2972 (Admin).
110 See, for example, *R (Nowak) v Nursing and Midwifery Council* [2013] EWHC 4341 (Admin).
111 See contrasting cases of *R (Shiekh) v General Dental Council* [2007] EWHC 2972 (Admin) and *Sandler v General Medical Council* [2010] EWHC 1029 (Admin).
112 NMC Guide ref INT-2b.
113 See, for example, *Christou v Nursing and Midwifery Council* [2016] EWHC 1947 (Admin).

5.87 Panels are required to take into account factors such as the impact on the registrant's right to practise; finances and reputation; seriousness of the allegation; nature and strength of the evidence; and likelihood of the alleged conduct being repeated. Where the registrant has been charged with a criminal offence, a regulatory body is not 'always obliged' to hear evidence or submissions as to the weaknesses of the case, the panel may assume that there was sufficient evidence to justify charges being brought by the Crown Prosecution Service[114]. An allegation that is manifestly unfounded or exaggerated should not be given weight. However, the panel is not permitted to decide the merits of disputed allegations.

5.88 If possible, the registrant should provide a reference from his or her employer setting out any mitigating factors and the extent to which a registrant has addressed any acknowledged failure. In a health case it may also be appropriate to provide an up to date medical report confirming a registrant's state of health and any compliance with medication or treatment regimes. References from other professionals, and evidence of the consequences for the registrant were they to be suspended should also be adduced. Any testimonials should include a statement that the writer is aware of the NMC proceedings and that they are aware of the nature of the allegations. The registrant may also consider providing the relevant training certificates and reflection pieces.

5.89 A suspension order should only be imposed if a panel considers that a conditions of practice order is not sufficient and proportionate. If there is a risk that the panel will consider that an interim order is necessary, and the registrant is willing and able to comply with conditions, the registrant, or his or her representative, can tactically propose suitable conditions. These should address the issues in question and be relevant, proportionate, workable and measurable. Examples include: training and supervision (either direct or indirect); auditing of patient records; an assessment of practice; temporary restrictions on an area or type of practice (for example, not to administer medication); agreement to undergo a medical or language assessment or to comply with suitable medical treatment or attend counselling. Conditions are most likely to be considered suitable where the registrant remains in employment as a registrant, or has identified such employment. In cases where there is an employer or prospective employer, they should be asked to provide a supportive statement confirming that they are willing to put in place the suggested conditions.

5.90 If the registrant is not in employment, then conditions which do not require third party engagement should be proposed. For example, a condition that the registrant only be permitted to practise in certain areas or roles, or until the registrant attended a suitable and accredited course, or that on obtaining employment the registrant formulate with his or her new employer a personal development plan with regular reviews. Any concern as to the lack of a named actual or prospective employer can be addressed by imposing a condition that the NMC be notified within a specified time period of employment being offered, and the registrant consenting to the potential employer being contacted by the NMC. All conditions of practice orders include a condition that the registrant

114 *Fallon v Horseracing Regulatory Authority* [2006] EWHC 2030 (QB).

informs his or her employer or prospective employer of the order, and informs the NMC if he or she changes employer.

5.91 An interim suspension order should not be imposed merely because there is no identifiable third party. Even in circumstances where the panel concludes that a high degree of supervision is required, it would not necessarily follow that, in the absence of a current employer, appropriate conditions cannot be formulated.[115]

5.92 In fraudulent or incorrect entry cases, the NMC guidance directs that panels should additionally consider 'the public interest in maintaining the integrity of the register', and evidence of this should be specifically identified.[116]

5.93 In English language cases, the NMC guidance suggests that relevant factors will include the severity of any clinical risk related to the lack of knowledge of English, the results of any language assessment and any refusal or persistent refusal to undergo a language assessment.[117] While a panel may direct that a language test be taken within a specified time as part of an interim conditions of practice order,[118] the NMC guidance suggests a more proportionate approach may be to impose supervision or observation if that would be sufficient to protect the public.[119]

Interim order notice

5.94 Article 31(15) provides that a registrant has the right to be afforded the opportunity to attend an interim order hearing or review,[120] and be represented.[121] Therefore a Practice Committee is required to provide a registrant with a written interim order notice prior to imposing or varying an interim order.[122] A Practice Committee is also required to provide a registrant with written notice where they intend to hold an interim order review hearing. Where a Practice Committee intends to hold an interim order review meeting, no such written notice is required (see para 5.103). The length of any notice period should be what is 'reasonable in all the circumstances'.[123] The NMC guidance suggest that a registrant will normally be provided with seven days' notice of an interim order hearing and 14 days' notice of an interim order review hearing, but it reserves the right to have a shorter period.[124]

5.95 The notice should:

- inform the registrant of the date, time and venue of the hearing and invite him or her to attend or submit written representations;

115 *Perry v Nursing and Midwifery Council* [2012] EWHC 2275 (Admin).
116 NMC Guide ref INT-2d.
117 NMC Guide ref INT-2e.
118 NMC (FTP) Rules 2004 r6B(3B).
119 NMC Guide ref INT-2e.
120 NMO 2001 art 31(15).
121 NMO 2001 art 31(16).
122 NMC (FTP) Rules 2004 r8(1).
123 NMC (FTP) Rules 2004 r8(4).
124 NMC Guide ref INT-3 and REV-2c.

- inform him or her of the right to be represented, the right to adduce evidence and witnesses, and the power of the panel to proceed in his or her absence.[125]

The notice should also set out why an interim order is being proposed.

5.96 No separate interim order notice is required where a substantive hearing notice has already been served.[126] This is because such hearing notices are separately required to inform registrants of the panel's power to impose interim orders. Further, no notice is required where a panel at a substantive hearing proposes to impose an interim order to cover any appeal period (see paras 5.331–5.333).

5.97 The panel at an interim order hearing or interim order review hearing or meeting has the power to make or vary an interim order in the absence of a registrant, or any written representations. This is where the panel is satisfied that all reasonable efforts have been made to serve the relevant notice, or the registrant has informed the NMC that he or she does not wish to attend.[127] If a registrant informs the NMC in advance of a hearing that he or she wishes to attend but is unable to do so on the date provided, then the panel will consider the merits of the interim order application in the registrant's absence, and if one is imposed list the matter for an early review hearing so that the registrant can attend. This will usually be within 14 days.[128]

5.98 There is no need for a registrant or his or her representative to attend a review hearing if the registrant is not contesting the order, and there is no other reason for the registrant to attend. A registrant who has been suspended may find it unduly onerous to attend six monthly hearings merely to have that order confirmed. The registrant should notify the NMC in writing of his or her intentions, in order to demonstrate that he or she is engaging with the regulatory process. In the absence of any representations or communication from the registrant, panels are likely to express concern about the lack of engagement. Any evidence of non-engagement, and therefore non-compliance with the NMC Code, during the NMC proceedings may be considered by the panel at the substantive hearing.

Interim order hearings

5.99 The normal procedure at an interim order hearing[129] is as follows:

- The NMC case presenter will make representations as to why it may be necessary to impose, revoke, confirm, vary or replace an interim order and may adduce relevant evidence.
- The registrant may then make representations and adduce relevant evidence. The registrant may give oral testimony. Registrants should

125 NMC (FTP) Rules 2004 r8(3).

126 NMC (FTP) Rules 2004 r8(2).

127 NMC (FTP) Rules 2004 r8(6).

128 NMC Guide ref INT-3.

129 A different procedure is applied whether the interim order is imposed following a decision on sanction pending appeal in accordance with NMC (FTP) Rules 2004 r24(14).

note that panels can receive evidence on the effect of an interim order on a registrant or evidence which establishes that an allegation is manifestly unfounded or exaggerated but not otherwise on the substance of the allegation. The panel can refuse to accept evidence which goes beyond its remit.

- The legal assessor may provide advice on questions of law.
- The panel will adjourn to deliberate in private and announce its decision with reasons.[130]

The procedures in NMC Rules 2004 Part 5 apply to interim order hearings.[131] This includes applications for the whole or part of a hearing to be heard in private (see paras 5.185–5.190).

5.100 The registrant will be notified of the decision, the reasons for imposing any interim order, and the right to apply to the High Court objecting to the order.[132] The High Court has power to revoke an interim suspension or conditions of practice order; reduce the length of the order; or vary a conditions of practice order.[133] This is by means of a High Court application, not an appeal (see chapter 10).

Interim order reviews and extensions

5.101 An interim order may be imposed for up to 18 months, and must be reviewed every six months, or if there is new evidence.[134] Therefore, where new evidence comes to light – for example, there is a change in employment – a registrant may apply for a review without waiting for the prescribed review hearing. A request for an early review should be made to the named NMC case officer. The case officer should agree to arrange an early review since determination of whether there has been a material change in circumstance is a matter for the reviewing panel to decide not the case officer.

5.102 The NMC guidance suggests that an early review would generally be scheduled where:

- there is information that the conditions imposed as part of an interim order are unworkable;
- the registrant was unable to attend the initial interim order hearing or provide detailed submissions to the panel, and is now in a position to do so;
- there is information that the interim order has been breached; or
- there is new information, that affects the previously identified risk.[135]

5.103 An interim order review can be conducted at a public hearing (for which the registrant must be provided with written notice) or a private meeting (where no notice will be provided). Interim suspension orders will usually

130 NMC (FTP) Rules 2004 r26(2).
131 NMC (FTP) Rules 2004 r16(a)(ii) and (b)(ii).
132 NMO 2001 art 31(14).
133 NMO 2001 art 31(12).
134 NMO 2001 art 31(2) and (6).
135 NMC Guide ref REV-2b

be reviewed at meetings, unless there has been a material changes in circumstances, or if the registrant requests a review hearing. Interim conditions of practice orders will usually be reviewed at public hearings, unless in all the circumstances, the NMC considers a meeting would be appropriate. Should a registrant wish to attend or supply written representations to the reviewing panel, the registrant is advised to contact their NMC case officer and request a review hearing. The review panel when conducting a six-month review or early review has the power to revoke, confirm or vary any condition, and replace an interim suspension order with a conditions of practice order and vice versa.[136]

5.104 The NMC guidance suggests that panels consider the following factors at interim order review hearings:

- the circumstances at the time the interim order was made, summarised in the decision of the panel;
- any other relevant documentation; and
- any change of circumstances since then.[137]

A panel can request a transcript of the previous interim order hearing to assist them reach their decision, but these are not provided as a matter of course.[138]

5.105 In order to extend an interim order beyond 18 months, the NMC must apply to the High Court.[139] The High Court may extend or further extend the interim order for up to 12 months, replace an interim suspension order with an interim conditions of practice order or vice versa.[140] The High Court applies the same test to an application for an extension as is applied by panels to the original interim order; namely the protection of the public, the public interest or the registrant's own interests.[141] The High Court has become increasingly critical of routine extensions being sought by regulatory bodies, and where an extension is sought a registrant may be able to successfully challenge it. For a discussion of High Court decisions concerning extensions see chapter 2 at paras 2.71–2.92.

5.106 Unless revoked or varied by a practice committee or the High Court, the interim order shall cease to have effect when a final decision in relation to the allegation in question has been reached. Where an order has been made to cover an appeal period, it will cease to have effect when the period has expired or any appeal finally disposed of.[142]

5.107 Where there is a new referral, the matter will be dealt with at a new interim order hearing rather than at a review hearing of the previous matters.[143]

136 NMO 2001 art 31(7); NMC Guide ref REV-2a.
137 NMC Guide ref REV-2a.
138 NMC Guide ref REV-2a.
139 NMO 2001 art 31(8).
140 NMO 2001 art 31(9).
141 *General Medical Council v Hiew* [2007] EWCA Civ 369, [2007] 1 WLR 2007.
142 NMO 2001 art 31(5).
143 NMC Guide ref INT-3.

Pre-hearing matters

Service of documents and notice

5.108 The NMC is required to keep the registrant informed of the progress of the proceedings. It will send out notices informing the registrant of the receipt of an allegation, and the referral of an allegation to the case examiners or a committee. It will also provide notice of hearings, notice of decisions and any other notice as from time to time may be required.

5.109 The NMC is required to send or deliver a notice of hearing by a postal or delivery service to the address recorded on the register, or last known address, if different.[144] It is important that registrants ensure that the NMC have their most recent address. The NMC requests that this be provided within 28 days of any change of details.[145] A registrant who fails to provide his or her professional body with his or her contact details, will have no grounds for complaining if he or she does not receive notice of any investigation or hearing.[146] If the registrant is represented then the notice of hearing may also be sent, delivered or emailed, to their solicitor, professional body or trade union.[147]

5.110 Any other notice or document may be sent by ordinary post or email to a previously notified address.[148]

5.111 Time limits run from the day after the notice was sent by delivery service, or the day on which it was left at the address or emailed.[149] The day after is the next calendar day, not the next business day.[150] In other words, the date the notice was received is irrelevant.[151] This is particularly important in relation to appeals (see paras 5.374–5.379 and chapter 10).

5.112 Service is proved by confirmation of posting issued by or on behalf of the post office or other delivery service, confirmation of receipt of email, or signed statement from the sender or person delivering the notice.[152] The NMC tends to use recorded delivery.[153]

5.113 To date, the courts have held that as long as the NMC has complied with the rules of service, the notice of hearing will be deemed to have been effectively served. This has been the case even where a nurse requested that notice of hearing be served by email because the nurse was going to be out of the country,[154] or where a notice served by recorded delivery letter was returned unopened and undelivered.[155] For discussion of these cases see chapter 2 at paras 2.346–2.349. Since the rules do not provide for a notice of

144 NMC (FTP) Rules 2004 r34(1).

145 NMC Guide ref HEA-2a.

146 *Adeogba v General Medical Council* [2016] EWCA Civ 162, [2016] 1 WLR 3867; *Jatta v Nursing and Midwifery Council* [2009] EWCA Civ 824.

147 NMC (FTP) Rules 2004 r34(2).

148 NMC (FTP) Rules 2004 r34(3).

149 NMC (FTP) Rules 2004 r34(5).

150 *Adesina v Nursing and Midwifery Council* [2013] EWCA Civ 818, [2013] 1 WLR 3156.

151 *Adesina v Nursing and Midwifery Council* [2013] EWCA Civ 818, [2013] 1 WLR 3156.

152 NMC (FTP) Rules 2004 r34(4).

153 NMC Guide ref HEA-2a.

154 *Jatta v Nursing and Midwifery Council* [2009] EWCA Civ 824.

155 *R (Raheem) v Nursing and Midwifery Council* [2010] EWHC 2549 (Admin).

hearing to be sent to a registrant by email, registrants who go abroad are advised to ensure that notice is provided to a legal or union representative.

Charges

> The particulars of the allegation and the facts upon which they are founded should be clear and settled in advance of any hearing.
>
> If in doubt, clarification and/or further and better particulars should be obtained.
>
> The panel may, having heard from both parties, amend either the allegation or the facts provided no injustice is caused but this should be the exception not the rule.

5.114 While a case is under investigation, the NMC refers to the matter as a regulatory concern which is considered in broad terms as fitness to practise being impaired. A charge will only come into existence at the point that the NMC serves the notice of hearing.[156] The NMC defines a charge as:

- an assertion that a registrant's fitness to practise is impaired with reference to one of the statutory grounds of impairment; and
- the schedule of alleged facts which 'particularises' the allegation.

5.115 Therefore, the charge contained in the notice of hearing is in three parts:

1) *The factual particulars, such as the date, the patient/person and the incident.* Often a single incident will give rise to a number of particulars – for example, 'on date X, when visiting patient A, the registrant failed to a) conduct a specified procedure; b) make a record of that procedure; c) notify the appropriate person'. Sometimes the factual particulars are set out in a schedule – this may occur where there are a large number of instances being relied upon, or where the facts of the charge relate to private (usually health) matters. In responding to a charge, the registrant will need to consider each separate particular and any sub-particular. It may also be necessary to address the introductory text (sometimes referred to as the 'stem' of the charge).
2) *Whether the factual particulars constitute lack of competence, misconduct, physical or mental health, not having necessary knowledge of English, police caution or conviction (the statutory ground).*
3) *Whether as a result of the statutory ground the registrant's fitness to practise is impaired.*

5.116 There is a considerable body of case-law in relation to the drafting of charges. The overriding principle is the requirement of fairness: that an accused must know the case against him or her, and be given sufficient notice of that case to enable him or her to prepare a defence. Where it is alleged that there is a long-standing pattern of incompetence, the thrust and detail of the allegations may be contained in the material before the panel[157] (for a fuller discussion, see chapter 1 at paras 1.82–1.157).

156 NMC Guide ref HEA-1a.

157 *Ogundele v Nursing and Midwifery Council* [2013] EWHC 2748 (Admin).

5.117 Another guiding principle is that of proportionality. There has been a purported shift in emphasis with the requirement on regulators to adopt a 'right touch' regulation.[158] This recognises that charges should only be brought where there is admissible evidence in support, and that the more serious the charge the stronger the evidence will need to be to prove. The NMC guidance on charging recognises that overcharging can be oppressive.[159] On the other hand, undercharging may mean that the NMC is not properly discharging its public protection duty and could lead to an appeal on the grounds of undue leniency or procedural irregularity. In considering proportionality, the NMC will consider whether the charge captures the overall seriousness of the allegation.

5.118 There are certain matters that must be alleged if they are to form part of the case against the registrant, namely:

- that the actions of the registrant caused or materially contributed to the death or serious harm of a patient;
- sexual and racial motivation, or other deliberate motivation; and
- dishonesty.[160]

5.119 In general, where a registrant's health condition led to the incidents in question, the charge will usually be impairment on the grounds of mental and/or physical ill health. However, in exceptional cases the charge may be one of misconduct where the alleged incident(s) are so grave that a striking off order may be required.[161]

5.120 NMC (FTP) Rules 2004 r28 provides the panel with the power to amend a charge set out in the notice of hearing any time prior to the findings of fact stage, unless having regard to the merits of the case and the fairness of proceedings the amendment would be unjust.[162] The parties are entitled to make representations prior to any decision.[163] Where a charge has been poorly drafted, is duplicitous or otherwise wrong, it is advised that representations be first made to the NMC case presenter either before or at the hearing, since an application to amend is more likely to succeed if the parties agree. Such representations can also be made prior to the hearing at a preliminary meeting and in pre-hearing correspondence with the NMC's in-house legal team. It is often advisable to make representations as early as possible since it demonstrates engagement and also strengthens a registrant's position if objections are raised at the substantive hearing.

5.121 Rule 29 provides the panel with the power to join allegations. It permits allegations against two or more registrants to be joined unless there is a risk of prejudice to the fairness of the proceedings. Joinder is permitted where the allegation against each registrant arises out of the same circumstances or a joint hearing is otherwise necessary.[164] Where two or more

158 NMC Guide ref HEA-1b.

159 NMC Guide ref HEA-1b.

160 NMC Guide ref HEA-1d.

161 This is in accordance with *Crabbie v General Medical Council* [2002] UKPC 45, [2002] 1 WLR 3104.

162 NMC (FTP) Rules 2004 r28(1).

163 NMC (FTP) Rules 2004 r28(2).

164 NMC (FTP) Rules 2004 r29(1).

registrants are to be heard in the same hearing, the panel will need to manage any resulting unfairness, and may in exceptional circumstances consider it no longer appropriate to keep the cases joined.[165]

5.122 Rule 29 also permits more than one category of allegation to be heard in a single hearing, with the exception of allegations involving a conviction or caution, which should only be heard after any allegation of misconduct has been determined.[166] The NMC guidance suggests that where there is an allegation of misconduct related to the conviction or caution, then such evidence can be heard together.[167] This guidance is not strictly in accordance with the letter of the rules although it makes sense where, for example, the misconduct was a failure to disclose the conviction or caution. More problematic, the NMC suggests that it may also be 'relevant and fair' to refer to it as evidence of fact or bad character.[168] This could be prejudicial to the registrant, and if possible should be subject to agreement between the parties before being referred to (see chapter 2 at paras 2.164–2.232 for a discussion on the case-law on character).

5.123 New allegations of a similar kind, or founded on the same facts, may be considered by the panel even if it is not included in the notice of hearing.[169] Where this is proposed, the registrant should be informed and given the opportunity to make written representations.

Disclosure

> The regulator must disclose unused material in its possession to the registrant. It should do so in sufficient time to allow the registrant to properly consider and/or use it. There is a continuing obligation of disclosure upon the regulator.
>
> While there is a duty to prevent inequality of arms, there is no positive duty on a disciplinary body to gather evidence to assist the practitioner.
>
> To allege unfairness under ECHR Article 6(3)(b), a complainant must demonstrate that a duty exists, that it has been breached and that this has caused an inequality of arms.
>
> Each case will depend on its own facts.

5.124 The NMC, along with other regulatory bodies, generally follow the rules of disclosure that exist in the criminal courts. These are explained in chapter 1 at paras 1.235–1.269. In general terms, the NMC is required to disclose evidence that not only supports its case but which could undermine its case or assist the case of the registrant. Evidence that the NMC do not propose to rely on is called 'unused material'.

165 NMC Guide ref HEA-4c.
166 NMC (FTP) Rules 2004 r29(2).
167 NMC Guide ref HEA-4.
168 NMC Guide ref HEA-4.
169 NMC (FTP) Rules 2004 r29(3).

5.125 The NMC council, practice committees or authorised person, may require any person, including a third party, to supply relevant information and/or produce relevant documentation.[170] The power is limited to that information and those documents that a party is required to disclose in civil proceedings,[171] and which are not otherwise prohibited by any enactment.[172]

5.126 If there are particular documents or evidence relevant to the registrant's case held by a third party, then a request should be made initially to the NMC, and if refused, to the relevant committee to obtain that information. Preliminary meetings can also be requested by the registrant for a direction that the NMC obtain the identified documentation (see paras 5.193–5.197). The NMC guidance states that it is not obliged to obtain third party information but may agree to do so if it considers the material to be relevant and essential, the registrant has unsuccessfully sought to obtain the information themselves, or the NMC is better placed to obtain this information.[173] The NMC will not however obtain witness statements on behalf of a registrant.

5.127 The NMC has no power under the rules to require the registrant to disclose information or documentation. The only power it has is to require registrants following referral to a practice committee to disclose the identity of any person by whom the registrant is employed to provide nursing or midwifery services, or with whom he or she has an arrangement to provide such services.[174] The registrant is also required to disclose details of any regulated body which authorises him or her to practise both in the UK and elsewhere.[175] However, registrants should note in relation to disclosure more generally, that the NMC Code requires them to engage with internal and external investigations, and that a failure to provide information when asked has the potential to be considered to be a failure to co-operate with an investigation.

5.128 A failure by the NMC to disclose may lead to an application to stay proceeding on the grounds of an abuse of process. However, a regulator is only required to disclose that evidence which is considered to be relevant, and an abuse of process argument is only likely to succeed if the registrant is able to establish that the failure to disclose the evidence in question was unfair. Thus in *R (Johnson) v Nursing and Midwifery Council*,[176] the failure by the nurse to take steps to obtain the documentation meant that the regulator could not be blamed and therefore there was no unfairness. Similarly in *R (Phillips) v Nursing and Midwifery Council*,[177] the failure of the NMC to call the patient named in the charge to give evidence was held not to be unfair because the nurse could have called the witness himself or herself.

170 NMO 2001 art 25(1).
171 NMO 2001 art 25(5).
172 NMO 2001 art 25(3).
173 NMC Guide ref HEA-3.
174 NMO 2001 art 25(2)(a).
175 NMO 2001 art 25(2)(b).
176 [2008] EWHC 885 (Admin).
177 [2008] EWHC 1698 (Admin).

Third party information

5.129 NMO 2001 article 25 provides the NMC with the power to anonymise documentation, or other evidence, that may lead to the identification of any person during the proceedings.[178] During a hearing witnesses will usually be referred to in accordance to a key, rather than by name or even their initials. Further, NMC (FTP) Rules 2004 r35 provides the NMC with the power to take 'such steps as it thinks fit' to prevent the disclosure of personal data which relates to individuals who are not a party to the proceedings, in order to avoid being in breach of data protection provisions.

5.130 Registrants should also be aware of the need to respect the privacy of those in their care, so if a registrant decides to disclose documents at any stage in the proceedings as part of his or her defence, then they should ensure that any references to third parties are redacted – in particular, references to patients. Particular caution should be exercised when disclosing, for example, patient notes, supervision records and practice development reviews. Further registrants are advised to obtain their employer's permission in writing to use such records. Of course this does not apply to documents obtained by and disclosed by the NMC. Failure to remove personal information could result in the registrant being in breach of data protection provisions, and allegations of breach of confidentiality. Further, it presents the registrant concerned in a poor light before the panel.

Admissibility of evidence

5.131 Under NMC (FTP) Rules 2004 r31(1) oral, documentary or other evidence is admissible as long as it is 'relevant and fair'. This includes evidence that would not otherwise be admissible in civil proceedings.

5.132 Panels should not consider prejudicial matters and matters which have not been charged.[179] This includes findings of fact made at some earlier investigation (usually as a result of an internal disciplinary process),[180] although if the panel places little weight on those findings then the fact that the panel knows about previous findings will not be grounds of any appeal.[181] A registrant is entitled to request that such evidence be redacted, and should do so. The NMC will usually agree to redact references to interim orders and disciplinary decisions by employers, and reference to other matters that have not been charged. Sometimes where there is an acceptable explanation for what would otherwise be prejudicial or irrelevant material, it may be preferable to adduce that explanation rather than seek redactions. This is a matter of judgment, but having large sections of a document blanked out, or witnesses alluding to other matters, can cause more prejudice since the panel may form the view that a registrant has something to hide.

5.133 Ideally any disputes over admissibility of evidence should be resolved prior to the hearing (if need be at a preliminary meeting), otherwise an

178 NMO 2001 art 25(4).

179 *Chauhan v General Medical Council* [2010] EWHC 2093 (Admin).

180 *Enemuwe v Nursing and Midwifery Council* [2015] EWHC 2081 (Admin).

181 *Georgieva v Nursing and Midwifery Council* [2017] GWD 11-156.

application to exclude evidence will need to be made before the very panel which the registrant wishes to exclude the evidence from. In some circumstances this may result in the panel that has seen the prejudicial evidence having to recuse itself resulting in the hearing being adjourned, sometimes for several months, to another date. Where there is a dispute over the admissibility of evidence, that evidence will not be included in the NMC hearing bundle but will be dealt with separately at the hearing.[182]

5.134 The panel is permitted to refuse to admit evidence from a registrant where there has been a failure to comply with directions issued at a preliminary meeting and there is no good cause for the failure to comply.[183] Therefore, if the registrant is seeking to adduce evidence which is subject to a direction then any reason for the non-compliance should be provided along with evidence.

Postponements and adjournments

5.135 NMC (FTP) Rules 2004 r32 sets out the provisions for postponements and adjournments. Where no notice of hearing has been issued, then this decision is made by a senior member of NMC staff.[184] Where a notice of hearing has been given, a party, or the chair of his or her own motion, may apply to postpone the hearing before the hearing begins.[185] Further, where a hearing has commenced, a party, or panel of its own motion, may apply to adjourn proceedings at any stage, provided that no injustice is caused and the parties are provided with the opportunity to make representations.[186] In considering whether or not to postpone or adjourn a hearing the chair or panel shall have regard to:

- the public interest in the expeditious disposal of the case;
- the potential inconvenience caused to a party or any witnesses to be called by that party; and
- the fairness to the registrant.[187]

This is a non-exhaustive list, and public interest and fairness will include consideration of the reasons for the adjournment and the history of the case (in particular whether there have been previous requests for an adjournment and by which party).

5.136 A postponement or adjournment may be sought for a variety of reasons – for example, to obtain certain evidence; to ensure a specified witness can attend; to ensure that the registrant can attend; to extend the length of the hearing; to put special measures in place; or to obtain or change legal representation. Whatever the reason, it is important that the application is made without delay and supported by relevant evidence. If time allows, the registrant should request a preliminary meeting to consider the application. An application is less likely to succeed if made at the commencement

182 NMC Guide ref HEA-12b.
183 NMC (FTP) Rules 2004 r31(8).
184 NMC Guide ref HEA-15a.
185 NMC (FTP) Rules 2004 r32(1).
186 NMC (FTP) Rules 2004 r32(2).
187 NMC (FTP) Rules 2004 r32(4). See also NMC Guide ref HEA-15a.

of a substantive hearing, due to the added factor of the inconvenience to any witness who has attended to give evidence. The extent to which the registrant has co-operated with proceedings to date and has engaged with the process will be a relevant factor.

5.137 Before adjourning proceedings, the chair or panel is required to consider whether or not to make an interim order.[188]

5.138 An application to adjourn may be linked to submissions as to whether to proceed in the absence of a registrant (see paras 5.150–5.162).

Cancellation of a hearing

5.139 NMC (FTP) Rules 2004 r33 provides a Practice Committee with the power to cancel a hearing and close a case on advice from a case presenter.[189] The NMC guidance suggests that this may occur where:

- a nurse or midwife's registration would have lapsed but for the fitness to practise proceedings, they do not intend to practise in the future, and there is no public interest in continuing;
- the evidence is not available to prove a factual charge although may be in future; or
- there is some other compelling reason, such as the ill-health of the registrant.[190]

Public interest considerations may include the need for a 'public marker' against the registrant concerned, but this is less important if the registrant has been subject to other public proceedings. It may also include whether the registrant is likely to work with vulnerable adults or children in future in any capacity.

5.140 Where a case is to be closed to enable registration to lapse, the registrant will be asked to sign a declaration that he or she will not seek to return to the register. The NMC guidance states that if they do seek to reapply at some later date the original allegation will be re-opened and they may face an additional allegation of misconduct, presumably for making a false declaration.[191] Unlike voluntary removal, the cancellation of a case does not require the registrant to admit the facts or admit impairment.

5.141 Usually where there is insufficient evidence to support a charge the NMC will offer no evidence (see paras 5.240–5.243). It is an essential requirement of the right to a fair trial that cases are brought without delay, and that there is finality so that the registrant concerned can continue with his or her life. However, the NMC guidance suggests that where the allegation is 'very serious' they may use the cancellation of hearing provision to, in effect, keep the case on ice.[192] The guidance states that this approach would be 'exceptional', and provides the example of a serious sexual assault with the complainant being too unwell to provide evidence within

188 NMC (FTP) Rules 2004 r32(5).
189 NMC (FTP) Rules 2004 r33(3).
190 NMC Guide ref HEA-9a.
191 NMC Guide ref HEA-9a.
192 NMC Guide ref HEA-9a.

a reasonable period of time, but where there is evidence that they are likely to recover in the future. The NMC claim that in such circumstances it may be in the public interest to cancel the hearing (presumably with the intention to resume the hearing at some point in the future). This approach, were it to be adopted, may find itself subject to a legal challenge on the grounds of a failure to provide a fair trial, and abuse of process.

5.142 If the NMC do propose to cancel a hearing, for whatever reason, a preliminary meeting will be held and the complainant will be provided with a reasonable opportunity to comment.[193] Where a case is closed there will be no entry made on the register. However, because there has been no final determination, the case can be reopened in the future. Since there has been no final determination, any interim order will need to be removed by the panel.

Delay

> ECHR Article 6 and domestic case-law confer a right to a hearing within a reasonable time, however to stay proceedings is an exceptional course and delay is not a ground unless there is material prejudice to the extent that no fair trial is possible.

5.143 There is no requirement under the NMC rules for a hearing to be held within a specified timescale. It has been held that both the legitimate expectation of complainants and the public confidence in the regulation of the medical profession require that the complaint should, in the absence of some special and sufficient reason, be publicly investigated.[194]

5.144 It may take months, or even years, for a case to be heard. However, the NMC, like other regulatory bodies, is subject to domestic and ECtHR case-law which confers the right to a hearing within a reasonable time under Article 6 and the right to a family and private life under Article 8. Where the delay becomes unreasonable, then a registrant may be able to apply for a stay of the proceedings on grounds of an abuse of process. In order to succeed in such an application, the delay must not be merely unreasonable but also prejudicial.[195] A stay of process will only be granted in exceptional circumstances where a fair trial is not possible.[196] Where the regulator or complainant is not responsible for the delay, then it is highly unlikely that such an application will succeed. However, delay may be taken into account as mitigation at the sanction stage (see para 5.307). For a consideration of the case-law on delay, see chapter 1 at paras 1.162–1.197.

193 NMC (FTP) Rules 2004 r33(4).

194 *R v General Medical Council ex p Toth* [2000] 1 WLR 2209.

195 *R v General Medical Council ex p Toth* [2000] 1 WLR 2209.

196 *R (Johnson) v Professional Conduct Committee of the Nursing and Midwifery Council* [2008] EWHC 885 (Admin).

Attendance at a hearing

Committee Panel and impartiality

> The question is whether the fair-minded and informed observer, having considered the facts, would conclude that there was a real possibility that the tribunal was biased.[190]

5.145 ECHR Article 6 provides the right to adjudication by an independent and impartial tribunal. Independence means separated from the executive and from the parties. Impartiality means both objective impartiality (the lack of actual bias), and subjective impartiality (the lack of the appearance of bias). The courts have accepted that the fact that disciplinary proceedings against registrants are determined by a body which includes members of the same profession does not of itself offend the requirement of 'independence' in Article 6(1).[198] Further, it accords with the principle that a governing body is best placed to judge what is right for its profession. For a fuller discussion of the case-law on this point, see chapter 2 at paras 2.264–2.291.

5.146 While it is accepted that there is an advantage to including members of the profession on Committee panels in order to assist with the task of assessing what is right for the profession, panel members should base their decision on the evidence before them and not rely on specialist expertise of a particular member that the parties have had no opportunity to challenge.[199]

5.147 Committee panels are administratively assisted by a Panel Secretary.

Representation and entitlement to be heard

5.148 Both the NMC case presenter and the registrant have a right to be heard in any hearing before a practice committee.[200] The registrant also has the right to be represented by a solicitor or barrister, professional or trade union representative or any other person.[201] The legal extent and limits of this entitlement is considered in chapter 2 at paras 2.302–2.327. Where a registrant is not represented, he or she has the right to be accompanied and advised by any person, save that such person is not entitled to address the panel without permission.[202] Further, a person who represents or accompanies a registrant shall not be called as a witness to the hearing.[203] Therefore, if a registrant is accompanied by a supportive colleague or employer who is intending to

197 *Porter v Magill* [2001] UKHL 67, [2002] 2 AC 357.

198 *Tehrani v United Kingdom Central Council for Nursing, Midwifery and Health Visiting* [2001] SC 581, [2001] SLT 879. See also *Stefan v General Medical Council (No 1)* [1999] 1 WLR 1293.

199 *Lawrence v General Medical Council* [2012] EWHC 464 (Admin).

200 NMC (FTP) Rules 2004 r20(1).

201 NMC (FTP) Rules 2004 r20(2).

202 NMC (FTP) Rules 2004 r20(3).

203 NMC (FTP) Rules 2004 r20(4).

provide evidence, including character evidence, then that person will be excluded until after he or she has given evidence. A representative may also be excluded from all or part of the hearing if his or her conduct has disrupted or is likely to disrupt proceedings.[204]

5.149 Where a case is complex and involves voluminous documentation, legal representation may be essential in order for the registrant's case to be properly presented.[205]

Absence of the registrant

> The panel has the discretion to proceed in the absence of the practitioner but: a) there must be strict adherence to the requirement that all reasonable effort at service has been met; and b) the decision to proceed must be taken with 'the utmost care and caution' and only after full consideration of the competing interests, with emphasis on those of the practitioner.

5.150 NMC (FTP) Rules 2004 r21 provides that where a registrant fails to attend a substantive hearing and is not represented, the panel may proceed in his or her absence. Rule 21 does not apply if the registrant is represented and the representative has clear instructions from the registrant to proceed, and is able to do so in compliance with any professional obligations. If the representative does not have clear instructions to proceed, then they may need to withdraw.

5.151 A panel may only proceed in a registrant's absence if it is satisfied that 'all reasonable effort' has been made to serve notice in accordance with the NMC (FTP) Rules 2004.[206] The rule explicitly requires the NMC case presenter to adduce evidence that all reasonable effort has been made to serve the notice of hearing.[207] Thus it is not sufficient for the panel to be informed that service has been attempted. The panel will expect service to be proved in accordance with the confirmation of service provisions under rule 34. This specifies that service may be proved by, for example, confirmation of posting issued by or on behalf of the post office, confirmation of receipt where notice was sent by email, or a signed statement from the sender or person delivering the notice[208] (see paras 5.108–5.113).

5.152 Even if the panel is satisfied that notice has been correctly served, the power to proceed in a registrant's absence is a discretionary power, and should only be exercised with 'utmost caution and care';[209] the alternative is to adjourn and issue directions.[210]

204 NMC (FTP) Rules 2004 r20(5).

205 *D v Nursing and Midwifery Council* [2014] CSIH 90; 2015 SC 282.

206 NMC (FTP) Rules 2004 r21(2).

207 NMC (FTP) Rules 2004 r21(2)(a).

208 NMC (FTP) Rules 2004 r34(4).

209 *R v Jones* [2002] UKHL 5, [2003] 1 AC 1 applied in disciplinary proceedings by *Tait v Royal College of Veterinary Surgeons* [2003] UKPC 34. For a recent NMC example see *Ward v Nursing and Midwifery Council* [2014] EWHC 16739 (Admin).

210 NMC (FTP) Rules 2004 r21(2).

5.153 In determining whether to proceed in the absence of a registrant a panel is required to take all the circumstances into account. Factors to take into account were identified in the criminal case of *R v Hayward*[211] which was approved by *R v Jones*[212] – and these factors have been applied to regulatory cases (see chapter 2 at paras 2.92–2.139 for the case-law regarding proceeding in absence).

5.154 The NMC guidance suggests that panels should take the following factors into account when deciding at a substantive hearing whether to proceed in absence:

- the public interest in the expeditious disposal of the case;
- the inconvenience to any witnesses that have attended or are due to attend;
- whether the registrant has engaged with the proceedings and his or her reason for non-attendance (and whether that reason is supported by independent evidence);
- the unfairness to the registrant if the proceedings were to continue, for example he or she will not have the opportunity to question evidence or provide his or her own evidence to the panel; and
- whether it is fair, appropriate and proportionate to proceed in the registrant's absence.[213]

5.155 The NMC guidance accepts that 'fairness to the registrant is a prime consideration', but then goes on to suggest that fairness to the regulator and the interest of the public should also be taken into account, that these are not criminal proceedings, and that the NMC has no power to enforce attendance at a hearing.[214] While this is undoubtedly correct, nevertheless the NMC's guidance should not be taken to mean that panels should proceed in cases where the registrant has been engaging with the proceedings, and has a good reason for their absence (either supported by evidence or with the potential of being supported by evidence).

5.156 The NMC guidance makes no reference to considering whether the absence was deliberate or voluntary, the likely length of the adjournment, and whether the adjournment may result in the registrant attending voluntarily on the next occasion. Arguably the NMC is seeking to encourage panels to proceed even where the absence is involuntary, whereas the case-law outlined in chapter 2 suggests that a hearing should rarely continue if the absence is truly involuntary.[215]

5.157 On the other hand, where a registrant has deliberately and voluntarily absented himself or herself from a hearing, or behaves in such a way as to obstruct the proper course of proceedings, it is likely that the panel will proceed in the registrant's absence. A more difficult question arises in relation to absence for ill-health or incapacity. Generally, if a registrant is unable to attend for an involuntary reason then the panel will agree to adjourn unless the defendant is represented and asks that the hearing

211 [2001] QB 862.
212 [2003] 1 AC 1.
213 NMC Guide ref HEA-13.
214 NMC Guide ref HEA-13a.
215 *R v Jones* [2002] UKHL 5; [2003] 1 AC 1.

continue. However, the mere fact that a registrant has claimed to be ill does not require an adjournment. If the registrant has failed or refused to provide medical evidence covering the relevant period, or the medical evidence is inadequate, then the panel may conclude that the registrant had voluntarily chosen not to attend or be represented and to proceed in his or her absence.[216] Therefore, it is always advisable, when applying to postpone or adjourn a hearing due to ill-health, to support the application with medical evidence specifically addressing the registrant's fitness to attend the hearing (a medical certificate stating that a registrant is signed off work sick may be not be sufficient, although a panel presented with a sick certificate should conduct further enquiries).[217]

5.158 It is important to refer panels to the legal tests and emphasise that it is only in rare and exceptional circumstances that the panel may proceed in the absence of the registrant. Fitness to practise hearings are significant hearings, the outcome of which could affect the registrant's livelihood and career – hence a registrant has the right to be present and represented. Usually a panel will agree to adjourn where there is evidence that the registrant is engaged with the proceedings and there has been no previous application to adjourn.

5.159 Where a registrant is unable to attend a hearing in person (for example, he or she is in custody) then it may be possible to apply to admit evidence via video-link or telephone-link either through the general discretion under rule 31(1) or by reference to ECHR Article 6 (right to a fair trial).

5.160 If it is known in advance of a hearing that a registrant is unable to attend, the NMC should be notified of this fact as soon as possible along with the reason for the non-attendance. The registrant should identify whether he or she will be applying for the hearing to be adjourned, or applying for measures to enable participation (for example telephone or video links). If time allows the registrant should request a preliminary meeting to consider the application.

5.161 If a panel does decide to proceed in a registrant's absence then it is under a duty to expose weaknesses in the NMC's case and to make such points on behalf of the registrant as the evidence permits, but the panel is under no duty to cross-examine witnesses.[218]

5.162 The rule applies to fitness to practise (and fraudulent and incorrect entry) hearings, review hearings, and restoration hearings.[219] It does not apply to interim order hearings,[220] which are subject to separate albeit similar provisions under rule 8(6) (see para 5.97). Rule 8(6) also requires the panel to be satisfied that all reasonable efforts have been made to serve an interim order notice, or notice of meeting or hearing, unless the registrant has informed the NMC that he or she does not wish to appear or be heard at the interim order hearing.

216 *Faulkner v Nursing and Midwifery Council* [2009] EWHC 3349 (Admin).

217 *Hayat v General Medical Council* [2017] EWHC 1899.

218 *McDaid v Nursing and Midwifery Council* [2013] EWHC 586 (Admin).

219 NMC (FTP) Rules 2004 r16.

220 NMC (FTP) Rules 2004 r21(1).

Witnesses

Overview

5.163 A panel may of its own motion require a person to attend a hearing to give evidence or produce a relevant document.[221] In addition a witness who is a nurse or midwife is required in any event under the NMC Code to co-operate with all investigations,[222] and may be subject to separate proceedings if they do not comply without reasonable excuse. If the registrant wants an NMC witness to attend the hearing this should be stated on the case management form. A registrant can of course call their own witnesses. If a witness is reluctant to attend, or their employer is reluctant to release them, the registrant may apply to the High Court for a witness order.

5.164 Witnesses are expected to attend the hearing in person. Where there is a good reason preventing a witness from attending, the panel may agree for evidence to be provided by Skype, video-link or over the telephone. Similarly, it may be agreed where a matter is not contentious and no disadvantage would be caused by accepting evidence remotely, and arguably would save considerable expense and time. However, it is a matter of discretion and panels vary as to whether they are prepared to accept evidence remotely. An application for evidence to be provided by Skype, video-link or telephone will need to be made either at a preliminary meeting or at the commencement of the hearing. The panel will expect to be informed of the reason for the non-attendance and be provided with details of the steps taken to contact the witness. It is always advisable to obtain agreement from the other party prior to making an application. Sometimes if a witness is unable to attend their evidence can be agreed, in which case there may be no need to call them at all.

5.165 A witness will be required to take an oath or affirm before giving evidence.[223] A witness will be examined by the calling party, cross-examined, re-examined and questioned by the panel.[224] Any further questioning is at the discretion of the panel.[225]

5.166 There is no express provision under the NMC (FTP) Rules 2004 as to how witness evidence is to be adduced. The NMC is not bound by the Civil Procedure Rules 1998,[226] which provide for statements to be tendered as evidence in chief, and arguably rule 31(1) only applies to the admission of evidence not the means by which it may be adduced (see para 5.131). Usually a witness will be asked to read their statement (or the statement will be taken as read) mirroring the practice for evidence in chief in civil courts. A registrant may request that evidence in chief be adduced orally through question and answer, for example in circumstances where there is a dispute of fact and the panel needs to assess the quality of the evidence. The giving of evidence should not be a memory test and a witness can always refer to their statement to refresh their

221 NMC (FTP) Rules 2004 r22(5).
222 NMC Code para 23.
223 NMC (FTP) Rules 2004 r22(1).
224 NMC (FTP) Rules 2004 r22(3).
225 NMC (FTP) Rules 2004 r22(4).
226 SI No 3132.

memory. If the registrant wants an NMC witness to give oral evidence in chief and not rely on their statement this should be stated on the case management form.

5.167 Witnesses are not permitted to attend the hearing until they have completed their evidence.[227] The panel may direct, on application by a party, that details that may identify a witness should not be revealed in public.[228] This is regularly used to protect the identity of patients.

Absence of a witness

> The panel has the discretion to proceed in the absence of a witness and to admit hearsay evidence, but the decision to proceed must be taken with 'the utmost care and caution' and only after full consideration of the competing interests with emphasis on those of the registrant.
>
> There must be compelling reasons to deprive a registrant of the opportunity to cross-examine a witness – this all the more so if the case or its consequences are serious.

5.168 The NMC rules on admissibility of evidence (see para 5.131), permits the panel to admit hearsay evidence and to allow witness statements to be read where a witness is unable to attend. The central requirement of 'fairness' in determining whether to admit evidence in such circumstances was emphasised in the Court of Appeal case of *Ogbonna v Nursing and Midwifery Council*.[229] It was held that rule 31(1) does not establish a more general principle to admit hearsay evidence, and that the determination of fairness is fact-sensitive. It will depend on the nature of the evidence and considerations such as the reason for the non-attendance of a witness and what steps were taken to secure the attendance of a witness.

5.169 Although there is no absolute right under ECHR Article 6 or common law to cross-examine a witness, there would need to be compelling reasons to deprive a registrant of the opportunity to cross-examine a witness whose evidence was central to the issues to be determined.[230] Where such evidence is admitted, it is likely to carry less weight by virtue of the fact that it has not been tested in cross-examination. However it may be probative if supported by other evidence.[231]

5.170 The NMC frequently seeks to rely on hearsay evidence, and subject to the requirement of fairness such evidence has been held to be admissible in principle. However, it is unlikely to be fair to admit significant anonymous hearsay evidence.[232] Where hearsay evidence is admitted, committees are required to properly assess the weight to be given to such evidence.[233]

227 NMC (FTP) Rules 2004 r22(6).
228 NMC (FTP) Rules 2004 r22(2).
229 [2010] EWCA Civ 1216.
230 *R (Bonhoeffer) v General Medical Council* [2011] EWHC 1585 (Admin), [2012] IRLR 37.
231 *Ward v Nursing and Midwifery Council* [2014] EWHC 1158 (Admin).
232 *White v Nursing and Midwifery Council* [2014] EWHC 520 (Admin).
233 *R (H) v Nursing and Midwifery Council* [2013] EWHC 4258 (Admin).

For a consideration of the case-law on absent witnesses and hearsay see chapter 2 at paras 2.92–2.139.

5.171 Sometimes a witness will become unavailable during the giving of evidence, usually because they have fallen ill. Whether the panel continues to take their evidence into account may depend on the reason for the absence and the extent to which, if at all, their evidence has been tested in cross-examination. The overriding consideration is whether there can be a fair trial were the evidence to be accepted, and in particular whether the panel are able to conduct a fair and proper assessment of the reliability of the evidence provided by that witness.

Vulnerable witnesses

5.172 Special measures may be made where a witness is vulnerable. NMC (FTP) Rules 2004 r23 defines a 'vulnerable witness' as any witness:

- under the age of 18;
- with a mental disorder or who is significantly impaired in relation to intelligence or social functioning;
- with physical disabilities who requires assistance to give evidence;
- who is the alleged victim where an allegation is sexual in nature; and/or
- who complains of intimidation.[234]

5.173 The panel has the power to adopt such measures as it considers necessary to enable it to receive the evidence of a vulnerable witness.[235] Such measures may include:[236]

- the use of video-links;
- pre-recorded evidence-in-chief, provided the witness attends for cross-examination and questioning (note: an unrepresented registrant is not permitted to cross-examine the alleged victim where the allegation is sexual in nature,[237] in such circumstances the panel will appoint an appropriate person.[238] There is no provision for the alleged victim to provide consent to be cross-examined by the registrant);
- the use of interpreters including signers; and
- the hearing of evidence in private, albeit in the presence of the parties and their representatives.[239]

This is a non-exhaustive list. The use of vulnerable witness orders in a sexual misconduct case has been recently supported by the courts.[240]

5.174 Before vulnerable witness measures can be imposed, the panel should seek representations from the parties and advice from the legal assessor. It is likely that such measures will be determined at a preliminary meeting. It is a discretionary power, and legal principles established by criminal

234 NMC (FTP) Rules 2004 r23(1).
235 NMC (FTP) Rules 2004 r23(2).
236 NMC (FTP) Rules 2004 r23(3).
237 NMC (FTP) Rules 2004 r23(4).
238 NMC (FTP) Rules 2004 r23(5).
239 NMC (FTP) Rules 2004 r23(6).
240 *Virdee v General Pharmaceutical Council* [2015] EWHC 169 (Admin).

cases are likely to be relevant to decisions on special measures, since the legal provisions are similar (see chapter 2 at paras 2.151–2.157).

Legal assessors

5.175 The NMC has the power to appoint a legal assessor, who must be a qualified lawyer.[241] The function of the legal assessor is to advise screeners, practice committees, Registrar or Council on questions of law, including procedural matters. All committee panels will be advised by a legal assessor, and this advice will be provided in front of the parties. The legal assessor will usually assist in drafting the panel's reasons for any decision, but does not participate in the decision making itself. For a fuller discussion of the role of the legal assessor see chapter 2 paras 2.302–2.327.

5.176 Legal assessors are a helpful source of information for the registrant and their advisers. The NMC case presenter should also be present (and vice versa) in any discussion with the legal assessor outside the hearing.

Medical assessors and registrant assessors

5.177 The NMC has the power to appoint registered medical practitioners to be medical assessors.[242] The function of the medical assessor is to advise the screeners, practice committees, Registrar or Council on any matter within their professional competence.

5.178 The NMC also has the power to appoint registered professionals to be registrant assessors.[243] The function of the registrant assessor is to advise the screeners, practice committees, Registrar or Council on matters of professional practice.

5.179 Unlike a legal assessor, a medical or registrant assessor can comment on the evidence but should only do so in open court and should not express a view on impairment[244] (see chapter 2 at paras 2.297–2.301).

Expert evidence

5.180 Unlike other regulators, the NMC rarely instructs experts, so it is only if a registrant instructs an expert that the panel will receive expert evidence. The NMC guidance suggests that an expert will only be considered where:

- there a need for specialised knowledge or expertise that cannot be provided by the NMC witnesses;
- there a need for an independent opinion;
- there has been a patient death or serious harm caused and expert evidence is required as to whether the registrant was directly responsible; or
- independent medical expert evidence is required in relation to a health matter, to determine issues such as diagnosis, prognosis and treatment, risk of relapse, and whether there is any risk to patients.[245]

241 NMO 2001 art 34.
242 NMO 2001 art 35.
243 NMO 2001 art 36.
244 *Watson v General Medical Council* [2005] EWHC 1896 (Admin).
245 NMC Guide ref INV-4.

5.181 If a registrant disagrees with the opinion of an NMC witness, he or she may wish to adduce evidence to undermine that opinion, instruct his or her own expert, or consider whether to apply for that evidence to be inadmissible on grounds of fairness. The panel is not obliged to admit this evidence and an expert's opinion is only admissible where the opinion is likely to furnish information that is outside the panel's experience and knowledge.

5.182 An expert should be provided with the hearing bundles and, if relevant, the registrant's medical records. If required, the expert should arrange for a consultation with the registrant.

5.183 An expert should be reminded of his or her duty to provide independent evidence irrespective of the party that calls him or her. Further, that the expert is only entitled to give opinion evidence within the expert's area of expertise.

5.184 The NMC has the power to order the author of an expert report to attend a hearing. This power can be exercised by a chair at a preliminary meeting.[246]

Public and private hearings

5.185 Under both common law and the ECHR it is viewed as an important safeguard that regulatory hearings be held in public, in order to ensure proper public scrutiny and the maintenance of public confidence in proceedings. The press and members of the public regularly attend fitness to practise hearings, so protecting the privacy of a registrant and their family can be an issue, and may affect the evidence that they are willing to give.

5.186 Under NMC (FTP) Rules 2004 r19, there is a rebuttable presumption that Practice Committee hearings will be held in public.[247] However, a hearing in whole or in part may be held in private, where the panel is satisfied that it would be justified in the interests of any party or of any third party (including the complainant, witness or patient), or in the public interest.[248] Conversely, there is a rebuttable presumption that where the case solely concerns a registrant's physical or mental health it will be held in private, unless the public interest or interests of any third party outweigh the need to protect the privacy or confidentiality of the registrant.[249] Before making a decision, the panel will provide the parties and any interested third party with the opportunity to make representations and obtain advice from the legal assessor.[250]

5.187 The 'private life' exception enables the panel to take into account the interests of the registrant and his or her family, and is regularly used where reference is to be made to private health matters; indeed, the NMC accepts that it would be 'extremely rare' for it to be appropriate to hear such evidence in public.[251] Further, it may be used if there is to be reference to other sensitive matters such as divorce proceedings, personal finances, or criminal proceedings of third parties. The only requirement is that of justification. The 'public interest' exception is likely to be more narrowly construed, and

246 NMC (FTP) Rules 2004 r18(5)(e).
247 NMC (FTP) Rules 2004 r19(1).
248 NMC (FTP) Rules 2004 r19(3).
249 NMC (FTP) Rules 2004 r19(2) and (2A).
250 NMC (FTP) Rules 2004 r19(2A) and (3).
251 NMC (FTP) Rules 2004 r19(2A) and (3).

limited to matters such as public interest immunity, national security, a witness whose identity needs protecting, and maintenance of public order.

5.188 The decision to hold a hearing in private must be consistent with ECHR Article 6(1) and therefore it must be a proportionate response to a legitimate aim. Representatives are advised to consider if there are alternatives, such as redacting information, anonymising information or concealing the identity of a third party. Further, where possible the application should be restricted to an application to hold only part of the hearing in private. This may be the case where medical conditions or personal information form part of the mitigating circumstances but do not relate to the facts of the allegation.

5.189 It may also be necessary to apply to have the rule 19 application in private; this is where the application would refer to the matter for which privacy is being sought. The decision, with reasons, will be given in public, subject to private information being appropriately redacted.

5.190 A registrant should note that these rules only apply to the hearing. The registrant's name and allegations, decision and any sanctions will still be made publically available if there is a finding of impairment. Usually, private information such as a health condition will be redacted (see paras 5.334–5.336).

Transcripts

5.191 NMC (FTP) Rules 2004 r27 provides that all hearings and preliminary meetings shall be recorded in writing or electronic form.[252] Either party may apply to be furnished with a transcript of the whole or part of any hearing that they were entitled to attend.[253] This is particularly useful where a case has gone part-heard, or at review and restoration hearings, since the transcript can be referred to in submissions to remind the panel of the evidence. Currently registrants are automatically provided with transcripts of part-heard substantive hearings but not of concluded substantive or interim hearings. Therefore, if a registrant requires a transcript they are advised to request it at the hearing.

5.192 There is no longer a transcriber present during hearings – the transcription is done electronically.

Preliminary meetings

5.193 NMC (FTP) Rules 2004 r18 provides committees with the power to hold a preliminary meeting where such a meeting would assist in the performance of its functions. This is a discretionary power and the decision whether or not to hold a preliminary meeting is for the relevant committee of the NMC to determine. If the committee declines to hold a preliminary meeting then any procedural matter can be raised at the substantive hearing. The NMC guidance suggests that preliminary meetings will only be arranged once the case examiners have determined that there is a case to answer.[254] Further, that once a final hearing has commenced any interim

252 NMC (FTP) Rules 2004 r27(1).
253 NMC (FTP) Rules 2004 r27(2).
254 NMC Guide ref HEA-6.

issues should be dealt with by that panel not the chair in a preliminary meeting.[255]

5.194 The chair of the relevant committee will preside over the preliminary meeting, with the legal assessor in attendance together with the parties, their representatives, and any other appropriate persons.[256] The parties shall be given not less than 14 days' notice of the hearing,[257] though this notice period can be waived by the registrant.

5.195 Preliminary meetings are held in private and are administrative in nature. NMO 2001 article 32 permits the chair to issue case management directions and to impose sanctions on non-compliance.[258] The NMC (FTP) Rules 2004 set out a non-exhaustive list of directions.[259] The chair has power to:

- issue directions regarding the service of expert evidence;
- consider an application for special measures for vulnerable witnesses under rule 23 (see paras 5.172–5.174);
- consider an application for failure to comply with directions under rule 31(8);
- consider an application for adjournment under rule 32 (see paras 5.135–5.138); and
- provide a preliminary view regarding admissibility of evidence, albeit the final decision is to be taken by the panel at the substantive hearing.

5.196 Preliminary meetings are only likely to occur where the nature of the case requires a lengthy hearing, or where there are particular evidential or legal issues that need to be resolved prior to the main hearing. If an issue arises that is likely to result in postponing or adjourning the main hearing, then it should usually be dealt with at a preliminary meeting in order to save costs and inconvenience for all concerned. Other issues that should properly be dealt with at preliminary meetings are: late service of documents; admissibility of evidence including hearsay; attendance and order of witnesses. However, preliminary meetings cannot address the costs of attending a hearing or change of venue.[260]

5.197 A preliminary meeting may be held by an Investigation Committee considering an interim order or a fraudulent or incorrect entry case, or by a FTP Committee.[261]

Fraudulent or incorrect entry onto the register

5.198 The NMC has the power to determine an allegation that an entry in the register has been fraudulently procured or incorrectly made.[262] This

255 NMC Guide ref HEA–6.
256 NMC (FTP) Rules 2004 r18(2).
257 NMC (FTP) Rules 2004 r18(4).
258 NMO 2001 art 32(3) and (4).
259 NMC (FTP) Rules 2004 r18(5).
260 NMC Guide ref HEA-6a.
261 NMC (FTP) Rules 2004 rr16 and 17.
262 NMO 2001 art 22(1)(b).

usually involves an allegation that a registrant does not have the necessary qualification to support his or her inclusion on the register. As the NMC guidance explains, this raises genuine public protection concerns because the person may lack the skills required and pose a risk to patient safety.[263]

5.199 The NMC defines an incorrect entry as 'wrong, false or inaccurate information'[264] – for example, mistakenly providing the wrong information about continuous professional development. An entry that is fraudulent is one which was deliberately misleading as to one or more of the entry requirements[265] – for example, provision of a false training certificate. The NMC guidance makes it clear that it is irrelevant whether the registrant was a party to the fraud or knew of the fraud.

5.200 The types of incorrect or fraudulent entries in question relate to those matters that a registrant is required to fulfil in order to be admitted to the register, namely incorrect or false information about:

- the approved qualification;
- the indemnity arrangements;
- good health and good character;
- payment of the registration or renewal fee;
- continuous professional development; or
- identity of the registrant.[266]

Where there is dual registration (ie as both a nurse and a midwife) and one of the entries to the register has been fraudulently obtained, there is likely to be a fitness to practise referral in relation to the other part of the register.[267]

5.201 If on initial receipt of an allegation the screeners consider that registration has been fraudulently procured or incorrectly made, the allegation will be automatically referred to the Investigating Committee to determine under rule 5.[268] The registrant will receive a notice of referral, which will include any relevant documents and invite him or her to provide representations within 28 days.[269] The registrant will be asked whether or not he or she wishes the allegation to be considered at a hearing.[270] The notice of referral will also be sent to a number of statutory persons including the registrant's employer or any other person to whom the registrant provides services, and any other body that authorises the registrant to practise a health or social care profession.[271]

5.202 Where a hearing has been requested by the registrant or is otherwise considered desirable,[272] the registrant will be sent a notice of hearing at least 28 days before the hearing, which will include notification of the charge particularising the allegation and the facts upon which the

263 NMC Guide ref GUI-3.
264 NMC Guide ref GUI-3.
265 NMC Guide ref GUI-3.
266 NMC Guide ref GUI-3a.
267 NMC Guide ref GUI-3b.
268 NMO 2001 art 22(5)(a) and NMC (FTP) Rules 2004 r2A(1).
269 NMO 2001 art 26(2)(a) and NMC (FTP) Rules 2004 r3.
270 NMC (FTP) Rules 2004 r3(2)(e).
271 NMC (FTP) Rules 2004 r3(3).
272 NMC (FTP) Rules 2004 r5(1).

allegation is based.[273] The notice should inform the registrant of the right to attend and be represented, adduce evidence and call witnesses, and cross-examine the NMC's witnesses.[274] The registrant is required to inform the NMC within 14 days of receipt of the notice of his or her intention to attend and whether he or she intends to be represented.[275]

5.203 If no hearing is requested or otherwise considered necessary, the NMC will invite written representations from the registrant and other interested parties,[276] and meet in private.[277] The Investigating Committee has the power to dispose of the matter in the absence of written representations from the registrant.[278]

5.204 If a hearing is arranged, then the procedure under NMC Rules 2004 Part 5 applies,[279] in particular rule 18 (preliminary meetings),[280] rule 22 (witnesses), rule 23 (vulnerable witnesses) and rule 24 (order of proceeding at initial hearing). The standard of proof is the civil standard (balance of probability) under rule 30.

5.205 The Investigating Committee has the power to determine whether an entry has been fraudulently procured or incorrectly made.[281] If it is satisfied that such an entry has been made, it has the power to order that the registrant's record on the NMC register be removed or amended.[282] The registrant and the complainant will be sent a notice of decision, informing him or her of the decision and the reasons.[283] The registrant will also be informed of his or her right to appeal to the High Court[284] (see paras 5.374–5.379). The order will not take effect during any appeals period,[285] and the panel may impose an interim order to cover this period.[286]

5.206 The Investigating Committee has the power to review an order imposed by it on receipt of new evidence.[287] This is also subject to an appeals process.

5.207 If the Investigating Committee concludes that there is no case to answer or no such entry has been made, it has the power to make a declaration and provide reasons with the consent of the person concerned.[288] The registrant has the choice as to whether he or she wishes the decision to be published on the website. Most registrants prefer not to.

273 NMC (FTP) Rules 2004 r5(2) and (3).
274 NMC (FTP) Rules 2004 r5(3)(e) and (f).
275 NMC (FTP) Rules 2004 r5(3)(g).
276 NMC (FTP) Rules 2004 r5(5)(a).
277 NMC (FTP) Rules 2004 r5(5)(b).
278 NMC (FTP) Rules 2004 r5(5)(b).
279 NMC (FTP) Rules 2004 r5(4)(b) and r16(a)(i).
280 See also NMC (FTP) Rules 2004 r5(4).
281 NMO 2001 art 26(2)(d)(ii).
282 NMO 2001 art 26(7).
283 NMC (FTP) Rules 2004 r5(6) and NMO 2001 art 26(5)(b).
284 NMO 2001 art 26(7).
285 NMO 2001 art 26(10).
286 NMO 2001 art 26(11).
287 NMO 2001 art 26(12).
288 NMO 2001 art 26(8) and (9).

Fitness to practise hearings

Remit

5.208 Allegations that a registrant's fitness to practise is impaired by reason of misconduct, lack of competence, criminal conviction or caution, not having the necessary knowledge of English and physical and mental ill-health are all dealt with by the FTP Committee. Allegations that a registrant's fitness to practise is impaired by reason of physical or mental health used to be dealt with by a Health Committee, but this has been abolished. The FTP Committee only considers those allegations referred to it following a determination of a case to answer, or exceptionally under the direct referral provisions (see para 5.40).

Initial referral

5.209 Upon receipt of a referral, the FTP Committee is required to send the registrant a notice of referral under NMC (FTP) Rules 2004 r9. The notice of referral will be served in accordance with the service provisions under rule 34(3) since it is not a notice of hearing (see paras 5.108–5.113). The notice will require the registrant to notify the NMC within 28 days if he or she would like the allegation to be considered at a hearing. If the registrant does not respond within this time period, then the NMC has the power to determine the matter without a hearing, so it is essential that registrants do respond promptly.[289] The notice of referral may be sent to the registrant's employer or any other person with whom he or she has arrangements to provide professional services, or other regulatory bodies that the registrant is registered with.[290]

5.210 The notice should contain any further disclosure and invite the registrant to submit written representations within 28 days.[291] The panel has the power to refer any representations received to the complainant for a response.[292] The panel has the power to require the registrant to submit to a medical, English or competence assessment, where the allegations relate to these matters.[293] Failure to submit to an assessment will be considered as non-engagement and can be taken into account by the panel.

5.211 The registrant is under no obligation to submit a response to the NMC at this stage, and the registrant should not be penalised for failing to respond. In recent years, a form referred to as a 'case management form' or 'standard directions response form' has been enclosed with the notice. This form covers various aspects of the hearing, including the number and names of witnesses that the NMC intends to call and the number of the days the hearing is expected to last. Completion of case management forms is important to evidence engagement with the NMC process, however the cautions expressed in paras 5.51–5.52 also apply to written representations

289 NMC (FTP) Rules 2004 rr9(2)(d) and 10(2).
290 NMC (FTP) Rules 2004 r9(3).
291 NMC (FTP) Rules 2004 r9(2)(b).
292 NMC (FTP) Rules 2004 r9(5).
293 NMC (FTP) Rules 2004 r9(4).

made at this stage. Registrants may wish to provide details of their witnesses or the evidence they intend to call, as requested within the form. However, again they are under no obligation to do so. Registrants are strongly advised to seek legal advice before completing this form.

Hearing or meeting

5.212 Under NMC Rules 2004 r10 the FTP Committee has the power to hold a hearing or meeting to consider a fitness to practise allegation (referred to in the rules as an initial hearing), or to review any order made by it (for example, an interim order or sanction), or to consider an application for restoration to the register.[294] A registrant is entitled to attend a hearing, but not a meeting. The committee is required to hold a hearing either where the registrant has requested a hearing within the specified 28-day limit or it considers a hearing to be desirable.[295] If no hearing is requested, or considered desirable, the committee has the power to consider the matter in the absence of the registrant or their legal representative.[296] The panel also has the power to make, vary, revoke or confirm an interim order at a meeting.[297] It is therefore important that registrants do respond within the 28-day period if they wish the matter to be dealt with at a hearing.

5.213 Where the matter to be determined is a registrant's fitness to practise the NMC will write to the registrant asking if they wish the case to be dealt with at a hearing. If no hearing is requested by the registrant, then the NMC will consider whether or not to hold a hearing or meeting. A meeting may be considered suitable where the registrant fully admits the allegation, or alternatively has failed to engage with the NMC and therefore is unlikely to attend any hearing.[298] A meeting is unlikely to be considered suitable in complex cases involving substantial evidence where the assistant of a case presenter is needed, or where the case raises a public interest issue that requires a hearing, or where the interests of the registrant require that the matter be dealt with at a hearing.[299] The final decision will be made by a panel of the FTP Committee.

5.214 Where the matter to be determined is a review of a substantive order, then the NMC will first decide whether or not a meeting should be arranged. If a meeting is considered to be suitable, then the registrant will be informed of this and given the opportunity to object and request a hearing within 14 days.[300] If no objection is received, then the registrant will receive a notice of meeting, but may still request a hearing after this point. Alternatively, the panel at the review hearing may consider that a hearing should be arranged. A meeting may be considered suitable where the case was considered at a meeting at the substantive stage, the

294 NMC (FTP) Rules 2004 r10(1).
295 NMC (FTP) Rules 2004 r10(2).
296 NMC (FTP) Rules 2004 r10(3).
297 NMC (FTP) Rules 2004 r10(3).
298 NMC Guide ref HEA-11c.
299 NMC Guide ref HEA-11c.
300 NMC Guide ref HEA-11c.

registrant failed to attend the substantive hearing, the registrant has not been in contact since the last hearing or has informed the NMC that they no longer wish to engage. Again, a meeting is unlikely to be considered suitable in complex cases.

5.215 The NMC guidance suggests that meetings are not suitable for restoration applications.[301]

Notice of hearing or meeting

5.216 Where a hearing is to be held, the committee is required to send the registrant a notice of hearing not later than 28 days before the hearing.[302] Where the hearing is a resumed hearing, the hearing having been adjourned, there is no requirement on the NMC to provide a written notice,[303] however the NMC will generally do so.[304] The notice will contain specified information. This includes the date, time and venue of the hearing,[305] and it will enclose any further relevant documentation or (if relevant) copies of any previous orders made.[306] The registrant should be informed of his or her right to be represented and that the committee has the power to proceed in their absence.[307] The registrant will be required to inform the NMC within 14 days of his or her intention to attend the hearing and/or be represented.[308] If the registrant is represented, then it is important that the NMC are informed as soon as possible so that the representative can be contacted by the NMC scheduling team to discuss the suitability of the proposed hearing dates.

5.217 Where the hearing is a fitness to practise hearing, the notice will contain a charge particularising the allegation.[309] It is likely that this will have already been provided in an earlier notice following the investigation stage. The notice will be accompanied with a notice to admit facts.[310] Any admissions can be taken into account at the main hearing.[311] Where the matter relates solely to the registrant's health, the registrant will be asked if he or she wishes the hearing to be conducted in public.[312] Registrants are strongly advised to seek legal advice before responding.

5.218 Where a meeting is to be held, the registrant will receive a notice of meeting no later than 28 days before the date of the meeting.[313] This will contain more limited information than a notice of hearing, but will still enclose any relevant documentation and inform the registrant of the committee's powers. If the matter relates to fitness to practise, it

301 NMC Guide ref HEA-11c.
302 NMC (FTP) Rules 2004 r11(1) and (2)(b).
303 NMC (FTP) Rules 2004 r32(3).
304 NMC Guide ref HEA-3f.
305 NMC (FTP) Rules 2004 r11(3)(a).
306 NMC (FTP) Rules 2004 r11(3)(c).
307 NMC (FTP) Rules 2004 r11(3)(d) and (e).
308 NMC (FTP) Rules 2004 r11(h).
309 NMC (FTP) Rules 2004 r11(3)(b).
310 NMC (FTP) Rules 2004 r11(3)(l).
311 NMC (FTP) Rules 2004 r11(3)(l).
312 NMC (FTP) Rules 2004 r11(3)(m).
313 NMC (FTP) Rules 2004 r11A(1).

will include the particulars of the allegation plus a notice to admit facts.[314] A registrant is not entitled to attend a meeting, but may make representations as to the documentation to be placed before the panel. This process may take some time and requests should be made as early as possible in the process. Registrants are again advised to seek advice.

Preparation

5.219 NMC fitness to practise hearings are public hearings, and if a registrant is representing himself or herself it is advisable for the registrant to attend another hearing to become familiar with the layout of the room and the process.

5.220 At the end of the investigation stage, the registrant will have received a bundle containing witness statements and documentation – referred to as exhibits. Prior to the substantive hearing, usually attached to the case management form, the registrant will receive the index to the proposed hearing bundle. This identifies the documents that the NMC intends to rely on at the hearing. It is important that the registrant considers this list carefully and notifies the NMC of any objections as soon as reasonably possible. If a registrant does not dispute the evidence provided by a witness, then the NMC should be notified that their statement can be agreed. If a statement or exhibit contains irrelevant or prejudicial material, then the NMC should be requested to redact that evidence. Early discussions with the NMC about evidence and documentation can prevent the need to have such discussions on the day of the hearing, and can therefore reduce unnecessary delay in the proceedings.

5.221 A registrant is advised to draft a witness statement or proof of evidence. The statement should have an introductory paragraph setting out his or her experience and/or expertise. The statement should then address the allegations, in particular identifying which, if any, facts are admitted and those that are denied, and setting out any mitigating circumstances. Where an allegation is admitted on the facts, the statement should include evidence of insight (see paras 5.287–5.292). Where an allegation is not admitted, the registrant is still advised to consider whether with hindsight he or she would have acted differently. Even where evidence-in-chief is to be given orally, it will assist the registrant if he or she has already set down his or her thoughts in writing. When considering admissions, insight and reflections, registrants may be assisted by reflection models such as Gibbs Reflective Cycle.

5.222 In addition to a witness statement, registrants are advised to produce their own bundle of exhibits, which should include: any additional documentation relevant to the allegations (and may include documents that the NMC have gathered that they are not relying on), documentation of subsequent employment, relevant training certificates, reflection pieces, testimonials and any other relevant documentation. Unless subject to a direction at a preliminary meeting (see paras 5.193–5.197), there is no requirement on a registrant to have served on the NMC evidence in advance of the hearing, and NMC Committee panels do not currently

314 NMC (FTP) Rules 2004 r11A(2)(a) and (e).

receive documents in advance of a hearing. Although the most recent NMC guidance suggest that this is an option,[315] and therefore may occur in future.

5.223 If a registrant is represented, a pre-hearing conference should be arranged to take full instructions and to ensure that he or she is fully prepared for the hearing.

Before the hearing commences

5.224 It is always advisable to get to a hearing at least 30 minutes before commencement. The first day is often a frustrating and bewildering experience. There will usually be housekeeping and documentary issues to resolve. Some hearing centres have no dedicated waiting room for registrants or their witnesses, so it is advisable to meet prior to the hearing to deal with confidential issues. Coffee, tea and lunch should be provided for registrants and NMC witnesses. Lunch will not be provided for the registrant's witnesses or other support persons. Registrants with specific dietary requirements may wish to advise the case officer of these prior to the hearing to ask if arrangements can be made to provide appropriate foods.

5.225 Currently there is no agreed hearing bundle (although the NMC is moving towards this). A registrant will often be served with a differently paginated hearing bundle or set of exhibits on the first day of the hearing – this should be only those documents previously disclosed, but the registrant may need to ask for extra time to check the documents before the hearing commences. If there are redactions, then these should be checked to ensure that the changes are agreed. If the registrant objects to any documents, the NMC cannot put the document before the panel but must first make an application to the panel for the document to be submitted. The registrant will be provided with an opportunity to explain their objections to the panel prior to a decision being made.

5.226 The registrant or representative should introduce himself or herself to the NMC case presenter, who is the person prosecuting the case on behalf of the NMC. The registrant should provide him or her with copies of any additional documentation he or she intends to rely upon, and if appropriate inform him or her of the registrant's response to the allegations or any change in position to the allegations. This provides an opportunity for the NMC to indicate its position – for example, any intention to offer no evidence, or a view that a particular allegation will be put on the grounds of lack of competence rather than misconduct. It may be that the parties can reach agreement on certain procedural issues, such as the wording of proposed amendments to the charges, an application to hold the hearing in private, or an application to adjourn.

5.227 The registrant or representative should also introduce himself or herself to the NMC panel secretary, who is the person responsible for the administration of the hearing, and may assist with reasonable requests to photocopy last-minute documents.

5.228 Finally, the registrant or representative should also introduce himself or herself to the legal assessor. Any legal issues should be discussed with

315 NMC Guide ref HEA-12c.

the assessor in the presence of the NMC case presenter. The legal assessor is often influential in the legal advice that he or she provides to hearings, and can provide invaluable assistance to representatives and registrants in resolving legal issues. However, there is no requirement for a representative to agree or accept the legal advice of an assessor. If the case raises a legal issue, it is always advisable to bring to the hearing copies of any case to be relied upon and it is good practice to provide a copy to the legal assessor and NMC case presenter prior to addressing the panel.

5.229 If the registrant or representative has failed to attend on time, or more time is needed to take instructions or to sort out documentary or other preliminary issues before the hearing commences, then the NMC panel secretary should be informed. The panel may require the parties to appear in front of them to explain the reason for the delay.

5.230 If the registrant or representative wishes to leave the hearing centre during an adjournment, it is always advisable to inform the NMC panel secretary in case the matter is called on, and leave contact details.

Overview of the procedure

5.231 Fitness to practise hearings should be conducted in accordance with the NMC's overarching objective – which is to safeguard the health and well-being of the public, promote and maintain public confidence in the profession and promote and maintain proper professional standards and conduct.[316] In exercising its function, the panel is required to have proper regard to both the interests of service users and those of the registrant.[317]

5.232 Present at a fitness to practise hearing will be:

- the committee panel, which will be made up of at least one registrant (a nurse or midwife), one non-registrant (lay person) and the chair who may also count as either the registrant or non-registrant;
- the legal assessor;
- the registrant and his or her representative;
- the NMC case presenter; and
- the NMC panel secretary.

5.233 Under NMC (FTP) Rules 2004 r24(1), the hearing shall be conducted in the following stages:

- the preliminary stage;
- the factual stage;
- the impairment stage;
- the sanction stage.

The preliminary stage

5.234 Following introductions, the registrant will be asked to confirm his or her name and personal identification number (PIN). Where a registrant has not attended, the panel will consider whether there has been correct service of the notice.

316 NMO 2001 art 3(4) and (4A).
317 NMO 2001 art 3(5).

5.235 The charges will then be read out and the registrant will be asked if there is any objection to the charge on a point of law.[318] Normally there will be no objection, however this is the point at which arguments over the wording of a charge or an application to amend a charge may be made. The case presenter and the registrant or representative may be asked to make representations and the legal assessor may be asked for advice. Unless the application is unopposed and straightforward, the panel will adjourn to deliberate in private and will then announce its decision and give reasons.[319]

5.236 Once the wording of the charge has been resolved, the registrant will be asked to indicate if he or she is making any admissions as to the alleged facts, whether it is accepted that any admitted facts amount to one of the statutory grounds – for example, misconduct, lack of competence, ill-health, lack of knowledge of English, criminal conviction or caution or determination by another regulator or licensing body. Second, whether it is accepted that the registrant's fitness to practise is impaired.[320]

5.237 If the facts are partially admitted, then this should be stated at the outset. Where there are multiple sub-particulars, care should be taken as to whether the registrant is admitting both the sub-particular and the stem. While partial admissions will not be recorded as an admission, it helps to identify which matters are in dispute. In many cases there will be mixed admissions and denials. There is no requirement on a registrant to admit or deny whether the facts if found proven amount to one or more of the statutory grounds or impairment. These are matters to be determined by the panel, and a registrant may just indicate that he or she is happy to rely on the panel's judgment. Admissions are often taken as an indication of insight (see paras 5.287–5.292), however a registrant should only admit those matters that he or she accepts.

5.238 Where facts are admitted, the chair shall announce that such facts have been found proved without further consideration.[321] Where a statutory ground and/or impairment is admitted, the panel will still proceed to consider the matter.

5.239 Other matters that may need to be raised at the preliminary stage are applications to hold the hearing in private, to adjourn, to address other evidential issues or to submit that the proceedings are an abuse of process.

Offer of no evidence

5.240 If the NMC offers no evidence against a registrant, it will mean that there is no finding made against them in relation to the whole or part of that allegation. The charge is in effect dismissed as unproven, and the matter cannot be reopened unless subject to an appeal.

5.241 There is no specific rule dealing with a decision by the NMC to offer no evidence, however this is addressed in the NMC guidance, and is a mechanism that has been accepted by the High Court,[322] albeit in rare

318 NMC (FTP) Rules 2004 r24(2)(c).

319 NMC (FTP) Rules 2004 r24(3).

320 NMC (FTP) Rules 2004 r24(4).

321 NMC (FTP) Rules 2004 r24(5).

322 *Professional Standards for Health and Social Care v NMC* [2018] EWHC 70 (Admin).

circumstances.[323] Once an allegation has been referred to a practice committee by a case examiner, the NMC has no power to withdraw a case. Therefore, the only mechanism by which a case may not proceed is with the permission of a FTP Committee panel. Permission is normally sought at the preliminary stage, although it could arise later in the hearing.

5.242 The NMC Guidance suggests that a case presenter may offer no evidence where:

- a particular charge or part of a charge adds nothing to the overall seriousness of the case;
- there is no longer a realistic prospect of some or all the factual allegations being proved (for example because new evidence has come to light or a witness has failed to attend); or
- there is no longer a realistic prospect of a panel finding impairment.[324]

5.243 Where the NMC proposes to offer no evidence, it should still fully open the case so that the panel can assess whether it is appropriate to offer evidence.[325] If the panel are not satisfied with the proposal to offer no evidence, then it can require a witness to attend to give evidence or produce relevant documents of its own motion.[326]

The factual stage

5.244 If all the charges are admitted on the facts, then the panel will move straight to the impairment stage. Otherwise, the NMC case presenter will open the NMC's case and present evidence in support of the allegations including those admitted by the registrant.[327] The panel does not see witness statements or documentation in advance of the hearing. Documents will be given exhibit numbers as they are adduced. The first exhibit is likely to be a document identifying any patients who are referred to in the evidence, by reference to a number or letter of the alphabet.

5.245 Unless there is a submission of no case to answer (see paras 5.273–5.274), the registrant will then present his or her case and present evidence in support.[328] There is no requirement on a registrant to give evidence at a hearing; the burden is on the NMC at all times to prove its case. If a registrant does give evidence, then he or she will be subject to cross-examination and questions from the panel. Whether the registrant gives evidence is a matter of judgment, and in most cases a registrant will be advised to do so, particularly where there are disputes of fact which the panel will need to resolve. Further, a registrant is advised to give evidence where there is mitigating and explanatory evidence or evidence of remorse, insight and understanding. If the registrant does give evidence, then this should be as full as possible – bare denials without explanation or insight are likely to be viewed negatively by the panel. If a registrant decides not to

323 NMC Guide ref HEA-10a.

324 NMC Guide ref HEA-10a.

325 *Professional Standards for Health and Social Care v NMC* [2018] EWHC 70 (Admin).

326 NMC (FTP) Rules 2004 r24(5). NMC Guide ref HEA-10b.

327 NMC (FTP) Rules 2004 r24(6).

328 NMC (FTP) Rules 2004 r24(9).

give evidence, there is a possibility that the panel may draw an adverse inference for a failure to give evidence.

5.246 Where a registrant does give evidence, then evidence-in-chief may be adduced either by oral questions or reading out his or her statement. Sometimes the panel will agree to accept the statement 'as read'. Even where a registrant has produced a statement, he or she may still provide further oral evidence-in-chief. The registrant will then be cross-examined by the NMC case presenter, and usually there will be questions from the panel. The panel may adjourn briefly in order to decide what questions to ask, and it is likely that the registrant member of the panel will ask questions about the registrant's practice. The registrant may then call any additional witnesses of fact to give evidence on his or her behalf.

5.247 Following completion of the evidence on the facts, the panel may invite both parties to make final submissions.[329] Such submissions may be oral and/or in writing. Written submissions are not expected, but are useful where there is a point of law that the panel need to consider, or where a case has gone part-heard. The panel, NMC case presenter and legal assessor should be provided with a copy of any cases referred to. If a case has gone part-heard and the panel are referred to evidence contained in the transcript, then the relevant page and line should be referred to. In general, the purpose of a closing submission is to persuade the panel to draw certain conclusions from the evidence they have heard by identifying consistencies in the registrant's case and inconsistencies in the NMC's case. The panel should be addressed on any evidential issues such as hearsay, witness credibility and relevance, along with any other legal points. There is no need to refer to cases where a legal principle or test is well-established. The fact-finding stage does not usually involve much law, and un-represented registrants will not be expected to have a detailed knowledge of legal issues (the legal assessor will usually inform the panel of any legal issues that they need to consider).

5.248 In all cases the panel will invite the legal assessor to advise on any question of law.[330] The legal assessor will usually remind the panel of the burden and standard of proof, identify any evidential issues that need to be resolved and identify the key legal authorities. The parties will then be given the opportunity to indicate if they agree with the advice of the legal assessor and to make further representations if they disagree.

5.249 In all cases, the panel will adjourn to deliberate in private, and then announce their decision with reasons.[331] The legal assessor sits in on these deliberations but plays no part in the decision-making. The legal assessor may at the request of the panel assist in drafting the decision. The legal assessor will inform the parties in open session of any advice given during these private deliberations.

5.250 The fact-finding stage is likely to be the lengthiest part of the hearing and will deal with whether the facts which make up the charge are proven to the required standard, and determine background facts.

329 NMC (FTP) Rules 2004 r24(10).

330 NMO 2001 art 34(2).

331 NMC (FTP) Rules 2004 r24(11).

5.251 In some cases it will be necessary to address not just the bare facts of the allegation, but also the conclusion to be drawn from that evidence. Two examples from recent cases are:

- *Record keeping errors*. If dishonesty is alleged, then the panel will need to determine whether any false representation made was done dishonestly, or whether it was an innocent or even a negligent mistake.[332]
- *Inadequate care*. If misconduct or lack of competence is alleged, then the panel will need to determine whether any failure in care was negligent or a mere error of judgment.[333] And, if misconduct is alleged, whether that negligence is gross negligence (see chapter 3 at paras 3.58–3.72).

These distinctions may be fine ones, but can be crucial in determining whether a particular charge is proven, and determining the level of culpability.

Conviction cases and determinations by another regulator

5.252 Convictions cases include those that occur in a court outside the UK, but where the offence is recognised as a crime in the UK,[334] as well as convictions by a Court Martial.[335] Where a registrant has been convicted of a criminal offence, a copy of the certificate of conviction is conclusive proof of the conviction, and findings of facts upon which the conviction is based is admissible on this basis.[336] The only evidence that a registrant may adduce in rebuttal is that he or she was not the person referred to in the certificate.[337]

5.253 On the other hand, determinations by another UK regulatory health or social care body or licensing body elsewhere are only admissible as prima facie evidence not as conclusive proof.[338] In other words a registrant can call evidence in rebuttal of the finding.

English language cases

5.254 The 'necessary knowledge of English' is defined as a knowledge of English which is necessary for safe and effective practice of nursing or midwifery in the UK.[339] Where the allegation is that a registrant's fitness to practise was impaired due to not having the necessary knowledge of English, and the registrant has been ordered to undertake a language examination or assessment the certificate stating the result and signed by the assessing or examining body is conclusive proof of the result achieved by the registrant.[340]

5.255 If the registrant fails to undertake an examination or other assessment and/or provide a certification of the results, then the panel may draw such

332 *Uddin v General Medical Council* [2012] EWHC 2669 (Admin). *Lavis v Nursing and Midwifery Council* [2014] EWHC 4083 (Admin).
333 *Johnson and Maggs v Nursing and Midwifery Council* [2013] EWHC 2140 (Admin).
334 NMO 2001 art 22(1)(a)(iii).
335 NMO 2001 art 22(2).
336 NMC (FTP) Rules 2004 r31(2).
337 NMC (FTP) Rules 2004 r31(3).
338 NMC (FTP) Rules 2004 r31(4).
339 NM0 2001 Sch 4 'Interpretation'.
340 NMC (FTP) Rules 2004 r31(4A).

inferences as seem appropriate in determining whether their fitness to practise is impaired.[341]

5.256 Guidance on English language tests and what is the pass score is provided on the NMC website.[342]

Competence cases

5.257 In a lack of competence case, if the registrant fails to submit to a competence assessment, then the panel may draw such inferences as seem appropriate in determining the matter.[343]

Health cases

5.258 Where the allegation is that fitness to practise was impaired due to physical or mental ill-health, the factual background will be relevant but is likely to be largely admitted. Therefore, the main focus will be on the particular health condition in question, and whether it caused or contributed to the alleged facts. If the expertise of an expert is required, and the registrant has been assessed by an NMC medical assessor, it is likely that he or she will be called to give evidence. The registrant may need to call his or her own medical expert if the NMC assessor's report is disputed.

5.259 If a medical expert is to be called, then the following evidence should be adduced:

- the expert's professional qualifications and area of specialisation;
- what documentation the expert has considered, whether the expert has personally assessed the registrant, and whether the expert has had any prior involvement with the registrant;
- diagnosis and prognosis, and whether the medical condition in question caused or contributed to the factual allegations; and
- whether a registrant's current fitness to practise is impaired by reason of ill health, and the likelihood and extent of recurrence of the medical condition, along with steps that the registrant has already taken to reduce recurrence and any further steps that can be taken.

5.260 If the registrant fails to submit to a medical examination when asked to do so, then the panel may draw such inferences as seem appropriate in determining the matter.[344]

Burden of proof

5.261 According to NMC (FTP) Rules 2004 r30,[345] the NMC has the burden of proving any facts relating to an allegation which is in dispute. The NMC Rules make this explicit, whereas for other regulators this is implicit. The rule relates only to the 'facts' of an allegation. The decision as to whether those facts amount to one or more of the statutory grounds, and whether a registrant's fitness to practise has been impaired, is a matter for the panel's judgment.

341 NMC (FTP) Rules 2004 r31(6A).
342 NMC Guide ref GUI-2e.
343 NMC (FTP) Rules 2004 r31(6).
344 NMC (FTP) Rules 2004 r31(5).
345 See also Health Act 1999 s60A.

5.262 The standard is the civil standard of balance of probabilities, ie whether the fact in issue more probably occurred than not. The civil standard of proof is a single standard and does not change with the seriousness of the allegation.[346] However, panels should have in mind when assessing probability that the more serious the allegation the less likely it is that the event occurred and, hence, the stronger should be the evidence before the panel concludes that the allegation is established on the balance of probability.[347] It is also recognised that the consequences for a registrant of being struck off can be more severe than a low-level criminal punishment and that 'the severity of the potential consequences is a factor that regulatory authority will need to bear in mind when applying the civil standards of proof'.[348] These cases are considered in chapter 2 at paras 2.371–2.383. There is an exception to the above in that there remains a very small number of 'legacy cases', ie cases which pre-date the change in the NMC (FTP) Rules in 2004 where the criminal burden of proof (beyond reasonable doubt) continues to apply.

Credibility of witnesses

5.263 Where there is a dispute of fact, the panel will need to determine which version of events it believes, which may involve assessing the credibility of the various witnesses. This means not just assessing whether an account is internally consistent (whether or not a witness is changing his or her story) but crucially whether it is consistent with other reliable witness evidence or documentary evidence.[349] Contemporaneous evidence can be particularly useful in testing evidence of a witness who otherwise comes across as convincing. For example, a witness may honestly believe a particular fact but could still be wrong. Conversely, a witness may be right even though their evidence is inconsistent (due to a poor memory or because they not telling the truth on a separate matter).[350]

5.264 Panels should take care not to equate lying or poor behaviour during a hearing with guilt (see chapter 2 at paras 2.233–2.238), although panels can take this into account at a later stage when determining insight. Further, panels have been warned against placing too much emphasis on demeanour of witnesses. While not irrelevant, it is an unreliable means of assessing the truth of any matter.[351] More reliable indicators are: whether the evidence fits with the agreed facts or with contemporaneous documentation, the inherent probability or improbability of the account, and any consistencies or inconsistencies both internally and with the evidence of others.

346 *Re B (children)* [2008] UKHL 35; quoted with approval in *Hosny v General Medical Council* [2011] EWHC 1355 (Admin).

347 *R (H) v Nursing and Midwifery Council* [2013] EWHC 4258 (Admin), applying the principle identified by Lord Nicholls in *Re H (minors) (sexual abuse: standard of proof)* [1996] AC 563.

348 *Moseka v Nursing and Midwifery Council* [2014] EWHC 846 (Admin).

349 *Duthie v Nursing and Midwifery Council* [2012] EWHC 3021 (Admin); *R (H) v Nursing and Midwifery Council* [2013] EWHC 4258 (Admin).

350 *Duthie v Nursing and Midwifery Council* [2012] EWHC 3021 (Admin).

351 *Suddock v Nursing and Midwifery Council* [2015] EWHC 3612 (Admin).

Character evidence

> Character is an integral part of the fitness to practise process. It is equally important when considering credibility and propensity, whether at the fact-finding stage, when judging the issue of impairment or when considering sanction.

5.265 Whether a registrant is of 'good character' (ie whether or not the registrant has been subjected to previous regulatory proceedings or criminal proceedings) is relevant both to the issue of credibility and propensity. This evidence can be adduced at the fact-finding stage, and the legal assessor should provide the panel with a good character direction.[352] Character evidence is also relevant at the impairment stage when assessing likelihood of recurrence; and at the sanction stage when considering mitigating factors.

5.266 In the context of regulatory proceedings, good character means no previous criminal convictions or cautions, no previous disciplinary sanctions imposed by a regulatory body, and may include no previous disciplinary action or incidents recorded on personnel files. In some circumstances, a registrant who has had a previous incident may still be considered to be of good character where the previous incident is old, minor in nature, or unrelated to the matter to be determined.

5.267 Evidence that a registrant is of 'bad character' may be admissible in certain circumstances. Reference to past conduct (criminal or otherwise) is usually redacted at the fact-finding stage but the NMC may seek to adduced it at the impairment stage.

5.268 Where a prosecution witness is of bad character then that evidence is admissible as long as it is relevant. Dishonesty convictions or convictions following a 'not guilty' plea are potentially relevant to the assessment of credibility, whereas evidence of more general bad character would be considered to be collateral and generally not relevant.

5.269 In all the above circumstances, what weight is to be placed on a person's character is a matter for the panel to determine. For a fuller discussion of the case-law on bad character, see chapter 2 at paras 2.164–2.232.

Mitigation evidence

5.270 Mitigation evidence relating to the circumstances in which the registrant found himself or herself may be relevant to the level of culpability, and therefore could be relevant to the issue as to whether the facts can be established at all or whether if established they amount to misconduct and/or lack of competence. Evidence of past or subsequent good practice may also be relevant, although more general character evidence is unlikely to be relevant at this stage.[353] Circumstances such as high workload or personal difficulties may explain why the conduct in question arose, but will seldom excuse the conduct because the provisions of the NMC Code

352 For an NMC example, see *Thorneycroft v Nursing and Midwifery Council* [2014] EWHC 1565 (Admin).

353 *Campbell v General Medical Council* [2005] EWCA Civ 250.

require registrants to act without delay if a situation arises that may prevent them from working within their code of practice. A registrant whose workload was too high would be expected to have raised this with his or her superiors and to have refused to do anything that could call the registrant's fitness to practise into question. A registrant experiencing difficult personal circumstances would be expected to have sought appropriate help or taken time off.

5.271 Further, too much emphasis on mitigating factors could undermine a registrant's ability to demonstrate insight. The approach to be adopted will depend on the facts of the case.

5.272 In almost all cases, complaints about the way the employer or service provider may have investigated an allegation will be of little relevance. The panel will not be interested in whether a fair investigation was conducted unless it affects the quality of the evidence that they are being invited to consider. For example, if the NMC seeks to draw inferences from certain evidence provided during an investigatory interview the way the interview was conducted may be relevant to explain why that evidence is unreliable. Another area may be the failure of an investigator to pursue an obvious line of enquiry.

No case to answer

> Submissions of no case to answer may be made in respect of a case or a specific allegation. They may be made where a) there is no evidence, or b) there is some evidence but it is weak, vague or inconsistent and, looked at 'in the round', a panel could not properly find the case (or fact) proved.

5.273 At the conclusion of the NMC's case, the registrant, or the panel on its own volition, may hear submissions that there is no case to answer on the basis of whether 'sufficient evidence' has been presented to find the facts of an allegation proved,[354] and/or to support a finding of impairment.[355] The panel will hear submissions from both parties and the legal assessor may give advice as to the appropriate test to be applied.

5.274 Prior to the change in the burden of proof from the criminal to the civil standard, it was well established that the test to be applied was that set out in the criminal case of *R v Galbraith*.[356] This is whether:

a) there was any evidence upon which a panel could find matters proved; or
b) there was some evidence, but of such an unsatisfactory nature that the panel properly directed could not find the matter proved.

This is the test applied by the other regulators, and has been recently upheld by the appellate courts.[357] In the past, some NMC case presenters

354 NMC (FTP) Rules 2004 r24(7).
355 NMC (FTP) Rules 2004 r24(8).
356 [1981] 1 WLR 1039, [1981] 2 All ER 1060. See also *Tutin v General Medical Council* [2009] EWHC 553 (Admin).
357 *R (Sharaf) v General Medical Council* [2013] EWHC 3332 (Admin).

have sought to argue that the *Galbraith* test no longer applies because fitness to practise proceedings have a civil burden of proof and suggest that the approach of the civil courts in *Benham Ltd v Kythira Investments Ltd.*[358] should be adopted. The test in *Benham* merely requires there to be a 'scintilla' of evidence from which an adverse inference could be drawn for there to be a case answer.[359] However, reliance on *Benham* arguably would not meet the requirement under the NMC's own rules for there to be 'sufficient evidence' (for further consideration of these cases, see chapter 2 at paras 2.384–2.401).

The impairment stage

5.275 The panel will only consider impairment if the facts of one or more allegations have been held to be well-founded. The impairment stage comprises two separate questions:[360]

a) Whether, on the basis of the facts admitted or found proved, the conduct in question amounts to one of the statutory grounds (misconduct, lack of competence, lack of necessary knowledge of English, ill-health, criminal conviction or caution, regulatory or licensing body determination)?
b) If so, whether the registrant's current fitness to practise is impaired?

5.276 These questions are a matter of judgment for the panel rather than fact, and therefore the burden of proof does not apply. Even where the statutory ground and/or impairment are admitted by the registrant, the panel is still required to exercise its own judgment. The panel can of course take into account the admission. The benefit to a registrant of making admissions at this stage is the demonstration of insight.

Misconduct and lack of competence

5.277 Misconduct is considered by the NMC to be conduct that falls short of what would be proper in the circumstances.[361] However, it is a word that is not defined by the NMC rules and is potentially a very wide concept comprising any departure from good professional practice whether or not it is covered by the NMC standards. It can involve conduct committed outside the professional role or work environment.

5.278 Lack of competence is considered by the NMC to be an unacceptably low standard of professional performance judged on a fair sample of the registrant's work[362] – although it could also comprise an 'exceptionally serious' single clinical incident.

358 [2003] EWCA Civ 1794.

359 [2003] EWCA Civ 1794.

360 *Cohen v General Medical Council* [2008] EWHC 581 (Admin); *Cheatle v General Medical Council* [2009] EWHC 645 (Admin).

361 NMC Guide ref GUI-2a. This is based on *Roylance v General Medical Council (No 2)* [2001] 1 AC 311.

362 NMC Guide ref GUI-2b. This is based on *Calhaem v General Medical Council* [2007] EWHC 2606 (Admin).

5.279 Not all breaches of NMC standards necessarily constitute misconduct and/or lack of competence. Further, not all misconduct or lack of competence will be of the level of seriousness to impair fitness to practise, ie to warrant action on the register that could affect a registrant's future practice and/or livelihood. Therefore, although the test does not refer to 'serious' conduct, a level of seriousness is required. For a discussion of the case-law (see chapter 3 at paras 3.14–3.57).

5.280 Further, there is a distinction to be made between misconduct and lack of competence.[363] This is important not only because lack of competence carries a lesser range of sanctions, but also because there is slightly less stigma attached to lack of competence. There is also a distinction to be made between negligence which would give rise to a civil liability but which is not otherwise sufficiently grave to constitute gross professional negligence. It is therefore possible in suitable cases to argue that the facts as found were either not sufficiently serious to constitute misconduct or lack of competence, or that they amount to lack of competence but not misconduct.

5.281 In determining the question of misconduct and/or impairment, the panel is entitled to take into account a breach of the standards set out in the NMC Code or other guidance or advice produced by the NMC.[364]

Impairment

5.282 Impairment is not defined by legislation or the NMC Code, however there is considerable case-law on this issue (see chapter 3 at paras 3.1–3.41). Crucially, it is well-established that it is a present-day test, since the wording of the NMO 2001 only provides powers to investigate an allegation that the registrant's fitness to practise '*is* impaired'.[365] Therefore, the purpose of fitness to practise proceedings is not to punish the registrant for past wrongdoings, but to protect the public or profession where a registrant's current fitness to practise is currently impaired. In reaching this decision, the panel can take into account the past wrongdoing, but it is also required to take into account other relevant factors, such as whether the conduct in question is easily remediable, whether it has been remedied and the likelihood of repetition.[366] Therefore, it is a forward-looking test.[367] However, in some cases even if the conduct in question is capable of remedy and has been remedied, the nature of the conduct may be such that such steps carry little weight.[368] This is where the conduct constituted a fundamental breach of professional standards, such that the need to

363 *R (Remedy UK Ltd) v General Medical Council* [2010] EWHC 1245 (Admin).

364 NMO 2001 art 22(4); NMC (FTP) Rules 2004 r31(7).

365 NMO 2001 art 22(1)(a).

366 *Cohen v General Medical Council* [2008] EWHC 581 (Admin).

367 *Meadow v General Medical Council* [2006] EWCA Civ 1390; *Cheatle v General Medical Council* [2009] EWHC 645 (Admin). See also *Sarkodie-Gyan v Nursing and Midwifery Council* [2009] EWHC 2131 (Admin).

368 *Council for Healthcare Regulatory Excellence v Nursing and Midwifery Council* [2011] EWHC 927 (Admin); for an example see *Odoi-Asare v Nursing and Midwifery Council* [2014] EWHC 1151 (Admin).

maintain public confidence in the profession overrides the interests of the registrant.[369]

5.283 NMC case presenters regularly refer to the factors in the case of *Council for Healthcare Regulatory Excellence v Nursing and Midwifery Council*[370] when determining whether impairment, namely whether the registrant:

a. has in the past acted and/or is liable in the future to act so as to put a patient or patients at unwarranted risk of harm; and/or
b. has in the past brought and/or is liable in the future to bring the medical profession into disrepute; and/or
c. has in the past breached and/or is liable in the future to breach one of the fundamental tenets of the medical profession; and/or
d. has in the past acted dishonestly and/or is liable to act dishonestly in the future.

Even if one or more of these factors do apply (and they often do) there is no presumption that this would impair fitness to practise. Each case should be considered on its own facts and merits. In relation to a criminal conviction the courts have held that not every conviction for a criminal offence will result in a finding of impairment. It will be a question of nature and degree.[371] Similarly, the courts have held that not every act of dishonesty results in impairment.[372] Arguably the same logic should apply to sexual misconduct cases.

5.284 Under NMC (FTP) Rules 2004 r24(12) the parties are given the opportunity to call evidence in relation to whether a registrant's fitness to practise is impaired and make further representations. It is unlikely at this stage that the NMC will call further witnesses, unless there is evidence of other past conduct that the NMC wish the panel to take into account when determining impairment (for example, previous disciplinary actions). Whether the registrant wishes to adduce further evidence may be a tactical decision. It will depend on whether there is further background evidence that he or she wishes the panel to take into account. It may also depend on whether or not the registrant has any insight into their conduct and/or is able to give evidence that his or her current fitness to practise is not impaired. It may also depend on whether sufficient insight has already been demonstrated at the fact-finding stage, or if the findings of fact identify issues that the registrant now needs to address (for example, a charge which had been denied being proved).

5.285 Again the parties will be invited to make closing submissions and the legal assessor will be invited to advise on legal matters. It is likely that there will be some reference to the legal tests and case-law by both the NMC case presenter and the legal assessor. Representatives and registrants who are representing themselves should familiarise themselves

369 *Council for Healthcare Regulatory Excellence v Nursing and Midwifery Council* [2011] EWHC 927 (Admin).

370 [2011] EWHC 927 (Admin).

371 *Farah v Nursing and Midwifery Council* [2014] EWHC 1655 (Admin).

372 *Professional Standards Authority v (1) General Medical Council; (2) Uppal* [2015] EWHC 1304 (Admin).

with the key legal issues. The Panel will adjourn to deliberate in private and will announce its decision and give reasons.[373]

5.286 Relevant evidence that the registrant may seek to adduce at this stage includes:

- written or oral evidence that explains the registrant's thought processes at the relevant time, and demonstrates an understanding of why the conduct constituted a statutory ground and/or impairment;
- what the registrant would do differently if in the same position again, including any evidence that the registrant has found himself or herself in a similar position and acted differently;
- evidence of remorse, such as an apology and if possible reparation;
- what, if any, steps the registrant has subsequently taken to change his or her practice or behaviour. This may include seeking medical assistance, attending counselling, direct or indirect supervision, audits/assessment of work, mentoring, self-reflection, personal research and/or training. If possible, provide documentary evidence in support, such as medical records, reports from counsellors, supervisors, mentors, appraisals and supervision sessions, training certificates and relevant documentation, evidence of research conducted and reflection pieces;
- character evidence relevant to the conduct in question, such as evidence that the registrant acted out of character or to demonstrate that the registrant is capable of learning from his or her mistakes (although more general character evidence is only relevant to the sanctions stage);
- relevant evidence of surrounding circumstances and mitigation, if not already adduced at the fact-finding stage; and
- oral or written evidence from other health professionals, supervisors, managers or other appropriate persons which confirms steps taken and that the registrant has insight.

Insight and remediation

5.287 An important consideration at this stage in the proceedings (and also at the sanction stage) is the issue of 'insight'. A minor matter may become more serious in the eye of the panel if the registrant fails to demonstrate insight,[374] by repeated denials or trivialising, whereas a serious matter may be made less serious if a registrant demonstrates insight.

5.288 The NMC guidance suggests that a registrant who shows insight will usually be able to:

- step back from the situation and look at it objectively;
- recognise what went wrong;
- accept his or her role and responsibilities and how they are relevant to what happened;
- appreciate what could and should have been done differently; and

373 NMC (FTP) Rules 2004 r24(12)(b) and (c).

374 *Nicholas-Pillai v General Medical Council* [2009] EWHC 1048 (Admin), but contrast *Nagiub v General Medical Council* [2011] EWHC 366 (Admin).

- understand how to act differently in the future to avoid similar problems happening.[375]

5.289 Where factual matters have been denied, it may be difficult for a registrant to demonstrate insight and therefore it is important that the basis of any denial is made clear and whether the registrant, despite the factual denials, accepts the findings that have been made against him or her. However, the NMC guidance does recognise that a denial should not be taken as a bar to showing insight.[376] Insight can be demonstrated in recognising that the incident in question could impair fitness to practise and steps to minimise recurrence. For example, a nurse who denies having made a medication error may nevertheless attend relevant training to demonstrate there is a low risk of recurrence.

5.290 The NMC suggests that evidence of insight may include early admissions, co-operation with internal or NMC proceedings, acknowledging the harm or risk of harm to patients, accepting that the conduct falls short of NMC standards, understanding the damage to the reputation of the profession, accepting personal responsibility without blaming others. It can include an apology, although this is not required, particularly where there may be good reasons for not offering an apology. Registrants should also bear in mind that at all times they are required to comply with the duty of candour.

5.291 Remedial steps may include attending relevant training; reflections including any examples of putting what he or she has learnt into practice; developing and complying with an action plan; supervised practice; and evidence from an employer of addressing concerns. Panels are looking to be reassured that a registrant fully understands what occurred, takes responsibility for his or her actions and takes steps to prevent recurrence. A wide range of evidence can be adduced to demonstrate remediation and insight, but it must withstand robust scrutiny (see the NMC guidance for what Panels are told to look for).[377]

5.292 The NMC guidance suggests that whereas it may be possible to remediate clinical failings through training courses and supervisions, it is more difficult to remediate where the case involved:

- criminal convictions that led to custodial sentences;
- inappropriate personal or sexual relationships with patients, service users or other vulnerable people;
- dishonesty, particularly if it was serious and sustained over a period of time, or directly linked to the registrant's practice; and
- violence, neglect or abuse of patients.[378]

However, even in such cases a registrant may be able to demonstrate genuine insight and understanding into their conduct and adduce evidence to persuade a panel that they have learnt from their failure and there is no risk of recurrence. Further, he or she may be able to adduce related evidence, for example evidence of subsequent honesty and

375 NMC Guide ref GUI-4b.

376 NMC Guide ref GUI-4b. See also *Professional Standards Authority v Health and Care Professions Council* [2017] EWCA Civ 319.

377 NMC Guide ref GUI-4b.

378 NMC Guide ref GUI-4a.

integrity, maintaining sexual boundaries, changed behaviour, attending counselling/therapy or other medical treatment.

Competence cases

5.293 NMC (FTP) Rules 2004 r31(6) provides that in determining whether fitness to practise is impaired by reason of lack of competence, the panel may take into account any refusal by a registrant to submit to a professional assessment of his or her practice. If there has been such a refusal, the registrant should explain reasons. The authors presently know of no case where a registrant has been asked to submit to a competency test.

Health cases

5.294 NMC (FTP) Rules 2004 r31(5) provides that in determining whether fitness to practise is impaired by reason of physical or mental health, the panel may take into account:

- a refusal by a registrant to submit to medical examination;
- the registrant's current physical or mental condition;
- any continuing or episodic condition suffered by the registrant; and
- a condition suffered by the registrant which although currently in remission may be expected to recur to the impairment of the registrant's fitness to practise.

This is a non-exhaustive list and other health matters may be taken into account, for example any reason why the registrant refused to submit to medical examination (see para 5.45 above), the extent to which a registrant is complying with medical or professional practitioners, the nature of the condition and the registrant's insight into that condition, the steps taken by the registrant to limit the impact of that condition on his or her work, the registrant's relationship with other health professionals and patient care.

5.295 If the registrant has a long-term or recurring condition, then it is likely that he or she will fall within the definition of disability under the Equality Act 2010.[379] The mere fact of having a disability does not mean that a registrant's fitness to practise as a midwife or nurse is impaired, and if possible registrants and their representatives should adduce medical evidence to this effect. The tricky area is where a registrant with a disability is perfectly fit to practise but only where reasonable adjustments are made by the employer or service provider. If the registrant is in employment, then evidence from an employer that they are willing to make such adjustments would be helpful. The registrant may be in a more difficult position where either an employer is not prepared to make the necessary reasonable adjustments or where the registrant is not in employment. The emphasis by health regulators on a registrant's health and fitness, without regard to the need for reasonable adjustments, could give rise in some circumstances to a claim for disability discrimination.

5.296 On a separate point, in some cases it may be necessary for the NMC to make reasonable adjustments to enable the registrant to fully participate

379 Discrimination law is outside the scope of this work.

in the process. If a registrant does require any special arrangement to be made, they or their representative should inform the NMC case officer.

The sanction stage

> The principal aims of sanctions are to protect the public, uphold the standards and reputation of the profession and to maintain public confidence.
>
> The punitive effect of sanctions is only one (and not the most important) factor to be borne in mind when assessing whether a sanction is proportional to the matters found proved against a registrant.

Introduction

5.297 Where a panel has concluded that a registrant's fitness to practise is impaired, the panel will proceed to consider what, if any, sanction to impose. The panel may decide to refer the matter for mediation or decide that it is not appropriate to take any further action.[380] Alternatively, if further action is required the panel must make one of the following sanctions:

a) a caution order for a period not less than one year and not more than five years;
b) conditions of practice order for a period not exceeding three years;
c) suspension order for a period not exceeding one year; or
d) striking-off order.[381]

In 2016/2017 fewer than one per cent of cases had no sanction imposed.[382]

5.298 When making, varying, replacing or revoking an order the panel shall direct the Registrar to record the decision on the register.[383]

Key principles

5.299 In considering sanction, the panel should take into account the NMC *Sanctions guidance*.[384] This has been accepted by the courts as a valuable reference point, and registrants and their representatives are advised to read it prior to making submissions. It emphasises that the panel can exercise its discretion when making a decision, but if it departs from the guidance it should explain and give reasons for its decision.

5.300 Panels are required to consider the least restrictive sanction first. However, once they have chosen a sanction they are advised to consider the next most serious sanction to that chosen, and explain why it was not considered necessary to impose the more severe sanction.

5.301 In considering which if any sanction to impose, the panel must have regard to the public interest. Public interest is defined as:

380 NMO 2001 art 29(4).
381 NMO 2001 art 29(5).
382 NMC *Annual fitness to practise report 2016–2017.*
383 NMO 2001 art 29(8).
384 NMC Guide ref SAN-1.

- protecting members of the public;
- maintaining public confidence in the professions; and
- declaring and upholding proper standards of conduct and behaviour.

Due to the primary consideration being public interest, the reputation of the profession is considered to be more important than the impact of any sanction on the individual.[385] However, public interest considerations may include consideration of the skills of the registrant,[386] and the safe return to practice of a nurse or midwife.[387]

5.302 While a sanction should not be punitive, it undoubtedly has that effect. Panels are required to have regard to the interests of the registrant and act proportionately. This requires panels to balance the interests of the public against those of the registrant. Thus any interference with a registrant's practice should be no more than is necessary in the public interest. A failure to act proportionately may breach a registrant's ECHR Article 8 right to respect for private and family life. The requirement to act proportionately also means that panels should take into account unintended consequences, such as a suspension order in effect terminating a career.

5.303 Panels should have careful regard to mitigating and aggravating factors. According to the sanctions guidance, mitigating factors include:[388]

- a registrant's insight and understanding and any attempts to redress his or her failings, for example early admissions, apologies and efforts to correct or prevent recurrence;
- a registrant's observance of good practice by keeping his or her knowledge up to date or their previous good character and history; and
- personal mitigation, such as stress or illness, personal and financial hardship, level of experience at the time in question, and level of support in the workplace.

5.304 The panel should assess mitigating factors not just in considering the length of the sanction but also which sanction to impose.[389] However, since the principal function of sanctions is not punitive but to protect the public interest, mitigation evidence carries less weight than in other jurisdictions. The converse of this is that where there is no risk to the public because a registrant has retired then this may be a highly material and relevant factor to take into account in determining sanction.[390] Arguably this could also apply where a registrant has demonstrably no intention of returning to nursing or midwifery.

385 *Bolton v Law Society* [1994] 1 WLR 512.

386 *Bijl v General Medical Council* [2001] UKPC 42; *Giele v General Medical Council* [2005] EWHC 2143 (Admin).

387 NMC Guides ref SAN-1 and SAN-2. This replaces the NMC *Sanctions indicative guidance for panels* (18 May 2012).

388 NMC Guide, ref SAN-3.

389 For a recent NMC example, see *Wisniewska v Nursing and Midwifery Council* [2016] EWHC 2672 (Admin).

390 *Clarke v General Optical Council* [2017] EWHC 521 (Admin).

5.305 Specific guidance is provided on 'cases with particular risk for public confidence':[391]

a) *Dishonesty* is considered to undermine the trust the public place in the profession, even if it occurred outside a professional role. The *Sanctions guidance* states that 'honesty, integrity and trustworthiness are considered to be the bedrock of any registrant's practice'. The guidance refers to the case of *Parkinson v Nursing and Midwifery Council*[392] which states that a nurse found to have acted dishonestly is always going to be at severe risk of having his or her name erased from the register. However, this case should not be read as requiring panels to impose a sanction of striking off unless there are exceptional circumstances. There are a wide range of different types of dishonesty, and it is important to differentiate between the more serious and less serious forms of dishonesty.[393] The guidance provides a list of what the NMC considers to be the more serious and the less serious forms of dishonesty.
b) *Sexual misconduct* covers both criminal convictions for sexual offences; and inappropriate relations with colleagues, patients or their relatives. It may also involve clinical conduct that has been found to be inappropriate due to a finding of sexual motivation. The *Sanction guidance* requires panels to have regard to the Professional Standards Authority's guidance on *Clear sexual boundaries*.[394] The *Sanctions guidance* suggests that in cases of serious sexual misconduct, a striking off order will often be the only proportionate sanction.
c) *Criminal convictions* cover both cautions and convictions. The *Sanctions guidance* reminds panels that the purpose of the sanction is not to punish the registrant for a second time. However, it also reminds panels that personal mitigation carries less weight in the regulatory context than in the criminal context. Therefore, the criminal sanction is not necessarily a reliable guide to how serious a conviction will be considered to be. The courts have held that as a general principle a registrant serving a current sentence should not be permitted to resume practice until he or she has satisfactorily completed that sentence.[395] This principle has been taken to apply both to custodial and community sentences, the period of a suspended sentence, and the period of any entry onto the sex offender's register. Of course if a conviction is subsequently overturned on appeal, then it may be possible to apply for the NMC to revoke the decision under the 'slip rule'[396] (see paras 5.384–5.385).

5.306 It is important to remind panels that the sanction imposed must be proportionate and that there is no tariff for dishonesty, sexual misconduct

391 NMC Guide, NMC ref SAN-5.

392 [2010] EWHC 1898 (Admin).

393 *Lusinga v Nursing and Midwifery Council* [2017] EWHC 1458 (Admin); *Watters v Nursing and Midwifery Council* [2017] EWHC 1888 (Admin).

394 See www.professionalstandards.org.uk/publications/detail/clear-sexual-boundaries.

395 *Council for the Regulation of Healthcare Professionals v General Dental Council and Fleischmann* [2005] EWHC 87 (QB).

396 *R (Jenkinson) v Nursing and Midwifery Council* [2009] EWHC 1111 (Admin).

or criminal convictions. Therefore, all sanctions are available to panels, and in less serious cases a caution order, conditions of practice order or suspension order may be sufficient to maintain public trust and confidence in the profession. For a fuller discussion of sanctions cases, see chapter 3 at paras 3.109–3.356.

5.307 If a registrant has been subject to an interim order, then that may be relevant to a) explain whether they have had an opportunity to address any identified failings; and/or b) to demonstrate compliance (or non-compliance) and insight. The length of time that a registrant has been subject to an interim order can be taken into account in a registrant's favour when determining sanction.[397] The *Sanctions guidance* cautions panels against applying a straight discount, since this may result in a sanction that is insufficient to achieve the stated purpose of public protection. Nevertheless, this is an important factor that should be taken into account when sanction is being determined. Similarly, where there has been an unreasonable delay in bringing proceedings, amounting to a breach of ECHR Article 6 (right to a fair trial), then the sanction should take that breach into account.[398]

No further action

5.308 Panels are not required to impose a sanction in every case. No further action may be appropriate where there is a relatively minor breach of the NMC Code, which has been fully admitted and remedied. It is only in rare cases that taking no action will be appropriate. In general registrants whose fitness to practise has been found to be impaired should be warned to expect a sanction of some sort to be applied. In 2016/2017 fewer than one per cent of cases had no sanction imposed. The NMC *Sanctions guidance* suggests that usually a finding of impairment would require some action to secure patients' safety or secure public trust and confidence in the profession or declare and uphold standards.[399] However, conversely it can be argued that in some cases the finding of impairment is a sufficient public declaration to mark the panel's disapproval.

Caution order

5.309 A caution order may be imposed for not less than one year and not more than five years.[400] The length will reflect the seriousness of the allegation. It has serious consequences for a registrant since any current or prospective employer will need to be informed of its existence, and the order will be recorded on the register and therefore be in the public domain. The advantage of a caution order over a conditions of practice or suspension order is that it does not place any other restrictions on a registrant's practice and does not require a review. Once the period has passed, the order lapses and no other action is required.

397 *Okeke v Nursing and Midwifery Council* [2013] EWHC 714 (Admin); *Kamberova v Nursing and Midwifery Council* [2016] EWHC 2955 (Admin).

398 *Okeke v Nursing and Midwifery Council* [2013] EWHC 714 (Admin).

399 NMC Guide, NMC ref SAN-4a.

400 NMO 2001 art 29(5)(d).

5.310 The *Sanctions guidance* suggests that a caution order may be appropriate where the case is at the lower end of the spectrum to mark that the behaviour was unacceptable. It would only be appropriate where there is no risk to the public or patients.[401]

Conditions of practice order

5.311 A conditions of practice order may be imposed for not more than three years at a time.[402] There is no restriction on what constitutes a condition, but it should address the panel's concerns about the registrant's practice. It can be restrictive, or remedial, or both. Conditions must be relevant, proportionate, workable and measurable. Suitable conditions may include a requirement to undertake further training, to be subject to supervision and reports, to comply with medical or professional assistance, or place a restriction on an area of practice. Until 28 July 2017 the NMC provided a list of model conditions, this is no longer in operation, but is still available from the NMC website and is a useful indicator of the type of conditions that may be considered by a panel.[403]

5.312 The *Sanctions guidance* states that the key consideration is whether imposing conditions is sufficient to protect patients and where necessary the wider public interest (ie maintaining public confidence and proper professional standards). The *Sanctions guidance* suggests that a conditions of practice order may be appropriate where:

- there is no evidence of harmful deep-seated personality or attitudinal problems;
- there are identifiable areas of practice in need of assessment and/or retraining;
- there is no evidence of general incompetence;
- there is potential and willingness to respond positively to retraining;
- there is insight into any health problems;
- patients will not be put in danger either directly or indirectly as a result of the condition;
- patients will be protected for the duration of the order;
- it is possible to formulate and monitor the conditions.

This list is non-exhaustive and not all factors have to be present.[404]

5.313 Where conditions of practice are being sought by a registrant (as the most appropriate or favourable outcome), it is advisable to adduce evidence that they are willing to comply with any proposed conditions. Further evidence from his or her employer, line manager or other appropriate professional should be provided confirming that they are aware of the proposed conditions, and willing and able to provide the necessary support or facilities to enable a registrant to comply with those conditions. Examples may include agreeing to provide a regular audit of patient notes done by a registrant or provide mentoring, supervision or training. In

401 NMC Guide, ref SAN-4b.

402 NMO 2001 art 29(5)(c).

403 NMC *Conditions of practice library* (January 2014), rescinded 28 July 2017.

404 NMC Guide ref SAN-4c.

many cases the employer or professional will be asked to provide a report to the NMC at appropriate intervals confirming the registrant's compliance and progress.

5.314 Where a registrant has been subjected to an interim conditions of practice order, the operation of that order and compliance may be relevant evidence. Unless the registrant has adduced this evidence at an earlier stage in the proceedings, the panel will be unaware of any such order.

5.315 Conditions of practice orders are usually subject to review and can be revoked, modified or replaced. The panel has the power to specify a period of time of up to two years within which no application to vary, replace or revoke may be made.[405] This power is rarely exercised. If for any reason the registrant is unable to comply with the conditions of practice order, the NMC should be informed as soon as possible. Unless the panel has imposed a restriction, an early review should be sought with an application to vary the terms of the order. A registrant who simply fails to comply with an order runs the risk that the order will be extended or replaced by a more severe sanction.

Suspension order

5.316 A suspension order is an order suspending the registrant's registration for a specified period of time of up to one year at any one time,[406] in other words, he or she cannot practise as a registrant during this period of time. The panel has the power to specify a period of time of up to ten months within which no application to vary, replace or revoke the order may be made.[407]

5.317 The *Sanctions guidance* states that key considerations are the seriousness of the case and whether the period of suspension will be sufficient to protect patients and is not fundamentally incompatible with continuing to be a registered registrant.[408] The guidance suggests that a suspension order may be appropriate where:

- there has been a single instance of misconduct but where a lesser sanction is not sufficient;
- there is no evidence of harmful deep-seated personality or attitudinal problems;
- there is no evidence of repetition of behaviour since the incident;
- there is insight and no significant risk of repetition of behaviour;
- in health cases and competence cases there would be a risk to patients were the registrant to continue to practise even with conditions.

This list is non-exhaustive and not all factors have to be present.[409]

5.318 A suspension order is often imposed where striking off is too harsh but no condition of practice can be devised or is appropriate. If a registrant is not working as a registrant, either because he or she has been subjected to an interim suspension order or for other reasons, then conditions of

405 NMO 2001 art 29(7)(c).
406 NMO 2001 art 29(5)(b).
407 NMO 2001 art 29(7)(b).
408 NMC Guide ref SAN-4e.
409 NMC Guide ref SAN-4e.

practice which require a supportive employer will often not be deemed suitable. Therefore, there is a risk that if a caution order is not appropriate then the only realistic alternative is a suspension order.

5.319 Short suspension orders are often used as a means of upholding standards in the profession; in order to demonstrate to the profession and the public that the registrant's actions are considered to be unacceptable. From the registrant's point of view, sometimes a short suspension order may be preferable to a lengthy conditions of practice order. Representatives should always discuss with registrants the approach to be adopted in relation to sanctions.

5.320 A panel is not permitted to impose conditions of practice alongside a suspension order. However, the *Sanctions guidance* advises panels to consider providing guidance on any expectations or actions that may be taken that may assist a panel in any subsequent review. While a registrant is not required to comply with this guidance, it is strongly suggested that he or she do so in order to achieve the most favourable outcome at the review, bearing in mind that the panel at any review will have the power to impose a further sanction, including a further period of suspension or even a striking off order.

Striking-off order

5.321 A striking-off order is an order removing the registrant from the register,[410] preventing them from working as a nurse or midwife. Under NMO 2001 article 33(2) the registrant may not apply for restoration for a period of five years, unless new evidence comes to light.[411]

5.322 A striking-off order may not be imposed where fitness to practise is impaired by reason of health, lack of competence or not having the necessary knowledge of English, unless the registrant has been continuously suspended and/or subject to a conditions of practice order for no less than two years.[412] Therefore, earlier in the proceedings, there may be advantages to admitting fitness to practise being impaired due to ill-health, lack of competence or lack of knowledge of English but denying misconduct. Time spent on an interim order is not to be included when calculating the two-year period under article 29(6).[413]

5.323 Striking-off orders should be reserved for the most serious cases. The *Sanctions guidance* states that key considerations are whether public confidence can be maintained if the registrant is not removed from the register; whether striking off is the only sanction which will be sufficient to protect the public interest; and whether the seriousness of the case is incompatible with ongoing registration. A striking-off order is likely to be appropriate when the conduct is fundamentally incompatible with being a nurse or midwife. The guidance suggests that this may occur where the conduct involves any of the following factors:

410 NMO 2001 art 29(5)(a).

411 NMO 2001 art 30(7).

412 NMO 2001 art 29(6).

413 *Okeke v Nursing and Midwifery Council* [2013] EWHC 714 (Admin).

- a serious departure from the relevant professional standards, guidance and advice;
- doing harm (physical, emotional or financial) to others or behaving in a way that could foreseeably result in harm to others, particularly patients and other professionals. This is regardless of whether the harm was caused deliberately, recklessly, negligently or through incompetence, although the seriousness of the harm should always be considered;
- an abuse of a position of trust or violation of the rights of a patient particularly vulnerable patients;
- serious misconduct of a sexual nature including involvement in child pornography;
- any violent conduct whether towards members of the public or patients, where the public interest can only be satisfied by removal;
- dishonesty, especially where persistent or covered up;
- persistent lack of insight into seriousness of actions or consequences;
- criminal convictions or cautions involving any of the conduct set out above.

This list is non-exhaustive and not all factors have to be present.[414]

5.324 The *Sanctions guidance* states that there is case-law that supports the removal of health professionals from the register where there has been a lack of probity, honesty or trustworthiness even where there are no concerns about their clinical skills or risk of harm to patients.[415] Further, that striking-off orders have been upheld on the basis that they are justified for reasons of maintaining trust and confidence in the profession. For a consideration of the case-law in this area, see chapter 3 at paras 3.275–3.319.

Process

5.325 The panel has the power to invite any person who has an interest in the proceedings to submit written representations.[416] This permits the panel to receive 'victim impact statements', although to date, as far as the authors are presently aware, this power has yet to be exercised. The panel may hear further evidence from the parties as to previous history (including previous findings of impairment) or mitigating circumstances or other relevant factors.[417] Unless the evidence is contentious, it is usually sufficient for it to be adduced by means of representations. Testimonials and character evidence should be adduced either in documentary form or by live evidence from witnesses.

5.326 There is no limit to the character evidence that may be adduced at this stage, but the most compelling will be that from other health and social care professionals with whom the registrant has worked. Other appropriate persons may be managers, patients, local dignitaries, other employers and neighbours. If the registrant is involved in charitable work, a reference

414 NMC Guide ref SAN-4f.
415 NMC Guide ref SAN-4f.
416 NMC (FTP) Rules 2004 r24(13)(a).
417 NMC (FTP) Rules 2004 r24(13)(c).

from that charity is advisable. Referees should state that they are aware of the allegations, set out their relationship to the registrant, and state how long they have known the registrant. An appropriate witness attending a hearing in order to show support for the registrant can be powerful evidence. In addition to character references, other evidence of character is also useful, such as 'thank you' letters from patients (with the patient's name redacted), or expressions of gratitude from colleagues. The absence of references or testimonials should not, however, count against a registrant.

5.327 The panel is required to provide the parties with the opportunity to make submissions identifying relevant factors which may affect the panel's decision.[418] Currently NMC case presenters take a neutral stance and do not seek to persuade the panel to adopt a particular sanction, although they may comment on the appropriateness of sanctions proposed by or on behalf of the registrant, and will remind the panel of the sanctions available and of any aggravating and mitigating circumstances. The legal assessor will then be invited to advise the panel on any legal issues. The panel will adjourn to deliberate in private and announce its decision and give reasons.[419]

5.328 In all cases, a finding of impairment may be taken into account in any subsequent proceedings, even if no further action is taken or any order imposed has lapsed. Moreover, NMC case presenters will ask panels to take into account any other relevant background matters such as allegations found proven at local disciplinary level, even if not referred to the NMC or which had been dismissed by the NMC following a submission of no case to answer.

Directions as to reviews

5.329 Under article 30(1), a conditions of practice order and a suspension order should be reviewed prior to the expiry of that order. The panel when imposing an order may specify a period within which no review should occur[420] (see paras 5.352–5.355). The panel may also specify that no review is necessary in which case the order will lapse on the expiry date.[421] The NMC suggests on the one hand that reviews will usually be necessary where a conditions of practice order has been imposed. On the other hand, a review may not be necessary where a suspension order is imposed in order to uphold the reputation of the profession but where there is otherwise no risk to patients.[422]

5.330 A striking off order cannot be reviewed, but the registrant can apply for restoration after five years (see paras 5.365–5.373).

418 NMC (FTP) Rules 2004 r24(13)(b).
419 NMC (FTP) Rules 2004 r24(13)(d) and (e).
420 NMO 2001 art 29(7).
421 NMO 2001 art 29(8A).
422 NMC Guide ref SAN-6.

Interim orders during the appeal period

5.331 The registrant has the right to appeal against any sanction order imposed within 28 days of the date that the notice of the order or decision is served (see paras 5.374–5.379). Therefore, no sanction order will have effect until the end of the 28-day appeal period, and if an appeal is lodged within that period, until the appeal has been finally disposed of. To cover this period, where the panel has imposed a conditions of practice order, a suspension order or a striking off order, the panel has the additional power to impose an interim order for up to 18 months.[423] The interim order will take effect during the 28-day period and any further appeal period. It is likely to be on the same terms as the substantive order. The test is the same as that which applies to other interim orders. Therefore, it may only be imposed where it is considered by the panel to be necessary for the protection of the public, or is otherwise in the public interest, or in the interests of the person concerned. The *Sanctions guidance* recognises that it is not an automatic decision in every case.[424]

5.332 An interim suspension order is often imposed where a suspension or striking-off order has been made. It is separate from, and additional to, the substantive order. Therefore, where a short suspension order has been made this may result in the interim order being longer than the suspension and in such cases it may be possible to argue that an interim order is unnecessary. Whether an interim conditions of practice order is considered necessary where a substantive conditions of practice order has been imposed will often depend on the particular circumstances and terms of the order. The terms of an interim conditions of practice order are likely to be the same as the substantive order, although representations should be made if such terms are not appropriate for an interim order.

5.333 Where a panel is considering imposing an interim order, then it is required to invite representations from the parties and take such representations into account.[425] The panel should be informed if there are any particular reasons why an interim order should not be imposed, for example if the registrant has patients booked or needs a period of time to arrange cover for his or her practice. The panel will adjourn to deliberate in private and then announce its decision and the reasons for that decision.[426]

Decisions

5.334 As soon as is practicable after the conclusion of a meeting or hearing (usually within seven days of the hearing) the panel is required to provide the registrant and the complainant with the decision, providing its reasons and informing the registrant of their right to appeal.[427] The NMC is also required to publish its decision and any orders imposed, including the

423 NMO 2001 art 31(1)(c) and (2).
424 NMC Guide ref SAN-7.
425 NMC (FTP) Rules 2004 r24(14)(a) and (b).
426 NMC (FTP) Rules 2004 r24(14)(c) and (d).
427 NMC (FTP) Rules 2004 r13(1) and (2).

issue of any undertaking or warning.[428] Publication is usually done via the NMC website and the decision and any order will be linked to a registrant's PIN and generally available to employers and the general public. Further the NMC may disclose to any person, information relating to a registrant's fitness to practise which it considers to be in the public interest to disclose.[429]

5.335 If an allegation is dismissed – either because the facts are not proved, or the facts as proved do not amount to a lack of competence or misconduct, or current impairment is not established – then no publication is required, and all references will be immediately removed from the NMC website, unless the registrant requests otherwise.

5.336 Where a hearing has been held partly in private, the information considered in private will not be included[430] – if necessary, two decisions may be produced: a public one and a private one.[431] The NMC advises that health matters and matters involving children should not be published, but accepts that there may be other evidence which should also not be put in the public domain. In all cases panels are advised to balance the need for transparent decision-making against protecting the interest of various parties including the complainant and the registrant. In exceptional cases, the panel may decide that a decision should not be published, in which case it should provide reasons for that decision.[432]

Consensual panel determination and voluntary removal

Consensual panel determination

5.337 In January 2013, the NMC introduced a process termed 'consensual panel determination', to be used in situations where the registrant is willing to admit most if not all the allegations and admit that their fitness to practise is impaired. The process is designed to encourage registrants to engage with the NMC earlier in the fitness to practise process to avoid the need for a full hearing of the facts. It will only be considered once a case has been referred to the FTP Committee. The NMC have published guidance on consensual panel determination.[433]

5.338 Consensual panel determination is a mechanism to allow the NMC and registrant to agree in writing the facts of the case and a provisional sanction. It can apply for the full range of sanctions, from caution orders to striking-off orders. The written agreement setting out the agreed facts is then put before a FTP Committee panel to make the final decision as to sanction. In reality, the final agreement is a process of negotiation. It can lead to disputed allegations being removed or amended, if they make little or no difference to the overall seriousness of the case, or there is no

428 NMO 2001 art 22(9).

429 NMO 2001 art 22(10).

430 NMC Guide ref HEA-14.

431 NMC Guide ref HEA-14b.

432 NMC Guide ref HEA-14b.

433 NMC Guide ref HEA-8 (for hearings commencing after 28 July 2017, otherwise see previous guidance: consensual panel determination (14 January 2013)).

realistic chance of the allegation being proved. It could include negotiation over the statutory grounds, if there is more than one alleged. Registrants should seek legal advice before entering into discussions, and any pre-agreement written communication between the registrant and the NMC should be labelled 'without prejudice' to ensure that the correspondence cannot be placed before a panel at a later stage.

5.339 The complainant will be provided with the opportunity to comment on any draft agreement, and it may be changed in the light of their comments. The complainant's comments may also be provided to the panel (if relevant) including whether or not they agree with the proposed outcome.

5.340 At any stage before the provisional agreement is submitted to a hearing or meeting, either party can decide that they no longer wish to proceed with consensual panel determination and the matter will proceed to a full hearing. A panel may consider the provisional agreement at either a hearing or a meeting. It has the power to accept or reject the agreement. In reaching its decision the panel can ask the parties to address it or to obtain further information. If the panel wishes to make a finding of no impairment or substitute a different sanction, this can only be done with the agreement of both parties.

5.341 Whether the panel accepts or rejects the consensual panel determination agreement, it should give its reasons. If the panel rejects the agreement, then the matter will be set down for a substantive hearing to be considered by a fresh panel. The new panel will not be informed that the registrant accepted impairment, unless the registrant himself or herself wishes the panel to know.

5.342 If the registrant is interested in a consensual panel determination, then he or she or their representatives should contact the NMC reviewing lawyer to discuss the feasibility of an application and what, if any, documentation the NMC would recommend submitting for a successful application. The NMC may also contact the registrant directly if they identify that consensual panel determination could be appropriate.

Voluntary removal

5.343 Nurses and midwives were previously not able to remove themselves from the register while they were the subject of an NMC referral. In January 2013, the NMC introduced the process of voluntary removal to allow registrants to apply to be removed from the register while subject to proceedings, or potential proceedings.[434] The NMC have published guidance on voluntary removal.[435] Voluntary removal will only be allowed by the NMC if the registrant accepts the details of the regulatory concern and provides evidence that they do not intend to continue practising. If the application is accepted by the NMC then it will conclude the proceedings.

5.344 Applications to be voluntarily removed from the register may be made by a registrant at any point in the referral process. There is no limit to the

434 Nursing and Midwifery Council (Education, Registration and Registration Appeals) Rules Order of Council 2004 SI 2004 No 1767 r14.

435 NMC Guide ref HEA-7 (for hearings commencing after 28 July 2017, otherwise see previous guidance: Voluntary Removal Decision-making (14 January 2013)).

number of applications that can be made, however it is unlikely to be granted on reapplication unless there has been a material change in circumstances.[436] The registrant will be asked to sign a voluntary removal declaration form confirming their intention not to apply for readmission within five years of the date of removal.

5.345 Applications will not be considered until there has been a determination of a case to answer – this is so that the NMC understands the extent of the referral. An application made during a substantive hearing will only be considered by the panel at the sanction stage following a finding of impairment. If the panel rejects the application, sanctions will be considered in the normal way.

5.346 When considering the application, the Registrar will have regard to a number of factors, including:

- the public interest, in particular whether there is a public interest in having a public hearing to determine the allegation;
- the interests and future plans of the registrant;
- the likelihood of seeking readmission to the register;
- the length of time since the registrant last practised;
- evidence of intention to practise in the UK or elsewhere in the future; and
- comments received from the complainant.

5.347 The NMC guidance suggests that voluntary removal is likely to be appropriate in health cases where it relates to a long-term health condition and the registrant accepts impairment as a result of his or her health condition. It may also be appropriate in competence and knowledge of English cases where the registrant concerned accepts that his or her fitness to practise is impaired for those reasons and they have already stopped practising and have no intention of returning to practice. Misconduct and conviction allegations are unlikely to be considered suitable for voluntary removal. Where an allegation covers more than one ground, the total allegation will be taken into account but it is unlikely to be granted where the allegation includes misconduct and may be suitable for a suspension or striking off order.[437]

5.348 A registrant or his or her representatives can contact the reviewing lawyer to discuss the feasibility of an application and what, if any documentation, the NMC would recommend submitting for a successful application.

5.349 Voluntary removal only applies to registrants who are subject to actual or potential fitness to practise allegations. There is a separate procedure for those who simply want to be removed from the register or let their registration lapse.

5.350 Voluntary removal is not permitted where the registrant is subject to undertakings. Nor is it permitted whilst a registrant is subject to a final conditions of practice or suspension order.[438] If the registrant is subject to

436 NMC Guide ref HEA-7a.
437 NMC Guide ref HEA-7d.
438 NMO 2001 art 12(3)(b).

an interim order, this will need to be revoked on the grounds that voluntary removal has been granted.[439]

5.351 Registrants can reapply to be readmitted to the Register five years after voluntary removal. The NMC have produced *Guidance on how fitness to practise allegations are considered as part of readmission applications.* Any application for readmission will be referred to the Registrar who will consider whether the registrant is:

- capable of safe and effective practice as a nurse or midwife; and
- meets the health and good character requirements.

This will include consideration of the fitness to practise allegations, including what matters the registrant had previously admitted or been found proved. The guidance requires the Registrar to 'exercise caution' in allowing a nurse or midwife to re-register where he or she had previously expressed an intention to cease to practise permanently.

Review hearings and restoration hearings

Review hearings

5.352 NMO 2001 article 30(1) provides that a review hearing will be held to review a conditions of practice order or suspension order prior to the end of the specified time period of that order, unless the panel has specifically stated at the time of making an order that a review will not be necessary.[440] Further, article 30(2) provides that a caution order, a conditions of practice order or a suspension order may be reviewed during the period it is in force, by an application from the registrant concerned or otherwise.[441] Finally, and exceptionally, a striking-off order may be reviewed if new evidence comes to light.[442]

Substantive order review hearings

5.353 A substantive order review hearing will usually take place within eight weeks prior to an order expiring.[443] At the review hearing, the panel has the power to:

- extend or further extend the current order, save that it must not extend a conditions of practice order by more than three years or a suspension order by more than one year at a time;
- replace the order with any order that it could have made at the initial hearing;
- impose a conditions of practice order on expiry of any suspension order.[444]

439 NMC Guide ref HEA-7b.
440 NMO 2001 art 30(1).
441 NMO 2001 art 30(2).
442 NMO 2001 art 30(7). NMC Guide ref REV-1d.
443 NMC Guide ref REV-1a.
444 NMO 2001 art 30(1) and (5).

The panel does not have power to revoke the existing order or make changes to an existing order. The panel can allow an existing order to expire on the expiry date. The NMC guidance to panels suggests that where exceptionally there is a need to change an order with immediate effect, then this can be done by using its early review powers.[445]

5.354 At the substantive order review hearing, the panel will not re-open the initial findings of fact or findings as to the statutory ground, but it will re-consider whether the registrant's practice remains impaired in the light of what has happened since the last hearing. The burden remains on the NMC in relation to any factual matters. However, the persuasive burden of demonstrating remediation, insight and compliance with any conditions or guidance from the previous panel is on the registrant concerned. The NMC suggests that in determining impairment, panels consider whether:

- the registrant has complied with any conditions imposed and the quality of evidence of compliance;
- the registrant shows insight into their failings or the seriousness of any past misconduct, and in particular whether that insight has improved or got worse;
- the registrant has taken effective steps to maintain their skills and knowledge;
- there has there been any further incident; and
- the registrant is safe to practise unrestricted or whether any risk to patient safety still remains.[446]

5.355 If the registrant's practice remains impaired, then a further sanction may be imposed – this may be an extension of the existing order or a new order. This will commence from the expiry of the old order unless an immediate change is necessary, which should only occur in exceptional cases.[447] There is always a risk that a more serious sanction will be imposed including a striking-off order if the registrant fails to address concerns identified by previous panels, fails to comply with conditions, or there is a further incident.[448]

Early review hearings

5.356 The NMC will generally arrange an early review hearing on request by a registrant. However, it will not schedule a hearing just because a registrant is dissatisfied with the outcome of a hearing, or if there is no new evidence to put before the panel.[449] If there is new evidence, then the NMC will schedule a review hearing. Examples of when an early review hearing may be scheduled include:

- information that the registrant is acting in breach of the order;
- where there are concerns that the registrant's fitness to practise has got worse;

445 NMC Guide ref REV-1c.
446 NMC Guide ref REV-1a
447 NMC Guide ref REV-1a.
448 See, for example, *M v Nursing and Midwifery Council* [2016] CSIH 95.
449 NMC Guide ref REV-1b.

- conditions have become unworkable (this may be because the registrant has changed employment or lost a supervisor); or
- the registrant has fully complied with the order and/or taken effective steps to address the problems (so presumably an order is no longer necessary).

5.357 Another situation that may occur is where the registrant was initially suspended because there were no workable conditions at the substantive hearing, but that there are now conditions that could be considered by the panel. Since any change to an order at an early review hearing will only take effect for the remaining period, a request for an early review within three months of the expiry of the substantive order will be treated as a substantive review hearing.[450]

5.358 At any early review hearing, the panel has the power to:

- confirm the current order;
- extend or further extend the current order, save that it must not extend a conditions of practice order by more than three years or a suspension order by more than one year at a time;
- reduce the period of the current order, save that a caution order may not be reduced to less than one year;
- replace the order with any order that it could have made at the initial hearing. Where an order is replaced it shall run for the remaining period of the order and then be reviewed at a substantive review hearing;
- vary any condition imposed by the current order; or
- revoke either the order or any condition imposed by the order.[451]

5.359 Unlike at a substantive review hearing, the panel has the power to make immediate changes to the order.

Procedure at review hearings

5.360 The review hearing is before the FTP Committee.[452] NMC (FTP) Rules 2004 r25 provides that the normal procedure at a review hearing is that:

- the NMC case presenter will inform the panel of the background to the case, the sanctions previously imposed, and refer to relevant evidence including transcripts from previous hearings;
- the registrant or their representative may then make representations and adduce relevant evidence; and
- the panel will adjourn to deliberate in private and announce its decision with reasons.[453]

5.361 The registrant has the right to attend the hearing and make representations.[454] This may include giving oral testimony at the hearing, calling witnesses and submitting evidence in support. A legal assessor will be in attendance to provide advice on questions of law. The provisions of Part 5

450 NMC Guide ref REV-1b.
451 NMO 2001 art 30(4) and (5).
452 NMO 2001 art 30(1).
453 NMC (FTP) Rules 2004 r25(2).
454 NMO 2001 art 30(9).

of the NMC Rules 2004 apply to review hearings[455] – for example, the provisions on preliminary meetings, private/public hearings, right to representation and witnesses.

5.362 Where a registrant's fitness to practise has been found to be impaired by reason of not having the necessary knowledge of English, the NMC may require the registrant to undertake an English examination or other assessment with the result provided to the panel.[456]

5.363 The panel may make the revocation of a suspension order subject to the registrant satisfying the NMC standards on additional education, training or experience.[457] This arises because if the registrant is suspended, he or she will have had a period of non-practice, and therefore may be in breach of the NMC standards were he or she to resume practice without undergoing additional education or training. If a registrant is in the position to comply with such education, training or experience requirements during the period of suspension, then the registrant should do so in order to avoid further delay at the end of the suspension period. This could include ensuring that his or her continuous professional development portfolio is up-to-date. Where a registrant cannot afford to attend training courses, online training may be freely available.

5.364 The power to extend an existing order at both early and substantive review hearings can result in the overall period being for longer than the period stated when the order was imposed. However, arguably the panel must have an evidential basis for repeated extensions, and such extensions should not amount to the equivalent of a striking-off order.

5.365 The panel may not impose an order which it could not have made at the time that the order being reviewed was made.[458] Therefore if the impairment was by reason of lack of competence, knowledge of English or ill-health, the panel will have no power to impose a striking off order at the review hearing unless the registrant has been continuously suspended and/or subject to a conditions of practice order for at least two years.[459] Interim orders do not count towards the determination of this period.[460]

5.366 In order to avoid an unfavourable outcome to the review hearing, registrants should adduce evidence of compliance with NMC orders, such as a report from their employer, further testimonials from colleagues and health professionals, or other steps taken to address the issues in question. If a registrant was able to continue to work as a practitioner, then clearly evidence as to his or her conduct since the NMC proceedings and further references and testimonials from health professionals and colleagues will be helpful. Even where a registrant has not been able to work as a health professional, a letter or statement from a current employer is still useful character evidence, particularly where the area of concern is not specific to his or her practice. Therefore, if the registrant had been

455 NMC (FTP) Rules 2004 r16(b)(iii).

456 NMC (FTP) Rules 2004 r25A.

457 NMO 2001 art 30(6).

458 NMO 2001 art 30(1)(b), which itself is subject to art 29(6) and (7).

459 NMO 2001 art 29(6).

460 *Okeke v Nursing and Midwifery Council* [2013] EWHC 714 (Admin). Note the wording of NMO 2001 art 30(1)(b) has been changed since the date of this decision.

found to be dishonest, evidence as to his or her honesty will be relevant along with evidence as to his or her general approach to the NMC proceedings and lessons learned. Where the registrant was found to be lacking in competence due to finding himself or herself in a stressful situation or with too much work, evidence of dealing with stressful situations or managing workload will be relevant.

5.367 If there is a further incident, this may be treated as a new referral and give rise to separate fitness to practise proceedings or it may be treated as a breach of an existing substantive order and dealt with at the review hearing.[461] If an interim order is imposed as a result of the new referral, then the reviewing panel will be informed, but panels have been advised to exercise caution and not change the substantive order merely to mirror the interim order.[462]

5.368 There is a right to appeal to the High Court within 28 days against an order or decision of the FTP Committee at a review hearing.[463]

Restoration hearings

5.369 A restoration hearing will be held to consider an application to restore a nurse or midwife onto the register following a striking-off order.[464] A nurse or midwife must wait at least five years after the striking-off order took effect before making an application for restoration to the register.[465]

5.370 The application will be considered by the FTP Committee.[466] In considering whether to grant an application to restore, the panel will have to satisfy itself that the applicant:

- holds an approved qualification as is required under NMO 2001 article 9(2)(a);
- is capable of safe and effective practice as required by article 9(2)(b);
- has the necessary knowledge of English as required by article 9(2)(ba); and
- is a fit and proper person to practise in the relevant profession, having regard to the circumstances that led to the nurse or midwife's removal.[467]

Thus the central question for the panel is the question of whether the applicant is safe to practise.[468] The panel also has the power to require that the applicant satisfies any additional post-registration education and training requirements imposed under article 19(3),[469] and has the power to impose a conditions of practice order.[470]

5.371 Rule 25 provides that the normal procedure at a restoration hearing is that:

461 NMC Guide ref REV-1e and REV-1f.
462 NMC Guide ref REV-1g.
463 NMO 2001 art 30(10) and (11).
464 NMO 2001 art 33(1).
465 NMO 2001 art 33(2)(a).
466 NMO 2001 art 33(3).
467 NMO 2001 art 33(5).
468 *Balamoody v Nursing and Midwifery Council* [2009] EWHC 3235 (Admin).
469 NMO 2001 art 33(6).
470 NMO 2001 art 33(7)(b).

- the NMC case presenter will inform the panel of the background to the case, the sanctions previously imposed, and refer to relevant evidence, including transcripts from previous hearings;
- the applicant or his or her representative may then make representations and adduce relevant evidence; and
- the panel will adjourn to deliberate in private and announce its decision with reasons.[471]

The applicant has the right to attend the hearing and make representations.[472] This may include giving oral testimony at the hearing, calling witnesses and submitting evidence in support. A legal assessor will be in attendance to provide advice on questions of law. The provisions of Part 5 of the NMC rules apply to restoration hearings,[473] for example the provisions on preliminary meetings, private/public hearings, right to representation and witnesses.

5.371 Where an application for restoration to the register has been rejected at a review hearing, a further application may not be made for the next 12 months.[474]

5.372 If a second or subsequent application for restoration is unsuccessful then the panel may direct that all further application be suspended indefinitely.[475] The applicant may apply for this direction to be reviewed but only after three years.[476]

5.373 There is a right to appeal to the High Court within 28 days of the decision refusing restoration to the register, imposing conditions of practice on that registration, or refusing to review a direction that all further applications be suspended indefinitely.[477]

Appeals

Appeal by the registrant

5.374 NMO 2001 article 38 provides a registrant with the right of appeal to the High Court against 'any order or decision' of the FTP Committee,[478] other than against an interim order made under article 31.[479] What constitutes a 'decision' is not defined under the order. However, it is clear that it is not limited to an appeal against an order imposing sanction. An appeal is also permitted in relation to any substantive finding of the FTP Committee,[480] and this would include a decision on facts, misconduct or impairment. Article 38 appeals would not apply to preliminary rulings on matters such as disclosure or the refusal to hold a preliminary hearing

471 NMC (FTP) Rules 2004 r25(2).
472 NMO 2001 art 33(4).
473 NMC (FTP) Rules 2004 r16(b)(iv).
474 NMO 2001 art 33(2)(b).
475 NMO 2001 art 33(9).
476 NMO 2001 art 33(10).
477 NMO 2001 art 33(12) and (13).
478 NMO 2001 art 38(1) and (4).
479 NMO 2001 art 31(12).
480 *Nowak v Nursing and Midwifery Council* [2013] EWHC 3335 (Admin).

because this does not involve a 'decision' by the panel (although judicial review may be available).[481]

5.375 The time limit for an appeal following imposition of a sanction is 28 days from the date the notice of order or decision was served on the person concerned.[482]. Most appeals are lodged following the final determination of a sanction.

5.376 The Notice of Decision is set out in NMC (FTP) Rules 2004 r13 (see paras 5.334–5.336) and is usually provided within seven days of the hearing that made the decision. Rule 34 sets out the provisions dealing with service (see paras 5.108–5.113). Under this rule, even though a registrant may be present at the hearing and be orally informed of the outcome, the clock only starts to tick once the written notice is served by the NMC. Registrants should note that if the notice is served by ordinary post, the clock will start to tick on the day after it was sent. A common mistake is to assume that time limits only start to run from the date of actual receipt.[483] That is not the case, and it is always advisable to seek legal advice. In exceptional circumstances a court may accept an appeal that has been served out of time.[484] Difficulties in instructing a lawyer and not having the finances to pay the court fee would not amount to an exceptional circumstance.[485] In a harsh decision the court has also held that a delay caused by the post office is not an exceptional circumstance (even where the posting was by guaranteed next-day delivery but there was a failure by the post office to deliver the next day).[486] Therefore, the best mode of delivery is to personally deliver the notice of appeal by hand to the relevant court and obtain a receipt, or otherwise post the notice of appeal in good time allowing for the possibility of a delay in the delivery process. For further information about time limits and discussion of relevant case-law, see chapter 10).

5.377 The appeal is one to which the Civil Procedure Rules 1998 apply, and the test is whether the decision in question was 'wrong'.[487] The High Court has the power to allow or dismiss the appeal, remit the appeal back to the FTP Committee or to substitute the decision with one that could have been made.[488] Therefore there is a risk that an appeal against a sanction could result in a harsher sanction being imposed. Further, if the appeal is unsuccessful, the original substantive order only comes into effect once the appeal has been decided. If an interim order has been imposed on the registrant to cover the appeal period, then the consequence of an unsuccessful appeal would be to prolong the period of time a registrant is suspended or on conditions of practice. It may also undermine the ability of the registrant to demonstrate insight at any subsequent review hearing. A further consideration is that civil courts are a costs jurisdiction, and usually costs follow the event, ie the losing party pays the

481 *Nowak v Nursing and Midwifery Council* [2013] EWHC 3335 (Admin).
482 NMO 2001 art 29(10); CPR Practice Direction 52D para 19.1(3).
483 *Adesina v Nursing and Midwifery Council* [2013] EWCA Civ 818, [2013] 1 WLR 3156.
484 *Adesina v Nursing and Midwifery Council* [2013] EWCA Civ 818, [2013] 1 WLR 3156.
485 *Daniels v Nursing and Midwifery Council* [2015] EWCA Civ 225 (Admin).
486 *Stevenson v General Optical Council* [2015] EWHC 3099 (Admin).
487 Civil Procedure Rules Part 52.
488 NMC 2001 art 38(3).

winning party's costs. This means that a registrant can recover his or her costs if he or she succeeds but is liable to pay the NMC's costs if he or she loses. Registrants are advised to seek legal advice before lodging an appeal.

5.378 In addition or as an alternative to the right of statutory appeal, a registrant may be able to apply for judicial review. For a discussion of the pros and cons of this option,[489] see chapter 10.

5.379 There is a limited right of appeal against a High Court decision to the Court of Appeal. This would require permission and will only be permitted if it raises an important point of principle or practice, or there is some other compelling reason for the Court of Appeal to hear the case.

Appeal by the Professional Standards Authority

5.380 The Professional Standards Authority (PSA) is an overarching body that regulates regulators including the NMC. It has power to refer disciplinary cases to the High Court when it considers that a decision made by that body is 'not sufficient' for the protection of the public.[490] The PSA may appeal both the final decision of a relevant committee and/or the sanction imposed.[491] The PSA may also appeal a decision to restore a nurse or midwife to the register.[492]

5.381 Whether a decision is 'sufficient' is considered in respect of whether it sufficiently:

- protects the health, safety and well-being of the public;
- maintains public confidence in the profession concerned; and
- maintains proper professional standards and conduct for members of that profession.[493]

The test to be applied is whether the decision was 'wrong'.[494] The High Court has the power to allow or dismiss the appeal, remit the appeal back to the relevant Committee or to substitute the decision by one that could have been made.[495]

5.382 The PSA is not permitted to submit an appeal during the appeal period for the registrant (ie the initial 28-day period following service of the Notice of Decision), but is required to submit any appeal within 40 days thereafter.

5.383 During any period of appeal by the PSA, a court order may be sought to prevent a registrant lapsing from the register, since there is no equivalent provision preventing lapse of registration under article 12 as there is under the fitness to practise provisions.[496] Registrants are advised to

489 For an example of an NMC case which was dealt with by judicial review, see *Johnson and Maggs v Nursing and Midwifery Council* [2013] EWHC 2140 (Admin).

490 National Health Service Reform and Health Care Professions Act 2002 s29(1)(i) and (4).

491 National Health Service Reform and Health Care Professions Act 2002 s29(2)(a) and (b).

492 National Health Service Reform and Health Care Professions Act 2002 s29(2)(c).

493 National Health Service Reform and Health Care Professions Act 2002 s29(4A).

494 Civil Procedure Rules 1998 Part 52.

495 NMO 2001 art 38(3).

496 *Profession Standards Authority for Health and Social Care v Nursing and Midwifery Council* [2013] EWHC 4369 (Admin).

seek legal advice before submitting any response to or attending the High Court in a PSA appeal. Any submissions made, if unsuccessful, may undermine the ability of the registrant to demonstrate insight at any subsequent remitted FTP hearing or review hearing. Registrants should also be aware that the civil courts are a costs jurisdiction and, should the registrant submit objections to the PSA appeal, the PSA regularly request costs orders against both the NMC and the registrant if the appeal is successful.

NMC corrective action

5.384 The NMC has no power to appeal the decision of a FTP Committee. However, it does have an inherent power to correct 'mistakes', characterised as 'slips, accidental mistakes or miscarriages of justice'. In such limited circumstances, the NMC may take corrective action without the need to submit an appeal to the High Court or apply for judicial review.[497] This power permits the NMC to reverse a finding of misconduct based solely on a flawed criminal conviction where all parties are in agreement and there was no room for speculation or uncertainty as to the outcome.[498] However, this power does not permit the NMC to overturn a finding at a substantive hearing of no case to answer which involved an exercise of judgment by the panel concerned.[499]

5.385 The inherent power is distinct from the power to review certain decisions specifically provided under the NMC rules, such as the power to review case to answer decisions by case examiners.

Registration appeals

5.386 These are separate, albeit related proceedings. As set out in para 5.3 above, registrants are required to apply to register with the NMC, and to renew their registration every three years. Registration will be granted if he or she satisfies the requirements of registration,[500] or the requirements of renewal/readmission.[501] If the application for registration or renewal is refused, the applicant has the right to appeal to the Council (called registration appeals).[502] The appeal will be heard by the Registration Appeals Panel. There is a further right to appeal the decision of the Registration Appeals Panel to the county court.[503]

5.387 The proceedings are governed by separate rules: Nursing and Midwifery Council (Education, Registration and Registration Appeals) Rules 2004 (NMC Registration Rules).[504] One of the key conditions of registration

497 *Jenkinson v Nursing and Midwifery Council* [2009] EWHC 111 (Admin); *R (B) v Nursing and Midwifery Council* [2012] EWHC 1264 (Admin).

498 *Jenkinson v Nursing and Midwifery Council* [2009] EWHC 111 (Admin).

499 *R (B) v Nursing and Midwifery Council* [2012] EWHC 1264 (Admin).

500 NMO 2001 art 9.

501 NMO 2001 art 10.

502 NMO 2001 art 37(1).

503 NMO 2001 art 37(10).

504 Nursing and Midwifery Council (Education, Registration and Registration Appeals) Rules 2004 SI No 1767, as amended.

and renewal is that the nurse or midwife is capable of 'safe and effective practice'.[505] The NMC has issued guidance to panels on how to assess a nurse or midwife's character and health in order to satisfy the safe practice requirements.[506]

5.388 The concepts that apply to fitness to practise hearings, particularly in relation to public protection and public interest, and the provisions of the NMC Code, equally apply to these proceedings. However, these are different and separate proceedings. Registration appeal panels only have a binary option available to them namely whether to admit or not admit to the register, whereas FTP Committees can adopt a more graduated approach due to the greater number of orders (sanctions) available to it. Therefore the fitness to practise *Sanctions guidance* does not apply to these hearings.[507]

Costs

5.389 Since the various healthcare regulators bring proceedings in the public interest, to protect the public or to uphold standards and so on, they are not in the position of an ordinary litigant prosecuting a claim. Unless a complaint is improperly brought, no order for costs is normally made against the regulator.[508]

505 NMO 2001 art 9(2)(b).

506 NMC *Character and health decision-making guidance* (October 2015).

507 *Doherty v Nursing and Midwifery Council* [2017] EWCA Civ 1344.

508 *Walker v Law Society* [2007] EWCA Civ 233.

CHAPTER 6

The Health and Care Professions Council

continued

Key points

- *Regulator:* Health and Care Professions Council (HCPC)
- *Professions regulated:* 16 including physiotherapists, paramedics and radiographers
- *Common sources of referral:* Patients, employers, police
- *Type of proceedings:* Fitness to practise
- *Relevant legislation:* Health and Social Work Professions Order (HSWPO) 2001 SI 2002 No 254
- *Fitness to Practise Rules:* Health and Care Professions Council (Investigating Committee) (Procedure) Rules 2003 (Schedule to SI No 1574); Health and Care Professions Council (Conduct and Competence Committee) (Procedure) Rules 2003 (Schedule to SI 2003 No 1575); Health and Care Professions Council (Health Committee) (Procedure) Rules 2003 (Schedule to SI 2003 No 1576)
- *Two-stage process:* Investigation and hearing
- *Investigating Committee:* Yes (HCPC (Investigating Committee) Rules 2003)
- *Hearing panels:* Conduct and Competence Committee or Health Committee
- *Key documents: Standards of performance, conduct and ethics* (2016) (apply to all registrants); *Standards of proficiency* (specific to each profession)
- *Location:* Main hearing centre: Health and Care Professions Tribunal Service, Kennington, London. Panels also sit outside London
- *Notice of hearing provision:* HCPC (Investigating Committee) Rules 2003 r5
- *Case management provisions:* HCPC (Investigating Committee) Rules 2003 r7
- *Procedure before a Fitness to Practise Panel:* HCPC (Investigating Committee) Rules 2003 r8; HCPC (Conduct and Competence Committee) Rules 2003 r10; and HCPC (Health Committee) Rules 2003 r10
- *Test:* Whether fitness to practise is impaired by reason of (in summary) a) misconduct; b) lack of competence; c) criminal conviction or caution; d) physical or mental health; e) determination by another regulator (HSWPO 2001 art 22(1)(a))
- *Interim order power:* Yes: interim conditions of practice or interim suspension (HSWPO 2001 art 31) heard by Interim Orders Panel
- *Interim order guidance:* Practice note on interim orders
- *General composition for final hearings:* Three-member panels, minimum one lay partner and one from the relevant profession
- *How to address panel:* Generally seated and 'Sir'/'Madam'
- *Independent legal assessor:* Yes
- *Evidence:* HCPC (Investigating Committee) (Procedure) Rules 2003 r8; HCPC (Conduct and Competence Committee) (Procedure) Rules 2003 r10; and HCPC (Health Committee) (Procedure) Rules 2003 r10; civil admissibility plus other evidence where necessary to protect the public

- *Half-time submission provision:* None specific, but permitted
- Sanction provisions: HSWPO 2001 art 29
- *Sanction documents: Indicative sanctions policy*
- *Review hearings:* HSWPO 2001 art 30
- *Restoration hearings:* HSWPO 2001 art 33
- *Appeal rule:* HSWPO 2001 art 38
- *Costs:* No general provision

Introduction

Establishment

6.1 The Health Professions Council (HPC) was first established in April 2002[1] as a successor to the Council for the Professions Supplementary to Medicine (CPSM). The CPSM had been established in 1960 and by the time of its demise was responsible for regulating 12 different professions. As of 1 August 2012 the HCP underwent a name change to the present Health and Care Professions Council (HCPC) to reflect its expanding scope with the addition of social workers in England to its jurisdiction. It now regulates 16 professions, including all of those that previously came under the jurisdiction of the CPSM (albeit with a name change in one case).

Current issues

6.2 At the time of writing (January 2018) there are plans to remove social workers from the HCPC's jurisdiction and bring them under a new, social work specific regulator, Social Work England. The rationale for the proposed change was set out in a policy statement jointly issued in June 2016 by the Department of Health and the Department for Education. The statement suggests that the HCPC approach is designed to maintain minimum standards of public safety, rather than to drive up standards in the social work profession. The enabling legislation, the Children and Social Work Act 2017, received Royal Assent in April 2017, but the timetable for transfer of the regulatory function from the HCPC to Social Work England is currently certain but projected for September 2018.

6.3 A more comprehensive overhaul of healthcare regulation is currently the subject of consultation by the Department of Health. A paper entitled *Promoting professionalism, reforming regulation* was published at the end of October 2017, and a consultation exercise closed at the end of January 2018. The paper refers to inefficiencies in the current system of nine separate health care regulators and suggests that a smaller number (three to four) is likely to be favoured. The stated aims are to achieve greater consistency of powers, efficiency and a proportionate approach to fitness to practise (FTP) concerns.

1 Under the Health and Social Work Professions Order (HSWPO) 2001 SI No 2002 254.

6.4 From April 2017, the HCPC established the Health and Care Professions Tribunal Service (HCPTS). While the HCPTS is not a separate organisation from the HCPC, the aim of the change is to reinforce role separation and to reassure registrants that the decision-makers in fitness to practise final hearings are at arm's length from those who investigated the allegation. The change is similar to that introduced by the General Medical Council (GMC) when it established the Medical Practitioners' Tribunal Service (MPTS). Most hearings are now held in a dedicated tribunal centre in Kennington which is separate (although geographically very close to) the HCPC's offices. The HCTPS also has its own website, which is where many of the very helpful resources such as practice notes are now available.[2]

Jurisdictional reach

6.5 The 16 professions currently regulated by the HCPC are:

1) arts therapists;
2) biomedical scientists;
3) chiropodists/podiatrists;
4) clinical scientists;
5) dieticians;
6) hearing aid dispensers;
7) occupational therapists;
8) operating department practitioners;
9) orthoptists;
10) paramedics;
11) physiotherapists;
12) practitioner psychologists;
13) prosthetists/orthotists;
14) radiographers;
15) social workers in England;
16) speech and language therapists.

6.6 The total number of professionals who (ie in the period 1 April 2015 to 31 March 2016, the most recent for which statistics are available[3]) come under the jurisdiction of the HCPC is in excess of 341,000 and the size of the individual professions ranges from the relatively small such as hearing aid dispensers (2442) and orthoptists (1,385) to the much more familiar physiotherapists (51,662) and paramedics (22,380). The largest profession numerically is social workers at 93,341. All of the professions have at least one legally protected title, and the HCPC regards it as part of its remit to prosecute cases of individuals infringing the relevant provisions.

6.7 In common with many of the other healthcare regulators, the HCPC's primary function is protection of the public, and it fulfils this by setting and publishing standards of proficiency for each of the registered professions as well as standards of conduct, performance and ethics that apply to all registrants, and by considering complaints against registrants.

2 See www.hcpts-uk.org/.

3 HCPC *Fitness to practise annual report 2016.*

6.8 As with other healthcare regulators, the HCPC's regulatory work is overseen by the Professional Standards Authority (PSA). In summary, the PSA has the power to challenge any fitness to practise decision of the HCPC (and of the other healthcare regulators it oversees) that it considers to be insufficient to protect the public[4] in the High Court or Court of Session.[5]

6.9 Complaints against registrants fall within the HCPC's jurisdiction, notwithstanding that the matters giving rise to the complaint occurred outside the UK, or that they pre-dated the registrant's registration.[6]

Approach to regulation

6.10 In its fitness to practise function, the HCPC adopts the same test as most other healthcare regulators: that a registrant's fitness to practise is impaired. Impairment can be alleged on the grounds of misconduct, lack of competence, physical or mental health, criminal conviction or caution or a determination of impairment by another health or social care regulator. The HCPC also has powers to investigate allegations of fraudulent or incorrect entry on the register.[7] Case-law from other regulatory bodies including the MPTS and Nursing and Midwifery Council (NMC) is applicable to decisions of the HCPC.

6.11 Again, in line with most of the other healthcare regulators, the regime followed by the HCPC involves complaints from whatever source (usually either patients or service users, or employers or former employers of the registrant in question) being initially referred to an Investigating Committee Panel which will consider, on the basis of the written complaint and any written response from the registrant, whether there is a case to answer. If there is, the case is referred to either the Conduct and Competence Committee (CCC) or the Health Committee, depending on the nature of the allegation.

6.12 After investigation (which can take many months, and in some cases years) a panel of the relevant committee will be convened to hear the complaint. It is upon this stage of the process that this chapter will primarily focus.

6.13 The matters covered in para 6.69 and onwards apply to health and conviction cases as well as to misconduct and competence cases. Matters specific to health and conviction cases are covered at paras 6.90–6.92 and 6.85–6.89 respectively.

Sources of law

6.14 The HCPC was established by the Health and Social Work Professions Order 2001 (HSWPO 2001),[8] which was made under the Health Act 1999 s60. HSWPO 2001 has been amended since its original enactment and,

4 Pursuant to NHS Reform and Health Care Professions Act 2002 s29(4) (as amended by the Professional Standards Authority for Health and Social Care (References to Court) Order 2015).

5 NHS Reform and Health Care Professions Act 2002 s29.

6 HSWPO 2001 art 22(3).

7 HSWPO 2001 art 22(1) and (2).

8 SI 2002 No 254.

helpfully, the HCPC website[9] contains a link to a consolidated version which includes all amendments up to October 2016. Although the website warns that this version is an internal working document and has no official status, it is plainly an extremely useful resource for registrants and representatives.

6.15 HSWPO 2001 covers all matters relating to the establishment of the HCPC, including the establishment and maintenance of the register and the HCPC's educational functions. The main provisions relating to fitness to practise are contained in Part V.

6.16 The specific rules governing the relevant committees are contained in:

- Health Professions Council (Practice Committees and Miscellaneous Amendments) Rules 2009;[10]
- Health Professions Council (Investigating Committee) (Procedure) Rules 2003;[11]
- Health Professions Council (Conduct and Competence Committee) (Procedure) Rules 2003;[12] and
- Health and Care Professions Council (Health Committee) (Procedure) Rules 2003.[13] Again there is a consolidated version on the HCPC's website which includes amendments to the rules up to October 2016.[14]

6.17 In addition to the statutory provisions set out above, the HCPC publishes a number of practice notes on matters of particular interest (for example, on making a finding of impairment and its indicative sanctions policy). Many of these contain references to relevant authorities and are a helpful starting point for registrants facing proceedings and representatives. All current practice notes are available on the HCPTS website.[15]

Fitness to practise – general and pre-hearing matters

Referrals

6.18 As indicated earlier, referrals to the HCPC can come from any source, but in the main come from individual patients or service users or their families, and from employers or former employers of the registrant in question. The HCPC annual report 2016 shows that 42.8 per cent of complaints came from members of the public and 25.2 per cent from employers (presumably including former employers).[16]

9 See www.hcpc-uk.org/aboutus/legislation/orders/.

10 Schedule to Health Professions Council (Practice Committees and Miscellaneous Amendments) Rules Order of Council 2009 SI No 1355.

11 Schedule to Health Professions Council (Investigating Committee) (Procedure) Rules Order of Council 2003 SI No 1574.

12 Schedule to Health Professions Council (Conduct and Competence Committee) (Procedure) Rules Order of Council 2003 SI No 1575.

13 Schedule to Health Professions Council (Health Committee) (Procedure) Rules Order of Council 2003 SI No 1576.

14 See www.hcpc-uk.org/Assets/documents/10004785HCPCCONSOLIDATEDPRACTICECOMMITTEERULES(July2104).pdf.

15 See www.hcpts-uk.org/legislation/rules/practicenotes.

16 HCPC *Fitness to practise annual report 2016.*

6.19 Standard 9 of the standards of conduct, performance and ethics,[17] which apply to all registrants, provides that they are under a duty to inform the HCPC if they are cautioned or charged with a criminal offence, have been the subject of a finding by another regulator or had any restriction placed on their practice by an employer, due to concerns about conduct or competence. The HCPC has powers under HSWPO 2001 art 22(6) to investigate a matter even if a complaint has not been raised in the usual way and these powers may be used in cases of self-referral, or where information has come from other sources, such as media reports.

6.20 No particular form is required for a complaint to be made to the HCPC, but it has standards of acceptance that require the complaint to:

- be in writing;
- identify the registrant concerned;
- provide sufficient detail of the concern and the surrounding circumstances for the registrant to understand and respond.

6.21 The HCPC states that it will not normally act on complaints that are made anonymously given its commitment to openness and transparency.

Historic complaints

> Article 6 (right to fair trial) of the European Convention on Human Rights (ECHR) and domestic case-law confer a right to a hearing within a reasonable time, however to stay proceedings is an exceptional course and delay is not a ground unless there is material prejudice to the extent that no fair trial is possible.

6.22 Unlike some other regulators, the HCPC's rules do not impose any time limit for the bringing of complaints, but both domestic case-law and the ECHR confer a right to the speedy and just resolution of disputes. While delay may, in certain circumstances, constitute a breach of Article 6 rights, mere delay is insufficient to stop proceedings. In the case of *R (Gibson) v General Medical Council*,[18] the court held that:

> . . . both the legitimate expectation of complainants and the public confidence in the regulation of the medical profession require that the complaint should, in the absence of some special and sufficient reason, be publicly investigated. It would undermine that important principle if mere unreasonable delay, absent prejudice, were to require a stay to be granted.

6.23 For the purposes of the ECHR, time runs from when a person is subjected to a 'charge', meaning that they are officially notified of or substantially affected by proceedings. In regulatory proceedings this is likely to be the date of the letter notifying the registrant of the allegations.

6.24 For a fuller discussion of the relevant authorities on this issue, and of the applicability of Article 6 to regulatory proceedings, see chapter 1.

17 HCPC *Standards of conduct, performance and ethics* (2016).

18 [2004] EWHC 2781 (Admin).

Double jeopardy

> Regulatory proceedings need not be stayed pending the outcome of criminal proceedings unless there are exceptional circumstances such as an impossible workload from which the defendant can demonstrate serious prejudice or injustice. Arguments regarding double jeopardy, privilege and publicity are otherwise unlikely to succeed.

6.25 In *Mote v Secretary of State for Work and Pensions and another*[19] the Court of Appeal reviewed the matter of concurrent proceedings and reaffirmed that the civil court continues to enjoy the discretion to adjourn but that civil proceedings could frequently continue *without* prejudicing the criminal trial. The criminal courts have the power to stay proceedings as an abuse of process and to control the admission of evidence. The fact that D may have to disclose his or her criminal defence during civil proceedings causes no prejudice since he or she is expected to disclose this in any event. For a fuller discussion of the authorities on this matter see chapter 1 at para 1.275.

Legal representation

6.26 A registrant is entitled to be represented by counsel, solicitor or other representative of his or her choice. In practice many registrants before the HCPC have legal representation provided through their trade union or professional body.

6.27 Once a representative has notified the HCPC that he or she is 'on the record', the case manager assigned to the case will normally be accommodating about arranging hearing dates to suit the representative's availability.

6.28 For a fuller discussion of the legal issues relating to representation see chapter 2.

Impartiality of the panel

> The question is whether the fair-minded and informed observer, having considered the facts, would conclude that there was a real possibility that the tribunal was biased.[20]

6.29 ECHR Article 6 provides the right to adjudication by an independent and impartial tribunal. Independence means separated from the executive and from the parties. Impartiality means both subjective impartiality (the lack of actual bias) and objective impartiality (the lack of the appearance of bias).

6.30 Currently the HCPC, like most healthcare regulators, appoints both the prosecutors and the adjudicating panels to judge cases. The fact that disciplinary proceedings against registrants are determined by a body which includes members of the same profession does not of itself offend

19 [2008] CP Rep 13.

20 *Porter v Magill* [2001] UKHL 67, [2002] 2 AC 357, at para 103, per Lord Hope.

the requirement of 'independence' in Article 6(1): see *Stefan v UK*[21] and accords with the principle that a governing body is best placed to judge what is right for its profession. For a fuller discussion of the applicable authorities on this point see chapter 1.

6.31 The HCPC's move in establishing the HCPTS is plainly designed to emphasise separation between the investigation and prosecution of complaints and the panel conducting the final hearing. As previously noted however, the HCPTS is part of the HCPC's organisation.

The role of the legal assessor

6.32 Panels of both the CCC and the Health Committee sit with a legal assessor, who must be a qualified lawyer.[22] The function of the legal assessor is to advise the panel on matters of law and procedure. Although often called upon to assist in the drafting of the panel's reasons for its decision, the legal assessor does not participate in the decision making itself. Legal assessors at the HCPC are experienced in regulatory law (many also sit as legal assessors on other regulatory bodies such as the NMC) and are a helpful source of information for the novice representative.

6.33 It is customary to ensure that the HCPC's representative is also present when a registrant's representative (and vice versa) wishes to speak with the legal assessor outside the hearing.

6.34 If any issues of admissibility of evidence cannot be resolved by agreement between the representatives a joint approach to the legal assessor prior to commencement of the hearing is advisable. Similarly, legal assessors welcome advance notification (on the day of the hearing but before the panel has formally convened) of any applications (for example, for the hearing to be held in private or for an adjournment) prior to the application being made.

6.35 For a fuller discussion of the role of the legal assessor see chapter 2.

Investigating Committee

Procedure

6.36 Once a complaint has been made to the fitness to practise department, if it meets the standards of acceptance, it will be allocated to a case manager. The case manager will notify the registrant that concerns have been raised, and may indicate that further investigations are to be carried out. Further investigation at this stage normally involves contacting the original complainant to seek further details or documentation.

6.37 Once this process is complete, the registrant will be notified of the allegation, as drafted by the HCPC, and provided with copies of all supporting documents. The registrant is invited to respond in writing and will normally have 28 days to do so, although this is often extended at the request of the registrant.

21 [1998] EHRR CD 130.

22 Health Professions Council (Functions of Assessors) Rules Order of Council 2003 SI No 1577 Sch 1.

6.38 The original complaint, together with any other material obtained in the course of investigation and any response from the registrant, is then considered by a panel of the Investigating Committee. Panels comprise three members, including one from the same profession as the registrant and at least one lay member (ie not registered with the HCPC). Panels meet in private and consider whether, if the matter were to proceed to a hearing, the allegations would be likely to be proven. The test applied by panels is whether there is a 'realistic prospect' of establishing that the registrant's fitness to practise is impaired. The realistic prospect test is applied to each part of the allegation ie facts, statutory ground and current impairment.

6.39 The panel can decide that there is a case to answer, in which case the matter is referred forward for a hearing, either to the CCC or the Health Committee, or that there is no case to answer, in which case no further action is taken other than to notify the registrant and complainant. Alternatively the panel may decide that more investigation is required. There is no right of appeal against a decision of the Investigating Committee panel.

6.40 In cases where they find no case to answer panels have the power to issue 'learning points' to a registrant, this is normally where the panel considers that there would be a realistic prospect of proving facts and statutory ground, but not of establishing current impairment. The annual report states that this power has been used on 56 occasions in 2015/16, up from 50 occasions the previous year. The HCPC states that the use of this power assists in taking a proportionate approach to cases where a registrant's conduct or competence may have fallen short of the required standards and enables it to provide advice to the registrant concerned as to how he or she can learn from the event.

6.41 For the most part panels do not regard it as possible to resolve conflicts of fact on the basis of the written complaint and submissions, so cases that turn on substantial conflicts of fact tend to be referred forward to a hearing in order that witnesses can be heard and their reliability and credibility tested.

6.42 In the year 2015/16, 787 cases were considered by ICPs, of which 48 were considered twice as the panel had requested further information. In 63 per cent of cases it was found that there was a case to answer.

Register entry allegations

6.43 The Investigating Committee has jurisdiction to consider allegations that an entry in the register has been fraudulently procured or incorrectly made.[23] Such cases normally relate to whether a registrant has the appropriate qualifications to entitle him or her to be a registered practitioner of the profession in question. In such cases the Investigating Committee will send a notice to the registrant who may request that the matter be considered at a hearing. If the registrant does not request a hearing the committee may hold one of its own volition.[24]

23 HSWPO 2001 art 22(1)(b).

24 HCPC (Investigating Committee) Rules 2003 r6(1)(a)(ii).

6.44 If a hearing is to be held, the registrant will be provided with a minimum of 28 days' notice, and has the right to attend and be represented as in other fitness to practise hearings.

Interim orders

> Interim orders may be made if they are necessary to protect the public or in the public interest or in the registrant's own interest prior to the substantive hearing on fitness.
>
> The threshold for an interim order is a high one because a registrant may be temporarily suspended or be subject to temporary conditions that limit or prevent his or her practice.
>
> No judgment is made regarding the facts of the allegation but the panel must be satisfied that, on a fair analysis, there *may* be a prima facie case. The registrant should be given the opportunity to make representations and may adduce evidence.

6.45 Under HSWPO 2001 art 31 the Investigating Committee and the practice committees have the power to apply to a panel of the relevant committee for an interim order. Such applications are made in cases where the severity of the allegations is such that the registrant may pose a risk to the public if permitted to continue to practise without restriction pending final disposal.

6.46 Interim orders fall into two categories: interim conditions of practice and interim suspension orders, and in either case may be made for a maximum period of 18 months. If the case has still not been disposed of within that period, the HCPC may apply to the High Court to extend the order.[25]

6.47 The test that a panel will consider in cases where an interim order is applied for is a high one: it must be necessary for the protection of the public, otherwise in the public interest or in the interests of the registrant.

6.48 The courts have considered the issue of wider public interest in this context. In *R (Shiekh) v General Dental Council*[26] (GDC), S, who had been given a suspended prison sentence for fraud, posed no direct risk to the safety of the public. The case concerned his character, not his clinical ability. Davis J overturned the GDC's suspension, finding that:

> It is a very serious thing indeed for a dentist or a doctor to be suspended. It is serious in many cases just because of the impact on that person's right to earn a living. It is serious in all cases because of the detriment to him in reputational terms. Accordingly, it is . . . likely to be a relatively rare case where a suspension order will be made on an interim basis on the ground that it is in the public interest.

6.49 The fact that the allegations do not raise issues of clinical competence does not mean that an interim order will never be required. In *Bradshaw v*

25 HSWPO 2001 art 31(8).
26 [2007] EWHC 2972 (Admin).

General Medical Council[27] a former Civil Aviation Authority medical officer was suspended on grounds of risk to the public, public interest and in his own interest. There was no criticism of his clinical competence, rather the case was one of dishonesty surrounding the investigation of an alleged affair with a colleague. While HHJ Kaye QC commented that absent any clinical or patient issues, suspension for an affair alone might well be disproportionate, here B had lied to an investigation, falsely accused a colleague and fabricated evidence. Despite there being no issues of clinical competence, the GMC was rightly concerned regarding the public perception of doctors and, of the risk that B may be persuaded to lie if he was accused of something by a patient.

6.50 For a fuller discussion of the authorities on interim orders, see chapter 2.

6.51 In cases where the application is made on grounds of protection of the public, it may be possible to oppose the application on the basis that an interim order is not necessary. Such arguments are most likely to succeed where, for example, the allegation relates to issues of competence and the registrant remains employed by an employer who is aware of the HCPC proceedings and who has in place measures to monitor the registrant's performance.

6.52 HSWPO 2001 art 31(5) requires that a registrant be given the opportunity to appear and be heard before any interim order is made. Due to the nature of interim orders, applications tend to be made at short notice, but it is essential that a registrant attends to give evidence and make submissions if an order is to be avoided or any restrictions on his or her practice are to be minimised. There are no specific provisions relating to notification to the registrant, but normal practice is around seven days. If a registrant wishes to attend a hearing but is unable to do so on the date specified, an application to adjourn may be made under the applicable rule,[28] but it must be borne in mind that the nature of interim orders is such that repeated or lengthy adjournments are unlikely to be granted.

6.53 If an adjournment application is to be made, it will be important to do so as soon as possible after notification is received and to provide as much information as possible about the reason why the adjournment is sought. Specific issues (such as the registrant's line manager being on leave for a period of days or weeks, from whom evidence about current supervision arrangements will be provided), are likely to be more persuasive than a vague reference to the registrant needing more time to gather evidence.

6.54 Supporting evidence from an employer in cases where the allegation relates to competence, confirming knowledge of the HCPC proceedings and setting out monitoring mechanisms, may also be determinative.

6.55 In health cases, an up-to-date report from a relevant medical practitioner may well be of assistance if it confirms good compliance with a medication regime or other forms of treatment so as to indicate that the health condition is sufficiently controlled.

27 [2010] EWHC 1296 (Admin).

28 HCPC (Investigating Committee) Rules 2003 r8(f).

6.56 Panels are required to consider conditions of practice before resorting to a suspension order, so if an order seems likely to be imposed it is worth considering what kind of conditions might be suggested that would adequately protect the public. The kind of interim conditions that may be considered include:

- not to practise a particular form of treatment;
- not to practise on a particular group of patients or service users;
- not to practise a particular form of treatment without a chaperone;
- not to practise above a given level of seniority;
- not to practise without a specified level of supervision (this is often tied to a requirement for the registrant to provided evidence or reports periodically to the HCPC);
- to notify the HCPC if changing employers.

6.57 Representatives will need to give considerable thought to the kind of conditions that might be suggested in the alternative to submissions opposing the application for a suspension order. Supporting evidence to show willingness to comply on the part of the registrant and any other party (for example, an employer) must also be adduced.

6.58 A 'bank' of commonly used conditions is annexed to the HCPTS' practice note *Drafting fitness to practise decisions*, which is a useful resource for representatives and is available on the HCPC website.[29] The bank conditions may be modified for application in a particular case.

6.59 Interim orders must be reviewed within six months of being made and every three months thereafter.[30] Once an interim order is in place, if the registrant does not require any change to conditions, or if there are no good grounds to apply for the removal of a suspension order, it is not necessary for the registrant to attend all review hearings. It is important, however, that registrants are seen to be engaging with the regulatory process and accordingly in most cases it will be appropriate for a letter to be sent to the HCPC prior to the review confirming compliance and that the registrant does not oppose the continuation of the existing order.

6.60 A registrant who is subject to an interim order may make an application for it to be reviewed where new evidence has become available which is relevant to the order.[31] This provision is particularly useful in cases where the registrant's employment status has changed during the currency of the interim order (for example, by the receipt of an offer of new employment or on the conclusion of an employer's investigation under its own disciplinary procedure into substantially the same matters as are before the HCPC and where the registrant has been mainly or wholly exonerated of any wrongdoing). As with initial interim order hearings, a registrant seeking to vary conditions of practice or to have a suspension order replaced with conditions should ensure that he or she provides as much

29 See www.hcpts-uk.org/assets/documents/1000535BDraftingDecisions.pdf.

30 HSWPO 2001 art 31(6).

31 HSWPO 2001 art 31(6)(b).

supporting evidence as possible demonstrating how any risk to the public will be managed by the proposed conditions.

6.61 In all hearings relating to interim orders, the panel will not consider whether the allegations are proven, but plainly if there is good evidence that this is unlikely (for example, where an employer's disciplinary investigation has exonerated the registrant on substantially the same matters) this should be put before the panel.

6.62 The HCPC's *Fitness to practise annual report 2016* shows that interim orders were applied for in 89 cases, and granted in 78 of those, which amounts to only four per cent of the total number of cases being investigated in the same period. It appears from these figures that the HCPC uses these powers sparingly and the majority of cases do not require an interim order.

Responding to the Investigating Committee Panel

6.63 If assisting a registrant to draft a response to an allegation at this stage, it is important to address the specific allegations directly. If the matters alleged are so minor that even if proven they are unlikely to amount to misconduct or lack of competence, this should be strongly emphasised from the outset as this will be a key consideration for the panel. The best chance for a registrant at this stage lies in responding in such way as to indicate that no finding of impairment at a full hearing would be likely because of the minor nature of the matter(s) alleged.

6.64 Of course in many cases it is not possible to make such an argument with credibility. It should also be borne in mind that, although a registrant's written representations to the Investigating Committee are not as a matter of course put before a CCC or Health Committee panel at a full hearing, they can be in the event that the registrant gives evidence at the hearing that is inconsistent with the contents of the earlier submissions. Great care needs therefore to be taken that any factual assertions set out in the submissions are correct. Similarly, it is unhelpful to express patently unrealistic views: for example, that an allegation of serious dishonesty is unlikely, if proven to lead to a finding of misconduct or impairment.

6.65 In cases where there are conflicts of fact between the complainant and registrant, it is important to refer to and provide copies of any documents that support the registrant's account. Often this will be contemporaneous records such as treatment notes, but could also include written statements from witnesses. In deciding whether the allegations can be proven, the panel must consider significant persuasive evidence that would be likely to undermine the complainant's account.

6.66 In many cases, however, where allegations of a serious nature are raised it is highly likely that the Investigating Committee Panel will refer the matter on to the Conduct and Competence Committee or the Health Committee as appropriate. Registrants should be made aware of this likelihood at an early stage and also that the timescale for completion of the process can be extremely protracted. The relevant case manager should be able to give some idea of timescales in any given case but most take more than a year from referral to final disposal.

Mediation

6.67 There is provision under HSWPO 2001 art 26(6) for the Investigating Committee, having decided that there is a case to answer, to refer a case for mediation. This can either be undertaken by the committee itself[32] or be referred to screeners for the mediation.[33] Given the consensual nature of disposal by mediation, panels will only refer cases where they are satisfied that, whatever the outcome, no other steps are necessary to protect the public.

6.68 A practice note sets out the relevant considerations and indicates that mediation may be an appropriate disposal in the following: in minor cases not resulting in harm; where an apology could resolve the issue; in cases involving overcharging or over-servicing but where no fraud has taken place; in cases concerning management or contractual arrangements where there has been no impropriety; and in those involving poor communication which is insufficiently serious to involve risk to service users.

Allegations

> The particulars of the allegation and the facts upon which they are founded should be clear and settled in advance of any hearing.
>
> If in doubt, clarification and/or further and better particulars should be obtained.
>
> The panel may, having heard from both parties, amend either the allegation or the facts provided no injustice is caused but this should be the exception not the rule.

Procedure

6.69 When an Investigating Committee Panel finds that there is a case to answer and refers it to either the CCC or the Health Committee, the registrant will be informed and will be provided with brief reasons as to why the panel reached its decision.

6.70 At this point, the allegation will be in draft form, but is likely to be sufficiently close to the final version that the registrant can begin to prepare his or her response to it.

6.71 The allegation is set out in three parts:

1) first, the factual particulars (eg on a specified date the registrant failed to provide adequate care to patient A in that he or she failed to record the findings of his or her assessment and treatment);
2) second, the statutory ground (eg that the conduct set out above amounted to misconduct and/or lack of competence); and
3) third, that, by reason of the misconduct or lack of competence set out, the registrant's fitness to practise is impaired.

32 HSWPO 2001 art 26(6)(a).
33 HSWPO 2001 art 26(6)(b).

6.72 The HCPC's practice note on the standard of acceptance for allegations requires the nature of the impairment alleged to be stated (presumably a reference to the need to identify the statutory ground) and the events and circumstances giving rise to the allegation in sufficient detail for that registrant to be able to understand and respond to that allegation.

6.73 In most cases, the drafting is sufficiently clear for the registrant to understand the allegation and be able to respond, but if not, this should be raised at the earliest opportunity with the case manager. Sometimes the matter can be easily rectified (for example, by providing the identity of particular patients/service users) but if not it should be pursued well in advance of the final hearing.

6.74 In *R (Wheeler) v Assistant Commissioner House of the Metropolitan Police*[34] it was alleged that W had failed to carry out duties 'to an acceptable standard' thereby breaching the code of conduct. Stanley Burnton J said:

> Vagueness is a ground for judicial review if it leads to unfairness in the proceedings, and the danger with a vague charge is that the parties, and in particular the respondent, do not know with some precision what is alleged against them, and therefore are not fully able to address those matters in the course of a hearing.[35]

6.75 His Lordship commented that while the particulars of a charge may be refined following an initial draft, it should be sufficiently particularised well before the hearing for the respondent to disciplinary charges to know what it is alleged he failed to do and, in what respects he failed.

6.76 In *Roomi v General Medical Council*[36] Collins J allowed R's appeal against a finding of impairment by reason of deficient professional performance (ie lack of competence) on the grounds that the finding by the panel went beyond the allegations contained in the notice of hearing. During the case, R called evidence to show that he had taken steps to improve his skills which led the panel to conclude that the deficiencies identified in the notice had been remedied. However, the panel still made an adverse finding relying on managerial matters out-with the original allegations. His Lordship was critical both of the panel for going beyond the matters alleged and of the assessor for failing to advise them of their error.

6.77 The application of ECHR Article 6 may be relied upon if necessary to achieve the appropriate level of particularisation. Certain matters are required to be explicitly stated in the allegation, including dishonesty and sexual motivation. For a fuller discussion of the law relating to the drafting of allegations see chapter 1.

6.78 The practice committee rules[37] allow for allegations to be joined where it would be just to do so. Joinder can apply to allegations against a single registrant or multiple registrants. Joinder is usually considered where there is a connection between the allegations (and the registrants) as

34 [2008] EWHC 439 (Admin).

35 [2008] EWHC 439 (Admin) at [6].

36 [2009] EWHC 2188 (Admin).

37 HCPC (Investigating Committee) Rules 2003 rr4(8) and 6(7); HCPC (Health Committee) Rules 2003 and HCPC (Conduct and Competence Committee) Rules 2003 r5(4).

hearing them together can save time, costs and the need for prosecution witnesses to attend on more than one occasion.

6.79 Allegations against a single registrant will normally only be joined where they are:

- of the same or similar character;
- based on the same acts, events or course of dealing; or
- based on connected or related acts, events or courses of dealing.

6.80 Allegations against more than one registrant will only be joined where:

- the registrants are subject to the same allegation;
- there is evidence that the registrants acted in concert; or
- the allegations against the registrants are linked in time or by other factors, for example where:
  - the allegations concern participation in the same act, event or course of dealing (or any series of them);
  - the allegations are based upon connected or related acts, events or courses of dealing; or
  - the allegations relate to actions taken in furtherance of a common enterprise.

6.81 Even where joinder appears to be appropriate based on the nature of the allegations, there may be other reasons why the discretion to do so should not be exercised. For example, where one registrant has failed to respond and joinder might cause delay or unfairness in dealing with another registrant or where it is apparent that registrants will present antagonistic or mutually exclusive defences.

6.82 In practice registrants are given the opportunity to oppose or consent to a proposal to join one or more allegations and representatives will need to give active consideration to what, if any, prejudice the registrant may suffer as a result. Many registrants find the lengthy period of uncertainty awaiting resolution of allegations to be particularly stressful, and the desirability of a quicker outcome is one of the factors to be taken into consideration.

6.83 If allegations are joined however this is not necessarily the end of the matter as panels have a similar discretion to sever in appropriate cases.

6.84 There is a practice note on joinder (also dealing with severance) available on the HCPTS's website.[38]

Conviction cases

6.85 HSWPO 2001 art 22(1)(a)(iii) provides that the HCPC has jurisdiction to consider cases where it is alleged that a registrant's fitness to practise is impaired by reason of a criminal conviction or caution. The procedure for dealing with such cases is broadly the same as for those on the other statutory grounds.

6.86 Conviction includes those which occur in a court outside the UK, but where the offence is recognised as a crime in the UK, as well as convictions by a court martial.[39] Binding over and discharge do not amount to

38 See www.hcpts-uk.org/assets/documents/10005361Joinder.pdf.

39 HSWPO 2001 art 22(2).

convictions, but the HCPC may in any event investigate the circumstances that led to the bind-over or discharge and deal with it as an allegation of misconduct.

6.87 The practice committee rules provide[40] that a certified copy of the certificate of conviction (or in Scotland, an extract conviction) is proof of the conviction and of the fact upon which it was based. Accordingly, in such cases it will not be open to registrants to suggest that they did not commit the offence in question, and representations will need to focus on any mitigating circumstances, insight, remorse and reparation.

6.88 Community sentences can present particular problems in light of the decision in *Council for the Regulation of Healthcare Professionals v General Dental Council and Fleischman*[41] as, if the conviction was for a serious offence and the sentence is still being served at the time of consideration by a fitness to practise panel, the registrant should not normally be permitted to resume practice until the sentence has been satisfactorily completed. In light of this unhelpful principle, representatives may wish to seek an adjournment of cases where a community sentence is ongoing until such time as it has been completed. For a more detailed discussion of the law on this point see chapter 3 at para 3.214.

6.89 There is a practice note on conviction and caution allegations which contains helpful information and which is available on the HCPTS website.[42]

Health cases

6.90 One of the statutory grounds under the HSWPO 2001[43] is impairment by reason of the registrant's physical or mental health. Such cases will be considered by the Investigating Committee initially and will, if there is a case to answer, then normally be referred to the Health Committee. The Health Committee rules and hearings are broadly similar to those of the Conduct and Competence Committee (CCC), however panels must include at least one registered medical practitioner[44] and may receive advice from a medical assessor.

6.91 Cases can be referred by the Health Committee to the CCC[45] where it appears that the allegation would be better dealt with by the CCC. The Health Committee's consideration is then suspended pending consideration by the CCC. Similarly, the CCC can refer cases to the Health Committee where it appears that it would be better dealt with by the Health Committee[46] and parallel provisions apply regarding suspension of consideration by the CCC.

40 HCPC (Investigating Committee) Rules 2003 r8((1)(d); HCPC (Conduct and Competence Committee) Rules 2003 and HCPC (Health Committee) Rules 2003 r10(1)(d).

41 [2005] EWHC 87 (QB).

42 See www.hcpts-uk.org/assets/documents/10005357Convictions.pdf.

43 HSWPO 2001 art 22(1)(a)(iv).

44 HSWPO 2001 Sch 1 para 19(6)(b).

45 HCPC (Health Committee) Rules 2003 r4(1).

46 HCPC (Conduct and Competence Committee) Rules 2003 r4(1).

6.92 A significant matter for representatives to consider in cases where referral to the Health Committee may be appropriate is that in health cases a striking-off order is not available as a sanction until the registrant has been suspended or subject to a conditions of practice order for a period of two years preceding the date of the decision to strike off.[47] Transfer to the Health Committee may not be agreed, however, in cases where the allegation is sufficiently serious that strike off may be the appropriate sanction.[48] An application for a case to be referred to the Health Committee should be made at an early stage in proceedings and well in advance of any hearing date being fixed, and should be supported by evidence from a medical practitioner.

Determination by another regulator

6.93 The HCPC also has jurisdiction to consider allegations on the ground of a determination by a body responsible for the regulation of a health or social care profession that a registrant's fitness to practise is impaired.[49] In practice, the approach to dealing with such cases will be similar to that applying to conviction cases.

6.94 Referral by another regulator does not infringe the principle of double jeopardy – see chapter 1 for a fuller discussion of the law.

Disposal by consent

6.95 The HCPC has discretion to deal with certain cases by consent. The HCPTS practice note[50] indicates that it will only be considered where the appropriate level of public protection is being secured and where doing it would not be detrimental to the wider public interest. Disposal by consent does not affect the panel's powers or the range of sanctions available, but may be used to expedite a case where a contested hearing is not necessary or desirable. A consent order is drawn up which is then presented to a panel, which may accept or reject it. In the event that a consent order is rejected by a panel, the matter will then proceed to a contested hearing and any admissions made by the registrant in the course of the attempted disposal by consent will be treated by the HCPC as being 'without prejudice' and will not be referred to at the contested hearing without the registrant's consent.

6.96 A registrant is not permitted to resign from the register while subject to an allegation or to a conditions of practice or suspension order,[51] but the HCPC can enter into a voluntary removal agreement allowing him or her to do so if it is satisfied that doing so will adequately protect the public. The terms of such an agreement will be similar to those applying had the registrant been struck off.

47 HSWPO 2001 art 29(6).

48 *Crabbie v General Medical Council* [2002] UKPC 45.

49 HSWPO 2001 art 22(1)(a)(v).

50 See www.hcpts-uk.org/assets/documents/1000535ADisposalbyConsent.pdf.

51 HSWPO 2001 art 11(3) and HPC (Registration and Fees) Rules 2003 r12(3).

Evidence

> While there is a duty to prevent inequality of arms, there is no positive duty on a disciplinary body to gather evidence to assist the registrant.
>
> To allege unfairness under HSWPO 2001 art 6(3)(b) a complainant must demonstrate that a duty exists, that it has been breached and this has caused an inequality of arms.
>
> Each case will depend on its own facts.

6.97 The HCPC has standard directions for case management, which provide that it will serve a copy of documents it intends to rely upon at the final hearing at least 42 days before the date of the hearing.

6.98 The HCPC bundles of documents for hearings are separated into two sections – one (core bundle) containing key documents such as the notice of hearing, certificate of service and witness statements; and the other (exhibits bundle) containing other documents exhibited by the witnesses.

6.99 The HCPC standard directions require the registrant to provide any documents he or she intends to rely upon 28 days before the date of the hearing.

6.100 In practice, many registrants are unable to comply with the 28-day rule, and extensions of time are frequently given. In cases where a significant volume of further documents is to be relied upon by the registrant, however, it is important to provide a paginated, indexed bundle sufficiently far in advance for it to be sent out to panel members in good time before the hearing.

6.101 In *R (Johnson) v Professional Conduct Committee of the Nursing and Midwifery Council*,[52] J applied for judicial review of the Professional Conduct Committee's refusal to stay proceedings on grounds (among others) of a failure to obtain relevant documents and other evidence. The NMC had agreed to do what they considered reasonable to obtain various records but they refused to obtain those they regarded them as irrelevant. Beatson J held that the ECHR Article 6 right to adequate facilities to prepare and equality of arms was case/fact-specific. There was a balance to be struck between the parties to ensure fairness. This did not include a positive duty on the part of the regulator to gather evidence for the defence, provided the registrant was not at a disadvantage in having to gather the evidence he or she wished to deploy.

6.102 For a fuller discussion of the law relating to regulators' duty to disclose evidence see chapter 1.

6.103 Character references do not need to be provided in advance of the hearing as they generally become relevant at the sanctions stage of proceedings, if a finding of impairment is made. Professional testimonials, however, should be provided if possible before the hearing, as this evidence is considered at the misconduct/impairment stage, and can be relevant at the facts stage as it may be argued that a practitioner of good character has less propensity to commit acts of misconduct. In practice,

52 [2008] EWHC 885 (Admin).

panels do not decline to consider evidence of this nature even if it is provided on the day of the hearing, but representatives should remember that this may delay proceedings, irritate the panel and generally not set the case off on a good footing, so should be avoided if at all possible. Clearly how much importance to place on this depends on the number and nature of the documents involved and any reasons why it has not been possible to provide them in advance, which should be brought to the panel's attention.

6.104 The standard directions also provide for a notice to admit facts to be served on the registrant at any time up until 21 days before the hearing. The practice note specifies that if a notice to admit facts is not responded to within 14 days indicating that the specified facts are disputed, the registrant will be taken to admit the facts set out in the notice. Care must therefore be taken to ensure that any such notice is responded to within the timescale.

6.105 Similarly, a notice to admit documents or witness statement(s) may also be served by the HCPC and must be responded to by the registrant in the same terms. It should be noted, however, that any admissions made through this process may be permitted to be amended or withdrawn where it is just to do so. This provision should not be relied upon though as, if a registrant has inadvertently admitted witness statements, witnesses may have been de-warned in the light of the registrant's admissions and late withdrawal may jeopardise the hearing date (or, potentially, lead to a refusal of the request to withdraw).

6.106 Generally registrants find the protracted timescale these cases take to reach a final hearing extremely stressful, and accordingly are keen for the matter to be progressed as speedily as possible, so it is important to avoid any action or omission that could inadvertently delay the final hearing.

Pleas

6.107 Irrespective of the notice to admit facts procedure, registrants are invariably asked at the outset of the final hearing to indicate their response to the allegation. In practice, the panel is likely to have prior indication from the registrant's witness statement that will have been provided together with documents in advance of the hearing. Admissions can be made in respect of any or all of the factual particulars, to the statutory grounds and to impairment.

6.108 In some cases, the registrant's position may be that while the factual particulars are not substantially disputed, there is a part of the wording that they object to. The most common circumstance is where particulars are drafted as 'on a specified date you failed to . . .'. The registrant may accept that he or she did not do the act in question, but not that it amounted to any failure on his or her part. In these circumstances panels are usually receptive to an indication of the position in precise terms at the start of the hearing. While any objection to the wording of a factual particular will prevent its being formally recorded as an admission, panels nevertheless find it helpful to have such matters clarified at the outset as it assists them in judging what matters are in dispute.

6.109 In practice, admitting to a particular that states that a registrant failed to take the specified action is not prejudicial to his or her position, as the issue of failure is really best addressed at the next stage of misconduct or lack of competence.

6.110 It is common practice for admissions to be partial – for example, some factual particulars but not others, and that some of those admitted particulars amount to misconduct and/or lack of competence but that others do not.

6.111 If significant factual admissions are to be made, it is helpful if this can be indicated to the HCPC at an early stage as it will ensure that witnesses are not warned to attend unnecessarily, which can reduce the overall time estimate for the hearing. More importantly though, registrants will gain credit in the later stages of the process if they have made admissions. Of course this does not suggest that registrants should admit to something they do not agree with, but careful scrutiny of the factual particulars will often reveal some that can without any difficulty be admitted, even if misconduct and/or lack of competence is not.

6.112 Pragmatism is appreciated by HCPC panels, and if the factual particulars that are to be admitted are of a serious and/or widespread nature then admissions in relation to misconduct/lack of competence and impairment should be considered. At sanctions stage, strike-off is not initially available in cases of lack of competence so if, as is often the case, an allegation is put on the alternative grounds of misconduct and/or lack of competence it is open to a registrant (and may be beneficial) to admit lack of competence but not misconduct in respect of the same factual particulars.

6.113 In common with the other main healthcare regulators, impairment is to be judged as at the time of the hearing (not at the time of the matters giving rise to the allegations) so in some cases it is possible to argue persuasively that, even though standards of conduct or competence were breached at the time in question, those deficiencies have since been rectified. This is most commonly seen in lack of competence cases where the registrant has subsequently undertaken further training or had supervision such that the level of competence has in the meantime reached the requisite standard. It may also succeed in cases of misconduct where the conduct in question was a one-off in an otherwise distinguished professional career, particularly where accompanied by expressions of remorse and insight.

6.114 For a full discussion of the law on misconduct, lack of competence and impairment see chapter 1.

Witnesses

> The panel has the discretion to proceed in the absence of a witness and to admit hearsay evidence but the decision to proceed must be taken with 'the utmost care and caution' and only after full consideration of the competing interests with emphasis on those of the registrant.
>
> There must be compelling reasons to deprive a registrant of the opportunity to cross-examine a witness – this all the more so if the case or its consequences are serious.

General rules and procedures

6.115 The HCPC will call whichever witnesses it considers necessary to prove the case (taking account of any prior notification from the registrant of facts or statements that will be admitted). Where a statement is agreed by the registrant, it will often, though not always, be considered unnecessary to call the witness, but simply to rely on the written statement. In some cases where the witness in question is key to the matter (for example, a manager who has conducted an investigation under an employer's own disciplinary procedure) they will be required to attend the hearing and give live evidence notwithstanding admissions by the registrant.

6.116 Hearsay evidence can be adduced at hearings,[53] and as in other courts, if statements are not agreed but the witness still does not appear in person, the panel will be advised by the legal assessor about the weight it can place upon their evidence given that it has not been tested in cross-examination, a matter the registrant's representative will need to address in submissions at the facts stage.

6.117 In *Nursing and Midwifery Council v Ogbonna*,[54] O faced three serious charges, all of which were found proved and she was struck off the register. On count one, the NMC placed sole reliance upon the statement of O's line manager P, with whom she was not on good terms. P did not give evidence, rather her statement was adduced as hearsay despite O's wish to cross-examine her. P had moved to the Caribbean. The NMC said that P was not available, even though they had made no enquiry regarding her availability, and said that no video-link was available at the panel hearing. On appeal, Davis J found that the panel had misdirected itself in finding that P was not available since no enquiry had been. The NMC rules required the panel to consider the overall fairness of the hearing before admitting hearsay and, given the misdirection, the test had not been met. The NMC appealed on the basis that his judgment curtailed the admissibility of hearsay statements. However, the Court of Appeal upheld Davis J's decision on the facts. No general principle was established other than to reaffirm the need to consider fairness before admitting hearsay. Fairness is required on both sides and it was commented that if, despite reasonable efforts the NMC could not arrange for P to be available for cross-examination, then the case for admitting her hearsay statement might well have been strong.

6.118 In *R (Bonhoeffer) v General Medical Council*[55] B faced several allegations of sexual misconduct while practising in Kenya. (See chapter 2 at paras 2.109–2.110 for a summary of the facts and fuller discussion of this decision and others on the admissibility of evidence.) In that case, the court upheld B's challenge and concluded, in essence, that:

> The admission of hearsay was not necessarily unfair. The key issue was whether admitting important evidence with no opportunity to cross-

53 HCPC (Investigating Committee) Rules 2003 r8(1)(b) and (c); HCPC (Health Committee) Rules 2003; and HCPC (Conduct and Competence Committee) Rules 2003 r10(1)(b) and (c).

54 [2010] EWCA Civ 1216.

55 [2011] EWHC 1585 (Admin).

examine a witness was fair at common law and/or under Art 6 given the seriousness of the case and any safeguards.

6.119 There is no absolute rule that a registrant must be afforded the opportunity to cross-examine a witness, even where the witness provides the sole or decisive evidence. However, a key point was the serious (criminal) nature of the allegations and the very serious consequences if proved. As a general rule, the more serious the charges or consequences, the greater the need for procedural safeguards to ensure a fair hearing. B's right to cross-examine a central witness could only be countered by *compelling* factors.

6.120 Hearsay evidence which is also anonymous is, however, likely to infringe the fairness requirement. In *White v Nursing and Midwifery Council; Turner v Nursing and Midwifery Council*[56] Mitting J held that anonymous letters alleging that the appellants had falsified discharge times to meet departmental targets should not have been relied on.

6.121 Registrants are of course entitled to call witnesses in support of their own case. Witnesses of fact will be called at the first stage of the hearing, whereas those providing evidence of professional standing or purely in relation to character will be called at misconduct/lack of competence or impairment stage and sanctions stage respectively.

6.122 It is worth giving careful consideration as to the most beneficial stage at which to call a supporting witness. In practice, at the hearing panels often agree to hear a single witness's evidence in one go (rather than splitting it into separate parts going to facts, misconduct/health/lack of competence/impairment/mitigation) for reasons of convenience. There is rarely any disadvantage to the registrant from taking this approach – generally the earlier a panel hears evidence of a registrant's good standard of practice the better.

6.123 Generally the HCPC and those who prosecute cases on its behalf are helpful to accommodating witness availability, so if there are constraints for a particular witness it is advisable to flag this up with the case manager in advance of the hearing, and with the case presenter and legal assessor on the first day of the hearing before it has formally commenced. Usually it is possible to agree a provisional timetable. Consideration may also be given to requests to hear supporting witnesses' evidence remotely, either by video-link or by telephone. If an application is to be made for one or more witnesses to give evidence by video-link, it must be raised with the case manager in advance of the hearing as the availability of the necessary equipment will need to be considered when the case is listed. A formal application may then be made to the panel at the start of the hearing.

6.124 Where a potential witness is unwilling to co-operate with an HCPC investigation, panels have powers[57] to require any person to supply information or provide any document which appears to be relevant to the discharge of the practice committees' fitness to practise functions. In practice the power is rarely used, as such information is usually in the possession either of the complainant or a current or former employer and

56 [2014] All ER (D) 107 (Feb).

57 HSWPO 2001 art 25(1); HCPC (Conduct and Competence Committee) (Procedure) Rules 2003 rr10(3) and 13(6); HCPC (Health Committee) (Procedure) Rules 2003 rr10(3) and 13(6).

those parties are usually willing to co-operate. The power is exercised through service of a requirement notice, which indicates that failure to comply without reasonable excuse amounts to a criminal offence punishable on summary conviction by a fine not exceeding level five on the standard scale.[58]

6.125 The power does not apply to the registrant who is the subject of the proceedings, however, although there is a more limited power[59] to require him or her to provide details of his or her employer, of any person with whom he or she has an arrangement to provide services and any other healthcare regulator by which he or she is authorised to practise. The enforcement provisions are the same as those set out in the previous paragraph applying to third parties.

6.126 In addition to the above, which apply during the investigation stage, practice committee panels have the power[60] to require any person (other than the registrant) to attend and give evidence at hearings or to produce documents. The power can be exercised by the panel of its own volition or on application by the parties.

6.127 Cases where the registrant may wish to use this provision are relatively rare, but may be appropriate in circumstances where, for example, only partial documentation has been provided to the HCPC by an employer and the registrant is aware of other documents in existence that would assist in his or her defence.

6.128 An application for such an order must be made in writing and must contain the following information:

- the name and address of the person concerned;
- the terms of the order sought;
- details of any information being sought;
- any steps the applicant has taken to secure the attendance of (or production by) that person on a voluntary basis; and
- evidence to show why the attendance of (or production by) that person is likely to support the case of the applicant.

In addition, a panel will normally require the party applying to indicate that they will meet the reasonable costs of the party providing/attending, accordingly an undertaking to this effect should be included in the application. Where the application is for documents to be produced, they must be identified individually or by reference to a class of documents, and must contain sufficient detail that the recipient is able to understand the obligation the order places upon them.

6.129 A copy of the application and any evidence in support of it should normally be sent to the person concerned. The panel may hold a hearing to consider the application or simply deal with the matter on paper if the parties agree or if a hearing is considered unnecessary.

6.130 If a witness order is granted, in order to be binding on the recipient, it must be served at least seven days before the hearing, so this timescale

58 HSWPO 2001 art 39(5).

59 HSWPO 2001 art 25(2).

60 HSWPO 2001 art 32(2)(m).

should be borne in mind when making any application for such an order. An HCTPS practice note provides more detail.[61]

6.131 The use of expert witnesses in fitness to practise proceedings is relatively rare, but may be necessary in certain cases. The need for expert evidence is most likely to arise in competency cases where the registrant wishes to defend his or her practice on the matter under scrutiny as being of an acceptable standard. There is a practice note on the use of expert witnesses which is available on the HCTPS website.[62] The practice note sets out detailed requirements to be observed if expert evidence is to be relied upon, which broadly mirror those applicable in the civil courts. In hearings it is not uncommon for witnesses to be a member of the same profession as the registrant and accordingly to have relevant knowledge and expertise to express a view on matters such as the adequacy of clinical reasoning or the standard of treatment notes. Such evidence is admissible. Findings from an investigation, however, are not normally admissible.[63] See chapter 2 for a fuller discussion of this issue.

6.132 Panels have discretion as to whether expert evidence is required in a particular case, the overriding principle being that it will assist the panel in dealing with the case.

Video-link

6.133 Video-links are used on occasion for convenience (eg where a key witness is out of the country for a prolonged period) as in other courts. From a registrant's perspective there is rarely any objection to the practice in these circumstances. Provided facilities can be accessed, the same can apply to witnesses in support of a registrant's case and can be helpful in overcoming limitations on availability. There are particular provisions in relation to the use of video-link and other measures for vulnerable witnesses, which are covered in paras 6.159–6.163 below.

Location

6.134 The HCPTS has a hearing centre in Kennington, London[64] which is the venue for most fitness to practise hearings, although the volume of cases means that on occasions hotels or business meeting venues in London are used. Panels also sit in Cardiff, Glasgow or Belfast where the registrant is resident in Wales, Scotland or Northern Ireland. Occasionally panels sit in other cities where it is appropriate to do so, for example to facilitate attendance by a large number of witnesses resident in that area or by a witness who has restricted mobility. Tea and coffee is provided for registrants, witnesses and representatives, and lunch for the registrant.

6.135 At the main hearing centre a small room is allocated to each registrant to enable consultation with any representative and witnesses in private.

61 See www.hcpts-uk.org/assets/documents/10005380HCPTSPracticeNotes-consolidated.pdf.

62 See www.hcpts-uk.org/assets/documents/10005380HCPTSPracticeNotes-consolidated.pdf.

63 *Enemuwe v Nursing and Midwifery Council* [2015] EWHC 2081 (Admin).

64 405 Kennington Park Road, London, SE11 4PT.

The HCPTS staff are generally very helpful, including about occasional requests for last-minute printing or photocopying (although of course this should not be relied upon and documents and statements should be provided within the stipulated timescales wherever possible). Where documents and statements have been served by email, it is prudent to check with the hearing officer prior to the start of the hearing that these have been received and forwarded to the panel members.

6.136 If a registrant has a particular reason for wanting the hearing held outside London, this should be raised at an early stage with the case manager and full reasons given in support of the request.

Preliminary meetings

6.137 The Investigating Committee and the practice committees, or their chair, may hold preliminary meetings in private with the parties, their representatives and any other person the committee or chair considers appropriate where such a meeting will assist the committee to perform its functions.[65]

6.138 At such meetings, the chair may make directions[66] and with the agreement of the parties, take any action the committee could take at such a meeting. In practice, preliminary meetings are usually held where the nature of the case is such that it is likely to require a lengthy hearing or where issues such as expert evidence need to be considered. Directions will be made to clarify the steps necessary prior to the final hearing. Such meetings often also deal with applications for witness orders, the joinder of allegations or vulnerable witness measures (on which see paras 6.159–6.163 below).

6.139 It is important to seek to resolve any preliminary issues prior to the final disposal hearing wherever possible, otherwise time taken to do so on the first day of the hearing can jeopardise the prospect of completing the case within the time allocated. Preliminary meetings are also a good opportunity to seek clarification of any issues relating to the drafting of the allegations.

Main hearings

Preparing for the main hearing

6.140 For all final disposal hearings it is advisable to prepare a full witness statement for a registrant, and for any other witness who intends to give evidence. Statements are drafted in the usual form and documentary evidence can either be exhibited and attached thereto or set out in a separate bundle with reference to the bundle pagination in the statement (remembering to distinguish the registrant's bundle from the HCPC bundle).

65 HCPC (Investigating Committee) Rules 2003, HCPC (Health Committee) Rules 2003 and HCPC (Conduct and Competence Committee) Rules 2003 r7.

66 HSWPO 2001 art 32(3).

6.141 As in all civil proceedings, statements should be full and set out all matters upon which the registrant seeks to rely. The form is a matter for the individual representative, but generally it will be helpful if the statement contains some introductory paragraphs setting out the registrant's route to qualification and a brief summary of their career to date. If appropriate, it would be helpful if it contains some general information about the surrounding circumstances in the course of the employment giving rise to the allegation (this is particularly important in cases where the registrant is asserting excessive workload, for example, or inadequate supervision). Each factual particular can then be set out with the registrant's response, then dealing with the issues of misconduct and/or lack of competence, impairment and finally issues going to mitigation.

6.142 The occasions when it is not beneficial to call the registrant to give evidence on his or her own behalf will be very rare indeed (this is most likely to arise in health cases, on which see paras 6.90–6.92 above, and see chapter 2 at para 2.402 for a discussion of the potential for adverse inference from silence) but in many cases the registrant is the only witness at the facts stage and others are called to give evidence more generally about the standards of the registrant's practice, hence their relevance tends to relate to misconduct/lack of competence, impairment or mitigation. Full witness statements should be provided for all witnesses, although the formalities are often relaxed in the case of professional witnesses at sanctions stage and these may be accepted in the form of a testimonial or letter addressed to the relevant committee. They should however be dated and signed and if possible presented on headed paper. It is also helpful if they contain confirmation that the writer is aware of the allegations the registrant faces.

Admissibility of evidence

6.143 The practice committee rules[67] provide that the civil rules of admissibility apply, although rules 8(1)(c)[68] and 10(1)(c)[69] provide that the committee may hear or receive evidence which would not be admissible in such proceedings if it is satisfied that admission of that evidence is necessary in order to protect members of the public. Accordingly, panels have wide discretion to admit evidence, though plainly any that is not relevant to the matters under consideration will not fall within the scope of the discretion. See paras 6.115 onwards regarding the admissibility of hearsay evidence.

6.144 Any issues about admissibility of evidence must be raised with the case manager at an early stage in proceedings and resolved well before the final hearing. Alternatively it may prove possible to resolve by approaching the legal assessor jointly with the HCPC's representative on the day of the hearing but before it has commenced.

67 HCPC (Investigating Committee) Rules 2003 r8(1)(b), HPC (Health Committee) Rules 2003 and HPC (Conduct and Competence Committee) Rules 2003 r10(1)(b).

68 Of the HCPC (Investigating Committee) Rules 2003.

69 Of the HCPC (Health Committee) Rules 2003 and HCPC (Conduct and Competence Committee) Rules 2003.

6.145 If the matter is not resolved prior to the hearing, the registrant's representative will be faced with the dilemma of making an application to exclude the evidence in question from the very panel from which he or she wishes to keep it. This may ultimately result in an application for a panel to recuse itself (if it has seen evidence that is argued to be prejudicial to the registrant and not properly admissible in the course of the application being made), resulting in adjournment of the hearing to another date. As most registrants have already waited many months and seek resolution to the uncertainty of facing proceedings, this is to be avoided, which reinforces the importance of resolving such issues at an early stage.

Public hearings

6.146 Under the practice committee rules[70] the presumption is that hearings are held in public. The rationale for this is clear: the importance of transparency and openness in regulatory proceedings to maintain public confidence in the process. There will, however, be occasions when evidence to be adduced will contain reference to personal matters which are not appropriate to be heard in public.

6.147 The rules make provision for the presumption of a public hearing to be disapplied where a panel is satisfied that it is in the interests of justice or for the protection of the private life of the health professional, the complainant, any person giving evidence or of any patient or client. On such occasions the public will be excluded from all or part of the hearing. Such applications are frequently granted where the evidence in question deals with matters such as the physical or mental health of the registrant. If an application is to be made on behalf of a registrant, the nature of the evidence should be made known to the panel and the particular ground relied upon (eg interests of justice or protection of private life). There is a practice note on conducting hearings in private which contains useful information for representatives which is available on the HCPTS website.[71]

6.148 Representatives should clarify to the registrant however that if the application is granted (and they are only granted in relation to a specific witness or part of a witness' testimony) this does not mean that all publicity will be avoided. The registrant's name and the allegation will already have been placed on the HCPC website and the final decision and any sanction will also be posted on the HCPC website in most cases.

6.149 In exceptional cases the HCPC may agree to limit the detail of allegations to be posted on the website. If agreement to such an approach is to be sought, an application must be made to the case manager at the earliest opportunity and supported by as much evidence as possible. Cases where such an approach may receive sympathetic consideration include allegations of child abuse or indecent images of children, where there may be fears of repercussions for the family of the registrant if details of the offence are made public. Such a request is unlikely to be granted, however,

70 HCPC (Investigating Committee) Rules 2003 r8(1)(a) and HPC (Conduct and Competence Committee) Rules 2003 r10(1)(a).

71 See www.hcpts-uk.org/assets/documents/10005356ConductingHearingsinPrivate.pdf.

if the information is already in the public domain (for example, as a consequence of criminal proceedings being reported in the press).

6.150 Registrants frequently find this aspect of the process particularly unpalatable and make comparisons with the treatment of complainants who are anonymised for the whole of the proceedings, so care must be taken to explain the position at the outset.

6.151 If at the final hearing the panel finds that the allegation is not well founded, the registrant will be given the choice of having the decision posted on the website or all reference to the case removed immediately. Most registrants opt for the latter, taking the view that they will inform anyone with a proper interest in the outcome and the less time their name remains publicly associated with proceedings the better.

Postponements, adjournments and absent registrants

> The panel has the discretion to proceed in the absence of the practitioner but a) there must be strict adherence to the requirement that all reasonable effort at service has been met and b) the decision to proceed must be taken with 'the utmost care and caution' and only after full consideration of the competing interests with emphasis on those of the practitioner.

6.152 A registrant facing an allegation has the right to attend the hearing and be represented, but in some cases the registrant does not wish to do so, or may be unable to do so on the dates fixed for the hearing. In the latter case, of course a postponement should be requested as soon as it becomes apparent that one is needed, giving full and detailed reasons as to why the postponement is needed. If the reason is related to the registrant's health, it is important to include supporting evidence from a medical practitioner.

6.153 There is a practice note, available on the HCPTS website,[72] which clarifies the distinction it draws between adjournments and postponements:

- postponement is an administrative action which may be taken on behalf of a practice committee by the HCPC's Head of Adjudication at any time up to 28 days before the date on which a hearing is due to begin; and
- adjournment is a decision for the panel or the panel chair, taken at any time after that 28-day limit has passed or once the proceedings have begun or are part heard.

6.154 An application to postpone or adjourn for more time to prepare the registrant's case is more likely to be granted if specific reasons can be given as to the further additional evidence needed and reasons why it has not been possible to obtain it within the usual timescales. Article 6 ECHR arguments can of course be used in support of such an application – on which see chapter 1.

72 See www.hcpts-uk.org/assets/documents/10005364PostponementsandAdjournments.pdf.

6.155 *Faulkner v Nursing and Midwifery Council*[73] demonstrated the importance of providing medical evidence to support an application to adjourn on health grounds. The decision to proceed in the absence of the registrant who failed to provide such evidence was upheld. Although F later gave evidence via a telephone link, he was restricted to addressing sanctions since the decisions on misconduct and impairment had already been made in his absence.

6.156 Panels have discretion to proceed in the absence of the registrant.[74] The discretion must be exercised with the utmost care and caution, given the potentially disastrous consequences for the registrant of an adverse finding in his or her absence. In exercising the discretion, panels are required to have regard to all of the circumstances known to them, including whether the absence is voluntary and amounting to a waiver of the right to attend. This underlines the importance of registrants engaging with the process at an early stage and making any application to adjourn at the earliest possible opportunity and supported by as much detail as is available.

6.157 In *R v Jones (Anthony)*[75] the following important observations were made:

> . . . the discretion to commence a trial in the absence of a defendant should be exercised with the utmost care and caution . . . If the absence of the defendant is attributable to involuntary illness or incapacity it would very rarely, if ever, be right to exercise the discretion in favour of commencing the trial, at any rate unless the defendant is represented and asks that the trial should begin.[76]

The applicability of these principles to regulatory proceedings was confirmed in *Tait v Royal College of Veterinary Surgeons*.[77]

6.158 There is a practice note, available on the HCPTS website, for panels considering proceeding in the absence of the registrant which sets out all of the factors to be considered, and provides a useful checklist as to matters to include in any application to adjourn.[78]

Vulnerable witnesses

6.159 Witness statements will have been provided by the HCPC along with the bundle of documents it proposes to rely upon and, unless their statements have been agreed by the registrant, witnesses will normally be called to give evidence at the hearing. In some cases, where the evidence to be given by a witness is not central to the HCPC case or the person is unavailable, the written statement will be relied upon alone. See paras 6.115 onwards on the admissibility of hearsay evidence to which the registrant has not agreed.

73 [2009] EWHC 3349 (Admin).

74 HCPC (Investigating Committee) Rules 2003 r9, HCPC (Health Committee) Rules 2003 and HCPC (Conduct and Competence Committee) Rules 2003 r11.

75 [2002] UKHL 5.

76 [2002] UKHL 5 para 13.

77 [2003] UKPC 34.

78 See www.hcpts-uk.org/assets/documents/10005365ProceedinginAbsence.pdf.

6.160 There are particular considerations regarding witnesses in cases where the allegations are of a sexual nature. Where the witness is the complainant, and where the registrant is representing him/herself the registrant is prevented from cross-examining the witness unless the witness has provided written consent. Where written consent is not given, the registrant must appoint a legally qualified person to cross-examine the witness on his or her behalf. If the registrant does not do so seven days before the hearing date, the HCPC will appoint a legally qualified person to do so.[79] This measure reflects similar provisions that apply in criminal cases.

6.161 There are also provisions under rules 8A and 10A for panels to adopt such measures as it considers desirable in relation to vulnerable witnesses. 'Vulnerable witnesses' are defined as:

- aged under 17;
- having a mental disorder;
- having a significant impairment of intelligence and social functioning;
- having physical disabilities who require assistance to give evidence;
- where the witness is the victim and the allegation against the registrant is of a sexual nature; and
- where the witness complains of intimidation.

6.162 A number of possible measures are set out in the rules and in the relevant practice note,[80] including video-links, pre-recorded evidence in chief, interpreters, screens and private hearings. In practice, the most commonly adopted measures are screens and video-links. Again, these measures reflect similar provisions used in the criminal courts. Applications for such measures are usually made at a preliminary meeting, but may on occasion be made on the first day of the final disposal hearing. The test as to whether such an application should be granted is that the quality of the witness's evidence is likely to be adversely affected as a result of his or her vulnerability.

6.163 A registrant or his or her representative may object to the use of such measures, but clear reasons need to be stated in support of the objection. It may be argued for example that where a case turns on a conflict of fact between the complainant and the registrant (as is often the case where the complaint is of a sexual nature) it is necessary for the panel to observe as closely as possible the demeanour of the witness in cross-examination and this is not possible through a video-link. Such an argument will not, of course, necessarily succeed, but panels may be persuaded to opt for screens rather than video-link. The registrant should be advised that requests for such measures in appropriate cases are often granted.

79 HCPC (Investigating Committee) Rules 2003 r8A(4) and (5); HCPC (Health Committee) Rules 2003 r10A and HCPC (Conduct and Competence Committee) Rules 2003 r10A(4) and (5).

80 See www.hcpts-uk.org/assets/documents/10005368SpecialMeasures.pdf.

Cross-examination

6.164 It is possible in many cases for the statements of some of the HCPC witnesses to be agreed. Where they are not, witnesses will be called to give evidence live, or via video-link.

6.165 The usual rules apply in cross-examination of witnesses, so the registrant's case must be put any factual conflicts challenged. There are tactical considerations in putting the registrant's case depending on the type of witness. For example, while robust cross-examination of a manager who has failed adequately to support a registrant facing allegations of unsatisfactory professional practice may be perfectly appropriate, such an approach might be less productive where the witness in question is a patient or service user, particularly if they are elderly, injured or otherwise vulnerable.

No case to answer

> Submissions of no case to answer may be made in respect of a case or a specific allegation.
>
> They may be made where a) there is no evidence or b) there is some evidence but it is weak, vague or inconsistent and, looked at 'in the round', a panel *could* not properly find the case (or fact) proved.

6.166 Although the HCPC's rules do not make specific provision for a submission of no case to answer at the conclusion of the HCPC's case (unlike, for example, those of the NMC), there is the opportunity to do so in appropriate cases, and the relevant practice note makes clear that it is entirely proper for panels to consider them.[81]

6.167 Such a submission is most likely to be considered appropriate in cases where either the factual basis has been significantly undermined in the course of cross-examination (for example, where a witness has retracted previous assertions, or otherwise shown to lack credibility or reliability) or where the facts set out in the particulars are of a low level of seriousness such that it is possible to argue that even if the HCPC's case is accepted in its entirety it will not amount either to the statutory ground (misconduct, lack of competence or health) or to impairment. A submission of no case to answer can also be appropriate where a key witness for the HCPC has failed to attend, although it should be borne in mind that his or her witness statement may in any event be admissible as hearsay evidence, so in the absence of any conflicting evidence from another witness (or contradictory documentary evidence) it may nevertheless be accepted.

6.168 There are tactical considerations to making such a submission, in particular if it is to be on the second basis. It must be borne in mind that, if the submission is not accepted and the case continues, it may affect the panel's willingness to accept that the registrant has insight into his or her

81 See www.hcpts-uk.org/assets/documents/1000535DHalfTimeSubmisisons.pdf.

failings or a full appreciation of the need to adhere to the requisite standards.

6.169 If such a submission is to be made the *Galbraith*[82] test is the relevant basis, being applicable in regulatory proceedings, on which see chapter 2.

Evidence-in-chief

6.170 As previously stated, it will be necessary to have drafted and submitted a full witness statement setting out the registrant's response to the allegations, together with other information that is relevant to consideration of the statutory ground and impairment. The usual practice is for the panel members to read the registrant's statement before the start of the hearing (although for certainty it is appropriate for a representative to check that they have done so) and generally panels take the statement as read. This means that having read it to themselves, it is unnecessary for the registrant to read the statement aloud. It should be explained to the registrant that his or her evidence will carry the same weight as if the registrant had read it aloud. There may be some supplementary questions from the registrant's representative to cover additional matters that have arisen in the course of evidence from the HCPC witnesses, and of course it may be necessary to take the panel to documents referred to in the statement, either in the HCPC bundle or in the registrant's if he or she has provided one.

6.171 The advantage of taking statements as read is that it saves time, and many registrants are keen to minimise the time they have to spend on the witness stand. Taking this approach can, however, feel to some registrants as though they have not told their side of the story to the panel, so in particular cases it may still be appropriate to ask the registrant to read the statement aloud. Panel chairs may be willing to accommodate the registrant's preference.

6.172 At the conclusion of evidence-in-chief (however taken) the registrant will be cross-examined by the HCPC's representative and usually there will be questions from the members of the panel. In cases concerned with aspects of professional practice it is likely that the majority of questions will be asked by the registrant member of the panel.

6.173 In cases where a supporting witness is being called on behalf of the registrant to give evidence either on issues of fact or of good professional performance, which is relevant to statutory ground and/or impairment, that witness will usually be called at this point. As with the registrant it is essential to have a full witness statement which can be taken as read. In most cases, unless the registrant's representative objects, the HCPC's practice is for the panel to withdraw to deliberate only once to decide on facts, statutory ground and impairment. Evidence given by witnesses which goes to both impairment and mitigation need not be called twice, panels are familiar with the overlap between the two and are content to be reminded at sanction stage of the evidence previously given which remains relevant.

82 *R v Galbraith* (1981) 73 Cr App R 124, CA.

Submissions

6.174 As previously indicated, the usual practice at the HCPC is to take submissions on facts, statutory ground and impairment all together and for the panel to withdraw to deliberate just once, although three separate decisions are taken with reasons given for each.

6.175 In most cases this practice has no particular disadvantage to the registrant, but occasionally there may be good reason for seeking a different approach. Any objection to the usual practice should be made known to the legal assessor and the HCPC advocate at the earliest opportunity.

6.176 The circumstances in which this can arise are where the registrant faces a number of allegations, where the facts are denied and where there is a significantly varying degree of seriousness in the factual particulars. In such cases, it may be helpful for the registrant's representative to know which of the factual particulars are proven before making submissions on statutory ground and impairment. So, for example, if the most serious factual particulars are found proven, the representative may wish to take a different approach in submissions on the remaining stages (or even take instructions as to whether admissions may be made).

6.177 In all cases it will be helpful to keep submissions focused on the three stages of the exercise and deal with each in turn. While it is common practice to refer to fundamental issues such as the burden and standard of proof, these will be covered by the legal assessor and referred to by the HCPC advocate in his or her opening statement. Written submissions or skeleton arguments are rarely necessary, but can be of assistance in cases where, for example, an unusual point of law is to be argued, or if a case has gone part heard, when it may be helpful to remind the panel of the evidence heard on the earlier occasion.

6.178 The panel will be taken through the key authorities on the statutory ground and impairment by the legal assessor. There is a practice note on impairment available on the HCPTS website to which panels are always urged to have regard.[83] Accordingly, it will not be necessary for the registrant's representative to set out the law on these matters (unless intending to rely upon an authority that is not referred to in the practice note) but simply to apply the tests derived from them to the facts of the case in hand.

6.179 See chapter 1 for a full discussion of the key authorities on impairment and the statutory grounds.

Mitigation and sanctions

> The principal aims of sanctions are to protect the public, uphold the standards and reputation of the profession and to maintain public confidence therein.
>
> The punitive effect of sanctions is only one (and not the most important) factor to be borne in mind when assessing whether a sanction is proportional to the matters found proved against a practitioner.

83 See www.hcpts-uk.org/assets/documents/1000535CFindingImpairment.pdf.

6.180 The panel will give its decision on facts, statutory ground and impairment with reasons for the decision reached at each stage. At the conclusion of the decision and reasons, further evidence and submissions will be invited from the HCPC's and the registrant's representatives.

6.181 In cases of misconduct, the panel may apply any of the sanctions set out in HSWPO 2001 art 29(4) and (5) which are:

- refer to screeners or undertake mediation;
- take no action;
- impose a caution order of between one and five years;
- impose a conditions of practice order up to a maximum of three years;
- impose a suspension order for a maximum period of one year; or
- make a striking-off order.

6.182 In cases of lack of competence and health, the same sanctions are available with the exception of a striking-off order, which may only be imposed after a registrant has already been suspended or subject to a conditions of practice order for a minimum period of two years preceding the date of the striking off order.[84]

6.183 This distinction in powers of sanction is an important consideration at earlier stages in the proceedings – for example, when deciding whether to make an application for a case to be referred to the Health Committee rather than to the CCC. Similarly there may be a tactical advantage to making admissions of lack of competence (but not misconduct) where allegations are put in the alternative, as is often the case.

6.184 The HCPC's advocates normally take a neutral stance on sanction and do not seek to persuade the panel that a particular sanction is appropriate in a given case. Usually he or she will simply bring the disposals available (depending on the statutory ground upon which impairment has been found) to the panel's attention and refer to mitigating and aggravating features.

6.185 Further evidence may be called by the registrant at the mitigation stage, although as referred to above, testimonials going to professional practice will have been adduced at impairment stage (unless current impairment is admitted). Purely personal character references are only relevant at sanctions stage. In many cases where the registrant is not practising their profession at the time of the hearing it will not be possible to obtain current professional testimonials, but panels are generally open to receiving relevant material in other forms such as 'thank you' letters or cards from former patients, or expressions of gratitude from colleagues.

6.186 The HCPTS has an indicative sanctions policy (updated March 2017) which is available on its website[85] and which helpfully sets out the purpose of sanction, the key principle of proportionality, the significance of insight and remorse, the procedure to be adopted by panels in deciding on sanction and an indication of the kind of factors that are likely to make a case suitable for each of the given sanctions. The policy is essential reading for

84 HSWPO 2001 art 29(6).

85 See www.hcpts-uk.org/assets/documents/10005520HCPCIndicativeSanctionsPolicy.pdf.

any representative, and will be of great assistance in deciding how to pitch submissions at the final stage of the process.

6.187 Panels are invariably reminded that the purpose of sanction is to protect the public, not to punish the registrant (although it is recognised that some, notably caution orders and suspension orders, will have a punitive effect). Protection of the public includes consideration of the deterrent effect, maintaining the reputation of the profession and upholding standards and public confidence in the regulatory process.

6.188 In addition to the factors set out in the policy, it will be necessary to give consideration to the impact of a particular sanction to the registrant in question. It should be noted that the policy amounts to guidance only and the appropriate sanction in any case is a matter of discretion for the panel. If a panel is departing from the guidance however, its reasons for doing so should be explained.[86]

6.189 A finding of impairment will not invariably lead to a sanction; there is an express power[87] for a panel to take no further action. Such disposals are rare, but arguments in support may be made in cases where the allegations raise low levels of concern and there has been full remediation of any deficiencies by the registrant prior to the hearing.

6.190 Mediation is rarely used and is only appropriate in cases where both parties (ie registrant and complainant) agree to its use and where the panel is satisfied that no other action is appropriate.

6.191 Caution orders are used in cases where the allegation represents an isolated lapse by the registrant or is of a minor nature. The advantage of a caution order over conditions of practice from a registrant's point of view (apart from the obvious absence of any restriction on the registrant's ability to practise) is that there is no requirement for review. Once the period has passed, the caution lapses and no other action is required. Registrants should however be advised that even once lapsed a caution may be taken into account if a further allegation is made against the same registrant.

6.192 Conditions of practice are often imposed in cases of lack of competence and health and may be restrictive or remedial or both. If conditions appear to be the appropriate (or most favourable) disposal it will be important to provide evidence to the panel of the registrant's willingness and ability to comply. If available, supporting evidence from another professional (for example, a manager or potential mentor) of their willingness to provide a particular form of support to the registrant will be very helpful.

6.193 Representatives should give careful consideration as to the kind of conditions that will be appropriate (in the sense of meeting the particular concerns) and workable in a given case. Such orders must be reviewed before the expiry of the original term[88] and registrants must be made aware that if, following imposition of such an order, there is any difficulty in complying with the specified conditions, the HCPC should be informed as soon as possible. In such cases, an early review should be sought to request a variation of the terms. A registrant who has simply failed to comply and not raised the matter before a mandatory review will be viewed

86 *Professional Standards Authority v HCPC and Doree* [2017] EWCA 319.

87 HSWPO 2001 art 29(4)(b).

88 HSWPO 2001 art 30(1).

much less sympathetically by any reviewing panel and will risk an extension of the order.

6.194 Panels should not confuse suspension and the imposition of conditions; and if imposing the latter, they must be reasonable and workable. In *Udom v General Medical Council*[89] the panel found U's fitness to practise impaired by reason of health and competence. It imposed a sanction which purported to be conditions that he was not to practise unsupervised for a period of nine months and was, during that period, to undergo a series of clinical attachments. The effect of the order was to suspend U from practice. Suspension and conditions of practice are separate mutually exclusive sanctions. Accordingly, the panel had been wrong to impose conditions which had the effect of being a 'backdoor' suspension of the registrant.

6.195 Suspension orders are used for cases where no conditions can be devised that will protect the public, but where repetition is unlikely and therefore striking off is not appropriate. Although the powers of sanction under HSWPO 2001 art 29 are alternatives and a combination (for example, of suspension with conditions) may not be imposed, in many cases a panel will, when suspending a registrant, provide an indication of the kind of steps that may be taken during the period of suspension that would assist a panel on review. Registrants who are subject to such an order should be made aware that compliance with the suggested steps is highly advisable in order to achieve a successful outcome to the review.

6.196 Striking-off orders are reserved for the most serious cases, and registrants who are struck off may not apply to be restored to the register for a period of five years following the order being made, unless new evidence relevant to the order has become available since the order was made.[90]

6.197 Cases that may merit a striking-off order include those that involve repeated and/or very serious allegations of abuse of trust or dishonesty, or ongoing persistent failures.

6.198 In most cases of conditions – and whenever suspension or strike-off orders have been made – after the panel gives its decision on sanction, the HCPC's advocate will make an application for an interim order to cover the period of 28 days (or longer if an appeal is lodged) during which the substantive order does not take effect. In cases of strike-off and suspension, the application will be for an interim suspension order, while in conditions cases the application will normally be for conditions replicating those in the substantive order, although this may not be necessary where conditions are purely remedial and have no restrictive effect.

6.199 Representatives will need to take instructions from the registrant if there are particular reasons for opposing the imposition of an interim order, for example if the registrant has patients booked in for the following days and needs time to arrange cover for his or her practice. Such a reason may, however, not find favour with a panel as the failure to make suitable alternative arrangements prior to the hearing may be regarded as indicative of a lack of appreciation of the seriousness of the allegations the registrant faces and the likelihood of strike-off or suspension. Although the

89 [2009] EWHC 3242 (Admin).

90 HSWPO 2001 arts 33(2)(a) and 29(7)(a).

panel will be advised that the making of an order in these circumstances is not automatic, realistically in many cases panels will feel that the public needs to be protected during the appeal period.

6.200 For a full discussion, authorities relevant to consideration of sanction and guideline cases, see chapter 2.

Reviews and challenges

Reviews

6.201 Conditions of practice and suspension orders must be reviewed before expiry.[91] In either case, the reviewing panel may extend the period of the order for a maximum period of three years for conditions and one year for suspension, or may replace with a different order of a kind that would have been available to the panel imposing the original order, or may make a conditions of practice order to take effect following expiry of a suspension order.

6.202 The importance of complying fully with conditions of practice has been referred to at para 6.119 above, and where recommended steps are brought to the registrant's attention by a panel imposing a suspension order, the importance of having followed them by the time of any review is clear if a subsequent extension of the suspension or stringent conditions of practice are to be avoided.

6.203 In addition to the mandatory review provided for under HSWPO 2001 art 30(1), a registrant subject to a caution, conditions or suspension is entitled to seek a review at any time.[92] Upon such a review, the panel is able to confirm the original order, extend or reduce the period for which it has effect, replace it with another order of a kind that would have been available to the original panel, revoke any condition imposed by the order or revoke the order itself.

6.204 The most common circumstances in which a registrant will wish to take advantage of this provision is where remedial conditions have been imposed which have been complied with well in advance of the normal expiry date of the order, or where there has been a material change to the registrant's status (for example, a change in employment). An application for such a review should be made in writing at the earliest opportunity setting out the reason why it is sought and supporting evidence of compliance with the conditions or the changed circumstances will need to be adduced at the review hearing.

Restoration

6.205 A registrant who is subject to a striking-off order may apply for restoration to the register, and there is a practice note that contains useful information for potential applicants and their representatives.[93]

91 HSWPO 2001 art 30(1).
92 HSWPO 2001 art 30(2).
93 Seewww.hcpts-uk.org/assets/documents/10005366Restoration.pdf.

6.206 The application must be made in writing to the registrar, although it will be referred for consideration to a panel of the practice committee that made the original order. No such application may be made for a period of five years following imposition of the original order unless new evidence that is relevant to the order becomes available. No further application may be made within a period of 12 months from a previous unsuccessful application for restoration.

6.207 The applicant must be given an opportunity to appear before a panel of the appropriate practice committee to argue his or her case. Restoration hearings follow a similar procedure as other fitness to practise hearings except that the applicant bears the burden of proof and therefore presents his or her case before any submissions are made by the HCPC's representative.

6.208 Panels in restoration hearings must ensure that the applicant has the requisite qualifications to be registered in the applicable profession and also that he or she is a fit and proper person to practise that profession. In applying the second requirement the panel is to have regard in particular to the circumstances that led to the making of the striking off order.

6.209 In presenting an application for restoration, it will be important to address matters such as the applicant's insight into the matters that led to the striking-off order and any remedial steps that have been taken in the interim as well as action taken to ensure his or her professional skills and knowledge have been kept up-to-date.

6.210 Panels may restore an applicant to the register with conditions or unconditionally. In order to avoid conditions therefore it is important to adduce as much evidence as possible of updated skills and knowledge at the restoration hearing.

6.211 If an application for restoration is unsuccessful on two or more occasions, the relevant practice committee may suspend the applicant's right to make further applications indefinitely. Where such a direction is made, the prospective applicant may apply for it to be reviewed after a period of three years has elapsed.

Appeals

6.212 Any order (other than an interim order) of the practice committees is subject to a right of appeal to the appropriate court, which is the High Court (England and Wales), the Court of Session (Scotland) or the High Court of Justice of Northern Ireland. The time limit for lodging and appeal is 28 days from the date when the notice of order or decision was served on the registrant.[94]

6.213 Where an appeal is lodged within the appropriate period, the order appealed does not take effect until the appeal is disposed of (hence the practice of imposing an interim order at the conclusion of a final disposal hearing as referred to in para 6.198 above) and the HCPC will be the respondent in the appeal proceedings.

6.214 The most likely grounds of appeal will be where the panel has imposed a sanction that is not within its powers (for example, conditions and

94 HSWPO 2001 arts 29(9) and 38.

suspension combined), otherwise made an error of law, failed to give adequate reasons for the decision or that the sanction imposed is too severe in the circumstances. Case-law from other regulatory bodies is of course applicable to appeals against decisions of the HCPC.

Challenge by the Professional Standards Authority

6.215 As referred to at para 6.8 above, fitness to practise decisions by the HCPC are subject to scrutiny by the Professional Standards Authority[95] (PSA). The PSA has four weeks from the last day of the appeal period (ie 28th day from service of the notice of order) to bring such a challenge. The PSA uses alternative dispute resolution (ADR) on occasions to dispose of such cases; others go to a full hearing in the appropriate court.

6.216 The prospect of challenge by the PSA takes some of the pleasure out of obtaining a good outcome for a registrant, but representatives should inform the registrant of the possibility.

95 NHS Reform and Health Care Professions Act 2002 s26.

CHAPTER 7

The General Dental Council

Key points

- *Regulator:* General Dental Council (GDC)
- *Professions regulated:* Dentists, clinical dental technicians, dental nurses, dental technicians, orthodontic therapists, dental hygienists
- *Type of proceedings:* Fitness to practise, fraudulent register entry hearings, restoration hearings, registration appeals
- *Relevant statute:* Dentists Act (DA) 1984
- *Fitness to practise rules:* General Dental Council (Fitness to Practise) Rules 2006 (Schedule to SI 2006 No 1663) (GDC (FTP) Rules 2006), recently amended by SI 2016 No 902
- *Case examiners:* Yes (GDC (FTP) Rules 2006 r5[1])
- *Investigating Committee:* Yes (GDC (FTP) Rules 2006 r7), most functions now performed by the case examiners
- *Notification of hearing:* Yes (GDC (FTP) Rules 2006 r13)
- *Interim Orders Committee (IOC):* Yes (GDC (FTP) Rules 2006 r15 and Part 5, r34–39)
- *Practice committees (for fitness to practise):* The Professional Performance Committee, the Professional Conduct Committee and the Health Committee. The Professional Performance Committee also hears fraudulent register entry hearings and restoration hearings
- *Registration appeals:* Heard by the Registration Appeals Committee
- *Key documents:* Standards for the Dental Team
- *Location:* 37 Wimpole Street, London W1G 8DQ
- *Preliminary meetings (commonly referred to as 'pre-meetings'):* GDC (FTP) Rules 2006 r51
- *Procedure before a Practice Committee:* GDC (FTP) Rules 2006 r14
- *Test:* Whether fitness to practise is impaired by reason of (in summary): a) misconduct; b) deficient professional performance; c) adverse physical or mental health; d) a conviction or caution for a criminal offence or agreement to pay a penalty as an alternative to prosecution under Social Security Administration Act 1992 s115A; e) determination by a regulator or by the Office of the Health Professions Adjudicator (OHPA) that fitness to practise is impaired; f) inclusion in an Independent Safeguarding Authority barred list (DA 1984 s27(2))
- *Interim order power:* Yes – interim conditions of practice or interim suspension (DA 1984 s32)
- *Interim order guidance: Interim orders guidance for the IOC* (updated 2 March 2017)[2]
- *General composition for final hearings:* At least three persons, to include at least one registered dentist, one lay person and (in any case concerning the registration of a dental care professional) one registered dental care professional
- *How to address panel:* Generally seated and 'Sir'/'Madam'
- *Advisers to the panel:* The panel is assisted by a legal adviser. The panel may also be advised by professional and medical advisers

1 The case examiner stage was instigated by SI 2016 No 902 and is discussed below.
2 See www.gdc-uk.org/about/who-we-are/committees/interim-orders-committee.

- *Sanction provisions:* DA 1984 s27B(6)
- *Sanction documents:* Guidance for the Practice Committees including indicative sanctions guidance; DC conditions bank (precedent for earlier conditions of practice)
- *Resumed hearings:* GDC (FTP) Rules 2006 r29. The purpose of a resumed hearing is to review conditions of practice or suspension orders which have been imposed at an earlier hearing (these hearings are known as 'review hearings' before other regulatory bodies)
- *Restoration hearings:* DA 1984 s28
- *Appeal rule:* DA 1984 s29

Introduction

Background

7.1 The General Dental Council (GDC) is the regulatory body which governs the dental profession and professions complementary to dentistry. It was originally created by the Dentists Act (DA) 1957. Its present powers derive from the Dentists Act (DA) 1984.

7.2 DA 1984 s1(1ZA) provides that:

> The over-arching objective of the Council in exercising their functions under this Act is the protection of the public.

7.3 The pursuit of the over-arching objective involves the following objectives:[3]

a) to protect, promote and maintain the health, safety and well-being of the public;
b) to promote and maintain public confidence in the professions regulated under the DA 1984; and
c) to promote and maintain proper professional standards and conduct for members of those professions.

7.4 In *Ivanova v General Dental Council*,[4] Jefford J observed that: 'Those obligations and functions therefore put front and centre the protection of the public.'[5] When appearing before a GDC committee (whether for the prosecution or for the defence) it is vital to keep the over-arching objective well in mind.

7.5 The key document upon standards of conduct, performance and ethics governing dental professionals is *Standards for the dental team*. This document is available on the GDC website[6] and replaces the previous standards document, the GDC *Standards for dental professionals*.

7.6 *Standards for the dental team* is supplemented by a number of additional guidance documents which all registrants are required to follow.[7] These documents include: guidance on advertising, guidance on commissioning

3 DA 1984 s1(1ZB).
4 [2017] EWHC 1992 (Admin).
5 [2017] EWHC 1992 (Admin), para 2.
6 See https://gdc-uk.org/professionals/standards/team.
7 See https://gdc-uk.org/professionals/standards/team/guidance_documents.

and manufacturing dental appliances, guidance on indemnity, guidance on prescribing medicines, guidance on reporting criminal proceedings, guidance on using social media, guidance on child protection and vulnerable adults and scope of practice.

7.7 The DA 1984 established six statutory committees to carry out the principal regulatory and disciplinary functions of the GDC. Three of these committees are collectively described as 'practice committees', namely: a) the Health Committee, b) the Professional Conduct Committee and c) the Professional Performance Committee. The other three committees are d) the Investigating Committee, e) the Interim Orders Committee and f) the Registration Appeals Committee. The work of the statutory committees will be considered in more detail later in this chapter.

7.8 The GDC's other functions (such as education, financial and business planning and policy) are carried out by non-statutory committees. An Appointments Committee exists to appoint members to the six statutory committees.

7.9 Hearings before a practice committee are divided into two parts: stage one is fact-finding (whether the charges are factually proved as alleged); and stage two comprises misconduct, impairment and sanction.

7.10 The quorum for each panel of a practice committee is three, of which there must be at least one registered dentist, one lay person and (in any case concerning a person's registration in the dental care professionals register) and one registered dental care professional. Any of the three members can act as the chair of the committee.

7.11 The committee is advised on questions of law by a legal adviser and may be advised by professional and medical advisers. Legal advisers must have a ten-year general qualification.[8] The role of the legal adviser (known in other areas of regulatory law as the legal assessor) is discussed in more detail in chapter 2 at para 2.292.

7.12 The layout of the hearing room is different from that of many other regulators: the panel, legal adviser and panel secretary sit at the front of the room facing the parties, rather than around a rectangular table.

7.13 The GDC's regulatory work is overseen by the Professional Standards Authority for Health and Social Care (PSA).[9] As for other regulators, the PSA has the power to challenge any fitness to practise (FTP) decisions that it considers to be unduly lenient in the High Court or Court of Session.

Current issues

7.14 *Shifting the balance*, a discussion document published by the GDC in March 2017, remains at the forefront of the GDC's strategic planning in relation to fitness to practise.

7.15 The key objectives of *Shifting the balance* include 'moving upstream' (ie focusing more energy upon prevention of complaints and on local complaint-handling), streamlining fitness to practise by channelling complaints elsewhere which do not relate to fitness to practise, making

8 DA 1984 Sch 4C para 1(5).

9 Formerly the Council for Healthcare Regulatory Excellence.

the present fitness to practise regime as efficient as possible and working towards legislative reform. These aims accord with a wider change in the regulatory climate, as seen in the PSA's publication *Regulation rethought*.[10] *Shifting the balance* also suggests that further reform of the current standards document (*Standards for the dental team*) may be necessary.

7.16 Following the publication and consultation on *Shifting the balance*, a consultation is underway (as of September 2017)[11] upon simplifying the initial stages of investigation into fitness to practise complaints.

Jurisdictional reach

7.17 The GDC regulates dentists and professions complementary to dentistry.

Dentists

7.18 Any person who is a graduate or licentiate in dentistry of a UK dental authority and who satisfies the registrar of his or her identity, good character and good physical and mental health, is entitled to be included in the register of dentists.[12]

7.19 Any 'exempt person' who holds an appropriate European diploma or who is a person to whom certain provisions of the European Communities (Recognition of Professional Qualifications) Regulations 2015[13] apply, and who is permitted to pursue the profession of dentistry in the UK by virtue of these regulations and who has passed any aptitude test or completed any adaptation period which is required, is entitled to be included in the register. Again, these persons must satisfy the registrar of their identity, good character and good physical and mental health. Under regulation 15(1) of the European Union (Recognition of Professional Qualifications) Regulations 2015, applicants may be required to inform the GDC of their intention to provide services by way of a declaration.

7.20 An 'exempt person', for these purposes, means a national of a relevant European state other than the UK, a national of the UK who is seeking access to, or is pursuing, the profession by virtue of an enforceable EU right or a person who is not a national of a relevant European state but who is, by virtue of an enforceable EU right, entitled to be treated, for the purposes of access to and pursuit of the profession, no less favourably than a national of a relevant European state.[14]

7.21 It remains to be seen how these provisions will be affected by Brexit.

7.22 Any person who holds a recognised overseas diploma and who satisfies the GDC of his or her requisite knowledge and skill, knowledge of English (except in the case of an exempt person), good character and good physical and mental health is entitled to be included in the register.[15] There are

10 4 October 2016.

11 See www.gdc-uk.org/news/news-and-blogs/news.

12 DA 1984 s15.

13 SI No 2059.

14 DA 1984 s53(1) (definition added by the European Qualifications (Health and Social Care Professions) Regulations 2007 SI No 3101).

15 DA 1984 s15.

also provisions for the inclusion of visiting dentists and temporary registrants.[16]

7.23 Under the DA 1984, the practice of dentistry includes the performance of any operation, treatment, advice or attendance as is usually performed or given by dentists. This includes operations, treatment, advice or attendance on persons in connection with the fitting, insertion or fixing of dentures, artificial teeth or other dental appliances.[17]

7.24 'Operation' means a surgical operation on the mouth of the patient.[18] 'Treatment, advice or attendance' includes taking an impression of the mouth for the purpose of repairing a denture.[19] It does not include the alteration of an existing denture that is unconnected with the fitting to the mouth itself.[20]

7.25 The performance of any medical task by a person who is qualified to carry out the task and is a member of any of the other regulatory bodies which are subject to the PSA is not deemed to amount to the practice of dentistry.[21] This work, therefore, falls outside the ambit of the GDC and is instead supervised by the appropriate regulatory body.

7.26 Appropriately supervised work undertaken by dental students, medical students or dental care professional students is not deemed to amount to the practice of dentistry.[22] Accordingly, this work also falls outside the ambit of the GDC (although the supervisor would be subject to the GDC's jurisdiction in his or her own right).

Professions complementary to dentistry

7.27 The DA 1984 defines professions complementary to dentistry as professions where the majority of members work in connection with the provision of dental care. This can either mean that they work with persons receiving dental care (ie patients), or with dentists or other dental care professionals.[23]

7.28 The definition of 'professions complementary to dentistry' *excludes* professions that are regulated by bodies other than the GDC that are themselves regulated by the PSA.

7.29 The following professions and job titles currently fall within the category of professions complementary to dentistry and are regulated by the GDC:[24]

16 DA 1984 s14.
17 DA 1984 s37.
18 *Hennan and Co Ltd v Duckworth* [1904–07] All ER Rep 862.
19 *Almy v Thomas* [1953] 1 WLR 1296, [1953] 2 All ER 1050.
20 *Twyford v Puntschart* [1947] 1 All ER 773.
21 DA 1984 s37(1A).
22 DA 1984 s37(2).
23 DA 1984 s36A.
24 General Dental Council (Professions Complementary to Dentistry) Regulations Order of Council 2006 SI No 1440 made under DA 1984 s36A(2) and (3) and s52(1A) and (1B); General Dental Council (Professions Complementary to Dentistry) (Dental Hygienists and Dental Therapists) Regulations Order of Council 2006 SI No 1667 made under DA 1984 s36A(2) and (3).

Profession	Job titles
Clinical dental technicians	Clinical dental technician, clinical dental technologist, denturist
Dental nurses	Dental nurse, dental surgery assistant
Dental technicians	Dental technician, dental technologist
Orthodontic therapists	Orthodontic therapist, orthodontic auxiliary
Dental hygienists	Dental hygienist

7.30 It is a criminal offence for a person who is not listed in the Dental Care Professionals Register to use any of the titles specified by regulations (as set out in the list of professions complementary to dentistry above). The offence is punishable on summary conviction by a fine up to the level five on the standard scale.[25]

7.31 The practice of dentistry is reserved to registered dentists and dental care professionals. It is illegal for persons who are not registered dentists or registered dental care professionals to hold themselves out, either directly or by implication, as practising or being prepared to practise dentistry. This is a criminal offence, punishable on summary conviction to a fine not exceeding the level five on the standard scale.[26] In *General Dental Council v Jamous*[27] the High Court held that tooth whitening was a treatment usually performed by dentists and therefore came within the meaning of the practice of dentistry identified in DA 1984 s37(1), so that a person not qualified as a dentist was prohibited from providing such treatment. There have recently been some successful prosecutions of persons other than dental professionals (eg beauticians) who have offered tooth whitening services.

Approach to regulation

7.32 In assessing fitness to practise, the GDC adopts the same test as other healthcare regulators: that a registrant's fitness to practise is impaired. Impairment can be alleged by:

a) misconduct;
b) deficient professional performance;
c) adverse physical or mental health;
d) a conviction or caution for a criminal offence or agreement to pay a penalty as an alternative to prosecution under Social Security Administration Act 1992 s115A;
e) determination by a regulator that fitness to practise is impaired;
f) inclusion in a Disclosure and Barring Service (DBS) barred list.

For full discussion of each of these issues see chapters 1 and 2. The case-law from other regulatory bodies, including the General Medical Council (GMC), Health and Care Professions Council (HCPC) and

25 DA 1984 s39.

26 DA 1984 s38.

27 [2013] EWHC 1428 (Admin).

Nursing and Midwifery Council (NMC) is applicable to decisions of the GDC.

7.33 Complaints against registrants will be considered even where the matter giving rise to the complaint occurred outside the UK or at a time when the registrant was not included on the register.[28]

7.34 A registrant who is the subject of an allegation and/or of proceedings before one of the committees, is known as a respondent. At hearings before a committee, respondents have the right to be legally represented or represented by a friend, family member or member of an organisation of which the respondent is a member.[29] For a fuller discussion of the legal issues relating to representation, see chapter 2 at para 2.302.

7.35 Fitness to practise proceedings often originate with a complaint made to the GDC from sources such as patients, employers or other official bodies. From 1 November 2016 onwards, new cases are referred to a pair of case examiners for investigation; the case examiners review the cases and decide whether or not to refer them to a practice committee. The role of the case examiners is considered below.

7.36 The GDC has three separate practice committees dealing with different types of fitness to practise issues: the Professional Conduct Committee, the Professional Performance Committee and the Health Committee.

7.37 Hearings before a practice committee are divided into two parts: stage one is fact-finding (whether the charges are factually proved as alleged), and stage two comprises misconduct, impairment and sanctions. Evidence relating to the charges is heard at stage one. Evidence relating to impairment and sanctions (for example, testimonial-type evidence) is heard at stage two. On occasion, permission can be sought for stage two evidence to be heard during stage one (for example, if the same witness is being called to give evidence in both areas). If this situation arises, the legal adviser will advise the committee to disregard the stage two evidence unless and until the matter reaches stage two.

7.38 All hearings before the statutory committees, including the Interim Orders Committee, are to be conducted in public except:

- where the interests of the parties or the protection of the private and family life of the respondent or any other person so requires; or
- to the extent that a committee is of the opinion that, in the special circumstances of the case, it is strictly necessary to do so as publicity would prejudice the interests of justice.

7.39 Before deciding whether or not to conduct a hearing (or part of a hearing) in private, the committee must invite representations from the parties and any other party whom a committee considers it appropriate to hear, and obtain the advice of the legal adviser.[30] There seems no reason why 'any other party' should not include the media.

7.40 Articles 6 and 8 (right to a fair trial and to private life, respectively) of the European Convention on Human Rights (ECHR) may be engaged by

28 DA 1984 s27(3).

29 GDC (FTP) Rules 2006 (Sch 1 to the General Dental Council (Fitness to Practise) Rules Order of Council 2006 SI No 1663) r52.

30 GDC (FTP) Rules 2006 r53.

the decision as to whether or not to conduct a hearing in private. Most hearings are held in public, as weight is typically given to the regulator's purpose of acting in the public interest and protecting the public. The case-law on human rights and regulatory law is discussed in more detail in chapters 1 and 2.

7.41 The practice committee is empowered to hold a preliminary meeting (commonly known as a 'pre-meeting') if it considers that it would assist in performing its functions. Pre-meetings are held in private. The parties and their representatives may attend. At a pre-meeting, the practice committee has a wide range of powers,[31] which include setting timetables for disclosure and expert evidence; time estimates for the hearing, joinder; statements of agreed facts; preparation of agreed bundles; and preparation of skeleton arguments. In a complicated case, legal representatives for the prosecution or the defence are advised to propose a pre-meeting in order to ensure that the final hearing runs as smoothly as possible. The GDC has published a guidance document: *Guidance for handling cases at preliminary meetings*. This is available on the GDC website.[32]

7.42 The practice committee may take any steps which it regards as necessary to protect vulnerable witnesses. Vulnerable witnesses may include:

- any witness under the age of 18;
- any witness with a mental disorder;
- any witness who is significantly impaired in relation to intelligence or social functioning;
- any witness with physical disabilities who requires assistance to give evidence;
- any witness where the subject matter of the hearing is of a sexual nature and the witness was the alleged victim; or
- any witness who complains of intimidation.[33]

Where appropriate, evidence can be given by video-link and/or pre-recorded evidence can be used as evidence-in-chief. Where proceedings concern a sexual allegation, respondents acting in person are not permitted to cross-examine the alleged victim directly in person.[34]

7.43 The three practice committees – the Professional Performance Committee, the Professional Conduct Committee and the Health Committee – may refer cases to each other or take advice from each other where appropriate.[35]

7.44 The practice committees must apply the civil standard of proof. The case-law relating to the standard of proof is discussed in more detail in chapter 2 (see para 2.371).

31 See GDC (FTP) Rules 2006 r51.

32 See www.gdc-uk.org/about/who-we-are/committees/professional-performance-committee.

33 GDC (FTP) Rules 2006 r56.

34 GDC (FTP) Rules 2006 r56.

35 GDC (FTP) Rules 2006 r26.

Sources of law

7.45 The GDC's powers derive from the DA 1984, which covers matters such as registration, the functions of the various committees, interim orders, sanction and appeals, and which empowers the GDC to make orders, rules and regulations in relevant areas.

7.46 The procedure followed in fitness to practise matters from the complaint stage onwards is governed by the General Dental Council (Fitness to Practise) Rules 2006 (GDC (FTP) Rules 2006).[36] The Registration Appeals Committee has its own procedure rules: the GDC (Registration Appeals) Rules 2006.[37]

7.47 The GDC has published new guidance for the practice committees, including indicative sanctions guidance (updated 1 March 2017). This is available on the GDC website.[38]

Proceedings

Referrals

7.48 Disciplinary proceedings against dentists and dental care professionals begin with a complaint or other information alerting the GDC to a potential issue. The complaint can come from any source, including other dental professionals, other professionals and members of the public.

7.49 A complaint or other information about a registrant (including a registrant whose registration is suspended) is initially passed to the registrar. The registrar determines whether a complaint or information amounts to an allegation.[39] Allegations are passed to the case examiners.

7.50 Where the registrar determines that a complaint or information amounts to an allegation, he or she must send a notification to the respondent and any maker of the allegation accordingly. The notification must:

- contain a summary of the allegation;
- be accompanied by a copy of the documents in the registrar's possession which relate to the allegation (however, the registrar shall not disclose to the maker of the allegation any evidence relating to the health or private and family life of the respondent or a third party, which has been provided by the respondent or a third party);
- invite the respondent to respond to the allegation with written representations addressed to the Investigating Committee within a period which the registrar shall specify in the notification; and

36 Schedule to the General Dental Council (Fitness to Practise) Rules Order of Council 2006 No 1663.

37 Schedule to the General Dental Council (Registration Appeals) Rules Order of Council 2006 SI No 1668.

38 See www.gdc-uk.org/about/who-we-are/committees/professional-performance-committee.

39 GDC (FTP) Rules 2006 r3.

- where the allegation has been made by a person, inform the respondent that representations received from him or her may be disclosed to that person for comment.[40]

7.51 Those advising registrants should take care from the earliest stage when corresponding with the regulator and disclosing further information. Any inconsistencies or inaccuracies can be used at the main hearing. Care should also be taken before suggesting that an allegation is minor or trivial in nature. On the one hand, it can be persuasive to emphasise that the matters alleged are too minor to amount to misconduct or lack of competence even if proven. On the other hand, this could be used to demonstrate a lack of insight or understanding of the seriousness of the allegation. The safest course of action for registrants is likely to be to take legal advice at the earliest opportunity.

7.52 *Standards for the dental team* provides that dental professionals have a duty to co-operate fully with any procedure for bringing concerns which applies to their work.[41] They have a duty to approach the GDC in relation to concerns about other dental professionals if taking action at a local level would not be practical or has failed, or if the problem is so severe that the GDC genuinely needs to be involved, or if there is a genuine fear of victimisation or a cover-up.[42]

7.53 Although the GDC does not impose any time limit for the bringing of complaints, both domestic law and the ECHR confer a right to the speedy and just resolution of disputes. However, unreasonable delay in itself is insufficient to stay proceedings against a respondent. The law on delay is discussed in more detail in chapter 1 (see paras 1.67 and 1.162).

7.54 Regulatory proceedings do not need to be stayed pending the outcome of criminal proceedings unless there are exceptional circumstances from which the defendant can demonstrate serious prejudice or injustice. The law relating to concurrent proceedings is discussed in more detail in chapter 1 at paras 1.275–1.279.

Case examiners and Investigating Committee

7.55 Following the changes to the GDC (FTP) Rules 2006 instigated by the GDC (FTP) (Amendment) Rules Order of Council SI No 902, most of the functions of the Investigating Committee have been delegated to the case examiners. Two case examiners consider each case: of these, one is a lay person, the other is a dentist or a dental care professional. The case examiners review the evidence and decide whether or not an allegation should be considered by a practice committee. They are also empowered to refer cases to the Interim Orders Committee.

7.56 According to current GDC policy,[43] case examiners should consider the following:

40 GDC (FTP) Rules 2006 r4.

41 See www.gdc-uk.org/Dentalprofessionals/Fitnesstopractise/Pages/Advice-on-raising-concerns.aspx.

42 See www.gdc-uk.org/Dentalprofessionals/Fitnesstopractise/Pages/Advice-on-raising-concerns.aspx.

43 See www.gdc-uk.org/about/who-we-are/committees/case-examiners.

1) whether there is a real prospect of the facts, as alleged, being found proved, and if so,
2) whether or not there is a real prospect of the statutory ground being established (eg misconduct), and if so,
3) whether or not there is a real prospect of a finding of current impairment being made.

7.57 The 'real prospect' test requires that the case examiners determine that there is a genuine (not remote or fanciful) possibility of establishing at a practice committee that the registrant's fitness to practise is currently impaired.

7.58 The case examiners are empowered to close the case, seek further information, issue a letter of advice, issue a warning (which can be published on the GDC website), request undertakings, or refer the matter to the Interim Orders Committee and/or practice committees.

7.59 Case examiners may review the decision to issue a warning upon the application of the respondent, the informant or the Registrar. They may also review a decision to refer a case to a practice committee upon referral from the relevant practice committee. They are also empowered to review a decision to close a case rather than referring it to a practice committee.[44]

7.60 In *R (P) v General Dental Council*[45] it was held that DA 1984 s27A(11), conferred a right upon registrants to seek a review of a decision to issue a warning, provided that registrants applied within two years of the decision.

7.61 Where the two case examiners fail to reach agreement, they must refer the allegation to the Investigating Committee for a determination. The Investigating Committee sits in the absence of the parties, and decides whether or not the allegation is to be considered by a practice committee. Written representations from the respondent and the maker of the allegation are taken into account.[46]

7.62 Where either the case examiners or the Investigating Committee decides that an allegation ought not to be considered by a practice committee, the GDC's registrar may review all or part of the determination, conduct his or her own investigations, seek representations and refer the matter for reconsideration by an Investigating Committee or case examiners.[47]

7.63 If the allegation proceeds to a practice committee, the respondent and the maker of the allegation must be given a reasonable opportunity to submit written representations commenting upon the allegation and upon the evidence (except evidence relating to the health or private and family life of the respondent or a third party which has been provided by the respondent or a third party).[48]

7.64 The particulars of the allegation and the facts upon which they are founded should be made clear in advance of any hearing. In *Gee v General*

44 DA 1984 ss27A(8) and 36O(8); GDC (FTP) Rules 2006 r6E.
45 [2016] EWHC 3181 (Admin).
46 GDC (FTP) Rules 2006 r7.
47 GDC (FTP) Rules 2006 r9.
48 GDC (FTP) Rules 2006 r7(2).

Medical Council[49] the court held it to be a requirement that the registrant had fair notice of the nature of the evidence to be led in support of the allegations, time to prepare for his defence and, that the panel should make plain which of the allegations of fact, if any, they had found proved. It is an aspect of ECHR Article 6 that a respondent should be made aware of the charges against him or her. Allegations should not be drafted in a vague or ambiguous manner. The case-law relating to the drafting of allegations is discussed in more detail in chapter 1 at paras 1.82–1.141.

Interim Orders Committee

> The Interim Orders Committee has the power to make an interim order for conditions of practice or for suspension.
>
> Weight is given to any risk to the public.

7.65 The Interim Orders Committee has the power to impose an interim order upon a respondent pending a hearing before one of the practice committees.[50] The Interim Orders Committee does not make findings of fact and does not make substantive decisions upon alleged impairment of fitness to practise. The relevant guidance document for Interim Orders Committee hearings is *Interim orders guidance for the IOC*.[51]

7.66 Interim orders may only be made in the following circumstances:

- where the Interim Orders Committee is satisfied that the order is necessary for the protection of the public;
- where it is otherwise in the public interest;
- where it is in the interests of the respondent.[52]

7.67 Interim orders can be appealed pursuant to DA 1984 s32(12). Appeals are heard by the High Court.

7.68 In *Manuel Nunez Martinez v General Dental Council*[53] Warby J considered an appeal against an interim order of conditions made by an Interim Orders Committee. His judgment includes the following important findings upon the role of the GDC's Interim Orders Committee:

- Where factual applications are disputed, it will normally not be possible for the Interim Orders Committee or the court to arrive at definitive conclusions of fact. What the Interim Orders Committee will normally have to determine is *whether the allegations are credible*.[54]
- The function of the Interim Orders Committee and the court in relation to an interim order *is one of risk assessment*.[55]

49 [1987] 1 WLR 564.

50 DA 1984 s32(4).

51 See www.gdc-uk.org/about/who-we-are/committees/interim-orders-committee.

52 DA 1984 s32(4) (for dentists) and s36V(4) for dental care professionals.

53 [2015] EWHC 1223 (Admin).

54 *Manuel Nunez Martinez v GDC*, above, para 18.

55 *Manuel Nunez Martinez v GDC*, above, para 20.

- There is no threshold other than the need to protect the public, the public interest and, where applicable, the interests of the registrant. It is not a question of a prima facie case.

7.69 Respondents have the right to attend an interim orders hearing and to be legally represented. They must receive notice of the reason why it may be necessary to impose an interim order in the notification of interim orders hearing.[56]

7.70 Evidence in an interim orders hearing is admissible whether or not that evidence would be admissible in any proceedings in a court, subject to the requirements of relevance and fairness.[57]

7.71 At the interim orders hearing, unless the committee determines otherwise, the GDC presenter makes submissions and presents evidence as to why it may be necessary to make, revoke, confirm or replace an interim order. After this the respondent, or his or her representative, may make submissions and present evidence. With the chair's permission, legal or professional advisers may question a witness. Those present at the hearing will be informed of any advice given to the committee, even if it was given during private deliberations.

7.72 After hearing the evidence, the Interim Orders Committee deliberates in private. A decision is then made in public.[58] Reasons must be given. Chapter 2 contains a discussion on the requirement to give reasons (see paras 2.39–2.40.

7.73 The Interim Orders Committee has the power to make the following orders:

- *Suspension:* Suspending a respondent's registration for a period not exceeding 18 months with six-monthly reviews.
- *Conditions:* Subjecting a respondent's registration to compliance with such conditions as the Interim Orders Committee may impose for a period not exceeding 18 months with six-monthly reviews.

7.74 Conditions should be clear; relevant; addressed to the registrant (not to third parties); necessary in order to protect patients, the public or in the interests of the registrant; proportionate to the allegations; formulated so that the conditions are not in effect a suspension; and written in such a way that compliance can be easily verified.

7.75 The guidance provides that conditions can only be adequate when there is reasonable confidence in the registrant's capacity to comply with them. If there is an issue between imposing conditions and suspension, suspension may be necessary to protect the public interest. If circumstances prevent the registrant from complying with the conditions, then suspension might be required.

7.76 Those advising registrants should obtain clear instructions from the client before proposing conditions to the Interim Orders Committee as an alternative to suspension. The GDC maintains a 'conditions bank' of standard conditions applicable in various types of interim orders cases.

56 GDC (FTP) Rules 2006 r35.
57 GDC (FTP) Rules 2006 r38.
58 GDC (FTP) Rules 2006 r36.

These are downloadable from the GDC website and can be used as a template where appropriate.

7.77 Interim orders may be reviewed at any time. An order must be reviewed if new evidence comes to light at any time, or if the registrant requests it. Review of an order by the request of the registrant can only apply after three months from the date of the order. The order must be reviewed every six months while it is in force as a minimum.[59]

7.78 Decisions of the Interim Orders Committee are published on the GDC website, with the exception of any confidential details relating to the respondent's physical or mental health. Where a hearing has been held in private, parties or witnesses who took part in the private hearing (or part of hearing) must not be identified.[60] The circumstances in which hearings are to be held in private are discussed at para 7.38 above.

Preliminary meetings

7.79 Before the substantive hearing a preliminary meeting ('pre-meeting') may be held if the committee members regard it as appropriate. A preliminary meeting is for case management purposes, and if necessary, the giving of directions. The parties attend the meeting, and a legal adviser is present. The preliminary meeting may also be attended by any person the committee thinks is appropriate – this can include a professional or medical adviser if the committee thinks this necessary.[61] The preliminary meeting may be held by the chair of a practice committee.

7.80 Directions may include:[62]

- time limits for the service of evidence and disclosure of expert evidence (if any);
- a requirement that each party provide an estimate of the length of the hearing and any dates on which they or any witnesses would not be able to attend the hearing;
- where the facts are not in dispute a requirement that the parties produce a statement of agreed facts;
- mutual disclosure of documents;
- the preparation of agreed bundles of documents to be distributed to the chair of a practice committee, members of a practice committee and the legal adviser in advance of the hearing;
- issues of joinder;
- the preparation of skeleton arguments where the parties are legally represented;
- a requirement that a party call the author of any expert report;
- where agreed between the parties, a direction that the witness statement of a witness shall stand as the evidence-in-chief of that witness;
- whether the hearing or part of it should be held in public or in private;
- special measures to be put in place at the hearing for vulnerable witnesses;

59 *Interim orders guidance for the IOC*, www.gdc-uk.org.

60 GDC (FTP) Rules 2006 r39.

61 See *Guidance for handling cases at preliminary meetings*, available at www.gdc-uk.org.

62 GDC (FTP) Rules 2006 r51.

- a direction for an adjournment of the preliminary meeting or that a further preliminary meeting should be held; and
- the date of any hearing or part of a hearing.

The fitness to practise hearing

Fitness to practise is assessed looking forward from the date of the hearing.

Much weight is given to the respondent's level of insight.

Practice committees

7.81 There are three practice committees: the Professional Conduct Committee; the Professional Performance Committee; and the Health Committee.

7.82 The Professional Conduct Committee deals with cases where it is alleged that a registrant's fitness to practise has been impaired by his or her conduct – eg cases of alleged assault, dishonesty or abuse of position. 'Misconduct' is not defined in the statutory materials. The case-law provides that it is conceptually separate from inadequate professional performance (*R (Calhaem) v General Medical Council*[63]). In *Remedy UK Ltd v General Medical Council*[64] the court identified two kinds of misconduct: a) sufficiently serious misconduct within the exercise of professional practice and b) morally culpable or disgraceful conduct outside the course of professional practice. Ultimately the decision as to whether a respondent's actions amount to misconduct in a particular case is a question for the panel (*Mallon v General Medical Council*[65]). It goes beyond negligence; however, in a particularly serious case negligence may amount to misconduct.

7.83 The Professional Conduct Committee also deals with cases where it is alleged that a registrant's fitness to practise has been impaired by reason of a criminal conviction, or by reason of the determination of another regulatory body. In the case of *Peckitt v General Dental Council*[66] Kerr J gave consideration to the question of the approach which should be taken to cases involving the determination of another regulatory body. The case concerned a maxillo-facial surgeon who had already faced proceedings before the GMC for allegedly punching a patient. The court addressed the following issue: should the GDC's Professional Conduct Committee reconsider the underlying facts in a case where another regulator has already made a determination? Kerr J found that:

> . . . it is not, at least other than in exceptional cases, for the second disciplinary panel to revisit the factual territory of the first. That seems to me to be the position, other than in rare and exceptional cases.[67]

7.84 The Professional Performance Committee deals with cases where it is alleged that a registrant's fitness to practise has been impaired by his or

63 [2007] EWHC 2606 (Admin).
64 [2010] EWHC 1245 (Admin).
65 [2007] CSIH 17.
66 [2016] EWHC 1803 (Admin).
67 *Peckitt v General Dental Council*, above, paras 37–38.

her inadequate professional performance (ie poor standard of work). 'Lack of competence', like misconduct, has not been defined by the regulators. In *R (Calhaem) v General Medical Council* (above) Jackson J observed that it connotes an 'unacceptably low' standard of professional performance which (save in exceptional circumstances) has been demonstrated by reference to a fair sample of work.

7.85 The Health Committee deals with cases where it is alleged that a registrant's fitness to practise may be impaired due to his or her own physical or mental health. The sanction of erasure from the register may not be imposed if the finding is one of impairment solely on health grounds.[68]

7.86 In all cases the panel must look to the future and focus upon the respondent's fitness to practise from the date of the hearing onwards (*Meadow v General Medical Council*[69]). Much weight is given to the insight or remorse demonstrated by the respondent in determining whether fitness to practise is likely to be impaired in the future. For a fuller discussion of the law relating to fitness to practise, see chapter 1 at paras 1.15–1.31.

Procedure – overview

7.87 The basic procedure at the hearing[70] is common to all three practice committees.

- The hearing begins with the preliminary stage – reading out the notification of hearing and amendment of the charge if appropriate.
- After this, 'stage one' begins:
  - First there is a factual enquiry.
  - The parties then make submissions on the facts.
  - The panel then makes a determination on whether the charges have been proved on the facts – the 'stage one' determination.
- Following the 'stage one' determination, the matter proceeds to 'stage two':
  - The parties make submissions on misconduct, impairment and sanction.
  - Further evidence can be adduced at stage two.
  - A determination on stage two is thereafter handed down.
- In relevant cases, the committee thereafter considers whether or not to make an immediate order.

Preliminary matters

7.88 At the preliminary stage, the notification of hearing is read out (unless both parties state that they do not desire it to be read out). The notification of hearing contains the charge or charges against the respondent. At any stage before making findings of fact, the practice committee may amend the charge set out in the notification of hearing unless, having regard to the merits of the case and the fairness of the proceedings, the required

68 DA 1984 s27B.

69 *Meadow v General Medical Council* [2007] QB 462.

70 GDC (FTP) Rules 2006 r14.

amendment cannot be made without injustice. The later the amendment, the more likely it is that injustice may be caused. Before making any amendment to the charge, the practice committee must consider any representations from the parties.[71] The case-law on allegations, charges and amendment applications is discussed in detail in chapter 1 at paras 1.82–1.157.

Stage one

7.89 The factual inquiry begins with the GDC presenter opening the case and presenting evidence. The respondent or the respondent's representative has the right to cross-examine any witness called by the presenter. After cross-examination, the witness can be re-examined. The committee members then have the opportunity to put questions to the witness. After the committee members have put questions to the witness, the representatives for the parties can put further questions to the witness arising out of the committee members' questions.

7.90 When the presenter has finished presenting the GDC case, the respondent or the respondent's representative may open the case for the respondent. This may commence with a submission that there is no case to answer.

7.91 In relation to submissions of no case to answer, it appears that the test set out in the criminal case of *R v Galbraith*[72] applies to submissions of no case to answer in regulatory law. The test in *R v Galbraith* is whether 1) there was any evidence upon which a panel could find matters proved, or 2) whether there was some evidence, but it was of such an unsatisfactory nature that the panel, properly directed, could not find the matter proved. The relevant law is discussed in more detail at chapter 2 at paras 2.384–2.401.

7.92 Where the respondent or the respondent's representative makes a submission that there is no case to answer, the practice committee must adjourn the hearing and deliberate in private for the purpose of determining whether to accept the submission. The chair of the practice committee shall announce whether the submission that there is no case to answer has been accepted. Where the practice committee has accepted the submission, they may make such orders as to costs and other matters as they consider necessary.[73]

7.93 If the hearing proceeds, the respondent or the respondent's representative shall present evidence. The GDC presenter may cross-examine any witness called by the respondent or the respondent's representative. After cross-examination, the witness can be re-examined. The committee members then have the opportunity to put questions to the witness. After the committee members have put questions to the witness, the representatives for the parties can put further questions to the witness arising out of the committee members' questions. The respondent or the respondent's representative shall set out or conclude the case for the respondent after the evidence has been set out.

71 GDC (FTP) Rules 2006 rr17 and 18.
72 [1981] 1 WLR 1039, [1981] 2 All ER 1060.
73 GDC (FTP) Rules 2006 r19.

7.94 At this stage, the evidence that may be presented should not include any evidence as to mitigation, but should be restricted to evidence relating to the facts alleged in the notification of hearing.

7.95 After the case for the respondent concludes, the practice committee must adjourn the hearing to deliberate in private as to their findings of fact. The practice committee must announce their findings of fact, by reference to the matters mentioned in the notification of hearing, in the presence of the parties.

7.96 Where a practice committee determines that *none* of the facts alleged in the notification of hearing have been proved against the respondent, they shall make the determination that the respondent's fitness to practise as a dentist or as a member of a profession complementary to dentistry is not impaired.[74]

7.97 Where a practice committee determines that *some or all* of the facts alleged in the notification of hearing *have* been proved against the respondent, the matter proceeds to stage two.

Stage two

7.98 At stage two, submissions are made by both the GDC representative and the respondent or respondent's representative upon impairment and sanctions. The submissions *must* cover the following matters:[75]

- the respondent's history;
- the question of whether, in the light of the facts found, the respondent's fitness to practise as a dentist or as a member of a profession complementary to dentistry is impaired; and
- where the GDC presenter's submission is that the respondent's fitness to practise as a dentist or as a member of a profession complementary to dentistry is impaired, what action should be taken (ie sanctions).

The respondent or representative may also adduce further evidence on stage two matters and may make submissions on mitigation by reference to the respondent's personal circumstances.

7.99 Following the submissions, the practice committee will withdraw to deliberate in private. The determination, together with reasons, is then given in public (except in the case of a private hearing as set out above). The practice committee must determine whether the respondent's fitness to practise is impaired and, if so, whether to impose any sanction against the respondent and what sanction to impose. Sanctions are considered in more detail below.

Immediate order

7.100 In a case where erasure, suspension or conditions of practice have been imposed at stage two, the practice committee will proceed to consider whether or not to impose an 'immediate order' of suspension or conditions.[76] An immediate order covers the 28-day period during which an

74 GDC (FTP) Rules 2006 r19.
75 GDC (FTP) Rules 2006 r20.
76 DA 1984 ss30 and 36U.

appeal can be brought and (if an appeal is brought) the period pending the hearing of the appeal in the High Court. If an immediate order is not made, the respondent will be free to practise during the appeal period.

7.101 An immediate order should be imposed if the practice committee is satisfied that it is a) necessary for the protection of the public, or b) otherwise in the public interest or c) is in the interests of the respondent.

7.102 In *Jonathan Davey v General Dental Council*[77] the court observed that 'the importance of the giving of reasons when an immediate order is made should not be underestimated'. An immediate order does not automatically follow from the making of a final order.

7.103 In *R (Rothschild) v General Dental Council* the court observed that the High Court should not interfere with the decision to impose an immediate order unless persuaded that the decision was wrong.

Sanctions

> The sanctions available to the GDC are: a) a reprimand, b) conditions of practice, c) suspension and d) erasure from the register.

Purpose

7.104 The purpose of sanctions is to protect the public, not to punish the registrant. However, the protection of the public includes consideration of the deterrent effect, the reputation of the profession and public confidence in the regulatory process. Even if impairment of fitness to practise has been proved, it is not mandatory to impose a sanction.[78]

Approach

7.105 In *Jonathan Davey v General Dental Council*[79] the High Court observed that the 'stepwise' approach to sanction (whereby the least restrictive sanction is considered before moving up in steps of severity to reach the appropriate level) is a matter of substance and not merely one of form.

Sanctions available

7.106 The sanctions available to the practice committees are as follows (in ascending order of gravity).[80]

a) *Reprimand:* This is a statement of the committee's disapproval, but the registrant is still fit to practise with no restrictions.
b) *Conditions:* Requirements (of a restrictive or a rehabilitative nature) are placed on the registrant's work for a set amount of time. The period

77 Before Deputy Master Bard, HQ15X02545, 8 October 2015 (unreported, but on Lawtel).
78 GDC (FTP) Rules 2006 r21(1)(b).
79 [2015] EWHC 3594 (Admin).
80 DA 1984 s27B.

will not exceed three years. The conditions usually have to be reviewed within a set period.

c) *Suspension:* The committee can suspend the dental professional's registration. This means that the registrant cannot work as a dental professional for that set period of time.

d) *Erasure:* This is the most serious sanction, as it removes a registrant's name from the register. This means that the registrant can no longer work in dentistry in the UK (unless and until he or she applies for re-inclusion).

Reprimand

7.107 A reprimand may be considered appropriate in circumstances where there is no risk to the public or to patients. It cannot be given in conjunction with another determination.[81]

Conditions

7.108 Conditions should be clear; relevant; addressed to the registrant (not to third parties); necessary in order to protect patients, the public or in the interests of the registrant; proportionate to the allegations; formulated so that the conditions are not in effect a suspension; and written in such a way that compliance can be easily verified.

7.109 The guidance provides that conditions can only be adequate when there is reasonable confidence in the registrant's capacity to comply with them. If there is an issue between imposing conditions and suspension, suspension may be necessary to give the public the protection expected. If circumstances prevent the registrant from complying with the conditions, then suspension might be required.

7.110 Representatives may wish to propose suitable conditions (on instructions from the respondent) as an alternative to suspension or erasure. The GDC maintains a conditions bank (separate from the interim orders conditions bank) which can be used as a source. Providing supporting evidence (eg a statement from a person who is willing to mentor the respondent) can be important in appropriate cases. Supervision of dentists can in some circumstances be undertaken by the dentist's local Deanery (postgraduate school of dentistry).

Suspension

7.111 Suspension is suitable where a committee finds that the withdrawal of registration is necessary for public protection, but does not need to last the five-year term that would be the minimum with erasure. Suspension will be for a given period of time, not exceeding 12 months. The determination must make clear whether the suspension will be automatically lifted at the end of the stated period or whether it will be reviewed.[82] Review hearings are dealt with below.

81 Guidance for the practice committees including indicative sanctions guidance.

82 Guidance for the practice committees including indicative sanctions guidance.

Erasure

7.112 Erasure from the register is obviously the most serious sanction. Following erasure a person cannot practise as a dentist or dental professional. The person can, however, apply for the restoration of his or her name to the register after a minimum of five years.[83] The guidance states that erasure is imposed in order to protect the public and maintain its confidence in the profession as a whole. Prior to erasure being considered, all other available sanctions should be considered in ascending order of seriousness to ensure that the case is being considered bearing in mind the principle of proportionality. No committee may erase purely on health grounds.[84]

7.113 The guidance provides that erasure is appropriate when the behaviour concerned is 'fundamentally incompatible' with being a dental professional.

Mitigation

7.114 Because disciplinary sanctions are not punitive in nature, personal considerations that would ordinarily weigh in mitigation of punishment have less effect than they would on sentencing in the criminal context. The guidance provides that in some situations the risk of harm to the public or the need to protect the public may properly override persuasive mitigation. In performance cases, evidence that failure to meet the expected standards was associated with particular circumstances which no longer exist may give some degree of reassurance. However, the chance of those circumstances recurring may be relevant to the evaluation of risk and to the disposal of the case.

7.115 Commonly, registrants provide testimonials in support of their character. These testimonials fall to be considered in the light of the factual findings made at the hearing. Greater weight is given to testimonials which demonstrate that the author was aware of the facts of the case.

7.116 It can consequently be useful to make referees aware of the factual background to the case prior to giving a testimonial. Care should, however, be taken to ensure that evidence is not provided which amounts to an admission contrary to the respondent's instructions.

Appeals from fitness to practise decisions

7.117 A right of appeal to the High Court lies from decisions of practice committees giving directions for erasure, suspension or conditional registration. An appeal must be lodged within 28 days of the day that the decision was served.[85] In *Darfoor v General Dental Council*[86] it was held that the time limit is strict and can only be extended by the discretion of the court in

83 DA 1984 s28.
84 DA 1984 s27B(7).
85 DA 1984 s29.
86 [2016] EWHC 2715 (Admin).

'exceptional circumstances' and where the appellant has personally done all that he or she could to bring the appeal in time.

7.118 The PSA can challenge decisions that they regard as unduly lenient. PSA appeals are dealt with in more detail in chapter 10 at paras 10.84–10.94.

Resumed hearings

7.119 A resumed hearing takes place when a direction for conditions or for suspension has previously been made. It usually takes place towards the end of the period of conditions or suspension.

7.120 At a resumed hearing the GDC presenter will inform the practice committee of the background to the case and the sanctions previously imposed on the respondent, direct the attention of the practice committee to any relevant evidence previously considered by the practice committee including transcripts of previous hearings, present any relevant evidence not previously considered by the practice committee, and make submissions as to the matters being considered by the practice committee. The respondent or representative may present evidence and make submissions.[87] The committee retires to deliberate and then gives the decision in public.[88]

7.121 As a matter of good practice, those representing registrants should provide evidence of compliance with conditions and of other steps taken to address the concerns raised at the earlier hearing (for example, any relevant continuing professional development). The committee will look for evidence of insight and for willingness to take on board lessons learnt from the original proceedings. They will ask what has changed since the date of the original proceedings. A resumed hearing should not be seen as an opportunity to challenge the original decision.

7.122 At a resumed hearing the practice committee has the following powers if a suspension order was originally imposed:[89]

- to terminate the suspension;
- to extend the suspension for a period not exceeding 12 months from the expiry of the original suspension;
- to replace the suspension with conditions of practice for a period of up to three years;
- to suspend registration indefinitely, provided that the registrant will have been suspended for at least two years on the date on which the direction takes effect, and the direction is made not more than two months before the date on which the period of suspension would otherwise expire. (In practice, this order will only be made at a second or subsequent resumed hearing, as DA 1984 s27B provides that practice committees are only able to impose a suspension order of up to

87 GDC (FTP) Rules 2006 r29.
88 GDC (FTP) Rules 2006 r29.
89 DA 1984 s27C.

12 months.) If this order is imposed, there is a provision for a review at the registrant's request after at least two years of the date of the order.[90]

7.123 If conditions of practice were originally imposed, the practice committee has the following powers at a resumed hearing:[91]

- to remove the conditions;
- to extend the conditions for a period of not more than three years;
- to vary, revoke or add to any of the conditions; or
- to suspend registration for not more than 12 months. Suspension of registration can also be imposed where a practice committee determines that a person has failed to comply with any condition.

7.124 There is the right of appeal to the High Court against resumed hearing decisions which result in conditions or suspension.[92] The appeal must be lodged within 28 days of the date of the decision.

Fraudulent register entry hearings before the Professional Conduct Committee

7.125 In addition to fitness to practise hearings, the DA 1984 provides that the Professional Conduct Committee hears cases where the registrar has reason to believe that an entry on the register has been procured by fraud.[93] The procedure is essentially the same as the fitness to practise procedure.[94]

7.126 If the Professional Conduct Committee determines that an entry has been fraudulently procured, it shall direct that that person's name be erased.[95]

7.127 There is a right of appeal to the High Court against fraudulent register entry decisions.[96] Appeals must be lodged within 28 days of service of the decision.

Restoration hearings before the Professional Conduct Committee

7.128 A dental professional whose name has been erased from the register following a practice committee hearing may apply for restoration to the register.[97] The Professional Conduct Committee also hears applications for restoration to the register following a determination that an entry on the register has been procured by fraud.[98] If the original complaint was

90 DA 1984 s27C(4).
91 DA 1984 s27C.
92 DA 1984 s29.
93 DA 1984 s24.
94 GDC (FTP) Rules 2006 r48.
95 DA 1984 s24.
96 DA 1984 s29.
97 DA 1984 s28.
98 DA 1984 s24.

made before 31 July 2006 (when the DA 1984 was amended), the application can be made ten months following erasure. If the complaint was made after 31 July 2006, the application can be made five years after erasure. No application may be made within 12 months of an earlier unsuccessful application. Where a second or subsequent application is unsuccessful during the same period of erasure, the Professional Conduct Committee may indefinitely suspend the right to make further applications.[99]

7.129 The application for restoration is dealt with by the Professional Conduct Committee. The evidence relating to the original erasure is considered. The applicant may address the committee and call witnesses. He or she may be legally represented. An applicant may be required to provide specific evidence as to fitness to practise and to undergo further requirements including education and training. Where an application is granted, the Professional Conduct Committee may impose conditions for a period of up to three years.[100]

7.130 There is a right of appeal to the High Court against a decision to refuse to restore a person's name to the register. There is also a right of appeal to the High Court against the decision to suspend the right to make further applications. Appeals must be lodged within 28 days of service of the decision.[101]

Registration Appeals Committee

7.131 The Registration Appeals Committee considers appeals from dental professionals made against the registrar in the following circumstances:

- where registration has been refused;
- where a person has been removed from the register (*except* by a practice committee);
- where a person has not been restored to the register (*except* by a practice committee).

7.132 If a decision is taken solely on the grounds that a person has failed to pay an appropriate fee or has failed to make the required application, this is not appealable.[102]

7.133 The Registration Appeals Committee is governed by its own rules of procedure – the GDC (Registration Appeals) Rules 2006. Under these rules, appeals are initiated by the registrant or would-be registrant. Appeals do not automatically proceed to a hearing unless either the appellant requests it or the GDC regards it as appropriate.[103]

7.134 If the matter proceeds to a hearing, a directions hearing may be scheduled for the purpose of case management.[104] Appeals are held in public unless the committee is satisfied that, in the interests of justice or for the

99 DA 1984 s28.
100 DA 1984 s28.
101 DA 1984 s29.
102 DA 1984 Sch 2A para 2 and Sch 4A para 2.
103 GDC (Registration Appeals) Rules 2006 r4.
104 GDC (Registration Appeals) Rules 2006 r9.

protection of the private or family life of the appellant or of any other person, the public should be excluded from all or part of the hearing. Appellants may be legally represented or represented by a professional colleague, officer or member of organisation or family member.[105]

7.135 At the hearing, the parties and their representative may address the committee, give evidence, call and examine witnesses and cross-examine witnesses called by the other party or their representative. The committee may also examine witnesses. The committee may admit any evidence which they consider fair and relevant to the case before them, whether or not this evidence was available to the registrar at the time of the appealable registration decision at issue or would be admissible in a court of law. The appellant has the right to address the committee last.[106]

7.136 The committee's determination is given in the presence of the parties, together with reasons.[107]

7.137 There is a right of appeal from decisions of the Registration Appeals Committee. Appeals are heard in the county court.[108] This is in contrast with appeals from the other committees, which are heard in the High Court.

Costs

7.138 There is a provision for costs orders to be made by a practice committee where a submission of no case to answer has been accepted.[109] In general, as for other regulators, costs orders are not typically made unless a complaint is improperly brought, as the regulators act in the public interest and are not in the position of the ordinary litigant (*Baxendale-Walker v Law Society*[110]).

105 GDC (Registration Appeals) Rules 2006 r14.
106 GDC (Registration Appeals) Rules 2006 r15.
107 GDC (Registration Appeals) Rules 2006 r16.
108 DA 1984 Schs 2A and 4A Part 6.
109 GDC (FTP) Rules 2006 r19(6).
110 [2007] EWCA Civ 233.

CHAPTER 8

The General Optical Council

continued

Key points

- *Regulator:* General Optical Council (GOC)
- *Professions regulated:* Optometrists, dispensing opticians, student opticians and optical businesses
- *Common sources of referral:* Registrant's employer, primary care organisations, professional or educational body, patients, members of the public, fellow registrants
- *Relevant statute:* Opticians Act (OA) 1989
- *Fitness to Practise Rules:* General Optical Council (Fitness to Practise) Rules Order Council 2013 SI No 2357 (GOC (FTP) Rules 2013)
- *Type of proceedings:* Fitness to practise; GOC (FTP) Rules 2013 Part 2
- *Investigation process:* GOC (FTP) Rules 2013 Part 2
- Case examiners: GOC (FTP) Rules 2013 Part 2 r3(b) provides for the registrar and case examiners to exercise the delegated function of the Investigation Committee under OA 1989 s13D(5)–(9)
- *Initial consideration and referral of allegations:* GOC (FTP) Rules 2013 r4 provides for initial consideration by the Registrar
- *Investigation Committee:* GOC (FTP) Rules 2013 Part 4 r13 sets out the process for consideration by the Investigation Committee of an allegation referred to it by the case examiners or to direct an assessment
- *Fitness to Practise Committee:* GOC (FTP) Rules 2013 Parts 6 and 7 sets out the hearings and procedure of the Fitness to Practise Committee
- *Location:* General Optical Council, 10 Old Bailey, London, EC4M 7NG
- *Notice of hearing provision:* GOC (FTP) Rules 2013 Part 7
- *Procedure before a Fitness to Practise Committee:* GOC (FTP) Rules 2013 Part 7
- *Test:* Whether fitness to practise is impaired by reason of (in summary): a) misconduct; b) deficient professional performance; c) a criminal conviction or caution; d) the registrant having accepted a conditional offer under the Criminal Procedure (Scotland) Act 1995 s302 (fixed penalty) or agreed to pay a penalty under the Social Security Administration Act 1992 s115A (penalty as alternative to prosecution); e) in Scotland, the registrant, in proceedings for an offence under the Criminal Procedure (Scotland) Act 1995 s246(2) or (3) (discharging him or her absolutely); f) adverse physical or mental health; g) a determination by a health regulatory body that fitness to practise is impaired (or a determination by a regulatory body elsewhere to the same effect (in accordance with OA 1989 s13D(2)–(3)).
- *Power to require a practitioner to undergo health or performance assessment?* Yes – GOC (FTP) Rules 2013 Part 3 rr6, 7, 8, 9, 10 and 11. Rule 11 provides for the Investigation Committee or the Fitness to Practise Committee to draw such inference as seems appropriate where the registrant fails to co-operate
- *Interim order power:* GOC (FTP) Rules 2013 Part 5 rr17–20, heard by Fitness to Practise Committee

- *Interim order guidance: Guidance Fitness to Practise Committee – Hearings and Indicative Sanctions Guidance – Interim Orders,* OA 1989 s13L
- *How to address panel:* Generally seated and 'Sir'/'Madam'
- *Legal Adviser:* appointed under OA 1989 s23D(1)(d); GOC (FTP) Rules 2013 r43
- *Evidence:* GOC (FTP) Rules 2013 r40(1). The Fitness to Practise Committee 'may admit any evidence it considers fair and relevant to the case before it, whether or not such evidence would be admissible in a court of law' subject to r40(2) and (3)
- *Sanction provisions:* OA 1989 s13F
- *Review hearings:* GOC (FTP) Rules 2013 Part 8 rr55–58
- *Registration Appeals:* General Optical Council (Registration Appeals Rules) Order of Council 2005 SI No 1477

Introduction

Establishment

8.1 The General Optical Council (GOC) was established by the Opticians Act (OA) 1958 to regulate the optical professions in the UK. The GOC currently registers around 29,000 optometrists and dispensing opticians, approximately 4,000 students and approximately 1,500 optical businesses. This legislation was consolidated to form the Opticians Act (OA) 1989 which includes all subsequent amending legislation. In 2005, a number of changes were made to the legislation. These included the introduction of mandatory continuing education and training (CET) for full registrants, and the introduction of registration for student optometrists and dispensing opticians.

Core functions

8.2 The GOC is the regulator for the optical professions in the UK. Its purpose is to protect the public by promoting high standards of education, performance and conduct among opticians and currently registers around 29,000 optometrists, dispensing opticians, student opticians and optical businesses.

8.3 The GOC has four core functions:

1) Setting standards for optical education and training, performance and conduct.
2) Approving qualifications leading to registration.
3) Maintaining a register of individuals who are qualified and fit to practise, train or carry on business as optometrists and dispensing opticians.
4) Investigating and acting where registrants' fitness to practise (FTP), train or carry on business is impaired.

8.4 This is achieved by setting and publishing standards of professional proficiency, as well as standards of conduct, performance and ethics that apply to all registrants, and by considering complaints against registrants. The

GOC publishes a code of conduct for individual registrants (optometrists, dispensing opticians and optical students) and a code of conduct for business registrants (companies and their employees). In order to promote safe and competent practice and to maintain public confidence in the profession, the GOC has the powers to take action where there is an impairment of the optometrists, dispensing opticians, student opticians and optical businesses.

Approach to regulation: the statutory grounds

8.5 The statutory grounds are set out in OA 1989 s13D(2)–(3) and cover allegations of misconduct, instances of deficient professional performance (although not in the case of a registered student), a previous conviction or caution, issues arising from adverse physical or mental health, or a determination by any other UK healthcare body[1] that fitness to practise is impaired. A finding of impaired fitness to practise against a business registrant can be based, among other things, on practises or patterns of behaviour within the business amounting to misconduct or deficient professional performance.

8.6 A registrant's fitness to practise may be impaired only on certain grounds which are set out at OA 1989 s13D(2) and (3). Those grounds vary, depending on whether it is a business registrant, a student registrant or an individual practitioner.[2] An allegation that an individual registrant's fitness to practise is, or may be, impaired, can relate to acts or omissions which occurred outside the United Kingdom or at a time when that registrant was not registered.[3] The GOC guidance[4] endorses established case-law and states the following principles regarding the concepts of 'misconduct' and 'deficient professional performance':[5]

- 'Misconduct' does not mean any breach of the duty owed by a business registrant or an individual registrant to their patient – it connotes a serious breach which indicates that the business registrant's or an individual registrant's fitness to practise is impaired.
- Mere negligence does not constitute 'misconduct' but negligent acts or omissions which are particularly serious may amount to 'misconduct'.
- A single negligent act or omission is less likely to cross the threshold of 'misconduct' than multiple acts or omission. However, there may be some circumstances in which a single negligent act or omission, if particularly grave, could be characterised as 'misconduct'.
- 'Deficient professional performance' connotes a standard of professional performance which is unacceptably low. A single instance of negligent treatment would be unlikely to constitute 'deficient professional performance' unless it was very serious indeed. Except in exceptional circumstances, 'deficient professional performance' should be based on consideration of a fair sample of work.

1 In Scotland only, an absolute discharge or a specified statutory penalty.
2 OA 1989 s13D(2) and (3).
3 OA 1989 s13D(3)(d).
4 *Guidance for case examiners* (July 2017).
5 *R (Caelhaem) v GMC* [2007] EWHC 2606 (Admin).

Sources of law

8.7 The OA 1958, under which the GOC was established, was consolidated and amended by the OA 1989 and the Opticians Act 1989 (Amendment) Order 2005.[6] Part 2A of the order governs fitness to practise.

8.8 The OA 1989 gives the GOC powers to make orders, rules and regulations in relevant areas, subject to approval by the Privy Council. These include the General Optical Council (Registration Rules) Order of Council 2005,[7] the General Optical Council (Registration Appeals Rules) Order of Council 2005[8] and the General Optical Council (Fitness to Practise) Rules 2013 (GOC (FTP) Rules 2103).[9] These replace the General Optical Council (Fitness to Practise) Rules 2005. The new FTP Rules came into force on 1 April 2014.[10]

8.9 The GOC can also take action if the laws in relation to the sale of optical appliances, or the testing of sight, are being broken and where there is a risk to the public. The GOC's Protocol on the *Investigation and prosecution of criminal offences* sets out the council's role in this process.

8.10 The GOC (FTP) Rules 2013 were designed to speed up the process, to allow the regulator to act faster to protect the public and reduce the stress that long investigations can cause for registrants. The main changes were:

- the introduction of case examiners as the principal decision-makers at the Investigation Committee stage;
- greater ability to screen out allegations which are not fitness to practise complaints;
- a new power vested in the Registrar to refer the most urgent cases directly to a fitness to practise hearing; and in addition a power to refer some cases to an interim order hearing.

8.11 The GOC maintains that after the changes the Rules remained as fair and rigorous as before. Registrants continue to have an opportunity to respond to all allegations made against them, and all final decisions are made by an independent panel with access to expert legal advice.

Starting the process

8.12 As with other healthcare regulators, the investigative and disciplinary process referrals to the GOC come from many sources, including a registrant's employer, a primary care organisation, the registrant's professional or educational body, self-declarations by the registrant. Every year, the GOC publishes a general report across all its activities, which includes a report dedicated to fitness to practise matters, with statistical information about the number and types of complaints that have been considered by the organisation. The GOC's annual reports are available online.

6 SI No 848.
7 SI No 1478.
8 SI No 1477.
9 SI No 2537.
10 SI No 2537.

8.13 Only a minority of the complaints that are made to the GOC result in a referral to the FTP Committee.[11] The GOC reports that in the majority of cases, case examiners decide that there is no need for any further action to be taken or that the matter can be appropriately dealt with by issuing a registrant with a warning or advice.

Initial consideration of cases

8.14 A major innovation introduced by the GOC (FTP) Rules 2013 was the delegation of powers of the Investigating Committee to the Registrar and case examiners. The Registrar initially considers all matters concerning fitness to practise received by the GOC.[12] The Registrar must consider whether or not to refer the matter to the FTP Committee for consideration as to whether an interim order should be made. Where the Registrar considers that the allegation does not fall within one of the grounds described in OA 1989 s13D, he or she shall notify the complainant and the case will be closed. Where the Registrar considers that the allegation does fall within one or more grounds described in OA 1989 s13D, he or she must refer the allegation to the case examiners for consideration under GOC (FTP) Rules 2013 r12. The Registrar must refer an allegation relating to a conviction which has resulted in a custodial sentence, whether immediate or suspended, to the FTP Committee.

8.15 Before the allegation is considered by the case examiners, further investigation and evidence gathering may have been undertaken by the GOC investigation team.

The investigation process

Case examiners

8.16 The GOC (FTP) Rules 2013 define a case examiner as an officer of the Council appointed by the Registrar on the Council's behalf for the purposes of exercising the functions of the Investigation Committee, in accordance with those rules, being a registered optometrist or dispensing optician, or a lay person.

8.17 The case examiners powers are set out in the GOC (FTP) Rules 2013.[13] The rules specify who can be a case examiner and their decision-making procedures. The case examiners undertake investigation into allegations referred by the Registrar. This may involve seeking additional information and in some circumstances expert reports and health and performance assessments.

8.18 At any stage, prior to making their final decision, the case examiners may adjourn their consideration of a case pending further investigation and inform the Registrar who will undertake that investigation. The Registrar has the task of providing any additional evidence obtained to the registrant and, where appropriate, to the maker of the allegation, giving

11 In 2016, 17–27 per cent of cases were referred to the FTP Committee.

12 GOC (FTP) Rules 2013 r4.

13 Created by delegation of the functions of the Investigating Committee under OA 1989 s13E(1).

them a reasonable opportunity to respond. The Registrar then provides the case examiners with all additional evidence, together with any further comments. The case examiners then resume their consideration of the matter.

8.19 If, during the course of considering the allegations, the case examiners consider that there may be evidence (either from the complaint made to the GOC or from any further investigation) of allegations not included by the Registrar, or that the allegations should be amended, the case examiners should adjourn their consideration of the case and inform the Registrar. The Registrar may then consider the matters raised and whether additional or alternative allegations should be drafted for consideration by the case examiners. The case examiners may then, after the registrant has had an opportunity to respond to any new or amended allegations/evidence,[14] resume their consideration of the matter.

Early disposal of cases

8.20 When considering an allegation, the case examiners may unanimously determine to close certain categories of case which, in the public interest, ought not to proceed through the fitness to practise procedure. The categories of case are as follows:

- an allegation which arises from events which occurred more than five years before the matter was brought to the attention of the GOC (except in exceptional circumstances);
- an allegation which is made by a complainant who wishes to remain anonymous or has indicated that they do not wish to co-operate further (although case examiners must bear in mind the GOC's own powers of investigation as set out in OA 1989 s13D); or
- any allegation which the case examiners consider is vexatious in nature.

Taking no further action

8.21 If the case examiners decide that an allegation does not need to be referred to the FTP Committee, or result in the issue of a warning, it may decide to close a case without taking any further action. The case examiners may decide to close a case and take no further action if:

- the allegation demonstrates no issue that could call into question a registrant's fitness to practise; or
- the alleged facts, even if proved, are not serious enough to result in that registrant's fitness to practise being impaired to the extent that would justify action being taken against their registration, and a warning is deemed unnecessary; or
- the alleged facts, if proved, may demonstrate that a registrant's fitness to practise is impaired, but there is no realistic prospect of being able to prove the alleged facts for evidential reasons, and a warning is deemed unnecessary.

14 GOC (FTP) Rules 2013 r12.

Informal advice

8.22 The case examiners may decide to issue advice to a registrant if the case is to be closed. Such advice has no formal status, it is simply advice. Such decisions may contain (but are not limited to) advice regarding future conduct, including advice about the appropriate handling of dissatisfied patients. In such situations, case examiners should draft the advice carefully so as to be clear that they are not issuing a warning. A warning is a formal response from the GOC to an allegation under OA 1989 s13D which is recorded against a registrant's entry in the register, whereas advice is an informal comment on the matter from the case examiners. Clear wording will also prevent any misinterpretation of the decision by a third party who is unfamiliar with the GOC's procedures. Where appropriate, the case examiners may also include positive comments in their advice.

Interim orders

8.23 If either of the case examiners is of the opinion that the FTP Committee should consider making an interim order in relation to a registrant, that case examiner must direct the Registrar who will refer the matter to the FTP Committee and notify the involved parties.[15]

8.24 An interim order can:

- suspend any registrant from practice completely; or
- temporarily remove an entry relating to a specialty or proficiency, or
- make their registration conditional on compliance with requirements imposed by the FTP Committee.

An interim order can last for a maximum of 18 months, unless extended by the relevant court, and will be subject to regular reviews during that period.

8.25 OA 1989 s13L states that the FTP Committee may make an interim order where they are satisfied that it is:

- necessary for the protection of members of the public; or
- otherwise in the public interest; or
- in the interests of a registrant.

8.26 In order to reach a decision about whether the FTP Committee should consider making an interim order, the case examiners will:

a) Take into account the circumstances, specified in the FTP Committee's guidance, as being likely to mean that an interim order is necessary.
b) Have regard to all the factors that will be taken into account by the FTP Committee when considering such a referral, including:
    i) the effect which any order might have on the registrant;
    ii) the requirement on the FTP Committee to balance the need for an order against the consequences which an order would have for the registrant, in order to satisfy themselves that the consequences are not disproportionate to the risk to the public;
    iii) that the primary purpose of an interim order is to protect the public from a real present or likely future risk. It will be relatively rare for

15 GOC (FTP) Rules 2013 r12(7) and OA 1989 s13D(9).

an interim order to be made only on the ground that it is in the public interest (for example, to maintain public confidence in the profession); and

iv) that an interim order might be made at an early stage of the investigation and, therefore, although the allegation ought to have been made in writing, it may not yet be supported by formal witness statements.

The public interest

8.27 The case examiners should always take into account the public interest. The wider public interest includes not just the protection of members of the public, but the maintenance of public confidence in the profession, and the declaring and upholding of proper standards of conduct and behaviour.

Equality and diversity

8.28 Paragraph 38 of the *Guidance for case examiners* expressly states that case examiners must be aware of and apply the GOC's Equality and Diversity Scheme. The guidance affirms the GOC commitment to promoting equality and valuing diversity and to operating procedures and processes which are fair, objective, transparent and free from discrimination. It acknowledges the GOC obligations in promoting equality as a positive requirement under the Equality Act 2010, and everyone who is acting on behalf of the GOC is expected to adhere to the spirit and letter of this legislation.

Potential outcomes of the case examiners consideration of an allegation

8.29 At the completion of the investigation stage there are a number of different, potential outcomes arising from the case examiners consideration of an allegation:[16]

- referral of the case to the FTP Committee;
- referral to the Investigation Committee where the case examiners are unable to reach a unanimous decision;
- the issue of a warning to the registrant;
- a decision to take no further action including issuing a registrant with advice about their future conduct; or
- a decision to take no further action.

Further information about each of these potential outcomes is set out later on in this chapter.

Decision making process

8.30 Disciplinary Committees are obliged under common law and pursuant to Article 6 of the European Convention on Human Rights (ECHR) (right to a fair trial), to give adequate reasons in any case in which a decision is

16 GOC (FTP) Rules 2013 r12(1).

made to impose a disciplinary order. The amount of detail will depend on the complexity of the case. The determination should clearly set out what the facts of the case are with sufficient detail to enable the reader to understand what has been decided and why.

8.31 When making their decision about a particular allegation, the case examiners are required to consider not only the original allegation, and any evidence that has been gathered by the Registrar, but also any written representations that have been received from the registrant concerned and the complainant where appropriate. The rules state that a registrant must be given copies of any information or documents received in support of the allegation and allowed 28 days in which to make any written representations before the case examiners commence consideration of the allegation(s).

8.32 The case examiners should also consider any comments received from the complainant, made once he or she has seen any written representations made by the registrant. Any comments from the complainant are also copied to the registrant.

8.33 There may be cases that involve concerns about a number of aspects of a registrant's fitness to practise. In making a decision, it is the cumulative effect of all potentially impairing factors that must be taken into account. Health and performance assessments are part of the process of collecting evidence (for individual registrants). Where the factual particulars relate to a number of aspects of a registrant's fitness to practise, the case examiners should include in their decision references to any specific representations or evidence they have considered that relate to their decision.

8.34 Where the case examiners' decision discounts, either fully or partially, an undisputed expert opinion, they must provide very clear reasons for this. The case examiners' role is not to make decisions on the facts, but only to determine whether the realistic prospect test has been met.

Recording decisions

8.35 All decisions made by the case examiners are recorded in writing, setting out full and detailed reasoning for the decision made, including:

- which factual particulars and allegations are being referred and on which ground of impairment;
- where documents have been submitted to support the allegation, the decision should refer to the specific document(s)/section(s) and set out how these relate to the decision;
- where the decision is not to refer the allegations due to evidence of insight and remediation. The case examiners should explain why there is no impairment;
- where the decision of the case examiners, which will not have resolved disputes of fact, appears to discount the findings of an expert opinion.

Notification

8.36 Following the case examiners' decision, the complainant(s) and the registrant(s) concerned receive a letter from the GOC setting out the case examiners' decision and the reasons for that decision. In the case of individual registrants, their employer is also informed of the case examiners' decision but are not provided with the full decision.

GOC referrals to third parties

8.37 The case examiners may instruct the GOC to refer an allegation to the police if it appears to relate to the commission of a criminal offence (or to refer the allegation to another enforcement agency, as appropriate) if it appears to relate to a non-GOC optical professional, for example, to the General Medical Council (GMC) if the allegation concerns laser eye surgery carried out by a doctor.

Code of conduct – GOC standards of behaviour and performance (1 April 2016)

8.38 The specific grounds for an allegation that a registrant's fitness to practise is impaired are set out under OA 1989 s13D(2) or (3). The ground of impairment will usually also constitute a breach of the standards of behaviour and performance expected of optical professionals, students and businesses. Until 31 March 2016 these standards were contained in the *Code of conduct for optometrists, dispensing opticians and optical students* and the *Code of conduct for business registrants.* Although there may be occasions where it is necessary to make reference to externally-produced guidance (for example, College of Optometrist guidance), wherever possible, decision makers and registrants should refer to apply GOC produced guidance, standards and competencies.

8.39 From 1 April 2016, the existing code of conduct relating to fully qualified individuals and students was replaced by new *Standards of practice for optometrists and dispensing opticians* and *Standards of practice for optical students.* This means that where the case examiners are considering a matter where the conduct complained of occurred after 1 April 2016, the new standards apply. For matters prior to that date, the code is applicable but decision makers will also make reference to the new standards where they consider that this will help to inform the registrant's future practice. The *Code of conduct for business registrants* remains in force unchanged.

Warnings

8.40 The GOC (FTP) Rules 2013 make provision for case examiners and the Investigation Committee to consider allegations of impairment of fitness to practise against a registrant and to make a number of decisions, one of which is to give a warning to the registrant.

8.41 The GOC has published guidance which aims to assist the GOC's investigatory decision makers (case examiners and the Investigation Committee) to determine when it is appropriate to issue a warning. The purpose of the guidance is to encourage consistent and appropriate decision making, whilst recognising that each case must be decided on its own facts. This guidance is also helpful to registrants and their representatives in formulating responses to allegations for consideration by the case examiners or Investigation Committee.

8.42 Warnings are available at both the investigation stage and the adjudication stage of the fitness to practise procedures. At the investigation stage, warnings can only be imposed where it has been decided that the matter should not be referred to the FTP Committee. At the adjudication stage, they can only be imposed when there has been a finding that the registrant's fitness to practise is not impaired.

When will a warning be considered?

8.43 A warning will be considered when the decision makers are satisfied that the alleged conduct or performance falls short of the threshold for the realistic prospect test for referral to the FTP Committee. However, there is evidence to suggest that his or her conduct or performance has fallen below the standard expected and to the extent that a formal response from the GOC is warranted. Examples of where the issuing of a warning may be considered appropriate include (but are not restricted to):

- where the matters complained of would, if proved, demonstrate a significant failure to meet the GOC core competencies or to follow the GOC codes of conduct or the guidance published by the professional bodies, but where a restriction on the registrant's registration would not be necessary;
- where the matters complained of would not amount, if proved, to an impairment of fitness to practise, but if repeated may do so;
- where there is a significant cause for concern following a performance assessment, but a restriction on the registrant's registration is not necessary;
- where the registrant accepts that she or he has acted improperly but can demonstrate that this is unlikely to occur again;
- where the registrant accepts that his or her standards have fallen below an acceptable level but can demonstrate that this is unlikely to happen again.

8.44 A warning is unlikely to be suitable where there is a substantial dispute as to the facts. This is because the decision makers must not resolve conflicts of evidence.

8.45 Once the decision makers are satisfied that the concerns raised are sufficiently serious to require a formal response by way of a warning, they must also have regard to the public interest.

8.46 Before a warning can be issued by the decision-makers, the registrant will be given the opportunity to make further written representations to them, having been advised of the nature of the warning being considered. These representations must be received within 28 days of the date they are written to. The decision-makers must consider any representation made by a registrant and decide whether or not to give a warning in the particular circumstances from the decision makers as to future conduct, training or standards of performance. These will be recommendations only and the GOC will not monitor them or seek to enforce compliance.

8.47 The fact that a warning has been issued will be confirmed to the initial complainant. Warnings will not be publicised and nor will their existence be disclosed to enquirers.

What happens if there is another complaint against the registrant?

8.48 Warnings will be in force for four years from the date that they are issued. Should the registrant be the subject of a further complaint of a similar nature within that period, the decision makers will take the original complaint into account in determining what action, if any, to take in respect of the new complaint. The registrant will be invited to provide representations on the relevance of the earlier warning in the context of the new complaint.

8.49 When considering a new allegation alongside the circumstances of an earlier warning, it is open to the decision makers to review the decision not to refer the earlier complaint to the FTP Committee. Again, this is a matter on which the registrant will be given the opportunity to make representations.

8.50 Once a warning has expired, the decision makers will not be entitled to take into account its previous existence.

Referral of cases from case examiners to the investigating committee

8.51 Where the case examiners decide that they require further information about the standard and quality of a registrant's work and an assessment is required before they can reach a decision on the case, they must refer the matter to the Investigation Committee requesting that an assessor (or assessors) be appointed and an assessment (or assessments) be directed. Also, if the Investigation Committee is, itself, considering a case where the case examiners have been unable to reach a unanimous decision about disposal of the allegation and the case has been referred to the Investigation Committee, it may decide that an assessment (or assessments) is required. Such assessments are commonly known as performance assessments. The case examiners will be able to deal with the majority of cases, however there are two situations where cases must be referred to the Investigation Committee by the case examiners:

1) where the case examiners decide to refer an individual registrant for a health and/or performance assessment, which can only be directed by the Investigation Committee;
2) where the case examiners are not unanimous in their decision about the appropriate disposal of the matter.

Both of those situations are explained further below.

8.52 The Investigation Committee must specify the matters on which the registrant is to be assessed. If more than one assessor is appointed in respect of a performance assessment, the assessors must together prepare a joint report for the Investigation Committee. In respect of a health assessment, each assessor will prepare a report. The registrant will be sent a copy of all reports prepared and may submit comments on the report(s) to the Registrar within 28 days of receipt.

8.53 Where a registrant co-operates and an assessment (or assessments) has taken place, the Investigation Committee must refer the allegation back to the case examiners. The case examiners receive a copy of the assessment report (or reports), together with any information provided by the registrant. The case examiners then resume their consideration of the matter under the provisions of GOC (FTP) Rules 2013 r12.

8.54 If a registrant fails to co-operate with, or submit to, an assessment (or assessments), the Investigation Committee shall not refer the allegation back to the case examiners for determination and shall instead proceed to consideration of the allegations itself. In these circumstances, the case examiners will cease to have any further involvement in the case.

Referral of cases to the Fitness to Practise Committee

8.55 When considering whether a case ought to be referred to the FTP Committee, the case examiners should keep in mind the GOC's overarching objective as set out in the legislation:[17]

> The over-arching objective of the Council in exercising their function is the protection of the public.

8.56 Further, the case examiners should ask themselves the following question: is there a realistic prospect of establishing that the registrant's fitness to practise is impaired to a degree that justifies action being taken against their registration (this is known as 'the realistic prospect test'). This involves consideration of two issues:

- Is there a realistic prospect of being able to prove the facts alleged against the registrant, if the allegation is referred to the FTP Committee?
- If the alleged facts were proved, are they so significant as to indicate that the registrant's fitness to practise is or may be impaired to a degree that justifies action being taken against their registration?

8.57 It is not the role of the case examiners to decide whether or not a registrant's fitness to practise is impaired – that is a decision for the FTP Committee to make (if the matter is referred onto that stage).

8.58 When considering the realistic prospect test, the case examiners should have regard to the following:

- They should proceed with caution (given that, among other considerations, the case examiners are working from documents alone and the evidence before them may be untested).
- It is not the role of the case examiners to make any findings of fact – it is for the FTP Committee to make factual findings.
- The FTP Committee will only find facts disputed by the registrant proved if, having heard the evidence, the committee considers it more likely than not to have happened (the 'civil standard of proof'); however, the case examiners must not (normally) resolve substantial conflicts of evidence.
- Where there is a plain conflict between two accounts, either one of which may realistically be correct, and on one account the matter would call into question the registrant's fitness to practise, the conflict should be resolved by the FTP Committee not the case examiners.
- If the case examiners are in doubt about whether to refer the matter to the FTP Committee, they should consider the complainant's version of events at their highest then apply the realistic prospect test.

17 OA 1989 s1(2A).

- It is not the case examiners' role to refer to the FTP Committee an allegation that is not supported by any evidence. There must be a genuine (not remote or fanciful) possibility both that the facts alleged could be found proved and that if they are, the registrant's fitness to practise could be found impaired by the FTP Committee.
- When determining whether the realistic prospect test is met in relation an allegation of culpable omission (ie that the registrant failed to do something that they should have done), the case examiners must consider whether i) there is a realistic prospect of proving that the registrant had a duty to do the specified thing *and* ii) that there is a realistic prospect of proving that the registrant failed to do the specified thing. If the realistic prospect test is not met for both i) and ii), it will not be met for the allegation overall.
- There is a public interest in both business registrants and individual registrants not being harassed by unfounded allegations.
- Where the realistic prospect test is met, there is a public interest in there being a public hearing before the FTP Committee.
- The case examiners should proceed with caution in reaching a decision not to refer a case where the decision may be perceived as inconsistent with a decision made by another public body (for example, a decision where there has been input from optical professionals, or a decision of an NHS body), in relation to the same or substantially the same facts. If the case examiners do reach such a decision, they should give reasons for any apparent inconsistency.
- The case examiners are entitled to assess the weight of the evidence.
- The presence of an interim order or previous interim orders is not relevant to considering whether the realistic prospect test has been met.
- The GOC's protocol on the handling of criminal convictions sets out a presumption against registration, restoration or retention on the GOC Register where an applicant discloses a conviction for an offence (included in the Criminal Justice and Court Services Act 2000 Sch 4).
- The case examiners should further note the factors identified within the FTP Committee's guidance as indicating that (if the case is considered by the FTP Committee) erasure is likely to be the appropriate sanction.

8.59 The case examiners should keep in mind the presence of mitigating factors which might result in a decision by the case examiners not to refer an allegation to the FTP Committee, but only where the mitigating factors:

a) are well-supported by credible evidence;
b) relate to the circumstances of the allegation rather than to matters that are personal to a business registrant or an individual registrant; and
c) are so significant that there is no realistic prospect of the FTP Committee finding that a registrant's fitness to practise is impaired.

Case examiners should also consider the likely impact on the FTP Committee's consideration of any evidence showing that:

a) a registrant's admitted failings are capable of being remedied;
b) have already been remedied; and/or
c) the level of any risk of repetition;

as well as the weight that can reasonably be given to that evidence.

8.60 Certain types of misconduct may be more capable of being remedied than others, for example, allegations concerning deficient professional performance. Such evidence may not always be available, and where it is available, it may not be clear or persuasive. Examples of types of misconduct which by their nature may be less capable of remediation include sexual misconduct or dishonesty.

Where case examiners are unable to reach a unanimous decision

8.61 Cases will be considered by a lay case examiner and a registrant case examiner. The case examiners must be unanimous in their decision about the disposal of an allegation. In the event that they are unable to reach a unanimous decision in a particular case, they must inform the Registrar and the Registrar will refer the matter to the Investigation Committee. The Investigation Committee will then determine how to dispose of the case.

Review of decision not to refer

8.62 At any time within five years of a decision not to refer having been made, the case examiners may review the original decision. However, a review can only take place if the case examiners consider that there is new evidence or information which makes a review necessary for the protection of the public, necessary for the prevention of injustice to a registrant, or otherwise necessary in the public interest. Alternatively, information is available to indicate that the GOC erred in its administrative handling of the case, and it is necessary in the public interest to review. If a review is to be undertaken, the Registrar will inform the registrant (and, in the case of individual practitioners, their employer) and the complainant that new information is available and, if appropriate, provide the same. The registrant and the complainant (if any) may provide representations. Thereafter, the case examiners will consider all the available information. The case examiners may determine:

- that the original decision should stand;
- that a warning may be given;
- to refer the matter to the FTP Committee; or
- to remove from a registrant's record any previous warning that has been issued.

Termination of a referral

8.63 Where an allegation has been referred to the FTP Committee, the case examiners may review the referral. If a review is to be undertaken, the Registrar will write to the complainant and give them the opportunity to comment. It is good practice to seek the registrant's comments also (both should be given 28 days within which to comment). The case examiners will then consider the available information and, if they decide that the case should not be considered by the FTP Committee, they will give a direction to the Registrar who will notify the relevant parties.

Allegations based on findings of other regulators

8.64 Under OA 1989 s13D(2), the only grounds on which the fitness to practise of an individual registrant, or the fitness to undertake training of a student registrant, can be 'impaired' are set out in section 13D(2)(a)–(g). These grounds include 'misconduct' at section 13D(2)(a); and, at section 13D(2)(g):

> . . . a determination by a body in the United Kingdom responsible under any enactment for the regulation of a health or social care profession to the effect that his fitness to practise as a member of that profession is impaired, or a determination by a regulatory body elsewhere to the same effect.

8.65 Under OA 1989 s13D(3), the only grounds on which the fitness to carry on business of a business registrant can be 'impaired' are set out in OA 1989 s13D(3)(a)–(g). These grounds include 'misconduct by the business registrant or by one of its directors' (section 13D(3)(a)); and, at section 13D(3)(g):

> . . . a determination by a body in the United Kingdom responsible under any enactment for the regulation of a health or social care profession to the effect that–
> (i) the business registrant's fitness to carry on business as a member of that profession is impaired; or
> (ii) the fitness of a director of the business registrant to practise that profession is impaired,
>
> or a determination by a regulatory body elsewhere to the same effect.

8.66 A determination about the fitness to practise of person by another UK health or social care regulator will be conclusive evidence of the facts found proved in relation to that determination. The only evidence which may be adduced in rebuttal of such a certified determination is evidence proving that the person is not the person referred to in the certificate. This is because the GOC takes the view that in the case of other UK health or social care regulators, the decision will have been reached by the disciplinary panel after a hearing conducted in accordance with due legal process. The regulator will have had the burden of proving the allegations to the required standard of proof. Legal representation is available to the parties and panels are independent and receive legal advice.

8.67 Adjudications made by the Advertising Standards Authority (ASA) are not treated by the GOC as a conclusive breach of the GOC code. The reason is that the ASA adjudication process is very different to that adopted in disciplinary hearings before other UK health and social care regulators.

The Investigation Committee

The Investigation Committee's membership

8.68 The legislation specifies the membership of the Investigation Committee and its decision-making procedures.[18] The Investigation Committee

18 GOC (Committee Constitution Rules) Order of Council 2005 and the GOC (Committee Constitution) (Amendment) Rules Order of Council 2008 SI No 3113.

has a mixture of lay and professional members. It has nine members in total, of which three must be registered optometrists, two must be registered dispensing opticians, three must be lay persons, and one must be a medical practitioner.[19] There must be a minimum of five[20] Investigation Committee members present in order for the committee to make decisions about an allegation (the committee's 'quorum'). This must include at least one optometrist, one dispensing optician and one lay member.

8.69 The Investigation Committee meets in private. It is able to obtain independent legal advice. The complainant, registrant and their representatives are not allowed to attend Investigation Committee meetings. The Investigation Committee takes its decisions by a simple majority vote (the Chair does not have a casting vote). No Committee member may abstain from voting and where the votes are equal, the legislation states that the committee must decide in favour of the registrant.[21]

Referral of cases to the Investigation Committee

8.70 All reports of fitness to practise which are received by the GOC are initially considered by the Registrar. Where the Registrar considers that the allegation falls within one of the grounds described at OA 1989 s13D, the matter shall be referred to the case examiners for consideration. The exception is where the allegation comprises a criminal conviction which has resulted in the imposition of a custodial sentence (immediate or suspended), where the matter will be referred straight to the FTP Committee).[22] Alternatively, if the Registrar does not consider that the allegation falls within any of the relevant grounds, he or she shall notify the complainant and the case will be closed.

8.71 The case examiners will consider the allegation and decide whether or not it should be referred to the FTP Committee for hearing. The case examiners will be able to deal with the majority of cases, however, there are limited circumstances in which cases must be referred to the Investigation Committee for further action. Cases will be referred to the Investigation Committee by the case examiners in two situations;

1) where the case examiners decide to refer an individual registrant for a health and/or performance assessment, which can only be directed by the Investigation Committee; or
2) where the case examiners are not unanimous in their decision about the appropriate disposal of the matter.[23]

19 GOC (Committee Constitution Rules) Order of Council 2005 r9 and the GOC (Committee Constitution) (Amendment) Rules Order of Council 2008.

20 GOC (Committee Constitution Rules) Order of Council 2005 r10 and GOC (Committee Constitution) (Amendment) Rules Order of Council 2008.

21 GOC (FTP) Rules 2013 r59(4).

22 GOC (FTP) Rules 2013 r4(5).

23 GOC (FTP) Rules 2013 rr12 and 13.

Assessment (health and/or performance)

8.72 Where the case examiners decide that they require further information about a registrant's health and/or the standard and quality of their work before they can reach a decision on the case, they must refer the matter to the Investigation Committee requesting that an assessor (or assessors) be appointed and an assessment (or assessments) be directed. Also, if the Investigation Committee is, itself, considering a case where the case examiners have been unable to reach a unanimous decision about disposal of the allegation and the case has been referred to the Investigation Committee, it may decide that an assessment (or assessments) are required.

8.73 In such circumstances, the Investigation Committee may direct that any one or more of the following investigative actions should be carried out (including, if required, more than one assessment):

- *A health assessment of an individual practitioner:*[24] This may be appropriate if the complaint (or an individual registrant's representations) raises questions as to whether his or her health (including any health condition relating to substance abuse) is having any impact on his or her work.
- *A performance assessment of an individual practitioner:*[25] This may be appropriate if it is considered that the complaint raises broad questions about the adequacy of the individual's standard of work in certain areas of practice, and that the decision-making would be assisted by a formal assessment of the registrant's work in those areas. The GOC has published guidance relating to performance assessment available online.

8.74 The Investigation Committee shall specify the matters on which a registrant is to be assessed. If more than one assessor is appointed to conduct a performance assessment, the assessors must together prepare a joint report for the Investigation Committee. In respect of health assessments, each assessor will prepare a report. The registrant will be sent a copy of all report(s) prepared and may submit comments on the report(s) to the Registrar within 28 days of receipt.

8.75 If the Investigation Committee directs, on its own behalf or on referral from the case examiners, that an assessment (or assessments) should be carried out, consideration of the case will be adjourned until the relevant further investigations are completed. Any additional evidence that is obtained as a result of further investigation will be provided to the registrant who will be given an opportunity to make additional written representations, which will be provided to the Investigation Committee or case examiners (and, if relevant, to the complainant).

8.76 Where a registrant co-operates with an assessment (or assessments) requested by the case examiners, the Investigation Committee must refer the allegation back to the case examiners, with the assessment report (or reports), together with any information provided by the registrant. The

24 GOC (FTP) Rules 2013 r7.
25 GOC (FTP) Rules 2013 r7.

case examiners will resume their consideration of the matter under the provisions of GOC (FTP) Rules 2013 r12.

8.77 If an individual registrant fails to co-operate with, or submit to, an assessment (or assessments) where the Investigation Committee has directed an assessment (or assessments) following a referral from the case examiners, the Investigation Committee shall not refer the allegation back to the case examiners for determination and shall, instead, proceed to consideration of the allegation itself. The Investigation Committee shall draw such inferences as seems fit, following an individual registrant's failure to co-operate with an assessment.

Further investigation

8.78 At any stage, prior to making their final decision, the Investigation Committee may adjourn their consideration of a case pending further investigation and inform the Registrar who will undertake that investigation. The Registrar will provide any additional evidence obtained to the registrant and, where appropriate, to the complainant, giving them a reasonable opportunity to respond. The Registrar will then provide the Investigation Committee with all additional evidence, together with any further comments. The Investigation Committee will resume its consideration of the matter.

8.79 If, during the course of considering the allegations, the Investigation Committee considers that there may be evidence (either from the complaint made to the GOC or from any further investigation) of allegations not included by the Registrar, or that the allegations should be amended, the Investigation Committee should adjourn its consideration of the case and inform the Registrar. The Registrar may then consider the matters raised and whether additional or alternative allegations should be drafted for consideration by the Investigation Committee. The Investigation Committee may then, after the registrant has had an opportunity to respond to any new or amended allegations/evidence, resume its consideration of the matter.[26]

Decision-making process

8.80 When making any decision about a particular allegation, the Investigation Committee will consider not only the original allegation and any evidence that has been gathered by the GOC, but also any written representations that have been received from the registrant concerned. The rules state that a registrant must be given copies of any information or documents received in support of the allegation, and allowed 28 days in which to make any written representations before the Investigation Committee considers the allegation(s).

8.81 The Investigation Committee will also consider any comments received from the complainant, made once the complainant has seen any written representations made by the registrant. Any comments from the complainant are also copied to the registrant.

26 GOC (FTP) Rules 2013 r12.

8.82 Where the Investigation Committee's decision discounts, either fully or partially, an undisputed expert opinion, it must provide very clear reasons for this. As with case examiners it is not the role of the Investigation Committee to make decisions on the facts, but only to determine whether the realistic prospect test has been met.

The public interest

8.83 The Investigation Committee should always take into account the public interest. The wider public interest includes not just the protection of members of the public, but the maintenance of public confidence in the profession and the declaring and upholding of proper standards of conduct and behaviour.

Equality and diversity

8.84 The GOC is committed to promoting equality and valuing diversity and to operating procedures and processes which are fair, objective, transparent and free from discrimination. Promoting equality is also a requirement under the Equality Act 2010 and everyone who is acting on behalf of the Council is expected to adhere to the spirit and letter of this legislation.

Potential outcomes of the Investigation Committee's consideration of an allegation

8.85 There are a number of different potential final outcomes arising from the Investigation Committee's consideration of an allegation:

- referral of the case to the FTP Committee;
- the issue of a warning to the registrant;[27]
- a decision to take no further action, including issuing the registrant with advice about their future conduct; or
- a decision to take no further action.

The provisions and guidance in respect of these potential outcomes are mirrored in those set out above in relation to outcomes available to case examiners.

Referral of an allegation to the FTP Committee

8.86 When considering whether an allegation ought to be referred to the FTP Committee, the Investigation Committee should keep in mind the GOC's overarching objective as set out in OA 1989 s1(2A):

> The over-arching objective of the Council in exercising their function is the protection of the public.

The overarching objective encompasses the following aims:

a) to protect, promote and maintain the health, safety and well-being of the public;

27 OA 1989 s13D(7).

b) to promote and maintain public confidence in the professions regulated under the OA 1989;
c) to promote and maintain proper professional standards and conduct for members of those professions; and
d) to promote and maintain proper standards and conduct for business registrants.

8.87 As with case examiners, the Investigation Committee is also required to consider whether is there a realistic prospect of establishing that the registrant's fitness to practise is impaired to a degree that justifies action being taken against their registration (this is known as 'the realistic prospect test'). The reader is referred to the paragraphs above setting out the decision-making process for case examiners, which is replicated for the Investigation Committee.

8.88 It is not the role of the Investigation Committee to decide whether or not a registrant's fitness to practise is impaired, as that is a decision for the FTP Committee to make (if the matter is referred on to that stage).

Warnings – guidance regarding warnings issued by the Investigation Committee

8.89 The Investigation Committee power to issue warnings replicates the power delegated to case examiners and hence reference should be made to paras 8.40–8.47 above. The key principles are summarised below:

- The Investigation Committee will only consider issuing a warning once it has decided that the matter should not be referred to the FTP Committee.
- When considering an allegation, the Investigation Committee must ensure that the potential ground for the allegation against a registrant under OA 1989 s13D has been identified, so that it can assess the prospects of being able to prove the necessary facts against the registrant in order to sustain the allegation.
- In giving reasons for issuing a warning, the Investigation Committee must avoid giving the impression that it has made a finding or determination of matters of fact on substantive issues arising from the complaint.
- The terms of any warning must be in clear terms, and must not seek to impose on a registrant a more onerous obligation than that required under the terms of the current GOC code or standards.
- A warning issued by the Investigation Committee is a record of a concern on the part of the Investigation Committee which, while not requiring referral to the FTP Committee, is potentially significant. A warning is not shown on the publicly available GOC Register, but it is recorded by the GOC for a period of four years from the date of the warning letter. Independent legal advice is available to the Investigation Committee.
- Warnings are only issued by the Investigation Committee once a registrant has been given an opportunity to make further written representations to the Investigation Committee, having been advised of the nature of the warning being considered. The Investigation Committee

shall consider any representations made by the registrant and decide whether or not to give a warning in the particular circumstances.

Taking no further action

8.90 If the Investigation Committee decides that an allegation does not need to be referred to the FTP Committee, or result in the issue of a warning, it may decide to close a case without taking any further action. The Investigation Committee may decide to close a case and take no further action if:

1) the allegation demonstrates no issue that could call into question a registrant's fitness to practise; or
2) the alleged facts, even if proved, are not serious enough to result in that registrant's fitness to practise being impaired to the extent that would justify action being taken against his or her registration, and a warning is deemed unnecessary; or
3) the alleged facts, if proved, may demonstrate that a registrant's fitness to practise is impaired, but there is no realistic prospect of being able to prove the alleged facts for evidential reasons and a warning is deemed unnecessary.

Recording decisions

8.91 All decisions made by the Investigation Committee shall be recorded (in writing) setting out full and detailed reasoning for the decision made. The Investigation Committee must always ensure that their reasoning is clear, and hence adopt the same approach as case examiners (see above).

Notification

8.92 Following the Investigation Committee meeting, the complainant(s) and the registrant(s) concerned receive a letter from the GOC setting out the Investigation Committee's decision and the reasons for that decision. In the case of individual registrants, their employer will be informed of the committee's decision but they will not be provided with the full decision.

Other parties

8.93 The Investigation Committee may instruct the GOC to refer an allegation to the police if it appears to relate to the commission of a criminal offence (or to refer the allegation to another enforcement agency, as appropriate) if it appears to relate to a non-GOC optical professional, for example, to the GMC if the allegation concerns laser eye surgery carried out by a doctor.

Interim orders

8.94 The Registrar and the Investigation Committee are also required to consider whether the FTP Committee should consider making an interim order suspending or placing conditions on the registration of a registrant who is the subject of an allegation.[28] An interim order can:

- suspend a registrant from practice completely;
- temporarily remove an entry relating to a specialty or proficiency; or
- make their registration conditional on compliance with requirements imposed by the FTP Committee.

An interim order can last for a maximum of 18 months, unless extended by the relevant court, and will be subject to regular reviews during that period. If the Investigation Committee is of the opinion that the FTP Committee should consider making an interim order, it will have regard to OA 1989 s13L. This process is also replicated for case examiners see para 8.23 above.

Investigation Committee considering findings by other regulators

8.95 By OA 1989 section 13D(5), the Investigation Committee is required to investigate an allegation (often referred to as a complaint) made to the GOC that the fitness to practise of an individual registrant, the fitness to carry on business of a business registrant, or the fitness to undertake training of student registrant is or may be impaired.[29]

8.96 The guidance set out above regarding consideration of such allegations by case examiners[30] is again identical as regards consideration by the Investigation Committee (which is logical given that case examiners exercise the delegated functions of the Investigation Committee). This guidance operates to assist decision-makers in deciding upon the evidential status of a determination of impairment of fitness to practise or carry on business by another UK health or social care regulator for the purpose of section 13D(2)(g) or (3)(g).

8.97 The main test to be applied when examining the status of such a determination is whether the process whereby the determination was reached was fair. In the case of other UK health or social care regulators, the decision will have been reached by the disciplinary panel after a hearing conducted in accordance with due legal process.

8.98 Therefore, in the case of a determination by another UK health or social care regulator, that determination will usually be relied upon by the Investigation Committee to provide a reliable basis for referring the allegation to the FTP Committee. This is on the basis that there is a realistic prospect of being able to prove the facts as found by the other regulator, and that such facts are so significant as to indicate that the registrant's fitness to practise is or may be impaired to such a degree that justifies action being taken against their registration.

8.99 It will be for the FTP Committee to determine whether there are exceptional circumstances in any particular case to question the determination of the other regulator, or to find that the findings of the other regulator

28 OA 1989 s13D(9).
29 OA 1989 s13D(1).
30 Para 8.16.

are not sufficient to find impairment of fitness to practise of a GOC registrant.

Allegations arising from adjudication by the Advertising Standards Agency

8.100 The ASA is the independent body responsible for regulating advertisers in the United Kingdom. Upon receipt of a complaint, it will consider and determine whether an advertiser has acted in breach of the *UK code of non-broadcast advertising, sales promotion and direct advertising* (CAP Codes). Its decision is published as an adjudication. An ASA adjudication can be reviewed at the request of the advertiser by the Independent Reviewer of ASA Adjudications.

8.101 If an ASA adjudication is sent to the Investigation Committee for investigation and consideration, the Investigation Committee must examine the status of that adjudication in relation to any allegation against the registrant on one of the grounds under OA 1989 s13D(2) or (3) (see also paras 8.16–8.19 regarding case examiners).

Fitness to Practise Committee

8.102 Allegations may be referred to the FTP Committee by the Registrar, case examiners and/or Investigating Committee.

Individual registrants

8.103 In the GOC's legislation the term 'individual registrant' refers to a registered optometrist or a registered dispensing optician. This includes those undertaking training as an optometrist or dispensing optician, and visiting optometrists and dispensing opticians from relevant European States. See section below on student registrants (para 8.104).

Student registrants

8.104 A student registrant is a person registered with the GOC as undertaking training as an optometrist or as a dispensing optician.

8.105 The GOC legislation states that only students currently in education or training can remain on the register. If a student is not studying (for example, taking a gap year), he or she is not able to remain registered. Students need to apply to be restored to the register when they recommence their studies.

8.106 All registered optometry and dispensing optics students must renew their registration each year. This is called 'student retention'. The GOC sends all existing student registrants a notification of retention in April each year. Applications must be completed and the retention fee paid by 15 July.

8.107 Anyone who fails to submit an application and pay their annual fees by the annual retention deadline may be removed from the student register.

Students who are not registered may be excluded from clinical training and examinations.

8.108 The GOC may not recognise qualifications of applicants for full registration who were not registered for all or part of their training.

8.109 The GOC has a legal duty to register and set the standards expected of optical students. From 1 April 2016 the existing *Code of conduct* has been replaced by new *Standards of practice for optical students.*

8.110 These standards define the standards of behaviour and performance the GOC expects of all registered student optometrists and student dispensing opticians.

8.111 The specific standards for optical students take account of the fact that they will develop their knowledge, skills and judgment over the period of their training. Once a student's training is complete and the students register as a practising optical professional, he or she will then be expected to meet the separate *Standards of practice for optometrists and dispensing opticians.*

Business registrants

8.112 A business registrant is a body corporate registered with the GOC as carrying on business as an optometrist, dispensing optician or both.

8.113 A body corporate is a limited company or limited liability partnership that has been incorporated with Companies House.

8.114 The GOC has a legal duty to set the standards expected of optical businesses. It does this in a *Code of conduct for business registrants.*

8.115 Certain areas of practice are restricted by legislation and rules. Listed below are the key areas that may affect the day to day running of business registrants, and about which the GOC has produced further guidance to assist registrants in applying their professional judgment to meet the standards:

- sight test;
- sale and supply of optical appliances;
- fitting of contact lenses;
- cosmetic (zero-powered) contact lenses;
- low vision aids;
- fluorescein.

8.116 Decisions taken against a business registrant must be about fitness to practise of the business as a whole and not about an individual involved in the business (eg a director), although the actions of an individual director may lead to fitness to practise allegations against the business registrant.

Impairment

8.117 Grounds for impaired fitness to practise are in accordance with OA 1989 s13D(2)–(3) for registered individuals (including students). A finding of impaired fitness to practise (fitness to undertake training in the case of students) against a registrant can be based on any of the following:

a) misconduct;
b) deficient professional performance (not in the case of a student registrant);
c) a conviction or caution in the British Islands for a criminal offence, or a conviction elsewhere for an offence which, if committed in England and Wales, would constitute a criminal offence;
d) the registrant having accepted a conditional offer under the Criminal Procedure (Scotland) Act 1995 s302 (fixed penalty: conditional offer by procurator fiscal) or agreed to pay a penalty under the Social Security Administration Act 1992 s115A (penalty as alternative to prosecution);
e) the registrant, in proceedings in Scotland for an offence, having been the subject of an order under the Criminal Procedure (Scotland) Act 1995 s246(2) or (3) discharging him or her absolutely;
f) adverse physical or mental health; or
g) a determination by any other UK health regulatory body that fitness to practise is impaired (or a determination by a regulatory body elsewhere to the same effect).

Business registrants

8.118 A finding of impaired fitness to practise against a business registrant can be based on any of the following:

a) misconduct (by the business registrant or a director);
b) practices or patterns of behaviour occurring within the business which:
   i) the registrant knew or ought reasonably to have known of; and
   ii) amount to misconduct or deficient professional performance;
c) the instigations by the business registrant of practices or patterns of behaviour within the business where that practice or behaviour amounts, or would if implemented amount, to misconduct or deficient professional performance;
d) a conviction or caution in the British Islands of the business registrant or one of its directors for a criminal offence, or a conviction elsewhere for an offence which, if committed in England and Wales, would constitute a criminal offence;
e) the registrant or one of its directors having accepted a conditional offer under the Criminal Procedure (Scotland) Act 1995 s302 or agreed to pay a penalty under the Social Security Administration Act 1992 s115A;
f) the registrant or one of its directors, in proceedings in Scotland for an offence, having been the subject or an order under the Criminal Procedure (Scotland) Act 1995 s246(2) or (3) discharging it or him or her absolutely;
g) a determination by any other UK health regulatory body that:
   i) the business registrant's fitness to carry on business as a member of that profession is impaired; or
   ii) the fitness of a director of the business registrant to practise that profession is impaired (or a determination by a regulatory body elsewhere to the same effect).

8.119 There is no statutory definition of impairment of fitness to practise. The GOC operates the three-stage decision making process. The decision on impairment is a separate decision from the decision on whether what has been found proved amounts to misconduct, deficient professional performance or adverse physical or mental health, etc. Having made that decision, the committee go on to determine whether, as a result, fitness to practise is impaired.

Misconduct

8.120 There is also no definition of misconduct in the GOC's legislation, and it is for the FTP Committee as an exercise of its judgment to determine whether an act or omission amounts to misconduct In *Roylance v GMC*[31] misconduct was described as:

> A falling short by omission or commission of the standards to be expected among [medical practitioners] and such falling short must be 'serious' . . . It is of course possible for negligent conduct to amount to serious professional conduct, but the negligence must be to a high degree.

8.121 The GOC guidance to FTP Committee states the view that although the terminology has changed since the *Roylance* case, the courts have been clear that it was 'inconceivable' that the change in language should signify a lower threshold for disciplinary intervention.

8.122 Misconduct can be found in relation to a single act where the conduct has been particularly serious. Where a registrant may have been negligent, misconduct may be constituted by a series of acts, unless the one act in question was particularly serious. The GOC guidance refers to *R (Vali) v General Optical Council*[32] that:

> Mere negligence does not of itself show that the act was misconduct. A higher degree of gravity than mere carelessness is required. I also note and agree that a single act is less likely to cross the threshold of misconduct but that depends of course on the gravity of the act.

See further above at paras 3.19–3.53.

Deficient professional performance

8.123 There is also no definition in legislation for deficient professional performance, although it is a separate concept to misconduct (or negligence). *R (Calhaem) v GMC*[33] explained the concept of deficient professional performance:

> (3) It connotes a standard of professional performance which is unacceptably low and which (save in exceptional circumstances) has been demonstrated by reference to a fair sample of the doctor's work.
>
> (4) A single instance of negligent treatment, unless very serious indeed, would be unlikely to constitute 'deficient professional performance'.

31 [1999] Lloyd's Rep Med 139.
32 [2011] EWHC 310 (Admin).
33 [2007] EWHC 2606 (Admin).

> (5) It is neither necessary nor appropriate to extend the interpretation of 'deficient professional performance' in order to encompass matters which constitute 'misconduct'.

See further above at paras 3.58–3.72.

8.124 The definitions of misconduct and deficient professional performance are distinct, any particular set of facts can only be decided as one or other category.

Health

8.125 Under OA 1989 s13D(2)(f), a registrant's fitness to practise may be impaired by reason of adverse physical or mental health.

8.126 To find an allegation of adverse physical or mental health proved, the FTP Committee must be satisfied that the registrant's health may put patient safety at risk. Expert evidence in the form of a medical report will normally be required.

8.127 Under GOC (FTP) Rules 2013 r46(22) when determining whether a registrant's fitness to practise is impaired by reason of adverse physical or mental health, the FTP Committee may take into account:

a) the registrant's current physical or mental condition;
b) any continuing or episodic condition suffered by the registrant; and
c) a condition suffered by the registrant which, although currently in remission, may reasonably be expected to cause a recurrence of impairment of the registrant's fitness to practise.

Determining impairment

8.128 In determining impairment, relevant factors for the committee to take into account include: whether the conduct which led to the allegation is remediable; whether it has been remedied; and whether it is likely to be repeated. Certain types of misconduct (for example, cases involving clinical issues) may be more capable of being remedied than others.

8.129 In coming to a conclusion on impairment, the committee must look forward, not back. When reaching a decision that fitness to practise is not impaired, the committee must make clear what remedial steps have been taken into account and why these mitigate against recurrence of the particular issues in question in the case.

8.130 The committee will also have regard to public interest considerations. In *Council for Healthcare Regulatory Excellence v Nursing and Midwifery Council (Grant)*,[34] the High Court said that, in deciding whether fitness to practise is impaired, the committee should ask themselves:

> Not only whether the registrant continued to present a risk to members of the public, but whether the need to uphold proper professional standards and public confidence in the registrant and in the profession would be undermined if a finding of impairment of fitness to practise were not made in the circumstances of this case.

34 *Council for Healthcare Regulatory Excellence v Nursing and Midwifery Council and Grant* [2011] EWHC 927 (Admin).

Interim orders (OA 1989 s13L)

8.131 Where the FTP Committee is satisfied that it is necessary for the protection of the public, or is otherwise in the public interest, or is in the interests of the registrant, for the registrant's registration to be suspended, or made subject to conditions, or an entry relating to a speciality or proficiency to be removed temporarily or made subject to conditions, it may make the following orders:

a) suspension of registration for a period not exceeding 18 months;
b) temporary removal of an entry relating to a speciality or proficiency for a specified period not exceeding 18 months (together with an interim suspension order); or
c) the registrant's registration or the entry relating to a speciality or proficiency made conditional on the registrant's compliance for a specified period not exceeding 18 months with such requirements as the committee think fit to impose (an order for interim conditional registration).

8.132 The High Court has considered the three 'limbs' of the grounds on which an interim order may be made – ie public protection, public interest and the interests of the registrant – and has considered whether a registrant can only be suspended on public interest grounds if this was 'necessary'. The High Court indicated that while the legislation allows an interim order on public protection grounds only if this is 'necessary', there is no such qualification to the public interest limb.[35]

8.133 The FTP Committee is required to explain how an order intended to safeguard public confidence is proportionate, bearing in mind the interim nature of the relief, as the public interest considerations could be fairly reflected by an appropriate decision at the final hearing.[36]

8.134 In considering an application for an interim order, the committee should first consider whether any order should be made. If the committee answers this affirmatively, then it should consider whether an interim order of conditions is the most appropriate response. Only if the committee are of the view that conditions will not meet the risks identified should it impose a period of suspension. When deciding whether to impose an interim order, the committee must take into account the following:

a) The effect which any order might have on the registrant. Interim orders have been described as a draconian measure, and the committee must balance the need for an order against the consequences which an order would have for the registrant and satisfy themselves that the consequences are not disproportionate to the risk from which they are seeking to protect the public.[37]
b) When considering an interim order, the committee is not making findings of fact, nor making findings as to whether the allegations are or

35 *Sandler v General Medical Council* [2010] EWHC 1029 (Admin).

36 *R (Sosanya) v General Medical Council* [2009] EWHC 2814 (Admin); *Patel v General Medical Council* [2012] EWHC 3688 (Admin); and *Houshian v General Medical Council* [2012] EWHC 3458 (Admin).

37 *Madan v General Medical Council* [2001] EWHC Admin 57; and *R (Scholten) v General Medical Council* [2013] EWHC 173 (Admin).

are not established. The committee can receive evidence from the registrant that an allegation is manifestly unfounded or manifestly exaggerated, but the committee should not decide on credibility or the merits of a disputed allegation; that is a matter for the substantive hearing. It is sufficient for the committee to act, if they take the view that there is a prima facie case and that the prima facie case, having regard to such material as is put before them by the registrant, requires that the public be protected by an interim order.[38]

c) As regards the amount of evidence before the committee, the High Court has indicated that it would expect the allegation to have been made or confirmed in writing, although it may not yet have been reduced to a formal witness statement. The committee will need to consider the source of the allegation and its potential seriousness. An allegation that is trivial or clearly misconceived should not be given weight.[39]

d) The High Court has also indicated that, where a registrant has been charged with a criminal offence, the committee will not always be obliged to hear evidence or submissions as to any alleged weaknesses in the criminal case. The committee can proceed on the basis that the Crown Prosecution Service has concluded there was sufficient substance in the matter to justify charges being brought.[40]

e) The primary purpose of an interim order is to protect members of the public. It will be relatively rare for an interim order to be made only on the ground that it is in the public interest (for example, to maintain public confidence in the profession).[41] Even in very serious cases, the committee must consider whether the public can be protected by conditions, such as restricting patient contact instead of a suspension order.[42]

8.135 When setting the length of an interim suspension or conditional registration order, the committee should bear in mind the length of time the GOC requires to bring the matter to a final substantive hearing which can, in some cases, be over 12 months. If a substantive hearing in the matter cannot be held before 18 months expires from the setting of the interim order (or before the expiry of an order that is imposed for less than 18 months), the GOC will be required to apply to the High Court for an extension. The maximum period should not be specified as a default, and the period must be justified on the individual facts of the case.[43]

8.136 Where an order is to be made, the committee should direct that a review be undertaken before the expiry of the six-month period. Under OA 1989 s13L(9)(b) following a High Court extension of an order, the committee must review the order within three months from the date of the HC extension.

38 *R (George) v General Medical Council* [2003] EWHC 1124 (Admin) para 42; *Perry v Nursing and Midwifery Council* [2013] EWCA Civ 145.

39 *General Medical Council v Sheill* [2006] EWHC 3025 (Admin).

40 *Fallon v Horse Racing Regulatory Authority* [2006] EWHC 2030 (QB).

41 *R (Shiekh) v General Dental Council* [2007] EWHC 2972 (Admin).

42 *Bawa-Garba v General Medical Council* [2015] EWHC 1277 (QB).

43 *Harry v General Medical Council* [2012] EWHC 2762 (QB).

Interim order review determinations

8.137 There must be a six-monthly review of ongoing interim orders. There may be an earlier review under section 13L(3)(a)(ii) or (b) if there is new evidence, or under section 15.14 if a case has an interim order, but it is no longer proceeding to a FTP Committee.

Powers on review of interim orders

8.138 Upon a review, the committee may:

a) continue the order;
b) revoke the order; or
c) vary conditions; or
d) replace an interim conditional order with an interim suspension order (and vice versa).

Revocation of interim orders

8.139 Any existing interim order will not automatically lapse on the making of a subsequent substantive order. The FTP Committee at a substantive hearing must, therefore, revoke any interim order immediately after it has determined the allegation.[44]

Interim orders when a referral has been terminated under rule 16

8.140 Where an allegation has been referred to the FTP Committee, under GOC (FTP) Rules 2013 r16, the case examiners may review the allegation and direct the Registrar that the allegation should not be considered. This may happen after the committee has already made an interim order against the registrant under rule 17.

8.141 If a referral to the committee is cancelled when it has already made an interim order against the registrant, the committee is required to hold a review hearing and should revoke the interim order using its powers in OA 1989 s13L.

8.142 If multiple allegations against the registrant have been referred to the committee but the case examiners have directed that only one or some of the allegations should no longer be considered by the committee, the committee must use the interim order review hearing to determine whether the remaining allegations meet the above requirements for an interim order. The committee may decide to continue, vary or revoke the interim order.

Fitness to practise hearings

8.143 Once the FTP Committee has heard the evidence, it must decide and prepare a written determination in respect of each decision as to:

44 OA 1989 s13L(11).

a) Whether the facts alleged have been found proved.
b) Whether, on the basis of the facts found proved, the registrant's actions amount to misconduct, deficient professional performance, or that he/she has adverse physical or mental health (where the allegation relates to a criminal conviction, stages a) and b) are in effect merged as a conviction is itself a ground for impairment.
c) Whether the misconduct, conviction, deficient professional performance, or adverse physical or mental health, leads to a finding that the registrant's fitness to practise is currently impaired.
d) What sanction (if any) is to apply.
e) Whether an immediate order should be imposed.

Private hearings

8.144 Where the FTP Committee is not considering a health allegation, GOC (FTP) Rules 2013 r25 states that committee hearings must be held in public, unless it considers it appropriate for the hearing to be held in private. When considering whether to hold all or part of the hearing in private, the committee must have regard to the interests of the maker of the allegation, any witness or patient concerned and the registrant, as well as the wider circumstances and the public interest.

8.145 Where the committee is considering the registrant's health, the hearing must be in private unless the committee considers it appropriate to meet in public, again having regard to the interests of the maker of the allegation, any witness or patient concerned and the registrant, as well as the wider circumstances and the public interest.

8.146 'Considering the registrant's health' may be broader than considering allegations of adverse physical or mental health, such as where the registrant raises health evidence in mitigation.

8.147 There may be certain types of allegations where the committee is more likely to consider a private hearing. For example, allegations that are of a particularly sensitive nature or involving sexual allegations. However, the committee should also consider its powers under rule 41 regarding vulnerable witnesses.

8.148 As with any public hearing, the hearing process will take care to respect the privacy of any patients involved in the allegations and not to refer to the names or personal details of individuals whose details have been redacted from the material being considered. It should be noted that, according to *GMC v BBC*,[45] a committee hearing cannot be considered a court for the purposes of the Contempt of Court Act 1981.

Bias

8.149 ECHR Article 6, as well as English common law, entitles everyone to a fair hearing by an independent and impartial tribunal. This also applies to registrants in professional regulatory hearings and the committee.

45 [1998] 1 WLR 1573.

8.150 It is important that committee members are aware of anything that might give rise to a bias on their part to ensure that the registrant receives an impartial hearing. It is the responsibility of the committee members to bring to the attention of the parties any potential conflict about which only they might know.

8.151 Whether a committee member should recuse themselves is a decision to be taken by the committee as a whole, and not by the individual member. The subjective views of the committee member in question as to whether he or she feels able to decide the case with impartiality are to be given limited weight.

Proceeding in the absence of the registrant and adjournments

8.152 GOC (FTP) Rules 2013 r22 states that:

> Where the registrant is neither present nor represented at a hearing, the Fitness to Practise Committee may nevertheless proceed if:
> (a) it is satisfied that all reasonable efforts have been made to notify the registrant of the hearing in accordance with section 23A and rule 61; and
> (b) having regard to any reasons for absence which have been provided by the registrant, it is satisfied that it is in the public interest to proceed.

This must be considered as a two-stage test. First, whether all reasonable efforts have been made to notify the registrant of the hearing; and then whether, in all the circumstances, it is appropriate to proceed in the absence of the registrant and any representatives.

8.153 *R v Jones*[46] sets out that the discretion to proceed in the absence of the registrant should be done with great care; that this discretion should be exercised in favour of proceeding in a registrant's absence only in rare and exceptional circumstances; and that in considering whether to proceed in those circumstances fairness to the registrant is paramount but fairness to the prosecution must also be considered.

8.154 Relevant factors to consider may include:

- the nature and circumstances of the registrant's absence, in particular whether he or she has voluntarily waived his or her right to attend;
- the seriousness of the allegation;
- whether an adjournment has been requested, the likely length of any such adjournment and whether an adjournment might result in the defendant attending future proceedings;
- the risks of reaching the wrong conclusion about either the registrant's absence or the wrong conclusion in the substantive case; and
- the general public interest and the interests of witnesses in ensuring that hearing should take place without undue delay.

8.155 The committee may also wish to consider practical steps such as the Hearings Officer contacting the registrant to confirm that he or she is not attending and to consider whether the registrant is represented.

46 [2002] UKHL 5.

8.156 If the registrant is absent due to ill-health, the committee should consider the registrant's evidence for this and any challenges to the evidence. The case-law suggests that, if on the balance of probabilities the committee considers that the registrant is unwell and his/her absence is involuntary, it will usually be appropriate for the committee to adjourn the hearing unless the registrant is represented and asks that the hearing should go ahead. It may be appropriate to make clear whether medical evidence will be required to support future applications.

Evidence and the standard of proof

8.157 GOC (FTP) Rules 2013 r38 establishes the standard of proof to be applied by the FTP Committee when making findings of fact:

> The standard of proof applicable to proof of any facts alleged by the Council at substantive hearings before the Fitness to Practise Committee is the standard applicable in civil proceedings.

8.158 There is only one civil standard of proof (ie proof that the fact in issue more probably occurred than not), and it is finite and unvarying. There is no 'sliding scale', and the standard of proof does not vary depending on the seriousness of the allegations.[47]

Admissibility of evidence

8.159 GOC (FTP) Rules 2013 r40 sets out what evidence the committee may hear. It may 'admit any evidence it considers fair and relevant to the case before it, whether or not such evidence would be admissible in a court of law'.[48] However, if the evidence would not be admissible in a civil court, the committee should not admit it unless, having considered the advice of the legal adviser, the committee believes that its duty to make due inquiry makes it desirable to hear the evidence.[49]

Hearsay

8.160 On many occasions a witness will attend a hearing in person, so that both the registrant and the case presenter can examine and cross-examine them and the committee may ask questions. However, if a witness cannot attend the hearing, the committee may decide to admit their written statement as hearsay evidence. Hearsay evidence can only be admitted when the committee is satisfied that it is fair to do so. What is fair will depend on the circumstances of each case and, in particular, on the seriousness and gravity of the allegations and the importance of the hearsay evidence to any disputed facts or allegations. The court in *R (Bonhoeffer) v GMC*[50] stated that:

> . . . in the absence of a problem in the witness giving evidence in person or by video link, or some other exceptional circumstance, fairness requires

47 *Re B (children)*[2008] UKHL 35; and *Re Doherty* [2008] UKHL 33.

48 GOC (FTP) Rules 2013 r40(1).

49 GOC (FTP) Rules 2013 r40(2).

50 [2011] EWHC 1585 (Admin).

> that in disciplinary proceedings a person facing serious charges, especially if they amount to criminal offences which if proved are likely to have grave adverse effects on his/her reputation and career, should in principle be entitled by cross-examination to test the evidence of his accuser(s) where that evidence is the sole or decisive evidence relied on against him.

The committee may decide to admit hearsay evidence but to give it less weight than evidence where both parties have been able to examine the witness.

Vulnerable witnesses

8.161 The committee should be aware that some witnesses before it may be considered vulnerable. This might include children, those with mental disorders or physical disabilities, or witnesses who were the victims in cases where the allegations are of a sexual nature.[51] In such cases, the committee may take measures to allow it to hear evidence from a vulnerable witness, including video-links, interpreters or screens. Where the allegations are of a sexual nature the registrant may not directly cross-examine a witness who was a victim without their written consent.

8.162 When considering what measures to put in place for a vulnerable witness, the committee will again need to consider what is fair for the parties involved. Cases involving vulnerable witnesses may be suitable for a procedural directions hearing.

Dishonesty

8.163 The GOC's code of conduct for individual registrants and the new standards document both state that the registrant must 'be honest and trustworthy'. Dishonesty is particularly serious as it may undermine trust in the profession. Examples of dishonesty may include:

- defrauding an employer, a colleague or an insurance company;
- defrauding the NHS;
- improperly amending or changing the detail on patient records;
- submitting or providing false references and information on a CV;
- research misconduct; or
- failure to disclose to the Council or employer or PCT criminal convictions and cautions.

8.164 There is a wide range of evolving case law in this area and, where the committee must determine whether the registrant was dishonest The question of whether or not a registrant's conduct is dishonest will be decided by the committee at the fact-finding stage, at which stage consideration will need to be given to: the nature of the alleged conduct and the evidence to suggest it took place; the registrant's state of mind and evidence of this; and what motivation there would be for the registrant to be dishonest.

51 GOC (FTP) Rules 2013 r41(1).

Mitigation

8.165 Mitigation evidence can include evidence about the circumstances leading up to the incidents in question, as well as evidence about the registrant's previous good character and history. It may include evidence about the time-lapse since the incidents occurred and evidence of actions taken to apologise for and/or address the concerns which resulted in the proceedings being brought. A demonstration of insight of those concerns coupled with actions taken to avoid repetition of them may also be regarded as mitigating factors. Whether a factor is a mitigating circumstance or not is entirely a matter for the committee to determine. In each case, the committee must consider both mitigating and aggravating features as set out in the evidence they have heard. They should also take into account any representations about these matters made on behalf of the GOC and the registrant, but bearing in mind always that representations are not evidence.

8.166 Testimonials prepared in advance of a hearing need to be evaluated in the light of the factual findings made at the hearing. The committee will consider whether the authors of the testimonials were aware of the events leading to the hearing and what weight, if any, to give to them. The committee should also consider how long the author has known the registrant; how recently the author has had experience of the registrant's behaviour at work; and whether there is any evidence that the author has a conflict of interest in providing the testimonial.

Sanction

Fitness to practise not impaired

Warning (OA 1989 s13F(5))

8.167 A warning may be given in a case where the fitness to practise of a registrant is found not to be currently impaired. When issuing a warning, the FTP Committee should consider setting a date of expiry of the warning. A warning does not directly affect a registrant's ability to practise or undertake training, but is published on the GOC's website and disclosed if anyone enquires about the registrant's fitness to practise history.

8.168 A warning may be appropriate where concerns raised by the case are sufficiently serious to require a formal response, but do not reach the threshold for impairment. The committee should explain why a formal response is required in the light of the finding of 'no current impairment' and the mitigating factors that may, therefore, be present. The committee will, therefore, need to record their reasons for issuing or not issuing a warning.

Fitness to practise impaired

Overview

8.169 Where fitness to practise is found to be currently impaired, available sanctions are set out in OA 1989 s13F(3)(a)–(c) and s13H. The purpose of any sanction is not to punish the registrant, but to protect patients and the wider public interest.

8.170 Where a committee finds that a registrant's fitness to practise is currently impaired, it can direct:

a) that no further action be taken;
b) a financial penalty (except in a health case); this may be imposed in conjunction with another sanction;
c) conditions (ordinarily to be followed by a review) for up to three years;
d) a period of suspension (ordinarily to be followed by a review) for up to 12 months;
e) erasure (except in a health case); or
f) entries relating to specialty or proficiency be subject to conditions or removal. Where impairment is found on the ground of deficient professional performance, and the deficiency relates to the performance of a specialty or proficiency, particulars of which are entered in the register, the committee may direct that the entry relating to that specialty or proficiency be subject to conditions (for up to three years), removed temporarily (for up to 12 months) or removed.[52]

8.171 The sanction should be proportionate. This means that the sanction must be appropriate, bearing in mind the interests of the public and the interests of the registrant and the seriousness of the allegations found proven against the registrant. Whatever sanction the committee decides on, it should be reached after considering all of the facts of the particular case. This includes taking account of any aggravating and mitigating features of the allegation, together with any personal mitigation put forward by the registrant.

8.172 In deciding what sanction is appropriate, the committee should consider them in ascending order, starting with the least severe. The committee must only then move on to the next sanction if the one under consideration is not sufficient in terms of dealing adequately with the issues identified.

Financial penalty orders (OA 1989 s13H)

8.173 The committee has the power to impose a financial penalty order of any sum not exceeding £50,000. The order may be made in addition to, or instead of, an erasure order, suspension or conditional registration order.

8.174 When making a financial penalty order, the committee must specify the period or date within which the sum is to be paid. Where the committee is considering making such an award it should take into account in relation to individual registrants their ability to pay and in relation to business registrants the size and financial resources of the business.

Conditions of practice

8.175 Conditions on the registrant's registration may be imposed up to a maximum of three years. Conditional registration allows a registrant to

52 OA 1989 s13F(4).

return to practice under certain conditions – for example, no longer being able to carry out certain procedures. Conditions may also make positive requirements of a registrant, such as a requirement to undergo training in a particular area of their practice.

8.176 The objectives of any conditions placed on the registrant must be relevant to the conduct in question and any risk it presents, and should be made clear so that the registrant understands what is expected of him or her.

8.177 Any conditions should be appropriate, proportionate, workable and measurable. The GOC sanctions guidance includes a detailed list of conditions which may be considered by a committee, which is a useful guide for registrants and representatives.

Suspension (maximum 12 months) (OH 1989 s13F(3)(b) or (4)(b))

8.178 This sanction may be appropriate when some or all of the following factors are apparent:

a) a serious instance of misconduct but where a lesser sanction is not sufficient;
b) no evidence of harmful deep-seated personality or attitudinal problems;
c) no evidence of repetition of behaviour since incident;
d) the committee is satisfied the registrant has insight and does not pose a significant risk of repeating behaviour;
e) in cases where the only issue relates to the registrant's health, there is a risk to patient safety if the registrant was allowed to continue to practise even under conditions.

8.179 The committee may direct a period of suspension, (or in cases based on deficient professional performance, temporary removal of an entry relating to a specialty or proficiency). The committee is only able to suspend a registrant for up to 12 months. Any future review hearing may extend the suspension for up to another 12 months.[53]

8.180 However, any extension of suspension must be based on the registrant's fitness to practise at the time of the review, rather than at the time of the initial finding of impairment and an extension cannot be exercised so as to reflect a conclusion by the original FTP committee that the gravity of the misconduct demanded a longer period of suspension.

Directing a review hearing

8.181 The committee should normally direct that there be a review of a conditional order or a suspension order before they expire. This is because before a suspension or conditions are lifted, the committee will need to be reassured that the registrant is fit to resume practice either unrestricted, or with conditions or further conditions. Also, where conditions have been imposed, the registrant must demonstrate to the committee that they have satisfied the conditions imposed at the previous hearing.[54]

8.182 Where it directs a review hearing, the committee may wish to give guidance, or clarify its expectations regarding the evidence or matters

53 OA 1989 s 13F(7); and *HK v General Pharmaceutical Council* [2016] UKSC 64.

54 *Bamgbelu v General Dental Council* [2013] EWHC 1169 (Admin).

the review panel may find useful to take into account in reconsidering the case. This is non-binding and cannot form the basis of an appeal against the decision, but may assist the registrant and the future committee.[55]

Erasure (OH 1989 section 13F(3)(a))

8.183 Erasure cannot be imposed in cases where impairment is only by reason of adverse physical or mental health. Erasure from the register is appropriate where this is the only means of protecting patients and/or maintaining public confidence in the optical profession. The Privy Council in *Bijl v GMC*[56] stated that a committee should not feel it necessary to remove:

> ... an otherwise competent and useful [registrant] who presents no danger to the public in order to satisfy [public] demand for blame and punishment.

However, this should be weighed against the words of Lord Bingham in *Bolton v Law Society*[57] that:

> The reputation of the profession is more important than the fortunes of any individual ember. Membership of a profession brings many benefits, but that is part of the price.

8.184 In deciding the committee's role in maintaining confidence in the profession, and in particular that erasure was appropriate despite a practitioner presenting no risk.

8.185 This sanction is likely to be considered appropriate when the behaviours in issue are fundamentally incompatible with being a registered professional and involve any of the following (this list is not exhaustive):

a) serious departure from the relevant professional standards as set out in the *Standards of practice for registrants* and the *Code of conduct for business registrants*;
b) doing serious harm to individuals (patients or otherwise), either deliberately or through incompetence, and particularly where there is a continuing risk to patients;
c) abuse of position/trust (particularly involving vulnerable patients) or violation of the rights of patients;
d) offences of a sexual nature, including involvement in child pornography;
e) offences involving violence;
f) dishonesty (especially where persistent and covered up); or
g) persistent lack of insight into seriousness of actions or consequences.

8.186 Where the committee directs erasure (or in cases based on deficient professional performance, removal of an entry relating to a specialty or proficiency), it will also consider whether erasure or removal should take effect immediately, and give reasons for its decision (see para 2.231 on immediate orders for conditions or suspension where direction made for conditional registration, suspension or erasure).[58]

55 *Ferguson v Nursing and Midwifery Council* [2011] EWHC 1456; and *Levy v GMC* [2011] EWHC 2351 (Admin).

56 [2001] UKPC 42.

57 [1994] 1 WLR 512.

58 OA 1989 s13I.

Determination

8.187 The amount of detail will depend on the complexity of the case. The determination should clearly set out what the facts of the case are with sufficient detail to enable the reader to understand what has been decided and why. If a decision turns on the credibility of one witness as opposed to another, then the reasons for the decision might be brief depending on the circumstances of a case. In cases where a finding may appear to be inexplicable in relation to the evidence received by the FTP Committee, then there would be a compelling need for detailed reasons. The courts have clarified that in 'exceptional' cases, eg where the factual background is complex or the evidence does not all go one way, more is required by way of explanation. In particular, the reasons why a witness is or is not found to be credible must be given where the witness evidence has been inconsistent, and where the committee considers a witness has been dishonest in the evidence they have given, this must be stated clearly and reasons given.[59]

Other types of hearing

Review hearing – by Fitness to Practise Committee

8.188 A substantive review hearing will always be treated as a substantive hearing and will commence at the impairment stage. As at the original hearing, orders for conditional registration (or orders varying conditions), suspension and erasure (including orders regarding entries relating to a speciality or proficiency) will not take effect until the end of the appeal period or, if an appeal has been made, before the appeal has been concluded.[60]

8.189 The registrant will need to satisfy the FTP Committee that he or she has fully appreciated the gravity of the offence, has not re-offended and has maintained his or her skills and knowledge, and that the registrant's patients will not be placed at risk by resumption of practice or by the imposition of conditional registration (following a period of suspension or more stringent conditions).

8.190 The registrant should produce information or objective evidence regarding these matters. If the committee considers that the registrant will not improve his or her performance through existing conditions without further supervision, the committee may impose further educational or training conditions.

8.191 All sanctions are available to a committee at a substantive review,[61] but the reasons for sanction must reflect the current situation and can only follow a finding that the registrant's fitness to practise remains impaired. Under OA 1989 s13F(8) and (9) where the original finding of impairment was by reason of adverse physical or mental health, and the review hearing is within two months of the period when the current suspension order

59 *Southall v General Medical Council* [2010] EWCA Civ 407; *Casey v General Medical Council* [2011] NIQB 95; and *Yaacoub v General Medical Council* [2012] EWHC 2779 (Admin).

60 OA 1989 s23H.

61 OA 1989 s13F(7) and (13).

would expire, and a registrant's name will have been suspended from the appropriate register for at least two years, then the committee may direct that a registrant's period of suspension be extended indefinitely. (Such directions are themselves subject to possible review.) Any period of interim suspension prior to a substantive sanction of suspension cannot count towards the two year period.[62]

Restoration – by Registration Appeals Committee

8.192 These cases are governed by the GOC (Registration Appeals Rules) 2005 which set out the procedure for considering applications for restoration to the register following erasure or removal by the FTP Committee, or where an entry relating to a speciality or proficiency has been removed.

8.193 The same rules set out the separate procedures which govern appeals against decisions to refuse entry to the register. Applications are made under OA 1989 s13K. The applicant cannot make an application until 22 months have passed since the order for erasure took effect, and the restoration hearing cannot take place until 24 months have passed. Prior to making the application the applicant must have acquired the required number of CET.

8.194 The Registration Appeals Committee can order health or performance assessments of individual applicants (but not bodies corporate). Failure to submit to or co-operate with any examination will result in the committee 'drawing such inferences as seem appropriate to them in respect of the appeal/application'.[63] The burden is on the applicant/appellant to satisfy the committee that they are 'fit' and that their name or entry should be restored.

8.195 The rules governing proceedings of the Registration Appeals Committee are essentially the same as those for a FTP Committee under the Fitness Appeals. However, hearings are conducted differently from a FTP hearing in that the appellant/applicant (registrant) should go first. However, in practice, committees find it useful for the respondent (the GOC case presenter) to address the committee first by setting out the framework of the decision making power and the evidence on which the GOC relies. If the committee proposes to follow this route, the appellant's/applicant's agreement should be sought.

8.196 The committee may direct the Registrar to restore the person's name or entry relating to a speciality or proficiency to the register.[64] Factors the committee may wish to consider for restoration cases are:

a) the original allegations;
b) the committee's reasons for the original sanction imposed;
c) whether the applicant has demonstrated insight;
d) what steps the applicant has undertaken towards rehabilitation;
e) whether the applicant kept up-to-date with professional knowledge and skills.

Decisions must be in writing with reasons.

62 *Okeke v Nursing and Midwifery Council* [2013] EWHC 714 (Admin).

63 GOC (FTP) Rules 2013 r13.

64 OA 1989 s13K(6).

8.197 Under rule 41 the committee may assess costs and order them to be paid by any party.

8.198 If during the same period of erasure, a second or subsequent application for restoration is unsuccessful, the committee may direct that the individual's or corporate body's right to make any further such applications be suspended indefinitely. However, the applicant can appeal against the suspension direction and after two years of the suspension of the right to apply the applicant can apply to the Registrar for that suspension direction to be reviewed by the Registration Appeals Committee.

Registration appeals – by Registrations Appeals Committee

8.199 These cases are also governed by the GOC (Registration Appeals Rules) 2005 which set out the procedure for considering appeals against decisions to refuse entry to the Register where the person/body concerned is referred to as the appellant.

8.200 Appealable decisions are listed in OA 1989 Sch 1A para 2. The most common decision appealed against is the refusal to register an individual or student (ie a decision on an application made under section 8 or section 8A). An appellant's notice of appeal must be made before the end of 28 days (starting with the date of the notice of the Registrar's decision), but an extension can be granted. The committee has the power to receive oral and documentary evidence that was not before the Registrar which means that the nature of the appeal is a fresh consideration of the issues.

8.201 The committee may:

a) dismiss the appeal;
b) allow the appeal and quash the decision appealed against;
c) substitute for the decision appealed against any other decision which could have been made; or
d) remit the case back to the Registrar/GOC to dispose of the case in accordance with the committee's directions.

8.202 The committee considering the appeal may make such enquiries as they consider appropriate.[65]

Appeals to the High Court

8.203 Appeals against the FTP Committee in respect of disciplinary orders lie to the High Court (or in Scotland, to the Court of Session) within 28 days beginning with the date on which notification was served.

8.204 Fresh evidence may be considered on appeal, if it was not available at the time of the original hearing.[66] However, the significance of fresh evidence is best considered by a Review Panel, and will not be considered by the court if a review has not taken place.[67]

65 OA 1989 Sch 1A para 4(6).

66 *Chandrasekera v Nursing and Midwifery Council* [2008] EWHC 3528 (Admin).

67 *Muscat v Health Professions Council* [2009] EWCA Civ 1090.

CHAPTER 9

The General Pharmaceutical Council

continued

Key points

- *Regulator:* General Pharmaceutical Council (GPhC)
- *Professions regulated:* Pharmacist and pharmacy technicians. It further regulates pharmacy premises
- *Common sources of referral:* Members of the public, Registrant's employers, other healthcare professionals and GPhC inspectors
- *Type of proceedings:* Fitness to practise, restoration hearings
- *Location:* 25 Canada Square, London, E14 5LQ
- *Relevant statute:* Pharmacy Order 2010 SI No 231
- *Fitness to Practise Rules:* The General Pharmaceutical Council (Fitness to Practise and Disqualification etc. Rules) Order of Council 2010 SI No 1615
- *Key document:* Standards for pharmacy professionals
- *Four-stage process:* Referral, investigation, adjudication and review
- *Investigation:* Conducted by the GPhC's Inspectorate (PO 2010 art 8 and GPhC (FTP) Rules 2010 r6(3))
- *Investigation Committee:* Yes, applies the 'real prospect test' when determining whether allegations 'ought to be' passed on (PO 2010 art 53)
- *Investigation Committee guidance:* 'Good decision making: investigating committee meetings and outcomes guidance'
- *Notice of hearing provision:* GPhC (FTP) Rules 2010 r16(1)
- *Case management provisions:* GPhC (FTP) Rules 2010 r21, 24 and 46 for non-compliance provisions
- *Test:* Whether fitness to practise is impaired by reason of (in summary): a) misconduct; b) deficient professional performance; c) adverse physical or mental health; d) a failure to comply with a professional performance assessment requirement; e) a criminal conviction or caution; or f) a determination by a another healthcare regulator (PO 2010 art 51(1))
- *Interim order power:* Yes – interim conditions of practice or interim suspension (PO 2010 art 56(1), GPhC (FTP) Rules 2010 r36) heard by an Interim Orders Committee
- *General composition for final hearings:* one chair and at least two other members (one lay and one registrant)
- *Addressing the panel:* Generally seated and 'Sir'/'Madam'
- *Independent legal adviser:* Yes (PO 2010 art 63(1))
- *Evidence:* GPhC (FTP) Rules 2010 r24(2) – subject only to the requirements of relevance and fairness, the Committee may receive any documentary evidence; and any oral evidence, whether or not such evidence would be admissible in any subsequent civil proceedings
- *Half-time submission provision:* GPhC (FTP) Rules 2010 r31(8) – whether 'sufficient evidence has been adduced to find the facts proved or to support a finding of impairment'
- *Sanction provisions:* PO 2010 art 54(2)(a)–(e)
- *Sanction document:* 'Good decision making: fitness to practise hearings and sanctions guidance'

- *Review hearings:* PO 2010 art 54(3)
- *Restoration hearings:* PO 2010 art 57 and GPhC (FTP) Rules 2010 r35
- *Appeal rule:* PO 2010 art 58(1)
- *Costs:* Power to make a costs award governed by GPhC (FTP) Rules 2010 r46

Introduction

Background

9.1 In February 2007 the Department of Health (DOH) published a government white paper entitled: *Trust assurance and safety: the regulation of health care professionals in the 21st century*. Within this paper the government set out its intentions to establish a new independent pharmacy regulator – the General Pharmaceutical Council (GPhC). This recommendation found favour with the now replaced Council for Healthcare Regulatory Excellence (CHRE), who in November 2008 published advice to the DOH in which it stated, 'the GPhC has the potential to become an exemplar of modern professional regulation: effective in protecting patients, agile in identifying and responding to change, and balanced in its approach to risk and regulation'.[1]

9.2 This public backing for reform in pharmacy regulation provided important political impetus for the creation of the Pharmacy Order (PO) 2010.[2] Designed to ensure that the pharmacy profession was regulated according to the same principles as other healthcare professions, the PO 2010 formally established the GPhC (which replaced the Royal Pharmaceutical Society of Great Britain) as the independent regulator for the 77,000 pharmacists and pharmacy technicians and the 14,000 pharmacy premises currently operating within England, Wales and Scotland.[3]

Function of the General Pharmaceutical Council

9.3 The statutory objective of the GPhC (set out in full under the provisions of article 6 of the 2010 Order) is to protect, promote and maintain the health, safety and well-being of the public, and in particular of those members of the public who use pharmacy services. To achieve this objective, in line with many other healthcare regulators, the GPhC is required to set and publish standards of proficient practice that are to be met by all those practising registered pharmacy.[4]

1 See Council for Healthcare Regulatory Excellence, *Advice to the Department of Health and the Pharmacy Regulation and Leadership Oversight Group on aspects of the establishment of the General Pharmaceutical Council* (November 2008), p2.

2 SI No 231.

3 For the precise figures, see GPhC, *Annual fitness to practise report / annual accounts 2016/17*, p7.

4 PO 2010 art 48(1)(a).

9.4 In May 2017, the GPhC published new *Standards for pharmacy professionals*,[5] setting out nine standards that all pharmacists and pharmacy technicians working in Great Britain are accountable for meeting.

9.5 These standards need to be met at all times and are not limited to working hours. They stipulate that pharmacy professionals must:

1) provide person-centred care;
2) work in partnership with others;
3) communicate effectively;
4) maintain, develop and use their professional knowledge and skills;
5) use professional judgment;
6) behave in a professional manner;
7) respect and maintain the person's confidentiality and privacy;
8) speak up when they have concerns or when things go wrong; and
9) demonstrate leadership.

9.6 Such standards, which are under continual review and may be subject to variation, can only be set following consultation with, among others, registrants themselves, service users, and professional bodies or organisations appearing to the GPhC to represent registrants' interests.[6]

9.7 To support pharmacists and pharmacy technicians to meet the above standards, the GPhC has also produced guidance in relation to various aspects of pharmaceutical practice. This includes guidance on:

a) obtaining consent;
b) maintaining sexual boundaries; and
c) preserving patient confidentiality.

All guidance can be found on the GPhC's website.

9.8 Article 4(3) of the PO 2010 sets out six core functions to be fulfilled by the GPhC. The setting and promotion of professional standards designed to ensure the safe and effective practice of pharmacy at registered pharmacies is one of these provisions. The other five listed functions are:

1) to establish and maintain a register of pharmacists, pharmacy technicians and premises at which a retail pharmacy business is, or is to be, carried on;
2) to set requirements by reference to which registrants must demonstrate that their fitness to practise (FTP) is not impaired;
3) to promote the safe and effective practice of pharmacy by registrants (including, for example, by reference to any code of conduct for, and ethics relating to, pharmacy);
4) to set standards and requirements in respect of the education, training, acquisition of experience and continuing professional development that it is necessary for pharmacists and pharmacy technicians to achieve in order to be entered in the Register or to receive an annotation in the Register and to maintain competence; and
5) to ensure the continued fitness to practise of registrants.

5 See GPhC, *Standards for pharmacy professionals* (May 2017).

6 PO 2010 art 5(2); and *Consultation on standards for pharmacy professionals* (2016), available on the GPhC website.

Jurisdictional reach

Regulation of individual professionals

9.9 The GPhC is responsible for the registration and regulation of all pharmacists and pharmacy technicians operating within England, Wales and Scotland.[7]

9.10 It is illegal to practise pharmacy without being registered to do so; accordingly anyone who is not registered with the GPhC but practises as a pharmacist or pharmacy technician, or refers to themselves as such, can be prosecuted.

9.11 The requirements of registration are set out in article 20 of the PO 2010 which is supplemented by the General Pharmaceutical Council (Registration Rules) Order of Council 2010.[8]

9.12 Additionally, in the case of pharmacists, the GPhC has published detailed *Criteria for registration as a pharmacist* (September 2012), detailing the education, training and experience requirements for initial registration as a pharmacist, including the criteria to be met where an applicant has obtained qualifications outside of the UK. This criteria can be downloaded from the GPhC's website.[9]

9.13 In order to be placed on the register, a pharmacist and pharmacy technician must:[10]

- Be 'appropriately qualified' (as defined by articles 21 and 22 of the PO 2010). In the case of pharmacists who have trained in Great Britain and Northern Ireland, this typically means having successfully completed an accredited four-year MPharm degree and a further 52-week programme of pre-registration training. In respect of pharmacy technicians, they must pass a knowledge and competency qualification and have completed a prescribed period of work experience.[11]
- Be fit to practise.
- Pay an annual registration fee.
- Meet any additional requirements relating to education, training or experience as the GPhC considers to be appropriate. For example, the GPhC reserves the right to require applicants who have trained outside of Great Britain and Northern Ireland, whose training is deemed to have been 'substantially different' from that which they would have received to successfully complete a period of adaptation with assessment, not exceeding three years.

9.14 The registration process also includes health, character and identity checks.

7 The Pharmaceutical Society of Northern Ireland, independent of the GPhC, is responsible for registering and regulating pharmacists and pharmacies in Northern Ireland.

8 SI 2010 No 1617 (in force since 27 September 2010).

9 See www.pharmacyregulation.org/registration/registering-pharmacist.

10 PO 2010 art 20(1)(a).

11 In the case of those who have qualified outside of Great Britain and Northern Ireland, registration may be achieved providing their qualifications falls within European Communities (Recognition of Professional Qualifications) Regulations 2015 SI No 2059 reg 3(9)(a) or (b).

9.15 The GPhC operates a 'rolling register', meaning that registration of both pharmacy professionals and pharmacies must be renewed every 12 months from the date of entry.[12]

9.16 Failure to apply for a renewed registration within two months of the existing registrations expiry will result in the registrant, and/or his or her pharmacy, being removed from the register. A renewal application by a pharmacist or pharmacy technician includes the making of a signed declaration that the applicant is fit to practise without restrictions.

Regulation of pharmacy businesses

9.17 Alongside its role as a regulator of individual professionals, the GPhC also acts as a systems regulator required to establish and promote standards for the safe and effective practice of pharmacy within registered pharmacies. The inclusion of a pharmacy business on the register is therefore dependent on (among other things) a declaration being made by the applicant that the standards set by the GPhC for safe and effective practice are to be met.[13]

9.18 The *Standards for registered pharmacies* (first published in September 2012) set out the requirements that must be met when operating a registered pharmacy. Grouped under five principles, all focused on safeguarding 'the health, safety and wellbeing of patients and the public', they apply to matters such as record keeping, staff training, the handling and storage of medicinal products and the condition of the premises.[14]

9.19 Pharmacy owners and superintendent pharmacists are responsible for ensuring that the required standards are met. Such are assessed during routine visits made by GPhC inspectors.

9.20 A failure to meet the relevant standards can lead to the issuing of an improvement notice setting out the measures that must be taken in order to rectify the failures within the practice that have been identified. A failure to comply with an improvement notice can lead to a criminal conviction and/or a fine.

Review

9.21 The Professional Standard Authority for Health and Social Care (PSA), previously known as the CHRE, is responsible for supervising and scrutinising the work of all nine of the healthcare regulators operating in the UK, including the GPhC. Among the many functions of the PSA is its power to review all fitness to practise decisions taken by the GPhC.

9.22 In circumstances where the PSA is of the view that a decision taken by a Fitness to Practise (FTP) Committee, in respect of a registrant's registration is 'unduly lenient' or 'should not have been made' at all and 'where it would be desirable for the protection of members of the public' for the PSA to take action, they may refer the case in question to the High Court of Justice in England and Wales, or to the Court of Sessions if the decision

12 PO 2010 art 25(1).

13 General Pharmaceutical Council (Registration Rules) Order of Council 2010 SI No 1617 r22(3)(c)(iv).

14 PO 2010 art 7(1).

was made under Scottish jurisdiction.[15] The decision to refer a case must be made within 40 days (excluding any appeal period) of the fitness to practise decision having been made.

Approach to regulation

9.23 The GPhC, through the provisions of the PO 2010 and the accompanying procedural rules founds within the General Pharmaceutical Council (Fitness to Practise and Disqualification etc Rules) Order of Council 2010[16] (GPhC (FTP) Rules 2010) adopt the same test as most other healthcare regulators when assessing whether a registrant's fitness to practise is impaired.

9.24 Impairment can be found (among other things) as a result of:

a) misconduct;
b) deficient professional performance;
c) the registrant suffering from adverse physical or mental health problems which impair his or her ability to practise safely and effectively;
d) a failure to comply with a requirement imposed following a professional performance assessment;
e) a criminal conviction or caution; or
f) a determination made by a another healthcare regulator that the registrants fitness to practise is impaired.[17]

Chapter 3 provides a detailed discussion of what constitutes some of the terms listed above, such as misconduct and deficient professional performance.[18]

9.25 The regulatory regime adopted by the GPhC in response to a complaint being made about a registrant's fitness to practise is procedurally similar to other health care regulators.

9.26 The process begins with all complaints about a registrant's practice being initially investigated by the GPhC's 'Inspectorate' – this may involve speaking with the individual who made the complaint as well as the registrant, and additionally visiting the premises where any incident that brought rise to the complaint took place, in order to gather further information relevant to the complaint made.

9.27 Additionally, the GPhC Inspectorate will periodically conduct visits irrespective of whether a complaint has been made about a registrant, as part of what the GPhC terms 'risked-based regulation', designed to monitor and secure compliance with relevant legal requirements and professional standards.

15 Pursuant to the provisions of National Health Service Reform and Healthcare Professions Act 2002 s29 – as amended by PO 2010 Sch 4 para 10(4).

16 SI No 1615.

17 PO 2010 art 51(1).

18 It is interesting to note the Law Commissions Draft Bill for the Regulation of Health and Social Care Professions seeks to replace 'misconduct' as a statutory ground for impairment with two new grounds: a) 'disgraceful misconduct' for conduct which may or may not be related to the exercise of professional skills, but which brings disgrace upon the practitioner and thereby prejudices the reputation of the profession; and b) a wider 'deficient professional performance' ground to encompass situations which would not have previously amounted to 'deficient professional performance' such as a single instance of negligent treatment.

9.28 It may be that the findings of an inspection visit raise concerns about the standards of care being provided by a registrant that in turn bring rise to a referral being made to the GPhC's Investigating Committee.

9.29 A fuller discussion of the responsibilities and powers of GPhC inspectors is found in para 9.56.

9.30 At the end of any initial investigation all the evidence gathered by a GPhC inspector will be assessed against a 'threshold criteria' to determine whether a complaint should be referred to the GPhC's Investigating Committee. This 'threshold criteria' is designed to act as a filter ensuring that relatively minor matters can be resolved expeditiously without the need to embark on a full fitness to practise investigation.

9.31 Any complaints referred to the Investigating Committee (which will include details of the initial complaint, any further information gathered by the Inspectorate, and any written response from the registrant) will be assessed to determine whether there is a 'real prospect' of the facts alleged being found proved and further whether there is a 'real prospect' of a registrant's fitness to practise being impaired as a result of such. If there is, the Investigating Committee will refer the case to the GPhC's FTP Committee.

9.32 The GPhC's FTP Committee is tasked with making a final determination on whether the facts behind the initial compliant have been found proved (based on the civil standard of proof), and if so, whether the registrant's fitness to practise is currently impaired. A positive finding in respect of such will then lead to a decision being taken on what sanction (if any) should be taken against the registrant. The procedures involved in such hearings will be focused on later within this chapter.

9.33 Unlike other healthcare regulators who have separate FTP Committees to deal with distinct issues relevant to the question of impairment – such as the registrant's health, professional conduct issues and clinical performance – the GPhC FTP Committee is not so divided, and accordingly any one panel could be tasked with dealing with any matter relevant to the issue of impairment.

Sources of law

Legislation and guidance

9.34 The GPhC derives most of its regulatory powers from the PO 2010, which was made principally under the provisions of sections 60 and 62 of the Health Act 1999 (as amended).

9.35 As previously noted, the PO 2010 brought about the transference of all of the regulatory functions of the Royal Pharmaceutical Society of Great Britain to the GPhC. Interestingly, the Health Act 1999 also allows for the future transfer of the regulatory functions of the Pharmaceutical Society of Northern Ireland to the GPhC, should the Northern Ireland Ministers approve such at a future date.

9.36 The PO 2010 covers a wide range of matters, including:

- setting out the GPhC's principal functions and general duties (found under Part 2 of the Order);

- setting out provisions for the registration of pharmacists and pharmacy technicians in Great Britain (found under Part 3);
- detailing provisions in respect of the education, training and continuing professional development of all registrants and prospective registrants (found under Part 5); and
- most significantly, for the purposes of this chapter, providing provisions relating to the fitness to practise of registrants and in particular the regulatory framework within which allegations of impairment are to be considered (found under Part 6).

9.37 The PO 2010 has been subject to some amendment since it was first enacted. Usefully, the GPhC website contains a link to a consolidated version where the original order has been appropriately reworded in line with various statutory amendments. However, the website notes that, 'the consolidated versions are not official text' and accordingly 'users should consult an official version of the legislation for the purpose of interpreting and applying the law'.

9.38 The provisions of the PO 2010 are supplemented by various rules governing more specific functions of the GPhC. Such rules are made under powers conferred upon the GPhC by the PO 2010 itself,[19] and are enacted subject to approval by the Privy Council. They include:

- General Pharmaceutical Council (Constitution) Order 2010;
- General Pharmaceutical Council (Registration Rules) Order of Council 2010;
- General Pharmaceutical Council (Statutory Committees and their Advisers Rules) Order of Council 2010;
- General Pharmaceutical Council (Appeals Committee Rules) Order of Council 2010;
- General Pharmaceutical Council (Continuing Professional Development and Consequential Amendments Rules) Order of Council 2011;
- General Pharmaceutical Council (2012 Registration and Renewal Fees) Rules 2011;
- General Pharmaceutical Council (Fitness to Practise and Disqualification etc Rules) Order of Council 2010, which sets out various matters relating to the procedures to be implemented, by the committees of the GPhC, when considering allegations that a registrant's fitness to practise is impaired or allegations that a person should be disqualified from inclusion on the register of pharmacy businesses.

9.39 In addition to the statutory provisions detailed above, the GPhC also publishes guidance in relation to its fitness to practise procedures, to assist its regulatory committees in making their decisions, such as:

- *Guidance on the General Pharmaceutical Council's threshold criteria policy* (last reviewed February 2016);
- *Good decision making: investigating committee meetings and outcomes guidance* (last revised March 2017); and

19 Such as PO 2010 art 48(1)(b), which stipulates rules must be made regarding the criteria to which FTP Committees must have regard in considering fitness to practise issues.

- *Good decision making: fitness to practise hearings and sanctions guidance* (last revised March 2017).

9.40 The GPhC also derives some of its regulatory powers directly from primary legislation. For example, under the provisions of section 80 of the Medicines Act 1968 (as amended by the PO 2010) the GPhC has the power to disqualify a body corporate involved in a retail pharmacy business from practising registered pharmacy, where, for example, such a body has been convicted of a particular offence or where the pharmacy premises for which the body corporate assumes control has failed to meet the standards required for safe practice as found under article 7 of the PO 2010.

9.41 Additionally, the provisions of section 9 of the Poisons Act 1972 allow for an inspector appointed by the GPhC to inspect pharmacy premises in order to ensure (among other things) compliance with the Poison Rules as set out in section 7 of the Poisons Act (which relate to the sale of non-medicinal poisons). Wilfully obstructing an appointed inspector in this task constitutes a criminal offence under the provisions of section 9(8) of the Act.

Case-law

9.42 Case law from other regulatory bodies – including the General Medical Council (GMC), Nursing and Midwifery Council (NMC) and Health and Care Professions Council (HCPC) – is applicable to decisions taken by the GPhC.

9.43 Additionally, the GPhC, as with other healthcare regulators, is a public authority, and as such is subject to the European Convention on Human Rights (ECHR), notably Article 6 (right to a fair trial). The decisions of the European Court of Human Rights (ECtHR) and the domestic courts, in respect of this right, are therefore relevant to fitness to practise procedures adopted by the GPhC.

Hearings location

9.44 Hearings of the GPhC's FTP Committee are open to the public and are held at 25 Canada Square, London, E14 5LQ.

Referrals

9.45 Disciplinary proceedings against pharmacists and pharmacy technicians will usually result from a complaint being made to the GPhC about their practice, or as a result of information gathered during a routine inspection of the premises where they operate, conducted by a GPhC inspector.

9.46 Complaints about a pharmacist's or pharmacy technician's practice may come from a variety of sources. For example, the GPhC's most recently published annual fitness to practise report,[20] notes that of the 1,889 cases dealt with by the GPhC between 2016 and 2017, most – 1,056 – were instigated by complaints made by members of the public; 107 were

20 Published pursuant to PO 2010 Sch 1 para 8.

as a result of concerns raised by a registrants employer, 201 came from other healthcare professionals and 177 were raised by GPhC inspectors.

9.47 Within these statistics, 148 of the concerns addressed by the GPhC stemmed from a registrant's own self-referral.

9.48 Self-referral to the GPhC is mandatory in certain circumstances. For example, rule 4(1) of the GPhC (FTP) Rules 2010 stipulates that a registrant must notify the council in writing (within seven days of the day on which the event occurred) of (among other things) any conviction he or she has received for any criminal offence, the acceptance of a police caution by him or her, and of any notification from another healthcare regulator of a determination that his or her fitness to practise is impaired.

9.49 Additionally, all registered pharmacists and pharmacy technicians are under a professional duty to report any concerns they have about another registrant's fitness to practise.[21]

9.50 In order to satisfy this duty, it is enough for a registrant to report a concern to his or her employers rather than to the GPhC directly. However, as highlighted in the GPhC *Guidance on raising concerns*,[22] failure of a registrant to report such concerns about a colleague may be considered out of line with the GPhC's standards for pharmacy professionals, and, significantly, 'may call into question their own fitness to practise'.

The initial investigation

The work of the Inspectorate

9.51 All complaints received by the GPhC initially go through a 'triage' process, which involves consideration of whether the GPhC has the power to investigate the complainant received. If the information received raises concerns about a pharmacy professional's fitness to practise, this will usually result in further 'inquiries' and/or an 'investigation' being conducted by its GPhC's Inspectorate.[23]

9.52 Currently, the GPhC employs 38 different inspectors, each tasked with covering different catchment areas throughout Great Britain.[24]

9.53 The GPhC is unique among healthcare regulators in having such a team of inspectors. Their responsibilities are multifarious, including:

- Being responsible for conducting initial investigations into any complaints raised – thus fulfilling one of their principal functions of assisting the GPhC in its investigation of all fitness to practise matters.[25]
- Visiting all registered pharmacies in Great Britain to ensure appropriate standards of care are being adhered to and that they are complying with the relevant provisions of the Medicines Act 1968 and the Poisons Act 1972.[26]

21 Following the provisions of the Public Interest Disclosure Act 1998.

22 See para 1.6.

23 Established under PO 2010 art 8.

24 The names, contact details and catchment areas covered by each GPhC inspector are provided on the GPhC website.

25 PO 2010 art 8(2)(b).

26 PO 2010 art 8(2)(a) and (c).

- Implementing enforcement proceedings when such standards are not being met – which may include initiating a criminal prosecution in certain prescribed circumstances.

9.54 The PO 2010 confers specific powers upon GPhC inspectors to facilitate both routine inspection visits and the initial investigations following a complaint being made about a registrant – if such is deemed appropriate to the proper consideration of the complainant.[27]

9.55 Article 10 of the PO 2010 allows inspectors to enter any registered pharmacy or other premises for the purposes of fulfilling its functions listed in part in para 9.53 above. Where entry is refused, then the inspector may apply for a court ordered warrant, authorising entry with the use of reasonable force if necessary.[28]

9.56 Inspectors' article 10 powers are supplemented by the provisions of article 11 of the PO 2010 which grant inspectors broad investigatory powers, invoked following entry into a registered pharmacy or other premise. They are statutorily permitted to 'do anything which is calculated to facilitate the discharge of the inspector's functions or which is incidental or conducive to the discharge of those functions'.[29] More specifically, an inspector's powers include the right to:

- inspect the premises and any plant, machinery or equipment at the premises;
- search the premises;
- inspect and remove from the premises any substance, article or product (whether or not appearing to the inspector to be a medicinal product);
- take and remove from the premises samples of any substance, article or product;
- require any person holding or accountable for any documents or records (whether or not kept at the premises being inspected) to produce them for inspection at the premises; and
- carry out any examinations and tests and make any enquiries (including such enquiries of any person as the inspector considers it appropriate to make) relating to the fitness to practise of a registrant who is or has been employed on the premises to provide pharmaceutical services.

9.57 Intentionally obstructing an inspector in exercising any of the above powers constitutes a criminal offence for which a registrant can be prosecuted.[30]

9.58 How an investigation is carried out will depends on the individual facts of a case, but may include:

- requesting that the informant provide a written statement or statutory declaration;
- speaking to the registrant about the complaint made;
- where the health of a registrant is questioned an inspector may require him or her to be medically examined by a registered medical practitioner;[31]

27 GPhC (FTP) Rules 2010 r6(3).
28 PO 2010 art 10(3).
29 PO 2010 art 11(5).
30 PO 2010 art 12.
31 GPhC (FTP) Rules 2010 r6(4).

- depending on the nature of the complaint, an inspector may interview a registrant under caution, under the relevant provisions and adjoining codes of practice of the Police and Criminal Evidence Act 1984. If such steps are taken a registrant is well advised to seek legal representation. Particular care must be taken in responding to the initial complaint before it has been formalised into specific charges, as the answers provided by the registrant may be used in evidence in any subsequent fitness to practise hearings.

Referral to the Investigation Committee

9.59 Once an initial investigation into a complaint made against a registrant has been completed, the GPhC's Inspectorate must decide whether to refer the complaint on to the GPhC's Investigating Committee.

9.60 The timescale for completing initial enquiries will naturally depend upon the seriousness and complexity of the complaint raised, although the GPhC aims to complete all initial enquiries within three to nine months of the concern being raised.

9.61 Under the provisions of article 52 of the PO 2010, there is a presumption that all allegations made against a registrant that his or her fitness to practise is impaired, or where the GPhC is in receipt of information that calls a registrant's fitness to practise into question, even when no explicit complaint has been made, will be referred to the Investigation Committee, subject to such conditions that the GPhC may prescribe. The conditions prescribed by the GPhC, that may act as a bar to referral, relate to the seriousness of the allegation, the timing of it and its source.

9.62 A complaint may not be referred where:

- it is of the type that according to the GPhC's published 'threshold criteria' should not be referred;[32]
- more than five years have elapsed since the most recent events referred to in the allegation (unless it is considered necessary for the protection of the public and in the wider public interest to refer the allegation);[33]
- the allegation is made by an anonymous informant and the allegation is not capable of independent verification, or where the informant is identifiable but he or she chose not to participate in the consideration of the allegation and the allegation is not capable of independent verification.[34]

The threshold criteria

9.63 The GPhC's 'threshold criteria', and the accompanying guidance on its application,[35] must be considered when determining whether an allega-

32 PO 2010 art 52(2)(a); and GPhC (FTP) Rules 2010 r6(2)(a).

33 GPhC (FTP) Rules 2010 r6(2)(b).

34 GPhC (FTP) Rules 2010 r6(2)(c).

35 See *Guidance on the GPhC's threshold criteria policy* (last reviewed in February 2016) available on the GPhC's website.

tion should be referred to the GPhC's Investigating Committee for further consideration.

9.64 The existing 'threshold criteria' (which has recently been the subject of a consultation, raising the possibility of future revision to ensure it is consistent with the new standards for pharmacy professionals)[36] was developed against seven key principles, which all registered pharmacy professionals must comply with.

9.65 Under each of these seven principles there are a series of statements of relevance to them. If one, or more, of the statements are deemed to be true in relation to any allegation, then it must be referred by an inspector to the Investigation Committee of the GPhC.

9.66 While many of these statements are self-explanatory, the GPhC has nonetheless published guidance designed to further clarify their meaning, as noted in para 9.39 above.

9.67 The guidance notes that is not a rigid set of rules, and that the threshold criteria must be considered on a case-by-case basis. It further notes that where investigators are in any doubt as to whether the threshold criteria is met, then the allegation should be referred to the Investigation Committee for further consideration.[37] Additionally, it states that in cases involving more than one allegation, where some are deemed to have passed the threshold criteria but others have not – all matters should be referred to the Investigation Committee.[38]

Where the threshold criteria is not met: no further action or advice

9.68 Where an inspector concludes that the complaint raised does not justify referral to the Investigating Committee on the grounds that the threshold criteria has not been passed, then the matter is formally closed.

9.69 In this scenario, no further action is taken against the registrant, or the registrant may receive advice on how to improve his or her practice. In both cases, both the registrant and the informant must be informed in writing as to the outcome.

9.70 When a case is closed, regardless of whether advice is given or not, it will not form part of a pharmacy professional's legal history. However, any case considered does provide so called 'soft intelligence' which may be used by the GPhC when assessing any future allegations against the threshold criteria.[39]

Bypassing the Investigation Committee

9.71 Not all complaints that are initially investigated by the GPhC's inspectorate that are found to satisfy the criteria for referral will next be considered by the GPhC's Investigation Committee. For example, where:

36 See the GPhC's *Consultation on revised threshold criteria* (December 2016).

37 *Guidance on the GPhC's threshold criteria policy* para 15.

38 *Guidance on the GPhC's threshold criteria policy* para 14.

39 *Guidance on the GPhC's threshold criteria policy* para 16.

- the GPhC forms the view that 'the public interest is best served by urgent consideration of the case';
- the allegation relates to a conviction for one or more criminal offences and the sentence imposed in respect of one or more of these convictions was a custodial sentence or a suspended sentence; or
- an allegation relates to a determination made by another regulatory body in the UK that the registrant's fitness to practise is impaired,

then the allegation *must* be referred directly to the GPhC's FTP Committee.[40]

Notification of referral

9.72 Once a decision has been taken to refer an allegation to the Investigation Committee, the registrant concerned must be sent:

- a notice of referral;
- copies of all documentation to be placed before the Investigation Committee;
- a copy of the GPhC's threshold criteria.[41]

9.73 The notice of referral must, among other things:

- contain particulars of the allegation made;
- contain any recommendations made by the GPhC relating to the disposal of the case;
- specify the date for the meeting of the Investigation Committee which will consider the allegation (which must be no less than 28 days after the date of service of the notice of referral);
- inform the registrant concerned of the Investigation Committee's powers; and
- invite the registrant to indicate whether the particulars of the allegation are admitted or denied, and provide written representations on the allegations made.[42]

9.74 Any indications/representations made by a registrant in relation to the allegations he or she faces must be served on the Investigation Committee within 21 days after the service of the notice of referral.[43]

9.75 Providing a written response to the allegation(s) made is not mandatory, but if done demonstrates that the registrant is actively participating in the regulatory process, something that may be considered by an FTP Committee when later addressing the question of the registrant's impairment.

9.76 Where a registrant wishes to provide a response, he or she is well advised to seek legal representation to assist in the drafting of such, given this response may be considered by the GPhC's FTP Committee if the allegation is referred to them by the Investigation Committee.

40 GPhC (FTP) Rules 2010 r6(5)(b) and (6)(a) and (b).

41 GPhC (FTP) Rules 2010 r7(1).

42 GPhC (FTP) Rules 2010 r7(2)(a)–(i).

43 GPhC (FTP) Rules 2010 r7(2)(e).

Additional powers of General Pharmaceutical Council inspectors: improvement notices

9.77 In circumstances where an inspector – either making enquiries into a complaint or when conducting a routine inspection visit – concludes that a pharmacy has failed to comply with standards listed under article 7 of the PO 2010, which all pharmacy owners must adhere to (relating to, among other things, the conditions in which drugs are stored, pharmacy security arrangements, record-keeping, the training of staff and the management of waste) an inspector may issue an improvement notice specifying the measures that the person to whom the notice applies must take to rectify the failure(s) detected.[44]

9.78 Failure to adhere to the terms of an improvement notice within a specified time period (not less than 28 days after service of such) is a criminal offence, which may result in removal or suspension from registration.[45]

The Investigation Committee

9.79 As stipulated by the provisions of article 53 of the PO 2010, the principal function of the GPhC's Investigation Committee is to decide whether the allegations referred it to it by the GPhC's Registrar 'ought to be' passed on to the GPhC's FTP Committee for further consideration.

The makeup of the Investigation Committee

9.80 The IC is made up of both lay[46] and registrant members. There are currently 13 members (and 15 reserve members), whose details can be found on the GPhC's website.

9.81 The GPhC rules[47] relating to the membership of its statutory committees stipulates that the IC must consist of a lay member who acts as a chair, two lay members who are deputy chairs, and not fewer than three and not more than 11 other members who may be lay or registrant members. The number of lay members must be at least the same as the number of registrant members.[48]

9.82 An IC meeting to consider a particular case, usually includes four people – a chair or deputy chair, two registrant members and a lay member. There must be at least three[49] members of the committee at an IC meeting

44 PO 2010 art 13.

45 PO 2010 art 14(1).

46 A lay member is defined as any person who is not and has never been entered in the register of not only the GPhC's register, but of any regulatory body, and is not entitled to be registered with the GPhC – see PO 2010 Sch 1 para 1(1)(b).

47 Note: PO 2010 Sch 1 para 5(1) states that the GPhC 'must by rules, as regards each statutory committee, make provision with regard to amongst other things their size, composition and procedures'.

48 General Pharmaceutical Council (Statutory Committees and their Advisers Rules) Order of Council 2010 r3(1).

49 General Pharmaceutical Council (Statutory Committees and their Advisers Rules) Order of Council 2010 r18.

before it can reach a decision, including at least one professional and one lay person.

9.83 Other people involved in IC meetings include:

- The IC secretary – responsible for the administrative arrangements of the committee. They do not take part in any decision-making, but must keep a record of all decisions reached and the reasons underlying them.[50]
- A legal adviser – responsible for advising the IC on questions of law.[51] They do not take part in decision-making, but must intervene in the decision-making process, where there is a possibility of a legal error being made, given their principal function of ensuring that the proceedings are fair. The GPhC's guidance states, 'because of the importance of the role, we believe that a legal adviser should be present at all IC meetings as this will support good decision-making'.[52] Should an IC reject the advice received by a legal advisor, they must record their reasons for doing so.[53]
- A clinical adviser – responsible for advising the IC on any issues within their area of medical expertise, in cases involving an assessment of a registrant's health. Importantly, their remit is restricted to explaining the medical evidence obtained in a case. They do not provide any opinion on a registrant's fitness to practise. Nor do they diagnose or dispute the diagnosis reached by a medical practitioner who has examined a registrant.[54] They do not take part in the decision making process. Should the IC reject the advice received by a clinical adviser, they must record their reasons.[55]
- In some cases, if deemed appropriate, the IC may also ask for advice from a specialist adviser.[56]

Impartiality of the panel

9.84 The IC operates, and makes decisions, independently of the GPhC. No member of the Investigation Committee can also sit as a member of the FTP Committee. Furthermore, in adherence to the rule 'against bias',[57] in order to ensure the impartiality of the GPhC's regulatory proceedings, 'no members of a statutory committee may sit as a member considering a case

50 General Pharmaceutical Council (Statutory Committees and their Advisers Rules) Order of Council 2010 r17.

51 General Pharmaceutical Council (Statutory Committees and their Advisers Rules) Order of Council 2010 r21.

52 See para 2.18.

53 General Pharmaceutical Council (Statutory Committees and their Advisers Rules) Order of Council 2010 r26.

54 *Sandra Watson v General Medical Council* [2005] EWHC 1896 (Admin).

55 General Pharmaceutical Council (Statutory Committees and their Advisers Rules) Order of Council 2010 r26.

56 General Pharmaceutical Council (Statutory Committees and their Advisers Rules) Order of Council 2010 r23.

57 The accepted test in making an assessment of potential bias is that laid down in in the leading case of *Porter v Magill* [2001] UKHL 67, that being (at para 103): 'whether the fair-minded and informed observer, having considered the facts, would conclude that there was a real possibility that the tribunal was biased'.

at any stage of the proceedings if that member has an actual or potential conflict of interest in relation to the case'.[58]

Investigation Committee procedure

9.85 Under rule 9 of the GPhC's FTP Rules, the IC meets in private to consider the allegations referred to it. This means that the person raising the concern, the Registrant and GPhC investigations staff do not attend its meetings.

9.86 Consequently, the IC's decisions will not be based on any oral evidence but rather all written 'documents and recommendations' placed before it by the Registrar and any written representations received from the registrant concerned.[59]

9.87 When reaching a decision, the IC should work within the framework set out in the GPhC's *Good decision making: Investigating committee meetings and outcomes guidance* (last revised in March 2017), which makes clear they are expected to:

> . . . behave in a fair and balanced way when reaching a decision. They are all equally responsible for the decision-making process and for the content of the IC's determination (its formal, written decision).[60]

Adjourning for further information

9.88 In circumstances where the IC is of the view that it has insufficient information to make a fully informed decision, it may direct that further investigation into the allegation is undertaken and adjourn its consideration of the allegation until such is done.[61]

9.89 Such further investigation may involve:

- inviting further comment from the maker of the initial allegation;
- when dealing with health allegations, requiring the registrant to undergo a medical examination; or
- in relation to 'knowledge of English' allegations, requiring the registrant to have to have a language assessment.

9.90 Should a registrant fail to fully comply with an assessment request made by the IC, this may be treated as a separate ground of misconduct and referred to the FTP Committee,[62] emphasising the importance of a registrant fully engaging in the investigatory process.

The 'real prospect' test

9.91 Where an IC is satisfied it has sufficient evidence to proceed, it must then address whether it considers that there is a 'real prospect' of the allega-

58 General Pharmaceutical Council (Statutory Committees and their Advisers Rules) Order of Council 2010 r19(1).

59 GPhC (FTP) Rules 2010 r7(2)(f).

60 GPhC's *Good decision making: Investigating committee meetings and outcomes guidance* para 2.9.

61 GPhC (FTP) Rules 2010 r9(3)(b).

62 GPhC (FTP) Rules 2010 r9(5) and (5A)(a).

tions under consideration being proven and furthermore, whether there is a real prospect that the registrant fitness to practise will be considered impaired by a future FTP Committee.[63]

9.92 The definition of 'realistic prospect' is considered in the case of *Swain v Hillman*[64] where Lord Woolf MR noted:[65]

> The words 'no real prospect of being successful or succeeding' do not need any amplification, they speak for themselves. The word 'real' distinguishes fanciful prospects of success or . . . they direct the court to the need to see whether there is a 'realistic' as opposed to a 'fanciful' prospect of success.

9.93 Consequently, the Investigation Committee acts as an important filter ensuring allegations without any proper evidential basis are not the subject of a full FTP hearing.

9.94 Importantly, however, the IC is not tasked with reaching a final determination in respect of allegations made against a registrant. As the GPhC's *Good decision making: investigating committee meetings and outcomes guidance* highlights:[66]

> The IC should consider all the information before it. It is entitled to assess the relevance and weight of the evidence, but should not try to resolve significant conflicts of – or disputes about – evidence. That is a matter for an FtPC.
>
> The IC should not try to consider what the FtPC will, or might, decide. The IC should only decide whether or not there is a real prospect of a matter being established before an FtPC. It should consider whether there is a real prospect that the FtPC will make a finding that the registrant's fitness to practise is currently impaired.

9.95 The real prospect test, applied by the IC consists of two parts:

1) First, the IC must assess whether there is a real prospect of the facts alleged being proved.
   - If the answer is no (in respect of all of the allegations), then no referral will be made to the FTP Committee.
   - If the answer is yes, then the IC should then ask:
2) Whether there is a real prospect that, based on those alleged facts, the FTP Committee will make a finding that the registrant's fitness to practise is impaired. (An analysis of what constitutes impairment is found later in this chapter.)
   - If the answer is yes, then the case will most likely be referred to the FTP Committee.
   - If the answer is no, but having found that they is a real prospect of the facts alleged being found proved, the IC may consider issuing the registrant with advice or a warning.[67]

9.96 The following 'key factors' 'should' be considered by the IC in deciding whether the real prospect test is satisfied.[68] They are:

63 See chapter 3 of the GPhC's *Good decision making: investigating committee meetings and outcomes guidance*.

64 [2001] 1 All ER 91.

65 At para 7.

66 At paras 3.3–3.4.

67 GPhC's *Good decision making: investigating committee meetings and outcomes guidance* para 3.11.

68 GPhC's *Good decision making: investigating committee meetings and outcomes guidance* para 3.12.

- all documents placed before it by the registrar;[69]
- the circumstances of the allegation;
- the registrant's behaviour, attitude and actions;
- the standards;[70]
- the registrar's recommendation[71] (although the IC is not bound by this nor are they restricted to only referring draft charges recommended by the registrar);
- any written representations received from the registrant concerned;
- any representations offered by a relevant patient or the person raising the concern;
- any relevant fitness to practise history;
- any guidance issued by the GPhC to the statutory committees; and
- any other guidance issued by the GPhC.

Considering onward referral

9.97 Where an IC concludes that the real prospect test has been satisfied, it does not automatically follow (although it is usual) that allegations considered will be referred to the FTP Committee.

9.98 Before reaching a decision on onward referral, the IC must address whether in all the circumstances of a case, the allegations 'ought to be' referred to the FTP Committee or whether another outcome is more appropriate. In doing so the IC must be mindful of the need to achieve a proportionate outcome.

9.99 In this context, a proportionate outcome is one that is no more serious than it needs to be to achieve the IC's aims.[72]

9.100 The factors that an IC should consider when addressing the question of onward referral are listed the GPhC's *Good decision making: investigating committee meetings and outcomes guidance*.[73] They include:

- the public interest: In reaching a decision on outcome, the IC should give appropriate weight to the wider public interest.[74] This involves consideration of the GPhC's role in protecting the public, maintaining public confidence in the profession and maintaining proper standards of behaviour;
- any aggravating or mitigating factors: As the GPhC's *Good decision making: Investigating Committee meetings and outcomes guidance* notes:[75]

> . . . although both mitigating and aggravating factors are important elements to consider, there are limits to how much the IC can consider them. This is because, unlike the FtPC, the IC cannot test any evidence before it. Therefore, the IC should not usually consider any purely personal mitigation – for example, character references or professional testimonials.

69 GPhC (FTP) Rules 2010 r9(3).
70 PO 2010 art 48(1).
71 GPhC (FTP) Rules 2010 r9(3)(a)(i).
72 *Chaudhury v General Medical Council* [2002] UKPC 41.
73 At para 4.6.
74 *Council for Healthcare Regulatory Excellence v Nursing and Midwifery Council* [2011] EWHC 927 (Admin).
75 At paras 4.10–4.11.

This is evidence that the FtPC will usually only consider once it has concluded that a registrant's fitness to practise is impaired.

However, as part of their decision-making, the IC can take account of any features of the case that would be considered by an FtPC as either aggravating or mitigating ones. These may include expressions of regret or apology, or evidence of remediation undertaken by the registrant.

- the circumstances of the allegation and whether there is an ongoing risk to members of the public;
- the registrant's behaviour, attitude and actions;
- all evidence placed before it by the registrar;
- the standards;
- the registrar's recommendation;
- any written representations received from the registrant concerned;
- registrants should be aware that theoretically any representations made to the IC could latterly be considered by a FTP Committee should the case be referred. Accordingly, registrants are well advised to seek legal representation to assist them in drafting a response to the allegations made;
- any representations offered by a relevant patient or the person raising the concern;
- any relevant fitness to practise history; and
- whether a lesser outcome would be appropriate.

9.101 If an IC is unsure whether the real prospect test has been met or whether it ought to refer allegations on, they should favour a decision to refer.[76]

Outcomes

9.102 The IC has a range of outcomes it can decide on, depending upon its assessment of the evidence. Unless the registrant has asked for the case to be referred to the FTP Committee,[77] the available outcomes include:

- taking no action;
- giving advice to the registrant (or to another person or body involved in the allegations);
- issuing a warning;
- agreeing undertakings with the registrant, if the registrant admits that his or her fitness to practise is impaired; or
- refer the case to a FTP Committee.

9.103 The GPhC's *Good decision making: investigating committee meetings and outcomes guidance* usefully details the above outcomes and the circumstances in which they may be considered appropriate.[78]

Taking no action

9.104 Where an IC decides that neither part of the real prospect test is met and no other outcome is needed, it can close an investigation by taking no

76 GPhC's *Good decision making: investigating committee meetings and outcomes guidance* para 4.5.

77 PO 2010 art 53(3)(a).

78 At chapter 5 of the guidance.

further action against a registrant. Consequently, nothing will be recorded against the registrant's name on the online register.

Advice

9.105 Where the IC is satisfied that there is a real prospect of proving the factual allegations, but not a real prospect of a finding of impairment, they may issue the registrant with a letter of advice about his or her future conduct or performance.

9.106 The advice given can be about 'any issue' the IC 'considers necessary', but it should be tailored to the individual circumstances of the case it is considering, with a view to ensuring future compliance with 'the relevant professional standards'.[79]

9.107 The fact a registrant has been issued with advice will not be recorded on the register. Furthermore, any advice provided does not place restrictions on their registration.

9.108 The IC can also give advice to any other person or body involved in its investigation of the allegation on any issue arising out of it.[80]

Warnings

9.109 If the IC is satisfied there is:

- a real prospect of proving the factual allegations;
- not a real prospect of a finding of impairment;
- the allegations do not need to be considered by a FTP Committee; and
- the behaviour involved in a particular case cannot be addressed solely by advice,

it may issue the registrant with a warning.[81]

9.110 When considering a warning, the IC will bear in mind the need to demonstrate to a registrant, and more widely to the profession and the public, that his or her conduct or behaviour fell below acceptable standards. While a warning places no restrictions on the registrant's ability to practise, it is recorded against the registrant's name on the register for a period of two years.[82]

9.111 According to the guidance issued:[83]

> A warning will not be appropriate if there is a risk to the public or patients which means that the registrant's registration must be restricted. Generally, warnings will not be appropriate if the allegation relates solely or mainly to the registrant's mental or physical health.

9.112 Where a warning is being considered by the IC, then the registrant concerned must be given an opportunity to comment on it, with a registrant entitled to ask for a referral to the FTP Committee instead.[84]

79 GPhC's *Good decision making: investigating committee meetings and outcomes guidance* p26.

80 See PO 2010 art 53(2)(a). Any registrant concerned and the person who made the initial allegation (if any) must be informed of advice or warning given under article 53(2) pursuant to the provisions of article 53(2)(b).

81 GPhC's *Good decision making: investigating committee meetings and outcomes guidance* p27.

82 GPhC's *Publication and disclosure policy* (last reviewed – December 2015) Table 1.

83 GPhC's *Good decision making: investigating committee meetings and outcomes guidance* p27.

84 PO 2010 art 53(3).

9.113 Where a warning is initially recommended by the referring registrar, they are required to inform the registrant of the recommendation and invite him or her to make representations about it in advance of an IC meeting taking place.

9.114 Where, however, the IC considers making a warning in the absence of an earlier recommendation then, in accordance with the guidance provided,[85] 'the IC must adjourn the meeting to allow the registrant to make written representations specifically on that warning'. Such representations must be made by a registrant no later than 21 days after the day of the issue of the letter inviting submissions. When the case then comes back to the IC, it must take into account any written representations made when deciding whether or not to issue the warning.[86]

Undertakings

9.115 Even where the IC is satisfied that both parts of the real prospect test are met, it may make use of its discretionary power not to refer an allegation to the GPhC's FTP Committee and issue undertakings instead.

9.116 This power is unlikely to be exercised where the allegations made against the registrant are of a serious nature and more serious sanctions need to be considered. Consequently, 'they will not be appropriate if patients will be put at risk, either directly or indirectly, as a result of continued registration with undertakings'.[87]

9.117 Undertakings are:

> . . . an agreement between the GPhC and a registrant about their future practice. The aim of undertakings is to allow the registrant to continue to practise, but with restrictions. They may include restrictions on a registrant's practice or a commitment to practise under supervision or to undergo retraining.[88]

9.118 Undertakings can only be issued in circumstances where the registrant has admitted that their fitness to practise is impaired and has agreed to comply with whatever undertakings the IC considers appropriate in their case.[89] Where a registrant has previously broken undertakings offered to them by the IC or conditions imposed by a FTP Committee, according to the GPhC's *Good decision making: undertakings bank*, undertakings should not be considered.[90]

9.119 The undertakings drafted should usually follow the standard format set out in GPhC's *Good decision making: undertakings bank*.[91] However, they should always be tailored to fit the specific circumstances of each case, dealing with the perceived risks involved in a proportionate way.

85 GPhC's *Good decision making: investigating committee meetings and outcomes guidance* paras 5.4–5.6.

86 GPhC's *Good decision making: investigating committee meetings and outcomes guidance* para 3.1.3.

87 GPhC's *Good decision making: investigating committee meetings and outcomes guidance* p28.

88 GPhC's *Good decision making: undertakings bank* para 2.2.

89 GPhC (FTP) Rules 2010 r10(1).

90 GPhC's *Good decision making: undertakings bank* para 2.7.

91 See pp10–18 setting out standard undertakings for all cases and those to be considered in cases including those involving health or substance misuse and performance cases.

9.120 The undertakings written should be clear, to avoid inadvertent non-compliance. So too should their aims so that if reviewed at a future date, the IC is in a position to decide whether these aims have been achieved.

9.121 All costs of compliance are to be met by a registrant, with undertakings set for up to two years. The fact that undertakings have been issued will be recorded on the register, for the duration that the undertaking are operative and two years following their expiry.[92]

9.122 Compliance with undertakings is monitored by the GPhC's 'monitoring and concerns team' who report back to the IC.

9.123 Where a registrant fails to comply with undertakings, the IC can either:

- refer the original allegation to the FTP Committee and treat the failure to comply with the undertakings as a separate allegation of misconduct and refer this allegation to the FTP Committee also; or
- refer the original allegation to the FTP Committee, but treat the failure to comply with the undertakings as a separate allegation of misconduct and refer that allegation to the FTP Committee alone.[93]

9.124 In contrast, where the IC receives information from the 'monitoring and concerns team' that the undertakings have been complied with or that they may no longer be appropriate, it may with the agreement of the registrant concerned, vary the original undertakings issued; or determine that those undertakings no longer apply.[94]

9.125 Following a decision to issue undertakings, the registrant must be notified in writing within ten days of the decision having been made. The notice must set out the undertakings to be fulfilled and warn the registrant of what steps the IC can take if they are not complied with.[95] If the registrant agrees to accept the undertakings, they must sign an 'undertakings form' and send it back to the IC secretary within 14 days of receipt. If they do not accept their undertakings, then the case may be referred to an FTP Committee.[96]

Referral to the Fitness to Practise Committee

9.126 Where the Investigation Committee determines that the allegation 'ought to be considered by the Fitness to Practise Committee' – or alternatively, in circumstances (be they unusual) where a registrant specifically requests a referral – the IC 'must' refer the allegation to the FTP Committee.[97]

9.127 When such a decision is taken the registrant concerned and the person who made the initial allegation (if any) must be informed of the decision in writing,[98] no later than ten days after the date upon which the decision was made. In some cases the registrant's employer will also be notified.

9.128 The notice must include the reasons for the decision and be accompanied by any legal advice considered by the IC.[99] The reasons provided do not

92 GPhC's *Publication and disclosure policy* (last reviewed – December 2015) Table 1.

93 GPhC (FTP) Rules 2010 r10(2)(a) and (b).

94 GPhC (FTP) Rules 2010 r10(3)(a) and (b).

95 GPhC (FTP) Rules 2010 r11(5)–(7).

96 GPhC's *Good decision making: investigating committee meetings and outcomes guidance* para 5.7.

97 PO 2010 art 53(3)(a).

98 PO 2010 art 53(3)(c).

99 GPhC (FTP) Rules 2010 r11(1) and (3).

need to be elaborate or lengthy, but they should tell everyone involved in broad terms why the IC reached its decision.[100]

Reconsideration of referral decision

9.129 Where the IC decides not to refer an allegation to the GPhC's FTP Committee, but within five years of this decision it receives a new allegation about the same registrant, the IC is entitled to have regard to the old allegation when deciding whether or not to refer the new allegation on, with such forming part of the registrant's fitness to practise history.[101]

9.130 In such circumstances, the IC may refer both the original and new allegation to the FTP Committee together, providing it is either necessary for the protection of the public; necessary for the prevention of injustice to the person concerned; or otherwise necessary in the public interest.

9.131 The IC also has the powers to reconsider a decision not to refer in circumstances where information is received showing the GPhC erred in its administrative handling of the case and accordingly it is now in the public interest that its original referral decision be reconsidered.[102]

Rescinding a referral decision

9.132 There may be circumstances when a decision to refer allegations to the FTP Committee has been made but a hearing has not yet taken place, when the GPhC's representative in the proceedings considers a hearing should not be held.

9.133 In such circumstances it is incumbent upon the GPhC's representative to inform the Investigating Committee of their opinion forthwith and of the reasons for it.[103] This opinion may be based on, for example:

- the evidence available;
- other information the council has; or
- new information about the case that has come to light after the case has been referred to the FTP Committee.

9.134 It is not unprecedented for those who are responsible for making an initial allegation against a registrant to latterly indicate that they do not wish to be involved in the proceedings. In such circumstances, without their evidence, the Investigation Committee may need to reconsider the real prospect of allegations being found proved and/or the public interest in proceeding to a full hearing without the support of the initial informant.

9.135 There may also be circumstances where new evidence comes to light that changes the complexion of the case brought against the registrant to such an extent that there is no longer a real prospect of the allegations against him or her being found proved.

100 *Lutton v GDC* [2011] CSOH 96.

101 Old allegations are often referred to as 'soft intelligence' when considering new ones against the same registrant.

102 GPhC (FTP) Rules 2010 r12(3) and (4).

103 GPhC (FTP) Rules 2010 r38.

9.136 Upon receipt of the presenter's opinion, the IC must consider such and revisit the real prospect test. Following this, it may direct that the original referral decision be cancelled / rescinded.

9.137 The IC may decide whether to rescind all of, or part of, the case against the registrant. Where a referral is fully rescinded the IC may decide to give advice, a warning, issue undertakings or take no further action. It must give reasons for its decision.

9.138 No decision can be taken by the IC without first giving the maker of the relevant allegation (if any) a reasonable opportunity to comment on the proposed rescission.[104]

Bypassing the Investigation Committee

9.139 While the IC acts as an important filter, scrutinising the strength and nature of an allegation made against a registrant or pharmacy owner in advance of any full fitness to practise hearing taking place, there may be circumstances where it is bypassed.

9.140 For example, allegations must be referred directly to the FTP Committee by the registrar where they considers 'the public interest is best served by urgent consideration of the case'.[105]

9.141 Similarly, direct referral to the FTP Committee must be done where the allegation made against a registrant relates to a conviction they have received and the sentenced imposes was one of either immediate custody or a suspended term of imprisonment.[106]

Recommendation for prosecution

9.142 If the IC believes that the GPhC should consider using its powers[107] to bring criminal proceedings, it must tell the registrar and give reasons for its decision.

Interim orders

9.143 At any stage of the fitness to practise process, the GPhC may refer allegations to the FTP Committee and request that they consider the imposition of an interim order.[108]

9.144 Typically, such a request will be made by the IC, following a decision to refer allegations to the FTP Committee, in circumstances where the IC believes an interim order 'should be made'.[109]

104 GPhC (FTP) Rules 2010 r38.

105 GPhC (FTP) Rules 2010 r6(5)(b).

106 GPhC (FTP) Rules 2010 r6(6)(a). Note: Further circumstances where referrals either must or may be referred directly to the GPhC's FTP Committee are found under rule 6(5)–(7A).

107 PO 2010 art 53(4).

108 Referral to the FTP Committee may be made by the registrar before an allegation has been considered by the Investigation Committee. See GPhC (FTP) Rules 2010 r6(5)(a).

109 PO 2010 art 53(3)(b); and GPhC (FTP) Rules 2010 r9(6)(b).

The test: necessity

9.145 The threshold for imposing an interim order is a high one. Given at the point of considering such, no facts will have been found proven against a registrant and given a decision to impose an interim order could significantly restrict a registrant's ability to practise, such decisions are not taken lightly.

9.146 As with other healthcare regulators, the test applied by the GPhC, is whether an interim order is 'necessary' (meaning more than merely desirable), 'for the protection of members of the public or is otherwise in the public interest or is in the interests of the registrant'.[110]

9.147 When considering such an order, regard should be had to the leading case of *R (Shiekh) v General Dental Council*,[111] where Davis J noted:[112]

> I think that, in the ordinary case at least, necessity is an appropriate yardstick. That is so because of reasons of proportionality. It is a very serious thing indeed for a dentist or a doctor to be suspended. It is serious in many cases just because of the impact on that person's right to earn a living. It is serious in all cases because of the detriment to him in reputational terms. Accordingly, it is, in my view, likely to be a relatively rare case where a suspension order will be made on an interim basis on the ground that it is in the public interest.

Notice

9.148 Where an interim order is to be considered the secretary to the FTP Committee must send an 'Interim Order Notice' to the registrant. This notice must be served on a date which provides the registrant with reasonable notice of the proposed hearing and must specify the following:

- the date, time and venue of the interim order hearing;
- inform the registrant of both his or her right to attend and to be represented; and
- inform the registrant that the hearing may proceed in his or her absence should the registrant not attend.[113]

9.149 An Interim Order Notice also requires the registrant to inform the secretary, by a specified date, whether he or she:

- intends to attend the hearing;
- opposes the making of the order; and
- will be represented (and if so, by whom).

9.150 The notice must also invite the registrant to submit written representations to the committee (in circumstances where the registrant will not be in attendance).

9.151 Where there is currently no order in place, an Interim Order Notice should further set out the reasons why an interim order is being sought.[114]

110 PO 2010 art 56(1).
111 [2007] EWHC 2972 (Admin).
112 At para 16.
113 GPhC (FTP) Rules 2010 r17(2)(a)–(c).
114 GPhC (FTP) Rules 2010 r17(2)(d)–(f).

Procedure

9.152 There is a presumption that interim orders hearings will be held in private unless having considered representations made by the parties the committee determines that the public interest of having the hearing ventilated in public outweighs the particular interests of the registrant concerned – or any third party involved (namely their rights to privacy under Article 8 of the ECHR).[115]

9.153 The precise procedure followed at interim order hearings is found under the provisions of rule 36 of the GPhC's FTP Rules.

9.154 Rule 36 stipulates that after any preliminary legal arguments have been made and the identity of the registrant concerned has been confirmed, the GPhC's representative must address the committee on the necessity of making an interim order. They may adduce evidence in support of any submissions made.

9.155 When considering the admissibility of any evidence relied upon by the GPhC, rule 36(9)[116] states that the committee may receive 'any evidence which appears to it to be fair and relevant to its consideration'.

9.156 The registrant may then make representations. Given the potentially significant impact on a registrant ability to practise this is usually done through submission made on their behalf by a suitably qualified legal representative.[117]

9.157 Where an order is opposed, such representations are likely to address the detrimental impact an order would have on the registrant, both professionally (loss of reputation, etc) and personally (the financial implications of not being able to practise, etc). Evidence may also be called in support of any submissions made on the registrant's behalf.

9.158 Only in very rare circumstances, where a committee considers such 'desirable' to discharge its functions, will any oral evidence be heard during an interim orders hearings.[118] A registrant's views on the order being proposed are usually heard through submissions made by their legal representative and may be presented in the form of a signed statement. Should any person give live oral evidence, on oath, then they may be subject to questioning from the committee members or opposing party.[119]

9.159 Any committee hearing an application for an interim order will be reminded by the legal assessor who sits in on the hearing that they are not a fact-finding tribunal, there to resolve substantial disputes on the facts alleged.

9.160 While the committee, when considering an interim order, makes no rulings on the facts alleged, they are however entitled to take into account the seriousness of the allegations made and the potential risks that emanate from such and further consider the relative strength / cogency of the evidence amassed in support of such when addressing whether or not an interim order is necessary.[120]

115 GPhC (FTP) Rules 2010 r39(2).

116 GPhC (FTP) Rules 2010.

117 PO 2010 art 61(2)(c).

118 GPhC (FTP) Rules 2010 r36(10).

119 GPhC (FTP) Rules 2010 r36(6).

120 As was explained by Pill LJ when giving judgment in the Divisional Court in *R (X) v General Medical Council* [2001] EWHC (Admin) 447.

Orders that can be made

9.161 Having heard representations and following legal advice on the test to be applied, provided by a legal advisor, the following outcomes are available to the Committee:

- impose no order, where it is not deemed necessary. For example, where no concerns have been raised about a registrants clinical competence and their risk to patient safety;
- impose conditions on their practice, known as an 'order for interim conditional entry';
- conditions may prevent a registrant from doing certain aspects of pharmaceutical work, or require that such be done under supervision. Where conditions are in place they must be proportionate, address the specific concerns and risks identified, be achievable and sufficiently clear to ensure compliance. When drafting conditions a Committee should consider the wording of those contained within the GPhC's *Good decision making: conditions bank* (published in January 2016);
- impose an 'interim suspension order', preventing the registrant from practicing as a pharmacist whilst such an order is operative.

9.162 In circumstances where an interim order is deemed to be 'necessary', an interim suspension order must only be considered where conditions are not deemed appropriate to address the particular risks identified. As noted by Sir Stephen Silber in the case of *Gulamhusein v General Pharmaceutical Council*:[121]

> A corollary of the test of necessity . . . is that an order for suspension should only be imposed if no other remedy would be appropriate and proportionate. Therefore, a disciplinary Committee should first consider whether any other remedy, such as the imposition of conditions, would ensure that the interests of the public and the profession were satisfied because an order for suspension would not be necessary if another remedy, such as the imposition of conditions, would be appropriate . . .

9.163 Whatever decision is made by the committee, they must provide written reasons for it.[122]

Length and review

9.164 Under the provisions of article 56(1) of the PO 2010, interim orders can last for no longer than 18 months, although an application to the High Court or Court of Session (in Scottish cases) may be made to extend their duration by up to 12 months.[123]

9.165 All interim orders made must be periodically reviewed. First, within six months after the date the order was first made; and thereafter, at three-month intervals.[124]

9.166 A review hearing may be listed before such times if new information is received impacting on the necessity of the particular order imposed

121 [2014] EWHC 2591 (Admin), at paras 4–25.
122 GPhC (FTP) Rules 2010 r36(8).
123 PO 2010 art 56(5).
124 PO 2010 art 56(2).

or at the registrant's request (although there should be good reason for such).

9.167 At a review hearing, a committee may either:

- rule that the existing interim order continues altered;
- revoke the existing order;
- in the case of orders for interim conditional entry – add to, remove or otherwise vary any condition in place; or
- if it considers it is necessary for protection of the public, or is otherwise in the public interest, replace an interim suspension order with conditions, or vice versa.[125]

9.168 Written notice must be provided to the registrant concerned of any decision to vary or revoke an order.

Appealing an interim order

9.169 The decision to impose an interim order and any subsequent decision taken at a review hearing can be the subject of appeal.

9.170 Where an appeal is upheld, the High Court or Court of Session (in Scottish cases) may terminate an interim suspension order, revoke an order for interim conditional entry or remove or vary particular conditions; and/or change the operational period of the interim order made.

9.171 The order that is subject to appeal will remain in place whilst the appeal is pending, unless the High Court otherwise directs.[126]

Revocation

9.172 Any interim order in place at the time of a substantive fitness to practise hearing must be revoked once a decision has been made whether or not a registrant's fitness to practise is impaired.[127]

Pre-hearing matters

Disclosure: notice

9.173 When an allegation is referred to the GPhC's FTP Committee, a registrant must be notified in writing of this decision within ten days from when the referral decision was made.[128] This written notification – known as a 'Referral Notice' – must also contain the reasons why the case was referred, along with any legal advice considered in making the decision. Additionally, the notice must 'particularise the matters to be referred'; and further, in circumstances where the GPhC is of the view an interim order should be considered, state the reasons for this view.[129]

125 PO 2010 art 56(3).
126 PO 2010 art 56(8).
127 PO 2010 art 56(10).
128 GPhC (FTP) Rules 2010 r11(1).
129 GPhC (FTP) Rules 2010 r11(3) and (8).

9.174 'As soon as is reasonably practicable' after the date on which the registrant has been served a Referral Notice, pursuant to the provisions of rule 14(1) of the GPhC's FTP Rules, the GPhC must also serve on the registrant:

- finalised particulars of the allegations;
- any time estimate for the duration of the GPhC's case;
- a list of witnesses whose evidence is (or whose oral evidence will be) relied upon by the GPhC in support of its case;
- any statements of evidence, expert reports or other documents relied upon by the GPhC in support of its case (not previously served upon the registrant); and
- in fulfilment of the GPhC's duty of disclosure, any evidence or documents that the GPhC has in its possession (other than documents for which privilege is claimed) which, whilst not relied upon by the GPhC, may assist the registrant in the preparation of their defence (otherwise known as unused material).

Document inspection

9.175 Rule 15 of the GPhC's FTP Rules stipulates that at any time after the service of a document, up until the commencement of the relevant hearing, the party that has been served with a document may serve notification on the other party in possession of the original version that they wish to inspect and examine it.

9.176 In circumstances where the GPhC is in possession of an original document and a request for inspection is made, they must provide facilities for its inspection within ten days of notice being served or as soon as is reasonably practicable if notified less than ten days before a hearing date.

Listing questionnaires

9.177 The GPhC must also serve on a registrant a 'listing questionnaire'.[130] A copy of the standardised questionnaire used by the GPhC can be found and downloaded off their website.[131]

9.178 The purpose of the listing questionnaire is to 'ensure that the GPhC is in a position to list fitness to practise cases for hearing efficiently'. Accordingly, the questionnaire requires[132] both the GPhC and a registrant (or those instructed on their behalf) to provide information relevant to the case to ensure it is dealt with as expeditiously as possible.

9.179 Information to be provided by the GPhC (found under section A of the questionnaire) must be served on the secretary to the FTP Committee no later than 12 weeks from the service of the Referral Notice. This includes:

- a proposed time estimate for the hearing;
- a list of the proposed witnesses relied upon by the GPhC, detailing those who will give live evidence and those that can be read and the details of any proposed experts.

130 GPhC (FTP) Rules 2010 r14(1)(e).

131 See www.pharmacyregulation.org/sites/default/files/Fitness%20to%20practice%20-%20Listing%20questionnaire.pdf.

132 GPhC (FTP) Rules 2010 r14(2)(b).

9.180 The information a registrant is expected to provide (found under section B of the questionnaire), must be served on the secretary no later than eight weeks after service of the questionnaire itself and the other documents listed in para 9.174 above.[133] This information includes:

- contact details of the registrant and their representative (where one is instructed);
- a list of the witnesses that they seek to rely upon and any expert evidence they propose to call;
- any admissions the registrants wishes to make in respect of any of the allegations faced; and
- notice of any legal argument that the registrant wishes to advance at the Fitness to Practise hearing.

9.181 Any proposed revisions to the information noted in a listing questionnaire must be sent to the FTP Committee secretary 'as soon as possible after becoming aware that the estimate or information has changed'.[134]

Notice of hearing

9.182 Following receipt of a completed listing questionnaire, the secretary to the FTP Committee, will list a hearing date. Once the dates for a hearing have been identified, the secretary will then issue a 'Notice of Hearing'[135] on the registrant no less than 28 days before the hearing date,[136] highlighting such dates. The notice should also:

- include the finalised particulars of the allegation(s) made;
- inform the registrant of his or her right to attend the fitness to practise hearing and to be represented;
- inform the registrant that the hearing may proceed in his or her absence (pursuant to rule 25 of the GPhC's FTP Rules);
- inform the registrant of the relevant procedural rules governing fitness to practise hearings;
- require the registrant concerned to inform the secretary within 14 days (beginning on the date on which the notice of hearing is served) whether he or she intends to attend the hearing, be represented and if so by whom, and whether he or she seeks to call witnesses and if so whom; and finally
- inform the registrant of the FTP Committees powers, such as the sanctions that they can impose following a finding of impairment.

133 GPhC's *Standard practice direction for case management* para 2.1(i) and (ii).

134 GPhC (FTP) Rules 2010 r24(5).

135 Please note that GPhC (FTP) Rules 2010 r3 stipulates that any document or notice required to be served by the GPhC must be in writing and served by post or electronic mail; or by leaving it at the address of the Registrant as it appears on the Register. A document is deemed to have been served a day after the day on which it was served or if served electronically deemed to have been served on date it was sent.

136 GPhC (FTP) Rules 2010 r16(1).

Hearing bundles

9.183 No later than 16 days before the Monday of the week in which the fitness to practise hearing is to take place, parties must serve on each other copies of the evidential bundles upon which they seek to rely.[137]

9.184 Discussion between the respective parties is likely to follow where there is to be a challenge to the admissibly of any of the evidence contained within these bundles. Such a discussion is important to identify what parts of the bundles can be served on the committee in advance of the fitness to practise hearing and what parts must not be disclosed until argument as to their admissibility has been heard.

9.185 No later than nine days before the Monday of the week in which the hearing is to take place, parties must serve on the secretary to the FTP Committee ten 'paginated' copies of any agreed bundles or the parts that are agreed.[138]

9.186 Where material contained in the respective bundles is disputed, the party who seeks to rely on such material must also provide the secretary with a written statement outlining why they seek to rely on it, and if necessary a skeleton argument addressing the materials admissibly.

9.187 No later than nine days before the Monday of the week in which the hearing is to take place, the parties must also serve on the secretary a list of all agreed witnesses to ensure they are de-warned (not required to attend the final hearing), and a list of those who need to be called to give live evidence.

9.188 It is important to note that theoretically, any material not served within the specified time frames shall not be admitted in evidence – except in 'exceptional circumstances'.[139]

Case management meetings

9.189 Any party to the proceedings may request a case management meeting,[140] providing such a request is served in writing on the other concerned parties and the secretary to the FTP Committee.

9.190 A written request must outline the reasons a case management meeting is being sought, and further state any directions that are being sought. Where directions are sought, it is preferable to serve draft directions in advance of a case management meeting on all parties and additionally state whether the presence of the other party is required.

9.191 Any request sent to the committee secretary will be forwarded on to the committee's chair. There is a legal presumption that the hearing will be agreed to by the chair unless they are of the view that the hearing is 'unnecessary' or the request for such is tantamount to 'an abuse of process'.[141]

9.192 The chair of a FTP Committee may also list a case management meeting of their own volition,[142] with the committee's secretary to notify

137 GPhC (FTP) Rules 2010 r18(2).
138 GPhC (FTP) Rules 2010 r18(3).
139 GPhC (FTP) Rules 2010 r18(4) and (5).
140 GPhC (FTP) Rules 2010 r19(1).
141 GPhC (FTP) Rules 2010 r19(4).
142 GPhC (FTP) Rules 2010 r20(1).

all concerned parties 'as is reasonable within the particular circumstances of the case' of such a decision.[143]

9.193 When case management meetings are held, they are held in private and conducted by a chair. Where the chair is not legally qualified, then a legal adviser must also be present at a case management meeting to provide the chair with appropriate legal advice.[144]

9.194 The physical attendance of all the parties at such meetings may not always be necessary. If possible, and as is occurring more frequently, such meeting may be conducted via video-link, over the telephone or using other methods as have been agreed by the parties.[145]

9.195 At the end of a case management meeting, directions may be issued by the chair[146] – either following a request for such by a concerned party, or of the chair's own volition. All directions made should be necessary to secure 'the just and expeditious management of the case'. Directions may include, but are not limited to:

- providing that either or both parties must comply with the provisions relating to disclosure and the inspection of documents within such period as may be specified in the direction;
- requiring the parties to obtain, and to disclose within a specified period, evidence and expert reports;
- requiring each party to provide an estimate of the length of the hearing and any dates on which they or any witnesses would not be able to attend the hearing;
- where facts are not in dispute or the allegation is admitted, requiring the parties to produce a statement of agreed facts;
- requiring the parties to state whether or not the health of the person concerned will be raised as an issue in the proceedings, and if so, whether, in their view, medical reports should be obtained;
- requiring a party to call the author of any expert report at the hearing;
- where agreed between the parties, directing that the witness statement of a witness is to stand as the evidence-in-chief of that witness;
- directing that special measures be put in place at the hearing for a vulnerable witness, including measures aimed at protecting the witness's identity;
- requiring chronologies and additional skeleton arguments to be produced by the parties;
- directing that a further case management meeting should be held; and
- obtaining rulings from the committee for the purpose of resolving questions of law or admissibility of evidence.[147]

9.196 When considering case management directions regard must also be had to the GPhC's practice direction: *Standard case management directions for*

143 GPhC (FTP) Rules 2010 r20(2).

144 General Pharmaceutical Council (Statutory Committees and their Advisers) Rules 2010 rr18(3) and 21(4).

145 GPhC (FTP) Rules 2010 r20(3).

146 GPhC (FTP) Rules 2010 r21.

147 GPhC (FTP) Rules 2010 r21(2).

principal fitness to practise hearings before the Fitness to Practise Committee. This practice direction is available to download from the GPhC's website.[148]

Non-compliance with case management directions

9.197 Where a party fails to comply with case management directions 'such inferences as the committee considered appropriate' may be drawn[149] by the FTP Committee at a final hearing.

9.198 More significantly, where evidence has not been served in accordance with the case management directions given, the FTP Committee may rule that such evidence cannot be adduced at the fitness to practise hearing,[150] and furthermore, at the conclusion of this hearing the committee may make an order that the party in default pay all or part of the other party's costs or expenses occasioned as a result of their default.[151]

The Fitness to Practise Committee, panels and hearings

Introduction

9.199 Pursuant to the provisions of article 54(1) of the PO 2010, the principal function of the GPhC's FTP Committee is to determine whether or not the fitness to practise of the registrant in respect of whom allegations are made is impaired.

9.200 A pharmacy professional is deemed fit to practise 'when they can demonstrate the skills, knowledge, character and health required to do their job safely and effectively'.

9.201 The GPhC furthers describe fitness to practise as:[152]

> . . . a person's suitability to be on the register without restrictions. In practical terms, this means: maintaining appropriate standards of proficiency ensuring you are of good health and good character, and you are adhering to principles of good practice set out in our various, standards, guidance and advice.

9.202 Accordingly, all registrants must complete a fitness to practise declaration with their registration renewal.[153] This must be done annually in order to remain on the GPhC register. This declaration requires registrants to inform the GPhC if there is any reason why their fitness to practise is impaired.

148 See www.pharmacyregulation.org/sites/default/files/Practice%20Direction%20 Standard%20Case.pdf.

149 GPhC (FTP) Rules 2010 r21(3).

150 GPhC (FTP) Rules 2010 r24(9).

151 GPhC (FTP) Rules 2010 r46.

152 See the GPhC's website: 'Definition of fitness to practise': www.pharmacyregulation.org/raising-concerns/registrants/definition-fitness-practise.

153 There are two occasions in which a registrant must declare issues about his or her fitness to practise to the GPhC. Once per year when renewing one's registration and again if there is a change in one's circumstances within a renewal year. See the GPhC's website for further details: www.pharmacyregulation.org/raising-concerns/registrants/definition-fitness-practise/declarations.

9.203 Additionally, those on the register are required to let the GPhC know within seven days if they become aware of an issue that may affect their fitness to practise.

9.204 Registrants are also required to complete continuing professional development, demonstrating their commitment to keeping up to date with developments in pharmacy practise.

Fitness to practise hearings: an overview

9.205 As with other healthcare regulators, there are three procedural stages involved in a full FTP hearing.[154] Once a committee has heard evidence it must decide:

1) whether the facts alleged have been found proved;
2) where all or some of the facts alleged are found proved, the committee must then decide whether as a result of such the registrant's fitness to practise is impaired;
3) where impairment is found, the committee must finally consider whether any action should be taken, by way of sanction, against the registrant's registration.[155]

The makeup of the committee

9.206 The GPhC's overall FTP Committee membership consists of a lay member who is the chair, not fewer than three and not more than eight lay members who act as deputy chairs and not fewer than eight and not more than fifty one other members who may be both lay and registrant members. Within this committee, the lay members must be at least equal in number to the registrant members.[156]

9.207 As is the case with the IC, the FTP Committee is independent of the GPhC, and is accountable for the decisions that it makes.[157]

9.208 Unlike other healthcare regulators who have distinct FTP Committees that sit depending on whether the fitness to practise of a registrant is considered to be impaired by reasons of professional competence and conduct or as a result of adverse health, the GPhC has one committee empowered to deal with all grounds upon which a registrant's fitness to practise can be considered to be impaired.

Fitness to Practise Panels

9.209 Individual panels are selected from the above committee pool to oversee fitness to practise hearings.

154 As identified by Silber J in the seminal case of *Cohen v General Medical Council* [2008] EWHC 581 (Admin).

155 PO 2010 art 54(2)(a).

156 General Pharmaceutical Council (Statutory Committees and their Advisers Rules) Order of Council 2010 r3(2).

157 GPhC's *Good decision making: Fitness to practise hearings and sanctions guidance* (last revised – March 2017) para 2.4.

9.210 Each FTP Panel must consist of one chair and at least two other members (one lay and one registrant).

9.211 More complex fitness to practise cases may require more than three panel members to sit. In such cases the chair is afforded wide powers to determine the composition and quorum of the committee, that they deem necessary to consider the case against the registrant 'fairly'.[158]

9.212 As is the case with the IC, in order to ensure the impartiality of a panel, no member of the FTP Committee may sit to consider a case 'if that member has an actual or potential; conflict of interest in relation to the case.'[159]

9.213 Other people that may also be present at an FTP hearing include:

- the panel secretary;
- a legal adviser;
- a medical adviser;
- the GPhC's representative; and
- the registrant's legal representative.

The panel secretary

9.214 Each statutory committee, including FTP Committees, are assisted by a secretary who is responsible for administrative arrangements. Some of their more important responsibilities include ensuring a record is kept of all the decisions made by the committee and the reasons for such, as well as ensuring copies of such are made available to the registrant and his or her legal representatives on request.

9.215 A panel secretary, however, forms no part in the actual decision-making process.[160]

9.216 In advance of any hearing, it is advisable for the registrant and his or her legal representative to identify themselves to the panel secretary to ensure that the evidence that they wish to be placed before the panel as part of the registrant's case has been received and sufficient copies have been made available for the hearing.

9.217 Additionally, in cases where there may be preliminary discussions between the GPhC's representative and the registrant's representative, about what material that can fairly go before the panel, it is worth speaking with the secretary to identify what material should not be disclosed until such discussions have taken place.

The legal adviser

9.218 Each FTP Committee is assisted by a legal adviser.[161] Their primary function is to ensure that all hearings are conducted 'fairly'. To achieve this they must:

158 General Pharmaceutical Council (Statutory Committees and their Advisers Rules) Order of Council 2010 rr18 and 18A.

159 General Pharmaceutical Council (Statutory Committees and their Advisers Rules) Order of Council 2010 r19(1).

160 General Pharmaceutical Council (Statutory Committees and their Advisers Rules) Order of Council 2010 r17.

161 PO 2010 art 63(1) states that legal advisers should be 'suitably qualified and experienced barristers, solicitors or advocates'.

- advise the committee on all questions of law that are referred to them by members of the committee (it is important that following such advice, be it given during the hearing or when the committee are in retirement, that the representative of the registrant and the Council's representative are afforded an opportunity to comment on such);
- intervene in circumstances where it appears an error of law has been made (during submissions made by either party for example, or during the course of a panels determination); and
- inform the committee of any procedural irregularities that they have noted.[162]

9.219 Additionally, at the request of the chair, the legal adviser must also advise the panel on the structure, format and presentation of the reasons behind any decision they come to. However the legal adviser must take no part in the decision making process itself.[163] Furthermore, to ensure their independence, a legal adviser cannot also sit as a member of the Council or any of its statutory committees.[164]

Clinical and specialist advisers

9.220 In cases where the registrant's fitness to practise is questioned on the grounds of adverse health, a clinical adviser must be appointed. In such health cases, this appointment must be made in advance of a fitness to practise hearing, as the clinical adviser appointed must also advise the IC in advance of any referral being made.[165]

9.221 The function of the clinical adviser is to advise the committee on any issues within the clinical adviser's areas of medical expertise and intervene to advise the committee on an issue where it appears to the clinical adviser that, without his or her intervention, there is a possibility of an error being made.[166]

9.222 In cases involving particular evidential complexities, a panel may also appoint a specialist adviser tasked with advising the panel on issues within the specialist adviser's areas of expertise.[167]

9.223 As with legal advisers, a clinical or specialist adviser must not participate in any of the decision-making of an FTP Committee.[168] Additionally, unlike legal advisers who may (at the request of the chair) be present

162 General Pharmaceutical Council (Statutory Committees and their Advisers Rules) Order of Council 2010 r21.

163 General Pharmaceutical Council (Statutory Committees and their Advisers Rules) Order of Council 2010 r21(4).

164 PO 2010 art 63(2).

165 PO 2010 art 64(1)(a); and General Pharmaceutical Council (Statutory Committees and their Advisers Rules) Order of Council 2010 r22(1)(a).

166 General Pharmaceutical Council (Statutory Committees and their Advisers Rules) Order of Council 2010 r22(2)(a) and (b).

167 PO 2010 art 64(2)(a); and General Pharmaceutical Council (Statutory Committees and their Advisers Rules) Order of Council 2010 r23(2).

168 General Pharmaceutical Council (Statutory Committees and their Advisers Rules) Order of Council 2010 rr22(4) and 23(4).

during the private deliberations of an FTP Committee, clinical and specialist advisers must not be.[169]

9.224 Any advice provided by a legal, clinical or specialist adviser must not only be tendered in the presence of all parties, but additionally a record of such must be maintained. Accordingly, in the case of a legal adviser who has given legal advice to a committee during the course of his or her private deliberations, such advice must 'at a convenient moment' be repeated before all parties when the hearing reconvenes.[170]

9.225 As previously noted above, this allow the legal representatives on both sides to comment on the accuracy / efficacy of the advice given.

9.226 While unusual, should a committee decide to reject the advice tendered to it by any of the above advisers, then the chair must announce its reasons for doing so. In such circumstances, the committee secretary must keep a record of both the advice given and the reasons provided by the committee for rejecting it. A copy of this record must then be sent to the parties involved in the proceedings.[171]

The General Pharmaceutical Council's representative

9.227 The GPhC's representative, sometimes referred to as the case presenter, is responsible for presenting the case being brought against the registrant.[172] Under the provisions of rule 40(1) of the GPhC's FTP Rules, he or she may be a barrister, solicitor or an employee of the GPhC.

The registrant

9.228 A registrant has a statutory right to be legally represented during the course of a FTP hearing. He or she may be represented by a barrister, solicitor or alternatively a representative from the registrant's trade union.

9.229 In circumstances where the registrant is not represented, they may be accompanied and advised by a so called 'supporter'. Given their lack of legal qualification, a supporter may only address the committee on the registrant's behalf with the permission of the chair.

9.230 A supporter must not be a member of the GPhC or of one of its statutory committees, an employee of the GPhC, or a witness at the hearing.[173]

Order of proceedings

9.231 Rule 31 of the GPhC's FTP Rules governs the order in which fitness to practise hearings are heard.

9.232 Rule 32 sets out a similar procedural framework for disqualification proceedings brought by the GPhC against a body corporate involved in a retail pharmacy business.

169 General Pharmaceutical Council (Statutory Committees and their Advisers Rules) Order of Council 2010 rr22(3) and 23(3).

170 General Pharmaceutical Council (Statutory Committees and their Advisers Rules) Order of Council 2010 rr24 and 25.

171 General Pharmaceutical Council (Statutory Committees and their Advisers Rules) Order of Council 2010 r26.

172 PO 2010 art 61(2)(c).

173 GPhC (FTP) Rules 2010 r40(2) and (3).

Preliminary legal arguments

9.233 Rule 31(2) stipulates that 'The Committee must hear and consider any preliminary legal arguments' at the outset of a hearing. Such arguments may include (but are not limited to), in cases where the registrant is neither present nor represented: whether the case should proceed in his or her absence; submissions on the admissibility of any evidence relied upon by either party to the proceedings; or whether any or all of hearing should be heard in private.

9.234 Given the timing of such arguments, it is advisable for the registrant and/or his or her legal representative(s) to turn up to the hearing well in advance of its scheduled start-time in order for discussion to take place with the case presenter and/or legal adviser about any preliminary arguments to be raised.

Preliminary arguments: proceeding in absence

9.235 While a registrant has a fundamental right to be present during a hearing where allegations are made against him or her, there will be occasions when a registrant is not in attendance.

9.236 Where a registrant fails to attend a hearing, and in circumstances where the committee is satisfied that there has been effective service of the Notice of Hearing or where all reasonable efforts have been made to serve such on the registrant,[174] the committee has a discretionary power to consider the case against the registrant in his or her absence.[175]

9.237 Such a decision is to be exercised with great caution, given the obviously detrimental impact on the registrant in not being able to challenge the evidence called against him or her, and not being able to positively state his or her case.[176]

9.238 Regard should be had to any known circumstances surrounding the registrant's absence. One key question for a committee to ask, is whether there is any evidence that the registrant has voluntarily absented himself or herself from the proceedings and can therefore be properly said to have waivered his or her right to appear, or alternatively whether there is any reason known to the committee for the registrant's absence that may render a decision to continue without the registrant unfair.

9.239 Where a registrant is unable to attend a hearing but does not wish for the case to proceed without him or her, it is vital that this position is relayed to the committee as soon as the reasons for their absence become known. Silence on the registrant's part may be construed as an unwillingness to engage in the process, making it more likely that the committee's will proceed without him or her.

Postponement and adjournments

9.240 If it is known that a registrant will not be in attendance, an application to postpone the hearing may be made by any party involved in the case or by

174 Pursuant to the provisions of GPhC (FTP) Rules 2010 r3.

175 GPhC (FTP) Rules 2010 r25.

176 See *R v Jones (Anthony)* [2002] UKHL 5; and the case of *Tait v Royal College of Veterinary Surgeons* [2003] UKPC 34.

the chair of the committee 'of their own motion'. Such an application may be granted in advance of the assigned hearing date.[177]

9.241 The committee also has the power to adjourn proceedings at 'any stage', again following an application by any party to the proceedings or of their own motion, providing:

- no injustice is caused to the parties; and
- the decision to adjourn is made after hearing representations from the parties party to the proceedings(where present).[178]

9.242 Rule 37(3) of the GPhC's FTP Rules contains a non-exhaustive list of some of the matters that a chair 'must' have regard to when considering an adjournment application. They are as follows:

- the public interest in the expeditious disposal of the case;
- the potential inconvenience caused to a party or any witnesses to be called by that party;
- the conduct of the party seeking the postponement or adjournment; and
- fairness to the parties.

An adjournment on grounds of ill-health

9.243 It may be that an adjournment request is made on the grounds that the registrant is not well enough to engage in the process. If this is the case, a 'proper medical certification is required in support of the application'. Where such evidence is not available, or the chair is not satisfied with that which has been produced, registrants should be made aware that the committee has intrusive powers allowing a chair to require them to make themselves available for a medical examination by a registered medical practitioner.[179]

9.244 Where a postponement or adjournment is granted, then the panel secretary must 'as soon as is practicable' notify the parties to the proceedings of the new date, time and venue for the postponed or resumed hearing.[180]

Admissibility of evidence

9.245 Under rule 24 of the GPhC's FTP Rules, a committee is afforded a wide discretion as to what evidence it may hear.

9.246 All questions as to the admissibility of evidence are to be decided by the committee themselves, having obtained legal advice from the legal adviser where appropriate. The committee may receive any evidence either orally or in documentary form providing it is satisfied that such evidence is both 'relevant' to the matters that have to be determined and that it would be 'fair' for such evidence to be adduced – 'whether or not such evidence would be admissible in any subsequent civil proceedings'.[181] Any legal challenge to the admissibility of evidence that may be made in advance of evidence being called should accordingly focus on these two principal factors.

177 GPhC (FTP) Rules 2010 r37(1).

178 GPhC (FTP) Rules 2010 r37(2)(a) and (b).

179 GPhC (FTP) Rules 2010 r37(4). See also the case of *Faulkner v Nursing and Midwifery Council* [2009] EWHC 3349 (Admin), which further highlights the importance of providing medical evidence in support of an application to adjourn on health grounds.

180 GPhC (FTP) Rules 2010 r37(5).

181 GPhC (FTP) Rules 2010 r24(2).

9.247 If a challenge to admissibility of a particular aspect of the GPhC's evidence is being considered by those acting on behalf of the registrant, then it is worth flagging up the arguments to be raised with the GPhC's representative and the legal adviser in advance of sitting. It may be that agreement can be made between the parties in relation to the exclusion of evidence. This has the obvious advantage of ensuring a committee is not made aware of prejudicial material, which they may then subsequently determine is inadmissible.

9.248 If strictly applied, evidence may only be heard providing it has been served in compliance with the GPhC's rules of service (addressed earlier in this chapter). However, even when not, the committee has a discretionary power to allow such evidence to be adduced 'in such exceptional circumstances as it may determine'.[182]

Hearing the case in public or private

9.249 There is a presumption that all fitness to practise hearings will be held in public.[183] Additionally, save for the private deliberations of the committee, all hearings must be recorded, with transcripts made available to any party to the proceedings, who applies for them (and pays the requisite fee).[184]

9.250 The position is different for cases involving consideration of a registrant's health – here there is a rebuttable presumption that the hearing will be held in private, in order to ensure that sensitive information about the registrant is not disclosed publically.

9.251 Even in such cases, the FTP Committee maintains a statutory right to have the hearings held in public, if having considered the representations of the parties involved and the advice of the clinical adviser, they form the view that 'the public interest in holding the hearing in public outweighs the interest of the registrant concerned . . . in maintaining their privacy'.[185]

9.252 In certain cases a hearing before the committee may be held wholly or partly in private if the committee, having heard representations from the parties, forms the view that the interests of maintaining the registrant's privacy (or an interested third party) outweigh the public interest in holding all of the hearing, or part of it, in public.

9.253 Even when a hearing is being held in public, the committee reserves the right to reject anyone in attendance, for all or part of the hearing, who has, or is likely to, 'disrupt' proceedings.[186]

Fact-finding

Allegations

9.254 Once all preliminary arguments have been made and ruled upon by the panel (following advice from the legal advisor), rule 31(3) of the GPhC's

182 GPhC (FTP) Rules 2010 r24(9).
183 GPhC (FTP) Rules 2010 r39.
184 GPhC (FTP) Rules 2010 r47.
185 GPhC (FTP) Rules 2010 r39(2).
186 GPhC (FTP) Rules 2010 r39(4).

FTP Rules requires the registrant concerned (if present) to confirm his or her name.[187] The panel secretary is then required to 'read out the allegation and the alleged facts upon which it is based'.

Admissions

9.255 Once all of the allegations have been read out, the chair of the panel is required to ask the registrant whether he or she wishes to make any admissions in respect of any of the allegations he or she faces. Where a registrant admits any of the facts alleged, the chair 'must announce that such facts have been found proved'.[188]

Opening the case and calling evidence

9.256 Where any of the facts alleged against a registrant are in dispute, the GPhC case presenter is required to open the case for the GPhC, outlining the allegations made and directing the panel to the evidence relied upon by the GPhC in support of them (as contained within the hearing bundle).

9.257 Following this, the case presenter may then formally adduce evidence and call witnesses in support of the allegations being made, subject to the provisions of rule 31(19) of the GPhC's FTP Rules. Such provisions afford the panel chair sweeping powers to refuse to allow a witness to give oral evidence, or to give oral evidence on a particular matter. This can be done where the panel are satisfied that the witness in question is not in a position to provide relevant testimony, or where all or part of the evidence that the witness is to provide, or is to provide on a particular matter, should have been disclosed to the party not calling the witness at an earlier stage in the proceedings.

Witnesses

Generally

9.258 Where evidence contained within a served witness statements cannot be agreed in advance of the hearing, then the maker of that statement will be required to attend the hearing so that their evidence can be tested under cross-examination.

9.259 Should a party fail to serve a statement that they intend to rely on (signed and containing an attestation of its truth[189]) on the other party to the proceedings, at least seven days before the hearing, they may not call the maker of that statement as a witness, unless the chair of the panel determines otherwise.[190]

9.260 While rule 43(2) of the GPhC's FTP Rules states explicitly that the GPhC 'may not compel the person concerned to be a witness',[191] under the provisions of article 62 of the PO 2010, the committee has the power to

187 This can also be done by the case presenter where the registrant is neither present nor represented: see GPhC (FTP) Rules 2010 r31(3)(b).

188 GPhC (FTP) Rules 2010 r31(6). This is in contrast to some other healthcare regulators who are required to make an independent assessment of the facts alleged irrespective of any admissions that have been made by a registrant.

189 As required under the provisions of GPhC (FTP) Rules 2010 r24(3).

190 GPhC (FTP) Rules 2010 r43(3).

191 GPhC (FTP) Rules 2010 r43(2).

compel witnesses other than the registrant concerned to give evidence. Accordingly, where parties have indicated that a witness is required to attend a hearing and there are concerns that they may not attend then the panel may issue the witness with a summons.[192] Failure to answer this summons could potentially lead to the witness being prosecuted for contempt.

9.261 Before giving evidence at the witness desk, witnesses are required to take an oath in line with their religious beliefs, or an affirmation. Where English is not a witness's first language, the committee may direct that their evidence be given through an interpreter.[193]

9.262 Having taken an oath or affirmation, the witness is then examined by the party calling him or her.

9.263 It is not uncommon for the case presenter to indicate that the contents of the witness's statement is be to adopted by him or her; he or she may then ask the witness supplementary questions in relation to the evidence contained within it.

9.264 Allowing a witness to adopt his or her statement as his or her evidence-in-chief, clearly has advantages so far as time-saving is concerned. That said, where a witness statement contains contentious content which is linked directly to the charges the registrant faces, then his or her representative may require the witness to give evidence, not simply by adopting his or her statement or even reading out its content verbatim, but to give evidence only in response to questions put to the witness by the case presenter. The advantage of adopting such a course is that were the witness to then give evidence during examination-in-chief, at odds with matters contained within his or her witness statement, such inconsistencies could be highlighted in cross-examination as a means of attacking the witness's reliability/credibility.

9.265 Following questions from the party calling a particular witness, he or she may be cross-examined. This will then be followed by any re-examination from the party calling the witness. The witness will then be questioned by members of the panel or by a clinical, legal or specialist adviser. Finally, the parties may then question the witness on matters arising out of the committee's questions, with the party calling the witness given the last opportunity to do so.

9.266 Except for expert witnesses and the registrant concerned, witnesses are not allowed to sit in the hearing room while evidence is being heard until after he or she has completed giving his or her evidence and having been formally released by the chair.[194]

Vulnerable witnesses

9.267 In order to ensure that all witnesses can give the best possible evidence, akin to the special measures afforded to vulnerable witnesses in criminal cases, the FTP Committee may 'adopt such measures as it considers necessary' to enable it to receive evidence from a witness it considers to be 'vulnerable'.

192 PO 2010 art 62(1)(b).
193 GPhC (FTP) Rules 2010 r43(1) and (5).
194 GPhC (FTP) Rules 2010 r43(6) and (10).

9.268 Under rule 44(1) of the FTP Rules, the following witnesses may be considered vulnerable and accordingly afforded special measures to assist them in the giving of their evidence:

- any witness under the age of 18;
- any witness with a mental disorder (within the meaning of the Mental Health Act 1983);
- any witness who is significantly impaired in relation to intelligence or social functioning;
- any witness with a physical disability who requires assistance to give evidence;
- any witness, where an allegation against a person concerned is of a sexual nature and the witness was the alleged victim; or
- any witness who complains of intimidation.

9.269 While there is no exhaustive list of the measures that may be used by a committee to assist vulnerable witnesses in giving their evidence, subsection (3) of rule 44 contains the measures that are most commonly adopted, such as:

- the use of video-links;
- allowing witnesses to give live evidence but from surroundings that are less intimidating than the hearing room itself;
- in certain circumstances the committee may also allow for the use of pre-recorded evidence as the evidence-in-chief of a witness, providing the witness is then present at the hearing for cross-examination and questioning.

9.270 Special measures may only be granted if the committee is satisfied that the legal test for allowing such is satisfied. They must be satisfied that the quality of the witnesses' evidence is 'likely to be adversely affected' without measures being in place to assist them.

9.271 It should not be assumed that special measures will automatically be granted where a witness is considered to be vulnerable. Measures can only be put in place having considered any representations from the parties to the proceedings as to the appropriateness of such.

9.272 For example, it may be argued that where a witness is to provide the only evidence in a case in relation to a significant factual dispute between him or her and the registrant, then it is particularly important that in order for the committee to accurately assess the reliability of this evidence they are afforded an opportunity to assess not only what the witness says, but the witness's overall demeanour. Allowing such a witness to give evidence via a live link, for example, may hamper a committee's ability to make such an assessment.

9.273 Where registrants are not legally represented, they should be made aware that specific protections are afforded to witnesses in cases where the allegations made against them are of a sexual nature. In such cases, where the witness is the alleged victim, the registrant concerned is barred from cross-examining the witness directly in person. In these circumstances, any questioning of the witness is to be undertaken by 'such person as the Committee considers appropriate'.[195]

195 GPhC (FTP) Rules 2010 r44(4) and (5).

Submissions of no case to answer

9.274 Once the case presenter has called all of the evidence relied upon by the GPhC, and in advance of the registrant adducing any evidence in response, rule 31(8)[196] of the GPhC FTP Rules make specific provision for the registrant or the legal representative acting on the registrant's behalf to make submissions regarding whether 'sufficient evidence has been adduced to find the facts proved or to support a finding of impairment'.

9.275 So-called 'submissions of no case to answer' may be made in respect of all or individual allegations made against the registrant.

9.276 A submission can be based either on the ground that there is no evidence in support of the allegation(s), or alternatively on the ground that what evidence has been adduced in relation to the allegation(s) is of such a weak and tenuous nature, on fair examination of such, a panel could not properly find the allegation proved. As considered in detail in chapter 2, the legal test to be applied when considering submissions of no case to answer is that outlined in the case of *R v Galbraith*.[197]

9.277 Submissions may be considered, for example, when a witness whose evidence brought rise to a particular allegation, either explicitly retracts previous assertions during the course of his or her evidence; or where the reliability and/or veracity of the witness's account has been significantly undermined during the course of his or her evidence to such an extent that reliance can no longer be fairly placed on the witness's testimony.

9.278 Additionally, a submission of no case to answer may be made in relation to a finding of impairment on the ground that even were the particular facts of the case to be found proved, such do not amount to the statutory ground alleged (such as misconduct), or impairment itself.

9.279 Caution should, however, be exercised when considering a submission of no case to answer in relation to a finding of impairment, as were a panel to find against a registrant, it may be felt that the making of the submission itself illustrates a lack of insight into the seriousness of the allegation(s) made against him or her.

The registrant's case

9.280 In the event that a submission of no case to answer is not made, or where following such the panel determines that there *is* a case to answer in respect of any of the allegations made, rule 31(9) of the FTP Rules allows for the registrant to then call evidence in support of his or her case.

9.281 As noted above, a registrant cannot be compelled to give evidence, although failure to do so (depending upon the particular circumstances of the case) may result in adverse inferences being drawn against him or her.

9.282 In the event that a registrant does give evidence, he or she, as with all other witnesses, is required to take an oath or affirmation. Failure to do so may result in less weight being attached to any evidence he or she provides.

196 GPhC (FTP) Rules 2010 r31(8).

197 *R v Galbraith* (1981) 73 Cr App R 124, CA.

9.283 In the event that the registrant is represented, the registrant will first be asked questions by his or her legal representative. This may involve the registrant adopting the contents of any written statement previously provided by him or her. Thereafter, the registrant may be cross-examined by the case presenter, and following this be asked questions by any or all of the panel members.

9.284 A registrant may also call witnesses to support his or her case (subject to the exclusionary provisions of rule 31(19) as outlined above).

9.285 In cases where the professional integrity of a registrant is being called into question, where allegations of dishonesty are being made, for example, a registrant may consider calling character witnesses, serving to highlight personal and professional characteristics in contrast to those being alleged.

9.286 A panel must not, however, be misled about a registrant's character. Calling character evidence in circumstances where a registrant has no previous FTP history or criminal convictions and/or cautions is unproblematic. However, where this is not the case, the use of character evidence is likely to be dependent on such history being disclosed to the panel in advance of any determination of the facts alleged. Use of character testimonials during the fact finding stage of a hearing should accordingly be carefully considered by a registrant and/or his or her representatives.

Findings of facts

Overview

9.287 Once all evidence relied upon by the GPhC and the registrant has been heard, the case presenter and then the registrant or his or her legal representative address the panel on the strength of the evidence heard. Submissions are akin to closing speeches in criminal cases, with the case presenter outlining why the allegations can be found proved and the registrant or representative emphasising why they cannot.

9.288 The legal advisor will then advise the panel on relevant matters of law, such as the burden and standard of proof applicable to fitness to practise hearings, before the panel retire to consider whether or not the facts alleged have been found proved.

The burden and standard of proof

9.289 Pursuant to the provisions of rule 42(1) of the GPhC FTP Rules, where facts at a principal hearing are in dispute, the burden of proving the facts rests on the GPhC.

9.290 The standard of proof that applies is the civil standard, namely the 'balance of probabilities'. This means that the committee will only find an alleged fact to be 'proved' if it decides, after hearing the evidence, that it is more likely than not to have happened.

Proof in the case of convictions

9.291 Where a registrant's fitness to practise is alleged to be impaired by reason of a criminal conviction, 'a copy of the certificate of conviction certified by a competent officer of the court or for a conviction in Scotland, an extract conviction, is admissible as conclusive proof of that conviction and the findings of fact on which it was based'.[198]

9.292 The only evidence which may be adduced by the person concerned in rebuttal of a conviction certified or extracted in accordance with the above is evidence for the purpose of proving that the person concerned is not the person referred to in the certificate or extract.[199]

The written determination – providing reasons

9.293 Once the panel has reached a decision at each stage of a hearing, it must provide a 'determination'. This determination is a formal statement made by the committee announcing its decision and explaining the reasons for it, as is required under the provisions of rule 31(14) of the GPhC FTP Rules.[200]

9.294 How much detail is contained in a determination will depend on the nature and complexity of the case under consideration. In every case:

> . . . the reasons should be adequate so that the decision can be easily understood by the registrant, the GPhC, the complainant and any other interested party. It should be clear why a particular decision has been made.[201]

9.295 The committee's determination should follow the GPhC's guidance on drafting fitness to practise determinations.[202] Further guidance is provided at paras 2.20–2.24 of the GPhC's *Good decision making: Fitness to practise hearings and sanctions guidance*, which notes the determination should use 'clear and direct language which leaves no room for misunderstanding or ambiguity'; and further, that:

> It is important, and in the interests of fairness, that the registrant is given proper reasons, so they can decide whether or not to appeal the decision. The GPhC, the complainant, the public, the Professional Standards Authority (PSA) and other pharmacy professionals must also be able to understand the reasoning behind the committee's decisions.

9.296 Complete and intelligible reasons for a decision are also required to ensure that any other committee that later considers the registrant's case (for example, at a review or restoration hearing) are able to understand the reasoning behind the original decision made in respect of a registrant's registration.

Impairment

Generally

9.297 Where a committee has found all or some of the facts alleged proved, and further, collectively judged that such constitute the statutory ground(s) upon which a finding of impairment is alleged, they must then go on to

198 GPhC (FTP) Rules 2010 r24(4).

199 GPhC (FTP) Rules 2010 r24(5).

200 GPhC (FTP) Rules 2010 r31(14).

201 GPhC's *Good decision making: Fitness to practise hearings and sanctions guidance* (last revised – March 2017) para 2.20.

202 Available on the GPhC's website.

separately decide whether or not the registrant's fitness to practise is impaired.

9.298 A detailed analysis of the statutory grounds that can be alleged in fitness to practise hearings, including deficient professional performance and misconduct, is found in chapter 3 of this book. Accordingly, such is not repeated here.

9.299 Reaching a decision on impairment is a matter for the collective judgment of the committee, there is no evidential standard of proof that needs to be satisfied.[203] Consequently, even when a registrant admits impairment, a committee must nonetheless reach a decision based on its own independent assessment of the case.

9.300 A decision on impairment must only be made once the committee has invited both parties to present further evidence and hear any further submissions from them as to whether, on the basis of any facts found proved, the registrant's fitness to practise is impaired.[204]

Character testimonials

9.301 In support of a submission that their fitness to practise is not currently impaired a registrant may wish to rely on character testimonials.

9.302 When considering what weight to attach to any testimonial provided, the committee must first consider whether they are genuine and then 'consider whether the authors of the testimonials were aware of the events leading to the hearing'.

9.303 The GPhC's *Good decision making: Fitness to practise hearings and sanctions guidance* further notes that:

> . . . any references and testimonials will need to be weighed appropriately against the nature of the facts found proved . . .
>
> Testimonials or other evidence which confirms the steps taken by the registrant to remedy the behaviour which led to the hearing (for example from professional colleagues) and evidence of the registrant's current fitness to practise may be relevant when the committee is considering the issue of impairment. This evidence should not be left to the sanction stage.[205]

The test

9.304 There is no statutory definition of impairment, although (as addressed in chapter 3) a significant body of case-law has emerged, assisting committees on the approach to take when determining impairment.

9.305 The principal question a committee must asked is: 'is' the registrant's fitness to practise impaired,[206] as opposed to 'was' it impaired. Consequently, it is open to a committee to conclude that while a registrant's conduct demonstrated that his or her fitness to practise *was* impaired in the past,

203 *Council for the Regulation of Healthcare Professional v General Medical Council and Biswas* [2006] EWHC 464 (Admin).

204 GPhC (FTP) Rules 2010 r31(11). See the GPhC's definition.

205 GPhC's *Good decision making: Fitness to practise hearings and sanctions guidance* (last revised – March 2017) and *Azzam v General Medical Council* [2008] EWHC 2711 (Admin), see para 5.20–5.22.

206 GPhC (FTP) Rules 2010 r31(12).

such is no longer case (by reason of corrective steps taken since, for example).

9.306 While the test for impairment is forward looking, involving an assessment of 'a person's suitability to be on the register without restrictions,[207] it is nonetheless permissible for a committee to take into account 'the way in which the person concerned has acted or failed to act in the past'.[208]

Important considerations

9.307 A committee should then have regard to what steps (if any) have been taken by a registrant since the conduct under review occurred. In doing so, they typically consider three questions:[209]

1) *Is the conduct which led to the charges easily remediable?* For example, attitudinal failings demonstrated in dishonesty cases may be considered more difficult to remediate than failings in clinical practice that can be corrected through appropriate re-training / education.
2) *Has it been remedied?* This will involve consideration of what corrective steps a registrant has taken in respect of his or her past failings – such as participation in training programs, completion of continuing professional development (CPD) courses and any relevant interaction with other professionals.
3) *Is it 'highly unlikely' to be repeated?* Here a committee may consider whether the registrant has made any expressions of remorse and/or offered an apology for his or her past conduct. Whether the registrant has shown insight into his or her failings may also be considered relevant to the likelihood of repeated behaviour in future.

Insight

9.308 When addressing the above questions, a committee is likely to consider what 'insight' the registrant has demonstrated into the failings identified in their respective case.

9.309 Insight 'is a key factor for committees to consider during fitness to practise proceedings',[210] involving an assessment of whether a registrant accepts and understands that he or she should have behaved differently, and that he or she will take steps to prevent any reoccurrence.

9.310 When assessing insight, the committee will need to take into account factors such as whether the registrant has 'genuinely' demonstrated insight, examining the registrant's conduct not only during the course of a hearing but also his or her actions outside of it.

9.311 GPhC guidance[211] also expects committees to:

207 See the GPhC's definition of fitness to practise: www.pharmacyregulation.org/raising-concerns/registrants/definition-fitness-practise.

208 See *Meadow v General Medical Council* [2007] EWHC 462 (QB) para 32.

209 Extracted from the case of *Cohen v General Medical Council* [2008] EWHC 581 (Admin) – see para 65.

210 GPhC's *Good decision making: Fitness to practise hearings and sanctions guidance* (last revised in March 2017) para 5.17.

211 GPhC's *Good decision making: Fitness to practise hearings and sanctions guidance* (last revised in March 2017) para 5.19.

> . . . be aware that there may be cultural differences in the way that insight is expressed, for example, whether or how an apology or expression of regret is framed and delivered. Sensitivity to these issues is important in deciding how a registrant frames their 'insight' and in judging their behaviour and attitude during the hearing.

Other factors to take into account

9.312 The GPhC's *Good decision making: Fitness to practise hearings and sanctions guidance*[212] further notes that when reaching a decision on impairment:

> The committee must also take into account relevant factors, which include whether or not the conduct or behaviour under consideration:
> a. presents an actual or potential risk to patients or to the public,
> b. has brought, or might bring, the profession of pharmacy into disrepute,
> c. has breached one of the fundamental principles of the profession of pharmacy,
> d. shows that the integrity of the registrant can no longer be relied upon.

Public interest considerations

9.313 In some cases, the facts found proved by a committee may be considered sufficiently serious, that notwithstanding a conclusion that the conduct involved has been remedied and is highly unlikely to be repeated, a finding of impairment is nevertheless justified. This may be done on public interest grounds.

9.314 In reaching a decision on impairment, the committee should give appropriate weight to the wider public interest. In the context of a fitness to practise hearing, public interest considerations include:

- protecting the public;
- maintaining public confidence in the profession; and
- maintaining proper standards of behaviour.

9.315 A finding of impairment may consequently be made on the basis that a failure to do so would undermine public confidence in the profession and/or fail to maintain proper standards of behaviour.

Impairment in cases involving knowledge of English

9.316 In cases where a committee is tasked with reaching a determination on whether a registrant's fitness to practise is impaired because they do not have a necessary knowledge of English, the GPhC's *Good decision making: Fitness to practise hearings and sanctions guidance* notes that they may take into account (among other things):

- whether the person concerned has complied with a direction, given under the rules, to have an examination or other assessment of their knowledge of English, or
- whether the person concerned has provided the registrar with evidence of the result of that examination or assessment.[213]

212 At para 2.13.
213 See para 2.15.

Sanction

9.317 Under the provisions of article 54(2) of the PO 2010, following a finding that a registrant's fitness to practise is impaired, a committee must then consider what sanctions (if any) should be imposed.

9.318 When doing so, a committee must have regard to the GPhC's guidance, *Good decision making: fitness to practise hearings and sanctions guidance* (last revised in March 2017). The guidance, however, is just that – it is not intended to interfere with a committee's power to impose whatever sanction it decides in individual cases.[214]

9.319 Following a finding of impairment, a committee may:

- agree undertakings;
- issue a warning;[215]
- impose conditions on the registrant's practice;[216]
- suspend the registrant from practising; or
- remove the registrant from the register.[217]

9.320 In rare cases, where impairment is found, but the registrant presents no risk to the public, and the committee conclude that there is no need for a sanction to be imposed, they may take 'no action' against the registrant. In such circumstances, no record of the case will be recorded on the register.[218]

9.321 Conversely, when a committee determines that a registrant's fitness to practise is not impaired, if they form the view that the concerns raised nonetheless are serious enough to 'need' a formal response, they may:

- issue a warning; or
- give advice to the registrant or any other person or other body involved in the investigation on any issue arising out of, or related to, the allegation.[219]

9.322 In such circumstances a committee should explain why a formal response is needed.

Further evidence

9.323 Under the provisions of rule 31(13), before a decision on sanction is reached:

> The Committee may receive further evidence and hear any further submissions from the parties or from any other person who has a direct interest in the proceedings where the registrant's fitness to practise is found to be impaired, as to the appropriate sanction, if any, to be imposed.

214 See *Council for the Regulation of Healthcare Professionals v GMC and Leeper* [2004] EWHC 1850 (Admin).

215 The Registrar must record any such warning in the Register in accordance with rule 5(5) of the GPhC (Registration Rules) 2010. Warnings remain on the register for a period of two years. After two years the warning will cease to be published on the public facing register but shall form part of the registrant's previous history.

216 Having regard to those set out in the GPhC's *Good decision making: conditions bank* (January 2016).

217 PO 2010 art 54(2)(a)–(e).

218 GPhC's *Good decision making: Fitness to practise hearings and sanctions guidance* (last revised in March 2017) p20.

219 PO 2010 art 54(5)(a); and GPhC's *Good decision making: Fitness to practise hearings and sanctions guidance* (last revised in March 2017) p20.

9.324 The GPhC case presenter will make submissions on sanction first. Ordinarily, they are instructed to adopt a neutral stance in respect of sanction and accordingly their submissions will usually focus on drawing the panel's attention to the relevant parts of the GPhC'S sanctions guidance they should have regard to.

9.325 Further evidence a committee may hear before reaching a decision on sanction, includes:

- any mitigating and/or aggravating factors involved; whether a factor amounts to mitigation or aggravation is entirely a matter for the committee to decide;[220]
- any relevant matters in the previous history of the registrant concerned (usually outlined by the case presenter);
- evidence of the registrant's behaviour and attitude before, during and after the incident in question and before and during proceedings. The committee may want to consider whether the registrant has shown any remorse or set out to put things right – including by offering an apology, demonstrated insight into the concerns in question and taken any steps to avoid repetition of them.[221]

9.326 When making a decision on sanction a committee 'must be sure that it has been presented with the evidence it needs to make a fair and proportionate decision'.[222] Consequently, the committee may, at any stage before making its decision as to a sanction, adjourn for 'further information or reports to be obtained in order to assist it in exercising its functions'.[223]

The purpose of sanction

9.327 When considering sanction, a committee must bear in mind that its purpose is not to punish the registrant concerned, but rather to 'protect patients and the wider public interest'.[224]

Proportionality

9.328 Any sanction imposed must be appropriate, proportionate[225] and in the public interest.

9.329 Being 'proportionate' in this context, means a 'sanction should be no more serious than it needs to be to achieve its aims.[226] Consequently, the committee should consider each available sanction, starting with the lowest and least restrictive, and decide if it is appropriate to the case.

220 GPhC's *Good decision making: Fitness to practise hearings and sanctions guidance* (last revised in March 2017) para 5.11.

221 GPhC's *Good decision making: Fitness to practise hearings and sanctions guidance* (last revised in March 2017) para 5.15.

222 GPhC's *Good decision making: Fitness to practise hearings and sanctions guidance* (last revised in March 2017) para 5.10.

223 GPhC (FTP) Rules 2010 r31(18).

224 GPhC's *Good decision making: Fitness to practise hearings and sanctions guidance* (last revised in March 2017) para 4.1.

225 *Chaudhury v General Medical Council* [2002] UKPC 41 para 21.

226 GPhC's *Good decision making: Fitness to practise hearings and sanctions guidance* (last revised in March 2017) para 5.1.

If it is not, the committee should consider the next available sanction, and so on, until it decides that a particular sanction is appropriate.[227]

9.330 When addressing the sufficiency of a sanction and its need to protect the wider public interest, a committee will considered:

- whether it is sufficient to protect the health, safety and wellbeing of the public;
- whether it is sufficient to maintain public confidence in the profession concerned; and
- whether it is sufficient to maintain proper professional standards and conduct for members of the profession concerned.

9.331 While a committee is entitled to give greater weight to the public interest, than to the consequences of a sanction to the registrant,[228] to ensure the sanction imposed is proportionate it must carefully consider the impact that it will have on the registrant (both professionally and personally). Any submissions made on behalf of a registrant should accordingly address such.

Available sanctions

Warnings

9.332 The imposition of a warning (which is recorded against a registrant's name on the register) is only likely to be considered appropriate in cases where there have been minor breaches of the GPhC's standards for which the registrant has shown genuine insight into his or her failings; and furthermore, where allowing the registrant to practise unrestricted would present no risk to patients and/or the public.[229]

9.333 A warning may also be given even where no finding of impairment has been made.

Conditions

9.334 According to the GPhC's sanctions guidance, circumstances in which the imposition of conditions of practice may be considered include where:

a. There is evidence of poor performance, or significant shortcomings in a registrant's practice, but the committee is satisfied that the registrant may respond positively to retraining and supervision,
b. there is not a significant risk posed to the public, and
c. it is safe for the registrant to return to practice but with restrictions.[230]

9.335 Conditions of practice, which may include those that are restrictive in nature (such as a requirement that the registrant can only perform certain aspects of his or her job under supervision or not at all), or those that are remedial in nature (such as a requirement that he or she complete training in an area of practice where his or her performance has been found to be deficient), may be imposed on a registrant's registration for a period of

227 *Giele v General Medical Council* [2005] EWHC 2143 (Admin).

228 *Marinovich v General Medical Council* [2002] UKPC 36.

229 GPhC's *Good decision making: Fitness to practise hearings and sanctions guidance* (last revised in March 2017) p21.

230 GPhC's *Good decision making: Fitness to practise hearings and sanctions guidance* (last revised in March 2017) p21.

up to three years.[231] Any conditions of practice imposed must therefore specify the duration that they are to be operative for.

9.336 There is no exhaustive list of the conditions that may be imposed, although the GPhC maintains a 'conditions bank'[232] providing examples of the type of conditions that may be suitable in certain cases.

9.337 Any conditions imposed must be designed to address the specific concerns a committee has about the registrant's practice. If considered appropriate they should not be so restrictive on a registrant's ability to practise as to be tantamount to a suspension,[233] nor should they be couched in terms that makes compliance with them unfeasible. In short, those imposed should be specific, measurable, achievable, relevant and, as already highlighted, time based (SMART).

9.338 In cases where a registrant seeks to argue that conditions are the most appropriate sanction to impose, evidence should be adduced demonstrating their willingness to comply with conditions. If they have already been subject to an interim conditions of practice order, their compliance with such is likely to be considered when addressing the suitability of imposing conditions as the final outcome.

9.339 In certain circumstances it may be of assistance to the panel for those appearing on behalf of the registrant to suggest the conditions that should be imposed. Prior to doing so, it may be advantageous to seek the approval of the case presenter as to the proposed conditions suitableness. Where the conditions proposed will involve others assisting the registrant – for example, where supervision of some/all of his or her practice is required or where there is a proposed condition to audit/monitor his or her work and report on its adequacy – then evidence from those who may be tasked to perform such work, highlighting their willingness to do such, should also be adduced when submissions on sanction are made.

Suspension

9.340 Following a finding of impairment, a committee may suspend a registrant from practice where it:

> . . . considers that a warning or conditions are insufficient to deal with any risk to patient safety or to protect the public, or would undermine public confidence . . . Also when public confidence in the profession demands no lesser sanction.[234]

9.341 A suspension order, temporarily removing a registrant's name from the register, may be made for a period of up to one year. Such a sanction will ordinarily be reserved for cases involving significant breaches of the professional standards where temporarily preventing the registrant from practising is necessary to protect service users and/or is in the wider public interest.

231 GPhC's *Good decision making: Fitness to practise hearings and sanctions guidance* (last revised in March 2017) p21.

232 See the GPhC's *Good decision making: conditions bank* (last updated in January 2016).

233 *Udom v General Medical Council* [2009] EWHC 3242 (Admin).

234 GPhC's *Good decision making: Fitness to practise hearings and sanctions guidance* (last revised in March 2017) p22.

9.342 Such a sanction should only be considered having first considered the suitability of a conditions of practice order. Consequently, a suspension order should only be imposed where no conditions can be adequately framed to protect the public and/or where conditions are not deemed appropriate to address the wider public interest concerns raised in a particular case.

Removal

9.343 A direction to remove a registrant's name from the register is be reserved for the most serious cases[235] where a registrant's behaviour is deemed to be fundamentally incompatible with continued registration and consequently public confidence in the profession demands no lesser sanction.

9.344 A registrant who has been removed from the register must wait at least five years (from the date the decision was made) before he or she can apply to be restored to registered practice.

9.345 For analysis of the case-law in supports of removal from a register, see chapter 3.

Health cases

9.346 Where a committee determines that a registrant's fitness to practise is impaired 'solely' by reason of adverse physical or mental health, it cannot direct that the registrant be removed from the register.[236] The chair may, however, require the registrant to agree to be medically examined by a registered medical practitioner nominated by the GPhC.

Guidance on particular areas of concern

9.347 Alongside providing general guidance on matters to be taken into consideration when addressing sanction in any given case, the GPhC's sanction guidance includes particular advice on the approach to be adopted in cases involving:

a) Sexual misconduct: Here the guidance notes that:

> The GPhC believes that some acts of sexual misconduct will be incompatible with continued registration as a pharmacist or pharmacy technician. Removal from the register is likely to be the most appropriate sanction in these circumstances, unless there is evidence of clear, mitigating factors that cause a committee to decide that such a sanction is not appropriate.[237]

b) Dishonesty: Here the guidance notes that whilst 'the GPhC believes that dishonesty damages public confidence, and undermines the integrity of pharmacists and pharmacy technicians', cases involving dishonesty can be complicated with the context in which the dishonesty took place an important consideration. Accordingly, whilst always considered serious, the guidance makes clear that 'there is not a presumption of removal in all cases involving dishonesty'.

c) Duty of candour.

d) Raising concerns.

235 GPhC's *Good decision making: Fitness to practise hearings and sanctions guidance* (last revised in March 2017) p22.

236 PO 2010 art 54(7).

237 GPhC's *Good decision making: Fitness to practise hearings and sanctions guidance* (last revised in March 2017) p30.

Interim measures following sanction

9.348 Any decision taken on sanction is an appealable decision. Accordingly, any sanction issued against a registrant's registration does not take effect until the period for bringing an appeal has expired (28 days from the date written notice of the decision was served on the registrant), or where an appeal is lodged until the date on which the appeal is finally disposed of.[238]

9.349 To cover this appeal period, a committee may impose an interim order (usually on the same terms as any sanction imposed) that takes effect immediately.[239]

9.350 An interim order must only be imposed if a committee considered it 'necessary for the protection of members of the public or is otherwise in the public interest or in the interests of the registrant'.

9.351 Before reaching a decision on whether or not to impose an interim order, the committee must invite representations from the parties on the necessity of such.[240] Instructions should be taken from the registrant concerned as to whether or not any opposition should be raised to the interim order proposed.

9.352 Whether or not a meritorious argument can be raised in opposition will depend on the reasons cited by the committee for the imposition of the sanction imposed. Where, for example, there are no concerns about patient/public safety, then it may be argued that a registrant be allowed to practise unrestricted during the appeal period, to allow him or her to make the necessary arrangements to have his or her work covered by others when the sanction imposed finally takes effect.

9.353 A committee must provide the reasons for any decision taken on whether or not to impose an interim order following a direction on sanction. This decision is itself appealable.[241]

Review hearings and restoration hearings

Review hearings

9.354 Where a registrant is made subject to a conditions of practise order or a suspension order following a fitness to practise hearing, the committee will usually direct that a review hearing take place before the expiration of any order made.

9.355 Review hearings should ordinarily take place towards the end of an orders operative period, unless there is good reason for the committee to review a case earlier, for example, if the GPhC has evidence that the registrant has practised while suspended or has failed to comply with conditions imposed upon his or her practice. In such circumstances, before a review hearing has taken place the GPhC may request case management

238 PO 2010 art 59(1).
239 PO 2010 art 60(2) and (4).
240 GPhC (FTP) Rules 2010 r31(15).
241 PO 2010 art 60(7).

directions, and the chair may direct that the new evidence of non-compliance be considered at the review hearing.[242]

9.356 Where a review hearing is ordered by a committee, they should explain to a registrant in their written determination on sanction, the type of evidence which the registrant would be expected to provide at the review hearing.[243] Typically, this will be evidence that demonstrates the steps the registrant has taken to address the particular concerns about their practice that have been considered in their particular case (eg reports from an appointed supervisor, evidence of CPD, written reflections from the registrants on the matters found proved against them etc).

9.357 Where a registrant has been made subject to a conditions of practice order, his or her compliance with the conditions imposed will be considered at a review hearing, with the committee at such a hearing tasked with determining whether the registrant's fitness to practise remains impaired. Depending on the determination made, a committee may then:

- extend the period for which the conditions shall remain operative (for such further period not exceeding three years and starting from the time when the original conditions of practice order would otherwise expire);
- add to, remove or otherwise vary the conditions to which a registrant is subject;
- direct that the registrant's practice be suspended (for example, where that person has failed, whether wholly or partly, to comply with his or her existing conditions), for a period no longer than 12 months; or
- direct that the registrant be removed from the register indefinitely (for example, in cases where the registrant has fundamentally failed to comply with conditions of practise previously ordered).[244]

9.358 Where a registrant has been made subject to a suspension order, at a review hearing a committee may:

- remove the registrant from the register;
- extend the suspension order (for a period not exceeding 12 months, starting from the time when the original period of suspension would otherwise expire);
- direct that the registrant's entry on the register be suspended indefinitely (providing the suspension has already been in force for at least two years);[245]
- in cases where the registrant's registration has already been indefinitely suspended, terminate that suspension; or
- replace the existing suspension order with a conditions of practice order (for a period not exceeding three years in duration) with conditions

242 GPhC (FTP) Rules 2010 r30.

243 GPhC's *Good decision making: Fitness to practise hearings and sanctions guidance* (last revised in March 2017) para 3.10.

244 PO 2010 art 54(3)(b)(i)–(iv).

245 Under the provisions of PO 2010 art 54(4), where a decision is taken to indefinitely suspend a registrant's registration then such a decision must itself be reviewed when the registrant concerned asks for such to be done; and at least two years have elapsed since the direction to indefinitely suspend took effect.

imposed that the committee 'thinks fit to impose for the protection of the public or otherwise in the public interest or in the interests of the person concerned'.[246]

9.359 Rule 34 of the GPhC's FTP Rules outlines the procedures adopted at a review hearing. This rule stipulates that once the committee has considered any preliminary arguments in relation to the hearing and the registrant concerned has been identified, then the case presenter for the GPhC must: inform the committee of the background to the case, and the sanction previously imposed; direct the attention of the committee to any relevant evidence, including transcripts of previous hearings; and further may adduce evidence and call witnesses[247] in relation to the registrant's fitness to practise, or as the case may be, the registrant's failure to comply with any requirement imposed as a condition of his or her registration.

9.360 Following this, the registrant concerned may then present their case, adducing evidence and where necessary calling witnesses in support of it.[248] The registrant's case should focus on addressing the registrant's compliance with the order he or she is subject to. Where appropriate, it is also advisable to highlight any further remedial steps they have taken to address the concerns in respect of their practice articulated by the previous FTP Committee.

9.361 The review hearing provides the registrant with an important opportunity to inform the committee as to what lessons he or she has learned since his or her registration was made subject to conditions or suspension. It should not, however, be seen as an opportunity to challenge the original decision taken. To do so would undoubtedly lead to questions being asked of a registrant's insight into his or her fitness to practise, which could result in the committee imposing a more restrictive order than the one the registrant is already subject to.

9.362 Once all evidence has been called in relation to the registrant's compliance with the original order made, in cases where they have been made subject to a conditions of practice order or a suspension order the committee must then hear submission from both parties as to what direction to now give in respect of the registrant's registration – namely whether the order should remain as it is, be extended, revoked or varied pursuant to the provisions of article 54(3) of the PO 2010. In disqualification cases they must hear submissions on whether or not the disqualification should be revoked.

9.363 Any decision the committee reaches at a review hearing, in respect of the registrant's registration, must be announced in public and the reasons for that decision must be provided.[249]

246 PO 2010 art 54(3)(a)(i)–(v).

247 Subject to GPhC (FTP) Rules 2010 r34(10), which states: 'The chair may refuse to allow a witness to give oral evidence, or to give oral evidence on a particular matter– (a) if not satisfied that the witness is in a position to provide relevant testimony; or (b) if satisfied that all or part of the evidence that the witness is to provide, or is to provide on that matter, should have been disclosed to the party not calling the witness at an earlier stage in the proceedings.'

248 See previous note.

249 Subject to GPhC (FTP) Rules 2010 r34(7).

Restoration hearings

9.364 A person whose entry has been removed from one or more parts of the register, in accordance with a direction by the committee, may apply to the registrar for restoration to the register, but only after the expiration of five years, starting from the date of his or her removal.[250]

9.365 The procedure adopted at restoration hearings – which to a large extent mimics that which is adopted at review hearings so far as the order in which evidence is heard is concerned – is governed by rule 35 of the GPhC's FTP Rules.

9.366 Additionally, the GPhC has recently published guidance for applicants and committee members on restoration to the register (issued in August 2017). This guidance sets out the steps that a registrant needs to take to apply for restoration, as well as outlining the procedure followed at restoration hearings.

9.367 Significantly, such guidance highlights that in applying for restoration to the register it is incumbent upon the applicant to satisfy a committee that he or she is fit to practise. In contrast to fitness to practise hearings, the burden of proof rests with the applicant. It is not for the GPhC to prove or provide evidence to show that an applicant should or should not be restored.[251]

9.368 The above guidance is available to download from the GPhC's website.[252]

Appealing a fitness to practise decision

9.369 A registrant may appeal to the High Court (or the Court of Sessions where the registrant making the appeal is domiciled in Scotland) the following decisions made by an FTP Committee:

a) a decision to remove a registrant from one or more parts of the register;
b) a direction for a registrant's registration to be suspended, or be made subject to conditions of practice (including a direction to extend a period of earlier suspension or conditional entry or making a period of suspension indefinite);
c) a decision to vary the conditions imposed under a conditions of practice order; and
d) a direction that no further applications for restoration may be made following a registrant's removal from the register.[253]

9.370 An appeal must be filed at the relevant court and served on the GPhC within 28 days, beginning with the date on which the written notice of the reasons for the decision was sent to the registrant (or within such longer period as the relevant court may, in accordance with rules of court, allow).

250 PO 2010 art 57(1) and (2).

251 GPhC's *Restoration to the register: Guidance for applicants and committees* (August 2017) para 3.3.

252 See www.pharmacyregulation.org/restoration.

253 PO 2010 art 58(1)(a)–(d).

9.371 Having considered the appeal, the relevant court may do one of the following:

a) dismiss the appeal;
b) allow the appeal and quash the direction in respect of which the appeal is made;
c) substitute for the direction in respect of which the appeal is made any other direction that the FTP Committee could have given; or
d) remit or refer the case to the registrar or the FTP Committee for disposal of the matter in accordance with the relevant court's directions as well as making such order as to costs as the court thinks fit.[254]

9.372 The Professional Standards Authority (PSA) in compliance with its statutory role of reviewing fitness to practise decisions, may also appeal the a decision taken by a FTP Committee of the GPhC on the grounds that such is 'unduly lenient'.[255]

Costs

9.373 While an FTP Committee has the power to award costs at the end of a hearing,[256] given the GPhC's justification for bringing proceedings is in order to protect the public, maintain public confidence in the profession and to ensure proper standards of registration are adhered to, they are not considered to be in the same position as other litigants bringing a claim. Consequently, unless there is evidence that the proceedings were brought inappropriately, no order for costs is usually made against them.[257]

The power to prosecute

9.374 Alongside its role in assessing the fitness to practise of all registered pharmacists and pharmacy technician, the GPhC as a public authority has the power to institute criminal proceedings for offences under PO 2010 and other legislation (such as the Medicines Act 1968 (as amended)).

9.375 When considering whether to exercise such powers, the GPhC should have regard to its *Prosecution policy* (last reviewed on 13 November 2015).

9.376 The policy encourages selecting the most proportionate and cost-effective approach to addressing any concern under consideration. Accordingly, in the case of criminal matters within the GPhC's remit this usually means seeking alternatives to prosecution, including securing voluntary compliance and non-criminal regulatory interventions such as fitness to practise proceedings.

254 PO 2010 art 58(5)(a)–(d).
255 National Health Service Reform and Healthcare Professions Act 2002 s29(4).
256 GPhC (FTP) Rules 2010 r46.
257 *Walker v Law Society* [2007] EWCA Civ 233.

CHAPTER 10

Appeals and judicial review

Key points

- Each regulator has a right of statutory appeal to a court on an error of law. Exactly which decision what can be appealed depends on the underlying statue that defines the power of the regulator.
- There are set time limits that control when an appeal can be brought. Anyone considering appealing should check the relevant time limits very carefully.
- The process for a statutory appeal is set out in Part 52 of the Civil Procedure Rules (CPR).
- Generally, the court will give some deference to the specialist nature of regulatory bodies.
- Some decisions of regulatory bodies may be amendable to judicial review. Judicial review is not an appeal from a decision. It is a claim that requires judicial scrutiny of administrative acts of public authorities.
- It is complex to decide when a decision can be reviewed by the court and specialist advice should be sought.
- The procedure for bringing a claim for judicial review is set out in CPR Part 54.
- The court must give permission for a claim for judicial review to proceed.
- Following CPR 54.5 a claim for judicial review must be issued by the court a) promptly and b) in any event not later than three months after the grounds to make the claim first arose.

Introduction

10.1 Certain decisions of healthcare regulators can be appealed. The process of appealing a decision made by any of the regulators mentioned in this book is by way of statutory appeal, meaning the right of appeal is set out in a statutory piece of legislation. This chapter sets out the statutory framework for appeals, identifies what type of decisions can be appealed; explains what orders can be made on appeal; the time limits for making an appeal; and finally the specific procedural rules that prescribe how such an appeal is made.

10.2 Certain decisions made by regulators can also be subjected to a claim for judicial review. This chapter sets out when a decision can be subjected to judicial review, summarises the possible grounds on which to bring such a claim for review and the process for doing the same.

Statutory appeals

What can be appealed?

10.3 Each of the healthcare regulators has specific statutory rules that set out which of the decisions they make can be appealed, which court the right of appeal lies to and the time period in which a decision must be appealed.

General Dental Council

10.4 Under section 29 of the Dentists Act (DA) 1984, only certain decisions made by the General Dental Council (GDC) can be appealed. Section 29 clearly sets out what decisions can be appealed:

> (1) The following decisions are appealable decisions for the purposes of this section–
> (a) a decision of the Professional Conduct Committee under section 24–
> (i) giving a direction for erasure of a person's name from the register under subsection (3) of that section, or
> (ii) refusing an application to restore a person's name to the register, or refusing to restore his name until the end of a specified period, under subsection (6) of that section;
> (b) a decision of a Practice Committee under section 27B or 27C giving a direction for erasure, for suspension, for conditional registration or for varying or adding to the conditions imposed by a direction for conditional registration; [. . .]
> (c) a decision of the Professional Conduct Committee under section 28–
> (i) refusing to grant an application to restore a person's name to the register,
> (ii) giving a direction for conditional registration under subsection (6)(b) of that section, or
> (iii) giving a direction under subsection (9) of that section suspending indefinitely the right to make further applications under that section [;][3]
> (d) a decision of the Council under regulation 67 of the General Systems Regulations to send an alert about a person.
> (1A) In subsection (1)—
> (a) a reference to a direction for suspension includes a reference to a direction extending a period of suspension and a direction for indefinite suspension; and
> (b) a reference to a direction for conditional registration includes a reference to a direction extending a period of conditional registration.

10.5 Under section 29(1B), a person in respect of whom an appealable decision is made must lodge any appeal before the end of the period of 28 days beginning with the date on which notification of the decision was served. However, there is one exception – under subsection (1C) a registrar can exercise a discretion to extend the period of time for appeal if the decision was served by post and the registrar is satisfied, on the application of that person, that he or she did not receive the notification within the period of 14 days beginning with the day on which the decision was made.

10.6 The DA 1984 prescribes that on appeal it is open to the High Court to order the following outcomes to an appeal:

a) that the appeal be dismissed;
b) that the appeal be allowed and that the determination or direction appealed against be quashed;
c) substitute for the decision appealed against any other decision which could have been made by the Professional Conduct Committee, the GDC, the Professional Performance Committee or (as the case may be) the Health Committee; or

d) that the case be remitted to the Professional Conduct Committee, the Health Committee or the Continuing Professional Development Committee to dispose to be dealt with under the relevant legislative provisions or in accordance with the directions of the court.

General Medical Council

10.7 Under section 40 of the Medical Act (MA) 1983 only certain decisions made by the General Medical Council (GMC) can be appealed. Section 40 states:

> (1) The following decisions are appealable decisions for the purposes of this section, that is to say–
> (a) a decision of a Medical Practitioners Tribunal under section 35D above giving a direction for erasure, for suspension or for conditional registration or varying the conditions imposed by a direction for conditional registration;
> (b) a decision of a Medical Practitioners Tribunal under section 41(9) below giving a direction that the right to make further applications under that section shall be suspended indefinitely.
> (1A) A decision under regulations made–
> (a) under section 31 above by virtue of subsection (8) of that section; or
> (b) under section 31A(1)(c) above,
> not to restore a person's name to the register for a reason that relates to his fitness to practise is also an appealable decision for the purposes of this section.
> (1B) A decision of the General Council under regulation 67 of the General Systems Regulations[1] to send an alert about a person is also an appealable decision for the purposes of this section.

10.8 The right of appeal for cases in England and Wales lies to the High Court (section 40(5)(c)). In Scotland the correct court is the Court of Session, and in Northern Ireland the right of appeal lies to the High Court of Northern Ireland.

10.9 Under subsections (4) and (4A) of section 40, a person in respect of whom an appealable decision falling within subsection (1) or (1A) has been made may, before the end of the period of 28 days beginning with the date on which notification of the decision was served under section 35E(1), or section 41(10), appeal against the decision to the relevant court.

10.10 On appeal it is open to the High Court to make one of the following orders: (section 40(7)):

a) dismiss the appeal;
b) allow the appeal and quash the direction or variation appealed against;
c) substitute for the direction or variation appealed against any other direction or variation which could have been given or made by a a medical practitioners tribunal; or
d) remit the case to the Medical Practitioners Tribunal Service (MPTS) for them to arrange for a medical practitioners tribunal to dispose of the case in accordance with the directions of the court.

1 European Union (Recognition of Professional Qualifications) Regulations 2015 SI No 2059.

General Pharmaceutical Council

10.11 Under article 58 of the Pharmacy Order (PO) 2010[2] certain decisions made by the regulator can be appealed, namely:

a) a decision of the Fitness to Practise Committee under article 54 to give a direction to remove the entry of a person from one or more parts of the Register;
b) a decision of the Fitness to Practise Committee under article 54 to give a direction for suspension or for conditional entry (including a direction extending a period of earlier suspension or of conditional entry or making a period of suspension indefinite);
c) a decision of the Fitness to Practise Committee under article 54 to give a direction to vary the conditions imposed by a direction for conditional entry; and
d) a decision of the Fitness to Practise Committee to give a direction under article 57(9) that a person may make no further applications under that article in respect of one or more parts of the Register.

10.12 Under article 58(3) the registrant has 28 days to appeal such a decision, beginning with the date on which the written notice of the reasons for the decision was sent, or within such longer period as the relevant court may, in accordance with the applicable rules, allow.

10.13 The right of appeal lies to the relevant court, which is the Court of Session in Scotland or the High Court in any other case (article 58(4)).

10.14 On appeal it is open to the court to make the following orders (article 58(5)):

a) dismiss the appeal;
b) allow the appeal and quash the direction in respect of which the appeal is made;
c) substitute the direction in respect of which the appeal is made with any other direction that the Fitness to Practise Committee could have given; or
d) remit or refer the case to the Registrar or the Fitness to Practise Committee for disposal of the matter in accordance with the relevant court's directions.

General Optical Council

10.15 Under section 23G(1) of the Opticians Act (OA) 1989 certain decisions made by the Regulator can be appealed. Those decisions are as follows:

(a) decision of the Fitness to Practise Committee:–
  (i) under section 13F above giving a direction for erasure, for suspension or for conditional registration or varying conditions imposed by a direction for conditional registration;
  (ii) under section 13F above in respect of an entry relating to a specialty or proficiency, giving a direction for removal (whether or not temporarily) or conditional inclusion or varying the conditions imposed by a direction for conditional inclusion; or
  (iii) under section 13H(1) above imposing a financial penalty order.

2 SI No 213. For the power to appeal decisions made by the Royal Pharmaceutical Society, see Pharmacy Order 2010 (Appeals – Transitional Provisions) Order of Council 2010 SI No 2150.

(b) a decision of the Fitness to Practise Committee under section 13J above giving a direction that a person's name or an entry relating to a specialty or proficiency be removed from the appropriate register;
(c) a determination of the Registration Appeals Committee under paragraph 4 of Schedule 1A to this Act other than a determination to allow the appeal and quash the decision appealed against; and
(d) a determination of the Registration Appeals Committee under section 13K(8) above directing that the right to make further applications under that section shall be suspended indefinitely.
(e) a decision of the Council under regulation 67 of the General Systems Regulations to send an alert about a person.

10.16 Under subsection (3) of section 23G, a person in respect of whom an appealable decision was taken has a period of 28 days, beginning with the day on which the decision was served on him or her, to appeal against the decision to the relevant court.

10.17 Under subsection (4) 'the relevant court' means:

(a) in any case falling within subsection (1)(a) above:
  (i) where the address of the person named in the appropriate register is, or if he were registered would be, in Scotland, means the Court of Session;
  (ii) where the address of the person named in the appropriate register is, or if he were registered would be, in Northern Ireland, means the High Court of Justice in Northern Ireland; and
  (iii) otherwise, means the High Court of Justice in England and Wales;
(b) in any case falling within subsection (1)(b) to (e) above (of section 23G) where the address of the person named in the appropriate register is, or if he were registered would be, in Scotland, the sheriff in whose sheriffdom that address is situated; or
(c) in any other case falling within subsection (1)(b), to (e) above (of section 23G), the county court.

10.18 On an appeal under this section from a decision of the relevant committee, the court may order the following outcomes (section 23G(6)):

(a) dismiss the appeal;
(b) allow the appeal and quash the direction or variation or order appealed against;
(c) substitute for the direction or variation or order appealed against any other direction or variation or order which could have been given or made by the relevant Committee; or
(d) remit the case to the registrar to refer it to the relevant committee to dispose of the case in accordance with the directions of the court.

Health and Care Professions Council

10.19 Under article 38 of the Health and Social Work Professions Order 2001[3] only certain decisions made by the Health and Care Professions Council (HCPC) can be appealed. Article 38(1) provides:

(a) any order or decision of the Health Committee or the Conduct and Competence Committee other than an interim order made under article 31, shall lie to the appropriate court; and
(b) a decision of the Council mentioned in paragraph (1A) or of the Investigating Committee under article 26(7) or (12) or of the Registrar

3 SI 2002 No 254.

under article 33(7)(a) as to whether he is satisfied as mentioned in article 10(4)(a) (which concerns renewal of registration) shall lie to a county court or, in Scotland, to the sheriff in whose sheriffdom the person's address in the register is (or if he were registered would be) situated.

10.20 The decisions that can be appealed falling under article 38(1)(b) are as follows:

- decisions of the Investigating Committee to order the registrar to remove or amend an entry in the register if it is satisfied that it has been fraudulently procured or incorrectly made (article 26(7)) or a review of such an order (article 26(12));
- decisions of the registrar to include the applicant on the register following the granting of an application to restore a registration (article 33(7)(a)).

10.21 Decisions under article 38(1A) are as follows:

- any decision of the HCPC under article 37 (appeals against decisions made by the Education and Training Committee[4]);
- a decision of the HCPC under Part 3 of the General Systems Regulations requiring an exempt person to complete an adaptation period, or pass an aptitude test, in connection with becoming entitled by virtue of that Part of those regulations to have access to, and to pursue, a relevant profession in the United Kingdom.

10.22 Additionally also a number of decisions concerning the General Systems Regulations, namely, a decision of the HCPC under regulation 67 of the General Systems Regulations to send an alert about a person; a decision of the Council to revoke, or not to issue, extend or vary a European professional card under Part 4 of the General Systems Regulations; and A failure by the Council to make a decision in relation to a European professional card within the time limit under regulation 51(1) or 56(1) of the General Systems Regulations.

10.23 On appeal, it is open to the court to order the following (article 38(3)):

(a) dismiss the appeal;
(b) allow the appeal and quash the decision appealed against;
(c) substitute the decision appealed against with any other decision the Practice Committee concerned or the Council, as the case may be, could have made; or
(d) remit the case to the Practice Committee concerned or Council, as the case may be, to be disposed of in accordance with the directions of the court or sheriff.

10.24 'Appropriate court' is defined by article 38(4), as being the High Court of England and Wales or the High Court of Northern Ireland or the Court of Session in Scotland, depending on which jurisdiction the decision was made in.

10.25 Note there are various specific professions relating to appeals concerning social workers within article 38, these are in the process of being

4 There are some exceptions as to which decisions can be appealed, and the entire of article 37 should be considered before any such decision is appealed.

revoked or repealed by the Children and Social Work Act 2017 (although at the time of publication there was no effective date for these changes to be brought into force). Therefore these specific provisions have not been set out in this book. Those advising social workers should consider the specific separate provisions.

Nursing and Midwifery Council

10.26 Under article 38 of the Nursing and Midwifery Order 2001[5] certain decisions made by the Regulator can be appealed:

a) Any order or decision of the Fitness to Practice Committee other than an interim order made under article 31.

b) A decision of the Council mentioned in paragraph (1A) (concerning the registrar removing a name from the register or refusing to add an entry to the register) or of the Investigating Committee under article 26(7) (the investigation committee's decision to remove or amend an entry on the register if it is satisfied that it is either incorrectly made or fraudulently procured) or of the Investigating Committee under article 12(12) (a review of a decision made under article 26(7)).

10.27 Any appeal under article 38(1)(a) shall be lodged in the appropriate court. Article 38(4) defines this as follows:

> (4) In this article 'the appropriate court' means–
> (a) in the case of a person whose registered address is (or, if he were registered, would be) in Scotland, the Court of Session;
> (b) in the case of a person whose registered address is (or, if he were registered, would be) in Northern Ireland, the High Court of Justice in Northern Ireland; and
> (c) in any other case, the High Court of Justice in England and Wales.'

10.28 Appeals under article 38(1)(b) shall lie to a county court or, in Scotland, to a sheriff.

10.29 Under article 38(3) the Court or sheriff may:

> (a) dismiss the appeal;
> (b) allow the appeal and quash the decision appealed against;
> (c) substitute for the decision appealed against any other decision the Practice Committee concerned, or the Council, as the case may be, could have made; or
> (d) remit the case to the Fitness to Practise Committee concerned or Council, as the case may be, to be disposed of in accordance with the directions of the court or sheriff.

10.30 Additionally, the article specifies that the court or sheriff may also may make such order as to costs (or, in Scotland, expenses) as it, or he or she, as the case may be, thinks fit.

5 SI 2002 No 253.

General Osteopathic Council

10.31 Under section 31 of the Osteopaths Act 1993 only certain decisions made by the General Osteopathic Council (GOsC) can be appealed. Section 31(1) provides that the following decisions can be appealed:

a) a decision of the Professional Conduct Committee made under section 8 (concerning restoration to the register after a strike off decision) or 22 (a decision of the Professional Conduct committee); or
b) a decision is made by an appeal tribunal hearing an appeal under section 30 (appeal of a decision by the Health Committee).

10.32 Any appeal must be lodged at the relevant court before the end of the period of 28 days beginning with the date on which notification of the decision is served on him or her.

10.33 The relevant court is defined as follows:

a) in the case of a person whose address on the register is (or if he were registered would be) in Scotland, means the Court of Session;
b) in the case of a person whose address in the register is (or if he were registered would be) in Northern Ireland, means the High Court of Justice in Northern Ireland; and
c) in the case of any other person, means the High Court of Justice in England and Wales.

10.34 The powers of the court on hearing an appeal are set out in section 31(8):

a) dismiss the appeal;
b) allow the appeal and quash the decision appealed against;
c) substitute for the decision appealed against any other decision which could have been made by the Professional Conduct Committee or (as the case may be) Health Committee; or
d) remit the case to the Committee or appeal tribunal concerned to dispose of the case in accordance with the directions of the court.

10.35 Additionally, the article specifies they court or sheriff may also may make such order as to costs (or, in Scotland, expenses) as it, or he or she, as the case may be, thinks fit.

How to appeal

Procedure for appealing

10.36 The procedure for an appeal is set out in the Civil Procedure Rules (CPR) 1998[6] and the accompanying Practice Directions (PDs). These are available both online and set out in the *White Book*.[7] The relevant rules are contained in Part 52, which concerns civil appeals. Prior to deciding to appeal, the complete civil procedural rules and practice directions contained within Part 52 should be read and carefully considered – what is set out below acts as a summary of the main procedural points.

6 SI No 3132.
7 Sweet & Maxwell.

Rules

10.37 CPR 52.21 sets out the fundamental rules concerning how the appeal will be conducted and the grounds of appeal. It states as follows:

> (1) Every appeal will be limited to a review of the decision of the lower court unless –
> (a) a practice direction makes different provision for a particular category of appeal; or
> (b) the court considers that in the circumstances of an individual appeal it would be in the interests of justice to hold a re-hearing.
> (2) Unless it orders otherwise, the appeal court will not receive –
> (a) oral evidence; or
> (b) evidence which was not before the lower court.
> (3) The appeal court will allow an appeal where the decision of the lower court was –
> (a) wrong; or
> (b) unjust because of a serious procedural or other irregularity in the proceedings in the lower court.
> (4) The appeal court may draw any inference of fact which it considers justified on the evidence.
> (5) At the hearing of the appeal a party may not rely on a matter not contained in his appeal notice unless the appeal court gives permission.

10.38 However, appeals from regulators are statutory appeals and the specific rules in relation to how to conduct this type of appeal are set out in PD D to CPR 52.

10.39 Under CPR 52.25, there are special provisions for statutory appeals (which would include those from regulatory bodies pursued under a statutory provision), any person may apply for permission to bring evidence to or make representations at a statutory appeal, but such an application must be made promptly. If an appeal is made by the Professional Standards Authority for Health and Social Care (PSA) then the registrant can seek to make representations at the hearing.

Practice Directions

10.40 A series of PDs supplement the rules. Compliance with these PDs is mandatory (rule 52.2). PD52A, PD52B and PD52C set out general rules that apply to nearly all appeals, while PD 52D deals specifically with statutory appeals. Set out below are some of the key points of procedure set out in the relevant PDs.

10.41 PD 52B contains considerable detail concerning how to start an appeal. It sets out requirements for the Appellant's Notice. The Appellant's Notice is called 'Form N161', and is the court form which must be completed to begin the process of an appeal. This is available online or from the High Court administrative offices in the Royal Courts of Justice. This form must be filed (presented to the court) and served (sent to the respondent and/or his or her legal representative). There is a fee that must be paid at court in order to file an Appellant's Notice.

10.42 At the same time as filing a completed notice of appeal, the registrant or his or her representative must file certain documents with the court. A description of these documents is set out in detail in PD 52B at para 4.2.

It includes a copy of the decision being appealed and three copies of the Notice of Appeal, with additional copies for each of the respondents. In statutory appeals from regulators it is likely there will only be one respondent, the regulatory body. In addition, Grounds of Appeal must be filed and served. This must contain a clear and simple statement of why the order of the lower court was wrong or unjust because of serious procedural or other irregularity (r52.21(3), supplemented by PD 52B para 4.2(d)).

10.43 It is necessary to serve the Notice of Appeal on any respondents in the appropriate manner and file a 'certificate of service' with the court to show that service has been properly effected.

10.44 PD 52A sets out the requirements for any skeleton arguments that are lodged with the court. Rule 5.1 states that 'The purpose of a skeleton argument is to assist the court by setting out as concisely as practicable the arguments upon which a party intends to rely'. It goes on to list the essential requirements of a skeleton argument. It must: be concise; define and confine the areas of controversy; be set out in numbered paragraphs; be cross-referenced to any relevant document in the bundle; be self-contained and not incorporate by reference material from previous skeleton arguments; and not include extensive quotations from documents or authorities. In addition, documents relied on must be identified and, where a case authority is cited, the skeleton must explain the proposition of law the authority demonstrates and identify the relevant parts of the case authority that support that proposition.

10.45 PD 52D para 20 deals specifically with statutory appeals and is relevant to any appeal being made under the following pieces of legislation:[8] Dentist Act 1984 ss29 and 44; Medical Act 1983 s40; Nursing and Midwifery Order 2001 art 38; Nurses, Midwives and Health Visitors Act 1997 s12; Opticians Act 1989 s23; Pharmacy Act 1954 s10; and Pharmacy Order 2010 art 58.

10.46 This Practice Direction requires that all appellants serve the Notice of Appeal on body whose decision is being appealed,[9] this repeats the provisions made in PD52B. The PD also confirms that the relevant Respondent to any statutory appeal of a decision of a healthcare regulator will be the regulatory body which made the decision under appeal.[10]

Deference to a specialist body

10.47 Advisors should consider that it is well recognised, when determining an appeal, that the High Court must have regard to the specialist nature of the tribunal making a fitness to practise decision. The specialist panel has an understanding of what the particular profession expects of its members in matters of professional practice – see, for example, *General Medical Council v Meadow*.[11] This deference suggests the High Court will be slow

8 PD 52D para 19.1.
9 PD 52D para 20.
10 PD 52D para 19.1(4).
11 [2007] QB 462 at [197].

to interfere with a decision of a fitness to practise body. This principle was more recently repeated in *Barnett v Solicitors Regulation Authority*.[12]

Judicial review

Introduction

10.48 The decisions of the various regulatory bodies may be the subject of a judicial review, which can in certain circumstances provide an alternative method to challenge the decisions of a regulator.

10.49 Judicial review is not an appeal from a decision. It is a claim that requires judicial scrutiny of administrative acts of public authorities. The court has a supervisory jurisdiction. As Sedley J put it in *R v Somerset CC ex p Dixon*:[13]

> Public law is not at base about rights, even though abuses of power may and often do invade private rights; it is about wrongs – that is to say misuses of public power.

10.50 A claim for judicial review is heard by the Administrative Court, which forms part of the Queen's Bench Division of the High Court. An application for review is started by issuing a claim form (see CPR 54.6). It is only those exercising public powers and performing public duties who can be the subject of a claim for judicial review. In *R v Insurance Ombudsman Bureau ex p Aegon Life Insurance Ltd*,[14] the court's approach as to who could be subjected to a judicial review was that it would not lie against a body whose 'constitution owed nothing to any exercise of government power', a body could only be classed a public if it 'had been woven into the fabric of public regulation or into a system of government control'. Generally, it is highly likely that decisions made by health care regulatory bodies while carrying out their regulatory functions could be the subject of a review.

Procedure

Pre-action protocol

10.51 There are various hurdles an application for judicial review must meet before it will be allowed to proceed by the court. Anyone considering a judicial review should first seek legal advice as to whether it is possible to bring a challenge. If it is, before issuing the claim, a letter before action must be sent and the parties must comply with the pre-action protocol. The details of the pre-action protocol are set out on the Ministry of Justice's website.[15]

12 [2016] EWHC 1160 (Admin). See commentary in *The White Book*, vol 1 on CPR 52x.3.11 (section concerning appeals before 3 October 2016) for relevant case-law on this point in the context of seeking permission to appeal.

13 [1997] COD 323, QBD.

14 *The Times*, 7 January 1994.

15 See www.justice.gov.uk/courts/procedure-rules/civil/protocol/prot_jrv.

Standing

10.52 The claimant will have to be deemed by the court to have sufficient interest in the decision being made in order to bring such a claim. Following section 31(3) of the Senior Courts Act 1981 provides as follows:

> No application for judicial review shall be made unless the leave of the High Court has been obtained in accordance with rules of court; and the court shall not grant leave to make such an application unless it considers that the applicant has a sufficient interest in the matter to which the application relates.

10.53 As stated in the recent case of *David Wylde and Others v Waverley Borough Council*,[16] it is important to note that mere interest alone in the matter in issue or the decision in question is not enough. The interest which must be established must be 'sufficient' so as to entitle a claimant to invoke the court's jurisdiction. Not every member of the public will have a right to bring a claim in relation to a breach of a statutory duty or an exercise of a statutory power or other public law error (see, for example, *R v Secretary of State for the Environment ex p Rose Theatre Company*;[17] *R v Tower Hamlets LBC ex p Thrasyvalou*[18]). In *Walton v The Scottish Ministers*[19] Lord Reed expressed himself in the following terms:

> In many contexts it will be necessary for a person to demonstrate some particular interest in order to demonstrate that he is not a mere busybody. Not every member of the public can complain of every potential breach of duty by a public body. But there may also be cases in which any individual, simply as a citizen, will have sufficient interest to bring a public authority's violation of the law to the attention of the court, without having to demonstrate any greater impact upon himself than upon other members of the public. The rule of law would not be maintained if, because everyone was equally affected by an unlawful act, no-one was able to bring proceedings to challenge it.

10.54 In regulatory cases, if the subject is the registrant against whom a fitness to practise decision has been made, it is very unlikely that this test will not be met; as the registrant has an obvious and direct interest in the outcome of any regulatory decision being taken concerning them.[20]

Permission

10.55 It is necessary to apply for and obtain permission from the court before a judicial review can proceed to a full hearing (see CPR 54.4 and Senior Courts Act 1981 s31(3)). The reason for this requirement to prevent the time of the court being 'wasted by busy bodies with misguided tor trivial complaints'.[21]

16 [2017] EWHC 466 (Admin).

17 [1990] 1 QB 504 at pp520B–E and 522C–E.

18 (1990) 23 HLR 38 at p47.

19 [2012] UKSC 44 at [20].

20 Whether an application has sufficient interest is a mixed question of law and fact and requires having regard to the relationship between the claimant and the matter to which the claim relates, see *R v Inland Revenue Commissioner ex p National Federation of Self-employed and Small Businesses Ltd* [1982] AC 617.

21 *R v Inland Revenue Commissioner ex p National Federation of Self-employed and Small Businesses Ltd* [1982] AC 617.

Alternative remedies

10.56 The basic principle is that judicial review is a remedy of last resort, so that where an alternative remedy exists that should be exhausted before any application for permission for judicial review is made.

10.57 As was recently emphasised in *Glencore Energy UK Limited v Commissioners of HMRC*,[22] permission to apply for judicial review should be refused where there are alternative remedies available to a claimant which are in substance adequate and appropriate. The High Court refused permission to apply for judicial review of a decision to impose diverted profits tax (DPT) as the statutory review and appeals process provided an effective and appropriate alternative.

10.58 The court held that as:

> Case law indicates that where a statutory alternative exists, granting permission to claim judicial review should be exceptional. The rule is not however invariable and where an alternative remedy is nonetheless ineffective or inappropriate to address the complaints being properly advanced then judicial review may still lie.
>
> . . .
>
> The first question will always be to determine whether the forum identified as the appropriate '*alternative*' is capable of amounting to a substitute for judicial review. To decide this, the Court has to (a) work out the scope and effect of the jurisdiction of the postulated '*alternative*' (which is a question of statutory construction) and then (b) work out whether the proposed Grounds for judicial review are capable of being adjudicated upon in that alternative forum. This second issue has two main strands to it which are whether the issues in dispute can be determined either in the public law *forum* set out in the proposed grounds for judicial review *or* in their pith and *substance*.
>
> The second issue: If there is an alternative, is it effective and appropriate? If the issues in dispute can *in principle* be determined in the '*alternative*' forum then there is a further stage in the analysis which is to determine, qualitatively, whether the alternative is as effective and appropriate as a judicial review in the High Court. There is no fixed or canonical list of criteria which apply to this exercise which by its nature is fact and context sensitive but, from case law, the following have been identified as potentially relevant to this comparative evaluation:
>
> The existence of non-judicial alternatives.
>
> Speed and expedition.
>
> Costs and expense.
>
> The need for fact finding.
>
> Utility and finality.
>
> The desirability of an authoritative ruling on the points of law arising.
>
> The strength of the issues.

Time limits – promptness

10.59 Following CPR 54.5 the claim form must be issued a) promptly and b) in any event not later than three months after the grounds to make the claim first arose. Advisors should be aware that failing to bring a claim promptly

22 [2017] EWHC 1476 (Admin).

could mean that the claim is refused by the court, even if the claimant is still within the three months of the decision under challenge (CPR 54.5). The court does have discretion under CPR 54.5 to allow a review after the three-month time period, but only if there is considered to be good reason for such an extension. The parties do not have the right to agree to extend time limits between themselves.

Duty of candour

10.60 One other feature of the procedure is the duty of candour. In claims for judicial review, parties rely upon one another to disclose relevant information to the court, since the court does not normally expect oral examination or cross examination of witnesses. There is a significant and onerous duty of candour on both parties. The defendant is expected to explain the full facts and reasoning underlying the decision challenged and to disclose the relevant documents. Claimants must also disclose all material facts and other matters that may hamper their case – for example, alternative remedies open to them, delay in bringing the claim etc. The importance of this was emphasised by the court in the case of *R (Banks) v Secretary of State for the Environment, Food and Rural Affairs*[23] in which the court emphasised that 'the obligation to be frank and honest lies on both parties, and a claimant who presents an incomplete or misleading claim may find this in itself is a good reason to reject that claim'.

Grounds of challenge

10.61 If these hurdles are surmounted then an advisor must consider if there are public law grounds upon which a decision could be challenged. There are only certain grounds upon which a decision can be challenged by way of judicial review. A full discussion of these grounds is outside of the scope of this work and therefore the following is only meant to provide a brief introduction.

10.62 The so-called *Diplock*[24] grounds are: illegality, irrationality and procedural impropriety. These are not exhaustive, and more recently further grounds have been developed, namely legitimate expectation and proportionality.

Illegality

10.63 Public bodies can only (generally) do what the law allows them to do. The law is set out in Acts of Parliament and in regulations, rules and orders made by government ministers. Public bodies may also have guidance and policy on the exercise of their legal powers. Guidance and policy do not have to be followed, but they should be followed unless there is good reason not to.

10.64 Public bodies must correctly understand and apply the law that regulates their decision-making powers. If they do not follow the law correctly their decision, action, or failure to act will be unlawful. An action

23 [2004] EWHC 416 (Admin).

24 As they were set out by Lord Diplock in *Council of Civil Service Unions v Minister* for the *Civil Service* [1985] AC 374.

or decision may be unlawful if the decision-maker had no power to make it or if it exceeds the powers given to him or her, or if it misapplies the law.

10.65 If a decision-maker fails to follow the law that regulates their decision-making, the decision will be 'illegal' or 'ultra vires' meaning beyond ones legal power or authority. Thus, a decision may be challenged on the basis that it is illegal where the public body has no power to take a particular action or decision, or has acted beyond its powers. This arises, for example, when the legislation relating to a public body does not include the necessary power or has precise limits on when the power can be used.

10.66 Where a regulator has power to exercise a discretion the courts have developed a range of principles in order to ensure its decision is not 'illegal' for example, a regulator must take into account relevant information; it must ignore irrelevant information; it must not delegate a decision for which it is exclusively responsible, and the decision-maker must ensure that it has not fettered its discretion by, for example, applying a very rigid policy. This latter point rests on the presumption that decision makers must give reasoned consideration in individual cases as to how to exercise a power or discharge a duty. In the case of *R v Port of London Authority, ex p Kynoch Ltd,*[25] Banks LJ observed that:

> There are on the one hand, cases where a tribunal in the honest exercise of its discretion has adopted a policy, and without refusing to hear an applicant intimates what its policy is, and that after hearing him it will in accordance with its policy decide against him, unless there is something exceptional in his case [. . .] On the other hand there are cases where a tribunal has passed a rule, or come to a determination, not to hear any application of a particular character by whomsoever made.

Irrationality

10.67 A decision may also be challenged on the basis that it is considered by the Courts to be so demonstrably unreasonable as to constitute 'irrationality' or 'perversity' on the part of the decision maker. As per Lord Greene, who stated in *Associated Provincial Picture Houses Ltd v Wednesbury Corporation:*[26]

> If a decision on a competent matter is so unreasonable that no reasonable authority could ever have come to it, then the courts can interfere . . . but to prove a case of that kind would require something overwhelming.

10.68 Irrationality as a ground of review rests on a presumption that different governmental decision makers could properly come to a range of different decisions. It is only when a given response exceeds the range of those permissible that the decision will be deemed to be irrational. For this reason, the threshold is extremely difficult to meet, which is why the Wednesbury ground is usually argued alongside other grounds, rather than on its own. The onus is on the claimant to establish irrationality or perversity.

25 [1919] 1 KB 176.
26 [1948] 1 KB 223, HL.

Proportionality

10.69 Claims may be brought on the basis that a public body has failed to act proportionately.[27] The concept of proportionality has been applied to test the justification for interferences with rights under, for example, European Conventions, the Human Rights Act 1998 and other common law rights.

10.70 There is argument that, depending on context, the threshold for review on the grounds of proportionality is lower than for the traditional grounds of review. Steiner comments when reviewing this strand of review that it 'puts the burden on an administrative authority to justify its action and requires some consideration of alternatives. In this respect, it is a more rigorous test than one based on reasonableness.[28]

10.71 The difference in approach was addressed by the court in *R (Daly) v Secretary of State for the Home Department*,[29] in which Lord Steyn indicated that:

> The differences in approach between the traditional grounds of review and the proportionality approach may therefore sometimes yield different results. It is therefore important that cases involving convention rights must be analysed in the correct way. This does not mean that there has been a shift to merits review.

He also reiterated that:

> [T]he intensity of review in a public law case will depend on the subject matter in hand [. . .] That is so even in cases involving Convention rights. In law context is everything.

10.72 In general terms, the concept of proportionality requires examination of the options open to a decision maker and a balancing exercise of the aim of the decision against the impact it may have on other competing interests in light of the available options. First, asking whether the public body's objective is legitimate? Then to ask, is the measure suitable for achieving it? And then finally, is it necessary, in the sense of there being a lesser intrusive means of achieving the aim?

10.73 Proportionality was recently considered in the case of *Wallace v Secretary of State for Education*.[30] In which Holgate J, emphasised that this does not require in every context for the decision to be the least intrusive means:

> The case law shows that the 'least intrusive means' test may be appropriate in certain specific contexts (e.g. *Samaroo v Secretary of State for the Home Department* [2001] UKHRR 1150) but not in others (see e.g. *R (Clays Lane Housing) v Housing Corporation* [2005] 1 WLR 2229 at paragraph 28).

10.74 He went on to hold:

> In many fields the 'least intrusive means' test is inappropriate and in such circumstances the Supreme Court has laid down a test of general

27 This may be argued to be a sub-heading within an argument regarding reasonableness of a decision. See *McGarth v Secretary of State for Work and Pensions* [2012] EWHC 1042 (Admin) at [33] 'an exercise of discretion which is disproportionate is indication of administrative action which is Wednesbury unreasonable'.

28 Steiner and Woods, *EC Law*, 3rd edn, 1992, p58.

29 [2001] UKHL 26.

30 [2017] EWHC 109 (Admin).

application, namely *whether a less intrusive measure could have been used without unacceptably compromising the achievement of the relevant objective(s)*, and whether having regard to these matters and the severity of the consequences for the individual, a fair balance has been struck between the rights of the individual and the interests of the public, *Bank Mellat v Her Majesty's Treasury (No. 2)* [2014] AC 700 at paragraphs 20 and 74–5.

Natural justice/procedural impropriety

10.75 There is a requirement that a public body should never act so unfairly that it amounts to an abuse of power. This means regulators must follow the proper procedure when reaching decisions – for example, they must follow any express procedures laid down by legislation in reaching their decisions – and in addition, they must not breach the rules of natural justice. One of the key issues here is the rule against bias, which requires the public body to be impartial and to be seen to be so. There must also be a 'fair hearing' before a decision is reached.

10.76 What constitutes a fair hearing will depend on the circumstances, and there is no set list of requirements. However, in the case of regulatory bodies it would require that:

- a registrant knows the case against him or her in advance of any hearing and has the opportunity to put his or her case properly;
- the decision-maker does not take into account evidence or factors which he or she was not aware of or does not refuse to hear evidence which might have led to a different decision;
- a registrant is not denied access to relevant documents;
- a hearing is not held in the absence of the registrant when he or she had a good reason for not being able to attend;
- finally, fairness may also demand that a regulator give reasons for their decision.

10.77 The healthcare regulatory bodies have their own procedural rules, which follow these principles, therefore if there is a failure of the part of the regulator to uphold its own procedure, it could be challenged on the both the grounds of illegality and a breach of the rules of natural justice.

10.78 Legitimate expectation emerged in the Court of Appeal's 1969 decision *Schmidt v Secretary of State for Home Affairs*.[31] Legitimate expectation can be broken down into two parts: a) procedural legitimate expectation – generally the obligation to consult before a policy of change of course of action is enacted; and also b) substantive legitimate expectation – which prevents the removal of a benefit which the individual enjoys.

Judicial review in practice: examples

10.79 Examples of recent judicial reviews which demonstrate the type of decisions made by Regulators that might be subject to judicial review and where such action is likely to succeed are found at:

31 [1969] 2 Ch 149, CA.

Name	Challenge
General Medical Council v Nwachuku and another; R (Nwachuku) v General Medical Council [2017] EWHC 2085 (Admin)	**Argument: decision-maker followed law incorrectly.** Argument that the medical practitioners tribunal had applied the wrong test in making a finding of dishonesty. **Outcome:** Permission for judicial review refused.
R (Pitt and another) v General Pharmaceutical Council [2017] EWHC 809 (Admin)	**Argument: policy challenge/human rights.** Challenge to wording of new professional standards published by the regulator engaged and breached Article 8 of the European Convention on Human Rights. **Outcome:** Claim refused.
R (AM) v GMC [2015] EWHC 2096 (Admin)	**Argument: policy challenge/human rights.** Challenge to the GMC's guidance (the 'Guidance') on assisted suicide which stated that doctors may have disciplinary proceedings brought against them, even though the Director of Public Prosecutions is unlikely to prosecute. The argument was that the Guidance breached Article 8 of the European Convention on Human Rights and was unreasonable in the public law sense.
	Outcome: Article 8 was engaged, but the application was refused as not contrary to Article 8 for the GMC to take as its starting point the principle that a doctor has a duty to obey the law and structure guidance accordingly. The purpose of professional regulation and criminal proceedings are different, therefore there is no reason to assume that the DPP's analysis of the public interest would be the same as that of the GMC.

British Dental Association v General Dental Council [2014] EWHC 4311 (Admin)	**Argument: policy challenge. Failure to consult/legitimate expectation.** Challenge to increase of fees. Following an earlier consultation, in June 2014 the GDC issued its 2014 Policy on retention fees in the light of the consultation responses. But many consultees had wanted more financial information than had been provided, particularly on the costs of fitness to practise cases. In response, a statement published alongside the 2014 Policy promised that in the forthcoming consultation document on 2015 fees the GDC would provide more detail on the Fitness to Practise process, and would build this into its public reporting on expenditure The 2015 fee consultation followed on 30 June 2014 and ended on 4 September 2014. The accompanying paper provided some details of the predictions which lay behind the cost increase. Broadly put, the BDA argued that the GDC had not published sufficient information to enable consultees to respond to the consultation in a fully informed manner The BDA's argued there was failure to consult. This argument had two limbs, the first that there was a general common law duty to consult, and the second that the GDC should be bound to its commitment to be transparent about its consultation process.
	Outcome: The judge rejected the first limb of the BDA's argument. The claim was allowed on the basis of the second limb of the argument. It held, the consultation was not transparent and was thus unlawful. The court attached importance to the statements by the GDC in its policy about transparency and that had created a legitimate expectation, 'To my mind specific public announcements such as this gave rise to a legitimate expectation among registrants that a transparent consultation would be conducted.'

	And that required consultees being put in a position to test the validity of the assumptions underlying the suggested fee increase, and to understand why alternatives had been rejected. This would enable them to make an informed and intelligent response and to propose alternatives. However, the judge applied *R (Edwards) v Environment Agency (No 2)*. Even though the claimant had won on a failure to consult, it would not follow that there should be a quashing order.
McCarthy v Visitors of the Inns of Court [2015] EWCA Civ 12	**Argument: procedural fairness.** The regulator did not disclose a witness statement. Argued that there was a potential for the first tribunal to reach a different conclusion had there been disclosure. **Outcome:** Permission for judicial review granted. At the substantive hearing, the court refused to quash decision. The matter was appealed to the Court of Appeal. This appeal was allowed.
Banerjee v General Medical Council [2017] EWCA Civ 78	**Argument: procedural unfairness** B appealed to the Court of Appeal from the order of Walker J dismissing her application for judicial review of the GMC's refusal to restore B to the medical register (see [2015] EWHC 2263 (Admin)).
	Outcome: The court rejected the overarching submission for B that the hearing before the panel was unfair in view of the number, nature, tone and content of questions asked by the panel members, in circumstances where the GMC had said it did not intend to revisit the probity of her conduct in relation to the voluntary erasure application.

Dryburgh v NHS Fife and General Dental Council (intervening party) [2016] CSOH 116	**Argument: procedural unfairness/ human rights** The Court of Session considered a claim for judicial review in a case where the registered dental care professional was not allowed representation at an NHS Trust disciplinary hearing. She was summarily dismissed. She sought a judicial review of the decision not to allow her legal representation. The dental nurse argued that the decision to refuse legal representation breached her right to a fair hearing under Article 6 of the European Convention on Human Rights, as the outcome of the disciplinary proceedings could, in practical terms, deprive her of the right to practise her profession; and because the findings of the disciplinary panel would influence proceedings before the practice committee of the General Dental Council. The respondents raised a preliminary issue arguing that the decisions were not susceptible to judicial review as this was a dispute about the party's rights and obligations within a contract between an employer and an employee and did not concern a public body. **Outcome:** The court rejected the claim for judicial review. The court concluded the decision was not amenable to judicial review. This is not a case where the decision was 'entrusted to a body other than the employer'. The matter was dealt with internally. The decisions were taken in the context of an employment dispute. While the decision not to allow the dental nurse legal representation was an administrative one, the dispute between the parties is essentially a contractual one in which she was seeking to defend her right to work in the face of allegations of misconduct. To deny her legal representation may raise an issue of natural justice but it did not elevate the contract into one within the domain of public administrative law.

R (British Medical Association) v General Medical Council [2016] EWHC 1015 (Admin)	**Argument: procedural unfairness/ challenge to procedure rules (set out in statutory instrument)/human rights.** The BMA brought a claim for judicial review challenging the legality of the General Medical Council (Legal Assessors and Legally Qualified Persons) Rules 2015 and specifically the fact these rules did not require a legally qualified chair, when he or she has provided advice to the other members of the tribunal in private, to repeat that advice before the parties and allow them to comment on it. **Outcome:** Claim refused. The 2015 rules were held not to be contrary to Article 6 (the right to fair trial), nor were they contrary to the requirements of common law fairness, nor otherwise unlawful. It was sufficient for the advice to be incorporated into the decision. Although there may be exceptions, for example where a new legal point arises during the panel's deliberations upon which the parties had had no earlier opportunity to comment on it.

Available remedies

10.80 There are specific remedies available in judicial review:

- A quashing order, which voids the decision made by the decision maker.
- A mandatory order which compels the decision maker, or body under challenge to fulfil their duties and to act in a certain way.
- A prohibiting order which prevents the decision maker, or body under challenge from acting in a certain way. A prohibiting order is similar to a quashing order in that it prevents a tribunal or authority from acting beyond the scope of its powers. The key difference is that a prohibiting order acts prospectively by telling an authority not to do something in contemplation.
- A declaration, which is a judgment by the Administrative Court that clarifies the respective rights and obligations of the parties to the proceedings, without actually making any order. Unlike the remedies of quashing, prohibiting and mandatory order the court is not telling the parties to do anything in a declaratory judgment.
- An injunction, which is an order made by the court to stop a public body from acting in an unlawful way. Less commonly, an injunction can be mandatory, that is, it compels a public body to do something.

- Damages are available as a remedy in judicial review in limited circumstances. Compensation is not available merely because a public authority has acted unlawfully. For damages to be available there must be either: a recognised 'private' law cause of action such as negligence or breach of statutory duty or; a claim under European law or the Human Rights Act 1998.

10.81 The discretionary nature of the remedies outlined above means that even if a court finds a public body has acted wrongly, it does not have to grant any remedy.

Judicial review or statutory appeal

10.82 The courts have emphasised the need to consider carefully whether or not a judicial review is appropriate, or whether the issue should in fact form the basis of an appeal at the end of a professional regulatory hearing.

Costs

10.83 A discussion of costs within the civil courts is outside of the scope of this publication. However there are likely to be cost consequences if an appeal is lodged in the High Court or the Court of Appeal and is not successful, or if a claim for judicial review is brought before the Administrative Court. Before pursuing any appeal, it is strongly advisable to seek legal advice in order to determine the merits of any argument being made on appeal and the possible cost consequences.

Professional Standards Authority for Health and Social Care[32]

10.84 The Professional Standards Authority for Health and Social Care (PSA) is a body corporate created by section 25 of the National Health Service Reform and Health Care Professions Act 2002, as amended.

10.85 This body is responsible for overseeing the nine health and care professional regulatory bodies. In relation to fitness to practise hearings the work of the PSA includes carrying out an audit of the initial stages of regulators' fitness to practise processes and looking at a sample of the decisions made by each regulator to close a case without referral to a formal hearing in front of an FTP Committee.

10.86 The power that enables them to do this is found within section 29 of the National Health Service Reform and Health Care Professions Act 2002.

10.87 When the PSA wants to refer a case to court, under section 29 they bring a statutory appeal of the regulatory body's decision.

32 See www.professionalstandards.org.uk.

10.88 Pursuant to section 29(7), where a case is referred to the High Court under section 29(4) it is to be treated as an appeal and accordingly CPR 52 applies. It follows that the court should allow an appeal where the decision was 'wrong' or unjust because of a serious procedural irregularity.

10.89 Section 29(8) makes provision for the court's powers on hearing the statutory appeal. The court may dismiss the appeal, allow it and quash the relevant decision, substitute any other decisions for the relevant decision or remit the case to the committee to dispose of in accordance with the directions of the court.

10.90 Pursuant to section 29(4) of the 2002 Act (as amended by the Professional Standards Authority for Health and Social Care (References to Court) Order 2015), the Authority may refer to the High Court where it considers that: 'the decision is not sufficient (whether as to a finding or a penalty or both) for the protection of the public'.

10.91 Section 29(4A) provides that:

> (4A) Consideration of whether a decision is sufficient for the protection of the public involves consideration of whether it is sufficient:
> (a) to protect the health, safety and well being of the public;
> (b) to maintain public confidence in the profession concerned; and
> (c) wto maintain proper professional standards and conduct for members of that profession.

10.92 The test of 'insufficiency' was introduced into the 2002 Act by an amendment made by the Professional Standards Authority for Health and Social Care (References to Court) Order 2015. Previously the wording of the test was 'undue leniency'. The court considered the difference between these tests in *Professional Standards Authority for Health and Social Care v (1) Nursing and Midwifery Council (2) Philomena Judge*:[33]

> The Court of Appeal considered the criteria to be applied by the court when deciding whether a relevant decision was 'wrong' in the case of *Ruscillo v Council for Regulation of Health Care Professionals* [2004] EWCA Civ 1356.
>
> The statutory test is no longer 'undue leniency' but is 'insufficiency' but I accept the submission advanced by both principal parties that the approach of this court should be the same as that indicated in Ruscillo at paragraph 73 in that case the court said this:
>
> > 'The task of the disciplinary tribunal is to consider whether the relevant facts demonstrate that the practitioner has been guilty of the defined professional misconduct that gives rise to the right or duty to impose a penalty and, where they do, to impose the penalty that is appropriate, having regard to the safety of the public and the reputation of the profession. The role of the court when a case is referred is to consider whether the disciplinary tribunal has properly performed that task so as to reach a correct decision as to the imposition of a penalty. Is that any different from the role of the council in considering whether a relevant decision has been "unduly lenient"? We do not consider that it is. The test of undue leniency in this context must, we think, involve considering whether, having regard to the material facts, the decision reached has due regard for the safety of the public and the reputation of the profession.'

33 [2017] EWHC 817 (Admin) at [8].

10.93 Under section 29(6) the PSA has a four-week time limit from the last date on which the practitioner concerned has the right to appeal against the relevant decision.

10.94 It is advisable for any registrant in the circumstance where such an appeal is brought by the PSA or a regulatory body to seek legal advice and assistance. Practitioners should be aware that, in certain circumstances, the PSA may be willing to enter into alternative dispute resolution (ADR) to agree an outcome with the registrant and the professional body and the PSA has a policy to the same.[34]

Appeals by regulators

10.95 In 2014, there was a consultation on proposed changes to the Medical Act (MA) 1983. It was proposed to permit the GMC to appeal against Medical Practitioner Tribunal decisions. Responses to the consultation were analysed and consequently amendments were made to the MA 1983 by the General Medical Council (Fitness to Practise and Overarching Objective) and the Professional Standards Authority for Health and Social Care (References to Court) Order 2015 ('the 2015 Order').[35]

10.96 The 2015 Order provides the GMC with a right of appeal pursuant to section 40A of the MA 1983. This mirrors the powers of the PSA:

> (3) The General Council may appeal against a relevant decision to the relevant court if they consider that the decision is not sufficient (whether as to a finding or a penalty or both) for the protection of the public.
> (4) Consideration of whether a decision is sufficient for the protection of the public involves consideration of whether it is sufficient–
> (a) to protect the health, safety and well-being of the public;
> (b) to maintain public confidence in the medical profession; and
> (c) to maintain proper professional standards and conduct for members of that profession . . .
> (5) On an appeal under this section, the court may–
> (a) dismiss the appeal;
> (b) allow the appeal and quash the relevant decision;
> (c) substitute for the relevant decision any other decision which could have been made by the Tribunal;
> (d) remit the case to the MPTS for them to arrange for a Medical Practitioners Tribunal to dispose of the case in accordance with the directions of the court . . .

10.97 The correct approach on such an appeal was considered by the divisional court in *General Medical Council v (1) Dr Nilesh Pravin Jagjivan (2) Professional Standards Authority for Health and Social Care*:[36]

> i) Proceedings under section 40A of the 1983 Act are appeals and are governed by CPR Part 52. A court will allow an appeal under CPR Part 52.21(3) if it is 'wrong' or 'unjust because of a serious procedural or other irregularity in the proceedings in the lower court'.

34 See www.professionalstandards.org.uk/library/document-detail?id=6f72e1f0–726a–44f6–89bd–3244041191e5.

35 SI No 794.

36 [2017] EWHC 1247 (Admin).

ii) It is not appropriate to add any qualification to the test in CPR Part 52 that decisions are 'clearly wrong': see *Fatnani* at paragraph 21 and *Meadow* at paragraphs 125 to 128.
iii) The court will correct material errors of fact and of law: see *Fatnani* at paragraph 20. Any appeal court must however be extremely cautious about upsetting a conclusion of primary fact, particularly where the findings depend upon the assessment of the credibility of the witnesses, who the Tribunal, unlike the appellate court, has had the advantage of seeing and hearing (see *Assicurazioni Generali SpA v Arab Insurance Group (Practice Note)* [2002] EWCA Civ 1642; [2003] 1 WLR 577, at paragraphs 15 to 17, cited with approval in *Datec Electronics Holdings Ltd v United Parcels Service Ltd* [2007] UKHL 23, [2007] 1 WLR 1325 at paragraph 46, and *Southall* at paragraph 47).
iv) When the question is what inferences are to be drawn from specific facts, an appellate court is under less of a disadvantage. The court may draw any inferences of fact which it considers are justified on the evidence: see CPR Part 52.11(4).
v) In regulatory proceedings the appellate court will not have the professional expertise of the Tribunal of fact. As a consequence, the appellate court will approach Tribunal determinations about whether conduct is serious misconduct or impairs a person's fitness to practise, and what is necessary to maintain public confidence and proper standards in the profession and sanctions, with diffidence: see *Fatnani* at paragraph 16; and *Khan v General Pharmaceutical Council* [2016] UKSC 64; [2017] 1 WLR 169, at paragraph 36.
vi) However there may be matters, such as dishonesty or sexual misconduct, where the court 'is likely to feel that it can assess what is needed to protect the public or maintain the reputation of the profession more easily for itself and thus attach less weight to the expertise of the Tribunal . . .': see *Council for the Regulation of Healthcare Professionals v GMC and Southall* [2005] EWHC 579 (Admin); [2005] Lloyd's Rep Med 365 at paragraph 11, and *Khan* at paragraph 36(c). As Lord Millett observed in *Ghosh v GMC* [2001] UKPC 29; [2001] 1 WLR 1915 and 1923G, the appellate court 'will afford an appropriate measure of respect of the judgment in the committee . . . but the [appellate court] will not defer to the committee's judgment more than is warranted by the circumstances'.
vii) Matters of mitigation are likely to be of considerably less significance in regulatory proceedings than to a court imposing retributive justice, because the overarching concern of the professional regulator is the protection of the public.
viii) A failure to provide adequate reasons may constitute a serious procedural irregularity which renders the Tribunal's decision unjust (see *Southall* at paragraphs 55 to 56).

10.98 To date, it is only the GMC of all the regulators considered in this publication that has the power to lodge an appeal.

Further rights of appeal

10.99 Once the statutory right of appeal has been exercised, either party to the appeal has a right of further appeal. The further right of appeal lies from the High Court to the Court of Appeal. However, CPR 52.13 requires the court to grant permission for second appeal. Permission must be granted by the Court of Appeal and will only be given where the appeal raises an important point of principle or practice or there is another completing reason for the Court of Appeal to hear it (CPR 52.13(2)). The procedural rules regarding appealing to the Court of Appeal are dealt with in PD 52C.[37]

37 See www.justice.gov.uk/courts/procedure-rules/civil/rules/part52/practice-direction–52c-appeals-to-the-court-of-appeal.

Index